Hidden
Pacific Northwest
The Adventurer's Guide

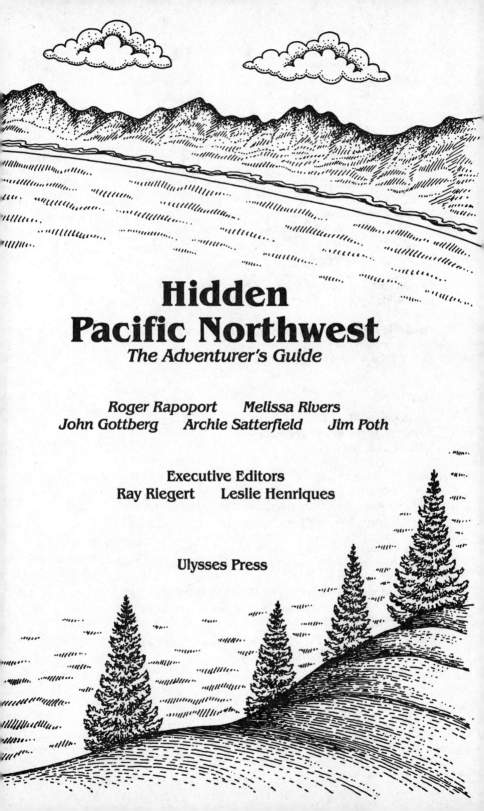

Hidden
Pacific Northwest
The Adventurer's Guide

Roger Rapoport   Melissa Rivers
John Gottberg   Archie Satterfield   Jim Poth

Executive Editors
Ray Riegert   Leslie Henriques

Ulysses Press

Published by: Ulysses Press
3286 Adeline Street   Suite 1
Berkeley, CA 94703
510/601-8301

Library of Congress Catalog Card Number 92-80234
ISBN 0-915233-62-2

Printed in the U.S.A. by the George Banta Company

10 9 8 7 6 5 4 3 2 1

Managing Editor: Claire Chun
Editorial Director: Roger Rapoport
Editor: Bob Drews

Maps: Wendy Ann Logsdon, Phil Gardner
Cover Designers: Bonnie Smetts, Leslie Henriques
Editorial Associates: Wendy Ann Logsdon, Laurie Greenleaf
Indexer: Sayre Van Young

Cover Photography: Front cover photo by Jan Butchofsky;
   back cover photos by Roger Rapoport, Lee Foster, Allan Seiden

Distributed in the United States by Publishers Group West, in Canada by Raincoast Books and in Great Britain and Europe by World Leisure Marketing

Printed on recycled paper

Contents

SPECIAL FEATURES

MAPS

Notes from the Publisher

Throughout the text, hidden locales, remote regions, little-known spots and special attractions are marked with a star (★).

* * *

An alert, adventurous reader is as important as a travel writer in keeping a guidebook up-to-date and accurate. So if you happen upon a great restaurant, discover a hidden locale, or (heaven forbid) find an error in the text, we'd appreciate hearing from you. Just write to:

Ulysses Press
3286 Adeline Street   Suite 1
Berkeley, CA 94703
510/601-8301

* * *

It is our desire as publishers to create guidebooks that are responsible as well as informative. The danger of exploring hidden locales is that they will no longer be secluded.

We hope that our guidebooks treat the people, country and land we visit with respect. We ask that our readers do the same. The hiker's motto, "Walk softly on the Earth," applies to travelers everywhere . . . in the forest, on the beach and in town.

CHAPTER ONE

The Pacific Northwest

The Why, Where, When and How of Traveling in Washington, Oregon and British Columbia

---

Why

The Pacific Northwest goes by many names, but perhaps "The Evergreen Playground" best captures its enchanting appeal. This is a land of intense beauty: gossamer mists on towering evergreens, icy summits that cast shadows on pastoral valleys and bustling cityscapes, wind-sculpted trees on wave-battered capes and inlets, warm breezes through juniper boughs. Powerful volcanoes, wondrous waterfalls, glistening waterways, even shifting desert sands.

The heavy rainfall for which the Pacific Northwest is famous is truly the heart that gives the region its majestic soul. The drizzle and clouds that blanket the coastal region during much of the winter and spring nourish the incredibly green landscape that grows thick and fast and soften the sharp edges of alpine peaks and jagged sea cliffs. But there's a flip side: Over half the region (meaning points east of the Cascade Range) is actually warm and dry through the year.

"The Evergreen Playground" fairly begs to be explored. While much of it remains undeveloped, vast expanses of wilderness are close by all metropolitan centers. Almost without exception, each city is surrounded by countless outdoor recreational opportunities, with mountains, lakes, streams and an ocean within easy reach. It's no surprise that residents and visitors tend to have a hardy, outdoorsy glow. After all, it is the proximity to nature that draws people here.

Asian populations lend an exotic feel to the bustling commercial centers of Seattle, Portland and Vancouver, while the distinctly British aura of Victoria imparts an entirely different foreign appeal. A montage of tiny ghost towns, towering totem poles, aging wooden forts, Scandinavian and

1

Bavarian communities, stage stops and gold-mining boomtowns and old-time fishing villages adds a frontier feel.

This book will help you explore this wonderful area, tell of its history, introduce you to its flora and fauna. Besides taking you to countless popular spots, it will lead you to off-the-beaten-path locales. Each chapter will suggest places to eat, to stay, to sightsee, to shop and to enjoy the outdoors and nightlife, covering a range of tastes and budgets.

The book sets out in Seattle, taking visitors in Chapter Two through this ever-popular city and the surrounding communities spread along South Puget Sound. Chapter Three heads up the Sound, taking in some small and some not-so-small coastal towns and the San Juans, an archipelago of evergreen-clad islands. Chapter Four covers moss-laden rainforests and historic port towns of Washington's Olympic Peninsula and southwestern coast while Chapter Five explores the numerous parks, forests, wildernesses and removed resort communities of the Washington Cascades.

Chapter Six heads to the arid plateau and desert region east of the Cascades in both Washington and Oregon. Portland, the "City of Roses," and the windy Columbia Gorge are the subject of Chapter Seven. Next we go on one of the nation's most scenic drives along the Oregon Coast in Chapter Eight and on to Mt. Hood, Mt. Bachelor, Crater Lake and other majestic peaks of the Oregon Cascades in Chapter Nine. Chapter Ten covers the cultural, learning and political centers lining the Heart of Oregon.

In Chapter Eleven we visit British Columbia, Canada's most westerly province, with stops in exotic Vancouver and the famous Whistler ski resort, followed by a motoring trip up the sleepy Sunshine Coast, an outdoors-lover's paradise. Chapter Twelve rounds out the book with a ferry trip to unspoiled Vancouver Island, its coasts lined with bucolic fishing villages, and to the very proper, very English Victoria, capital of the province.

What you choose to see and do is up to you, but don't delay; things are changing here. The Pacific Northwest is no longer the quiet backwater of a decade ago. Growth and expansion continue in the major population centers strung along the long, black ribbon of Route 5. While Northwesterners are vociferous advocates for preserving nature, rapidly increasing population and growing economic demands are taking a toll.

Sadly, it's becoming difficult to miss the horrid clear-cut swaths through the evergreen background, evidence of the logging industry that feeds the local economies. Salmon that once choked the many streams and rivers have dwindled in number, as have numerous forest creatures such as the spotted owl.

Tourism has also had an impact. As the beauty of the area has been "discovered" by travelers who've taken home tales of this don't-spread-it-around secret vacationland, it's become a hot destination, especially among international visitors. It's getting harder and harder to find those special hidden spots—go soon before "hidden" no longer applies.

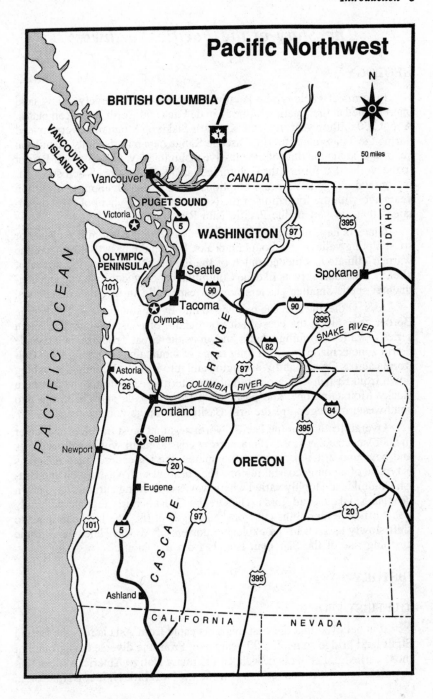

Pacific Northwest

BRITISH COLUMBIA

VANCOUVER ISLAND

Vancouver

CANADA

PUGET SOUND

Victoria

WASHINGTON

OLYMPIC PENINSULA

Seattle

Spokane

Tacoma

Olympia

RANGE

SNAKE RIVER

IDAHO

Astoria

COLUMBIA RIVER

Portland

Salem

Newport

OREGON

Eugene

Ashland

CASCADE

PACIFIC OCEAN

CALIFORNIA

NEVADA

N

0   50 miles

The Story of the Pacific Northwest

GEOLOGY

In terms of geology, the Pacific Northwest is a relatively young land mass formed at the junction of the Juan de Fuca and North American plates. About 200 million years ago, the Klamath-Siskiyou Mountains were created during the Triassic uplift. The Cascade Range began to rise only 20 million years ago, about the time of the massive Columbia lava flow, second-largest in the world, that formed the Columbia Plateau which spreads across Washington and Oregon. Volcanic eruptions reached a peak about two million years ago with the formation of the Northwest's long chain of "fire mountains" that are part of the Pacific Rim Ring of Fire.

Glaciers have also played a major role within the last million years or so, sculpting valleys and mountain peaks. Within the past 10,000 years, the warmer climate has melted much of the ice mass, adding to the power of already formidable rivers like the Columbia that carved the plateau and continental shelf. Smaller glaciers remain, especially in the high mountains.

As a whole, the area can be divided into five distinct zones. The Pacific Border zone along the coast includes a chain of coastal mountains and a series of valleys forming what's known as the Great Trough. The Cascade Sierra zone is made up of the long range of mountains stretching from California across Oregon and Washington and into British Columbia. Reaching down from British Columbia into northeastern Washington is the Northern Rocky Mountain zone, and pushing up from Nevada and California into southwestern Oregon are the arid Basin and Range zones.

Overall features of the Pacific Northwest that most travelers encounter include spectacular sea cliffs, a narrow coastal plain with small estuaries and bays and a major range of mountains, the Cascades, miles inland as is typical of a young coastal region. The coastlines of Washington and British Columbia are highly varied where waves and strong currents have hewn headlands, islands and fjords. The Oregon Coast is fairly regular, with only a few offshore monoliths cut from the jagged cliffs. The land continues to shift slowly as seen in the explosive powers of Mt. St. Helens and in the creeping rise of the San Juan Islands from the Pacific.

HISTORY

THE FIRST PEOPLE

It is believed that the first migrants came from Asia across the Bering Strait land bridge some 25,000 years ago. From the diverse background of those earliest inhabitants descended the many Native American tribes that populated the North American continent. Kwakiutl, Haida, Bella Coola,

Tlingit, Salish, Yakima, Nez Perce, Paiutes, Shoshone, Umpqua and Rogue are but a few of the Northwest tribes.

The verdant land of the Pacific Northwest both provided for and dictated the lifestyles of the various tribes. Those that lived inland east of the mountain ranges were forced to live nomadic lifestyles, depending primarily on foraging and hunting game for survival, moving along as the climate and animal migrations demanded. They generally lived in caves during hunting migration and constructed large pit houses for winter camp.

The mild climate and abundant resources of the valley and coast led to a fairly sedentary life for the tribes that lived west of the mountain ranges. They constructed permanent villages of longhouses from the readily available wood, fished the rich waters of the coast, foraged in lush forests and had enough free time to develop ritualized arts, ceremonies and other cultural pursuits along with an elaborate social structure. The potlatch, a complex ceremony of gaining honor by giving away lavish gifts to the point of bankruptcy, is one of the more renowned ritualized traditions of the Northwest tribes.

Arrival of the white man brought many changes to the generally peaceful natives. Introduction of the horse made life easier for a period, facilitating hunting and travel for the nomadic tribes. However, disease, drugs (namely alcohol) and distrust accompanied the newcomers and eventually added to the decline of the Native American population. Land grabbing by European settlers forced the tribes onto ever-shrinking reservations.

Resurgence in Native American arts and crafts is evident in galleries and museums throughout the Northwest. While most natives no longer live on the reservations but have integrated into white society, many have banned together to fight for change. Tribal organizations are now reclaiming lands and fishing rights; nations such as the Sechelt Band in British Columbia have won the legal right to independent self-government. There are even a growing number of native-owned-and-operated resorts such as Ka-Nee-Tah, a hot spring and golf retreat in central Oregon.

EARLY EXPLORATION

In terms of white exploration and settlement, the Pacific Northwest is one of the youngest regions on the continent. The Spanish began to arrive in the Northwest by sea as early as the mid-1500s; the Strait of Juan de Fuca, Heceta Head, Fidalgo Island, Cape Blanco, Quadra Island and other prominent landmarks bear witness to Spanish exploration and influence. Spanish interest waned when other pressing matters required the attention and money needed to chart the Northwest, and all claims to the area were dropped in 1819 as part of the negotiations regarding Florida.

The Russians also made their way into the region beginning with the explorations of Vitus Dane in 1741. Soon afterward, Russian trappers trekked from Siberia down through Alaska and into the Northwest. As a result of losses brought on by the Napoleonic Wars, Russia renounced all claims to the area south of 54° 40′ in 1824.

Sir Francis Drake passed briefly along the Northwest Coast in 1579, but it was explorer James Cook's expedition in the late 1700s in search of the legendary "Northwest Passage" that resulted in British claim to the region. When passing through China on their homeward bound trip, he and his men discovered the high value of the pelts they carried, leading to an intense interest on the part of the British government in the profitable resources of the Northwest.

The government later commissioned Captain George Vancouver to chart the coastal area between 45° and 60° north latitude which includes Oregon, Washington, British Columbia and Alaska. Mt. Baker, Whidbey Island, Puget Sound, Vancouver Island, Burrard Inlet and many other geographical features retain the names he gave them on his meticulously drawn maps completed between 1791 and 1795.

Captain Robert Gray was also plying Northwest waters at this time, making certain that the United States could lay claim to parts of the lucrative new territory. During his journey, he discovered the mighty Columbia River while searching for the same fabled waterway between the Pacific and Atlantic oceans.

Early explorers like Alexander McKenzie and Simon Fraser were actually the first Europeans to explore land routes, but it was not until Meriwether Lewis and William Clark explored and mapped overland passages, returning with stories of the area's fabulous beauty and natural bounty, that interest in settling the Northwest began in earnest.

THE NEWCOMERS

Trading posts were established to facilitate the fur enterprises; large firms like the Hudson Bay Company and the North West Company vied for control of the profitable region. Settlements sprang up around these posts and continued to grow as the trickle of pioneers swelled into a wave with the opening of the Oregon Trail in the mid-1800s.

Tensions began to mount between American and British settlers who occupied the same territory and came to a head in the San Juan Islands in what's known as the bloodless "Pig War." An uneasy stand-off between the nations held until successful negotiations divided American and British-controlled territory in 1872.

Homesteading, fishing, logging, ranching and other opportunities kept the flow of settlers coming, as did a series of gold strikes. Stage routes were established, and river traffic grew steadily. There were enough residents to warrant separation of the Oregon Territory by the 1850s, and Washington and Oregon attained statehood by the turn of the century. British Columbia was officially accepted as a Canadian province in 1871. Railroads pushed into the region, reaching Portland and Puget Sound by 1883 and British Columbia in 1885, ushering in the modern age.

Rapid industrial development came with the world wars, and the Northwest emerged as a major player in the shipbuilding and shipping industries. Expansion in lumber, agriculture and fishing continued apace. Growth industries today include banking, high technology and Pacific Rim trade. Modern residents are for the most part rugged individualists, fiercely proud of their natural setting and protective of the environment.

FLORA

While it's generally the coniferous trees that everyone equates with the Pacific Northwest, there is much more to the flora of the region than its abundance of redwoods, Western hemlock and white pine, red cedar and other evergreens. Each of the distinct geologic zones hosts its own particular ecosystem.

In the moist woodlands of the coastline, glossy madrone and immense Coast redwoods tower over Pacific trilliums and delicate ladyslippers. Bogs full of skunkcabbage thrive alongside fields of yellow Scotch broom and hardy rhododendrons in a riot of color. Unique to the region are pristine rain forests with thick carpets of moss and fern beneath sky-scraping canopies of fir, cedar and spruce.

In the lowland valleys, alders, oaks, maples and other deciduous trees provide brilliant displays of color against an evergreen backdrop each spring and fall. Daffodils and tulips light up the fields, as do azaleas, red clover and other grasses grown by the many nurseries and seed companies that prosper here. Wild berry bushes run rampant in this clime, bringing blackberries, huckleberries, currants and strawberries for the picking. Indian paintbrush, columbines, foxglove, butter cups and numerous other wildflowers are also abundant.

The verdant parks and forests of the mountain chains contain some of the biggest trees in the world, holding records in height and circumference, with fir, pine, hemlock and cedar generally topping the charts. Thick groves filter the sunlight, providing the perfect environment for mushrooms, lichens, ferns and mosses. The elegant Tiger lily, beargrass, asters, fawnlily, phlox, columbine, valerian and a breathtaking array of alpine wildflowers thrive in high meadows and on sunny slopes.

With the dramatic decrease in rainfall in the plateaus and deserts zone comes a paralleling drop in the amount of plantlife, though it is still rich in pine, juniper, cottonwood and sagebrush. Flowers of the area include wild iris, foxfire, camas, balsam root and pearly everlasting.

FAUNA

It was actually the proliferation of wildlife that brought about white colonization of the Pacific Northwest, beginning with the trappers who came in droves in search of fur. It turns out that beaver and otter pelts were highly valued in China during the 1800s, so these creatures were heavily hunted. Nearly decimated colonies, now protected by law, are coming back strong. Playful otters are often spotted floating tummy up in coastal waters, while the shy beaver is harder to spot, living in secluded mountain retreats and coming out to feed at night.

Fish, especially salmon, were also a major factor in the economic development of the region, and remain so to this day, though numbers of spawning salmon are dropping drastically. Nonetheless, fishing fanatics are still drawn here in search of the five varieties of Pacific salmon along with flounder, lingcod, rockfish, trout, bass and many other varieties of sportfish. Those who don't fish will still be fascinated by the seasonal spawning frenzy of salmon, easily observed at fish ladders in Washington, Oregon and British Columbia.

Among the more readily recognized creatures that reside in the Pacific Northwest are the orca (killer whales), porpoises, dolphins, seals and sea lions often spotted cavorting in the waters just offshore. Twice-yearly migrations of grey whales on the trip between Alaska and California are much anticipated all along the coastline. Minke whales are more numerous, as are Dall's porpoises, often mistaken for baby orca because of their similar coloration and markings. Special museums and exhibits throughout the coastal zone attest to the importance of these marine animals in the region.

Of the varieties of bear living in the Northwest's remote forests, black bear are the most common in Oregon and southern Washington. Weighing upwards of 300 pounds and reaching six feet tall, they usually feed on berries, nuts and fish and avoid humans unless provoked by offers of food or danger to a cub. Grizzly and brown bear are more prevalent farther north. Big-game herds of deer, elk, antelope along with moose, cougar and mountain goats range the more remote mountainous areas. Scavengers such as chipmunks, squirrels, raccoons, opossums and skunks are abundant as well.

Over 300 species of birds live in the Pacific Northwest for at least a portion of the year. Easily accessible mud flats and estuaries throughout the region provide refuge for tufted puffins, egrets, cormorants, loons and other migratory waterfowl making their way along the Pacific Flyway. Hundreds of pairs of bald eagles nest and hunt among the islands of Washington and British Columbia and winter along the Oregon coast, along with great blue herons and cormorants. You might also see red-tailed hawks and spotted owls if you venture quietly into the region's old-growth zones.

With a proliferation of protected refuges and preserves providing homes for great flocks of Canadian and snow geese, trumpeter swans, great blue herons, kingfishers, cranes and other species, birdwatchers will be in seventh heaven in the Pacific Northwest, one of the fastest-growing birder destinations on the continent.

On a smaller scale, we find the slimy slug that thrives in the moist climate. Not quite large enough to be mistaken for a speed bump, they leave telltale viscous trails. While the slug is the bane of gardeners, it is still regarded as a sort of mascot for the region; souvenir shops stock plush toy replicas and gag cans of slug soup.

Where to Go

The number of tourists visiting the Pacific Northwest continues to grow as the secrets of its beauty and sunny summer and fall weather get out. Because the landscape is so widely varied, each area with its own appeal, here are brief descriptions of the regions presented in this book to help you decide where you want to go. To get the whole story, read the more detailed introductions to each chapter, then delve into the material that interests you most. We begin in Washington, head to Oregon, then up to cover British Columbia.

Seattle, recently rated the most liveable city in the United States, offers a comfortable mix of cultural sophistication and natural ruggedness. The clustered spires of its expanding skyline hint at the growth in this busy seaport, the shipping and transportation hub of the Northwest. Nearby communities stretched along South Puget Sound, including Tacoma, Olympia, the state's capital, and the Kitsap Peninsula, are also covered.

Puget Sound and the San Juan Islands, regarded in this book as the coastal area stretched between Seattle and Blaine on the Canadian border, is entirely enchanting, from sea-swept island chains to pastoral coastline. The entire region is punctuated by rich farming tracts, picturesque, forest-covered islands, quaint fishing villages and a shoreline of sloughs and estuaries. The arts are strong in the region, perhaps because of the preponderance of artists drawn by its natural beauty to live here.

Native Americans were probably the first to discover the beauty and bounty of the **Olympic Peninsula and Washington Coast,** with lush rain forests, stretches of driftwood-cluttered beach, tumbling rivers and snow-capped mountains. Several tribes still live in the area on the outskirts of the massive Olympic National Park alongside fishing villages such as Sequim and Port Angeles and the Victorian-styled logging town of Port Townsend.

National parks, forests and wildernesses, including the North Cascades, Snoqualmie and Wenatchee National Forests, Mt. Rainier National Park and the Mt. St. Helens National Volcanic Monument, make up the bulk of the spectacular **Washington Cascades.** Fascinating Leavenworth, a Bavarian-style village, and several small resort towns are also important features here.

The majestic Cascade Range parallels the West Coast running through Oregon and Washington to British Columbia. Once past the slopes, you'll find sagebrush-filled high desert country with shoot-'em-up Western towns and quiet Indian reservations scattered through Washington and Oregon in the **East of the Cascades** zone. Commercial Spokane, pastoral Yakima and industrial Pendleton (home of the famous Pendleton Wools) are also described in this section.

Bounded by an evergreen forest, productive greenbelt and the mighty Columbia River, **Portland and the Columbia River Gorge** remain as close to nature as a growing metropolis can be. Portland, the "City of Roses," reflects a pleasant mix of historic buildings decorated in glazed terra cotta and modern smoked glass and brushed steel structures in the downtown core intersected by the Willamette River and numerous parks. The sense of hustling enterprise dampens as you head east into the gorge where you'll find smaller communities such as The Dalles and Hood River along with breathtaking treasures like Multnomah Falls.

The awe-inspiring beauty of the **Oregon Coast** includes 400 miles of rugged coastline dotted by small, artsy communities such as Yachats and Bandon and larger fishing villages such as Astoria, Newport and Coos Bay connected by Route 101, one of the most beautiful drives in the nation. Foresight on the part of the state legislature preserved the coast from crass commercial corruption, so great stretches remain untouched and entirely natural.

The **Oregon Cascades** hold a bevy of treasures including world-famous rivers like the Rogue and the Umpqua (fishing haunt of Zane Grey), Mt. Hood and Mt. Bachelor ski resorts and the sapphire splendor of Crater Lake, the deepest lake in the country. As with the Washington Cascades, it is a region of national forests and wildernesses.

Cradled between the Coastal and Cascade mountain ranges is the **Heart of Oregon**, a pastoral valley of historic stage stops, gold-mining boomtowns and small farming communities. Sheep-covered meadows, cloud-shrouded bluffs and striped pastures line Route 5, the primary artery traversing the valley. Salem, the state capital, Eugene, home of the University of Oregon, and Ashland, site of the world-famous Shakespeare Festival, are included in this section.

Stretched above Washington and the United States border, British Columbia boasts delights that are hard to match. Extraordinary natural beauty surrounds **Vancouver and the Sunshine Coast**, seen in the caressing Pacific, soaring, protective mountains and vast tracts of forest. Bustling Vancouver sparkles and excites, with more than enough sightseeing, shopping, dining and entertainment opportunities to please one and all. The scenic Sunshine Coast entices with a broad range of recreational opportunities including hiking, biking, boating, camping, diving and fishing. The glacier-covered peaks of Garibaldi Provincial Park and alluring Whistler resort round out the territory.

Visitors to **Victoria and Vancouver Island** will find civility, gentility and a bit of pomp surrounded by one of the greatest outdoor vacation destinations around. Managing to retain the stately air of the British Empire outpost it once was, charming Victoria, the capital of British Columbia, rests at the southernmost tip of the island. Few roads connect the scattered seaport settlements and rugged provincial parks strewn across the remainder of the island, which is rather wild and wooly.

When to Go

SEASONS

The Pacific Northwest isn't the rain-soaked, snow-covered tundra many imagine it to be. In fact, summer and fall days (June-September) are generally warm, dry and sunny. Overall temperatures range from the mid-30s in winter to the upper 80s in summer. There are distinct seasons in each of the primary zones, and the climate varies greatly with local topography.

The enormous mountain ranges play a major role in the weather, protecting most areas from the heavy rains generated over the Pacific and dumped on the coastline. Mountaintops are often covered in snow year-round at higher elevations, while the valleys, home to most of the cities, remain snow-free but wet during the winter months. East of the mountain ranges are temperature extremes and a distinct lack of rain. Travelers spend time at the rivers, lakes and streams during the hot, dry summers and frolic in the snow during the winter.

The mountainous zones are a bit rainy in spring but warm and dry during the summer when crowds file in for camping, hiking and other outdoor delights. Fall brings auto traffic attracted by the changing seasonal colors, while winter means snow at higher elevations that provides the perfect playground for cold-weather sports.

The coastal region is generally soggy and overcast during the mild winter and early spring, making this the low season for tourism. However, winter is high season among Northwesterners drawn to the coast to watch the fantastic storms that blow in across the Pacific. Summers are typically warm and dry in the coastal valleys and along the crisp, windy coast, making it the prime season for travelers who show up in droves, clogging smaller highways with recreational vehicles.

CALENDAR OF EVENTS

Festivals and events are a big part of life in the Northwest, especially when the rains disappear and everyone is ready to spend time outdoors enjoying the sunshine. Larger cities throughout the region average at least one major event per weekend during the summer and early fall. Below is a sampling of some of the biggest attractions. Check with local chambers of commerce (listed in the regional chapters of this book) to see what will be going on when you are in the area.

JANUARY

Seattle: Colorful parades take to the streets of the International District to celebrate **Chinese New Year** in late January or early February.

East of the Cascades: In addition to seeing mushing and snowmobiling contests, you'll hear Carillon bells and perhaps munch wienerschnitzel at the **Great Bavarian Ice Fest** in Leavenworth. There are also ice sculptures, ski competitions and dogsled races at the **Deer Park Winter Festival**.

Vancouver and the Sunshine Coast: A quick plunge into frigid English Bay during the **Polar Bear Swim** on New Year's Day is said to bring good luck throughout the year.

FEBRUARY

Seattle: **Fat Tuesday** is a week-long Mardi Gras-style festival with parade, arts and crafts and plenty of jazz and food.

Olympic Peninsula and the Washington Coast: **Hot Jazz Port Townsend** brings jazz greats to the Olympic Peninsula.

Oregon Coast: Munch crustaceans to your heart's content at the annual **Crab Feed** in Coos Bay and Charleston, or if you'd rather, cheer on the crabs at the **Pacific Northwest Crab Races** in Garibaldi. The **Seafood and Wine Fest** in Newport, the oldest and largest wine fest in the Northwest, promises plenty of seafood, wine and live entertainment.

Vancouver and the Sunshine Coast: **Chinese New Year** lights up Vancouver's Chinatown with fireworks, food and a boisterous dragon parade.

MARCH

Seattle: Judges under umbrellas count as contestants lure gulls in Port Orchard's **Seagull Calling Contest**.

The Washington Cascades: Snow-castle and sculpture competitions are the highlight of the **White Pass Winter Carnival**.

Portland and the Columbia River Gorge: Horse lovers will enjoy **Equestrian Elegance**, a noncompetitive horse exhibition in McMinnville.

The Oregon Coast: There's plenty of Nordic food, music, dance and crafts at Tillamook's **Swiss Fest**. Highlight of the **Beachcombers Festival** in Brookings is the contest of artworks constructed from materials collected on the beach.

Vancouver and the Sunshine Coast: Vancouver's Granville Island comes to life with **Spring Celebration**, a crafts-and-food fair.

Victoria and Vancouver Island: All eyes are on the water during the **Pacific Rim Whale Watching Festival** in Ucluelet and Tofino.

APRIL

Seattle: The music, dance, crafts and foods of over 20 different cultures are represented at **Worldfest**. Enjoy some of the first blossoms of spring at the **Daffodil Festival Grand Floral Parade** which passes through Tacoma, Puyallup and nearby communities.

Puget Sound and the San Juans: If you'd rather catch those early-spring colors in all their natural glory, queue up for the drive through the rich farmlands of La Conner and Mt. Vernon during the **Skagit Valley Tulip Festival**.

The Washington Cascades: Enjoy over 40 different apple-oriented events during the 11-day **Washington State Apple Blossom Festival** in Wenatchee.

East of the Cascades: Taste the best of local wines at the **Spring Barrel Tasting** in Yakima Valley.

Portland and the Columbia River Gorge: Delicate pink-and-white apple blossoms of the area orchards steal the show during the **Hood River Blossom Festival**.

Victoria and Vancouver Island: There's a lot of toe-tapping going on as top entertainers perform at the **TerriVic Dixieland Jazz Party** in Victoria.

MAY

Seattle: An international array of crafts and folktales, food, costume, music and dance is the focus of the **Northwest Folklife Festival**.

Puget Sound and the San Juans: A salmon barbecue and beauty pageant are held in conjunction with the 85-mile **Ski-To-Sea Relay Race** between Mt. Baker and Bellingham.

Olympic Peninsula and the Washington Coast: Many of Port Townsend's grand Victorian homes are open to the public during the **Historic Homes Tour**.

East of the Cascades: The ten-day **Spokane Lilac Festival** features a carnival, bed race, torchlight parade, food booths and more. There's also a **Hot Air Balloon Stampede** with over 50 balloons in Walla Walla. In Oregon, loggers parade and compete in log rolling and tug-of-war contests at the **Central Oregon Timber Carnival** in Prinville.

The Oregon Coast: Participants from around the globe come to sculpt magical creations in the **Cannon Beach Sandcastle Contest**, ranked one of the top competitions in the world. The **Spring Kite Festival** takes off in Lincoln City, the "kite capital of the world."

The Heart of Oregon: A hydroplane boat race, waterskiing show, parade and skydiving competition are part of the fun at **Boatnik** in Grants Pass.

Vancouver and the Sunshine Coast: **Children's Festival**, with food and festivities geared to please the little ones, takes place in Vancouver.

Victoria and Vancouver Island: **Victoria Days** are the big event of the season, topped off by a grand parade in mid-May.

JUNE

Seattle: You'll enjoy hearty servings of strawberry shortcake and performances by Norwegian dancers at the **Strawberry Festival** in Poulsbo.

Puget Sound and the San Juans: Traditional war-canoe races and ceremonial songs and dances are the highlight of the **Lummi Water Festival** held on the Lummi Indian Reservation northwest of Bellingham. In addition to a range of nautical events there are a carnival, parade, art show and grand pyrotechnics display during Everett's **Salty Sea Days.**

Olympic Peninsula and the Washington Coast: Booths sell sausage, doughnuts, ice cream, baskets and dolls made of garlic at the **Garlic Festival** in Ocean Park (Long Beach Peninsula).

East of the Cascades: **Kam Wah Chung Days** in John Day, Oregon, celebrates the city's Chinese heritage with rickshaw races, a parade, Chinese checkers tournament and more.

Portland and the Columbia River Gorge: Portland's biggest party of the year, the **Rose Fest**, is a month-long celebration with parties, pageants and a "Grand Floral Parade" second only to California's Rose Parade. **Fort Vancouver Days**, a city-wide celebration with rodeo, chili cook-off and jazz concert takes place, in Vancouver, Washington.

The Oregon Cascades: The High Cascades play host to the **Sisters Rodeo and Stampede Run** in Sisters.

The Heart of Oregon: Outstanding jazz, bluegrass and gospel performances as well as classical concerts mark the month-long **Oregon Bach Festival** at the University of Oregon in Eugene. A similarly outstanding event is the **Peter Britt Music Festival** in Medford which features an array of music, dance and theatrical performances and runs through early September.

Vancouver and the Sunshine Coast: Vancouver pulls out all the stops in June with the **North Vancouver Folkfest**, the colorful **Dragon Boat Races** on False Creek and the ten-day **Du Maurier International Jazz Festival** with its performances of world-class musicians. You'll also find **Canada Day Celebrations** taking place throughout British Columbia the end of June.

Victoria and Vancouver Island: Not to be outdone, Victoria has its fair share of summer events in June including the **Oak Bay Tea Party**, the **Jazz Fest** and the **International Folkfest.**

JULY

Seattle: Kimono-clad dancers take center stage in **Bon Odori**, a Japanese festival celebrated in the International District as part of the multicultural events of **Seafair**, one of Seattle's biggest celebrations. Northwest talent is showcased in the **Bellevue Jazz Festival**, the oldest jazz fest in the region.

Olympic Peninsula and the Washington Coast: **Splash!** in Aberdeen features Indian canoe races, a grand parade, a street dance and fireworks.

East of the Cascades: At the **Sweet Onion Festival** they celebrate Walla Walla, Washington's famous produce. Cowboys and Indians turn out in force to take part in the rodeo and Native American exhibition that are the centerpieces of the **Chief Joseph Days** in Joseph, Oregon. Gliders come from the world over to take part in the **Hang Gliding Festival** in Lakeview, Oregon.

Portland and the Columbia River Gorge: The **Robin Hood Festival** in Sherwood brings a parade, live music and, what else, an archery competition.

The Oregon Coast: The **Astoria Scandinavian Festival** celebrates the area's heritage. Coos Bay and North Bend join forces to present the **Oregon Coast Music Festival.** The **Dory Festival** in Pacific City offers dory-boat races, a fish fry, parades and lots of crafts and food.

The Heart of Oregon: The **International Pinot Noir Celebration,** attracting top winemakers from around the world, is held in conjunction with the **Annual Antique Show** in McMinnville. Minstrels, jesters, acrobats and craftspeople from all over Oregon gather in Grants Pass and don Olde English garb to show their stuff at the **Renaissance Art Festival.** History comes to life during the **Oregon Trail Pageant** in Oregon City.

Vancouver and the Sunshine Coast: The **Vancouver Sea Festival** stages the famous Nanaimo-to-Vancouver bathtub race along with fireworks, sailing regattas, musical entertainment and barbecues. The **Whistler Country and Blues Festival** brings more music to the mountains. The Sunshine Coast pulls out all the stops during July with **Roberts Creek Daze,** the **Halfmoon Bay Country Fair** and the **Sea Cavalcade** in Gibsons, all good, old-fashioned fairs with booths, games, competitions and parades.

Victoria and Vancouver Island: **B.C. Open Sandcastle Competition** takes the spotlight in Victoria, while the loggers compete in climbing and chopping in **All Sooke Days.**

AUGUST

Seattle: The **Gig Harbor Jazz Festival** is a venue for big names in jazz and blues. **Olympia Harbor Days,** one of the largest arts-and-crafts fairs in the Northwest, also offers a fascinating tugboat race. There's great fun at **Art in the Park** in Everett, with a juried art show, medieval fair, jousting, a Shakespearean play and lots of food and live music.

Puget Sound and the San Juans: Many of the Northwest's finest artists display their work at top local shows like the **Coupeville Arts and Crafts Festival** on Whidbey Island. Friday Harbor is the site of the **San Juan County Fair,** with arts and crafts, agricultural and animal exhibits, a carnival and food booths featuring the bounty of the islands.

Olympic Peninsula and the Washington Coast: Salmon-fishing competitions, a street fair and a couple of parades highlight the **Derby Days Festival** in Port Angeles. World champions descend on Long Beach to compete in the **International Kite Festival.**

East of the Cascades: Sagebrush roping, a ten-kilometer run, a street dance, barbecue and beer garden are part of the fun during **Steens Mountain Days** in Frenchglen, Oregon.

Portland and the Columbia River Gorge: The renowned **Mt. Hood Festival of Jazz** is an eagerly awaited weekend of big-name musicians performing in the great outdoors.

The Oregon Coast: Fresh blackberries and quality arts and crafts draw large crowds to the **Annual Blackberry Arts Festival** in Coos Bay.

The Heart of Oregon: A carnival, agriculture and craft exhibits, lots of entertainment and plenty of junk food await at the **Oregon State Fair** in Salem. Junction City's Danish roots are celebrated during the **Scandinavian Festival** with folk dancing, food and crafts.

Vancouver and the Sunshine Coast: The popular **International Airshow** takes flight in Abbotsford just above the U.S. border, and the **Pacific National Exhibition**, a massive agricultural and industrial fair with everything from top-name entertainment to lumberjack contests, is a happening from mid-August through Labor Day in Vancouver. In Whistler, the **Whistler Classical Music Festival** brings soothing strains to the mountains.

Victoria and Vancouver Island: The glory of flight is celebrated at the **Aircraft Festival** on Salt Spring Island. Once again, hot jazz hits the spotlight in Victoria's **Market Square Jazz Festival and Sunfest.**

SEPTEMBER

Seattle: The **Bumbershoot Arts Festival** brings music, plays, art exhibits and crafts to Seattle Center. "Do the Payallup" is the catch phrase of the **Western Washington Fair** in Payallup, one of the country's largest agricultural fairs.

East of the Cascades: Bronco busting awaits at the **Ellensburg Rodeo**, ranked among the top ten rodeos in the nation. Tour the biergarten and German food circus at the **Odessa Deutches Fest**. In Oregon, the main event is the **Pendleton Roundup**, a major rodeo along with a historical parade of covered wagons and buggies and a pageant of Native American culture.

Portland and the Columbia River Gorge: Portland's **Artquake** shakes up the city with dance, music, theater performances and visual-art displays. Classic cars and planes are showcased in the **Vintage Festival** in Newberg.

The Oregon Coast: Vast quantities of salmon are slow baked over an open alderwood fire at the **Indian Style Salmon Bake** in Depoe Bay. The **Cranberry Festival** in Bandon celebrates the autumn harvest with a cranberry foods fair, crafts and a parade.

Vancouver and the Sunshine Coast: Celluloid delights from around the world are the focus of the **Vancouver International Film Festival**. Alternative performance arts take center stage during the **Vancouver Fringe Festival**. The streets of Whistler fill with clowns, jugglers, musicians and comedians who descend for the **International Festival of Street Entertainment**.

Victoria and Vancouver Island: There's a flotilla of pre-1955 wooden boats in the **Classic Boat Festival** in Victoria's Inner Harbour. Salmon is king at the **Salmon Festival** in Port Alberni.

OCTOBER

Seattle: **Salmon Days** in Issaquah features a salmon bake, races, live entertainment, arts and crafts and a parade.

Olympic Peninsula and the Washington Coast: There's plenty of seafood and entertainment along with a shucking contest at the **Oysterfest** in Shelton. Make your way through a cranberry bog and enjoy special taste treats at the **Cranberry Festival** in Long Beach.

East of the Cascades: Leavenworth is ablaze during the **Washington State Autumn Leaf Festival** complete with oompah bands and Bavarian costumes. See prize-winning livestock, produce and crafts, nibble cotton candy and enjoy a ride or two at the Central Washington State Fair in Yakima.

Portland and the Columbia Gorge: Pie eating, pumpkin carving, apple peeling and other fruit-related contests highlight the **Hood River Valley Harvest Fest.**

The Oregon Coast: Stunt flyers compete in the **World Cup Kite Competition** in Seaside. The **Cranberry Festival**, Bandon's major event, offers a football game, parade and crafts fair.

Vancouver and the Sunshine Coast: **Octoberfest** brews and oompah bands seem right at home in Whistler's Bavarian-style village.

Victoria and Vancouver Island: Victoria's proud heritage is celebrated during **British Fortnight**.

NOVEMBER

Seattle: Seattle Center is all decked out with an ice-skating rink, Christmas train display and a few arts-and-crafts booths during **Winterfest**, which runs through early January. **Zoolights** lends a festive spirit to the famous Tacoma Zoo from late November through Christmas.

The Oregon Coast: Artists, musicians, writers and craftspeople gather for the **Stormy Weather Festival** in Cannon Beach. At the **Christmas Bazaar** in Lincoln City you can pick up homemade food items suitable for gifts.

DECEMBER

Puget Sound and the San Juans: The little town of Lynden is decorated like an old Dutch community during the **Dutch Sinterklaas Celebration,** complete with gingerbread and visits with old St. Nick. **Christmas ships** cruise the Swinomish Channel in La Conner.

East of the Cascades: The Bavarian village of Leavenworth looks like a scenic Christmas card during the **Christmas Lighting Festival.** Horse-drawn wagons, barbershop quartets and carolers in costumes of the 1800s are part of the fun at the **Dicken's Old-Fashioned Christmas** in Soap Lake, Washington.

The Oregon Coast: Victorian teas, lamplighting ceremonies and productions of *The Christmas Carol* are part of the **Dickens Festival** in Cannon Beach.

The Heart of Oregon: The works of regional artists are on display at the **Umpqua Valley Christmas Artfest,** a good place to pick up those last-minute gifts.

Vancouver and the Sunshine Coast: On the 31st you can choose between two alcohol-free parties, the **New Year's Bash** with entertainment on the village square at Whistler or **First Night,** a night-long theatrical and musical series hosted by the merchants of downtown Vancouver.

Victoria and Vancouver Island: **Butchart Gardens** puts on the holiday finery with Christmas light displays throughout the month. There's also a **Christmas Ships Parade** in Victoria's Inner Harbour.

How to Deal With...

VISITOR INFORMATION

For a free copy of *Destination Washington,* contact the **Washington Tourism Division** (Department of Trade and Economic Development, 101 General Administration Building, Mail Stop AX-13, Olympia, WA 98504).

Oregon: The Official Travel Guide is available from the **Oregon Tourism Division** (Economic Development Department, 775 Summer Street Northeast, Salem, OR 97310; 800-547-7842 outside Oregon, 800-543-8838 inside Oregon).

Travel information on British Columbia is available from **Tourism British Columbia** (802, 865 Hornby Street, Vancouver, BC V6Z 2G3; 604-660-2861).

Large cities and small towns throughout the region have chambers of commerce or visitor information centers; a number of them are listed in *Hidden Pacific Northwest* under the appropriate chapter.

For visitors arriving by automobile, Washington and Oregon provide numerous **Welcome Centers** at key points along the major highways where visitors can pull off for a stretch, a cup of coffee or juice and plenty of advice on what to see and do in the area. The centers are clearly marked and are usually open during daylight hours throughout the spring, summer and fall.

PACKING

Comfortable and casual are the norm for dress in the Northwest. You will want something dressier if you plan to catch a show, indulge in high tea or spend your evenings in posh restaurants and clubs, but for the most part your topsiders and slacks are acceptable garb everywhere else.

Layers of clothing are your best bet since the weather changes so drastically depending on which part of the region you are visiting; shorts will be perfectly comfortable during the daytime in the hot, arid interior, but once you pass over the mountains and head for the coastline, you'll appreciate having packed a jacket to protect you from the nippy ocean breezes, even on the warmest of days.

Wherever you're headed, during the summer bring some long-sleeve shirts, pants and lightweight sweaters and jackets along with your shorts, T-shirts and bathing suit; the evenings can be quite crisp. Bring along those warmer clothes—pants, sweaters, jackets, hats and gloves—in spring and fall, too, since days may be warm but it's rather chilly after sundown. Winter calls for thick sweaters, knitted hats, down jackets and snug ski clothes.

It's not a bad idea to call ahead to check on weather conditions. Sturdy, comfortable walking shoes are a must for sightseeing. If you plan to explore tidal pools or go for long walks on the beach, bring a pair of lightweight canvas shoes that you don't mind getting wet.

Scuba divers will probably want to bring their own gear, though rentals are generally available in all popular dive areas. Many places also rent tubes for river floats and sailboards for windsurfing. Fishing gear is often available for rent as well. Campers will need to bring their own basic equipment.

Don't forget your camera for capturing the Pacific Northwest's glorious scenery and a pair of binoculars for watching the abundant wildlife that live here. And pack an umbrella, just in case.

HOTELS

Lodging in the Northwest runs the gamut, from rustic cabins in the woods to sprawling resorts on the coastline. Chain motels line most major thoroughfares and mom-and-pop enterprises still vie successfully for lodgers in every region. Large hotels with names you'd know anywhere appear in most centers of any size.

Bed and breakfasts, small inns and cozy lodges where you can have breakfast with the handful of other guests are appearing throughout the region as these more personable forms of accommodation continue to grow in popularity. In fact, in areas like Ashland in southern Oregon and the San Juans in Washington, they are the norm rather than hotels and motels.

Whatever your preference and budget, you can probably find something to suite your taste with the help of the regional chapters in this book. Remember, rooms are scarce and prices rise in the high season, which is generally summer along the coastline and winter in the mountain ranges. Off-season rates are often drastically reduced in many places. Whatever you do, plan ahead and make reservations, especially in the prime tourist seasons.

(Text continued on page 22.)

High Adventure in the Northwest

Whether you're an expert or a novice, a fanatic or simply curious, there's a sport here with your name written on it. Remember, the Pacific Northwest is known as "Evergreen Playground," not "Evergreen Couch Potato." So if what turns you on is dropping through the sky, paddling alongside whales or keeping your feet firmly on the ground, just do it!

For heart-stopping thrills, the newest madness to hit the Northwest is *bungee jumping*. Jumpers strapped into a full-body harness with three to five connecting bungee cords swan dive off a 180-foot-high bridge, the highest commercial bungee bridge in the Western Hemisphere. If this sounds great until you actually eyeball the 20-story drop, **Bungee Masters** (9656 Southwest Beaverton-Hillsdale Highway, Beaverton, OR 97005; 503-520-0303) will refund the jump fee. Those who make the plunge are awarded membership in the Dangerous Sports Club.

Still want to take a flying leap? *Para-gliding*, an exercise involving climbing a mountain, stepping off the edge, then gliding down in a parachute-like rig, is growing in popularity, too. In most cases, participants learn to fly in just one day. The **Oregon Paragliding Association** (1012 Northwest Wall Street, Bend, OR 97701; 503-389-5411) and **Parawest Paragliding** (Blackcomb Mountain, Whistler, BC V0N 1B0; 604-932-7052) provide qualified instruction and services.

Heli-sports, from skiing untouched powder or blue glaciers to hiking spongy, moss-covered alpine fields, are currently all the rage in the high reaches of British Columbia. The helicopter ride to inaccessible areas is the highlight for many, while others appreciate the ease of having gear packed in for them. **Canada Heli-Sports Inc.** (P.O. Box 460, Whistler, BC V0N 1B0; 604-932-2070) can provide further details.

With so many majestic ranges in the Northwest, *mountaineering* abounds. Rock and ice climbing are big draws in both the Cascades and Rocky Mountains. Climbers should be familiar with cold-weather survival techniques before tackling Northwest heights, which are tricky at best. For climber's guidelines and further information, turn to the **National Park Service** (Pacific Northwest Regional Office, 83 South King Street, Seattle, WA 98104; 206-442-4830) and the **Outdoor Recreation Council of B.C.** (1367 West Broadway, Vancouver, BC V6H 4A9). Mountaineering clubs like the **Mazamas** (909 Northwest 19th Avenue, Portland, OR 97209; 503-227-2345) and **Ptarmigans** (P.O. Box 1821, Vancouver, WA 98668) conduct classes and guided tours of Northwest peaks.

Mountain bike descents—racing down alpine slopes on two wheels—is a growing sport in resort areas of British Columbia. Participants usually take high-

performance mountain bikes on the gondola to the heights, then follow experienced guides down mountain faces that are the winter domain of skiers. **Whistler Outdoor Experience** (P.O. Box 151, Whistler, BC V0N 1B0; 604-932-3389) can tell you more.

Rest assured: There are tamer outdoor adventures here. In fact, many swear that the best way to soak in the beauty of the Pacific Northwest is to travel slowly by bike or foot. Extensive guided *bicycling and walking tours* of the scenic mountains, forests, coastline and islands of the region last anywhere from two days to weeks. Top operators include **Backroads Bicycle Touring** (1516 5th Street, Suite 1C10, Berkeley, CA 94710; 800-245-3874) and **The Sierra Club** (Outing Department, 730 Polk Street, San Francisco, CA 94109; 415-923-5630).

In this realm of lakes, streams, rivers and ocean, it's no surprise that many of the top adventure sports are water related. *Whitewater rafting* is one of the best-known adventure activities in the region, with challenging rapids on the Lewis, Snoqualmie and White rivers in Washington, the Rogue, Deschutes and McKenzie in Oregon and the Fraser and Green rivers in British Columbia. If you aren't acquainted with these rivers join a guided trip or chat with outfitters who know the treacherous spots to look out for. The **Northwest Rafter's Association** (P.O. Box 19008, Portland, OR 97219) is a good source for further information.

Kayaking and *canoeing* are also popular ways to shoot the rapids. Paddlers ready to take on the open ocean gain access to spectacular places like the various marine parks in British Columbia (Desolation Sound and the Pacific Rim National Park) and Washington (numerous protected islands among the San Juans). Other placid bodies of water suitable for kayak and canoe exploration include the Hood Canal in Washington, the Willamette and Columbia rivers in Oregon and the Powell River Canoe Route on British Columbia's Sunshine Coast. The folks at **Ebb and Flow Kayak and Canoe** (0604 Southwest Nebraska Street, Portland, OR 97201; 503-245-1756) can tell you more about the waters and outfitters of the area.

Squeezed between the border of Washington and Oregon, the breezy Columbia Gorge is reputed to be the *windsurfing* capital of the continent, with championship competitions held annually. English Bay in Vancouver and Washington's San Juan Islands are also popular destinations for the sport, with numerous outfits set up to teach would-be windsurfers or just rent the sailboards and wetsuits. The **Boardsailing Association** (P.O. Box 209, Newport, RI 02840; 401-849-5200) can put you in touch with top schools in the region.

For additional information and lists of outfitters, turn to the sports headings of each regional chapter.

Accommodations in this book are organized by region and classified according to price. Rates referred to are for two people during high season, so if you are looking for low-season bargains, it's good to inquire. *Budget* lodgings are generally less than $50 per night and are satisfactory and clean but modest. *Moderate*-priced lodgings run from $50 to $90; what they have to offer in the way of luxury will depend on where they are located, but they often offer larger rooms and more attractive surroundings. At a *deluxe* hotel or resort you can expect to spend between $90 and $130 for a double; you'll usually find spacious rooms, a fashionable lobby, a restaurant and a group of shops. *Ultra-deluxe* properties, priced above $130, are a region's finest, offering all the amenities of a deluxe hotel plus plenty of extras.

Whether you crave a room facing the surf or one looking out on the ski slopes, be sure to specify when making reservations. If you are trying to save money, keep in mind that lodgings a block or so from the waterfront or a mile or so from the ski lift are going to offer lower rates than those right on top of the area's major attractions.

RESTAURANTS

Seafood is a staple in the Pacific Northwest, especially along the coast where salmon is king. Whether it's poached in herbs or grilled on a stake Indian-style, plan to treat yourself to this regional specialty often. While each area has its own favorite dishes, its ethnic influences and gourmet spots, Northwest cuisine as a whole tends to be hearty and is often crafted around organically grown local produce.

Within a particular chapter, restaurants are categorized geographically, with each entry describing the type of cuisine, general decor and price range. Dinner entrées at *budget* restaurants usually cost under $8. The ambience is informal, service usually speedy and the crowd a local one. *Moderate*-priced restaurants range between $8 and $16 at dinner; surroundings are casual but pleasant, the menu offers more variety and the pace is usually slower. *Deluxe* establishments tab their entrées from $16 to $24; cuisines may be simple or sophisticated, depending on the location, but the decor is plusher and the service more personalized. *Ultra-deluxe* dining rooms, where entrées begin at $24, are often gourmet places where the cooking and service have become an art form.

Some restaurants change hands often while others are closed in low seasons. Efforts have been made to include in this book places with established reputations for good eating. Breakfast and lunch menus vary less in price from restaurant to restaurant than evening dinners. If you are dining on a budget and still hope to experience the best of the bunch, visit at lunch when portions and prices are reduced.

TRAVELING WITH CHILDREN

The Pacific Northwest is a wonderful place to bring the kids. Besides the many museums, boutiques and festivals set aside for them, the region also has hundreds of beaches and parks, and many nature sanctuaries sponsor children's activities, especially during the summer months. A few guidelines will help make travel with children a pleasure.

Many Northwest bed and breakfasts do not accept children, so be sure of the policy when you make reservations. If you need a crib or cot, arrange for it ahead of time. A travel agent can be of help here, as well as with most other travel plans.

If you're traveling by air, try to reserve bulkhead seats where there is plenty of room. Take along extras you may need, such as diapers, changes of clothing, snacks and toys or books. When traveling by car, be sure to carry the extras, along with plenty of juice and water. And always allow extra time for getting places, especially on rural roads.

A first-aid kit is a must for any trip. Along with adhesive bandages, antiseptic cream and something to stop itching, include any medicines your pediatrician might recommend to treat allergies, colds, diarrhea or any chronic problems your child may have.

When spending time at the beach or on the snow, take extra care the first few days. Children's skin is especially sensitive to sun, and severe sunburn can happen before you realize it, even on overcast days. Hats for the kids are a good idea, along with liberal applications of sunblock. Be sure to keep a constant eye on children who are near the water or on the slopes.

Even the smallest towns usually have stores that carry diapers, baby food, snacks and other essentials, but these may close early in the evening. Larger urban areas usually have all-night grocery or convenience stores that stock these necessities.

Many towns, parks and attractions offer special activities designed just for children. Consult local newspapers and/or phone the numbers in this guide to see what's happening where you're going.

BEING AN OLDER TRAVELER

The Pacific Northwest is a hospitable place for senior citizens to visit, especially during the cool, sunny summer months that offer respite from hotter climes elsewhere in the country. Countless museums, historic sights and even restaurants and hotels offer senior discounts that can cut a substantial chunk off vacation costs. The national park system's Golden Age Passport, which must be applied for in person, allows free admission for anyone 62 and older to the numerous national parks and monuments in the region.

The **American Association of Retired Persons** (AARP) (921 Southwest Morrison, Room 521, Portland, OR 97205; 503-227-5268) offers membership to anyone over 50. AARP's benefits include travel discounts with a number of firms; escorted tours and cruises are available through AARP Travel Experience/American Express (400 Pinnacle Way, Suite 450, Norcross, GA 30071; 800-927-0111).

Elderhostel (75 Federal Street, Boston, MA 02110; 617-426-7788) offers reasonably priced, all-inclusive educational programs in a variety of Pacific Northwest locations throughout the year.

The federal government offers an informative brochure, *Travel Tips for Senior Citizens* (Superintendent of Documents, Government Printing Office, Washington, DC 20402; 202-783-3238) for a nominal fee.

Be extra careful about health matters. In addition to the medications you ordinarily use, it's a good idea to bring along the prescriptions for obtaining more. Consider carrying a medical record with you—including your medical history and current medical status as well as your doctor's name, phone number and address. Make sure your insurance covers you while you are away from home.

BEING DISABLED

Oregon, Washington and British Columbia are striving to make more destinations accessible for the disabled traveler. For information on the areas you will be visiting, contact the **Resource Center for the Handicapped** (20150 45th Avenue Northeast, Seattle, WA 98155; 206-362-2273) and **Access Oregon** (2600 Southeast Belmont Street, Suite A, Portland, OR 97214; 503-230-1225).

Evergreen Travel (4114 198th Street Southwest #13, Lynnwood, WA 98036-6742; 800-435-2288 or 206-776-1184) specializes in tours of the Pacific Northwest for the handicapped.

For more specific advice on traveling in the region, turn to the *Oregon Guide To Accessibility* or the *Oregon Coast Access Guide* available from the **Spinal Cord Association** (825 Northeast Multnomah Street #1075, Portland, OR 97232; 503-239-9148), *Access Seattle* from the **Easter Seal Society** (521 2nd Avenue West, Seattle, WA 98119; 206-284-5706) and *British Columbia Travel Guide for the Disabled* available from the **Ministry of Tourism** (802 Hornsby Street, Vancouver, BC V6Z 2G3; 206-660-2861).

The **Society for the Advancement of Travel for the Handicapped** (347 5th Avenue, Suite 610, New York, NY 10016; 212-447-7284), **Travel Information Service** (Moss Rehabilitation Hospital, 1200 West Tabor Road, Philadelphia, PA 19141-3099; 215-329-5715), **Mobility International USA** (P.O. Box 3551, Eugene, OR 97403; 503-343-1284) and **Flying Wheels Travel** (P.O. Box 382, Owatonna, MN 55060; 800-533-0363) offer general information. Also providing assistance is **Travelin' Talk** (P.O. Box 3534, Clarksville, TN 37043; 615-552-6670), a networking organization.

BEING A WOMAN TRAVELING ALONE

It is sad commentary on life in the United States, but women traveling alone must take precautions. It's entirely unwise to hitchhike and probably best to avoid inexpensive accommodations on the outskirts of town; the money saved does not outweigh the risk. Bed and breakfasts, youth hostels, college dorms and YWCAs are generally your safest bet for lodging.

If you are hassled or threatened in some way, never be afraid to scream for assistance. It's a good idea to carry change for a phone call and to know the number to call in case of emergency.

Women alone will usually feel much safer in British Columbia, especially in the well-populated areas. However, it's a good idea to remain cautious just the same.

BEING A FOREIGN TRAVELER

PASSPORTS AND VISAS   Most foreign visitors are required to obtain a passport and tourist visa to enter the United States. Contact your nearest United States Embassy or Consulate well in advance to obtain a visa and to check on any other entry requirements. Entry into Canada calls for a valid passport, visa or visitor permit for all foreign visitors except those from the United States, Commonwealth countries or Western Europe, who should carry some proof of citizenship (driver's license, voter's registration or birth certificate), including two pieces with photo identification. The necessary forms may be obtained from your nearest Canadian Embassy, Consulate or High Commissioner.

CUSTOMS REQUIREMENTS   Foreign travelers are allowed to bring in the following: 200 cigarettes (or 100 cigars), $400 worth of duty-free gifts, including one liter of alcohol (you must be at least 21 years of age) and any amount of currency (amounts over U.S. $10,000 require a form). Americans who have been in Canada over 48 hours may take out $400 worth of duty-free items ($25 worth of duty-free for visits under 48 hours). Carry any prescription drugs in clearly marked containers; you may have to provide a written prescription or doctor's statement to clear customs. Meat or meat products, seeds, plants, fruits and narcotics are not allowed to be brought into the United States. The same applies to Canada, with the addition of firearms.

DRIVING   If you plan to rent a car, an international driver's license should be obtained prior to arrival. United States driver's licenses are valid in Canada and vice versa. Some rental car companies require both a foreign license and an international driver's license along with a major credit card and require that the lessee be at least 25 years of age.

CURRENCY   American and Canadian money is based on the dollar. Bills in the United States generally come in six denominations: $1, $5, $10, $20, $50 and $100. Every dollar is divided into 100 cents; in Canada the $1 coin is generally used. Coins are the penny (1 cent), nickel (5 cents), dime (10 cents) and quarter (25 cents). You may not use foreign currency to purchase goods and services in the United States and Canada. Consider buying traveler's checks in dollar amounts. You may also use credit cards affiliated with an American company such as Interbank, Barclay Card, VISA and American Express.

WEIGHTS AND MEASUREMENTS   The United States uses the English system of weights and measures. American units and their metric equivalents are as follows: 1 inch = 2.5 centimeters; 1 foot = 0.3 meter; 1 yard = 0.9 meter; 1 mile = 1.6 kilometers; 1 ounce = 28 grams; 1 pound = 0.45 kilogram; 1 quart (liquid) = 0.9 liter. British Columbia now uses metric measurements.

The Sporting Life

CAMPING

Parks in the lush Pacific Northwest rank among the top in North America as far as attendance goes, so plan ahead if you hope to do any camping during the busy summer months. Late spring and early fall present fewer crowds to deal with and the weather is still fine.

Though much of Washington's scenic coastline is privately owned, there are a few scattered parks along the shore and even more situated inland in the mountains. It is possible to reserve campsites at 12 state parks from Memorial Day through Labor Day; contact the **State Parks and Recreation Commission** (7150 Cleanwater Lane, Olympia, WA 98504; 206-753-2027) for details.

You'll find a multitude of marvelous campsites along Oregon's protected coast and in its green mountain ranges. Sixteen of the 50 state parks with campgrounds are open year-round. Reservations are accepted at 13 parks between Memorial Day and Labor Day and are essential if you hope to get a spot during July and August. The **State Parks and Recreation Division** (525 Trade Street Southeast, Salem, OR 97310) maintains a **Campsite Information Center** (503-238-7488 or 800-452-5687 outside Portland) to provide updated campsite availability.

For information on camping in the various national parks and forests of Washington and Oregon, contact the **National Park Service** (Pacific Northwest Regional Office, 83 South King Street, Seattle, WA 98104; 206-442-4830).

Many of British Columbia's prime wilderness areas, both marine and interior, are protected as provincial parks. Except for those that are day-use only areas, most parks are set up with some sort of camping facilities, from primitive sites with pit toilets to pull-through recreational vehicle pads (with nearby sani-stations but no electrical, water or sewage hook-ups). There is a minimal fee for use of the campsites available on a first-come, first-served basis throughout the year. For further information, contact **Ministry of Parks** (1610 Mount Seymour Road, North Vancouver, BC V7G 1L3; 604-929-1291) or the **Outdoor Recreation Council of B.C.** (1367 West Broadway, Vancouver, BC V6H 4A9).

For information on camping at the Pacific Rim National Park on Vancouver Island's western shore and other national parks in British Columbia, contact **Parks Canada West Region** (134 11th Avenue Southeast, Calgary, Alberta T2G 0Y5; 403-231-4401).

WILDERNESS PERMITS

Wilderness camping is not permitted in the state parks of Oregon and Washington, but there are primitive sites available in most parks. Permits are required for wilderness camping in parts of the Alpine Lakes wilderness area of the Mt. Baker-Snoqualmie and Wenatchee national forests in Washington and in the Mt. Jefferson, Mt. Washington and Three Sisters wilderness areas of Oregon between May 24 and October 31; permits are available at the ranger stations. Permits are not required in all other national park and forest areas.

Follow low-impact camping practices in wilderness areas; "leave only footprints, take only pictures." When backpacking and hiking, stick to marked trails or tread lightly in areas where no trail exists. Be prepared with map and compass since signs are limited to directional information and don't include mileage. Guidelines on wilderness camping are available from the **USDA Forest Service** (Pacific Northwest Region, P.O. Box 3623, Portland, OR 97208; 503-326-2877).

In British Columbia, wilderness camping is allowed in Garibaldi, Manning, Strathcona and Cape Scott provincial parks. No permit is required, but it's always best to check in with a ranger station to let someone know your plan before heading into the back country. A new BC Parks regulation states that wilderness camping is now permitted in any large provincial park provided that it is done one kilometer inland from any roadway. Contact the **Ministry of Parks** (1610 Mount Seymour Road, North Vancouver, BC V7G 1L3; 604-929-1291) for details.

Wilderness camping is also permitted in British Columbia's national parks. Write to the **Canadian Parks Service** (Western Region, #220 Fourth Avenue Southeast, P.O. Box 2989, Stations M, Calgary, Alberta T2P 3H8) for more information.

BOATING

With miles of coastline and island-dotted straits to explore, it's no wonder that boating is one of the most popular activities in the Northwest. Many of the best attractions in the region, including numerous pristine marine parks, are accessible only by water and have facilities set aside for boaters.

Write to the **State Parks and Recreation Commission** (7150 Cleanwater Lane, KY-11, Olympia, WA 98504) for a boater's guide to Washington. The **Oregon State Marine Board** (3000 Market Street Northeast #505, Salem, OR 97301; 503-378-8587) will furnish information on boating throughout the state.

Boaters heading into British Columbian waters from the United States must clear customs at the first available port of entry; **Tourism British Columbia** (802, 865 Hornby Street, Vancouver, BC V6Z 2G3; 604-660-2861) can provide further information on customs as well as details on reserving moorage space during the busy summer months.

There are several waterways suitable for extended canoeing and kayaking trips. The **Recreational Canoeing Association of B.C.** (1367 West Broadway, Vancouver, BC V6H 4A9; 604-275-6651) can provide more information as can the **American Canoe Association** (P.O. Box 190, Newington, VA 22120; 703-550-7523), publishers of *Canoe Magazine*.

Whitewater rafting is particularly popular, especially on the Rogue and Deschutes in Oregon and the Fraser River in British Columbia where you will find outfitters renting equipment and running tours throughout the summer months. The *White Water River Book* (Pacific Research, 1982) is a good guide to techniques, equipment and safety.

WATER SAFETY

The watery region of the Pacific Northwest offers an incredible array of watersports to choose from, be it on the ocean, a quiet lake or stream or tumbling rapids. Swimming, scuba diving, walking the shoreline in search of clams or just basking in the sun are options when you get to the shore, lake or river.

Shallow lakes, rivers and bays tend to be the most popular spots since they warm up during the height of summer; otherwise, the waters of the Northwest are generally chilly. Whenever you swim, never do so alone, and never take your eyes off of children in or near the water.

FISH AND FISHING

With its multitude of rivers, streams, lakes and miles of protected coastline, the Pacific Northwest affords some of the best fishing in the world. The waters of British Columbia alone hold 74 known species, 25 of those sportfish. Salmon is the main draw, but each area features special treats for the fishing enthusiast that are described in the individual chapters of *Hidden Pacific Northwest*.

Fees and regulations vary, but licenses are required for salt and freshwater fishing throughout the region and can be purchased at sporting-goods stores, bait-and-tackle shops and fishing lodges. You can also find leads on guides and charter services in these locations if you are interested in trying a kind of fishing that's new to you. Charter fishing is the most expensive way to go out to sea; party boats take a crowd but are less expensive and usually great fun. On rivers, lakes and streams, guides can show you the best place to throw a hook or skim a fly. Whatever your pleasure, in saltwater or fresh, a good guide will save you time and grief and will increase the likelihood of a full string or a handsome trophy.

For further information on fishing in Washington, contact the **Washington Department of Fisheries** (115 General Administration Building, Olympia, WA 98504; 206-586-1425) concerning shellfish, bottomfish, salmon and saltwater sportfish and the **Washington State Department of Wildlife** (600 North Capitol Way, Olympia, WA 98501; 206-753-5700) concerning freshwater game fish.

The **Oregon Department of Fish and Wildlife** (P.O. Box 59, Portland, OR 97207; 503-229-5403) can supply information on fishing in the state.

For updated details and regulations for freshwater fishing in British Columbia, contact the **B.C. Fish Branch** (Ministry of Environment, 810 Blanshard Street, Victoria, BC V8V 1X5; 604-387-4573) or the **Recreational Fisheries Division** (Department of Fisheries and Oceans, 555 West Hastings Street, Vancouver, BC V6B 5G3; 604-666-3271) for saltwater fishing.

SKIING

As winter blankets the major mountain ranges of the Pacific Northwest, ski season heats up at numerous resorts. Ski enthusiasts head for Mt. Adams, Mt. Rainier and Mt. Baker in Washington, Mt. Hood, Mt. Bachelor and Mt. Ashland in Oregon and Mt. Seymour, Grouse Mountain and the Whistler/Blackcomb mountains in southwestern British Columbia. Specifics on the top resorts are listed in each regional chapter.

For additional ski information on Washington and Oregon, contact the **Pacific Northwest Ski Association** (640 Northwest Gilman Boulevard #104, Issaquah, WA 98027; 206-392-4220). For information on skiing in British Columbia, obtain a copy of *Ski With Us!* from **Tourism British Columbia** (Parliament Buildings, Victoria, BC V8V 1X4).

CHAPTER TWO

Seattle and Southern Puget Sound

Rain city? Not today. Last night's storm has washed the air clean, swept away yesterday's curtain of clouds to reveal Mt. Rainier in all its astonishing glory. From your hotel room window you can see the Olympics rising like snow-tipped daggers beyond the blue gulf of Puget Sound. Below, downtown Seattle awakens to sunshine, espresso and the promise of a day brimming with discovery for the fortunate traveler.

The lesson here is twofold: Don't be daunted by Seattle's reputation for nasty weather, and don't limit yourself to anticipating its natural setting and magnificent greenery, awesome as they may be. For this jewel surrounded by water, earning it the nickname "The Emerald City," sparkles in ways too numerous to count after a decade or more of extraordinary growth.

Both greater Seattle and Southern Puget Sound, which we also explore in this chapter, have changed dramatically. The city, squeezed into a lean, hour-glass shape between Elliott Bay and Lake Washington, covers only 92 square miles, and its population is still under 600,000. But the greater metropolitan area, reaching from Everett to Tacoma and east to the Cascade foothills, now boasts some 2.6 million, and the entire Puget Sound basin claims perhaps three million of the state's nearly five million residents.

While most newcomers have settled in the suburbs, Seattle's soaring skyline downtown is the visual focus of a region on the move. No longer the sleepy sovereign of Puget Sound, Seattle today is clearly the most muscular of the Northwest's three largest cities. Its urban energy is admired even by those who bemoan Seattle's freeway congestion, suburban sprawl, crime and worrisome air and water pollution. Growth has been the engine

31

of change, and although the pace has slowed in the '90s, the challenges posed by too rapid an expansion remain persistent topics of discussion.

Seattle offered no hint of its future prominence when pioneers began arriving on Elliott Bay some 140 years ago. Like other settlements around Puget Sound, Seattle survived by farming, fishing, shipbuilding, logging and coal mining. For decades the community hardly grew at all. One whimsical theory has it that because the frontier sawmill town offered a better array of brothels to the region's loggers, miners and fishermen, capital tended to flow into Seattle to fund later investment and expansion.

Whatever the reason, the city quickly rebuilt after the disastrous "Great Fire" of 1889. But it would be another eight years before the discovery of gold in Alaska put Seattle on the map. On July 17, 1897, the ship *Portland* steamed into Elliott Bay from Alaska, bearing its legendary "ton of gold" (actually, nearly two tons), triggering the Klondike Gold Rush. Seattle immediately emerged as chief outfitter to thousands of would-be miners heading north to the gold fields.

Today, Seattle remains tied to its traditions. It's so close to the sea that 20-pound salmon are still hooked in Elliott Bay, at the feet of those gleaming, new skyscrapers. It's so near its waterfront that the boom of ferry horns resonates among its buildings, and the cries of gulls still pierce the rumble of traffic. But the city's (and the state's) economy has grown beyond the old resource-based industries. International trade, tourism, agriculture and software giants like Microsoft now lead the way. The spotlight has passed from building ships to building airplanes, from wood chips to micro-chips, from mining coal to cultivating the fertile fields of tourism.

In the process, one of the nation's most vibrant economies has emerged. You can see that energy in Seattle's highrises, feel it in the buoyant street scene fueled in part by locals' infatuation with espresso (you'll find an espresso bar on nearly every downtown street corner, and drive-through espresso spots in the suburbs). And there is fresh energy beneath your very feet. A "new underground" of retail shops (as distinguished from the historic Pioneer Square Underground) is taking shape around stations in the downtown Metro Transit Tunnel, opened in fall 1990.

Civic energy has produced a glorious art museum downtown, a small but lively "people place" in Westlake Park, a spacious convention center and additions to Freeway Park. Private enterprise has added hotels, office towers with grand lobbies brimming with public art, shopping arcades, restaurants, nightclubs and bistros.

During the late '80s, as locals struggled with construction chaos, Seattle's downtown briefly suffered the nickname "little Beirut." Thankfully, that disruption has passed. For now, downtown is relatively peaceful, accessible and rich in discoveries for visitors.

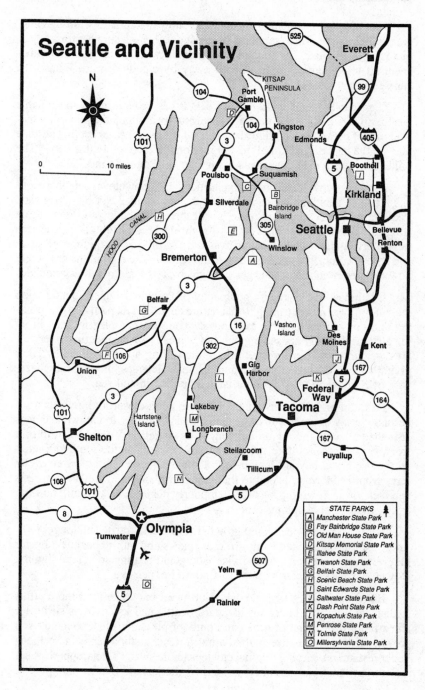

Seattle and Vicinity

N

0   10 miles

525
Everett

KITSAP PENINSULA

104
Port Gamble
D

104
Kingston

3
Edmonds

99

101

405

5
Boothell
I

Poulsbo
Suquamish
C
Kirkland

Silverdale
B
Bainbridge Island

HOOD CANAL
H

305

E
Seattle

Bellevue
Renton

300

Winslow

Bremerton
A

3

Belfair
G

16

Vashon Island

Des Moines
J
Kent

302

167

F 106
Union

Gig Harbor
L

K
Federal Way

164

3

Lakebay
M
Longbranch

Tacoma

101

Shelton

Steilacoom

167
Puyallup

108

101

N

Tillicum

5

8

Olympia
Tumwater

O

Yelm
507

5
Rainier

STATE PARKS
A	Manchester State Park
B	Fay Bainbridge State Park
C	Old Man House State Park
D	Kitsap Memorial State Park
E	Illahee State Park
F	Twanoh State Park
G	Belfair State Park
H	Scenic Beach State Park
I	Saint Edwards State Park
J	Saltwater State Park
K	Dash Point State Park
L	Kopachuk State Park
M	Penrose State Park
N	Tolmie State Park
O	Millersylvania State Park

Historically, weather bureau statistics show that mid-July through mid-August brings the driest, sunniest, warmest weather—a sure bet for tourists, or so you'd suppose. But in the last decade or two, that mid-summer guarantee all too often has been washed away by clouds or rain. What's the sun-seeking tourist to do?

Consider September. In recent years it has brought modestly reliable weather. Or, simply come prepared—spiritually and practically—for whatever mix of dreary and sublime days that fate delivers. An accepting attitude may be the best defense of all in a region once described in this way: "The mildest winter I ever spent was a summer on Puget Sound."

Have goofy weather, growth, gentrification of downtown neighborhoods and a tide of new immigrants eradicated the old Seattle? Not by a long shot. Pike Place Market's colorful maze is still there to beguile you. Ferry boats still glide like wedding cakes across a night-darkened Elliott Bay. The central waterfront is as clamorous, gritty and irresistible as ever. Pioneer Square and its catacomb-like underground still beckons. The soul of the city somehow endures even as the changes wrought by regional growth accumulate.

It is indeed the changing geography of the wider Puget Sound region that may appear more striking. What nature created here, partly by the grinding and gouging of massive lowland glaciers, is a complex mosaic. From the air, arriving visitors see a green-blue tapestry of meandering river valleys weaving between forested ridges, the rolling uplands dotted by lakes giving way to Cascade foothills and distant volcanoes, the intricate mazeway of Southern Puget Sound's island-studded inland sea.

From on high it seems almost pristine, but a closer look reveals a sobering overlay of manmade changes. Even as Seattle's downtown becomes "Manhattanized," the region is being "Los Angelized" with the birth of a freeway commuter culture stretching from Olympia on the south to Everett on the north and beyond Issaquah on the east. Some commuters arrive by ferry from Bainbridge Island to the west. Farmlands and wetlands, forests and meadows, are giving way to often poorly planned, hastily built housing tracts, roads and shopping centers.

For the traveler, such rapid growth means more traffic and longer ferry line-ups; more crowded campgrounds, parks and public beaches; busier bikeways and foot trails; more folks fishing and boating and clam-digging. Downtown parking can be hard to find and expensive.

But despair not. The legendary Northwest may take a bit more effort to discover, but by almost any standard Seattle and its environs still offer an extraordinary blend of urban and outdoor pleasures close to hand. And growth seems only to have spurred a much richer cultural scene in Seattle—better restaurants serving original cuisines, more swank hotels, superb opera and a vital theater community, more art galleries and livelier shopping in a retail core sprinkled with public plazas that reach out to passers-by with summer noon-hour concerts.

In this chapter we will point you to familiar landmarks, help you discover some "hidden" treasures and find the best of what's new downtown as we look at a region that reaches from Olympia to Everett, Bremerton to Issaquah.

Downtown Seattle

Flying in to Seattle, the central part of this lush region looks irresistible. From the air you'll be captivated by deep bays, harbors, gleaming skyscrapers, parks stretching for miles and hillside neighborhoods where waterskiing begins from the backyard. Central Seattle's neighborhoods offer a seemingly inexhaustible array of possibilities from the International District to Lake Union and the waterfront to Capitol Hill. Eminently walkable, this area can also be explored by monorail, boat and bike. From the lofty heights of the Space Needle to the city's unique underground tour this is one of the Northwest's best bets.

Downtown Seattle (Pioneer Square to Seattle Center, the waterfront to Route 5) is compact enough for walkers to tour on foot. Energetic folks can see the highlights on one grand loop tour, or you can sample smaller chunks on successive days. Since downtown is spread along a relatively narrow north-south axis, you can walk from one end to the other, then return by public transit via buses in the new Metro Transit Tunnel or aboard the Waterfront Streetcar trolleys, each of which have stations in both Pioneer Square and the International District. The Alweg Monorail also runs north-south between Westlake Center and Seattle Center.

A good place to orient yourself is the **Seattle-King County Tourism Development Office** (520 Pike Street, Suite 1300; 206-461-5840). There's also a visitors' information center on the baggage level of Sea-Tac International Airport (206-433-5217).

Pioneer Square and its "old underground" remain one of Seattle's major fascinations. It was at this location that Seattle's first business district began. In 1889 a fire burned the woodframe city to the ground. The story of how the city rebuilt out of the ashes of the Great Fire seems forever intriguing to visitors and locals alike.

To learn exactly how the underground was created after the new city arose, then was forgotten, then rediscovered, you really need to take the one-and-a-half-hour **Underground Tour** (from Doc Maynard's Tavern, 610 1st Avenue; 206-682-4646). Several of these subterranean pilgrimages are offered daily to the dark and cobwebby bowels of the underground—actually the street-level floors of buildings that were sealed off and fell into disuse when streets and sidewalks were elevated shortly after Pioneer Square was rebuilt (in fire-resistant brick instead of wood).

Above ground, in sunshine and fresh air, you can stroll through 88 acres of mostly century-old architecture in the historic district (maps and directories to district businesses are available in most shops). Notable architecture includes gems like the **Grand Central Building** (1st Avenue South and South Main Street), **Merrill Place** (1st Avenue South and South Jackson Street), the **Maynard Building** (1st Avenue South and South Washington Street), the cast-iron **Pergola** in Pioneer Square Park and facing buildings such as the **Mutual Life and Pioneer buildings** (1st Avenue and Yesler Way). More than 30 art galleries are located in the Pioneer Square area. Here you can shop for Native American art, handicrafts, paintings and pottery.

1st Avenue and Yesler Way is at the heart of the district. **Yesler Way** itself originated as the steep "Skid Road" for logs cut on the hillsides above the harbor and bound for Henry Yesler's waterfront mill, and thence to growing cities like San Francisco. Later, as the district declined, Yesler Way attracted a variety of derelicts and became the prototype for every big city's bowery, alias "skid row."

The new city boomed during the Alaska Gold Rush. For a look back at those extraordinary times, stop by the Seattle office of the **Klondike Gold Rush National Historical Park** (117 South Main Street near Occidental Park; 206-553-7220) where you can see gold-panning demonstrations, a collection of artifacts, films and other memorabilia.

The main pedestrian artery is **Occidental Mall and Park**, a tree-lined, cobbled promenade running south from Yesler Way to South Jackson Street allowing pleasant ambling between rows of shops and galleries (don't miss the oasis of **Waterfall Park** off Occidental on South Main Street).

For an overview of the whole district, ride the rattling, old, manually operated elevator to the observation level of the 42-story **Smith Tower** (2nd Avenue and Yesler Way) built in 1914.

Sharp ethnic diversity has always marked the **International District**, next door to Pioneer Square to the southeast (South Main to South Weller streets, 5th to 8th avenues South). The polyglot community that emerged on the southern fringes of old Seattle always mixed its Asian cultures and continues doing so today, setting it apart from the homogeneous Chinatowns of San Francisco or Vancouver across the border in British Columbia.

Chinese began settling here in the 1880s, Japanese around 1900, and today the "I.D." as it's commonly known is also home to Koreans, Filipinos, Vietnamese and Cambodians. For all its diversity, the district clearly lacks the economic vitality, bustling street life and polished tourist appeal of other major Chinatowns. Yet some find the International District all the more genuine for its unhurried, even seedy, ambience.

A variety of mom-and-pop enterprises predominates—specialty-food and grocery stores, herbal-medicine shops, dim sum palaces and fortune-cookie factories. You're welcome to poke in for a look at how cookies, noodles, egg rolls and won ton wrappers are made at the **Tsue Chong Co.** (801 South King Street; 206-623-0801). To see a variety of ethnic foodstuffs, drop by **City Produce** (South Lane Street and 7th Avenue South; 206-682-0320), a wholesale vegetable market with retail sales. The district's single major retail store is **Uwajimaya** (6th Avenue South and South King Street; 206-624-6248); it's not only the largest Japanese department store in the Northwest but also a worthwhile experience of Asian culture even if you're not shopping.

Wing Luke Asian Museum (407 7th Avenue South; 206-623-5124; admission) offers a well-rounded look at the district's history and cultural mix with presentations that include an early-day Japanese store, historical photography and rotating exhibits from Asian countries. You'll also see paintings, ceramics, prints, sculpture and other art.

The **Nippon Kan Theater** (620 South Washington Street; 206-624-2151) is the centerpiece of the **Kobe Park Building National Historical Site** and offers occasional dramas and other cultural presentations. The park and community gardens adjacent to it offer pleasant strolling. **Hing Hay Park** (South King Street and Maynard Avenue South) is the scene of frequent festivals—exhibitions of Japanese martial arts, Chinese folk dances, Vietnamese food fairs, Korean music and the like. Its colorful pavilion comes from Taipei in Taiwan.

The old **waterfront** beginning at the western edge of Pioneer Square remains one of the most colorful quarters of the city and what many consider Seattle's liveliest "people place." The waterfront grows more interesting by the year, a beguiling jumble of fish bars and excursion-boat docks, ferries and fireboats, import emporiums and nautical shops, sway-backed old piers and barnacle-encrusted pilings that creak in the wash of wakes. On sunny summer days, the waterfront's the most popular tourist draw in the city.

The action's concentrated between Piers 48 and 60, and again around Pier 70. Poking around by foot remains the favorite way to explore, but some folks prefer to hopscotch to specific sites aboard the **Waterfront Streetcar** which runs from Pioneer Square to Pier 70 (you also can climb into a horse-drawn carriage here for a narrated tour). Still another way to do it is via boat (see "Hey! The Water's Fine" below). Here's a sampler of attractions: As you stroll south to north, you'll encounter a harbor-watch facility, a dozen historical plaques that trace major events, a public boat landing, the state-ferry terminal at Coleman Dock and the waterfront fire station whose fireboats occasionally put on impressive, fountain-like displays on summer weekends. Ye Olde Curiosity Shop houses a collection of odd goods from around the world, Ivar's is the city's most famous fish bar, and cavernous shopping arcades include pier-end restaurants, outdoor picnic areas and public fishing. **Central Waterfront Park** is a crescent-shaped retreat from commercialism presenting sweeping views over the harbor.

The **Seattle Aquarium** (Piers 59 and 60; 206-386-4320; admission) allows you to descend to an underwater viewing dome for up-close looks at scores of Puget Sound fish. Next to the aquarium is the **Omnidome Theater** (Pier 59; 206-622-1868; admission). This highly recommended program features the 1980 Mt. St. Helens eruption as well as an overview of the devastation you can see on your own Northwest tour.

Across Alaskan Way is the 155-step Pike Hillclimb leading past cliff-side shops up to Pike Place Market. You'll also pass some piers whose sheds have been leveled to provide public access, the last vestiges of working waterfront on the central harbor—fish-company docks and such—as well as the Port of Seattle headquarters.

The venerable market, born in 1907, has proved itself one of the city's renewable treasures. Saved from the wrecking ball by citizen action in the early '70s, the market was later revitalized through long-term renovation. Today, the seven-acre **Pike Place Market National Historic District**, and the surrounding neighborhood, are in many respects better than ever. The main historic market (Virginia to Pike streets, 1st to Western avenues) now offers 400 different products in 40 categories, some 600 businesses, about 250 farmers, 225 craftsworkers and a good 50 restaurants and eateries. In all, a market experience unparalleled in the nation! To learn more, take the **Market Classroom Tour** (206-682-7453).

There are so many ways to enjoy the market that we can scarcely begin to list them. Come early for breakfast and wake up with the market (at least a dozen cafés open early). Come at noon for the ultimate experience of marketplace clamor amid legions of jostling shoppers, vendors hawking salmon and truck-farm produce, and street musicians vying for your contributions. Come to explore the market's lower level, often missed by tourists, a warren-like collection of second-hand treasures, old books, magazines, posters and vintage clothing. Come to shop for the largest collection of handmade merchandise in the Northwest on handcraft tables at the market's north end. Come to browse all the "nonproduce" merchandise surrounding the main market—wines, exotic imported foods, French kitchenwares, jewelry and avant garde fashions.

One of the most valuable Pacific Northwest museums of the '90s is the **Seattle Art Museum** (1320 2nd Avenue; 206-625-8969; admission) east of Pike Place Market, designed by the husband/wife architectural team of Robert Venturi and Denise Scott. The five-story, limestone-faced building highlighted with terra-cotta and marble has quickly become a regional, Post-Modern landmark. You'll enter via a grand staircase lined with Chinese Ming and Qing dynasty statuary. The catch is that this is the stairway to nowhere. To see the collection you'll have to descend an elevator to the galleries. Known for its Northwest Coast Native American, Asian and African art, the museum also features Meso-American, Andean, modern and contemporary art, photography and European masters. Do not miss the superb collection of African masks.

City center, or **Downtown**, has undergone a remarkable rejuvenation. It's a delightful place to stroll whether you're intent on shopping or not. Major downtown hotels are clustered in the retail core, allowing easy walks in any direction. Here's one way to sightsee:

Start at the south end of **Freeway Park** (6th Avenue and Seneca Street). The park's many waterfalls and pools create a splashy, burbling sound barrier to city noise. Beds of summer-blooming flowers, tall evergreens and leafy deciduous trees create a genuine park feeling, inspiring picnics by office workers on their noon-hour break. Amble north through the park, and take a short detour beneath a street overpass toward University Street (steps next to more waterfalls zigzag up to Capitol Hill and dramatic views of city architecture). Continue north as the park merges with similarly landscaped grounds of the **Washington State Convention and Trade Center** (800 Convention Place; 206-447-5000) with occasional exhibits as well as maps and tourist information.

Head west through linking landscaping that leads you past yet more waterfalls and flowers in the main plaza of **Two Union Square**. Cross 6th Avenue and enter **Pacific First Center** on the corner of Union Street. This handsome, new building's lower levels are lined with upscale shops and a theater complex, bold sculptures and stunning exhibits of colorful art glass. Wander and admire for a bit, stop for a meal or an espresso, then continue by leaving the building at the 5th Avenue and Pike Street exit. Cross 5th Avenue past the striking Coliseum Theater to Nordstrom. Head west on Pike Street to 4th Avenue and turn right, shortly entering triangular **Westlake Park** (4th Avenue and Pine Street), which offers a "water wall" against street noise, a leafy copse of trees and an intriguing pattern of bricks that replicate a Salish Indian basket weave design best observed from the terraces on the adjoining **Westlake Center**.

The center is an enormously popular, multilevel shopping arcade, a people place offering cafés and espresso, a brew pub, flower vendors, handicrafts and access to what's been heralded as downtown's "new underground." The marbled, well-lighted, below-street-level arcades were created as part of the city's new downtown transit tunnel. Metro buses (propelled electrically while underground) rumble by on the lowest level. Just above it are mezzanines full of public art, with vendors and shops, and underground access to a string of department stores.

Walk south on 4th Avenue a few blocks to **Rainier Square** (4th and 5th avenues, University and Union streets) and discover another burgeoning underground of upscale enterprises. Follow its passageways eastward past a bakery, restaurants and access to the venerable **Fifth Avenue Theater**. Continue east, up an escalator back to Two Union Square and Freeway Park.

DOWNTOWN SEATTLE HOTELS

Lodgings vary widely in style and price throughout the Seattle area. Downtown, there's a thick cluster of expensive luxury hotels interspersed with a few at moderate and even budget rates.

The **Alexis Hotel** (1007 1st Avenue; 206-624-4844) is an elegant, little haven a block from the waterfront and close to downtown stores and business centers. The 54 rooms have soft colors and contemporary furnishings mixed with a few antiques, all done in good taste. Some of the roomy suites have fireplaces. Breakfast is complimentary, and the service is unmatched in this renovated historic hotel. Ultra-deluxe.

Seattle has only one place to stay that is directly on the waterfront: the **Edgewater Inn** (2411 Alaskan Way; 206-728-7000). It began as a top-flight hotel on Pier 67 in the 1960s, later slid into decay and was recently renovated in "mountain lodge" style—meaning plaid comforters and peeled-log furniture in the rooms and an antler chandelier in the lobby. Half the 238 rooms and suites have stunning views of Elliott Bay, West Seattle and the Olympic Peninsula. Rooms are comfortable, and the staff is accommodating. The restaurant has a fine water view. Deluxe to ultra-deluxe.

A retreat from the throngs in Pike Place Market is **Inn at the Market** (86 Pine Street; 206-443-3600). The hotel, several shops and a restaurant are centered by a brick courtyard with a 50-year-old cherry tree. Small (65 rooms), light and airy and furnished in French country style, the ultra-deluxe-priced inn is one of Seattle's best. Rooms have views of the city, courtyard or water.

Pensione Nichols (1923 1st Avenue; 206-441-7125) is a rare find—European-style lodging within a block of Pike Place Market. Nine rooms on the third floor of a historic building share three baths and a large common space with a stunning view of the bay. Most of the rooms, painted a cheerful yellow, have skylights but no windows and are furnished simply; there are some antiques. The front two are larger and have windows facing 1st Avenue. A continental breakfast is served. Moderate.

The **Seattle International Youth Hostel** (84 Union Street; 206-622-5443) is a low-priced establishment on the edge of Pike Place Market. In addition to 126 sleeping units, the bright, clean hotel has a kitchen, dining room, lounge and small library. Its closure between 11 and 4 daily and a midnight curfew on weekends might make it inconvenient for some people. Budget.

The **Four Seasons Olympic** (411 University Street; 206-621-1700) is the place to stay for classic grandeur and luxury. Priced in the ultra-deluxe range, it offers spacious, well-furnished rooms with a subtle oriental flavor. There are three restaurants, a stately marble lobby, meeting rooms and a myriad amenities. The Italian Renaissance hotel, built in 1924, stands in the heart of the downtown business district.

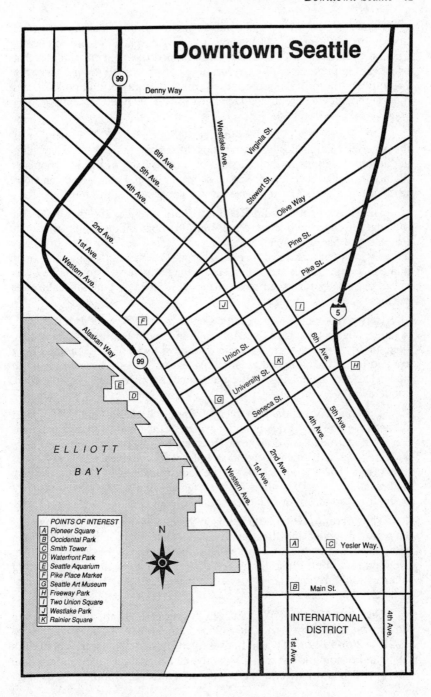

Downtown Seattle

POINTS OF INTEREST
A	Pioneer Square
B	Occidental Park
C	Smith Tower
D	Waterfront Park
E	Seattle Aquarium
F	Pike Place Market
G	Seattle Art Museum
H	Freeway Park
I	Two Union Square
J	Westlake Park
K	Rainier Square

ELLIOTT BAY

INTERNATIONAL DISTRICT

Considered a luxury hotel some 60 years ago, the **Pacific Plaza** (400 Spring Street; 206-623-3900) is now a dignified, quiet, downtown classic. Though updated, it hasn't lost its old-fashioned flavor, with windows that open, ceiling fans and traditional furniture in rather small rooms. There are 160 moderately priced rooms and 16 suites. A continental breakfast and morning newspaper are provided in a lounge off the multitiered lobby. The concierge is very helpful.

The **Seattle YMCA** (909 4th Avenue; 206-382-5000), a member of the American Youth Hostels Association, offers straightforward, clean, budget accommodations in the heart of downtown. Each of the 198 rooms is plainly furnished with a bed, phone, desk and lamp. Four people can sleep in each dorm unit. The hotel includes a pool and health club.

The **WestCoast Camlin Hotel** (1619 9th Avenue; 206-682-0100), on the edge of downtown and a block from the convention center, was built in 1926 and has been renovated in recent years. The 136-room hotel has a lovely lobby of marble with oriental carpets, a restaurant on the 11th floor and a new Japanese casual restaurant on the lobby level. Most of the oversized, classically furnished rooms have work areas, a popular feature for business travelers. Deluxe.

Between downtown and Seattle Center is **Sixth Avenue Inn** (2000 6th Avenue; 206-441-8300), a five-story motor inn with 167 rooms. The rooms, done in crisp blue and cream, are a cut above those in most motels. They contain blond furniture and assorted plants and books. Those on the north and in back are the quietest. There's a restaurant overlooking a small garden. Moderate.

The **Inn at Virginia Mason** (1006 Spring Street; 206-583-6453) is an attractive, nine-story, brick building owned by the medical center next door. On the eastern edge of downtown, it caters to hospital visitors and others looking for a convenient location and pleasant accommodations at reasonable prices. The 79 rooms have dark-wood furnishings in a burgundy, gray and mauve decor. Two suites have a fireplace and whirlpool tub. There's a small restaurant by a brick terrace. Moderate.

The **Sorrento Hotel** (900 Madison Street; 206-622-6400) is known for its personal service and attention to detail. A historic building that has been remodeled, Sorrento is on a hilltop a few blocks above the downtown area. Beyond the quiet, plush lobby are a notable restaurant and an inviting lounge. All 76 rooms and suites have a warm, traditional, European atmosphere. Ultra-deluxe.

On a grassy hill in West Seattle, facing east toward Elliott Bay and downtown, is **Hainsworth House** (2657 37th Avenue Southwest; 206-938-1020 or 206-932-0654). The impressive, Tudor-style home was built in 1906 and restored in the mid-1980s. It contains antiques, Persian rugs and lots of polished woodwork, but the atmosphere is unassuming. Guests make popcorn in the kitchen, play with the dogs and ask for scrambled tofu for breakfast if they don't want eggs. There are two well-furnished rooms upstairs; one has a fireplace and a grand view. Moderate to deluxe.

DOWNTOWN SEATTLE RESTAURANTS

The fine **al Boccalino** (1 Yesler Way; 206-622-7688) serves some of the city's best Italian dinners. Located in a brick building near Pioneer Square, the restaurant's atmosphere is unpretentious and intimate, the antipasto imaginative (quail baked with prosciutto and cognac; beans with swordfish and fennel) and the entrées cooked and sauced to perfection. Saddle of lamb with brandy, tarragon and mustard is a favorite. There are daily specials for every course. Moderate.

For a romantic dinner, try **Il Terrazo Carmine** (411 1st Avenue South, Pioneer Square; 206-467-7797) in the Merrill Place Building. For patio diners, a cascading reflecting pool drowns out some, but not all, of the freeway noise. Entrées include ravioli with venison or the half chicken roasted with an oregano sauce. The restaurant also features an extensive Italian wine list. Deluxe.

White-linen tablecloths, black-rattan furnishings and loads of plants greet you at **Linyen** (424 7th Avenue South; 206-622-8181), an upscale Cantonese restaurant in the International District. In the foyer, you are greeted with the specials posted on the blackboard, such as hot and smokey jumbo prawns in lobster sauce, red-pepper beef, Linyen fishcakes with vegetables or clams in black-bean sauce. Moderate.

Just a few blocks away is **Hanil** (409 Maynard Avenue South; 206-587-0464) set in the Bush Asia Center, up above a park. The interior of this Korean restaurant is filled with wood paneling, green plants and flowers. The restaurant serves great lunch specials in lovely lacquered boxes and classic Korean barbecue prepared on gas burners at your table. Barbecued chicken, pork or beef are excellent. Budget.

For great Vietnamese food at low prices, try **Hien Vuong** (502 South King Street; 206-624-2611). After the green oilcloths and the white-lace curtains, there's no decor to speak of—just hungry patrons eager for a dish of shrimp, sugar cane and rice paper, Cambodian noodle soup or papaya with beef jerky. Shrimp rolls here are some of the best in town. Budget.

On the outskirts of the International District you'll find **Chau's Chinese Restaurant** (310 4th Avenue South; 206-621-0006), a small, unpretentious restaurant that offers great seafood such as Dungeness crab with ginger and onion, clams in hot garlic sauce, bird's-nest scallops and rock-cod fillets with corn sauce. Choose the fresh seafood entrées over the standard Cantonese entrées. Budget.

Hidden away is **Place Pigalle** (5 Pike Place Market; 206-624-1756). Wind your way past a seafood vendor to this restaurant with spectacular views of Elliott Bay. The dark-wood trim, handsome bar and other touches make for a European-bistro atmosphere. The restaurant makes the most of fresh ingredients from the market's produce tables. Dine on duck with rosemary polenta, gingered calamari in cream or salmon in a brandy sauce. The dishes are artfully presented, but the service is sometimes uneven. Priced in the deluxe range.

Across the cobbled street, you can observe the eclectic mix of shoppers and artists in the Pike Place Market at **Three Girls Bakery** (1514 Pike Place; 206-622-1045), a popular hangout. This tiny lunch counter and bakery with a few seats serves good sandwiches—the meatloaf sandwich is popular—and hearty soups, including chili and clam chowder. You have more than a hundred kinds of bread to choose from. The sourdough and rye breads are recommended. If you don't have room for pastries, buy some to take home. You won't regret it. Budget.

In Post Alley behind some of the market shops you will find more than just a wee bit of Ireland at **Kells** (1916 Post Alley; 206-728-1916). This traditional Irish pub will lure you to the Emerald Isle with pictures and posters of splendid countryside. A limited menu includes salmon with an Irish dill sauce, rack of lamb, Irish stew and meat pies. From the heavy, dark bar comes a host of domestic and imported beers. Irish music is piped in all the time, and live musicians play Irish tunes Wednesday through Saturday. Moderate.

Talk about hidden—this place doesn't even have a sign. You enter through the pink door off of Post Alley. **The Pink Door** (★) (1919 Post Alley; 206-443-3241), with its Italian kitsch decor, is lively and robust at lunch time. Especially good are the spinach fettucine with salmon and cream, lasagna and a delicious cioppino. In the evening, the pace slows, the light dims and it's a perfect setting for a romantic dinner. In the summer, rooftop dining offers views of the Sound. Dinners are *prix-fixe* for a four-course, set menu. Moderate.

Off a brick courtyard above Pike Place Market, **Campagne** is one of the city's top restaurants. Diners enjoy French country cooking in an atmosphere both warm and elegant. Entrées include grilled veal sweetbreads on handmade fettuccine and a rich cassoulet with duck confit, garlic sausage, pork and lamb. The simply prepared dishes are usually the best: grilled chicken with roasted garlic, for example, or ahi tuna with artichoke hearts and a dollop of aioli. Deluxe to ultra-deluxe.

Every meal served at **El Puerco Lloron** (Pike Place Market Hillclimb, 1501 Western Avenue; 206-624-0541) includes wonderfully fresh tortillas, made by hand while hungry diners watch from the cafeteria line. The *chile rellenos* compares with the best. Tamales, enchiladas and tacos are all authentic and of good quality. There's a Mexican fiesta atmosphere in the warm, steamy room. Budget.

Tucked into a hillside in Pike Place Market, **Il Bistro** is a cozy cellar spot with wide archways and oriental rugs on wooden floors. Light jazz, candlelight and well-prepared Italian food make it an inviting spot on a rainy evening. Several pastas are served; the entrées include rack of lamb, veal scallopine, fresh salmon and chicken stuffed with mozzarella. Deluxe to ultra-deluxe.

On the Pike Place Market hill, **Takara Restaurant and Sushi Bar** (1501 Western Avenue; 206-682-8609) serves Japanese food in a casual atmosphere. Chicken and salmon teriyaki, fried flat noodles with vegetables and pork and sashimi on a bed of grated radish are a few of the delicately flavored, budget-priced dishes.

Septieme (2331 2nd Avenue; 206-448-1506) is Kurt Timmermeister's re-creation of small Parisian cafés that catered to the literati and students. This café carries plenty of reading material and turns out cups of good coffee and lattes that attract students from nearby Antioch University as well as business folks and shoppers in the Belltown area. A favorite luncheon sandwich is eggplant with roasted peppers. Desserts include shortbread, carrot cake, a variety of cookies and other mouthwatering treats. In summer, there is a small outdoor courtyard. Budget.

You might not expect a restaurant on the top floor of a small office building, but **Kaspar's by the Bay** (2701 1st Avenue; 206-441-4805) is certainly worth knowing. From tables near the windows you can watch ferries traversing the water from Winslow and Bremerton. The menu emphasizes Northwest seafood but includes beef, pork, lamb, chicken and quail. The Pike Street Market Grill dish features an array of seafood with a ginger-butter sauce. The desserts are innovative. Moderate.

Artists and others without a lot of money for eats hang out at the **Two-Bells Tavern** (2313 4th Avenue; 206-441-3050) in Belltown. Local artwork on the walls changes every two months. This funky bar with 25 kinds of beer and a host of inexpensive good food is a busy place. You can always find good soups, sandwiches, salads and cold plates. Some favorites are an italian-sausage soup and the hot beer-sausage sandwich. Prices fall in the budget category.

A favorite among downtowners is the **Botticelli Café** (101 Stewart Street; 206-441-9235). The four-table café is known for its panini—little sandwiches made of toasted focaccia bread and topped with olive oil, savory herbs, cheeses and vegetables. The espresso and ices are good, too. Budget.

Contemporary, international cuisine prepared with imagination is served at the **Dahlia Lounge** (1904 4th Avenue; 206-682-4142) near the shops of Westlake Center. Bright-red walls and ceiling, a neon sign and paper-fish lampshades create a celebratory atmosphere. The chef draws upon numerous ethnic styles and uses Northwest products to develop such dishes as roasted eggplant and garlic dip with grilled pita and green apples. Moderate in price.

Original Northwest art hangs above the booths in **Fullers** (1400 6th Avenue; 206-624-0541), an internationally acclaimed restaurant in the Sheraton Seattle Hotel and Towers. The decor is plush and sophisticated and the cuisine still top quality, though there's a new chef at the helm. Monique Barbeau is adhering to the path created by the Pences, featuring Continental dishes with an Asian flair. Thai ravioli in coconut broth, roast duck with a plum glaze and salmon in a rhubarb-orange compote are examples. Deluxe to ultra-deluxe.

Now at home in the Westin Hotel is **Nikko** (1900 5th Avenue; 206-322-4905), where longtime sushi chef Shiro Kashiba demonstrates his skills. Tempura, sukiyaki, sushi and sashimi are among the Japanese delicacies served. Moderate.

The decor is spare and clean in **Wild Ginger** (1400 Western Avenue; 206-623-4450), and the menu is Pacific Rim. Dark-wood booths fill the big, open room; at one end is a satay bar where skewered chicken, beef and fish are grilled, then served with peanut sauce. The wondrous Seven Elements Soup, an exotic blend of flavors, is a meal in itself. Prices are in the moderate range.

Spend a perfect summer day at Alki Beach in West Seattle, then take in dinner at the **Alki Bakery & Café** (2726 Alki Drive Southwest; 206-935-0616) where a well-rounded menu includes great salads (the wilted spinach and bacon is a favorite), seafood, meat, chicken and pasta dishes. Try the eggplant in a marinara sauce, topped with cheese. Specials of the evening are listed in the two dining areas. Be sure to leave room for dessert—a lovely fruit torte or delicious cheesecake made in the bakery. Also a popular place for breakfast, the Bakery offers up hearty omelettes, french toast and a host of muffins, cinnamon rolls and danishes from the bakery. Coffee, espressos and lattes are good, too. If you've overindulged, you can always take another stroll on the beach. Moderate.

DOWNTOWN SEATTLE SHOPPING

The oldest and loveliest structure in Pioneer Square is the **Pioneer Building** (600 1st Avenue; 206-624-1783). Here is Seattle's first electric elevator, and the **Pioneer Square Mall** (600 1st Avenue; 206-624-1164) in the basement has over 10,000 square feet of space devoted to antiques and maintained by some 80 dealers.

Grand Central Arcade Building (216 1st Avenue South; 206-623-7417) houses 17 shops. Visitors can also enjoy drinks and baked goods at lobby tables adjacent to a brick fireplace. **Millstream NW** (214 1st Avenue South; 206-233-9719) sells Northwest sculpture and jewelry by local artisans. **Adjiri Arts** (214 1st Avenue South; 206-464-4089) has African masks, silk-screened African T-shirts and musical instruments resembling marimbas made of wood and gourds.

For ten years **The Prints and The Pauper** (112 South Washington Street; 206-624-9336) has been dealing in photographic art, paintings and sculptured works produced by up-and-coming Northwest artists. Prices are reasonable, and you might get a masterpiece with a signature that one day will be highly valued.

In the heart of the Pioneer Square district is the **Elliott Bay Book Company** (101 South Main Street; 206-624-6600) featuring over 125,000 titles, including an outstanding stock of Northwest books and a newly added section for professional, business and health-science subjects. You're bound to enjoy browsing, snacking in the on-premises café or listening in on frequently scheduled readings by renowned authors.

Seattle's connection with the Pacific Rim is legendary, and **Uwajimaya** (516 6th Avenue South; 206-624-6428) demonstrates the tie with shoji screens and lamps, kotatsu tables (with heaters underneath to warm feet) lacquerware music boxes, goldimari ceramic pieces and Japanese, Chinese, Thai, Vietnamese, Philippine and American canned and frozen foods.

Known as an "Oriental Woolworth's," **Higo Variety Store** (604 South Jackson Street; 206-622-7572) has all kinds of small toys, bowls and sundries in the five-and-dime category. Also on hand are some more expensive articles such as hapi coats, kimonos and obi sashes.

Along the waterfront, Piers 54 through 70 are shoppers' delights. You'll love **Ye Olde Curiosity Shop** (Pier 54; 206-682-5844), a Seattle landmark where the mummy "Sylvester" presides over souvenirs, Native American totem poles and masks, Russian stacking dolls, lacquerware and Ukrainian eggs. **Kalole's Bye N'Bye** (Pier 70; 206-448-8937) is noted for its Hawaiian lace, seashells, freshwater pearls, straw hats and hula shirts.

Called the "Soul of Seattle," the **Pike Place Market** (85 Pike Street; 206-682-7453) has been in business for 85 years. The corridors are lined with fresh produce, seafood stalls and quaint specialty shops. The **Pure Food Fish Market** (1511 Pike Place Market; 206-622-5764) ships fresh or smoked salmon worldwide. **Hands of the World** (Main Arcade; 206-622-1696) specializes in ethnic jewelry, masks and home accessories such as carved picture frames and folkloric art.

In the Downtown area, 5th Avenue, Seattle's fashion street, is lined with shops displaying elegant finery and accessories. **Rainier Square** (1333 5th Avenue; 206-628-5050) houses several prestigious retail establishments. **Totally Michael's** (1333 5th Avenue; 206-623-2528), a 78-year-old Seattle tradition, is a treasure house of antique, estate and contemporary pieces. **Biagio** (1312 4th Avenue; 206-623-3842) specializes in handsome leather goods—handbags, luggage, business and attaché cases.

At the **Westlake Center** (4th Avenue and Pine Street; 206-467-1600), colorful pushcarts loaded with jewelry, scarves and other small trappings lend a European flavor to the 77 retail establishments here. **Kekko Eastern Imports** (206-682-3398) deals in Middle Eastern bangles, pendants and other jewelry. **Fireworks** (206-682-6462) takes its name form unusually fired sculptures, wallhangings and plates.

DOWNTOWN SEATTLE NIGHTLIFE

There are many fine nightclubs in Pioneer Square, and on "joint-cover" nights one charge admits you to seven places within a four-block radius. Among them is **Doc Maynard's** (610 1st Avenue; 206-682-4649), heavy on rock-and-roll. The **New Orleans Creole Restaurant** (114 1st Avenue South; 206-622-2563) offers jazz and blues nightly. Over at the **Fenix Café** (111 Yesler Way; 206-447-1514) there's live music Thursday through Monday. And at **Comedy Underground at Swannies** (222 South Main Street; 206-628-0303), comics entertain Wednesday through Sunday. There's an open-mike Monday and Tuesday.

Along the waterfront you'll find rock aplenty at **Pier 70** (foot of Broad Street and Alaskan Way; 206-728-7071), a good dance spot. Live bands play Top-40 tunes and heavy metal. Cover.

Belltown, near the Pike Place Market, has lots of activity after dark. **The Vogue** (2018 1st Avenue; 206-443-0673) features modern dance music with bands. Cover. Nearby, **Café U-Betcha** (2212 1st Avenue; 206-441-1989) offers karaoke and vocal entertainment.

Dimitriou's Jazz Alley (6th Avenue and Lenora Street; 206-441-9729) is a downtown dinner theater and premier jazz club with international acts. Cover.

Last Laugh Comedy Club (75 Marion Street; 206-622-5653) will do anything (anything?) for a laugh. Cover. The **Mystery Café** (206-324-8895), located in the same building, serves up a murder mystery with your dinner. Cover.

For satirical/comical revues try the **Cabaret de Paris** (Rainier Square, 1333 5th Avenue; 206-623-4111). Food and drink are available. Cover.

At the **Off Ramp Music Café** (109 Eastlake East at Denny Way and Stewart Street; 206-628-0232) there's alternative rock every night as well as regularly scheduled entertainers.

Timberline (2015 Boren Avenue; 206-622-6220) draws a largely gay crowd, with everyone enjoying country-and-western dancing. Cover on the weekends.

Seattle Center/Queen Anne Area

Northwest of downtown a familiar landmark rises skyward—the Space Needle. Thirty years after the 1962 World's Fair, the fairgrounds, long since renamed **Seattle Center**, frankly need renovating. For some time, politicians and planners have been debating what to do with the site (two miles north of the retail core between Denny Way and Mercer Street; 206-684-7200), but no firm plan has emerged. Meanwhile, locals and visitors continue to flock to the **Space Needle** (206-443-2111; admission) for the view or a meal, to summer carnival rides at the **Fun Forest**, to the **Food Fair's** short-order ethnic eateries, to see opera and live theater at the center's many stages, to see wide-ranging exhibits and demonstrations at the **Pacific Science Center** (206-443-2001; admission).

Kids will also enjoy visiting the center's **Seattle Children's Museum** (206-441-1767) on the ground floor of Center House. The collection features a kid's-size neighborhood that includes a grocery, doctor's office, café, bus and fire engine. There are also a giant Lego room, a small lagoon for children and a drop-in art studio.

For a rewarding, spur-of-the-moment visit, drop by the center on a summer evening for a contemplative quarter-hour of gazing at the **International Fountain**. The combination of changing lights and waterworks against a rose-tinted summer sunset can lull you into a dreamy state.

SEATTLE CENTER/QUEEN ANNE AREA RESTAURANTS

For good sandwiches, omelettes, *frittatas* and soup, consider **A. Jay's** (2619 1st Avenue; 206-441-1511) in the Queen Anne Hill district. This deli is a place to linger over the Sunday newspaper and enjoy a casual breakfast. If you are there for lunch, try the shrimp salad—it's fresh and flavorful. Other deli items include latkes, blintzes and bagels with lox and loaded with cream cheese. Coffee is plentiful. Service is helpful and friendly. Breakfast and lunch. Budget.

Near the Seattle Center, **Le Tastevin** (19 West Harrison Street; 206-283-0991) has been a standard-bearer for lighter French food in Seattle for more than a decade. In the bar, there's a lighter, ten-item menu with $12 entrées that are fine for lunch. Dinner here is an experience. Start with a flavored vodka, then an order of oysters on the half shell. Entrées include bouillabaisse, salmon in puff pastry, flambéed sweetbreads with port, mushrooms and cream, and prawns in a Pernod-flavored sauce. Desserts, such as a variety of soufflés, a mousse torte and cherries jubilee, are to die for. Deluxe.

SEATTLE CENTER/QUEEN ANNE AREA NIGHTLIFE

Home of the 1962 World's Fair, the **Seattle Center** (305 Harrison Street; 206-684-7200) still offers innumerable night-time diversions.

Sharing facilities at the **Seattle Center Opera House** (along Mercer Street between 3rd Avenue North and Nob Avenue; 206-389-7676) are the **Seattle Opera Association** (206-389-7600) famous for summer performances of Wagner's "Ring of the Niebulong"; **Pacific Northwest Ballet** (206-547-5900) where the *Nutcracker* production is a Christmas tradition; and the **Seattle Symphony** (206-443-4747) where the repertoire ranges from baroque to contemporary.

The **Seattle Repertory Theatre** (along Mercer Street between Warren Avenue and 2nd Avenue North; 206-443-2222) plays at the adjacent Bagley Wright Theatre, while the **Intiman Theatre** (206-626-0782) presents plays by the great dramatists at the nearby Playhouse.

At the **Space Needle Restaurant** (203 6th Avenue North; 206-443-2150) the entertainment—from 500 feet up—in either the restaurant or the observation deck is seeing metropolitan Seattle, its environs, Puget Sound, the Olympic Mountains and Mt. Rainier, the Queen of the Cascade Range, as you rotate in a 360-degree orbit.

For new renditions of classics, contemporary plays and musicals, try the **Bathhouse Theater** (7312 West Greenlake Drive North; 206-524-9108) on the shores of Green Lake.

A Contemporary Theater (100 West Roy Street; 206-285-5110) and **The Empty Space Theater** (107 Occidental Avenue South; 206-467-6000) specialize in works by new playwrights.

Seattle Neighborhoods

While downtown is the city's magnet, some of Seattle's best parks, sightseeing and nightlife can be found in nearby neighborhoods. Arboretums and science museums, lakeside dining and shopping worth a special trip are all in this region.

The six miles or so of shoreline circling **Lake Union** present an incredibly varied admixture of boat works and nautical specialty shops, street-end pocket parks, boat-in restaurants, seaplane docks, rental-boat concessions, ocean-research vessels, houseboats, flashy, new condo developments and office complexes. You could spend a day exploring all the byways and funky, old warehouses and oddball enterprises. The lake's south end offers extensive public access to the shore behind a cluster of new restaurants, a wooden-boat center and new park.

One of Seattle's most cosmopolitan neighborhoods, **Capitol Hill** is the place to toss back an exotic wheatgrass drink at a vegetarian bar, sip a double espresso at a sidewalk café, shop for radical literature at a leftist bookstore or hit a straight or gay nightclub. If you can't find it on Capitol Hill, Seattle probably doesn't have it. Broadway Avenue is the heart of this region known for its boutiques, yuppie appliance stores and bead shops.

Home of some of the city's finest Victorians, this neighborhood includes **Volunteer Park** (East Ward Street from 11th to 17th avenues). Be sure to head up to the top of the water tower for a great view of the region.

Few guidebooks look at the Lake Washington Ship Canal as a single unit. Yet it ties together a wondrous diversity of working waterfront and recreational shoreline along eight miles of bay, lake and canal between Puget Sound and Lake Washington. Construction of the locks and canal began in 1911 and created a shipping channel from Lake Washington to Lake Union to Puget Sound. Along its banks today you can see perhaps the liveliest continuous boat parade in the West: Tugs gingerly inching four-story-tall, Alaska-bound barges through narrow locks; rowboats, kayaks, sailboards and luxury yachts; gill-netters and trawlers in dry dock; government-research vessels; aging houseboats listing at their moorings; and seaplanes roaring overhead.

In all, the ship canal presents a splendid overview of Seattle's maritime traditions. But you'll also discover plenty that's new—rejuvenated neighborhoods like the Fremont District and south Lake Union's upscale shoreline, a renovated Fisherman's Terminal and a handful of trendy, waterside restaurants. Amid the hubbub of boat traffic and ship chandlers, you'll also encounter quiet, street-end parks for birdwatching, foot and bike paths, the best historical museum in the city and one of the West's renowned arboretums. Here's a summary, west to east.

Hiram M. Chittenden Locks in Ballard is where all boats heading east or west in the ship canal must pass and thus presents the quintessential floating boat show; it's one of the most-visited attractions in the city. Visitors crowd railings and jam footbridges to watch as harried lock-keepers scurry to get boats tied up properly before locks are either raised or lowered, depending on boats' direction of passage. Terraced parks flanking the canal provide splendid picnic overlooks. An underwater fish-viewing window gives you astonishing looks at several species of salmon, steelhead and sea-going cutthroat trout on their spawning migrations (June into November). Lovely botanical gardens in a park-like setting offer yet more diversion.

Fisherman's Terminal (on the south side of Salmon Bay about a mile east of the locks) is home port to one of the world's biggest fishing fleets, some 700 vessels, most of which chug north into Alaskan waters for summer salmon fishing. But you'll always be able to see boats here—gill-netters, purse-seiners, trollers, factory ships—and working fishermen repairing nets, painting boats and the like. Here, too, are net-drying sheds, nautical stores and shops selling marine hardware and commercial fishing tackle. One café opens at 6 for working fishermen; there's a fish-and-chips window and one good seafood restaurant (Chinook's) overlooking the waterway.

The Fremont District is locally famous for the sculpture "Waiting for the Interurban," whose collection of life-like commuters is frequently seen adorned in funny hats, scarves and other castoff clothing. Centered around Fremont Avenue North and North 34th Street at the northwest corner of Lake Union, the district is top heavy with shops proffering the offbeat (handmade dulcimers, antiques and junk).

Gas Works Park (foot of Wallingford Avenue North off North 34th Street) occupies property that dangles like a giant, green tonsil from Lake Union's north shore. Until 1956, the park's namesake "gas works" produced synthetic natural gas from coal and crude oil. Some of the rusting congeries of pipes, airy catwalks, spiraling ladders, tall towers and stubby tanks was torn down during park construction, but enough remains (repainted in snappy colors) to fascinate youngsters and old-timers alike.

On the south side of Union Bay, 175-acre **Washington Park** (Lake Washington Boulevard East and East Madison Street) presents enough diversions indoors and out to fill a rich day of exploring in all sorts of weather. Most famous is the **Washington Park Arboretum** (which occupies most of the park), at its best in the spring when thousands of rhododendrons and azaleas—some 10 to 15 feet tall—and groves of spreading chestnuts, dogwoods, magnolias and other flowering trees leap into bloom. Short footpaths beckon from the **Visitor Center** (Arboretum Drive East; 206-543-8800). But two in particular deserve mention—Azalea Way and Loderi Valley—which wend their way down avenues of pink, cream, yellow, crimson and white blooms. The arboretum's renowned **Japanese Garden** is especially rewarding in spring, and both arboretum and garden present splendid fall colors in October and early November.

Miles of duff-covered footpaths lace the park. For naturalists, the premier experience will be found along the one-and-a-half-mile **Arboretum Waterfront Trail** at the north end of the park on Foster Island behind the Museum of History and Industry (see below). This footpath takes you on an intriguing bog-walk over low bridges and along boardwalks through marshy wetlands teeming with ducks and wildfowl, fish and frogs and aquatic flora growing rank at the edge of Lake Washington.

In summer, you can join the canoeists paddling the labyrinth of waterways around Foster Island, sunbathers and picnickers sprawling on lawns, anglers casting for catfish and trout and the swimmers cooling off on hot August afternoons.

On rainy days the **Museum of History and Industry** (2700 24th Avenue East; 206-324-1125; admission) is a fitting retreat. It's the city's best early-day collection and pays special tribute to Puget Sound's rich maritime history, as befits any museum located next door to this vital waterway.

The **University of Washington Campus** (45th Street Northeast and 15th Avenue Northeast; 206-543-9198) borders the canal north of Montlake Cut (part of the waterway) and is a haven for anyone who enjoys the simple pleasure of strolling across a college campus. It boggles the mind to think of what awaits you on its 694 acres—handsome, old buildings in architectural styles from Romanesque to modern; Frosh Pond; the **Burke Museum** (206-543-5590) and its famous collection of Northwest Indian Art; the **Henry Art Gallery** (206-543-2280) with its marvelous textiles; red-brick quads and expanses of lawn and colorful summer gardens; canal-side trails on both sides of the Montlake Cut; access to the Burke-Gilman Trail; and a lakeside **Canoe House** with rentals (206-543-9433).

A mile or so north of the ship canal, **Green Lake Park** and **Woodland Park** straddle Aurora Avenue North (Route 99) and together offer 530 acres of park, lake and zoo attractions. The star is **Woodland Park Zoo** (Phinney Avenue North and North 55th Street; 206-684-4820), which since 1979 has won praise for its program of converting static exhibits into more natural, often outdoor environments. Most notable are the African Savannah, Gorilla Exhibit, the Marsh and Swamp and the Elephant Forest where you can see Thai elephants working at traditional tasks. A Tropical Rain Forest, heralded as a "journey through different levels of forest," is scheduled to open in fall 1992.

Green Lake Park, enormously popular with all ages and classes of Seattlites, is simply the best outdoor people-watching place in the city. Two loop trails circle the shore (the inner trail is 2.8 miles long, the outer 3.2 miles) and welcome all-comers. On summer days, both paths are filled with strollers and race-walkers, joggers and skaters, bikers and nannies pushing prams. On the lake you'll see anglers, canoeists, sailboarders, swimmers, birdwatchers and folks floating in inner tubes.

SEATTLE NEIGHBORHOODS HOTELS

Seattle's neighborhoods offer several hotels and numerous bed-and-breakfast accommodations. A bed and breakfast can be a great value, offering a casual atmosphere, homecooked food included in the room rate and personal contact with an innkeeper who usually knows the city well. Contact the **Washington State Bed & Breakfast Guild** (509-938-3658) or **Pacific Bed & Breakfast Agency** (206-784-0539).

The **MV Challenger** (1001 Fairview Avenue; 206-340-1201) is a "bunk and breakfast" on Lake Union. The opulent interior of the renovated, 96-foot tugboat is done in mahogany and oak. It has a bar, a salon with a fireplace and seven cabins with nautical furnishings. They all overlook the lake and city skyline. Captain's Cabin, the largest, is in the former pilothouse. Moderate in price.

Three Capitol Hill buildings with housekeeping accommodations make up the **Baker Guest Apartments** (528 15th Avenue East; 206-323-5909). They're a good choice for families or for travelers who want the privacy and amenities of apartment living at moderate rates. Kitchens are well equipped, and laundry facilities are provided. Apartments range from studios to two-bedroom, two-bath units. They're spotlessly clean and furnished in a simple, residential style.

Bellevue Place (1111 Bellevue Place East; 206-325-9253) is a bed and breakfast in a tony residential area on Capitol Hill. The big home, built in 1905, has three comfortable, tastefully furnished rooms that share a divided bath. The bed and breakfast caters to a mixed gay and straight clientele. It has three parlors (one with a grand piano, one with a fireplace), and a solarium where breakfast is often served. Moderate.

Also in the popular, busy Capitol Hill area, **Gaslight Inn** (1727 15th Avenue; 206-325-3654) is a moderately priced bed and breakfast with urban flair. The 1906 house is furnished with oak, maple and glass antiques. Various period styles have been effectually combined with modern amenities in the nine guest rooms. Most have private baths, and two have fireplaces. Gaslight has a heated, outdoor swimming pool and serves a continental buffet breakfast. Gay-friendly.

Expect a friendly welcome and lots of conversation at **Roberta's Bed & Breakfast** (1147 16th Avenue East; 206-329-3326). The comfortable, traditional home on Capitol Hill has four rooms on the second floor and a fifth under the eaves on the third floor. There are cozy window seats, gleaming woodwork, skylights, shelves full of books, a piano and a full, meatless breakfast. Moderate.

The owners' collection of rocking horses adds a whimsical touch to **Rocking Horse Inn** (2011 10th Avenue East; 206-322-0206) on Capitol Hill, behind a high fence and courtyard. The friendly innkeepers welcome both gay and straight visitors. They have a cozy living room with a fireplace, a television room, an outdoor hot tub and three guest rooms that share a bath. A spacious suite and a room with a Santa Fe decor occupy the second floor. Above them is a sunny, yellow room with panoramic view. A generous continental breakfast is served. Moderate.

From the **Capitol Hill Inn** (1713 Belmont Avenue; 206-323-1955) it's an easy walk downtown and to the convention center. The Queen Anne-style home dating back to 1903 has been beautifully restored as a bed-and-breakfast inn and furnished with antiques and reproductions of Victorian wallpaper and tiffany light fixtures. There are five guest rooms and two comfortable parlors. An abundant breakfast is served. Moderate. Gay-friendly.

A favorite of visitors to the University of Washington, both gay and straight, the **Chambered Nautilus Bed & Breakfast Inn** (5005 22nd Avenue Northeast; 206-522-2536) is only a block from the campus. Breezily casual, the spacious home has a family atmosphere. Games and books, soft chairs by the fireplace and an all-day coffeepot add to the homeyness. Six guest rooms on the second and third floors have antique furnishings. Four have private baths. A full buffet breakfast is served, sometimes on the sun porch. Moderate.

Also in the University District is **Meany Tower Hotel** (4507 Brookley Avenue Northeast; 206-634-2000), a 15-story tower with 180 corner rooms. All units have views of the mountains or the lake and cityscape. Standard hotel furnishings are in the spacious, peach-and-green rooms. A handsome restaurant and lounge are on the floor below the lobby. Moderate.

The **University Plaza Hotel** (400 Northeast 45th Street; 206-634-0100) is a three-story motor hotel adjacent to Route 5, west of the University of Washington. There are 135 comfortably furnished rooms centered around a pool courtyard. Rooms on the freeway side can be noisy. On the ground floor, behind a mock-medieval England facade, are a restaurant, lounge, gift shops and beauty salon. Moderate.

SEATTLE NEIGHBORHOODS RESTAURANTS

Bicycles hang from the rafters. T-shirts are on sale in the lobby. **Cucina! Cucina!** (901 Fairview Avenue; 206-447-2782) is an open, spacious, noisy Italian restaurant with a large deck overlooking Lake Union where you can watch float planes land and take off or see kayakers gently paddling by. Diners can see into the open kitchen to watch the staff making pizzas large and small for baking in the woodburning ovens. One of the most interesting is spicy chicken. You will find a variety of pasta dishes, such as salmon linguine, lasagna, and good spinach and Caesar salads. Moderate.

Ayutthaya (727 East Pike Street; 206-324-8833) is a corner restaurant in Capitol Hill renowned for its Thai cookery. Small, clean-lined and pleasant in blue and lavender, Ayutthaya features plenty of chicken and seafood dishes along with soups and noodles. Flavors blend deliciously in the curried shrimp with green beans, coconut milk and basil. Or try the chicken sautéed in peanut-chili sauce. Budget.

Near Seattle University, **Kokeb** (926 12th Avenue; 206-322-0485) is a pleasant restaurant offering the hotly spiced dishes of Ethiopia. The finger food is eaten with chunks of a large, flat bread. The atmosphere is rustic, with an open-beamed ceiling. Budget.

One of the world's great clam chowders is served at **Rain City Grill** (2359 10th Avenue East; 206-325-5003). That's just the start. There are other appetizers (butternut-squash ravioli with bleu cheese and pecans is a happy choice), several salads and about a dozen entrées. Pork tenderloin with spicy peanut sauce, a mixed-seafood grill and roast duckling with marionberry and ginger sauce are among the outstanding dishes. The festive Capitol Hill restaurant has a weather theme, complete with colorful umbrellas suspended from the ceiling. The service is attentive. Moderate to deluxe.

At **Mamounia** (1556 East Olive Way; 206-329-3886), a Moroccan restaurant, patrons sit on the floor, nestled in mounds of pillows in the dim light with music of the sitar and panpipes dancing in the darkness. Dishes, such as roast chicken or curried lamb and bread, arrive and then the fun really begins. There are no utensils, so diners must tear off hunks of the meat and bread and eat with their fingers. At the least, it's a gastronomic adventure, or it could be your own rendition of *Tom Jones*. Moderate.

Born in Italy, reared in Argentina and trained in Spain, Marco Casabeaux pours his international experience into a relatively new, colorful and lively, Spanish-eclectic restaurant in the Madison Park area. Start your meal at **Cactus** (4220 East Madison Street; 206-324-4140) with one of the most unusual items on the menu—a declawed prickly pear cactus salad. On weekends, there is a tapas bar. Some of the more unusual entrées are cinnamon chicken or the pork stick *adobo*, a fiery-hot pork steak. Moderate.

Not too far away, in a small house surrounded by gardens, is **Rover's** (2808 East Madison Street; 206-325-7442), which specializes in French cuisine and is just the place for those romantic occasions. Chef Thierry Rautureau creates the ever-changing menu based on locally available, fresh produce. Entrées include rabbit, venison, pheasant and quail in addition to seafood, beef and chicken in imaginative sauces. A good selection of Northwest and French wines is available. Service is friendly and helpful. Moderate in price.

After visitors watch the ships go through the locks in the Ballard area, they stop at **Hiram's At-The-Locks** (5300 34th Northwest; 206-784-1733) for seafood and views of the channel. Northwest specialties dominate the menu, though the preparation is standard. They include local clams, oysters on the half shell, whole steamed crabs and salmon cooked in several ways. Deluxe.

Scandies (2301 Northwest Market Street; 206-783-5080) is appropriately located in Ballard, a community with Scandinavian roots. Open all day every day, the restaurant serves such Scandinavian specialties as open-faced sandwiches (pickled herring, Jarlsberg cheese, spiced lamb), crêpe-style pancakes with lingonberries, Denmark's *frickadeller* (pork meatballs) and *scorpa* (cardamom cookies). Beers from Norway and Denmark are available in the informal, blue-and-white restaurant. Budget to moderate.

A favorite seafood place for tourists is **Ivar's Indian Salmon House** (401 Northeast Northlake Way; 206-632-0767) with its dugout canoe hung overhead and Northwest Native American longhouse-style architecture and decor. The restaurant also features views of the kayak, canoe, tugboat, windsurfer and yacht activity on Lake Union. The menu includes alder-smoked salmon and black cod, Northwest Native American style, and prime rib. Prices are budget.

Near the University of Washington, make a beeline for the **Beeliner Diner** (2114 North 45th Street; 206-547-6313). Upbeat and lively, this is the place to go for generous portions of well-prepared American food: footlong grilled hot dogs, cheeseburgers, turkey pot pie and roast chicken with mashed potatoes. Each evening there's a blue-plate special. It's a friendly café, like the 1940s diners it resembles. Budget.

Truffles (3701 Northeast 45th Street; 206-522-3016) is just what it claims to be: "a neighborhood bistro, bakery and deli." In the big, cheerful, open room, customers line up at a deli case to order cheeses, salads and meats or sit at tables with red-and-white checkered cloths and order homemade soups, chicken-curry salad, pasta and thick sandwiches. It's a good breakfast spot, with oversized croissants and homemade granola. Budget.

Union Bay Café (3505 Northeast 45th Street; 206-527-8364) serves Northwest regional foods with a Mediterranean influence. The entrées include grilled sturgeon with roasted garlic, tomato and dill and hazelnut chicken on sautéed spinach with lemon butter. More unusual is the venison sausage with huckleberries, caramelized onions and sage. Lighter entrées are available in the simple, classic café. The appetizer list is almost as long as the regular menu. Moderate.

On a busy commercial street between the University and Ravenna districts is **Ciao Bella** (5133 25th Avenue Northeast; 206-524-6989). The authentic Italian cuisine has been drawing raves since the little, L-shaped ristorante opened. On the menu are several classic pizzas, veal and chicken entrées and delectable pasta dishes. Chicken breast sautéed with gorgonzola cheese and fish soup with clams, mussels, calamari and prawns are flavored with artistry. Moderate.

Even if you are down to your last six bucks, you can get a meal at **Greenlake Vietnamese Food** (7906 East Greenlake Drive North; 206-525-0842) located in the, you guessed it, Green Lake area. This little hole-in-the-wall is nothing on atmosphere, but the food is good and cheap. The sweet-and-sour chicken is a refreshing change from the lumpy, breaded, fried rendition found in many Chinese restaurants. Preschoolers will enjoy the two bilingual children's books on the counter—in English and Vietnamese. Budget.

Next door is **Guido's Pizza** (7902 East Greenlake Drive North; 206-522-5553), another small, funky, unpretentious place, the aromas from which send joggers across the street at Green Lake into Pavlovian salivation. You can buy pizza by the whole or slice, delicious salads and good cappucinos. The artichoke pizza is wonderful. Budget.

SEATTLE NEIGHBORHOODS SHOPPING

If you're in the market for a potato gun, would like to lunch on instant jellyfish, crave a glow-in-the-dark squid or are searching for a popping Martian, head on over to **Archie McPhee's** (3510 Stone Way; 206-545-8344) near Lake Union, west of the university. This novelty-and-toy store offers more than 10,000 exotic items from all over the world.

Capitol Hill's Broadway Market is filled with popular shops like **Urban Outfitters** (401 Broadway Avenue East, Suite 101; 206-322-1800). Featuring casual urban ware, this shop offers new and vintage clothing, jewelry, housewares and shoes for the hip crowd. Another good place to shop for men's and women's clothing, shoes and accessories is **The Cramp** (219 Broadway Avenue East; 206-329-3392).

Chocoholics can get their fix in the Capitol Hill area at **Café Dilettante/Dilettante Chocolates** (416 Broadway Avenue East; 206-329-6463).

Madison Park Pharmacy (4200 East Madison Street; 206-323-6422) is popular with international travelers. A wide array of moneybelts, world time clocks, neck pillows, adjustable clothing line and guidebooks is found here.

At the **Washington Park Arboretum Visitor's Center Gift Shop** (2300 Arboretum Drive East; 206-543-8800) are gardening books, cards, china, earrings, necklaces, serving trays and sweatshirts. You can also buy plants from the arboretum greenhouse.

Dominated by the UW campus is the University district, a commercial neighborhood overflowing with a vast array of retail shops. One that attracts many tourists is the **La Tienda Folk Art Gallery** (4138 University Way Northeast; 206-632-1796). Here you'll find handpicked craft items from all over the world including those made by 200 selected American artisans.

SEATTLE NEIGHBORHOODS NIGHTLIFE

In the Capitol Hill area, **Matzoh Mamma's** (509 15th Avenue East; 206-324-6262) features folk music and comedy.

Capitol Hill also offers a number of popular gay and lesbian clubs and bars including the following:

Brass Connection (722 East Pike Street; 206-322-7777) is a popular gathering spot featuring deejay dance music.

Night Mary's (401 Broadway East; 206-325-6565) is a lesbian-oriented disco located in the Broadway Market. Weekend cabaret and big band shows also attract a mixed crowd. Cover. It's adjacent to **Hamburger Mary's,** a popular restaurant with a mixed clientele.

A 3000-square-foot dance club, **Changes Too** (1501 East Olive Way; 206-322-6356) is in an older, brick building. The gay crowd rocks to deejay music four nights a week.

A rustic, cedar-paneled establishment, **Hombres Saloon** (1413 14th Avenue; 503-323-2158) features a deejay, pool and darts. Hombres also has a comfortable fireplace where you can warm yourself on those cold Seattle nights.

One of the biggest gay clubs in the area is **R Place** (619 East Pine Street; 206-322-8828). Depending on your mood, you can plunk down at the sports bar, throw darts, enjoy a music video, shoot pool, enjoy tunes from the jukebox or play a low-stakes gambling game called pull tabs.

Another popular spot is **Neighbors Disco** (1509 Broadway; 206-324-5358) offering progressive rock.

Over in the Ballard district, you'll enjoy both the dinner and live jazz, rock or comedy shows at **The Backstage** (2208 Northwest Market Street; 206-781-2805). At the **Owl Café** (5140 Ballard Avenue; 206-784-3640) live blues bands perform nightly.

Near the University of Washington you'll find an array of clubs and places to park yourself at night.

There are cocktail service, full dinner and lots of laughs at **Giggles Comedy Niteclub** (5220 Roosevelt Way Northeast; 206-526-5347) Friday, Saturday and Sunday. Cover.

Well-known rock groups keep **The Far Side** (10815 Roosevelt Way Northeast; 206-362-1480) on their itineraries. Cover.

At the **University Sports Bar and Grill** (5260 University Way Northeast; 206-526-1489) you can dance weekends to live reggae, ska or rock. Popular with the college crowd, the club features big-screen television, an upstairs deck and darts.

SEATTLE NEIGHBORHOODS
BEACHES AND PARKS

Discovery Park—With two miles of beach trail and nine miles of footpaths winding through mixed forest and across open meadows, this bluff-top preserve (Seattle's largest at 535 acres) protects a remarkable "urban wilderness." Here are sweeping vistas, chances to watch birds and study nature, the Daybreak Star Indian Cultural Center with exhibits from various tribes, four miles of road for bicycling and an 1881 lighthouse (oldest in the area). Fort Lawton Historic District includes Officers' Row and military buildings surviving from the park's days as an Army fort.

Facilities: Picnic areas, restrooms, fitness trail and visitors' center at park's east gate; restaurants and groceries nearby; information, 206-285-4425, or 206-386-4236 for guided walks.

Getting there: Located a quarter-hour drive north of downtown in the Magnolia district; main entrance at West Government Way and 36th Avenue West.

Boren/Interlaken Parks—A secret greenway (★) close to downtown is preserved by these neighboring parks on Capitol Hill; it's just right for an afternoon or evening stroll.

Facilities: None; restaurants and groceries nearby.

Getting there: The park is located from East Roanoke Avenue to Lake Washington Boulevard East and Washington Park.

Seward Park—This 278-acre peninsula jutting into Lake Washington encompasses Seattle's largest virgin forest. Walking through it on one of several footpaths is the prime attraction, but many come to swim and sunbathe, launch a small boat, fish or visit a fish hatchery. Best introductory walk is the two-and-one-half-mile shoreline loop stroll; to see the large Douglas firs add another mile along the center of the peninsula.

Facilities: Picnic areas, restrooms, play areas, fishing pier and nature trails; restaurants and groceries nearby; information, 206-722-6342. *Swimming:* The swimming beaches' gentle surf is ideal for children, and there are lifeguards in summer. *Fishing:* From the pier.

Getting there: Located on the west shore of Lake Washington, southeast of downtown Seattle, at Lake Washington Boulevard South and South Orcas Street.

Carkeek Park—Tucked into a woodsy canyon reaching toward Puget Sound, this 216-acre wildland protects Piper's Creek and its resurrected runs of salmon and sea-going trout. Natural-history exhibits explain how citizens helped clean up the stream and bring the salmon back. Trails lead past spawning waters, to the top of the canyon and through a native-plant garden.

Facilities: Picnic areas, restrooms, play areas, beachcombing, pioneer orchard and brickyard; restaurants and groceries nearby; information, 206-386-4237.

Getting there: Located north of downtown, at Northwest Carkeek Park Road and 9th Avenue Northwest.

Warren G. Magnuson Park—This 212-acre site carved from the Sand Point Naval Air Station presents generous access to Lake Washington and wide views across the lake. It's a favorite place to launch a boat, swim or toss a frisbee.

Facilities: Picnic areas, restrooms, softball fields, boat ramp, tennis courts and swimming beaches with summer lifeguards; restaurants and groceries nearby.

Getting there: Located on Lake Washington, northeast of downtown Seattle, at Sand Point Way Northeast and 65th Avenue Northeast.

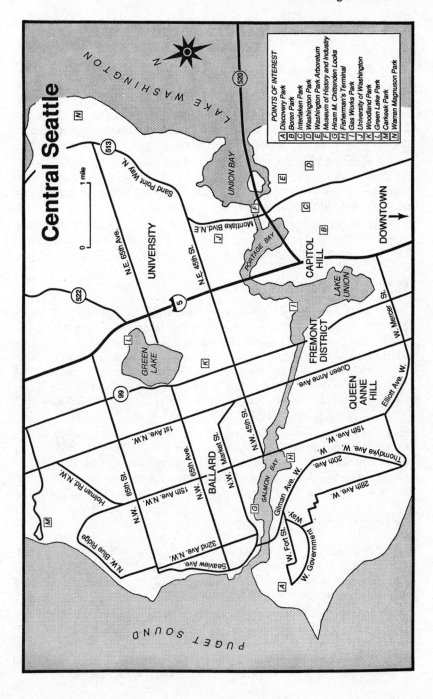

Central Seattle

LAKE WASHINGTON

N

UNION BAY

PUGET SOUND

PORTAGE BAY

LAKE UNION

SALMON BAY

DOWNTOWN →

UNIVERSITY

FREMONT DISTRICT

CAPITOL HILL

QUEEN ANNE HILL

BALLARD

GREEN LAKE

DOWNTOWN

Sand Point Way N.

N.E. 65th Ave.

N.E. 45th St.

Montlake Blvd. N.E.

W. Mercer St.

W. Mercer St.

Queen Anne Ave.

1st Ave. N.W.

N.W. Market St.

N.W. 45th St.

15th Ave. N.W.

N.W. 65th St.

N.W. 85th St.

Holman Rd. N.W.

32nd Ave. N.W.

Seaview Ave.

N.W. Blue Ridge

Elliott Ave. W.

15th Ave. W.

Thorndyke Ave. W.

20th Ave.

28th Ave. W.

W. Fort St.

W. Government Way

Gilman Ave. W.

520

513

522

5

99

A
B
C
D
E
F
G
H
J
K
L
M
N
T

0 | 1 mile

POINTS OF INTEREST

A | Discovery Park
B | Boren Park
C | Interlaken Park
D | Washington Park
E | Washington Park Arboretum
F | Museum of History and Industry
G | Hiram M. Chittenden Locks
H | Fisherman's Terminal
I | Gas Works Park
J | University of Washington
K | Woodland Park
L | Green Lake Park
M | Carkeek Park
N | Warren Magnuson Park

Seattle North

Catching a glimpse of history is popular here. To the northeast of Seattle is **Edmonds**, a longtime mill town. A historic walk will take you past the site of the old shingle mills, Brackett's Landing where the earliest pioneers settled, and numerous homes and buildings constructed in the late 1800s or early 1900s. The Edmonds Chamber of Commerce (5th Street; 206-670-3973) has a brochure covering the historic sites around town.

A visit to the **Edmonds Museum** (118 5th Avenue; 206-774-0900) with its working shingle-mill model and collections of logging tools and household furnishings will give you a better understanding of the pioneer heritage and industrial history of Edmonds.

You'll find tidepools, three stretches of public beach, a long fishing pier, an underwater park and summer beach walks hosted by the Edmonds Beach Rangers (206-775-2525) on the **Edmonds waterfront**.

SEATTLE NORTH RESTAURANTS

If you venture up to Edmonds, try **Ciao Italia** (512 5th Avenue South; 206-771-7950). This small restaurant on the main drag doesn't look like much from the outside—thankfully the lace curtains block out most of the traffic view—but the food prepared by the robust owner/chef from Ischia (a small island near Naples) is outstanding. Best choices here include spaghetti *muruchiaro* (a garlicky seafood pasta in white-wine sauce) and *vittello alla siuliana* (stuffed veal like they do it in Sicily). Dinner only. Moderate.

A moderately priced French deli and bakery, **Brusseau's** (117 5th Avenue South, Edmonds; 206-774-4166) features country-style breakfasts, smoked salmon sandwiches, torta rustica, seafood gumbo and a wide variety of desserts. Decorated like grandma's kitchen with calico wallpaper, the restaurant has a pleasant courtyard with planters and picnic tables. Be sure to arrive early for the light supper because Brusseau's closes at 7 p.m.

SEATTLE NORTH SHOPPING

Our favorite shop in Edmonds is **Vision Quest** (508 Main Street; 206-778-4333) offering an array of local art (jewelry, masks, woodwork, prints) and Native American music and artifacts. The store also features a variety of intriguing workshops, gatherings and drum circles.

There are a number of good shops in the renovated **Old Mill Town** (5th Avenue South, Edmonds; 206-771-4515) including the **Edmonds Antique Mall** (206-771-9466), **Basketta** (206-775-1002) overflowing with baskets and windsocks and the **Old General Store** (206-771-2561) with Native American jewelry, baskets, pottery and Pacific Rim folk art.

Seattle West

Out west of Seattle you'll find some rare treasures such as a company town operating in the time-honored manner, a fascinating Indian cultural show, a marine-science center and inns that look like they were created for a James Herriott book. From the islands of Puget Sound west to Hood Canal this is also a region rich in parks and natural areas. You'll also want to tour the Kitsap Peninsula, Bremerton's Naval Heritage and the parks of Southern Puget Sound.

Since you can reach pastoral **Vashon Island** (★) by state ferry from the Fauntleroy dock in West Seattle (a 15-minute crossing), we include it in this section of the book. However, Vashon stretches south for 13 miles toward Tacoma (accessible by another 15-minute ferry from Tahlequah), creating a lovely Seattle-to-Tacoma country-road alternative to Route 5. The ferry to Tacoma lands next to one of the city's highlights, splendid Point Defiance Park (see "Tacoma and Olympia" below).

The Vashon Island Highway will take you fairly directly down the island, through the town of Vashon. Just south of town is the **Country Store and Farm** (20211 Vashon Highway; 206-463-3655) where you can peruse merchandise grown or produced on the island—cider, fruit and syrups, berries and preserves and a variety of gardening tools, natural-fiber clothing, kitchen wares and such.

Side roads beckon from the highway to a handful of poorly marked state beaches and county parks. **Point Robinson County Park** on Maury Island (linked to Vashon via an isthmus at the hamlet of Portage) is easier to find and particularly interesting since it's next door to the Coast Guard's picturesque Point Robinson Lighthouse (not open to the public).

To the north, **Winslow** offers a much more attractive destination for most travelers, and you can see it on foot. The picturesque town is on Bainbridge Island, a 35-minute ferry ride from Coleman Dock (pick up a self-guiding brochure with map, *Leave Seattle Behind*, before boarding). To see more than obvious attractions (restaurants, shops, a winetasting room), head for the mile-long waterfront footpath called **Walkabout** to the left of the ferry landing. Follow it along the shoreline, past shipyards and hauled-out sailboats under repair, to **Eagle Harbor Waterfront Park** and its fishing pier and low-tide beach. Carry on to a ship chandler and pair of marinas. Return as you came, or through the Winslow business district. At our press time, the town was considering a name change to Bainbridge Island.

Another interesting loop trip west of Seattle begins in the Navy town of Bremerton. You can explore some of the region's history as well as the remote reaches of southern Puget Sound.

Take the ferry or drive to Bremerton and visit the **Puget Sound Naval Ship Yard** (Burwell Street and Pacific Avenue, near the ferry dock; 206-

476-3711) in Bremerton. The best way to get here is the Washington State Ferry (cars and walk-ons; one hour) or state foot-ferry (50 minutes) from Seattle's Coleman Dock (Pier 52) through Rich Passage to Bremerton. The shipyard's major attraction is the famous World War II battleship *U.S.S. Missouri*, on whose decks the peace treaty ending the war with Japan was signed. Other ships come and go; call ahead. **Bremerton Naval Museum** (a half-block north of the ferry dock on Washington Avenue; 206-479-7447) looks back to the days of Jack Tar and square-riggers.

Only an hour from the heart of Seattle, the Kitsap Peninsula is framed on the east side by Puget Sound and the west by Hood Canal. Historic company towns, naval museums and remote parks make this area a fine retreat from the city.

A good place to learn about the region's Native American heritage is the town of Suquamish. Chief Seattle and the allied tribes he represented are showcased at the **Suquamish Museum** (★) (Route 305, Suquamish; 206-598-3311) in an outstanding collection of photographs and relics along with mock-ups of a typical Indian dwelling and the interior of a longhouse and several award-winning video presentations shown in a small theater.

Old Man House, site of the Suquamish Village and one of the last longhouses in the Pacific Northwest, and **Chief Seattle's Grave**, set under a canopy of dugout canoes in a hillside graveyard overlooking Seattle (his namesake), are just a few miles further down Suquamish Way. Follow the road signs.

"Velkommen til Poulsbo" is an oft-repeated phrase in "Washington's Little Norway." There are some wonderful samples of historic architecture on a **walking tour** of town; the Poulsbo Chamber of Commerce (19044 Jensen Way Northeast; 206-779-4848) can provide a guide map. At the brand new **Marine Science Center** (18743 Front Street Northeast, Poulsbo; 206-779-5549) you can learn about the various forms of marine life that inhabit the waters of Southern Puget Sound; they even have a touch tank of friendly sea creatures.

The **Thomas Kemper Brewery** (★) (22381 Foss Road Northeast; 206-697-1446) one mile north of Poulsbo off the road to Kingston offers informal, 30-minute tours of the facility, has a small pub and beer garden with live music and sponsors a grand Oktoberfest celebration every year.

Among our favorite villages in the Pacific Northwest is **Port Gamble** (★), one of the West's last company towns. Situated on a bluff at the intersection of Admirablty Inlet and Gamble Bay, this century-old community is owned by the Pope and Talbot lumber firm.

The town is home to about 150 sawmill workers and their families who rent homes from the company. Picturesque frame houses, towering elms and a church with Gothic windows and a needle spire give the community a New England look. Don't miss the mock-ups of Captain Talbot's cabin and A. J. Pope's office at the **Pope and Talbot Historical Museum** (206-297-3341; admission) or the **Sea and Shore Museum** on the second floor of the quaint, 1853 **Port Gamble Country Store** (Rainier Avenue; 206-297-2623). Renovations are underway on the 1887 **Walker Ames Mansion** next door. Other historic homes and buildings are occupied by current Pope and Talbot employees but can be viewed from the outside; a walking-tour guide can be obtained at the Country Store.

SOUTHERN PUGET SOUND On a map, Southern Puget Sound looks like a fistful of bony fingers clawing at the earth. This maze of inlets, peninsulas and islands presents plentiful saltwater access and invite days of poking around. Here are three representative experiences:

South of Bremerton is the **Longbranch Peninsula** (★), a showcase of Southern Puget Sound's outdoor treasures. Quiet coves and lonely forests, dairy farms, funky fishing villages with quiet cafés, shellfish beaches and oyster farmers, a salmon hatchery, fishing piers and wharves all await leisurely exploration. Take Route 16 to Route 302, proceeding west until you reach Key Center. The **Key Peninsula Highway**, running south from this community, is the main road bringing you to most attractions.

To visit the hamlet of **Lakebay** on Mayo Cove, turn east from Peninsula Highway three-and-a-half miles south of Home (the town, not your Home Sweet) onto Cornwall Road and follow it to Delano Road. On the south side of the cove is **Penrose Point State Park** with 145 acres of forest, two miles of beaches, hiking trails, fishing, picnicking and camping. At the end of the highway is another bayside village, **Longbranch**, on the shores of Filucy Bay, one of the prettiest anchorages in these waters.

Hartstene Island (★) (northeast of Shelton via Route 3 and Pickering Road) is connected to the mainland by a bridge, providing auto access to a quintessential Southern Puget Sound island experience. Many of the island's public beaches are poorly signed, but **Jarrell Cove State Park** (at the foot of Wingert Road, off North Island Drive; 206-426-9226) and a marina on the other side of the cove are easily found at the island's north tip. You'll see plenty of boats from both sides of the cove, and at the park you can stroll docks, fish for perch, walk bits of beach or explore forest trails. Main roads loop the island's north end, or head for the far southern tip at Brisco Point with views overlooking Peale Passage and Squaxin Island.

The eastern shore of **Hood Canal** (★) is a mere mile or two from the western side of the channel, but in character it's worlds apart. Beach access is limited, but views across the canal to the Olympic Mountains are splendid, settlements few and quiet and back roads genuine byways—few tourists ever get here. This is also where the canal bends like a fishhook to the east, called the "Great Bend."

To see the east shore in its entirety, begin at Belfair, leaving Route 3 for Route 300. At three miles, watch for Belfair State Park on the left.

The road now narrows and traffic thins on the way to the modest resort town of Tahuya; shortly beyond, the canal makes its great bend. The road dives into dense forest, bringing you in about 11 miles to a T-junction; bear left, then left again to the ghost town of Dewatto. Take Dewatto Bay Road eastward out of town, then turn north and follow signs 12 miles to a left turn into the little town of Holly, or continue north 15 miles more to **Seabeck**, founded in 1856 as a sawmill town and popular today with anglers, scuba divers and boaters.

SEATTLE WEST HOTELS

On Bainbridge Island, **The Beach Cottage** (5831 Ward Avenue Northeast; 206-842-6081) is a complex of four cottages on a landscaped hillside above the water. The cottages have kitchens (with breakfast ingredients in the refrigerator), private decks, fireplaces and views of the Olympic Mountains, the Seattle skyline or the marina. They accommodate up to four people. Deluxe.

Serenity and comfort in the countryside characterize **Bombay House** (8490 Northeast Beck Road, Bainbridge Island; 206-842-3926). The five-room bed and breakfast has moderate prices and a bright, cheery atmosphere. The rooms, which vary in size and decor, view the sea or the lavish flower and herb gardens.

Rooms at the **Poulsbo's Cypress Inn** (19801 7th Avenue Northeast, Poulsbo; 206-697-2119), part of a small chain in the Northwest, are modern and comfortably furnished with big beds, satellite television, individual air conditioning and other basic amenities; a few are equipped with kitchenette or jacuzzi. Moderate.

If you can afford the high tariff, a stay at the **Manor Farm Inn** (★) (26069 Big Valley Road Northeast, Poulsbo; 206-779-4628) is like stepping onto the set of *All Creatures Great and Small*, complete with a working farm attended by an Englishman, owner Robin Hughes. Plush rooms are country cozy, and the food can't be beat, but the best thing about this place is the chance to stroll among the calves, kittens, chickens, piglets, sheep, rabbits, doves and horses in the farm's white-fenced pastures or the opportunity to pull on a pair of rubber boots and head to the quiet trout pond to drop a line and wait for a nibble. Prices are ultra-deluxe; book well in advance.

SEATTLE WEST RESTAURANTS

Café Tosca (9924 Southwest Bank Road, Vashon Island; 206-463-2125), in the heart of downtown, is Vashon's newest restaurant with Italian-opera posters on the walls. Entrées include calamari steak, chicken marsala, se tortellini in a pesto cream sauce and the very popular capellini *pomi-*

doro, angel-hair pasta with tomatoes, garlic, olive oil and basil. Don't forget to save room for a piece of homemade cheesecake and Italian caffe. Moderate.

The old island hangout is **Sound Food Restaurant** (20312 99th Avenue Southwest, Vashon Island; 206-463-3565). The restaurant is known for its casual atmosphere—windows overlooking the gardens and lots of wood inside. Saturday and Sunday brunches result in long waits, but the food—whole-wheat waffles, blintzes with fresh fruit, potato pancakes, omelettes with wonderful sauces and breads and pastries from the bakery—is usually worth it. A variety of soups, salads and sandwiches of baked bread is available for lunch. Dinner entrées include a vegetable linguine, seafood dishes and even meatballs a la Mexico. Desserts—sigh—come fresh from the bakery. Moderate.

In a large Tudor house nestled in the trees is the **Pleasant Beach Grill** (4738 Lynwood Center Northeast, Bainbridge Island; 206-842-4347). The white-linen tablecloths and low lighting bespeak a comfortable island elegance. The chef specializes in Northwest seafood but includes a couple of succulent chicken dishes, pastas and aged-beef entrées. The white fish in a curry sauce with mushrooms and red, green and yellow peppers comes recommended. Dinner only. Moderate.

What you won't find at the **Four Swallows** (4569 Lynwood Center Road, Bainbridge Island; 206-842-3397) you can order at a standard restaurant. What you will find are exotic combinations of mouth-watering fare scribbled on a tablet in the foyer each evening. How about kiwi fruit, pears and feta cheese dipped in pine nuts and served with crackers and roasted garlic? The salads are tasty mixes of greens with flavorful dressings. Dinner only. Budget.

Locals swear by the omelettes, sandwiches and clam chowder at **Judith's Tearoom and Rose Café** (18820 Front Street Northeast, Poulsbo; 206-697-3449), but we found the staff to be abrupt to the point of rudeness. Anyway, try something from the daily dessert tray where the selections often include fruit, nut or cream pies, bread pudding and cheesecake. Breakfast, lunch and formal tea. Budget.

The **New Day Seafood Eatery** (325 Hostmark Street Northeast, Poulsbo; 206-697-3183) is actually the outlet for the fresh catch brought in every day by the vessel *New Day* and features fast and cheap fish and chips (or clams, shrimp, scallops, oysters or chicken and chips). Diners choose from booths inside or picnic tables on the large deck overlooking Liberty Bay and the wharf. Lunch and dinner. Budget.

SEATTLE WEST SHOPPING

Looking like a lane in far-away Scandinavia, the main street of Poulsbo is lined with wonderful galleries and boutiques. You'll find paintings, pottery, weavings, cards, rosemaling, baskets, even food products created by local artists at the **Verksted Co-operative Gallery** (18820 Front Street Northeast, 2nd floor; 206-697-4470), while **Gallery Potlatch** (18830-B Front Street Northeast; 206-779-3377) carries a fine selection of prints, glasswork, pottery, jewelry and Native American art.

For merchandise from the five Scandinavian countries, visit **Five Swans** (18846 Front Street Northeast; 206-697-2005) or **Sluys Gifts** (18924 Front Street Northeast; 206-779-7171). For sweets head to **Boehm's Chocolates** (18864 Front Street Northeast; 206-697-3318) and **Sluys Bakery** (18924 Front Street Northeast; 206-779-2798) for pastries and cookies.

SEATTLE WEST BEACHES AND PARKS

Manchester State Park—This one-time fort overlooking Rich Passage includes abandoned torpedo warehouses and some interpretive displays explaining its role in guarding Bremerton Navy Base at the turn of the century. The park is infamous for its poison oak—stay on the two miles of hiking trails, or try the 3400 feet of cobbled beach.

Facilities: Picnic areas, restrooms and showers; restaurants and groceries nearby; information, 206-871-4065. *Diving:* Rocks off Middle Point attract divers.

Camping: There are 50 sites plus three walk-in sites.

Getting there: Located at the east foot of East Hilldale Road off Beach Drive, east of Bremerton.

Fay Bainbridge State Park—A small park (17 acres), it nevertheless curls itself around a long sandspit to present some 1400 feet of shoreline. The only campground on Bainbridge Island is here.

Facilities: Picnic areas, restrooms, showers, play area, boat ramp, horseshoe pits and volleyball courts; restaurants and groceries nearby; information, 206-842-3931. *Swimming:* Chilly waters, no lifeguard.

Camping: There are 36 sites including ten walk-in.

Getting there: At Sunrise Drive Northeast and Lafayette Road about six miles north of Winslow at the northeast tip of Bainbridge Island.

Old Man House State Park—This day-use only park was once the site of a longhouse used as a meeting place by Chief Seattle and the Suquamish Indians. Check out the interpretive and historical displays. A small, sandy beach overlooks the heavy marine traffic that cruises through Agate Passage.

Facilities: Pit toilet and picnic tables; groceries nearby.

Getting there: Located on the Kitsap Peninsula just north of Agate Pass off Route 104.

Point No Point Beach Resort (★)—This private resort with beach access sits on the northern tip of the Kitsap Peninsula overlooking Admiralty Inlet and mid-Puget Sound. The waters off the point teem with salmon, attracting anglers from the world over. Other sites of interest include the Point No Point Lighthouse and the 35-acre Point No Point Nature Park with trails, viewpoints for watching eagles and a beach for clam digging.

Facilities: Restrooms, showers, laundromat and picnic tables; boat rentals, launch and groceries nearby in Hansville; information, 206-638-2233. *Fishing:* Outstanding. *Swimming:* Good.

Camping: There are four tent sites and 38 RV hookup sites.

Getting there: Located at 8708 Northeast Point No Point Road; from Kingston follow Route 104 to Hansville Road, then to Point No Point Road just east of Hansville.

Buck Lake County Park—Near Hansville on the northern tip of the Kitsap Peninsula, picturesque Buck Lake is a good spot for quiet, contemplative fishing or a relaxing summer swim.

Facilities: Restrooms, bath house, boat launch, picnic tables and playground. *Fishing:* Excellent either on the lake or from the shore. *Swimming:* Permitted.

Getting there: Located on Buck Lake Road; take Route 104 from Kingston to Hansville Road and follow it north.

Salisbury Point—This tiny, six-acre park with small stretch of saltwater beach is next to Hood Canal Floating Bridge and gives views of the Olympic Mountains across the canal. Though camping here is very limited, this is the closest you'll come to accommodations near historic Port Gamble, just seven miles west.

Facilities: Restrooms, picnic shelters, boat launch, playground; restaurant and groceries nearby; information, 206-779-3756. *Fishing:* Good. *Swimming:* Good.

Camping: In the parking lot, in a self-contained vehicle.

Getting there: North of Hood Canal Floating Bridge turn left on Wheeler Road and follow the signs.

Kitsap Memorial State Park—This 58-acre park four miles south of Hood Canal Floating Bridge has a quiet beach well suited for collecting oysters and clams. Between the canal, beach and playground facilities there's plenty to keep the troops entertained, making this a good choice for family camping.

Facilities: Restrooms, showers, shelter, tables and stoves, boat moorage, playground with horseshoe pits and baseball diamond; some facilities wheelchair accessible; restaurant and groceries nearby; information, 206-779-3205. *Fishing:* Excellent off the beach. *Swimming:* Good.

Camping: There are 43 sites but no RV hookups; trailer dump.

Getting there: From Kingston take Route 104 (which turns into Bond Road) to Route 3, then follow it north until you reach the park.

Illahee State Park—Wooded uplands and 1700 feet of saltwater shoreline are separated by a 250-foot bluff at this site. Steep hiking trails connect the two park units. On the beach is a fishing pier; at the south end are tide flats for wading.

Facilities: Picnic area, restrooms, showers, baseball field, play area, horseshoe pits and boat ramp; information, 206-478-6460. *Fishing:* From the pier.

Camping: There are 25 sites.

Getting there: Located at the east foot of Sylvan Way (Route 306) two miles east of Route 303 northeast of Bremerton.

Twanoh State Park—With many amenities of a city park, Twanoh's 175 acres also include the forests, trails and camping of a more remote site. A two-mile hiking trail takes you through a thick forest of second-growth conifers next to Twanoh Creek; or explore a half-mile of saltwater beach.

Facilities: Picnic areas, restrooms, showers, boat launch and dock, tennis, horseshoe pits and concession stand; information, 206-275-2222. *Swimming:* Saltwater wading pool and beach. *Diving:* Good.

Camping: There are 39 tent sites and nine hookups; closed in winter.

Getting there: Eight miles southwest of Belfair on Route 106.

Belfair State Park—Two creeks flow through the 63-acre park en route to Hood Canal, affording both fresh and saltwater shorelines. Along its 3700 feet of beach the saltwater warms quickly across shallow tide flats, but pollution makes swimming here risky; shellfish are usually posted off-limits.

Facilities: Picnic areas, restrooms and showers; restaurants and groceries nearby; information, 206-275-0668. *Swimming:* There's a lagoon with a bathhouse.

Camping: There are 147 tent sites and 47 RV sites; dump station.

Getting there: Located three miles west of Belfair on Route 300.

Scenic Beach State Park—Well named it is, with glorious views across Hood Canal to the Olympics and north up Dabob Bay. Nearly 1500 feet of cobblestone beach invites strolls; scuba divers also push off from here. In May, 88 acres of native rhododendrons burst into bloom.

Facilities: Picnic areas, restrooms, showers, play area, horseshoe pit, volleyball and community center; restaurants and groceries nearby; information, 206-830-5079. *Fishing:* Good for salmon and bottom-fish at nearby artificial reef; boat launch next to park.

Camping: There are 50 sites; closed October through April.

Getting there: Located just west of Seabeck on Miami Beach Road Northwest about 13 miles northwest of Bremerton.

Seattle East

Seattle East, extending from the eastern shore of Lake Washington to the Cascade foothills, blends urban and rural assets of this metropolitan region. Here you'll find wineries and archaeological sites, prime birdwatching areas and homey bed and breakfasts.

Château Ste. Michelle in Woodinville (on Route 202 south of town; 206-488-1133) is the state's largest winery with daily tasting and tours. Situated on a turn-of-the-century estate, it also offers greenswards, duck and trout ponds, experimental vineyards and frequent outdoor concerts on summer weekends.

Renowned as Seattle's foremost suburb, **Bellevue** boasts a surprisingly diverse network of parks (206-455-6881) embedded within its neighborhoods. **Mercer Slough Nature Park** (stretching north from Route 90 off Bellevue Way) is the biggest and may be the best with some 300 acres of natural wetland habitat and ten miles of trails. **Wilburton Hill Park** will be centered around a new botanical garden of native and ornamental Northwest plants. To see what Bellevue used to be like before the coming of freeways, commuters and office towers, stroll the short stretch of shops along Main Street westward from 104th Avenue Southeast in **Old Bellevue**.

South of Bellevue, Seattle's rock legend Jimi Hendrix is buried. A caretaker can show you the guitarist's grave at **Greenwood Cemetery** (350 Monroe Avenue Northeast, Renton; 206-255-1511).

SEATTLE EAST HOTELS

The **Shumway Mansion** (11410 99th Place Northeast, Kirkland; 206-823-2303) is a historic mansion with a New England flavor. To save it from demolition, the present owners had it moved to a knoll in north Kirkland, where it now accommodates guests, weddings and social functions. When a group takes over, overnight visitors can retreat to a tiny reading alcove on a second floor. The formal inn contains European furnishings, rugs out of the Orient, lace curtains and silk floral arrangements. Each of the seven guest rooms has a queen bed and antiques and easy chairs. The innkeepers serve a full breakfast on crystal and china. Moderate.

Twelve acres of evergreen trees surround the **Wildflower** (25237 Southeast Issaquah-Fall City Road, Issaquah; 206-392-1196). This two-story, log home has a gracious hostess and four guest rooms named for plants common in the area: daisy, rose, fern and strawberry. Knotty-pine walls, antiques, dried flowers and heirloom quilts create an old-fashioned, country flavor. The downstairs living room is equally cozy with a woodstove, braided rugs, a wicker rocker and shelves of books. A wide verandah overlooks the lovely natural landscaping. Moderate.

In a quiet wooded area southeast of Seattle is the **Maple Valley Bed and Breakfast** (★) (20020 Southeast 228th Street, Maple Valley; 206-432-1409). The two-story, contemporary home has open-beamed ceilings, peeled-pole railings, cedar walls and detailed-wood trim. Guests like to lounge on sheepskin-covered couches by the huge, stone fireplace. The two guest rooms are individually decorated and color coordinated. On cool nights, heated, sand-filled pads ("hot babies") are used to warm the beds. A full breakfast is served on Northwest-crafted pottery in a dining area that overlooks trees, wandering peacocks and ponds with ducks. Budget to moderate.

SEATTLE EAST RESTAURANTS

The open kitchen at **Andre's Gourmet Cuisine** (14125 Northeast 20th Street, Bellevue; 206-747-6551) is as entertaining as the food. This restaurant offers a menu with Vietnamese specialties like spring rolls or pork with lemon grass, as well as Continental selections, such as lamb with garlic. Vietnamese chef Andre Nguyen comes with experience from some of Seattle's best restaurants. Moderate.

You wouldn't expect to find a good restaurant in this little shopping strip, but here it is. At **Pogacha** (119 106th Avenue Northeast, Bellevue; 206-455-5670), a Croatian version of pizza is the mainstay. The pizzas, crisp on the outside but moist inside, are baked in a brick oven. Because the saucing is nonexistent or very light, the flavor of the toppings—pesto and various cheeses, alone or over vegetables or meat—is more apparent. Other entrées include soups, salads and pastas. Moderate.

One of the best Japanese restaurants in all of Puget Sound is hidden in the Totem Lake West shopping center in suburbia. **Izumi** (★) (12539 116th Avenue Northeast, Kirkland; 206-821-1959) features an excellent sushi bar. Entrées are fairly standard—beef, pork, chicken sukiyaki and teriyaki— but the ingredients are especially fresh and carefully prepared. Service is friendly. Moderate.

A couple of local residents who grew up in Pakistan and Bangladesh have opened **Shamiana** (10724 Northeast 68th Street, Kirkland; 206-827-4902). The food is cooled to an American palate but can be spiced to a full-blown, multistar *hot*. A buffet of four curries, salad, nan and dal is offered at lunch. Dinners are a la carte, and include entrées such as lamb curry with rice *pulao* or fish *tikka*, smokey cod with rice *pulao*. Moderate.

SEATTLE EAST SHOPPING

Domus (141 Bellevue Square, Northeast 8th Street and Bellevue Way, Bellevue; 206-454-2728) carries ever-changing design items for the home. Expect extensive selections of bric-a-brac, paintings, furniture, chinaware and some jewelry. **Fidalgo's** (172 Bellevue Square, Bellevue; 206-455-

8888) has artificial flowers, plants and trees so well done they rival nature's productions. **Bellevue Square** (206-454-2431) also has 200 other unique shops, department stores and restaurants.

One of the most elegant shops in Bellevue is **Alvin Goldfarb** (305 Bellevue Way Northeast; 206-454-9393). Specializing in 18-carat gold pieces crafted by an in-house goldsmith who also works with precious and semi-precious gems, this is a mecca for discriminating people who desire a one-of-a-kind item.

Five miles north of Bellevue is the downtown **Kirkland Square** (215 Central Way, Kirkland; 206-822-2290), a mini-mall easily identified by its handsome, ten-foot-high clock. If you're tired of shopping till you drop, kids (and some adults) rave about **Quarters** (206 Main Street, Kirkland; 206-889-2555) where they can don helmets and ride the only two Virtuality machines in the United States at this writing. They can also play such video games as Dragonslayers and Starblades.

Refurbished farmhouses, a barn and a feed store are stocked with handicrafts and artful, designer clothing at Issaquah's **Gilman Village** (317 Northwest Gilman Boulevard; 206-462-0594). Among the 40-plus shops clustered in these historic structures is **Northwest Gallery** (206-391-4221), owned by 34 woodworkers and stocked with handicrafts such as boxes, toys, furniture, custom cabinetry and screens. **Made in Washington** (206-392-4819) handles only vases, perfume bottles, dinnerware and wood carvings. A combination bookstore and restaurant, the **Oasis Book Company** (206-462-0594) stocks all your favorite literary needs.

SEATTLE EAST NIGHTLIFE

Bellevue has the best pickings for nightlife in Seattle East. At **Bailey's Comedy Penthouse** (821 Bellevue Way Northeast; 206-455-2445; dinner reservations, 206-455-4494) diners enjoy preferred seating for the shows.

Papagayo's (2239 148th Avenue Northeast; 206-641-6666) features dance fests, karaoke, blues and rock. Cover.

Daniel's Broiler (Bellevue Place, 10500 Northeast 8th Street; 206-462-4662) has piano Tuesday through Saturday and a Sunday jazz showcase.

The **New Jake O'Shaunnessey's** (401 Bellevue Square, Bellevue; 206-455-5559) is a sports bar with four televisions in the lounge. With a welcoming fireplace and large dancefloor, the **Greenwood Inn** (625 116th Avenue Northeast; 206-455-9444) features live bands playing Top-40 and rock-and-roll in the lounge. Cover.

Good things come in small packages, and the **Village Theater** (120 North Front Street, Issaquah; 206-392-2202) proves it. The local casts here will tackle anything, be it Broadway musicals, dramas or comedy.

Kilgore's (17626 Northeast 140th Street, Woodinville; 206-481-3400) is a popular country-and-western club with a good dancefloor. Karaoke is also offered. Cover on weekends.

For progressive, industrial or Top-40 music, make your way to **The Backdoor** (2207 Bel-Red Road, Redmond; 206-746-7918). There's dancing Friday and Saturday. Cover.

SEATTLE EAST BEACHES AND PARKS

Saint Edwards State Park—This former Catholic seminary still exudes the peace and quiet of a theological retreat across its 316 heavily wooded acres and 3000 feet of Lake Washington shoreline. Except for a handful of former seminary buildings, the park is mostly natural, laced by miles of informal trails. To reach the beach, take the wide path just west of the main seminary building. It winds three-fourths mile down to the shore, where you can wander left or right. Side trails climb up the bluff for the return loop.

Facilities: Picnic areas, restrooms, soccer and baseball fields; for information, 206-823-2992. *Swimming:* Beach (no lifeguard) and indoor pool year-round.

Getting there: On Lake Washington's eastern shore, between Kenmore and Kirkland on Juanita Drive Northeast at Northeast 145th Street.

Marymoor County Park—This roomy, 485-acre preserve at the north end of Lake Sammamish in Redmond is a delightful mix of archeology and history, river and lake, meadows and marshes, plus an assortment of athletic fields. A one-mile footpath leads to a lakeside observation deck, and there's access to the eight-mile Sammamish River Trail. The 1904 Marymoor Mansion houses a historical museum, with a pioneer windmill nearby.

Facilities: Picnic areas, restrooms, play areas, baseball and soccer fields, tennis courts, model-airplane airport, bicycle velodrome with frequent races and archeological site; restaurants and groceries nearby; information, 206-296-2964.

Getting there: Located on Bellevue-Redmond Road (Route 901) off Route 520 just south of Redmond city center.

Lake Sammamish State Park—A popular, 431-acre park at the southern tip of Lake Sammamish near Issaquah, it offers plenty to do, including swimming, boating, picnicking, hiking and birdwatching along 6858 feet of lake shore and around the mouth of Issaquah Creek. Look for eagles, hawks, great-blue heron, red-wing blackbirds, northern flickers, grebes, kingfishers, killdeer, buffleheads, widgeon and Canada geese.

Facilities: Picnic areas, restrooms, showers, soccer fields, jogging trail and boat launch; restaurants and groceries nearby; information, 206-455-7010. *Swimming:* Two beaches but no lifeguards.

Getting there: Located at East Lake Sammamish Parkway Southeast and Southeast 56th Street, two miles north of Route 90 in Issaquah (15 miles east of Seattle) via exit 17.

Luther Burbank County Park—At the northeast corner of Mercer Island in Lake Washington, this little jewel presents some 3000 feet of shoreline to explore along with marshes, meadows and woods. You can tour the entire 77-acre site on a loop walk.

Facilities: Picnic areas, restrooms, play area, tennis courts and amphitheater with summer concerts; restaurants and groceries nearby; information, 206-296-4438. *Fishing:* Good from pier for salmon, steelhead, trout and bass. *Swimming:* Beach with summer lifeguard.

Getting there: Entrance is at 84th Avenue Southeast and Southeast 24th Street, via the Island Crest Way exit from Route 90 on Mercer Island, east of Seattle.

Gene Coulon Beach Park—At the south tip of Lake Washington in Renton, this handsomely landscaped site is most notable for the loads of attractions within its 55 acres: one-and-a-half miles of lakeside path, the wildfowl-rich estuary of John's Creek and a "nature islet," a lagoon enclosed by the thousand-foot floating boardwalk of "Picnic Gallery," a seafood restaurant and interesting architecture reminiscent of old-time amusement parks. A logboom-protected shoreline includes a fishing pier.

Facilities: Picnic grounds and floats, restrooms, play areas and volleyball; restaurant on park grounds and others nearby; information, 206-235-2568. *Boating:* A boat harbor with rentals and ramp. *Fishing:* Good from pier for trout and salmon. *Swimming:* Bathing beach protected by a concrete walkabout with summer lifeguard.

Getting there: Bordered by Lake Washington Boulevard North in Renton, north of Route 405 via exit 5 and Park Avenue North.

Seattle South

Meander from the heart of the city south to the Tacoma line and you'll find one of the world's great aviation museums, the historic coal-mining town of Black Diamond and beautiful river gorges. Inviting fresh and salt-water beaches provide a convenient retreat from urban living. With an ample array of outdoor activities, Seattle South serves as the city's back door to the wilderness.

About ten miles to the south, off Route 5 at Boeing Field, is the **Museum of Flight** (9404 East Marginal Way South; 206-764-5720; admission). Centered in a traffic-stopping piece of architecture called the Great Gallery, the museum is a must. In the glass-and-steel gallery, 22 aircraft hang suspended from the ceiling, almost as if in flight. In all, some 45 aircraft (many rare) trace more than 70 years of aviation. You'll see a 1916 B & W float plane, 1917 Curtis Jenny biplane, 1929 Boeing 80-A bi-plane, 1932 Yakima Clipper sail plane, 1935 DC-3, 1962 A-12 Blackbird, 1968 Aerocar III (flying car) and many homebuilts.

The 1909 **Red Barn** houses one wing of the museum. The so-called "barn" was originally the Boeing Co.'s boat-building factory on the banks of the nearby Duwamish River. Later it was converted to aircraft production, the company's original plant. Since relocated several times, it now houses exhibits on Boeing's early days in the airplane business, a far cry from today's mammoth factories.

Black Diamond (about 35 miles southeast of Seattle on Route 169) is an old coal-mining town with the odds and ends of its mining, logging and railroading history on display at the **Black Diamond Historical Society Museum** (Baker Street and Railroad Avenue; 206-886-1168), housed in an 1884 railroad depot. But the real reason most folks stop here—on their way to Mt. Rainier, the Green River Gorge or winter ski slopes—is the famous **Black Diamond Bakery** (32805 Railroad Avenue; 206-886-2741). At last count, the bakery and its wood-fired ovens produced some two dozen varieties of bread, along with doughnuts and cookies.

Green River Gorge is less than an hour from downtown Seattle but is worlds away from the big city. The heart of the gorge covers only some six miles on the map but is so twisted into oxbows that it takes kayakers 12 river miles to paddle through it. Just 300 feet deep, the steep-walled gorge nevertheless slices through solid rock (shale and sandstone) to reveal coal seams and fossil imprints and inspire a fine sense of remoteness. State and county parks flank the gorge (see "Beaches and Parks" below), but for the ultimate experience walk trails at the privately owned **Green River Gorge Resort** (four miles east of Black Diamond on Green River Gorge Road; 206-886-2302). Sandstone cliffs crowd the earnest, endless rush of the river, waterfalls pour from fern-clad ledges, and pools sparkle next to moss-lined grottoes.

SEATTLE SOUTH HOTEL

A stone's throw from Sea-Tac Airport, the **Seattle Marriott** (3201 South 176th Street; 206-241-2000) is a wonderfully luxurious hotel featuring a 20,000-square-foot tropical atrium five stories high. Around it are 459 freshly renovated guest rooms. There are a restaurant, jazz club, whirlpools, health club and gameroom. Airport shuttle is provided. In the moderate to deluxe price range.

SEATTLE SOUTH RESTAURANT

An excellent Thai restaurant convenient to Sea-Tac Airport is **Bai Tong** (★) (15859 Pacific Highway South, Sea-Tac; 206-431-0893). Located in a former A&W drive-in (the root beer barrel is still on the roof) this eatery is known for its steamed curry salmon, grilled beef with Thai sauce and marinated chicken. The carpeted dining room is lush with potted plants, and the walls are adorned with photos of mouthwatering dishes. Prices are in the budget range.

SEATTLE SOUTH BEACHES AND PARKS

The **Green River Gorge Conservation Area** (206-931-3930) includes six state parks and some 50 miles of hiking trails. Here we pick the two developed parks at the entrance and exit of the gorge and one nearby state park on a lake.

Flaming Geyser State Park—Once a resort, this 667-acre park downstream from the exit of Green River Gorge offers ten miles of hiking trails and nearly five miles of riverbank. Pick up a trail map and brochure in the main parking lot.

Facilities: Picnic areas, restrooms, play areas, volleyball, horseshoe pits and kayaking for skilled paddlers; restaurants and groceries in Black Diamond; information, 206-931-3930. *Fishing:* Steelhead in season (check posted regulations).

Getting there: Located on Green Valley Road three miles west of Route 169, south of Black Diamond.

Kanaskat-Palmer State Park—Lovely walking on riverside paths, especially in summer, is the hallmark of this 320-acre park upstream from the entrance to Green River Gorge.

Facilities: Picnic areas, restrooms, showers, and rafting and kayaking for experienced whitewater boaters; information, 206-886-0148. *Fishing:* Steelhead in season (check posted regulations).

Camping: There are 50 sites, including 19 with RV hookups and four walk-ins.

Getting there: Located on Cumberland-Kanaskat Road off Southeast 308th Street, 11 miles north of Enumclaw and Route 410.

Nolte State Park—Surrounding Deep Lake, 117-acre Nolte Park is famous for its huge Douglas firs, cedars and cottonwoods. A one-and-a-half-mile path circles the lake taking you around nearly 7200 feet of shoreline and past the big trees; a separate nature trail interprets the forest.

Facilities: Minimal picnic area; groceries and restaurants in Enumclaw; information, 206-825-4646. *Boating:* No motor boats. *Fishing:* For trout. *Swimming:* At the lake; no lifeguards.

Getting there: Located on Veazie-Cumberland Road just south of Southeast 352nd Street, six miles north of Enumclaw and Route 410.

Ed Munro Seahurst County Park—A well-designed, 140-acre site where landscaping divides 4000 feet of saltwater shoreline into individual chunks just right for private picnics and sunbathing. A nature trail and some three miles of primitive footpath explore woodsy uplands and the headwaters of two creeks.

Facilities: Picnic areas, restrooms, showers, playground and marine laboratory with fish ladder and outdoor viewing slots; restaurants and groceries nearby; information, 206-296-2959. *Diving/fishing:* An artificial reef just offshore is popular with divers and anglers with boats.

Getting there: Located at 13th Avenue Southwest and Southwest 144th Street, via exit 154B from Route 5.

Saltwater State Park—You'll share this busy park with lots of locals, nearly 800,000 visitors a year, so don't expect solitude. But among the 88 acres, do revel in the fine views, some 1500 feet of shoreline and quiet woods with two miles of hiking trails.

Facilities: Picnic areas, restrooms, showers, play areas and concession stand; restaurants and groceries nearby; information, 206-764-4128. *Swimming:* Tolerable in saltwater tide flats at south end of beach. *Diving:* A sunken barge about 150 yards offshore from a prominent sandspit attracts a variety of fish and divers.

Camping: There are 52 sites.

Getting there: Located on Marine View Drive (Route 509) about halfway between Seattle and Tacoma, west of Route 5 via exit 149.

West Hylebos Wetlands State Park (★)—A rare chunk of urban wetland tucked between industrialization and subdivisions, the 68-acre park offers examples of all sorts of wetland formations along a one-mile boardwalk trail—springs, streams, marshes, lakes, floating bogs and sinks. You'll also see remnants of ancient forest, plentiful waterfowl, more than a hundred species of birds and dozens of mammals.

Facilities: Portable toilets; restaurants and groceries nearby; information, 206-593-2206.

Getting there: Located on South 348th Street at 4th Avenue South, northeast of Tacoma just west of Route 5 and exit 142.

Tacoma and Olympia

The Tacoma/Olympia region southwest of Seattle is rich in history, parks, waterfalls and cultural landmarks. Tacoma features numerous architectural gems; nearby villages like Gig Harbor are ideal for daytrippers. One of the nation's prettier capital cities (and there you may have thought Seattle was the capital of Washington!), Olympia is convenient to the wildlife refuges of Southern Puget Sound as well as to Native American monuments and petroglyphs.

Despite a lingering mill-town reputation, Tacoma, the city on Commencement Bay, has experienced a lively rejuvenation in recent years and offers visitors some first-rate attractions. Before the Alaska Gold Rush thrust Seattle into prominence at the turn of the century, Tacoma was Puget Sound's leading city. Charles Wright, president of the Great Northern Railroad, chose it as the western terminus of his railroad, and he wanted more than a mill town at the end of his line. Some of the best architects of the day were commissioned to build hotels, theaters, schools and office buildings.

Today, Tacoma is the state's "second city" with a population of 177,500 and jealously protects its treasure of turn-of-the-century architecture in a pair of historic districts overlooking the bay on both sides of Division Avenue. The 1893 **Old City Hall** (South 7th and Commerce streets) was modeled after Renaissance Italian hill castles. The 1889 **Bostwick Hotel** (South 9th Street and Broadway) is a classic example of a triangular Victorian "flatiron." The 1911 **Union Depot** (Pacific Avenue and South 19th Street) was designed by the same architects who created New York's Grand Central Station.

The restored **Pantages Theater** (901 Broadway; 206-591-5894), designed by Marcus Priteca in 1918, is a classic of the vaudeville circuit (W.C. Fields, Mae West, Will Rogers and Houdini all performed here) and offers dance, music and theater productions.

Wright Park (Division Avenue and I Street) is 30 acres of serene landscaping with an onion-domed 1907 Conservatory housing a wide-ranging botanical collection. **Washington State Historical Society Museum** occupies the 1891 Ferry Museum building (315 North Stadium Way, 206-593-2830) and has a respected collection of Northwest Indian art.

A treat for the kids as well as adults is **Point Defiance Park** (Pearl Street off Ruston Way), which offers a zoo with an outstanding aquarium featuring polar bears you can watch from an underwater window. You'll also see an outdoor railroad museum with steam engine; Fort Nisqually, a reconstruction of the original 1833 Hudson's Bay Company post; a children's fantasy land; rhododendron, rose, Japanese and native Northwest gardens; and numerous scenic overlooks.

Gig Harbor across the Tacoma Narrows off Route 16 is a classic Puget Sound small town. The community that arose around this somewhat-hidden harbor was founded as a fishing village by Croatians, Slavs and Austrians. Gig Harbor still looks like a haven for fishermen, but today you're more likely to see every sort of pleasure craft here; it's one of the best boat-watching locales on Puget Sound. The tight harbor entrance funnels boats single-file past dock-side taverns and cafés where you can watch the nautical parade. Or, rent a boat from Rent-A-Boat (off North Harborview Drive; 206-858-7341) and join the flotilla.

Steilacoom (★) about five miles south of Tacoma is a quiet counterpoint to Gig Harbor's bustle. Founded by Yankee sea captains in the 1850s, it exudes a museum-like peacefulness and preserves a New England look among its fine collection of clapboard houses. Get a self-guiding brochure at **Steilacoom Historical Museum** (112 Main Street; 206-584-4133). Don't miss the **Nathaniel Orr Home and Pioneer Orchard** (1811 Rainier Avenue) and its nice collection of handmade furniture. At the 1895 **Bair drugstore** (Lafayette near Wilkes streets) you can order an old-fashioned float from the 1906 soda fountain.

At the southern tip of Puget Sound, **Olympia**'s state capitol dome rises boldly as you approach on Route 5, a tempting landmark for travelers and an easy detour from the busy freeway. But this community of some 38,000 offers visitors more to peruse than government buildings and monuments. Nevertheless, the capitol campus may be the best place to begin your explorations.

You can take a guided tour through the marbled halls of the Romanesque **Legislative Building** (206-586-8684), recently remodeled, and see other buildings on the grounds—**Temple of Justice, Governor's Mansion** and **State Library**. The nearby **State Capitol Museum** (211 21st Avenue West; 206-753-2580) includes a fine collection of Northwest Coast Indian artifacts.

Downtown, the handsomely restored **Old Capitol** (7th Avenue and Washington Street across from stately Sylvester Park) will catch your eye with its fanciful architecture. But most of downtown is a potpourri of disparate attractions—the new **Washington Center for the Performing Arts** (Washington Street near Legion Way; 206-753-8586), galleries, the **Capitol Theater** (5th Avenue and Washington Street) with its old films and local theater, a summer **Farmers' Market** (North Capitol Way and Thurston Avenue) and a bit of Bohemia along 4th Avenue West.

Percival Landing (★) (foot of State Avenue at Water Street) is an inviting, harbor-side park with observation tower, kiosks with historical displays, picnic tables, cafés and boardwalks next to acres of pleasure craft. For a longer walk, head south on Water Street, cross 4th and 5th avenues, then turn west and follow the sidewalk next to the Deschutes Parkway (or get in your car and drive) around the park-dotted shores of manmade **Cap-**

itol Lake two-and-a-half miles to the town of Tumwater and a pair of parks rich in history.

Tumwater marks the true end of Puget Sound. Before Capitol Lake was created, the Sound was navigable all the way to the Deschutes River. Tumwater Falls Historical Park, at the meeting of river and lake, is rich in both history and recreation. One of two pioneer houses here was built in 1860 by Nathaniel Crosby III (Bing Crosby's grandfather). Down by the river you can fish, launch a canoe, have a picnic, explore fitness and hiking trails, watch birds in reedy marshes and see more historical exhibits. Across the river, a handsome, six-story, brick brew house built in 1906 marks an early enterprise that lives on in a 1933 brewery a few hundred yards south.

Follow Deschutes Parkway south to Tumwater Falls Park where the main attraction is the namesake falls, twisting and churning through a rocky defile. Feel the throb of water reverberating through stream-side footpaths. Listen to its sound, which the Indians called "Tumtum." You'll find lovely walking next to the river and plenty of history in the headquarters exhibit, including an Indian petroglyph and a monument recounting the travails of the first permanent settlement north of the Columbia River here in 1845.

Ten miles south of Olympia are Mima Mounds (Wadell Creek Road, Littlerock; 206-743-2400), an unusual group of several hundred hillocks spread across 120 acres. Scientists think they could have been created by glacial deposits or even, believe it or not, giant gophers. A self-guided interpretive trail offers a close look at this geologic oddity.

TACOMA AND OLYMPIA HOTELS

The Pillars (★) (6606 Soundview Drive, Gig Harbor; 206-851-6644), on a hillside overlooking Puget Sound, offers views of Mt. Rainier and Vashon Island. The gracious home has three attractive rooms, two with water views and one giving a bird's-eye look at the garden. Guests may play the piano in the large living room, relax and read by the stone fireplace, or swim in the covered heated pool. The hosts offer a warm welcome but don't intrude on their visitors' privacy. Their breakfast includes home-baked breads. Deluxe in price.

No Cabbages Bed and Breakfast (7712 Goodman Drive Northwest, Gig Harbor; 206-858-7797) is a comfortable, old-fashioned beach house built against a wooded hillside. It has two guest rooms, which have their own entrance and share a bath. They feature knotty-pine walls and great views of the deck terrace and harbor. The house is filled with eclectic art and interesting conversation. The innkeeper serves an outstanding breakfast. Budget.

The Harbinger Inn (1136 East Bay Drive, Olympia; 206-754-0389) is a restored, 1910 mansion with period antiques and a manicured lawn and garden. The living room, a first-floor porch with wicker furniture and a second-floor veranda overlook the marina, capitol building and the Olympic Mountains. Two of the four well-furnished rooms also have views. The owners lend bicycles, as this is a choice area for bicycling, and serve a continental breakfast. Moderate.

TACOMA AND OLYMPIA RESTAURANTS

Do you enjoy good tempura? Then don't walk, run to **Fujiya** (1125 Court C, Tacoma; 206-627-5319) downtown. Masahiro Endo, owner and chef, is a great entertainer with his knife at the sushi bar. Chicken sukiyaki is delicious. Moderate.

If you've a hankering for barbecued ribs, fried chicken or catfish, try **Lessie's Southern Kitchen** (1716 6th Avenue, Tacoma; 206-627-4282). This is no antebellum mansion, just a plain, well-lighted café with good food. Just as good as the entrées are the greens, grits, yams, biscuits and melt-in-your-mouth corncakes served up alongside. Lessie is Southern stock herself, so you can count on this fare being authentic. Breakfast is served all day. Budget.

Don't come to **Pacific** (823 Pacific Avenue, Tacoma; 206-572-3651) for exotic decor but for good, authentic Vietnamese food. Try some of the noodle dishes, such as stir-fried with chicken and vegetables, or shrimp rolls with a rich, brown, peanut sauce. The coffee is strong and good. Budget.

Mandarin and Szechuan fare is the specialty at **Ya Shu Yuen** (757 38th Street, Tacoma; 206-473-1180), a small, family-run establishment. The chicken in plum sauce and Szechuan beef are especially good. The vegetarian dishes also are mouth-watering. Budget.

One of the best views in Olympia is from **Falls Terrace** (106 Deschutes Way; 206-943-7830), through huge windows overlooking the Tumwater Falls on the Deschutes River. Start your meal with some Olympia oysters. The menu features pasta dishes, an excellent bouillabaisse and an array of chicken, lamb and beef entrées. Desserts are more ice-cream theatrics than tasty morsels. Moderate.

Hidden across from the Farmer's Market is **Gardner's Seafood and Pasta** (111 West Thurston Street, Olympia; 206-786-8466). It is no secret to locals, who flock to this small restaurant. While seafood is the specialty here, there are several pastas that are very good, too. Try the pasta primavera. The Dungeness crab casserole is rich with cream, chablis and several cheeses. Homemade ice cream fills out the meal. Dinner only. Moderate.

Patrons don't usually go for the water, but at **The Spar** (114 East 4th Avenue, Olympia; 206-357-6444) it truly is exceptional because it comes from the restaurant's own artesian well. Once a blue-collar café, the restaurant features large photographs of loggers felling giant Douglas firs. On the menu are thick milkshakes, giant sandwiches, prime rib and Willapa Bay oysters. Budget.

In downtown Olympia, the **Urban Onion** (116 Legion Way, Olympia; 206-943-9242) serves sizable breakfasts, good sandwiches and hamburgers and a thick, hearty lentil soup. Dinners include chicken, seafood and *gado gado*, a spicy Indonesian dish of sautéed vegetables in tahini and peanut sauce. The restaurant is part of a complex of shops in the former Olympian Hotel. Budget to moderate.

TACOMA AND OLYMPIA SHOPPING

In the Proctor District in north Tacoma you can find souvenirs, gifts and handmade clothing at the **Pacific Northwest Shop** (2702 North Proctor Street; 206-752-2242). Fine Irish imports are in stock at **The Harb & Shamrock** (2704 North Proctor Street; 206-752-5012). The **Old House Mercantile** (2717 North Proctor Street; 206-759-8850) offers a variety of gifts. Educational toys are found at **Teaching Toys** (2624 North Proctor Street; 206-759-9853). The **Washington State Historical Museum** (315 North Stadium Way; 206-593-2830) features gifts, jewelry, games and books.

Tacoma's best bookstores include **Fox Book Company** (737 St. Helens Street; 206-627-2223), **O'Leary's Books** (3828 Southwest 100th Street; 206-588-2503), **Book Feire** (3818 North 26th Street; 206-759-4680) and **McCarver Street Books** (2123 North 30th Street; 206-383-4030).

For sportswear and outdoor gear in Tacoma, try **Basecamp Adventure Gear** (38th Street and Pine Street; 206-472-4404), **Sportco** (4702 East 20th Street; 206-922-2222) or the **Duffle Bag** (8207 South Tacoma Way; 206-588-4433).

In Gig Harbor, **The Beach Basket** (4102 Harborview Drive; 206-858-3008) features, of course, baskets and other gifts. Scandinavian utensils, books and gifts can be found at **Strictly Scandinavian** (7803 Pioneer Way; 206-851-5959). **Kelly's Toys & Gifts** (7806 Pioneer Way; 206-851-8697) features stuffed animals, games and handcrafted items. **Mostly Books** (3126 Harborview Drive; 206-851-3219) stocks books (you're kidding) and gift items.

You can pick up souvenirs, handcrafted items and produce outdoors at Olympia's **Farmers' Market** (401 North Capitol Way; 206-352-9096). Contemporary women's clothing and accessories are found at **Juicy Fruits** (113 5th Avenue West; 206-943-0572). **Olympic Outfitters** (414 4th Avenue East; 206-943-1997) is housed in a restored, brick-and-metal building with a climbing wall inside and is stocked with everything from backpacking to kayaking gear.

TACOMA AND OLYMPIA NIGHTLIFE

For live jazz, rhythm and blues, blues and alternative music, **Prosito Italian Restaurant** (3829 6th Avenue, Tacoma; 206-752-0676) is a popular spot. Cover. **Christie's Lounge** (in the Best Western Executive Inn, 5700

Pacific Highway East, Fife; 206-922-0080) features live bands playing Top-40 music. **C. I. Shennanigan's Restaurant & Lounge** (3017 Ruston Way, Tacoma; 206-752-8811) has a piano bar called the Broker's Pub and upstairs the upscale Club Rio with a deejay. Cover at Club Rio.

The **Tides Tavern** (2925 Harborview Drive; 206-858-3982) in Gig Harbor features live bands playing '50s and '60s rock and some rhythm and blues. Cover for live shows.

For Top-40 sounds in the Lakewood area try **Leslie's Restaurant & Night Life** (9522 Bridgeport Way Southwest, Tacoma; 206-582-4118) with live bands or the **Lakewood Bar & Grill** (10009 59th Avenue Southwest, Tacoma; 206-582-1196) featuring a deejay. Cover at both clubs.

The **Columbia Street Pub** (200 4th Avenue West, Olympia; 206-943-5575) features a number of good, locally brewed beers and live jazz, bluegrass or Irish folk music.

TACOMA AND OLYMPIA BEACHES AND PARKS

Dash Point State Park—Nearly 400 acres of forested wildland with 3300 feet of saltwater shoreline preserve a bit of solitude just barely outside the Tacoma city limits. Six miles of trail ramble through mixed forest of second-growth fir, maple and alder. The park's beach is one of the few places on Puget Sound where you'll find enjoyable saltwater swimming—shallow waters in tide flats are warmed by the summer sun. Tides retreat to expose a beach front nearly a half-mile deep.

Facilities: Picnic areas, restrooms and showers; restaurants and groceries nearby; information, 206-593-2206. *Fishing:* From the pier at Dash Point County Park south of the state park. *Swimming:* Good in tide flat shallows (no lifeguard). *Diving:* Investigate two shipwrecks just offshore.

Camping: There are 108 sites; RV hookups available.

Getting there: Located just northeast of Tacoma on Southwest Dash Point (Route 509).

Point Defiance Park—Jutting dramatically into Puget Sound, this 700-acre treasure is hailed by some as the finest saltwater park in the state, by others as the best city park in the Northwest. Here are primeval forests, some 50 miles of hiking trails, over three miles of public shoreline and enough other attractions to match almost any visitor's interests. Five Mile Drive loops around the park perimeter with access to trails, forest, beach, views, attractions and grand overlooks of Puget Sound.

Facilities: Picnic areas, restrooms, play areas, tennis and volleyball courts, snack bar and concession stands, restaurant at boathouse; other restaurants and groceries nearby; information, 206-591-3681. *Boating:* Marina, boat rental, boathouse, boat launch. *Fishing:* From the pier at the boathouse or in a rented boat.

Getting there: Entrance located at Pearl Street, off Ruston Way in Tacoma.

Kopachuk State Park—Boasting lovely views across Carr Inlet toward the Olympic Mountains from its half-mile of shoreline (some low-tide clamming and fishing), Kopachuk also invites the car-top boater to launch from the beach and paddle out to Cutts Island Marine State Park a half-mile away.

Facilities: Picnic areas, restrooms and showers; restaurants and groceries are nearby; information, 206-265-3606. *Diving:* Artificial reef in nine fathoms about 200 yards offshore designated as an underwater park.

Camping: There are 41 sites.

Getting there: Located on Kopachuck Drive Northwest at Northwest 56th Street about six miles west of Gig Harbor and Route 16.

Penrose Point State Park—With nearly two miles of saltwater shoreline, this 145-acre park provides some of the most accessible public clamming in Southern Puget Sound. Try the half-mile of sandspit in Mayo Cove exposed at low tide. You can also hike along two miles of trail, launch a canoe or kayak for shoreline explorations, picnic and camp.

Facilities: Picnic areas, restrooms and showers; restaurants and groceries nearby; information, 206-884-2514. *Swimming:* On sandy, shallow-water beaches.

Camping: There are 83 sites.

Getting there: Located off Delano Road at the foot of 158th Avenue near Lakebay on the Longbranch Peninsula west of Tacoma.

Nisqually National Wildlife Refuge—Within this 3780-acre refuge lies one of the last pristine river deltas in the United States. The eco-system is a diverse mix of conifer forest, deciduous woodlands, marshlands, grasslands and mud flats and the meandering Nisqually River (born in Mt. Rainier National Park). Here, the river mixes its fresh waters with the salt chuck of Puget Sound. An important stop for migratory wildfowl on the Pacific Flyway, the refuge also is home to deer, otter, coyote and some 50 other species of mammals, over 200 kinds of birds and 125 species of fish. Trails thread the refuge; longest is the five-mile, dike-top loop that circles a pioneer homestead long since abandoned. You can also kayak or canoe.

Facilities: Picnic sites, education center and restrooms; restaurants and groceries nearby; information, 206-753-9467.

Getting there: Located about 25 miles south of downtown Tacoma via exit 114 from Route 5.

Tolmie State Park—A salt marsh with interpretive signs separates 1800 feet of tide flats from forested uplands overlooking Nisqually Reach. The sandy beach is fine for wading or swimming; at low tides you may find clams. A two-and-a-half-mile perimeter hiking trail loops through the park's 106 acres.

Facilities: Picnic areas, restrooms and showers; restaurants and groceries are nearby; information, 206-753-1519. *Diving:* An artificial reef 500 yards offshore and almost-nonexistent current make underwater park popular.

Getting there: Located on Hill Road Northeast, northeast of Olympia via exit 111 from Route 5.

Millersylvania State Park—Some 840 acres of primeval conifer forest and miles of foot trail are this park's big appeals. But visitors also come to enjoy its 3300 feet of shoreline along Deep Lake where you can swim, launch a small boat or fish for trout.

Facilities: Picnic areas and restrooms; restaurants and groceries are nearby; private resort across the lake; information, 206-753-1519.

Getting there: Located at exit 95 just east of Route 5, ten miles south of Olympia.

The Sporting Life

SPORTFISHING

Salmon is the Sound's most famous fish, but scores of other species make sportfising a signature attraction here. A combination of migratory and "resident" stocks offer angling for Chinook and Coho almost year-round. And when salmon fishing slows, you can try your luck for some 200 types of bottom-fish that also populate these waters—colorful fellows like the Red Irish Lord and copper rock fish, as well as greenling, halibut and many varieties of cod. The Edmonds Marina, just across the Sound, is home to the West Coast's largest fleet of charter vessels. To sign up for a Seattle charter trip (usually all day, $50 and up) call **Angling Unlimited** (Shilshole Marina, Seattle; 206-789-8335), **Ballard Salmon Charters** (Shilshole Marina, Seattle; 206-789-6202), **All Seasons Charter Service** (Port of Edmonds, Edmonds; 206-743-9590) and **Glen Jarstad Charters** (Kingston Marina, Kingston; 206-377-5362).

SEA KAYAKING AND SMALL BOATING

In a city rich in waterways and boating, Lake Union just north of downtown Seattle offers a good sampler of small boats for rent, including sea kayaks. Novices may want to try their first paddle on the lake's calmer waters before taking to the real "sea." For instruction and rentals try **Northwest Outdoor Center** (2100 Westlake Avenue North; 206-281-9694). For sailboats, stop by **Kelly's Landing** (1401 Northeast Boat Street; 206-547-9909)

Hey! The Water's Fine

Even if you're a diehard landlubber, do not fail to at least once go sightseeing here by boat. Simply put, if you leave Seattle without plying its surrounding waters your trip will be incomplete. So don't hesitate, dear traveler: Head to the downtown central waterfront and make some waves.

On a clear day you can see forever, or so it would seem aboard one of the **Washington State Ferries.** Headquartered at Coleman Dock (Pier 52; 206-464-6400), the ferries make frequent departures to Bremerton and to Winslow on Bainbridge Island, both across Puget Sound to the west. But getting there is much of the fun because from your watery perch you'll be treated to grand views of Mt. Rainier, Mt. Baker and the Olympics (the Mountains, not the Games, silly). Up closer you'll see pleasure boats and other craft, and you may even catch a glimpse of an orca (killer) whale. To Bremerton, you can ride the car-and-passenger ferry or the passenger-only boat. At Pier 50 next door, you can board a passenger-only ferry to Vashon Island.

This is your captain speaking. That's just part of the show on **Seattle Harbor Tours** (Pier 55; 206-623-1445), which offer at least one tour every day year-round and more in mid-summer. On the harbor spin you'll get grand mountain views and see boat traffic like you won't believe: freighters, tugboats, sailboats, ferries, you name it. The captain's live narration spices up the trip.

Gray Line Water Sightseeing (Pier 57; 206-623-4252) goes north to Shilshole Bay, eastward through the Hiram M. Chittenden Locks into the Lake Washington Ship Canal and then on to the south tip of Lake Union. You return to the waterfront by bus. Going through the locks is an experience in itself, plus you'll get to see zillions of other boats doing the same. And along the way you might even see salmon jumping.

For something different, **Spirit of Puget Sound** (Pier 70; 206-443-1442) presents half-hour "mini-cabaret" performances as the highlight of its cruises, all of which serve meals. Lunch, dinner, Sunday brunch and moonlight cruises go throughout the week, and longer tours feature live music and dancing.

A narrated harbor tour is included in the **Tillicum Tours-Blake Island** (Piers 55 and 56; 206-443-1244) excursion to 55-acre Blake Island Marine State Park, which has tons of things to see and do.

S.S. Virginia V (206-624-9119) is the last of the legendary "Mosquito Fleet," the motley flotilla of steamboats that once carried foot-passengers and cargo around Puget Sound before the coming of highways and autos. Today, the *Virginia V* offers evening tours that include dinner, live music (mostly jazz) and dancing.

or **Sailboat Rentals and Yacht Charters Inc.** (2046 Westlake Avenue North; 206-281-9176). For classic wooden rowing dories see the **Center for Wooden Boats** (1010 Valley Street; 206-382-2628). To try out a sleek rowing shell, stop by **Rowing Northwest** (3304 Fuhrman Avenue East; 206-324-5800). To rent a "kicker boat" for do-it-yourself sportfishing, you'll have to leave the lake. Try **Seacrest Boat House** (1660 Harbor Avenue Southwest, West Seattle; 206-932-1050).

The beautiful waters of Admiralty Inlet and Hood Canal offer plenty to interest the boater. If you didn't bring your own, contact **Kingston Rentals** (Kingston Marina; 206-297-8320) or **Poulsbo Sea Kayaking Co.** (17791 Fjord Drive Northeast, Poulsbo; 206-697-2464).

SCUBA DIVING

Puget Sound's hundreds of miles of shoreline, scores of public beaches, extraordinary marine life and numerous underwater parks offer considerable opportunities for diving. But the Sound's average temperature of around 55 degrees means wet suits are *de rigeur*, and full scuba gear is the frequent choice of divers. Of the many exciting dive spots in the area, two standouts are Bracket's Landing Underwater Park in Edmonds and Hood Canal Floating Bridge on the Kitsap Peninsula. Numerous dive shops with equipment rentals and lessons are located around major population centers. Some of the bigger outfitters include **Underwater Sports Inc.**, with shops in Seattle (10545 Aurora Avenue North; 206-362-3310), Bellevue (12003 Northeast 12th Street; 206-454-5168), Federal Way (34428 Pacific Highway South; 206-874-9387), Tacoma (9608 Southwest 40th Street; 206-588-6634) and Edmonds (264 Railroad Avenue; 206-771-6322); **Lighthouse Diving Centers,** with shops in Seattle (8215 Lake City Way Northeast; 206-524-1633), Lynnwood (5421 Southwest 196th Street; 206-771-2679) and Midway (24860 Pacific Highway South; 206-839-6881); **Northwest Sports Divers Inc.** (8030 Northeast Bothell Way, Bothell; 206-487-0624); and **Underwater Sports** (264 Railroad Avenue, Edmonds; 206-771-6322).

In Tacoma, also try **Nautilus Dive** (3630 South Cedar Street; 206-475-1316), **Northwest Divers Inc.** (4815 North Pearl Street; 206-752-3973) and **The Scuba Locker** (10518 South Tacoma Way; 206-582-8460). In Bellevue, **Silent World** (13600 Northeast 20th Street; 206-747-8842) is the place to go. In Kirkland, try **American Sport Diver** (12630 120th Avenue Northeast; 206-821-7200).

GOLF

Greater Seattle boasts nearly a score of private golf courses and two-score public courses. The Southern Puget Sound region covered here has dozens more. In Seattle, consider **Jackson Park Golf Club** (1000 Northeast 135th Street; 206-363-4747), **Jefferson Park Golf Club** (4101 Beacon Avenue South; 206-762-4513) and **West Seattle Golf Course** (4470 35th Avenue Southwest; 206-935-5187). Some better public courses outside Seattle include **The Classic Golf Course** (Spanaway; 206-847-4440), **Capitol City Golf Club** (Yelm; 206-491-5111), **North Shore Golf Course** (Federal Way; 800-447-1375) and **Tall Chief Public Golf Course** (Fall City; 206-222-5911).

TENNIS

Seattle alone has some 60 parks and other sites with tennis courts, about two dozen of them lighted. The region offers nearly 600 courts at perhaps 200 sites. Given the city's unreliable weather, you may be looking for an indoor court. Try the **Seattle Tennis Center** (2000 Martin Luther King Jr. Way; 206-684-4764).

HORSEBACK RIDING

Equestrians will find a good selection of horse ranches, riding academies and stables scattered throughout this region. One of the best places for a ride is **Bridal Trails State Park** in Bellevue (off Route 405, exit 17; 206-827-2900). Crisscrossed with 28 miles of riding trails used mainly by local riders, the park has no rental mounts. However, nearby outfitters offer trail rides here. One is **Eastside Equestrian Center** (Kirkland; 206-827-2992).

Another popular location is Tiger Mountain State Forest near Issaquah. Saddle up at **Tiger Mountain Stables** (24508 Southeast 133rd Street, Issaquah; 206-392-5090). Other east-of-Seattle outfitters include **Aqua Barn Ranch** (15227 Southeast Renton-Maple Valley Road, Renton; 206-255-4618) and **Have Ponies Will Travel** (Renton; 206-271-3794).

In the Tacoma and Olympia area are **Su Dara Riding** (Puyallup; 206-531-1569), **Happy Trails Horseback Riding Ranch** (10126 Case Road Southwest, Olympia; 206-753-8700) and **Forest View Stables** (12915 Marksman Road Southwest, Olympia; 206-943-0462).

BICYCLING

Often praised in national media as the capital of bicycle commuting, Seattle also is friendly to the recreational cyclist. The three-mile loop around **Green Lake** is the most leisurely and rich in recreational detours. The **Alki Bike Route** in West Seattle offers six miles of shoreline pedaling—half on separated bike paths—and changing views of the city, Sound and mountains from Seacrest Park to Lincoln Park.

The nine or so gentle miles between Seward and Washington parks along **Lake Washington Boulevard South** offer wonderful views of the lake. Best long-distance path is the **Burke-Gilman Trail**, stretching north 12 level miles from Gas Works Park on Lake Union, through the university campus, past lovely neighborhoods next to Lake Washington and on to Logboom Park at the lake's northern tip.

Pedal past Puget Sound parks, beaches and the bustling Edmonds port, home of the largest charter fleet on the West Coast, on the three-mile **Edmonds Waterfront Trail** running between Edmonds Underwater Park and Deer Park Reserve.

The moderately difficult **Poulsbo-Port Gamble Loop** features 20 hilly miles with outstanding views of Hood Canal, the Cascade Range and the Olympic Mountains.

As easygoing as the Burke-Gilman Trail but quite rural is the eight-mile long **Sammamish River Trail** beginning farther east in Redmond's Marymoor Park. It winds north past the **Château Ste. Michelle Winery** (open for tours and tasting; 206-488-4660) before linking with the Burke-Gilman in Bothell to create a city-center to farmlands tour.

For more biking details and a free *Seattle Bicycling Guidemap* call 206-684-5087. For county-wide information, contact the King County Bike Hotline (206-296-7433).

BIKE RENTALS   Rental shops are spotted near good pedaling. Try the **Alki Bicycle Company** in West Seattle (2722 Alki Avenue Southwest,; 206-938-3322), **Gregg's Greenlake Cycle** in the University of Washington area (7007 Woodlawn Avenue Northeast; 206-523-1822), **The Bicycle Center** near the Burke-Gilman Trail (4529 Sand Point Way Northeast; 206-523-8300) and **Sack's Feed and Cycle** (10991 Route 104 Northeast, Kingston; 206-297-2443).

HIKING

Nearly every park mentioned in the "Beaches and Parks" sections of this chapter offers at least a few miles of hiking trail through forest or along a stream or beach. Some are outstanding, such as Nisqually National Wildlife Refuge, Green River Gorge, Point Defiance Park in Tacoma and Discovery Park in Seattle.

DOWNTOWN SEATTLE TRAILS   For short strolls in downtown Seattle, try **Freeway Park** and the grounds of the adjoining Washington State Convention Center (.5 mile) and **Myrtle Edwards** and **Elliott Bay parks** (1.25 miles) at the north end of the downtown waterfront. Just across Elliott Bay, West Seattle offers about four miles of public shoreline to walk around Duwamish Head and Alki Point.

SEATTLE NORTH TRAILS   For a longer walk, the **Burke-Gilman Trail** (12 miles) extends from Gas Works Park in Seattle to Logboom Park in Kenmore.

The **Shell Creek Nature Trail** (.5 mile) in Edmond's Yost Park off Main Street is an easy walk past a series of dams, along a salmon-filled stream and through a cool grotto. Contact Edmonds Parks and Recreation (700 Main Street; 206-775-2525) for a guide to the area's flora.

SEATTLE WEST TRAILS   Located southwest of Bremerton, **Gold Mountain Hike** (4 miles) is a moderate-to-strenuous climb with a 1200-foot elevation gain. You will survey the twisting waterways of Southern Puget Sound and Hood Canal from a 1761-foot point that also offers vistas from the Olympics to the Cascades and Edmonds to Olympia. The walk begins at a gate on Minard Road, about one-and-a-half miles from old Belfair Valley Road, five-and-a-half miles west of Route 3.

SEATTLE EAST TRAILS   Three foothills peaks nicknamed the "Issaquah Alps" (Cougar Mountain County Park, Squak Mountain State Park and Tiger Mountain State Forest) south of Issaquah (about 15 miles east of Seattle) include miles and miles of trail and road open to hikers year-around. Cougar Mountain Regional Wildland Park (206-296-4258) is the best bet for visitors. One representative hike is the 2.2-mile route via **Lakemont Gorge and Peggy's Trail** up to 1470-foot Anti-Aircraft Peak and great views. Since the route may change, don't try it without an *Issaquah Alps Trails Club Guidebook* available in bookstores and outdoor shops. Just west of Issaquah, leave Route 90 at exit 13 (Southeast Newport Way), and on the south side of the freeway follow the very short stub road to concrete barricades at the road-end; park here and locate the trailhead beyond the barriers.

SEATTLE SOUTH TRAILS   The trail along **Big Soos Creek** (5 miles), now protected in two parks, is an inviting ramble on a blacktop path next to one of the few wetland streams still in public ownership hereabouts. In Kent, south of Seattle, follow signs off Route 516 (Kent-Kangley Road) at 150th Avenue Southeast.

TACOMA AND OLYMPIA TRAILS   A wonderful river-delta walk, **Brown Farm Trail** (5 miles) loops through Nisqually National Wildlife Refuge. You may see bald eagles, coyotes, deer, great blue heron, red-tail hawks and a variety of waterfowl such as wood, canvasback and great-scalp ducks, as well as mallards and pin tails. Views stretch from Mt. Rainier to the Olympics. You'll also see many of the islands in the south, Steilacoom and the Tacoma Narrows Bridge.

Transportation

BY CAR

Seattle lies along Puget Sound east of the Olympic Peninsula in the state of Washington. **Route 5** enters Seattle from Olympia and Tacoma to the south and from Everett from the north. **Route 90** from Eastern Washington goes near Snoqualmie and Fall City and through Bellevue on its way into Seattle. **Route 405** serves the Eastside suburban communities of Bellevue, Kirkland and Redmond. **Route 169** leads from Route 405 southeast of Renton to Maple Valley, Black Diamond and Enumclaw. **Route 16** leads north from Tacoma, across the Tacoma Narrows Bridge toward Gig Harbor and further north toward Bremerton. On Bainbridge Island, the main thoroughfare is **Route 305** that goes from Winslow northwest across the island and onto the Kitsap Peninsula to Poulsbo.

BY FERRY

The **Washington State Ferry System** (206-464-6400) serves Seattle, Southworth, Vashon Island, Winslow, Bremerton, Kingston, Edmonds, Mukilteo, Columbia Beach, the San Juan Islands and Sidney, B.C. The **Victoria Clipper** passenger catamaran service (206-448-5000) operates daily trips between Seattle and Victoria, B.C. **SeaCat Victoria** (206-343-5555) travels between downtown Seattle and Victoria's Inner Harbour, carrying 450 passengers and 80 cars in just over two hours.

BY AIR

In Sea-Tac, about 20 miles south of downtown Seattle, is **Seattle-Tacoma International Airport,** served by Air B.C., Air Canada, Alaska Airlines, American Airlines, America West Airlines, British Airways, Continental Airlines, Delta Air Lines, Hawaiian Airlines, Horizon Air, Japan Air Lines, Northwest Airlines, Trans World Airlines, Thai Airways International, Time Air/Canadian Airlines International, United Airlines and USAir.

Shuttle service to the northern Kitsap Peninsula is available through the **Bremerton-Kitsap Airporter** (206-876-1737).

BY TRAIN

Rail service in and out of Seattle is provided by **Amtrak** (206-464-1930) on the "Empire Builder."

BY BUS

Greyhound/Trailways Bus Lines (206-624-3456) serves Seattle. The terminal is at 8th Avenue and Stewart Street.

CAR RENTALS

Most major car-rental businesses have offices at Seattle-Tacoma International Airport. Rental agencies include **Allstar Rent A Car** (206-431-3368), **Avis Rent A Car** (206-433-5231), **Budget Car and Truck Rental** (206-682-2277), **Dollar Rent A Car** (206-433-6777), **Hertz Rent A Car** (206-433-5262), **Mini-Rate Rent A Car** (206-244-1701), **Practical Rent A Car** (206-241-4645), **Sears Car and Truck Rental** (206-224-7888), **Ten**

Dollar Rent A Car (206-878-4700), **Thrifty Car Rental** (246-7565) and **XtraCar Inc.** (206-246-7510).

PUBLIC TRANSPORTATION

Bus transportation provided by **Metropolitan Transit** (206-553-3000) is free in downtown Seattle. Metro Transit provides service throughout the Seattle-King County area.

The **Monorail** (206-684-7200) is 30 years old and still going. Deemed transportation for the future, the Monorail was built for the 1962 World's Fair. It runs between downtown and the Seattle Center every 15 minutes.

Waterfront Streetcar trolleys (206-553-3000) run along the waterfront from Seattle's historic Pioneer Square to Pier 70. In the Kitsap Peninsula area, the **Poulsbo-Kitsap Transit** (206-373-2877) provides routed service in Poulsbo; otherwise, you will have to depend on taxis for transportation around the peninsula.

TAXIS

In the greater Seattle area are **Checker Cab** (206-622-1234), **Farwest Taxi** (206-622-1717), **North End Taxi** (206-363-3333), **Rainier Taxi** (206-241-7735) and **Yellow Cab** (206-622-6500).

CHAPTER THREE

Northern Puget Sound
and the San Juan Islands

"Every part of this land is sacred to my people. Every shining pine needle, every sandy shore, every mist in the dark woods, every clearing and humming insect is holy in the memory and experience of my people . . . . We are part of the earth and it is part of us. The perfumed flowers are our sisters; the deer, the horse, the great eagle, these are our brothers. The rocky crests, the juices in the meadows, the body heat of the pony, and man—all belong to the same family." This was part of Chief Seattle's poignant reply when in 1854 the "Great White Chief" in Washington pressed to purchase some of the land around Puget Sound then occupied by several Northwest Indian tribes. And those sentiments still ring true today as the natural beauty and appeal of Northern Puget Sound and the San Juan Islands remain undiminished.

The Indians had good reason to hold this awe-inspiring land in such high regard. It supported them, providing for all their needs with verdant woods full of deer and berries and crystal waters full of salmon, letting them live in peaceful co-existence for hundreds of years. Even the weather was kind to them here in this "rain shadow," shielded by the Olympic and Vancouver mountain ranges protecting them from the torrential rains regularly dumped not far inland.

Things slowly began to change for the Northwest Indian tribes and the land with the arrival of Juan de Fuca in 1592, exploring the coastline under the Spanish flag. The flood gates of exploration and exploitation weren't fully opened, however, until Captain George Vancouver came in 1792 to chart the region for the British, naming major landmarks such as Mt. Baker, Mt. Rainier, Whidbey Island and Puget Sound after his compatriots.

Establishment of trade with the Indians and the seemingly inexhaustible quantity of animals to supply the lucrative fur trade drew many pioneers. Before long, industries such as logging, mining, shipping and fishing began to flourish, supporting the early settlers (and still supporting their ancestors today).

The geographical layout of the 172 islands of the San Juan archipelago made for watery back alleys and hidden coves perfect for piracy and smuggling, so the history of the area reflects an almost Barbary Coast type of intrigue where a man could get a few drinks, a roll in the hay and be shanghaied all in one night. Chinese laborers were regularly brought in under cover of night to build up coastal cities and railroads in the 1800s. This big money "commodity" was replaced by opium, silk and then booze during Prohibition.

Smuggling has since been curbed, and while things are changing as resources recede, logging and fishing are still major industries in the region. However, current booms in real estate and tourism are beginning to tilt the economic scale as more and more people discover Northern Puget Sound and the San Juan Islands.

The area referred to as Northern Puget Sound begins just beyond the far outskirts of Seattle, where most visitors will arrive, and extends northward up the coast to the Canadian border. Communities along the coast such as Everett, Bellingham and Blaine are more commercial in nature, heavily flavored by the fishing industry, while other small towns such as La Conner and Mount Vernon are still very pastoral, dependent on an agriculturally based economy. Springtime along this stretch of land is particularly lovely, especially when the fields are ablaze in daffodils, iris and tulips.

Of the 172 named islands of the San Juans, we concentrate on the six largest. These also are very pastoral, with rich soil and salubrious conditions perfectly suited to raising livestock or growing fruit. The main islands are not interconnected or connected to the mainland by bridges but are reached by limited ferry service, an inhibiting factor that helps preserve the pristine nature here.

The ferry system is severely overtaxed during the busy summer season when the San Juans are inundated with tourists, making it difficult to reach the islands at times and absolutely impossible to find accommodations if you haven't booked months in advance. The crowds drop off dramatically after Labor Day, a pleasant surprise since the weather in September and October is still lovely and the change of seasonal color against this beautiful backdrop is incredible.

Serpentine Whidbey Island, with its thick southern tip reaching toward Seattle, is the longest island in the United States. Situated at its northern tip is Fidalgo Island, home of Anacortes and the ferry terminal gateway to the San Juans. Lopez is by far the friendliest and most rural of the islands,

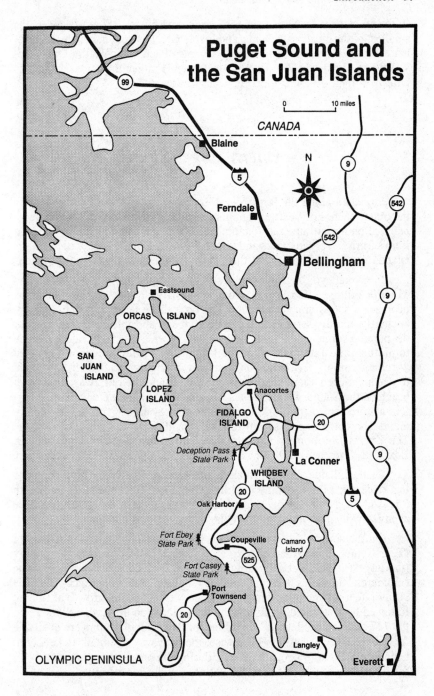

Puget Sound and the San Juan Islands

0   10 miles

CANADA

N

Blaine

Ferndale

Bellingham

Eastsound

ORCAS   ISLAND

SAN JUAN ISLAND

LOPEZ ISLAND

Anacortes

FIDALGO ISLAND

Deception Pass State Park

La Conner

WHIDBEY ISLAND

Oak Harbor

Fort Ebey State Park

Coupeville

Camano Island

Fort Casey State Park

Port Townsend

Langley

Everett

OLYMPIC PENINSULA

followed closely by San Juan, the largest and busiest. Shaw Island is the smallest of the clustered islands, and lovely Orcas Island, named after Spanish explorer Don Juan Vincente de Guemes Pacheco y Padilla Orcasitees y Aguayo Conde de Revilla Gigedo (whew!) rather than orca whales, is tallest, capped by 2400-foot Mt. Constitution.

Northern Puget Sound

Stretched along the fertile coastline between the Canadian border and the outer reaches of Seattle, communities along North Puget Sound are dependent on agriculture and fishing, so the distinct pastoral feel of the area is no surprise. Verdant parks and vista spots taking in the beauty of the many islands not far offshore head the list of sightseeing musts in the region.

In Everett you'll find your best vantage point from the dock behind **Marina Village** (1728 West Marine View Drive), a sparkling new complex of upscale shops and restaurants. The boxy little temporary building opposite the marina serves as an interpretive site and information center for the popular summertime Jetty Island Days, when a free ferry ride takes you to picturesque **Jetty Island** for sail regattas, guided nature walks, bird watching, campfires, a hands-on "Squirmy, Squiggly and Squishy" program to teach children about small marine animals and the only warm saltwater beach on the Sound. **Firefighter's Museum** (13th Street Dock, Everett) offers a storefront display of antique turn-of-the-century firefighting equipment. The collection is set up for 24-hour, through-the-window viewing. The **Everett/Snohomish County Convention and Visitor Bureau** (P.O. Box 1086, Everett, WA 98206; 206-252-5181) can provide more information.

On the hillside above the marina, ornate **mansions** of the lumber barons that once ruled the economy here line Grand and Rucker streets from 16th Street north. None are open to tour, but a slow drive up and down these avenues will give you a feel for the history of the city.

On the south side of town you'll find a free industrial tour at **Boeing** (Tour Center, State Road 526, Everett; 206-342-4801), a massive facility (the largest in the world by volume) where they construct those gigantic commercial airplanes that carry over one million passengers every day. The 90-minute tours include films on the history of flight and growth at Boeing followed by a narrated walk viewing the production lines where they build the 747 and 767 models. Reservations for these popular tours are available for groups of ten or more; otherwise, the best way to obtain tickets is to be in line at the tour center by 8 a.m. during the busy summer months. Call for directions and tour times; no children under ten admitted.

Another fascinating tour is available at the **Millstone Coffee Plant (★)** (729 100th Street South East, Everett; 206-347-3848), where you'll learn first hand how they sample, select, roast, flavor and package some of the Northwest's favorite specialty coffees. Call the plant manager about schedules for the 30-minute tour.

If you plan to catch the Mukilteo ferry to Clinton on Whidbey Island, be sure to allow enough time to visit the historic **Mukilteo Lighthouse** (206-355-2611; weekends only, 12 to 4 p.m.) built in 1905. There are picnic tables above a small rocky beach cluttered with driftwood and a big grassy field for kite-flying adjacent to the lighthouse in little Mukilteo State Park.

Strategically located at the crossroads of Puget Sound, midway between Seattle and Vancouver, B.C., **La Conner** got its start as a trading post. It remains a fine example of American life at the turn of the century, with many well preserved homes and buildings from the mid to late-1800s. You can obtain a historical walking tour guide from the **La Conner Chamber of Commerce** (P.O. Box 644, La Conner, WA 98259; 206-466-4778).

Many of those historic structures along the waterfront now house boutiques, galleries and restaurants while others in town such as the **Gaches Mansion** (703 South 2nd Street; 206-466-4446; admission), a grand Victorian structure filled with period furnishings, are preserved as museums. A walk through the collection of automobiles, farm and fishing equipment, vintage clothing, household furnishings and photographs at the **Skagit County Historical Museum** (501 4th Street; 206-466-3365; admission) gives a further lesson on the history of the region.

Each spring the fields of La Conner and neighboring Mount Vernon are alive with color as the iris, tulips and daffodils, the major cash crop grown in the area, begin to appear. **The Skagit Valley Tulip Festival Office** (P.O. Box 1007, Mount Vernon, WA 98273; 206-428-8547) can provide a guide to events and tour map of the nurseries and display gardens.

There are interesting gardens to view year-round. The prettiest is **RoozenGaarde** (1587 Beaver Marsh Road, Mount Vernon; 206-424-8531) with display gardens and a great little gift shop.

Located west of Burlington, **Padilla Bay National Estuarine Research Reserve** (1043 Bay View Edison Road, Bay View; 206-428-1558) is the place to find bald eagles, great blue herons and dozens of other species. The interpretive center offers exhibits on the region's natural and maritime history.

Early growth in **Bellingham** centered around the industries of mining and logging. To this day the city retains an industrial nature with thriving ports, home to a large fishing fleet and, more recently, the Alaska Marine Highway Ferry System terminal, tempered by a firm agricultural base. Perhaps it is because of this outward appearance that visitors are often amazed at the array of cultural arts and international dining experiences to be enjoyed here.

Bellingham has two noteworthy museums. The **Children's Museum Northwest** (227 Prospect Street; 206-733-8769; admission) has several hands-on, career-oriented theme centers (fire station, television station, dental room, science center, etc.) to delight the kids. Just down the street, the red-brick Victorian architecture of the **Whatcom Museum** (121 Prospect Street; 206-676-6981) is as interesting as the fine collections of Northwest art and regional history housed inside. It's also a good point to start a walking tour of the many outdoor sculptures scattered around downtown. A Sculpture Walk route guide is available from the **Bellingham/Whatcom County Visitor and Convention Bureau** (904 Potter Street; 206-671-3990).

At the **Maritime Heritage Center** (1600 C Street; 206-676-6806), you can tour the hatchery, watch fish make their way up the ladder, learn about the life cycle of salmon, or just toss a line into the abutting creek for steelhead or cutthroat trout.

No visit to Bellingham is complete without a trip to the **Big Rock Garden** (★) (2900 Sylvan Street; 206-734-4167), a fantastic, open-air gallery of Northwestern and Japanese art set in a serene Japanese garden with patio and deck areas where visitors can sit and take it all in.

Don't miss the opportunity to stroll through the grounds of **Western Washington University** (South College Drive; 206-676-3963) to enjoy the many fountains, sculptures and tremendous variety of architecture on this rich green campus. Immediately adjacent to the campus is **Sehome Hill Arboretum** (25th Street, Sehome Hill District; 206-676-6985), laced with fern-lined footpaths under a cool green canopy of moss covered trees; only the hum of traffic and the view from the observation tower remind you that you are in the city rather than some forest primeval.

Hovander Homestead Park (5299 Neilsen Road, Ferndale; 206-384-3444; admission) features a 19th-century farmhouse and handsome Victorian residence. Laced by the Nooksak River, the 720-acre park also includes **Tenant Lake,** where you'll find a boardwalk leading out over the lake and a fragrance garden with braille signs. There's also an interpretive center.

Another Ferndale stop is **Pioneer Park** (1st Avenue at Cherry Street; 206-384-6461). Here is the largest collection of original log homes in the state. Each of the ten buildings is a mini-museum. You'll see a post office, stagecoach inn, granary, veteran's museum, school house and a residence. Don't miss the little log church.

Another site in the Northern Puget Sound area worth taking in is **Peace Arch State Park** (Follow the signs off Route 5). The large, white arch, flanked by American and Canadian flags, is surrounded by bountiful formal gardens and symbolizes the ongoing friendship between the two countries. The park is meticulously groomed, and spills across the international boundary.

NORTHERN PUGET SOUND HOTELS

In addition to its outstanding waterfront location, the friendly 28-room **Marina Village Inn** (1728 West Marine View Drive, Everett; 206-259-4040) is loaded with special touches. The spacious harborside rooms have sunken sitting areas with custom sleeper sofas, cushioned seats built into large bay windows and personal telescopes for viewing Whidbey, Hat and Jetty Islands. One room with a view of the village fits into the moderate range, while those with harbor views are deluxe to ultra deluxe; reservations are suggested.

There are plenty of budget-priced accommodations in Everett, but most appear a bit worse for wear. However, the new **Homeport Motor Inn** (2385 Route 99, Everett; 206-771-8008) is a good deal. Rooms in this three-story motel are comfortably appointed and clean, with soft pastel carpets, curtains and bedspreads and cable television; there are even a few kitchenette and jacuzzi units. Other amenities include hot tubs and continental breakfast.

The Hotel Planter (715 1st Street, La Conner; 206-466-4710), originally built in 1907, is right in the thick of things when it comes to shopping and dining in historic downtown La Conner. This 12-room hotel was recently renovated; new sunlights, lighter paint and carpeting, floral chintz comforters and pine furnishings in the tight bedrooms brighten and update its look. There's also a new jacuzzi under the gazebo on the garden terrace out back. Moderate to deluxe.

White Swan Guest House (1388 Moore Road, Mount Vernon; 206-445-6805) offers moderate-to-deluxe accommodations in a country setting. The rooms are country casual and there's a superb collection of samplers spread across the house. The English country garden features a big orchard where you're welcome to pick your own apples and plums, as well as strawberries. A separate cottage offers kitchen facilities.

As you might guess from the name, **Schnauzer Crossing** (★) (4421 Lakeway Drive, Bellingham; 206-733-0055) is presided over by a delightful pair of schnauzers. Choose from a spacious master suite with fireplace, library room, jacuzzi tub and double shower, a smaller lakeview room done in iris motif or a recently completed cottage, perfect for families or couples seeking romantic seclusion. Well-thought-out amenities in each room include thick terry robes for the trip to the hot tub in the Japanese garden; other extras are the gourmet breakfast, a tennis court and a canoe for paddling around nearby Lake Whatcom. Deluxe.

If you're looking for an escape from the everyday bustle or a cozy home base for skiing Mt. Baker, book a room at the **Anderson Creek Lodge** (5602 Mission Road, Bellingham; 206-966-2126), a tranquil retreat 15 minutes northeast of downtown Bellingham. Each of the six rooms in the inviting wooden lodge has a personality of its own; some feature family heirlooms, others have floral chintz or a distinctly oriental decor. There are even horseback riding and nature trails on the 65-acre spread, and a heated indoor pool with spa. Moderate.

Tucked into the rose garden near the north end of picturesque Chuckanut Drive is the **Fairhaven Rose Garden AYH-Hostel** (107 Chuckanut Drive, Bellingham; 206-671-1750). You'll find this your typical hostel-environment: men's and women's dorms, private couple rooms, showers and laundry facilities. All the action of the Fairhaven district is within walking distance. Budget.

Housed in the old Blaine Air Force Base a few miles from the Canadian border, the **Birch Bay AYH Hostel** (4639 Alderson Road, Building 630, Blaine; 206-371-2180) provides 50 beds in bare, shared rooms. Pluses here include a sauna, cable television and the hostel's proximity to Birch Bay State Park. Budget.

There is something for everyone at the sumptuous **Inn at Semi-ah-moo** (9565 Semiahmoo Parkway, Blaine; 206-371-2000), located on the tip of the sandy spit stretched between Semiahmoo Bay and Drayton Harbor. History buffs will enjoy browsing through the inn's collection of early photography, romantics will delight in a walk on the beach or a leisurely sunset meal in one of the restaurants or lounges, and sports fanatics will flip over the array of activities. The 196 guest rooms are spacious and nicely appointed; some rooms have decks or patios, and others have fireplaces. Ultra-deluxe.

NORTHERN PUGET SOUND RESTAURANTS

The history of **Charles at Smugglers Cove** (★) (8340 53rd Avenue West, Mukilteo; 206-347-2700) is as good as the food, making it doubly worth the drive to Mukilteo. This red-brick mansion-turned-restaurant was purportedly owned at one time by Mafia kingpin Al Capone. Today the owners traffic in fresh seafood and steaks with French flair; their bouillabaisse, châteaubriand, rack of lamb, prawns in tarragon butter and baked Alaska are outstanding, and the setting in the elegant dining rooms or on the sheltered deck is splendid. Deluxe.

Anthony's Home Port (1726 West Marine View Drive; 206-252-3333) is the spot for seafood when it comes to waterfront dining in Everett. Prime picks on the menu include six varieties of fresh oysters, steamed Discovery Bay clams or Whidbey Island mussels, grilled steak and prawns, Dungeness crab cakes and pan fried scallops sprinkled with gremolata. Their four-course Sunset Dinner (served from 4:30 to 6 p.m.) is a bargain and includes everything from appetizer to dessert. Here you can dine al fresco on the deck or pick a spot in the considerably less breezy dining room or lounge. Moderate.

The Norwegian proprietors of the **Farmhouse Inn** (Whitney Road and Highway 20, Mount Vernon; 206-466-4411), a large restaurant with country decor dominated by heavy oak tables and chairs, believe in serving up solid, old country-style portions of meat and potato classics—fried chicken and french fries, roast turkey with mashed potatoes and gravy, rib eyes and baked potatoes—along with a hearty selection of daily baked goods thrown in for good measure. The lunch buffet is a real bargain. Budget.

The same people own and operate the **Lighthouse Inn** (1st Street; 206-466-3149) in nearby La Conner, so you can expect extra-large servings here as well, though the fare of this waterfront location is primarily seafood. Favorites include lobster, clam strips and prime rib, with fish and chips and burgers thrown in to please the little ones. The simple nautical decor leaves something to be desired, but the fresh flowers and dim lamps on the tables lend a slight air of romance. Moderate.

Best bet for breakfast or lunch in La Conner is the **Calico Cupboard** (720 South 1st Street; 206-466-4451) at the south end of the main drag, where they serve hearty and wholesome baked goods, soups, salads, sandwiches and vegetarian fare as good for the heart as for the taste buds. Don't be surprised if there is a line to get in to this modest café. Budget.

In addition to coffees and teas, the coffee shop in **Tony's Coffees & Teas** (1101 Harris Avenue, Bellingham; 206-733-6319) serves up fresh daily soups, salads, sandwiches and pastries to an eclectic crowd of regulars sporting unusual hairstyles (a mohawk shaped like a question mark!). It's almost too bohemian, but the bagels with cream cheese and sprouts, Greek salad and cocoa mocha at budget prices make it worth the trip.

Paper lanterns and fans add a dash of color to liven up the bare-bones decor of the new **Tokyo House** (1222 North Garden Street, Bellingham; 206-733-6784) with its industrial-style tables and chairs. Patrons don't come here for the atmosphere but for tasty Japanese standards with interesting additions to the menu such as kim chee and sweet and sour pork. Service is prompt, and this budget eatery is as neat as a pin.

If the columns, sconces and etchings adorning the walls of this cavernous, restaurant aren't enough to impart a classic Euro feel, the authentic Italian cuisine of **Il Fiasco** (★) (1309 Commercial Street, Bellingham; 206-676-9136) certainly is. The seasonal menu features a variety of salads, antipasto, pastas and *piatti forti* (usually fish, veal or duck) highlighted by whatever special the imaginative chef creates each day. Regulars come back often for the calamari or lamb lasagna. Ask any resident and they'll invariably tell you that this is *the* place for fine dining in Bellingham. Deluxe.

The few booths and barstools in the long, narrow dining area of tiny **Café Toulouse** (133 East Holly Street, Bellingham; 206-733-8996) are always full, a testament to the quality breakfast, lunch and dessert selections served here. Favorites include fresh fruit pancakes, curried chicken salad, roast pork loin with mint jelly or smoked turkey with cranberry-apple cream cheese sandwiches and anything from the fresh daily dessert board accompanied by piping espresso or latte. Budget.

For budget-to-moderate Mexican dining try **Tres Sombreros** (5694 3rd Avenue, Ferndale; 206-384-5820). Decorated with Mexican murals, paintings and parrot sculptures, the dining room offers booth and table seating. There's also patio dining outside in the summer. Popular specialties are fajitas, *carne asada*, sopas and a wide variety of combination plates.

Since it is always so busy, locals would probably prefer not to share the **Vista Pizza, Rib and Steak House** (★) (442 Peace Portal Drive, Blaine; 206-332-5155). Rumor has it that the amazingly low-priced one pound-steak dinner brings in enough business to this smoke-filled little diner to generate $1.4 million a year. Though it's not made clear on the menu, the generously proportioned luncheon special of lasagna, spaghetti or pizza and a trip to the salad bar is still available in the evenings, making it possible to get a substantial meal for under $5 per person, tip included. Budget.

For romantic waterfront dining, it's hard to beat the Inn at Semi-ah-moo's elegant dining room, **Stars** (9565 Semiahmoo Parkway, Blaine; 206-371-2000). Soft piano music fills the room as diners feast on parchment-wrapped salmon, sautéed langoustinos, venison scallops, prime rib, pheasant in morrel sauce and other rich entrées. For lighter fare, try the livelier Packers Oyster Bar just down the corridor for fresh steamer clams, coconut salmon, Fisherman's stew or homestyle burgers. Stars is deluxe. Packers is budget.

NORTHERN PUGET SOUND SHOPPING

Antique hounds will want to make the quick 15-minute trip east of Everett to Snohomish, antique capital of the Northwest and home to **Star Center** (829 2nd Street; 206-568-2131), a five-level mall with over 100 dealers, and dozens of other antique shops to browse through.

Shopping is a major drawing card of little La Conner, with most of the boutiques and galleries concentrated along 1st and Morris streets. Focus on **Earthenworks** (713 1st Street; 206-466-4422) and **The Scott Collection** (Pier 7 Building, 1st Street; 206-466-3691) for fine art, **Bunnies By The Bay** (617 East Morris Street; 206-466-5040) and **The Barbershop Exchange/The Cat Attic** (705 South 1st Street; 466-3602) for collectibles and unique gifts, and **Chez La Zoom** (2nd and Morris Street; 206-466-4546) and **The Town Clothier** (721 South 1st Street; 206-466-3086) for men's and women's fashionable attire. If gardening, greenery or dried flowers are your thing, you'll enjoy the **Bonsai Grove** (6th and Morris streets; 206-424-3984) and the historic **Tillinghast Seed Company** (623 East Morris Street; 206-466-3329).

The best shops and galleries in Bellingham are generally located in the Fairhaven District. In the renovated **Marketplace Building** (12th Street and Harris Avenue) you'll find an eclectic collection of goods including steins, home brewing supplies, beerabilia and 300 varieties of beer at **Bullie's Beer Emporium Shoppe** (206-734-2855); music, potpourri, jewelry and Arabic clothing at **East of Egypt** (206-733-5495); and high tea served in the **Rosewood Tearoom** (206-671-0602).

Other boutiques of interest in the area include **The Crystal Dolphin** (1209 11th Street; 206-671-5034) selling New Age crystals, jewelry, books, music and artwork; **Artwood** (1000 Harris Avenue; 206-647-1628), a co-op gallery of fine woodworking by Northwest artists; and **Inside Passage** (355 Harris Avenue, Suite 103; 206-734-1790) for gifts of the Pacific Northwest.

NORTHERN PUGET SOUND NIGHTLIFE

Bacchus By The Bay (1728 West Marine View Drive, Everett; 206-258-6258) is an English-style pub with an extensive wine list and occasional live jazz on warm summer evenings. Things are also jumping a few doors down at **Anthony's Homeport** (1728 West Marine View Drive, Everett; 206-252-3333), with great happy hour prices and a nice sheltered deck overlooking the marina. For country-and-western music and dancing, visit **Gerry Andal's Ranch Restaurant** (620 South East Everett Mall Way; 206-355-7999).

The **La Conner Tavern** (702 South 1st Street; 206-466-9932), housed in a waterfront structure that was at one time Brewster's Cigar Store, is the primary watering hole in La Conner and does a booming business through the wee hours of the morning.

In Bellingham, you'll find great happy hour specials and the best sunset views in the little bar of **Le Chat Noir** (★) (The Marketplace, Suite 301, Fairhaven; 206-733-6136). With an interior reminiscent of an old speakeasy, **Speedy O'Tubb's Rhythmic Underground** (1305 11th Street, Fairhaven; 206-734-1539) features a range of live music (rock, blues, reggae, jazz, etc.) and attracts a younger crowd from nearby Western Washington University.

Bob's Tavern (★) (1434 Peace Portal Drive, Blaine; 206-332-6789) is packed to the rafters every evening by 9 because of "cowboy karaoke." Buffalo and moose heads and a tribute to Loretta Lynn, who got her start here years ago, grace the walls of this straight-off-a-movie-set country-and-western bar.

NORTHERN PUGET SOUND BEACHES AND PARKS

Mukilteo State Park—Mukilteo State Park, a swath of beach adjacent to the Whidbey Island-Mukilteo Ferry facilities on Possession Sound, is a day-use-only facility known primarily as a prime fishing spot with public boat launch. Noble little Elliott Point Lighthouse on the tip will keep shutterbugs happy; it's also a fine spot for beachcombing or picnicking while waiting for the ferry to Whidbey Island.

Facilities: Restrooms, picnic grounds, boat launch, floats. *Fishing:* Excellent. *Swimming:* Fair, but chilly at times.

Getting there: Take the Mukilteo exit off Route 5 and follow the signs to the ferry.

Bay View State Park—This tiny park on the north side of the town of Bay View overlooks the **Padilla Bay National Estuarine Sanctuary,** an ecological pocket of 11,600 acres of marsh and tidelands snuggled between Fidalgo and Guemes islands and the mainland. The Breazeale Padilla Bay Interpretive Center, half a mile north on Bay View-Edison Road, is a good place to get better acquainted with the many forms of wildlife that inhabit the area. A nature trail winds through parts of the wildlife habitat area just beyond the center.

Facilities: Restrooms, showers, fireplaces, picnic tables and shelter, kitchen, laundromat, playground; restaurants and groceries in Bay View; information, 206-428-4044.

Camping: There are 90 sites, RV hookups are available.

Getting there: Take exit 230 off Route 5 just north of Mount Vernon, follow Route 20 west until it intersects with Route 237, then follow the signs to Padilla Bay Sanctuary.

Larrabee State Park—This 1966-acre park on Samish Bay offers eight miles of hiking trails, including two steep trails to small mountain lakes (Fragrance and Lost lakes), and a stretch of beach with numerous tide pools for views of the local marine life. The Nature Conservancy maintains a wildlife refuge on tiny Chuckanut Island at the center of Chuckanut Bay.

Facilities: Restrooms, showers, picnic tables and shelters, fireplaces, kitchens, playground, amphitheater, boat launch; restaurant and groceries nearby; information, 206-676-2093. *Fishing:* Good freshwater fishing in either of the mountain lakes and saltwater fishing in Chuckanut, Pleasant and Samish bays. *Swimming:* Good.

Camping: There are 74 tent sites and 26 hookups.

Getting there: Located seven miles south of Bellingham on scenic Chuckanut Drive (Route 11).

Teddy Bear Cove (★)—There's been talk of making a public beach of this secluded, narrow stretch of sand bordered by thick trees just south of the Bellingham city limits, but for now it remains the well-hidden haunt for nudists seeking summer fun on the Washington coastline. The beach area curves out around the shallow cove, like a thumb jutting out toward Chuckanut Bay.

Facilities: None. *Swimming:* Very cold.

Getting there: Tricky to find since it's not marked in any way. It is four miles south of Fairhaven Park on Chuckanut Drive near a slight widening in the road; if you've reached Larrabee State Park you've gone too far. With luck on your side, there will be a string of cars parked on the side of the road next to concrete embankments and a crowd trooping down the long pebble trail and across the railroad tracks to the beach.

Birch Bay State Park—The highlight of this 192-acre park with 6000 feet of shoreline is the warm, shallow bay, suitable for wading up to half a mile out in spots, bordered by a mile-long stretch of driftwood and shell-strewn beach edged by grassland. The camping area is located inland in a stand of old-growth cedar and Douglas Fir; nestled in the lush greenery it's hard to tell that the park sits in the shadow of Arco's Cherry Point Refinery. Birdwatchers frequent the park to visit the marshy estuary at the south border that attracts over 100 varieties of birds.

Facilities: Restrooms, fireplaces, picnic tables and shelters, trails, underwater park; some facilities for disabled; restaurants, groceries and boat launch nearby; information, 206-371-2800. *Fishing:* Good. *Swimming:* Excellent.

Camping: There are 147 sites, some with RV hookups.

Getting there: It's eight miles south of Blaine off Birch Bay Road.

Semiahmoo Park—This long, slender spit dividing Semiahmoo Bay and Drayton Harbor is a favorite among beach lovers, who can comb sandy, narrow beaches on both sides of the spit, and of birdwatchers who come here to observe bald eagles, loons, heron and other species supported by this protected, nutrient rich habitat. The spit was at one time home to the Semiahmoo Indians (thus its name) and later the site of a fish cannery; the history of both are reviewed in the park's museum.

Facilities: Restrooms, picnic tables, fire pits, bike path; information, 206-371-5513. *Fishing:* Outstanding clamming on both sides of the spit.

Getting there: Located near Blaine. Take the Birch Bay-Lynden Road exit west off Route 5, turn north onto Harbor View Road then west onto Lincoln Road, which becomes Semiahmoo Parkway and leads into the park.

Whidbey Island

Whidbey Island, stretched north to south along the mainland, is the longest island in the continental United States. This slender, serpentine bit of land is covered in a rolling patchwork of loganberry farms, pasturelands, sprawling state parks, hidden heritage sites and tiny farming and fishing villages. The artistic hamlet of Langley near Whidbey's southern tip is a current hot spot for weekend escapes from Seattle.

Most of the sights in **Langley** are concentrated along 1st and 2nd streets, where falsefront shops house small galleries, boutiques and restaurants.

There's a lovely stretch of public beach flanked by a concrete wall adorned in Northwest Indian motifs just below **Seawall Park** (look for the totem pole on 1st Street), and a wonderful bronze statue by local artist Georgia Gerber above a second stairwell leading down to the beach.

In the spring months you'll find a colorful tulip display at **Holland Gardens** (500 Avenue West and 30th Street Northwest, Oak Harbor). During the balance of the year come to see the beautiful floral displays that make this small garden a local favorite.

With 1500 native and hybrid species spread across 53 acres, **Meerkerk Rhododendron Gardens** (Resort Road, Greenbank; 206-321-6682) is a must. Magnolia, maple and cherry trees add to the beauty of this spot that is also a test garden.

At **Whidbeys Greenbank Loganberry Farm** (★) (Wonn Road, Greenbank; 206-678-7700) they produce Whidbey's, Washington's only liqueur. A self-guided tour of their small facility followed by a visit to their gift shop and tasting room makes a great afternoon outing.

The **Ebey's Landing National Historical Reserve**, the first such reserve in the country, lies midway up Whidbey Island taking in 17,000 acres that include Fort Ebey and Fort Casey state parks and the historic town of Coupeville, where authentic falsefront buildings line Front Street above the wharf. Here you'll find **Alexander Blockhouse** (Alexander and Front streets) and **Davis Blockhouse** (Sunnyside Cemetery Road), built by early settlers for protection against possible Indian attacks, and a good collection of Indian and pioneer artifacts in the new **Island County Historical Museum** (Alexander Street, Coupeville; 206-678-3310). Contact the Ebey's Landing National Historical Reserve (P.O. Box 774, Coupeville, WA 98239; 206-678-6084) for more information.

Built in 1897, **Admiralty Head Lighthouse** at Fort Casey State Park (1280 South Fort Casey Road, Coupeville, Whidbey Island; 206-678-5419) features an interpretive center offering history on the region's military past. You'll also enjoy excellent views of Puget Sound.

WHIDBEY ISLAND HOTELS

The beautiful **Inn at Langley** (★) (400 1st Street, Langley; 206-221-3033) has perfected the fine art of hospitality at a polished property worthy of its magnificent waterfront setting. With a decorator's color palette taken directly from the beach, rooms in shades of grey, cream, tan and brown accented by lots of natural wood are elegant, presenting a delicate balance of modern art and furnishings, and are decked out with every possible amenity (fireplace, jacuzzi, Krups coffee set and large deck to take advantage of the view). A serene oriental garden set in front of the grand dining room is an added touch. If you can afford the ultra-deluxe tariff, this is the most luxurious selection available in the region.

Gallery Suite (★) (1st Street, Langley; 206-221-2978) on Puget Sound includes a bedroom, parlor, kitchen and private deck. Furnished with contemporary pieces and an antique Japanese chest, the inn also offers great views from a private deck. This gay-friendly inn is convenient to good shopping and restaurants in turn-of-the-century Langley. Deluxe.

Though it's only a few miles north of downtown Langley, the **Log Castle Bed and Breakfast** (Saratoga Road; 206-321-5483) somehow feels like a retreat hidden away on a gorgeous, sandy beach far from everything. This colossal log home crowned by an eight-sided turret was been built bit by bit over the years. The four rooms are warm and inviting, with private baths and comfortable furnishings; a couple even have private decks with grand views. Moderate.

Cliff House (5440 Windmill Road, Freeland; 206-321-1566) is an architecturally stunning, two-story structure of wood and sweeping panes of glass set on a wooded bluff overlooking Admiralty Inlet. Guests have the run of the entire two-bedroom house, with its open central atrium, wonderful gourmet kitchen, sunken sitting area and wrap-around cedar deck with large jacuzzi. Ultra-deluxe.

Captain Whidbey's Inn (2072 West Whidbey Island Inn Road, Coupeville; 206-678-4097), a well-preserved and maintained log inn on Penn Cove, is a fine example of the type of Northwest retreat all the rage 50 years ago and now coming back into fashion. This walk into the past offers several cozy, antique furnished rooms that share two baths and waterfront views; more recent additions to the property include two rows of spacious, pine-paneled rooms with baths and a few private cottages with fireplaces. Continental breakfast is served in the dining room where the wooden floors creek nostalgically and the massive stone fireplace chases away the chill. This is one of only a handful of waterside accommodations in the region; to fully enjoy the water, arrange for an afternoon sail with Captain John Colby Stone, the third-generation innkeeper. Moderate.

The **Auld Holland Inn** (5861 Highway 20, Oak Harbor; 206-675-2288) is a moderately priced roadside motel with flair, from the flowering window boxes on the European exterior to the immaculately clean, antique-filled rooms. Some rooms even have fireplaces and princess canopied beds topped with windmill quilts. For those seeking budget prices there are 24 mobile home units with two or three bedrooms tucked behind the full-sized windmill housing the motel's office.

WHIDBEY ISLAND RESTAURANTS

Since 1989, **Café Langley** (113 1st Street, Langley; 206-221-3090) has served Greek favorites like spanikopita, moussaka, dolmades and lamb shish kabobs along with fresh seafood (Penn Cove mussels, grilled salmon and halibut), pastas and steaks. The atmosphere here is airy Mediterranean, with stucco-like walls, exposed beams and an assortment of exotic fish etched on a glass partition. There are often people waiting in the park across the street for a table in this popular café. Moderate.

The **Doghouse Tavern** (230 1st Street, Langley; 206-321-9996) is the place to go for great ribs, burgers, fish and chips and chowder. A totem on the side of this waterfront building points the way to their separate family dining room in case you've got the kids along. Budget.

The **Star Bistro Café and Bar** (201½ 1st Street, Langley; 206-221-2627), a trendy little café with art deco decor, is a popular meeting spot for lunch, dinner and drinks. Their pastas, salads and espressos are particularly good, and the grilled pesto King salmon on a french roll is inventive and tasty. On a calm day you can dine al fresco on the second floor deck with a great view of the Saratoga Passage. Moderate.

Whidbey Fish (★) (Route 20, Greenbank; 206-678-3474) is another don't-blink-or-you'll-miss-it find that's developed a strong local following. Best items on the short menu are the outstanding crab cakes, fragrant smoked salmon and fresh loganberry pie. Mix-and-match wooden tables and a long bar share space with the kitchen in this boxy roadside diner. Hours are erratic; budget.

Award-winning **Rosi's Garden** (606 North Main Street, Coupeville; 206-678-3989) serves a blend of Northwest and European cuisine highlighting the many fresh products of Whidbey Island. On the menu you'll find Penn Cove mussels, prime rib with crab béarnaise, halibut florentine and poached salmon in hollandaise; save room for the decadent desserts. Seating in the peach and mauve front room of this tiny seaside cottage is very limited, so reservations for dinner, the only meal they serve, are highly recommended. Deluxe.

Kasteel Franssen (5861 Highway 20, Oak Harbor; 206-675-0724) is the showcase for the culinary arts of Jean Paul Combettes, who for years was chef to the stars at Lake Tahoe's famous House of Lords. Lace table dressings, antiques, tapestries and fine art reproductions of Rembrandt and other masters set a romantic European tone well suited to dishes such as coquille St. Jacques, *hollandaise biefstuk* (beef steak in hollandaise), rack of lamb and chicken breast in champagne sauce. Dinner only; moderate.

WHIDBEY ISLAND SHOPPING

There's plenty to keep shoppers and browsers busy on Whidbey Island, especially in artsy Langley and historic Coupeville. The best art galleries are concentrated in Langley By The Sea; the **Childers/Proctor Gallery** (302 1st Street; 206-221-2978) showcases bronzes, paintings, sculpture and pottery; **Soleil** (308 1st Street; 206-321-0383) carries Nambe ware, double-sided aluminum pieces by Arthur Court and jewelry by local craftspeople; **Line of the Spirit Gallery** (220 2nd Street; 206-321-0989) features an array of

Southwest Indian arts and artifacts; and the **Hellebore Glass Studio** (308 1st Street; 206-221-2067) has fine hand-blown glassworks and a studio where you can watch them work.

Other noteworthy shops in town include **The Star Store** (201 1st Street; 206-321-5223), a modern mercantile selling fun clothing and housewares; **Island Gift Baskets** (220 2nd Street, Suite 107; 206-321-1960) for gift items of the Pacific Northwest; and the two shops of **Whidbey Island Antiques** (2nd Street and Anthes Avenue; 206-221-2393).

In the revitalized waterfront district of Coupeville you'll find wonderful antiques and collectibles at **Salmangundi Farms** (12 Front Street; 206-678-5888); fine imported clothing and jewelry from Scotland and Ireland at **Tartans and Tweeds** (4 Front Street; 206-678-6244); and nautical gifts, artifacts and sportswear at **Nautical 'N' Nice** (22 Front Street; 206-678-3565).

WHIDBEY ISLAND NIGHTLIFE

If you're looking for a little dance action, head to **Hong Kong Gardens** (4643 East State Highway 525, Clinton; 206-221-2828) where, on the weekends, they clear the dinner tables off the dancefloor and hit the switch for the disco lights as the band plays popular rock tunes.

For local color in a friendly tavern try the cozy pub in **Captain Whidbey's Inn** (2072 West Captain Whidbey Inn Road, Coupeville; 206-678-4097) where the walls are adorned with university pennants and business cards, or **Toby's Tavern** (Front Street, Coupeville; 206-678-4222) where they filmed the bar scene from the movie *War of the Roses.*

WHIDBEY ISLAND BEACHES AND PARKS

South Whidbey State Park—There are 340 acres with 4500 feet of rocky shoreline to explore in this lovely state park. Hikers will enjoy the one-and-a-half-mile loop trail through an old growth stand of fir and cedar. Black-tailed deer, bald eagles and osprey are among the many creatures here. Campsites on the wooded bluff above the beach are very secluded. *Facilities:* Restrooms, showers, picnic tables and shelters, fireplaces; restaurants and groceries nearby; information, 206-321-4559. *Swimming:* Only the hardy will venture into the cold waters of Admiralty Inlet.

Camping: There are 54 standard sites and 6 primitive ones.

Getting there: Take Route 525 nine miles north of Clinton to Bush Point Road, which eventually becomes Smuggler's Cove Road.

Fort Casey State Park—History buffs and children enjoy exploring the military fortification of this 137-acre park. While most of the big guns are gone, you'll still find panoramic views of the Olympic Mountains across the Straight of Juan de Fuca from the top of the concrete bunkers built into the escarpment. Wild roses and other flowers line the paths to the museum housed in pretty Admiralty Head Lighthouse and the beachside campground that overlooks the Keystone Harbor ferry terminal. Scuba enthusiasts swarm to the underwater trail through the park's marine wildlife sanctuary off Keystone Harbor.

Facilities: Restrooms, showers, picnic tables, fireplaces, underwater marine park; restaurants and groceries nearby; information, 206-678-4519. *Fishing:* Good salmon, steelhead and bottom fishing. *Swimming:* Excellent.

Camping: There are 35 sites.

Getting there: At Coupeville turn south off Route 20 onto Engle Road and follow the Keystone Ferry signs to the park.

Fort Ebey State Park—Massive guns are long gone from this coastal World War II fortification, but there are still bunker tunnels and pillboxes to be explored. The picturesque beach at Partridge Point is the hands-down favorite of the islanders; at low tide it's possible to walk the five-mile beach stretch to Fort Casey.

Facilities: Restrooms, showers, picnic tables, fireplaces, nature trails: restaurants and groceries nearby; information, 206-678-4636. *Fishing:* Good bass fishing on Lake Pondilla. *Swimming:* Good.

Camping: There are 50 sites. Secluded campsites under a canopy of Douglas fir are much nicer than the crowded sites at nearby Fort Casey.

Getting there: From Route 20 turn west onto Libbey Road then south onto Valley Drive and follow the signs.

Oak Harbor City Beach Park—A full-scale windmill is the centerpiece of this day-use park on Oak Harbor Bay next to the sewage processing plant (not a deterrent, believe it or not). A sandy beach slopes down from the lighted walking path bordering expansive green fields suitable for flying kites or playing frisbee.

Facilities: Bathhouses, picnic tables, ball fields, tennis courts, playground. *Swimming:* There's a wading pool and protected swimming area.

Getting there: Located in downtown Oak Harbor off Pioneer Parkway, east of Route 20; watch for the windmill.

Deception Pass State Park—The most popular state park in Washington, it encompasses over 3000 acres laced with eight-and-a-half miles of hiking trails through forested hills and wetland areas and along rocky headlands. There are several delightful sandy stretches for picnics or beachcombing. Breathtaking views from the 976-foot steel bridge spanning the pass attract photographers from around the world. At Cranberry Lake's south shore you'll find beaver dams and muskrats.

Facilities: Restrooms, showers, bathhouse, picnic tables, kitchens, shelters, fireplaces, boat rentals, concession stand, boat launches (salt and freshwater), environmental learning center, underwater park; restaurants nearby; information, 206-675-2417. *Fishing:* Fly-fishing for trout on Pass Lake. *Swimming:* Supervised swimming on Cranberry Lake in the summer. *Camping:* There are 240 sites at Deception Pass and 16 at Bowman Bay.

Getting there: Take the Mukilteo ferry to Whidbey Island and follow Route 525 and Route 20 to the park on the northern tip of the island.

Fidalgo Island

An easy drive from Seattle, Fidalgo Island is a good place to enjoy folk art, ride a charming excursion train and see impressive murals. Quiet inns and waterfront restaurants make this island a pleasant retreat.

Because of its ferry terminal, **Anacortes** on Fidalgo Island is known as "the gateway to the San Juans," but don't just zip on through because there's plenty to see and do here. One of the best ways to get acquainted with the city and its history is to make a walking tour of downtown to view the 40 life-sized murals attached to many of the historical buildings. As part of the **Anacortes Mural Project**, these murals are reproductions of turn-of-the-century photographs depicting everyday scenes and early pioneers of the town. A tour map is available from the **Anacortes Chamber of Commerce** (1319 Commercial Avenue; 206-293-3882).

Other reminders of earlier days are the **W. T. Preston** (7th Street and R Avenue), a drydocked stern-wheeler that once plied the waters of the Sound breaking up log jams, and next door the refurbished **Burlington Northern Railroad Depot** (6th Street and R Avenue; 206-293-2670), now a community arts center and the spot to catch the **Anacortes Railway**, an elaborate miniature steam locomotive with three passenger cars built by a local resident and operated on summer weekends.

At the **Anacortes Museum** (1305 8th Street; 206-293-1915) you'll find an entertaining collection of regional memorabilia, and in front of the building a highly amusing drinking fountain with varying levels suited for dogs, cats, horses and humans donated to the city by the Women's Temperance Union.

Even if you don't plan to stay in Anacortes at the **Majestic Hotel (★)** (419 Commercial Avenue; 216-293-3355), stop by for a 360-degree view of Fidalgo and surrounding islands from the fantastic cupola above fourth-floor suites and ogle the amazing skylight and collection of art and antiques.

If you have an interest in **totems**, drive by 2102 9th Street to see the display in front of the home of another talented resident, former State Senator Paul Luvera, Sr., who carved thousands of totems during his retirement before passing away recently.

FIDALGO ISLAND HOTELS

At the **Holiday Inn** (2903 Commercial Avenue, Anacortes; 206-293-6511), one of the only motels that falls into the budget category even during high season, you get what you pay for. Aging rooms are very basic but tidy, with nicked furnishings in both the cramped bedroom and separate sitting room.

A lot of care and expense went into the painstaking renovation of the historic 1889 McNaught building, now the new **Majestic Hotel** (★) (419 Commercial Avenue, Anacortes; 216-293-3355) which specializes in European elegance, from the plush feather bedding and antique furnishings to the warm and inviting mahogany-paneled library and grand English garden. Guests are treated to croissants and coffee each morning. The highly individual guest rooms vary in price from moderate to ultra-deluxe.

At the **Nantucket Guest House Inn** (3402 Commercial Avenue, Anacortes; 206-293-6007), the proprietress was welcoming weary travelers into her home long before bed and breakfasts came into fashion. Each of the comfortable guest rooms is furnished in lovingly polished family antiques and cozy quilts; two of the rooms share a bath and a third has a bath across the hall. Moderate.

FIDALGO ISLAND RESTAURANTS

Since 1935, the **Bridgeway Café** (1541 Highway 20, Anacortes; 206-293-9250) has served up fresh, hand-breaded oysters and prawns, grilled burgers and mouth-watering pies. Look for this unpretentious roadside establishment located on the hill two miles north of Deception Pass. Budget.

While it's not particularly well decorated or romantic, **La Petite** (3401 Commercial Avenue, Anacortes; 206-293-4644) is the only dinner spot in town fancy enough to have tablecloths. The fare here is solid Dutch gourmet, with often repeated favorites such as *gemarinder de lam* (marinated lamb in herbs and red wine) and *kippige knoflock* (chicken breast over parmesan pasta). The traditional Dutch breakfast of egg cup, thinly sliced ham and cheese and piping hot loaves of bread draws a crowd. Deluxe.

Potted plants, taped classical music and tablecloths soften the rough edges of **Charlie's** (Ferry Terminal Road, Anacortes; 206-293-7377), a roadside hash house next to the ferry terminal. Captive diners, here during the long wait for the ferry, choose from soups, salads, sandwiches and seafood at lunch and pasta, steak and seafood for dinner. Moderate.

FIDALGO ISLAND SHOPPING

Most of the great shops on Fidalgo Island are scattered along Anacortes' Commercial Avenue. At fascinating and fun **Bunnies By The Bay**

(2916 Commercial Avenue, Suite B 266; 206-293-8037) they create designer stuffed animals to complement any decor scheme. **Left Bank Antiques** (1904 Commercial Avenue; 206-293-3022), housed in a renovated church, absolutely bulges with American and European antiques and gift items. At **Potlatch Gifts** (708 Commercial Avenue; 206-293-6404) you'll find an intriguing collection of Native American jewelry, prints, woodcarvings, basketry, weavings and woolens sharing space with the Samish tribal offices and a cultural interpretive center. The historic **Marine Supply and Hardware Co.** (202 Commercial Avenue; 206-293-3014) is packed to the rafters with nautical antiques and memorabilia.

Resist the temptation to buy smoked salmon to take home for friends and family until you visit **Specialty Seafoods** (★) (605 30th Street, Anacortes; 206-293-4661) for alderwood smoked oysters, King, North Pacific or Sockeye salmon. Discount prices are terrific at the difficult-to-locate warehouse (take 22nd Street east toward the Anacortes Marina, turn right onto T Avenue and you'll find the warehouse in an industrial complex a block down on the right).

FIDALGO ISLAND NIGHTLIFE

If a quiet conversation over drinks in refined surroundings is your style, visit the **Rose and Crown Pub** (The Majestic Hotel, 419 Commercial Avenue, Anacortes; 206-293-3355).

Lopez Island

Life on pastoral Lopez Island is much slower and friendlier; here residents wave to everyone and are truly disappointed if you don't take the time to wave back. The history of the island is well mapped out at the **Lopez Historical Museum** (Lopez Village; 206-468-2049) with its exhibit of pioneer farming and fishing implements. While you're there, pick up a historical landmark tour guide to the many fine examples of Early American architecture scattered around the island.

Pick up some bread and wine at the Village Market in Lopez Village before heading out to **Glencorra Farm** (★) (Mud Bay Road; 206-468-3848) to tour the dairy where they make delicious sheep-milk cheeses that you can purchase in the gift shop. Then take your goodies out to **Agate Beach Park** (MacKaye Harbor Road) to feast on while watching the sunset. Another good sunset view spot is **Shark Reef Park** (Shark Reef Road) where you might see some harbor seals, heron and, if you're lucky, a whale or two.

If you like horses, pull off the road at the bend on Center Road between Cross and Hummel Lake roads to admire the large herd of **Shetlands** frolicking in rolling pastures.

Most visitors to the San Juans miss **Shaw Island**, a short ferry ride from Lopez Island. Those who do make the trip are in for a treat. Stop by the general store near the ferry landing (both operated by Franciscan nuns) for picnic supplies before heading out to **South Beach County Park** (Squaw Bay Road) two miles to the south. Afterward continue east along Squaw Bay Road, turn north on Hoffman Cove Road and make your way to the picturesque little red school house. Park by the school and cross the street to see the **Shaw Island Historical Museum** (Schoolhouse Corner; 206-468-3351), a tiny log cabin housing a hodgepodge of pioneer memorabilia.

LOPEZ ISLAND HOTELS

Best bet here is the **Inn At Swifts Bay** (★) (Port Stanley Road; 206-468-3636), a delightful bed and breakfast in an elegant Tudor home. Posh best describes the interior, with a comfortable mix of modern, William Sonoma-style furnishings and antique reproductions adorned in crocheted antimacassars and needlepoint pillows. Two rooms sharing one bath fall into the moderate cost category, and two suites with private entrances and baths are deluxe in price. The leisurely gourmet breakfast is without a doubt the most delicious morning repast available in the islands. Gay-friendly.

Edenwild (Lopez Village; 206-468-3238), newest addition to the scant list of lodgings on the island, is a two-story Victorian. The seven guest rooms are pretty, with blond-wood floors, claw-foot tubs and antique furnishings; two rooms have romantic fireplaces, one is handicap accessible and those on the west side of the structure have views of Fisherman's Bay and San Juan Channel. Included in the deluxe price is breakfast served in the sunny dining nook or on the delightful garden terrace where they also serve afternoon tea and dessert.

There are three budget-priced rooms on the island. The **Lopez Lodge** (206-468-2500) above Lopez Video in the village has two no-frills, motel-like rooms with a shared bath across the hall. The **Island Farm House** (Hummel Lake Road; 206-468-2864) offers a more cozy and comfortable room with bath overlooking a field of sheep.

LOPEZ ISLAND RESTAURANTS

The **Bay Café** (Lopez Road; 206-468-3700) has an imaginative menu of ethnic cuisine featuring fresh Northwest products. There are always daily specials to choose from, with often-repeated favorites like scallops in Thai curry, marinated lamb kabobs in mint yogurt sauce, beef satay with peanut sauce and wok-seared beef with pinenuts, wild mushrooms and jasmine rice. Reservations are essential, especially during summer. Deluxe.

The hole-in-the-wall **Wildflower Café** (Lopez Road; 206-468-2114), with diner-style bar and kitchen up front and small dining area in the back, doesn't offer much in the way of decor, but the selections of baked, broiled and fried seafood, chicken and steaks are quite a draw. Favorites here include the thick Lopez Pizza, rich pecan chicken and burgers. Moderate.

Set off to one side in the **Lopez Island Pharmacy** (★) (Fisherman Bay Road; 206-468-2644) is an old-fashioned, pink and grey soda fountain, the best spot in town for lunch on Lopez. Grab a stool at the bar and order a sandwich, bowl of soup or chili or slice of pie to go with your phosphate, malt, float, or other fountain treat. Budget.

LOPEZ ISLAND SHOPPING

For the most part, shopping here is limited to those establishments located in sleepy little Lopez Village. **Archipelago** (206-468-3222) sells natural fiber clothing and a line of tourist T-shirts; **Panda Books** (206-468-2132) stocks an admirable selection of new and used books and regional music. For fine art visit **Chimera Gallery** (206-468-3265), the cooperative showcase for prints, paintings, weaving, pottery and jewelry produced by local artists.

LOPEZ ISLAND BEACHES AND PARKS

Spencer Spit State Park—This long stretch of silky sand on Lopez Island encloses an intriguing salt-water lagoon. The mile-long beach invites wading and swimming during warm summer months and beachcombing and clamming year-round.

Facilities: Restrooms, beach bonfire pits, picnic shelters; restaurants and groceries nearby in Lopez Village; information, 206-468-2251. *Fishing:* Excellent crabbing, shrimping and bottom fishing. *Swimming:* Good.

Camping: There are 35 sites, 10 of which are walk-in only.

Getting there: Take the ferry from Anacortes to Lopez Island, then follow the ten-mile route to the park on the eastern shore of the island.

San Juan Island

San Juan Island, the namesake of the archipelago, is a popular resort destination centered around the town of Friday Harbor. This 20-mile-long island has a colorful past stemming from a boundary dispute between the United States and Great Britain. The tension over who was entitled to the islands was embodied in American and British farmers whose warring over, get this, a pig, nearly sent the two countries to the battlefield. When an American farmer shot a British homesteader's pig caught rooting in his garden, ill feelings quickly escalated. Fortunately, cooler heads prevailed so that what is now referred to as the "Pig War" of 1859 only resulted in one casualty: the pig. The history of this little-known war is chronicled through interpretive centers in the **San Juan Island National Historic Park** (206-378-2240), which is divided into **English Camp** (West Valley Road) on the north end of the island, with barracks, a formal garden, cemetery, guardhouse, hospital and commissary left in tact, and **American Camp** (Cattle Point Road) on the south end of the island where the officers and laundress's quarters, a cemetery and the Hudson Bay Company Farm Site remain.

San Juan Historical Museum (405 Price Street, Friday Harbor; 206-378-3949) is a charming turn-of-the-century frame building with a good collection of Native American baskets and stone implements, antique diving suits, period furniture and clothing. A place to learn about the region's maritime history, the museum also features an excellent collection on this region's proud past.

On a sunny afternoon, a stroll through the fragrant herb gardens at **Giannangelo Farms** (★) (5500 Limestone Point Road, Friday Harbor; 206-378-4218) on the north end of San Juan Island is hard to beat.

Afterglow Vista (★) (Roche Harbor Road) is the mausoleum of one of the region's wealthy families. The structure itself is fascinating; an open, Grecian-style columned complex surrounds six inscribed chairs, each containing the ashes of a family member, set before a round table of limestone. A seventh chair and column have obviously been removed, some say as part of Masonic ritual, other believe because a member of the family was disinherited.

Oyster-lovers and birdwatchers should make the trip down the dusty road to **Westcott Bay Sea Farms** (★) (4701 Westcott Drive, Friday Harbor; 206-378-2489) where they'll find saltwater bins of live oysters and clams and an array of birds attracted to the oyster beds stretched out in the bay.

SAN JUAN ISLAND HOTELS

Named for its view, **Olympic Lights** (4531-A Cattle Point Road, Friday Harbor; 206-378-3186) is a remodeled 1895 farmhouse set on five grassy, breeze-tossed acres overlooking the Olympic Peninsula across the Strait of Juan de Fuca. Guests kick off their shoes before heading up to the cream-carpeted second floor with four comfortably appointed, pastel-shaded rooms sharing two baths; a fifth room on the ground floor has a private bath. You'll find no frilly, Victoriana clutter here, just a peaceful night snuggled under down comforters topped off by a farm-fresh breakfast. Priced in the moderate range.

If you've dreamed of life on the water, you'll appreciate the **Wharfside Bed and Breakfast** (Port of Friday Harbor; 206-378-5661), a 60-foot, two-masted sailboat with two guest rooms. The forward stateroom with double bed and two bunks feels a bit cramped, while the aft stateroom with queen bed seems roomier. The moderate price includes a three-course breakfast.

The **Elite Hotel** (35 1st Street, Friday Harbor; 206-378-5555) is more a hostel than a hotel, with clean, bare-bones, dorm-style family and group rooms conveniently located in the heart of Friday Harbor. Budget.

Set in the rolling West Valley near English Camp National Park and surrounded by a working ranch, **States Inn** (2039 West Valley Road, Friday Harbor; 206-378-6240) is a bit of Sleepy Hollow in San Juan. Each of the nine rooms have decor schemes that hint at their namesake states—tiny Rhode Island comes closest, with shells and brass dolphins on the fireplace mantle, various renditions of ships on the walls and copies of the New England publication *Yankee* to peruse. The friendly and informative innkeeper

and the multicourse country breakfasts make up for the slight sulphur odor that emanates from the tap water. This deluxe-priced inn is also handicap accessible, hard to find in the islands.

Roche Harbor Resort (4950 Tarte Memorial Drive, Roche Harbor; 206-378-2155) has something for everyone. You can check in to the century-old **Hotel de Haro** where gingerbread trim, parlor beds, antiques and a roaring fireplace bring back the good old days at budget to deluxe prices. In addition to this three-story, 20-room establishment, ten former workers' cottages provide moderate-to-deluxe two-bedroom accommodations, ideal for families. Furnished with Salvation Army pieces, the cottages are convenient to the swimming pool. For contemporary lodging at deluxe prices choose one of the condominiums.

SAN JUAN ISLAND RESTAURANTS

When locals look for a romantic spot, they usually make a reservation at **Café Bisset** (170 West Street, Friday Harbor; 206-378-3109). Dim lighting, candles and fresh bouquets of flowers add romance to the already intimate surroundings. The basics remain the same on the menu—lamb, duck, beef and three seafoods—but the method of preparation changes daily utilizing fresh local produce. Dinner only by reservation; deluxe.

Roberto's (★) (1st and A streets, Friday Harbor; 206-378-6333) sits on the hill overlooking the ferry landing. You'll find no fancy decor, but the Italian fare served here is a culinary escape. Try the "past tour of Italy" (with pesto, bolognese and alfredo sauces) or the Sicilian salmon in capers and onions followed up by homemade cheesecake or fresh fruit tarts. Moderate.

Another recent addition to Friday Harbor's dining scene is **What's Cooking** (1st Street; 206-378-6616), an unpretentious diner serving hearty portions of home-cooked breakfast and lunch favorites like biscuits and gravy, blueberry pancakes, chicken fried steak and juicy burgers. Budget.

SAN JUAN ISLAND SHOPPING

Most of the shops are located within blocks of Friday Harbor, giving you plenty to do while waiting for the ferry. Cannery Landing, next to the ferry terminal on Front Street, houses **Friday Harbor Studio and Design** (206-378-3531), selling original screenprint art on cotton sportswear.

Art-lovers visiting Friday Harbor will want to stop by **El Picaflor** (40A Spring Street; 206-378-3051) for their collection of Latin American handicrafts; **Garuda & I** (225 A Street; 206-378-3733) for an amazing selection of ethnic arts, crafts, musical instruments and jewelry from India and Asia; and the **Sunshine Gallery** (85 Nichols Street; 206-378-5819) to view the locally produced basketry, sculptures, watercolors, ceramics and jewelry.

SAN JUAN ISLAND NIGHTLIFE

On San Juan Island, **Herb's Tavern** (80 1st Street, Friday Harbor; 206-378-9106) is the local sidle-up-to-the-bar joint with the only pool tables in town. You'll find live music and dancing each weekend at the **Riptide** (175 Spring Street, Friday Harbor; 206-378-4747) and the **Roche Harbor Resort Lounge** (Roche Harbor Road, Roche Harbor; 206-378-2155).

SAN JUAN ISLAND BEACHES AND PARKS

San Juan County Park—Orca whales frequently pass by the rocky shoreline of this ten-acre park on the western edge of San Juan Island. Because of its locations on Smallpox Bay, the park is a haven for kayakers and scuba divers who enjoy the easy waters in the shallow bay or the more challenging shelf that drops steeply off about 80 feet out.

Facilities: Restrooms, picnic tables, fire pits; information 206-378-2992. *Fishing:* Fair. *Swimming:* Good in the shallow, protected bay.

Camping: There are 18 standard sites and one for groups.

Getting there: Located on Westside Road just north of Lime Kiln Point State Park.

Lime Kiln Point State Park—Situated on a rocky bluff overlooking Haro Straight, this is the prime whale-watching spot on San Juan Island. A footpath takes you to picturesque Lime Kiln Lighthouse, listed on the National Register of Historic Places. The site is named for an early lime kiln operation, with remnants of old structures still visible to the north of the lighthouse.

Facilities: Restrooms, picnic tables, interpretive displays.

Getting there: Located just off Westside Road on the western shore of San Juan Island.

Cattle Point Picnic Area (★)—Though it takes a precarious scramble down a rocky ledge to reach it and picnic tables on the bluff above lend little privacy, this gravelly half-moon is arguably the prettiest public beach on San Juan Island.

Facilities: Picnic tables, shelter, interpretive signs, nature trail. *Swimming:* Cold, but safe in shallows.

Getting there: Follow Cattle Point Road through American Camp and on to the southern tip of the island.

Fourth of July Beach—This secluded, sandy crescent is where the locals head when they're looking for privacy on San Juan Island. There are often bald eagles nesting in the nearby trees, a poignant sign of this aptly named stretch.

Facilities: Pit toilets, picnic tables, fenced grassy area off the parking lot suitable for frisbee. *Swimming:* The shallow, little bay area extends out a long way and is suitable for wading on hot days.

Getting there: Located on the northeastern edge of American Camp.

Orcas Island

Trendy, artsy-craftsy and lovely to look at, Orcas Island is a resort that caters to everyone from backpackers to the well-to-do. A nature sanctuary pocketed with charming towns, the island also boasts more sun than some of its neighbors.

One of Orcas Island's leading landmarks is Rosario Resort. Even if you're not planning to stay here during your trip, make sure to visit **Moran Mansion** (★) (One Rosario Way; 206-376-2222) for a fantastic evening show that includes music performed on a 1910 Steinway grand piano and an amazing pipe organ along with entertaining narration and slides of life on the island in the early 1900s.

Of the many small historical museums in the San Juans, the **Orcas Island Historical Museum** (North Beach Road, Eastsound; 206-376-4840) is our favorite. A fine assemblage of relics and antiques stored in four interconnected log cabins of prominent early settlers maps the history and growth of industry on the island.

Madrona Point (★), a pretty Madrona tree-dotted waterside park saved from condo development by the Lummi Indian tribe, is a fine spot for a picnic. It's at the end of the unmarked road just past Christina's Restaurant in Eastsound.

ORCAS ISLAND HOTELS

A stay at **Turtleback Farm Inn** (Route 1, P.O. Box 650, Eastsound, WA 98245; 206-376-4914) is like stepping into the much-loved story *Wind in the Willows*, surrounded as it is by acres of forest and farm tracts full of animals as far as the eye can see. Rooms in this lovely, 100-year-old farmhouse vary in size and setup, but all seven guest rooms have a charming mix of contemporary and Early American furniture, cozy quilts and antique fixtures in private baths. Deluxe.

It's not unusual to find semi-tame deer roaming around the ample grounds of **Rosario Resort** (1 Rosario Way, Eastsound; 206-376-2222) tucked away on Cascade Bay on the east side of the horseshoe of Orcas Island. The motel-style rooms scattered along the waterfront or perched on the hillside overlooking the bay are clean and comfortable but could use a decorating overhaul; best choices are the newer rooms in the 2300 or 2400 building. Deluxe.

Accommodations at the funky **Doe Bay Village Resort** (Star Route 86, Olga; 206-376-2291) range from bunk houses to rustic cabins to tents. There are shared central bathrooms, a community kitchen and a small café on the grounds of this large retreat along with a splendid three-tiered steam sauna and three mineral baths perched on a covered deck. Budget.

ORCAS ISLAND RESTAURANTS

La Famiglia (A Street, Eastsound; 206-376-2335), an inviting, wood-paneled restaurant decorated with distinct Northwest accents, has been the preferred choice of islanders since opening in 1976. The lunch and dinner menus feature Italian classics with island flair—pasta primavera with salmon, seafood linguini, steamer clams in garlic and wine. There are even pizza and sandwiches to please the younger set. Moderate.

Bilbo's Festivo (North Beach Road, Eastsound; 206-376-4728) specializes in Tex-Mex fare. A margarita or cerveza on the tiled garden patio surrounded by adobe walls rounds out the experience. Bilbo's serves dinner only, but is opening **La Taqueria**, a lunch outlet in the courtyard. Budget.

The Deer Harbor Inn (Deer Harbor Road, Deer Harbor; 206-376-4110), tucked away in an expanse of orchard grove peering out over Deer Harbor and the Olympic Range, is where locals come for that special night out. The daily menu is chalked on the board; rock cod, Coho salmon and choice steaks are prime picks. For diners on the deck, this is a great spot to watch the sunset. Dinner only; reservations recommended. Deluxe.

ORCAS ISLAND SHOPPING

On Orcas Island you'll find several interesting shops congregated in Eastsound. **Darvill's Rare Print Shop** (206-378-2351) carries antique maps, etchings and fine prints and has a connected bookstore that will please avid readers. For casual wear try **Orcas North West** (206-376-2386), and for souvenirs and handicrafts of the island visit **Gulls & Buoys Gifts** (206-376-2199) or the **Green Dragon Company** (206-376-5366).

Don't spend all your time and money in Eastsound because you won't want to miss **Orcas Island Pottery** (★) (off West Beach Road; 206-376-2813), the oldest existing craft studio on Orcas. You can even watch potters at work through the windows of the studio.

The Right Place (off West Beach Road; 206-376-4023) has more pottery strewn about the garden and in the showroom. An intriguing spinning and weaving shop, **The Naked Lamb** (206-376-4606), is also on the grounds.

At a bend in Horseshoe Highway as you reach the town of Olga is **Orcas Island Artworks** (★) (206-376-4408), the cooperative art gallery showcasing stained glass, woodworking, jewelry, leatherwork and furniture all produced by local hands. Tucked away in the attic is the **Nebula Bookstore** (206-376-4666) with metaphysical books, crystals and incense.

ORCAS ISLAND NIGHTLIFE

Vista Lounge (Rosario Resort, 1 Rosario Way, Eastsound; 206-376-2222) is the place to go for live entertainment and great sunset views, with an occasional comedy night and special theme dance weekends thrown in for good measure.

ORCAS ISLAND BEACHES AND PARKS

Moran State Park—Washington's fourth-largest park consists of almost 5000 verdant acres flanked by 1800 feet of saltwater shoreline and crowned by sweeping Mt. Constitution. The view from the stone platform at the peak takes in the San Juans, Mt. Baker and Vancouver, B.C. There are miles of forest trails connecting the four mountain lakes, numerous waterfalls and five campgrounds.

Facilities: Restrooms, showers, kitchen shelters, picnic tables; some facilities wheelchair accessible; restaurants and groceries nearby; information, 206-378-2044. *Fishing:* There is fresh water fishing on several lakes, with fishing supplies and boat rentals available. *Swimming:* Good.

Camping: There are 135 sites.

Getting there: Located near Eastsound, accessible by state ferry from Anacortes.

Obstruction Pass Multiple Use Area (★)—This primitive, heavily forested locale on the southeastern tip of Orcas Island is tricky to get to, so the crowds are kept to a minimum, a reward for those who care to search it out. The area is laced with hiking trails, has several free campsites and a beach.

Facilities: Vault toilets, picnic tables, buoys, trails; restaurants and groceries in Olga. *Fishing:* Good. *Swimming:* Good.

Camping: There are nine primitive sites; hike-in only.

Getting there: From the town of Olga follow Doe Bay Road east, turn right on Obstruction Pass Road and keep right until you hit the parking area. From there it's a half-mile hike to the campground.

OTHER PARKS Many of the smaller islands are preserved as state parks including **Doe, Jones, Clark, Sucia, Stuart, Posey, Blind, James, Matia, Patos** and **Turn**. They are accessible by boat only and in most case have a few primitive camp sites, nature trails, a dock or mooring buoys off secluded beaches, but no water or facilities.

The Sporting Life

SPORTFISHING

With thousands of miles of tidal coastline, Puget Sound and the San Juan Islands boast some of the best sportfishing opportunities in North America. In addition to five varieties of pink salmon (chinook, coho, chum, pink and sockeye), anglers can try for cod, flounder, halibut, ling, rockfish, sea perch, squid and sturgeon. Scuba divers often concentrate their efforts on harvesting abalone, crab, octopus, shrimp and squid, while shellfishers are rewarded with butter and razor clams. Clamming and fishing licenses are required and are available in sporting goods stores throughout the area.

Experienced fishing charter operators in the North Puget Sound region include **Everett North Sound Charters** (2815 West Marine View Drive, Everett; 206-339-1275), **Sea King Salmon Charters** (2812 McLeod Road, Bellingham; 206-671-7231) and **Jim's Charters** (P.O. Box 464, Blaine, WA 98230; 206-332-6724).

Operators in the islands include **Deception Pass Charters** (565 West Cornet Bay Road, Oak Harbor; 206-675-9597), **Buffalo Works Fishing Charters** (P.O. Box 478, Friday Harbor, WA 98250; 206-378-4612), **Moby Max Charters** (Route 1, P.O. Box 1065, Eastsound, WA 98245; 206-376-2970) and **Bounty Charters** (Orcas Island; 206-376-2165).

SCUBA DIVING

The protected inland sea waters of Puget Sound hold treasures untold for the diver, where the craggy rock walls, ledges and caves of this sunken mountain range and enormous forests of bull kelp provide homes for a multitude of marine life. It is also the site of some of the most tremendous tidal changes in the world; the strong currents and rip tides can be treacherous, so plan to use local dive charters or talk in detail with another diver experienced in the area.

There are literally hundreds of great dive spots to choose from, some little known and others crowded with divers. Favored dive sites in the San Juans are just off Henry, Stewart and Waldron islands. There are also several easily accessible protected underwater marine reserves in Fort Casey State Park, Deception Pass State Park and Birch Bay State Park.

Underwater Sports Inc. (4809 Evergreen Way, Everett; 206-252-7334), the **Whidbey Island Dive Center** (8636 80th Street Northwest, Oak Harbor; 206-675-1112) and **Emerald Seas Aquatics** (180 1st Street, Friday Harbor; 206-378-2772) provide air fills, rentals and lessons as well as dive charters.

BOATING

Spending time on the water is a part of daily life here, and certainly something that visitors should not miss. In fact, many of the 100-plus islands of the San Juans are accessible only by boat. Rental options are numerous, from tiny skiffs to sleek sailboats to five-foot yachts. On the mainland contact **La Conner Rent-A-Boat** (612-C North Dunlap, La Conner; 206-466-3533), **Rainbow Rentals** (329 North 1st Street, La Conner; 206-466-4054) or **Fairhaven Boatworks** (501 Harris, Bellingham; 206-647-2469).

In the islands try **North Island Sailing** (2550 North Swantown Road, Oak Harbor; 206-675-8360), **Penmare Marine Co.** (1806 Q Avenue, Anacortes; 206-293-4839), **Wind & Sails** (P.O. Box 337, Friday Harbor, WA 98250; 206-378-5343) or **Deer Harbor Charters** (P.O. Box 303, Orcas Island, WA 98280; 206-376-2970).

Kayaking is also immensely popular. Turn to **Sea Kayak Rentals** (1120 L Avenue, Anacortes; 206-293-3692), **Sea Quest Expeditions** (P.O. Box 2424, Friday Harbor, WA 98250; 206-378-5767), **Shearwater Adventures** (P.O. Box 787, Eastsound, WA 98245; 206-376-4699) or **Island Kayak Guides** (Doe Bay Resort, Olga, Orcas Island; 206-376-4755) for lessons, tours and rentals.

If you'd rather have someone else do all the work on a leisurely sunset cruise between Everett and Langley, call **Mosquito Fleet Enterprises** (P.O. Box 196, Langley, WA 98260; 206-321-0506).

HORSEBACK RIDING

Because of soaring insurance costs, many horseback riding outfits have had to drop out of the business. However, **Anderson Creek Lodge** (5602 Mission Road, Bellingham; 206-966-2126), **Lang's Pony and Horse Rides** (4565 Little Mountain Road, Mount Vernon; 206-424-7630), **Virginia Knapp** (4212 Sandy Point Road, Langley; 206-221-7106) and **Madrona Ridge Ranch** (Madrona Way, Coupeville; 206-678-4124) have managed to hang in there.

GOLF

Enthusiasts will be pleased with the abundance of beautiful golf courses in the region, many offering unparalleled views of the Sound. With an average annual rainfall of 50 inches, courses in this temperate climate zone are lush and green.

Good choices along North Puget Sound include **West E. Hall Memorial Golf Course** (1226 Southwest Casino Road, Everett; 206-353-4635), **Kayak Point Golf Course** (15711 Marine Drive, Stanwood; 206-652-9676), **Overlook Golf Course** (1785 Route 9, Mount Vernon; 206-422-6444), **Lake Padden Municipal Golf Course** (4882 Samish Way, Bellingham; 206-676-6989) and the **Sudden Valley Golf and Country**

Whale Watching in the San Juan Islands

Here in the waters of the San Juan archipelago there are three resident pods, or extended families, of *Orcinus Orca*, otherwise known as "killer" whales. Because they are so frequently and easily spotted in the protected waters, these gentle black and white giants have been carefully studied by scientists since 1976.

You'll find their research documented at the **Whale Museum** (62 1st Street, Friday Harbor; 206-378-4710; admission) where you can learn more about whales and other marine animals found in the area. A photo collection with names and pod numbers will help you identify some of the 90 or so resident orcas, distinguished by their grayish saddle patches and nicks, scars or tears in the dorsal fins and tails. Displays and videos explain the difference between breaching, spy hopping, tail lobbing and other typical orca behavior and the many vocalization patterns that scientists can only guess at the significance.

The Whale Museum also has an adopt-an-orca program set up to help fund the ongoing research and all sorts of whale-related educational material, art and souvenirs available in their gift shop. They operate a 24-hour hotline (800-562-8832) for whale sightings and marine mammal strandings as well.

In June, July and August you can often see the whales from shore when they range closest to the islands to feed on migrating salmon. The best shoreline viewing spots are **Lime Kiln Point** on San Juan Island or **Shark Reef Park** on Lopez Island. Sightings drop dramatically in the winter as the pods travel up to 100 miles per day out to the open ocean for food.

If you want to get a closer look, put on your parka and sunglasses, grab your binoculars and camera and climb aboard one of the **wildlife cruises** that ply the waters between the islands. Even if you don't see any orca during the trip, you will almost certainly spot other interesting forms of wildlife such as sleek, grey minke whales, Dall's porpoises (which look like miniature orca), splotchy brown harbor seal, bald eagles, great blue heron, cormorants or tufted puffin.

Island Mariner Cruises (5 Squalicum Esplanade, Bellingham; 206-734-8866) offers day-long nature and whale watching expeditions with commentary on the history, flora and fauna of the San Juans as you cruise through the islands. **Western Prince Cruises** (Friday Harbor; 206-378-5315) has similar naturalist-accompanied wildlife tours on a half-day basis; admission to the Whale Museum in Friday Harbor is included. You can also try **San Juan Boat Rentals and Tours** (Friday Harbor; 206-378-3499) for a three-hour whale-sighting excursion.

Happy spotting!

Club (2145 Lake Whatcom Boulevard, Bellingham; 206-734-6435). Perhaps the most famous course is the **Semiahmoo Golf and Country Club** (8720 Semiahmoo Parkway, Blaine; 206-371-7005), designed by the legendary Arnold Palmer.

On Whidbey Island visit **Lams Links** (Ducken Road, Oak Harbor; 206-675-3412) or **Island Greens Golf** (3890 East French Road, Clinton; 206-321-6042), a Scottish-style, nine-hole course. On Fidalgo Island head for the **Similk Beach Golf Course** (1250 Christiansen Road, Anacortes; 206-293-3444).

In the San Juan Islands try **Lopez Island Golf Course** (Airport Road, Lopez Island; 206-468-2679), **San Juan Golf and Country Club** (2261 Golf Course Road, Friday Harbor; 206-378-2254) and **Orcas Island Golf Club** (Route 1, P.O. Box 85, Eastsound, WA 98245; 206-376-4400).

TENNIS

No need to leave your racket at home with so many public courts to take advantage of. In Everett you'll find courts at **Clark Park** (240 Lombard). In Bellingham your best bets are the courts at **Lake Padden Park** (4882 Samish Way; 206-676-6989) or **Fairhaven Park** (107 Chuchanut Drive; 206-676-6985) downtown.

On Whidbey Island you can use the lighted courts at **Coupeville High School** (South Main Street) or those at **Oak Harbor City Park** (70th Street West). On Fidalgo Island head to the **Anacortes High School** facility (20th Street and J Avenue). **Lopez High School** (Center Road) is your only option on Lopez Island. On San Juan try the courts at the **Friday Harbor High School** (Guard Street) or head out to the **Roche Harbor Resort** (Roche Harbor Road).

BICYCLING

The **Waterfront Loop** in Everett takes you past the majestic old homes of early lumber barons and through the Everett Marina Village. There are no designated bike lanes along the dusty rural roads of **Mount Vernon**, but you'll see rich fields and quiet lanes for miles. Bellingham offers several bike routes, some arduous, some easy, all highlighting the scenery and history of the area. The best of the bunch is the fairly easy, 45-minute **Lake Padden Loop**. For a map of bike routes, contact the Bellingham Visitors Bureau (P.O. Box 340, Bellingham, WA 98226; 206-671-3990).

Those looking for a long-distance ride will enjoy the 50-mile **Island County Tour**, which begins at Columbia Beach on Whidbey Island and continues on to Deception Pass at the northern tip of the island. This trip is moderately strenuous, with high traffic on a good portion of the ride, but the spectacular views of the Strait of Juan de Fuca and the Saratoga Passage are reward enough.

In the San Juans there are several routes to choose from. The easiest and most popular is the **Lopez Island Perimeter Loop**, 32 miles of gently rolling hills and narrow, paved roads passing by Fisherman's Bay, Shark Reef Park, MacKaye Harbor and Agate Beach on the west side of the island and Mud Bay, Lopez Sound and Shoal Bay on the east side. Slightly more difficult is the 20-mile **San Juan Island Loop** along hilly, winding roads through Friday Harbor, Roche Harbor, San Juan Island National Historic Park and along the San Juan Channel. The **Horseshoe Route** on Orcas Island is by far the most difficult, with 16 miles of steep, twisting roads beginning at the ferry landing in Orcas, continuing through Eastsound, then on to Olga. An alternative route for the very hardy starts in Olga, passes through Moran State Park, over Mt. Constitution and ends in Doe Bay.

Contact the **Washington State Department of Transportation** (Transportation Building KF-01, Olympia, WA 98504-5201; 206-753-6005) for a state trails directory and map. The *Puget Sound Cyclist* (105 West John Street, Seattle, WA 98119) is a helpful periodical with detailed information.

BIKE RENTALS   For bike rentals in the North Puget Sound region contact **The Bicycle Center** (4718 Evergreen Way, Everett; 206-252-1441), **Rainbow Rentals** (329 North 1st Street, La Conner; 206-466-4054), **Fairhaven Bicycle and Ski** (1103 11th Street, Bellingham; 206-733-4433) or the **Semiahmoo Marina** (9565 Semiahmoo Parkway, Blaine; 206-371-2000).

You'll find more options in the islands: **The Pedaler** (56031/2 South Bayview Road, Langley; 206-321-5040), **Dean's Sports Plus** (8118 80th Northwest, Oak Harbor; 206-679-7145), **Anacortes Cyclery** (2012 Commercial, Anacortes; 206-293-6205), **Lopez Bicycle Works** (Fisherman's Bay Road, Lopez Island; 206-468-2847), **Island Bicycles** (380 Argyle, Friday Harbor; 206-378-4941), **Orcas Bicycle Company** (Orcas Ferry Landing, Orcas Island; 206-376-4517) and **Wildlife Cycles** (P.O. Box 1048, Eastsound, WA 98245; 206-376-4708).

HIKING

NORTHERN PUGET SOUND TRAILS   On the **Langus Riverfront Park Nature Trail** (3.2 miles) in Everett, hikers are likely to spot red-tailed hawk or grey heron as they make their way through towering spruce, red cedar and dogwood trees along the banks of the Snohomish River, past Union Slough and on toward Spencer Island, a protected haven for nesting ducks.

The Padilla Bay National Estuarine Sanctuary in the tiny town of Padilla Bay a few miles north of Mount Vernon offers the best hikes in the area. Stringent rules on noise guide hikers on the **Padilla Bay Shore Trail** (2.2 miles) so that they do not disturb the migratory waterfowl that nest in the estuary, mudflat, sloughs and tidal marsh viewed along this path.

An additional interpretive route tying into the roadside trail brings you to the Breazeale Interpretive Center, bringing the distance to 6 miles. Binoculars and field guides can be checked out at the center to aid your exploration of the forest and meadow habitat of the **Upland Trail** (.8 mile).

There are several good choices for hikes in Bellingham. The **Interurban Trail** (6 miles) begins near the entrance to Larrabee State Park, hugs the crest above Chuckanut Drive overlooking the bay and the San Juan Islands, then passes the rose gardens of Fairhaven Park into the revitalized Fairhaven District of the city.

There are three-and-a-half miles of rolling trails through the lush **Sehome Hill Arboretum**, crowned by incredible views of Mt. Baker, the San Juans and the Canadian Rockies seen from the observation tower at the summit. Since no motorized boats are allowed on **Lake Padden**, the path (1.5 miles) around the glistening lake and through some of the park's 1008 acres is both peaceful and rejuvenating.

In Birch Bay State Park in Blaine, the gently sloping **Terrell Marshall Trail** (1.5 miles) winds through a thickly wooded area of birch, maple, red cedar, hemlock and fir, home to pileated woodpeckers, bald eagle, ruffed grouse, muskrats and squirrel, and on to Terrell Marshall Swamp, the halfway point on the loop, before passing back through the forest to the trailhead. Pick up a flora and fauna guide to the interpretive trail at the contact station just inside the park gate.

WHIDBEY ISLAND TRAILS The most picturesque hikes on Whidbey Island are found in and around Fort Ebey State Park. The **Ebey's Landing Loop Trail** (3.5 miles) has some steep sections on the bluff above the beach, but carry your camera anyway to capture the views of pastoral Ebey's Prairie in one direction and Mt. Rainier and the Olympics framed by wind-sculpted pines and fir in the other. Trimmed in wild roses, the trail swings around Perego's Lagoon and back along the driftwood-strewn beach.

The **Partridge Point Trail** (2 miles) connecting Fort Ebey State Park and the Department of Natural Resources' Partridge Point campsite climbs through a mix of coastal wildflowers on a windswept bluff 150 feet above the water with wide views of Port Townsend, Admiralty Inlet, Protection Island and Discovery Bay. A fenced path at the southern end drops down the headland to the cobbly beach below.

There are numerous trails to choose from in Deception Pass State Park. Locals prefer **Rosario Head Trail** (.3 mile) on the Fidalgo Island side, stretching over the very steep promontory between Rosario Bay and Bowman Bay with sweeping views of the San Juans, Rosario Strait and the Strait of Juan de Fuca, and continuing on the **Lighthouse Point Trail** (1.5 miles) which passes further along the rocky bluff, past the lighthouse and into a dense stand of fir and cedar. On the Whidbey Island side of the bridge, climb the steep switch back on **Goose Rock Perimeter Trail** (1.2 miles) and you might see great blue heron on Coronet Bay, then follow the path down under the bridge next to the swirling waters of the pass and on to quiet North Beach to see the totem pole. Heartier hikers might want to tackle the **Goose Rock Summit Trail** (1.2 miles), with an altitude gain of some 450 feet for an unparalleled view of Deception Pass and the Cascades.

FIDALGO ISLAND TRAILS   In Anacortes, your best bet is to head for the **Washington Park Loop Road** (2.3 miles), located on Fidalgo Head at the end of Sunset Avenue four miles west of downtown. Rewarding views on this easy, paved path with a few moderate slopes include incredible glimpses of the San Juans, Burrows Pass and Burrows Island. You'll also find quiet, cool stretches through dense woods and access to beaches and romantic, hidden outcroppings suitable for a glass of champagne to toast the breathtaking sunsets.

LOPEZ ISLAND TRAILS   On Lopez, ideal hiking choices include the **Shark Reef Park Loop Trail** (.5 mile), a mossy path that meanders through a fragrant forest area and along a rock promontory looking out over tidal pools, a large kelp bed, a jutting haul out spot for seals and across the channel to San Juan Island. Spencer Spit State Park's **Beach Trail** (1 mile) travels down the spit and around the salt marsh lagoon alive with migratory birds; at the end of the spit is a reproduction of a historic log cabin built by early settlers, a fine spot for a picnic or brief rest stop with a nice view of the tiny islands offshore.

SAN JUAN ISLAND TRAILS   Two of the best hiking alternatives on San Juan are the established hiking trails of the San Juan Island National Historical Park. The **Lagoon Trail** (1 mile) in American Camp is actually a couple trails intertwined, starting from a parking area above Old Town (referred to on maps as First) Lagoon and passing through a dense stand of Douglas fir connecting the lovely, protected cove beaches of Jakle's Lagoon and Third Lagoon. The highlight of the **Bell Point Trail** (1.5 miles) in English Camp is the observation platform with compass plates identifying the many islands dotting the waters as far as the eye can see.

ORCAS ISLAND TRAILS   Unless you plan to spend an extended period of time here, there's little chance of covering the many hiking trails that twist through Moran State Park on Orcas Island connecting view spots, mountain lakes, waterfalls and campgrounds. The **Mountain Lake Trail** (3.6 miles) takes you from the summit of Mt. Constitution along a rocky ledge to Twin Lakes and the Mountain Lake Campground, with occasional views glimpsed through the thick trees. The **Around-the-Lake Trail** (4 miles) is fairly easy and takes in sights such as drooping log cabins and a dam and footbridge at the south end of Mountain Lake; for a little more challenge, try the **Twin Lakes Trail** (2.1 miles) that heads up the valley at the north end of Mountain Lake. If you're a waterfall lover, take the **Cascade Falls Trail** (2.7 miles) from the south end of Mountain Lake past Cascade and Rustic Falls and on to Cascade Lake.

Transportation

BY CAR

Route 5, also known as the Pacific Highway, parallels the Northern Puget Sound coastline all the way up to the Canadian border. Route 20 from Burlington takes you into Anacortes, the main jump-off point for ferry service to the San Juan Islands. Route 16 leads from Tacoma across The Narrows and onto the Kitsap Peninsula where it connects to Route 3 skirting the Sinclair Inlet and continuing north to Port Gamble.

BY AIR

Visitors flying into the Northern Puget Sound area usually arrive at either Bellingham International Airport or the much larger and busier Seattle-Tacoma International Airport (See Chapter 2 for further information). Carriers serving the Bellingham airport include Alaska Airlines, Horizon Air and United Express.

The Bellingham/Sea-Tac Airporter (206-733-3600) provides express shuttle service between Bellingham, Mount Vernon, Marysville and Sea-Tac airport.

Charter and regularly scheduled commuter flights are available into the tiny Friday Harbor Airport through Air San Juan, Harbor Airlines and West Isle Air. Small commuter airports with limited scheduled service include Anacortes Airport, Eastsound Airport and Lopez Airport; all are served by Air San Juan and West Isle Air.

BY BOAT

Washington State Ferries (206-464-6400), which are part of the state highway system, provide transportation to the four main islands of the San Juans—Lopez, Orcas, Shaw and San Juan—departing from the Anacortes Ferry Terminal (Ferry Terminal Road; 206-293-8166). Schedules change several times per year, with added service in the summer to take care of the heavy influx of tourists. The system is burdened during peak summer months, so arrive at the terminal early and be prepared to wait patiently (sometimes three hours or more) in very long lines if you plan to take your car along; walk-on passengers seldom wait long.

Private, walk-on ferry service among the islands is available through Fairweather Water Taxi and Tours (P.O. Box 1237, Friday Harbor, WA 98250; 206-378-2826). Island Shuttle Express (119 North Commercial Street, Bellingham; 206-671-1137) runs between Bellingham and the San Juan Islands.

BY BUS

Greyhound/Trailways provides regular service into Bellingham (1329 North State Street; 206-733-5251), Blaine (1300 Boblet Road), Everett (1503 Pacific Avenue; 206-259-7294) and Mount Vernon (1101 South 2nd Street; 206-336-5111).

BY TRAIN

Amtrak (2900 Bond Street, Everett; 800-872-7245) offers service into Everett on the Puget Sound shoreline via the "Empire Builder" which originates in Chicago and makes its final stop in Seattle before retracing its route. West Coast connections through Seattle on the "Coast Starlight" are also available. There's direct service from Portland, Oregon, the Columbia Gorge, Idaho, Denver and Chicago to Seattle via the "Pioneer."

CAR RENTALS

At Bellingham International Airport you'll find **Avis Rent A Car** (206-676-8840), **Budget Rent A Car** (206-671-3802), **Dollar Rent A Car** (206-733-5590), **Freedom Rent A Car** (206-733-2510), **Hertz Rent A Car** (206-733-8336), **National Car Rental** (206-734-9220) and **Thrifty Rent A Car** (206-676-2633). **U-Save Auto Rental** (206-671-3688), located downtown, offers free airport pickup.

Less-expensive local rental agencies in the islands include **A#1 Rent A Car** (206-259-5058) in Everett, **Friday Harbor Rentals** (206-378-4351), **Pacific Rent A Car** (206-293-7632) in Anacortes and **U-Save Auto Rental** (206-293-3105) also in Anacortes.

PUBLIC TRANSPORTATION

Whatcom County Transportation Authority (206-676-7433) provides public transit in Blaine, Bellingham and Lummi Island. In Everett you can get just about anywhere for 30 cents via **Everett Transit** (206-353-7433). **Island Transit** (206-678-7771) covers Whidbey Island, with scheduled stops at Oak Harbor, Coupeville, the Keystone Ferry, Greenbank, Freeland, Langley and the Clinton Ferry. In smaller towns like La Conner and Mount Vernon and on most of the islands there are no public transportation systems set up; check the yellow pages for taxi service.

TAXIS

Cab companies serving the Bellingham International Airport are **Bellingham Taxis** (206-676-0445) or **Superior Cabs** (206-734-3478). For service from the Friday Harbor Airport contact **Primo Taxi Service** (206-378-3550). **Patsy's Taxi** (206-293-3979) serves the Anacortes Airport.

CHAPTER FOUR

Olympic Peninsula
and Washington Coast

One of the most spectacular sights for many Pacific Northwest visitors is sitting by the dock of the bay (Seattle's Elliott Bay, that is) watching the sun set behind the stark profile of the Olympic Mountains. The area is even more memorable looking from the inside out.

The Olympic Peninsula is a vast promontory bounded on the east by Puget Sound, the west by the Pacific Ocean and the north by the Strait of Juan de Fuca. With no major city—the largest town is Port Angeles, a community of only 12,000 people—it retains a feeling of country living on the edge of wilderness, which indeed it is. The Olympic National Park, which dominates the peninsula, is a primeval place where eternal glaciers drop suddenly off sheer rock faces into nearly impenetrable rain forest, where America's largest herd of Roosevelt elk roams unseen by all but the most intrepid human eyes, where an impossibly rocky coastline cradles primitive marine life forms as it has done for millions of years. No fewer than five Indian reservations speckle sections of a coast famed as much for its shipwrecks as for its salmon fishing.

South of the national park, the Washington coast extends down the Northwest's finest sand beaches and around two enormous river estuaries, to the mouth of the Columbia River and the state of Oregon. Ocean Shores and Long Beach have become major resort centers.

The Washington coast is known for its heavy rainfall, and justifiably so. Though the Olympics are not high by many standards—its tallest peaks are under 8000 feet—they catch huge amounts of precipitation blowing in from the Pacific Ocean. So much snow falls that more than 60 glaciers survive at elevations as low as 4500 feet. Even greater amounts fall on the windward slopes: 140 inches a year and more in the Forks area. Not only does this foster the rapid growth of mushrooms and slugs, but it has also led to the creation of North America's greatest rain forest in the soggy Hoh River valley. Yet a mere 40 miles away as the raven flies, Sequim—in the Olympic rain shadow—is a virtual desert with only about 15 inches of rain per year.

The first residents of the peninsula and coast were tribes like the Makah, Ozette and Quileute, whose descendants still inhabit the area today. A seafaring people noted for their woodcarving, they lived in series of longhouses facing the sea and are known to have inhabited this region for as long as 2500 years.

Their first contact with Europeans came in 1775, when they massacred a Spanish landing party. Three years later, the ubiquitous British Captain James Cook sailed the coast and traded for sea otter furs with Vancouver Island natives; his report opened the gates to the maritime fur trade.

American entrepreneur John Jacob Astor established a fort at the mouth of the Columbia River in 1803, and two years later Meriwether Lewis and William Clark led a cross-country expedition that arrived at Cape Disappointment, on the Washington side of the Columbia, in late 1806. White settlement was at first slow, but by the mid-19th century Port Townsend had established itself as Puget Sound's premier lumber-shipping port, and other communities sprang up soon after.

Olympic National Park was annexed to the national park system in 1938. But long before that, Washingtonians had discovered its natural wonders. A fledgling tourism industry grew, with lodges constructed at several strategic locations around the park, including lakes Crescent and Quinault, Sol Duc Hot Springs and Kalaloch, overlooking the Pacific. Coastal communities were also building a visitor infrastructure, and quiet beach resorts soon emerged.

Today, typical Olympic Peninsula visitors start their tour in Port Townsend, having traveled by ferry and car from Seattle or Whidbey Island, and use Route 101 as their artery of exploration. Port Townsend is considered the most authentic Victorian seacoast town in the United States north of San Francisco, and its plethora of well-preserved 19th-century buildings, many of them now bed and breakfasts, charms all visitors. Less than an hour's drive west, the seven-mile Dungeness Spit (a national wildlife refuge) is the largest natural sand hook in the United States and is famed for the delectable crabs that share its name. Port Angeles, in the center of the north coast, is the headquarters of Olympic National Park and its primary gateway. The bustling international port town also has a direct ferry link to Victoria, Canada, across the Strait of Juan de Fuca.

Neah Bay, the northwesternmost community in the continental United States, is the home of the Makah Indian Museum and Cultural Center and

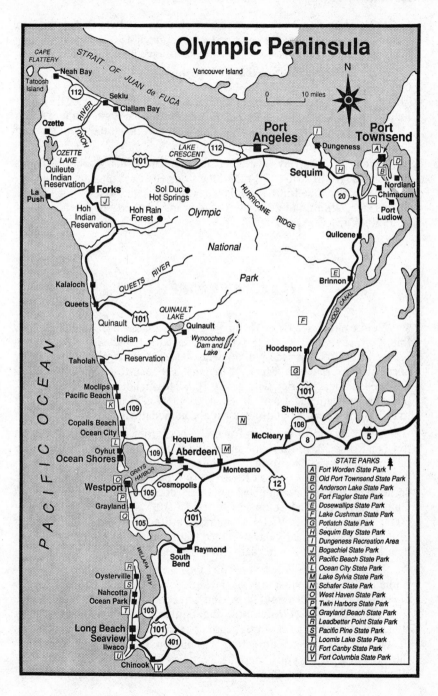

Olympic Peninsula

CAPE FLATTERY

STRAIT OF JUAN de FUCA

Vancouver Island

N

0   10 miles

Tatoosh Island

Neah Bay

112

Sekiu

Clallam Bay

Ozette

HOKO RIVER

OZETTE LAKE

Quileute Indian Reservation

La Push

Forks J

Sol Duc Hot Springs

Hoh Indian Reservation

Hoh Rain Forest

Olympic

LAKE CRESCENT

112

101

Port Angeles

I

Dungeness

Sequim

H

20

Port Townsend

A

B

D

Nordland

Chimacum C

Port Ludlow

HURRICANE RIDGE

Quilcene

National

Park

QUEETS RIVER

E

Brinnon

Kalaloch

Queets

101

Quinault

Indian

Reservation

QUINAULT LAKE

Quinault

Wynoochee Dam and Lake

F

HOOD CANAL

Hoodsport

G

101

Taholah

Moclips

Pacific Beach

K 109

Copalis Beach

Ocean City

L

Oyhut

Ocean Shores

109

Hoquiam

Aberdeen M

Montesano

Shelton

108

McCleary

8

N

5

O

GRAYS HARBOR

Westport

P

Grayland

Q

105

Cosmopolis

101

105

12

PACIFIC OCEAN

Raymond

South Bend

WILLAPA BAY

Oysterville R

Nahcotta S

Ocean Park

T

103

Long Beach

Seaview

Ilwaco

U

401

101

Chinook V

STATE PARKS

A	Fort Worden State Park
B	Old Port Townsend State Park
C	Anderson Lake State Park
D	Fort Flagler State Park
E	Dosewallips State Park
F	Lake Cushman State Park
G	Potlatch State Park
H	Sequim Bay State Park
I	Dungeness Recreation Area
J	Bogachiel State Park
K	Pacific Beach State Park
L	Ocean City State Park
M	Lake Sylvia State Park
N	Schafer State Park
O	West Haven State Park
P	Twin Harbors State Park
Q	Grayland Beach State Park
R	Leadbetter Point State Park
S	Pacific Pine State Park
T	Loomis Lake State Park
U	Fort Canby State Park
V	Fort Columbia State Park

an important marina for deep-sea fishing charters. Clallam Bay, to its east, and La Push, south down the coast, are other sportfishing centers. The logging town of Forks is the portal for visitors to the national park's Hoh Rain Forest.

Route 101 emerges from the damp Olympic forests to slightly less moist Grays Harbor, with its twin lumber port towns of Aberdeen and Hoquiam. Though these towns combined have a population of over 25,000, they have limited appeal to travelers, who typically head over the north shore of Grays Harbor to the hotel resort strip of Ocean Shores, or down the south shore of the harbor to the quaint fishing village of Westport.

Serene Willapa Bay is another huge riverine estuary south of Grays Harbor. The resort strip of 28-mile-long Long Beach Peninsula, which provides a seaward dike for the bay, is older and less contrived than the Ocean Shores area. Wildlife refuges, oyster farms and cranberry bogs lend it a sort of 1950s Cape Cod ambience.

Port Townsend Area

Before either Seattle or Tacoma were so much as a tug on a fisherman's line, Port Townsend was a thriving lumber port. Founded in 1851, it has retained its Victorian seacoast ambience better than any other community north of San Francisco. Much of the city has been designated a national historic landmark district, with nearly 70 Victorian houses, buildings, forts, parks and monuments. Many of the handsomely gabled homes are open for tours and/or offer bed-and-breakfast accommodations.

The best way to see Port Townsend is on foot. When you drive into town on Route 20, you'll first want to stop at the **Port Townsend Chamber of Commerce** visitor information center (2437 East Sims Way; 206-385-2722). Then continue east on Route 20 as it becomes Water Street. At the corner of Madison Street, opposite the ferry dock, you'll find the **Jefferson County Historical Museum** in City Hall (210 Madison Street; 206-385-1003; admission), with Victorian antiques, artifacts and hundreds of photos of Port Townsend's early days. Guided historical walking tours leave from here at 10 a.m. and 2 p.m. daily, May through October.

Heading west on Water Street by foot, note the elegant stone and wood-frame buildings on either side of the street, most of them dating from the 1880s and 1890s. Turn right on Adams Street; halfway up the block on the right is the **Enoch S. Fowler Building**, built in 1874, the oldest two-story stone structure in Washington. A former county courthouse, it now houses the weekly newspaper. Turn left at Washington Street and five blocks farther, on your right, you'll see the **Francis Wilcox James House** (1238 Washington Street; 206-385-1238), built in 1891. It has five chimneys and a commanding view of the harbor—and in 1973 became the Northwest's first bed and breakfast.

Turn right up Harrison Street, then right again at Franklin Street. Two blocks farther, at Franklin and Polk streets, the **Captain Enoch S. Fowler Home**, built in 1860, is the oldest surviving house in Port Townsend and is typical of New England homes. Two more blocks ahead, the **Rothschild House** (Franklin and Taylor streets; 206-385-4730; admission) was built in 1868 by an early Port Townsend merchant. Notable for its outstanding interior woodwork, it's maintained by the State Parks Commission for public tours.

A block north, at Jefferson and Clay streets, **Trinity Methodist Church** (1871) is the state's oldest standing Methodist church. Its small museum contains the Bible of the church's first minister. A block east, the 1889 **George Starrett House** (744 Clay Street; 206-385-3205; admission), now a bed-and-breakfast inn, offers public tours. At Clay and Monroe streets, the **Lucinda Hastings Home** was the most expensive house ever built in Port Townsend when it was erected in 1889 at a cost of $14,000. Turn right here, and return down Monroe to Water Street and your starting point at City Hall.

Get back in your car and drive north on Monroe Street. (The arterial staggers a half-block right at Roosevelt Street onto Jackson Street, then turns right onto Walnut Street.) All roads flow into W Street, the south boundary of **Fort Worden State Park** (206-385-0854). If the fort looks familiar, it could be because it was used in the filming of the Richard Gere-Debra Winger movie, *An Officer and a Gentleman*. Authorized in 1896, it includes officers' row and a refurbished **Commanding Officer's House** (admission), the **248th Coast Artillery Museum** (admission), gun emplacements, a balloon hangar, marine interpretive center and **Point Wilson Light Station**. Fort Worden offers long stretches of beach that command impressive views of the Cascades and nearby islands.

On the dock at Fort Worden is the **Port Townsend Marine Science Center** (206-385-5582; admission). Of special interest are its four large touch tanks, representing different intertidal habitats, and a "wet lab" where creatures like starfish, anemones and sea cucumbers can be handled by curious visitors.

Road visitors to Port Townsend typically cross the one-and-a-half-mile **Hood Canal Floating Bridge** on Route 104 from the Kitsap Peninsula. Located 30 miles southeast of Port Townsend, it is the world's only floating bridge erected over tidal waters and one of the longest of its kind anywhere. Constructed in 1961, the bridge was washed away during a fierce storm in February 1979 but was rebuilt in 1982.

Traveling south from Port Townsend, Route 20 joins Route 101 at Discovery Bay. Twelve miles south of the junction is the town of **Quilcene** on the Hood Canal, a serpentine finger of Puget Sound. The town is especially noted for its oyster farming and processing and is the location of a state shellfish research laboratory (not open to the public). The **Mount Walker Observation Point**—five miles south on Route 101, then another five miles on a gravel road that starts at Walker Pass—offers a spectacular view of the Hood Canal and surrounding area.

In Brinnon, 12 miles south of Quilcene on Route 101, the **Whitney Gardens** boast an extensive collection of rhododendrons, Washington state's official flower. They are in bloom in May and June.

PORT TOWNSEND AREA HOTELS

The **James House** (1238 Washington Street, Port Townsend; 206-385-1238) claims to have been the Pacific Northwest's first bed-and-breakfast. Just a few steps from shops and restaurants at the foot of the bluff that stands behind lower downtown, it dates from 1891, though it's only been a bed and breakfast since 1973. The house is unmistakable for its five chimneys; inside, the floors are all parquet. Some, but not all, of the 12 rooms have private baths. There are a fireplace and library, and ample continental breakfasts are served. Kids are welcome, but only if they're over six (as in age, not height). Moderate to deluxe.

For those less than enthralled with bed and breakfasts, the **Palace Hotel** (1004 Water Street, Port Townsend; 206-385-0773) provides historic accommodation in a former seafarers' bordello. Though nicely renovated, this is a bit rustic: After checking in next door at the Tibbles Gallery, you must climb a long flight of stairs (or two) to your room. There are 15 guest chambers, each with antiques recalling the red-light flavor of the past. The madam's former room even has a kitchenette. Moderate.

For students and budget travelers, there are two **youth hostels** in eastern Jefferson County—one at **Fort Worden State Park** (Port Townsend; 206-385-0655), open year-round except the Christmas holiday period, the other at **Fort Flagler State Park** (Nordland; 206-385-1288), open May-September or by appointment.

South of town about 20 miles, **The Resort at Port Ludlow** (9483 Oak Bay Road, Port Ludlow; 206-437-2222) is one of the Northwest's premier family resorts. It boasts a championship golf course, tennis courts, two swimming pools, a marina, hiking and bicycling trails and 1500 acres of land. There are 180 suites with fireplaces, kitchens and decks and a restaurant with marvelous views of water and mountains. Ultra-deluxe.

PORT TOWNSEND AREA RESTAURANTS

For an evening of fine dining, it would be hard to top the **Manresa Castle** (7th and Sheridan streets, Port Townsend; 206-385-5750). Located in an 1897 hilltop inn that overlooks the town and bay like a German castle on the Rhine River, it combines an elegant restaurant and an Edwardian pub. Two gourmet menus are offered: a moderately priced "light dining" menu featuring everything from pastas and curries to baked quail and coquilles St. Jacques, and a deluxe full-dinner menu that offers the likes of grilled salmon, Cajun beef and scampi, and pork tenderloin Normandy.

Ask locals where to eat, and chances are they'll recommend the **Fountain Café** (920 Washington Street, Port Townsend; 206-385-1364). You'll probably have to stand in line for a seat, but the wait will be worth it. Occupying the ground floor of a historic building (is there anything else in downtown Port Townsend?), the Fountain serves outstanding seafood and pasta dishes, including oysters as you like 'em. Soups and desserts are homemade. The decor is in keeping with the eclectic penchant of many young local artists. Moderate.

The **Lido Restaurant** (925 Water Street, Port Townsend; 206-385-7111) is an equally casual spot. Right on the main street beside the water, it's a place to watch the ferries come and go while enjoying a sandwich or a seafood crêpe. Moderate.

Breakfasts draw full houses at the **Salal Café** (634 Water Street, Port Townsend; 206-385-6532). On Sunday, in fact, breakfast is served all day, perhaps to give customers time to peruse the newspaper. Huge omelettes and various seafood and vegetarian recipes get oohs and ahs. Lunch features gourmet homestyle cooking, along with pizzas and sandwiches. Budget.

Some folks say the **Shanghai Restaurant** (Point Hudson, Port Townsend; 206-385-4810) serves the best Chinese food this side of Vancouver's Chinatown. Forget the view of the RV park across the street, and enjoy the spicy Szechuan and northern Chinese cuisine. Budget.

The **Chimacum Café** (★) (4900 Rhododendron Drive, Chimacum; 206-732-4631), nine miles south of Port Townsend, is a local institution. This is food like grandma should have made—country-fried chicken dinners, baked ham and so forth, followed of course by homemade pies brimming with fresh fruit. Breakfast is also served. Budget.

PORT TOWNSEND AREA SHOPPING

Port Townsend offers the most interesting shopping on the peninsula with its array of galleries, antique and gift shops, bookstores, gourmet restaurants and cafés and all-purpose emporiums. Proprietors have paid particular attention to historical accuracy in restoring commercial buildings. Many shops feature the work of talented local painters, sculptors, weavers, potters, poets and writers.

For antiques, try the **Port Townsend Antique Mall** (802 Washington Street; 206-385-2590) or any of the many other shops along the 600 through 1200 blocks of Water or Washington streets. A couple of the better galleries for contemporary arts and crafts are the **Pacific Northwest Retreat for the**

Arts (517 Polk Street; 206-385-6353), with artists in residence, and the **Art Center Gallery** (1034 Water Street; 206-385-7494).

PORT TOWNSEND AREA NIGHTLIFE

In Port Townsend, you'll find live rock music weekends at the **Back Alley** (Tyler and Water streets; 206-385-2914), **Lanza's** (1020 Lawrence Street; 206-385-6221) and the **Lido** (925 Water Street; 206-385-7111). All three are rustic establishments, popular with locals.

PORT TOWNSEND AREA BEACHES AND PARKS

Fort Worden State Park—A 446-acre estate right in Port Townsend, this turn-of-the-century fort includes restored Victorian officers houses, barracks, theater, parade grounds and artillery bunkers. A beach and boat launch are on Admiralty Inlet, at the head of Puget Sound.

Facilities: Restrooms, picnic areas, lodging; restaurants and groceries are in town; information, 206-385-4730. *Fishing:* Try the dock or beach.

Camping: There are 80 sites with RV hookups.

Getting there: Entrance located on W Street at Cherry Street, at the northern city limits of Port Townsend.

Kah Tai Lagoon Nature Park—This midtown park, which features 50 acres of wetlands and 35 acres of grasslands and woodlands, is a great place for birdwatching: more than 50 species have been identified here. There are two-and-a-half miles of trails, a play area for kids and interpretive displays.

Facilities: Restrooms, picnic areas; restaurants and groceries in town; information, 206-385-2722.

Getting there: Located on 12th Street near Sims Way in Port Townsend.

Old Port Townsend State Park—Decommissioned in 1895 when Indian attacks on Port Townsend (the town) were no longer a threat, the park has seven miles of trails and a beach on Port Townsend (the inlet).

Facilities: Restrooms, picnic areas; restaurants and groceries in town; information, 206-385-3595. *Fishing:* From the shore.

Camping: There are 40 sites.

Getting there: Located on Old Port Townsend Road, three miles south of the town of Port Townsend off Route 20.

Fort Flagler State Park—The long-abandoned fort building, which dates from 1898, is a minor attraction here: bigger is the saltwater beach on Admiralty Inlet, popular for clamming and beachcombing. There are also a boat launch and hiking trails.

Facilities: Restrooms, picnic areas, lodging, groceries; restaurants are in Nordland, three miles south, and Hadlock; information, 206-385-1259. *Fishing:* Good for salmon, halibut, sole, crab and shellfish.

Camping: There are 116 sites.

Getting there: Located on north tip of Marrowstone Island, eight miles northeast of Hadlock off Oak Bay Road.

Dosewallips State Park—At the mouth of the Dosewallips River on the Hood Canal, a long, serpentine arm of Puget Sound, this 425-acre park is especially popular among clam diggers and oyster hunters during shellfish season. There are a pleasant beach and hiking trails.

Facilities: Restrooms, picnic areas; restaurants and groceries in nearby Brinnon. *Fishing:* Good for winter steelhead in river; salmon and bottomfish in Hood Canal.

Camping: There are 33 sites.

Getting there: Located at Brinnon, 37 miles south of Port Townsend on Route 101.

Olympic National Forest—Surrounding Olympic National Park on its east, south and northwest sides, this national forest provides ample recreational opportunities. It includes five wilderness areas on the fringe of the park.

Facilities: Restrooms, picnic areas; restaurants and groceries in towns around perimeter of forest; information, 206-956-2300. *Fishing:* Best bets are Lakes Cushman and Wynoochee and the Dosewallips, Dungeness and Soleduck rivers.

Camping: There are numerous campgrounds throughout the forest.

Getting there: Numerous access roads branch off Route 101, especially south of Sequim, and between Quilcene and Hoodsport, on the east side of the Olympic Peninsula.

Port Angeles Area

The northern gateway to Olympic National Park as well as a major terminal for ferries to British Columbia, the Port Angeles area is one of northwest Washington's main crossroads. Sequim on Route 101, 31 miles west of Port Townsend, and nearby Port Angeles are two of the peninsula's more intriguing towns. On the Strait of Juan de Fuca at the foot of the Olympic Mountains, this region often may be dry when it's pouring rain just a few miles south.

The town of **Sequim** (pronounced "Squim") is graced with a climate that's unusually dry and mild for the Northwest: it sits in the Olympic rain shadow. A major attraction just north of town is the **Olympic Game Farm** (383 Ward Road; 206-683-4295; admission), whose animals—lions, tigers, bears, buffalo and many others—are trained for film roles. Walking and driving tours of the farm, including a studio barn, are available year-round.

In Sequim itself, the **Sequim-Dungeness Museum** (175 West Cedar Street; 206-683-8110) preserves the native and pioneer farming heritage of Sequim and the surrounding area. For visitor information, contact the **Sequim-Dungeness Chamber of Commerce** (P.O. Box 907, Sequim, WA 98382; 206-683-6197).

North off Route 101, the Dungeness Valley is dotted with strawberry and raspberry fields. Weathered barns left over from the dairy farming days are still visible. Pay a visit to the **Cedarbrook Herb Farm** (986 Sequim Avenue South; 206-683-7733), where 150 different varieties of herbs and spices fill the air with a marvelous (but undefinable!) aroma and inspire many a gourmet chef to go on a culinary buying spree.

Opposite the mouth of the Dungeness River is one of the Olympic Peninsula's most remarkable natural features: the **Dungeness Spit**, almost seven miles long, the largest natural sand hook in the United States. A short trail within the adjacent **Dungeness Recreation Area** provides access to this national wildlife refuge. The spit and the surrounding bay and estuary are teeming with wildlife, including seabirds, seals, fish, crabs and clams.

Seventeen miles west of Sequim on Route 101 is the fishing and logging port of **Port Angeles**, the Olympic Peninsula's largest town. A major attraction here is the **City Pier** (206-452-9277). Adjacent to the ferry terminal, it boasts an observation tower, promenade decks, a picnic area and the **Arthur D. Feiro Marine Laboratory** (206-452-9277; admission), where visitors can observe and even touch samples of local marine life.

As the gateway to Olympic National Park, Port Angeles is home to national park headquarters. At the **Olympic National Park Visitor Center and Pioneer Memorial Museum** (3200 Mount Angeles Road, Port Angeles; 206-452-4501), you'll find an excellent slide show and exhibits on the natural and human history of the park.

The **Clallam County Museum** (223 East 4th Street; 206-452-7831) in the old county courthouse building has a variety of interesting regional historical displays. For tourist information, contact the **North Olympic Peninsula Visitor & Convention Bureau** (121 East Railroad Avenue, Port Angeles; 206-452-8552).

PORT ANGELES AREA HOTELS

You'll feel good right down to your cockles—as well as your steamer clams, butter clams and horse clams—after shellfishing on the saltwater beach outside the **Sequim Bay Resort** (662 West Sequim Bay Road, Sequim; 206-681-3853). The fully equipped housekeeping cottages here are suitable for vacationing families and shoreline lovers, including those with pets. A playground has swings, tetherball and horseshoes, and there's a guest laundry. There's also space for tents and hookups for RVs. Budget.

Just a spit from the Spit—Dungeness, that is—is the **Groveland Cottage** (★) (1673 Sequim-Dungeness Way, Dungeness; 206-683-3565), by the coast north of Sequim. The turn-of-the-century building has four rooms with private baths above a country craft shop. The rooms may be simple, but service is not: coffee and the morning paper are delivered to your room in anticipation of the four-course gourmet breakfast. Moderate.

Perhaps the nicest motel-style accommodation in these port communities is the **Red Lion Bayshore Inn** (221 North Lincoln Street, Port Angeles; 206-452-9215). A modern gray building that extends along the Strait of Juan de Fuca opposite the ferry dock, it offers rooms with private balconies overlooking the water. A private strand of beach and swimming pool beckon bathers. Moderate to deluxe.

Victoria, across the strait on Vancouver Island, is said to be "more British than the British"—but the same slogan could almost apply to **The Tudor Inn** (1108 South Oak Street, Port Angeles; 206-452-3138). Hosts Jane and Jerry Glass serve a traditional English breakfast and afternoon tea in the restored Tudor-style home. Most of their antique collection is Old English, and the well-stocked library will steer you to books on the United Kingdom. One bedroom has a private bath; four others share two baths. Moderate.

PORT ANGELES AREA RESTAURANTS

One-and-a-half miles west of Sequim is **Casoni's** (104 Hooker Road, Sequim; 206-683-2415), the north coast's best Italian eatery. Mamma Casoni herself is queen bee of the kitchen, which dishes up generous portions of pastas, seafood, veal and chicken dishes, as well as some remarkable cheesecakes for dessert. Dinner only. Moderate.

If retired physicist Tom Wells and his Cambodian-born wife, Lay Yin, aren't off studying a solar eclipse somewhere around the globe, you'll find them at the **Eclipse Café** (★) (144 South 5th Avenue, Sequim; 206-683-2760). Yin's culinary touch dominates: Southeast Asian taste tempters stand out. This one's for hungry adventurers. Breakfast and lunch only. Budget.

The undisputed winner in the northern Olympic Peninsula fine-dining sweepstakes is **C'est Si Bon** (2300 Route 101, four miles east of Port Angeles; 206-452-8888). The decor is modern and dramatic, with handsome oil paintings and full picture windows allowing panoramas of the Olympic Range. The cuisine, on the other hand, is classical French: tournedos with crabmeat and a shallot sauce, coquilles St. Jacques, veal Normande with apples and calvados. There are French wines and desserts, too, of course. Dinner only. Deluxe.

You'll find bistro-style food, service and ambience at **The Greenery** (117-B East 1st Street, Port Angeles; 206-457-4112), including homemade soups and pastas. Fresh fish specials are served throughout the day, and Caesar salads are prepared tableside, "the old way." Moderate.

Practically next door is the **First Street Haven** (107 East 1st Street, Port Angeles; 206-457-0352), one of the best places around for quick and tasty breakfasts and lunches. Have a homemade quiche and salad, along with the house coffee, and you'll be set for the day. No dinners. Budget.

PORT ANGELES AREA SHOPPING

There are good antique dealers in Sequim. Try the **Country Cottage Antique Mall** (233–243 West Washington Street; 206-683-8983) or **Today's and Yesterday's** (531 West Washington Street; 206-683-5733).

PORT ANGELES AREA NIGHTLIFE

You didn't come to this part of the state for its nightlife, and that's good. What little there is usually exists only on Friday and Saturday nights.

Your best bet in Port Angeles may be the lounge of the **Red Lion Bayshore Inn** (221 North Lincoln Street; 206-452-9215) for Top-40 music.

PORT ANGELES AREA BEACHES AND PARKS

Sequim Bay State Park—Water sports and hiking, both along the shore and up the Jimmycomelately River (that's its name, honest), are the main attractions at this park on Sequim Bay, sheltered from rough seas by two spits at its mouth and from heavy rains by the Olympic rain shadow. There are a beach and boat launch.

Facilities: Restrooms, picnic areas; restaurants and groceries in Sequim; information, 206-683-4235. *Fishing:* Satisfactory.

Camping: There are 60 sites.

Getting there: Located on Route 101, four miles east of Sequim.

Dungeness Recreation Area—The Dungeness Spit is a national wildlife refuge, but a recreation area trail provides access. Marine birds and seals are among the impressive wildlife to be seen; the Dungeness crab is internationally famous as a fine food.

Facilities: Restrooms, showers, picnic areas; restaurants and groceries in Dungeness three miles east, or Sequim eight miles southeast; information, 206-683-5847. *Fishing:* Good from the shore.

Camping: There are 65 sites.

Getting there: Located at the base of the Dungeness Spit, five miles west of Sequim on Route 101, then four miles north on Kitchen-Dick Road.

Salt Creek Recreation Area—One of the finest tidepool sanctuaries on the Olympic Peninsula is this three-mile stretch of rocky beach (★). Starfish, sea urchins, anemones, mussels, barnacles and other invertebrate life can be observed . . . but not removed.

Facilities: Restrooms, picnic areas; restaurants and groceries in Joyce; information, 206-928-3441.

Camping: There are 80 sites.

Getting there: Located two miles east from Joyce (or ten miles west from Port Angeles) on Route 112, then three miles north on Camp Hayden Road.

Olympic National Park

The Olympic Peninsula's dominant attraction—in fact, the reason most tourists come here at all—is Olympic National Park. Rugged, glaciated mountains dominate the 1400-square-mile park, with rushing rivers tumbling from their slopes. But the rainier western slopes harbor an extraordinary rain forest, and a separate 55-mile-long coastal strip preserves remarkable tidepools and marvelous ocean scenery. Wildlife in the park includes the rare Roosevelt elk, as well as deer, black bears, cougars, bobcats, a great many smaller mammals and scores of bird species.

The most direct route into the park from Port Angeles is the Heart of the Hills/Hurricane Ridge Road. It climbs 5200 feet in just 17 miles to the **Hurricane Ridge Lodge** (206-928-3211), where there are breathtaking views to 7965-foot Mount Olympus, the highest peak in the Olympic Range, and other glacier-shrouded mountains. Visitors to Hurricane Ridge can dine in the day lodge, picnic, enjoy nature walks or take longer hikes. In winter, enjoy the small downhill ski area here and many cross-country trails.

Twenty miles west of Port Angeles on Route 101 is **Lake Crescent**, one of three large lakes within park boundaries. Carved during the last Ice Age 10,000 years ago, it is nestled between steep forested hillsides. A unique subspecies of trout lures anglers to its deep waters. There are several resorts, restaurants, campgrounds and picnic areas around its shores. From National Park Service-administered Lake Crescent Lodge, on the southeast shore, a three-fourth-mile trail leads up Barnes Creek to beautiful **Marymere Falls**.

West of Lake Crescent, the Soleduck River Road turns south to **Sol Duc Hot Springs**, 14 miles off Route 101. Long known to the Indians, the therapeutic mineral waters were discovered by a pioneer in 1880 and like everything else the white man touched, soon boasted an opulent resort. But the original burned to the ground in 1916 and today's refurbished resort, nestled in a valley of old-growth Douglas fir, is more rustic than elegant.

The springs remain an attraction. Sol Duc is a major trailhead for back-packing trips into the park; also here are a fish hatchery and ranger station (206-374-6522).

On the west side of the national park are three more major points of entry. The **Hoh Rain Forest** is 19 miles east of Route 101 via the Hoh River Road, 13 miles south of Forks. For national park information here, call the Forks Ranger Station (206-374-5450). There's a less well-known rain forest at the end of the **Queets River Road**, 14 miles off Route 101, 17 miles west of Quinault. Finally, **Quinault Lake**, on Route 101 at the southwestern corner of Olympic National Park, is the site of several resorts and camp-grounds, including the venerable Lake Quinault Lodge. Watersports of all kinds are popular at this glacier-fed lake, surrounded by deep fir forest.

OLYMPIC NATIONAL PARK HOTELS

The rustic **Lake Crescent Lodge and Log Cabin Resort** (6540 East Beach Road, 21 miles west of Port Angeles; 206-928-3325) is a historic landmark on the shores of gorgeous Lake Crescent along Route 101. Bud-get-watchers can stay in the main lodge (bathrooms are down the hall from guest rooms); more upscale are lakeshore chalets and cabins with fireplaces. There are also an RV park with full hookups and a campground on Log Cabin Creek. The handsome log lodge has a broad veranda on the lake, a restaurant and popular bar and a gift shop; all manner of boats are rented at the marina. The resort is open May to October. Budget to moderate.

The **Sol Duc Hot Springs Resort** (Soleduck River Road, 44 miles west of Port Angeles; 206-327-3583) is another historic property, this one built in 1910 around a series of hot sulphur pools 14 miles south of Route 101. The 32 cabins (half with kitchens) have undergone occasional renovations since then, including indoor plumbing! The best plunge, however, after a day of hiking or fishing, remains the springs, kept at 98 to 104 degrees. Camping sites and RV hookups are available. The resort is open May to October. Cabin prices are moderate.

OLYMPIC NATIONAL PARK RESTAURANTS

The best choice for dining in the park is the **Lake Crescent Lodge** (6540 East Beach Road, 21 miles west of Port Angeles; 206-928-3325). Enjoy the view from the veranda onto beautiful Lake Crescent, where an-glers dip their lines for the unique crescenti trout, a subspecies of rainbow trout that may wind up on your platter in the restaurant. Northwest cuisine is a specialty. Open May to October. Moderate.

There's another dining room at the **Sol Duc Hot Springs Resort** (Sole-duck River Road, 44 miles west of Port Angeles; 206-327-3583), just behind the hot sulphur springs. As at Lake Crescent, the food is solid Northwest

The Hoh Rain Forest

No matter where you may wander on this earth, there's only one Hoh Rain Forest. It's said to be the only coniferous rain forest in the world. Graciously spared the logger's blade, it's been undisturbed since time began. In other words, it's a natural wonder to be embraced and cherished.

Reached by traveling 13 miles south from Forks on Route 101, then 19 miles east on the Hoh River Road, this is the wettest spot in the contiguous 48 states. In fact, wet isn't the word: even the air drips like a saturated sponge. The average annual precipitation here is 145 inches, more than 100 inches of which fall between October and March. But temperatures at this elevation, between 500 and 1000 feet, rarely fall below 40 degrees in winter or rise above 70 in summer. The legacy of this mild climate is dense, layered canopies of foliage.

The forest floor is as soft and thick as a shag carpet, cloaked with mosses, bracken ferns, huge fungi and seedlings. Hovering over the lush rug are vine maple and alder, Nootka cypress and black cottonwood, some hung with moss, stretching wiry branches to taste any slivers of sunlight that may steal through the canopy. Above them, Douglas fir, Sitka spruce, Western hemlock, Western red cedar and other gigantic conifers rise 200 to 300 feet, putting a lid on the forest, lichen dripping from their boughs and blanketing their trunks like hair suits. In all, 300 plant species live here, not counting 70 epiphytes (mosses, lichens and such).

Some compare this environment to a cathedral. Indeed, the soft light is like sun filtered through stained glass, and the arching branches could pass for a vaulted apse. To others, it's simply mystical. The ancient coastal Indians would have agreed.

Though there are similar rain forests in Washington, the rain-forest ecology is most conveniently studied at the **Hoh Rain Forest Visitor Center** (206-374-6925) and on the nature trails that surround it. The **Hoh River Trail** extends for 19 miles to the river's source in Blue Glacier, on the flank of Mount Olympus, but the rain forest can be appreciated by most visitors on a two-and-a-half-mile (one-way) day hike.

About three-fourths of a mile in, you'll see enormous old-growth firs, some over nine feet in girth and at least 500 years old. At about one mile, the trail drops to Big Flat, the first of several grassy, open areas. The winter grazing of Roosevelt elk, whose survival was a major reason for the creation of Olympic National Park, has opened up the forest floor.

Keep your eyes open, too, for wildlife. Besides the elk, you may spot river otter or weasel. Black bears, coyotes and cougars also inhabit these forests. Bald eagles and great blue heron feed on the salmon that spawn seasonally in the Hoh.

fare, including Dungeness crab from the north Olympic Coast. Open May to October. Moderate.

A mile high in the Olympic Range, 17 miles south of Port Angeles, the **Hurricane Ridge Lodge** (Hurricane Ridge Road; 206-928-3211) frames glaciers in the picture windows of its coffeeshop. Come for the view, but the standard American fare served here isn't half-bad either. Open daily mid-May through September, weekends mid-December to April. Moderate.

OLYMPIC NATIONAL PARK

Olympic National Park—This spectacular national park, 900,000 acres in area and ranging in elevation from sea level to nearly 8000 feet, contains everything from permanent alpine glaciers to America's lushest rain forest (the Hoh) to rocky tidepools rich in marine life. Wildlife includes goats and elk in the mountains, steelhead in the rivers and colorful birds everywhere. Three large lakes, Crescent (near Port Angeles), Ozette (on the coast) and Quinault (on the southwestern edge), are especially popular visitor destinations.

Facilities: Restrooms, picnic areas, hotels, restaurants and groceries; information, 206-452-4501 (Port Angeles); ranger stations in Forks (206-374-5450), Quilcene (206-765-3368) and Sol Duc (206-374-6522). *Fishing:* Trout and steelhead in rivers and lakes. *Swimming:* The lakes are cold.

Camping: Permitted; some for tents only, some closed in winter.

Getting there: Route 101 circles the national park. The numerous access roads are well marked.

Olympic Coast

Largely undeveloped, the rough-and-tumble Olympic Coast is one of the Northwest's hidden gems. Home to America's finest Native American research centers, this region is also famous for its archaeological preserves, maritime sanctuaries and pristine beaches. It features some of the finest wilderness hiking in the region.

Fifty miles west of Port Angeles via Route 112, where the Strait of Juan de Fuca approaches the Pacific Ocean, are the sister communities of **Clallam Bay** and **Sekiu** (pronounced "C-Q"). These are prime sportfishing grounds for salmon and huge bottomfish, especially halibut. If you're spending time at a fishing resort in one of these towns, don't miss the wonderful tidepools northeast of Clallam Bay at **Slip Point**. Just west of Sekiu, at the mouth of the Hoko River, visitors can view the remains of a 2500-year-old Makah Indian fishing village at the **Hoko Archeological Site**.

For more than 2500 years, **Neah Bay**, in the Makah Indian Reservation 18 miles west of Sekiu on Route 112, has been the home of the Makah tribe. The **Makah Museum, Cultural and Research Center** (P.O. Box 95, Neah Bay, WA 98357; 206-645-2711; admission) houses the prehistoric artifacts discovered at the Hoko and Lake Ozette digs, including baskets, whaling and sealing harpoons, canoes and a replica of a 15th-century longhouse. Visitors can enjoy excellent charter-fishing excursions from the harbor, which is also home to a commercial fishing fleet.

A winding, scenic coastal drive to the end of Route 112 climaxes at **Cape Flattery**, the northwesternmost corner of the contiguous United States. The road at times runs within feet of the water, providing spectacular blufftop views of the Strait of Juan de Fuca and Tatoosh Island—a great location for whale watching between March and May. A short trail leads to the shore. Beach hikers can find some of the last wilderness coast in Washington south of here.

Returning on Route 112 toward Sekiu, Lake Ozette Road branches south at the Hoko River. The road leads 20 miles to the northernmost of three tiny Indian reservations (the Ozette) surrounded by the coastal strip of Olympic National Park. **Ozette Lake** is the largest of the national park's three lakes; a strip of land just three miles wide separates it from the ocean. Two trails lead from here to the sea. The Indian Village Trail to **Cape Alava**, the westernmost point of the continental United States, leads to the **Ozette Dig** (★), a 500-year-old Indian village excavated by archaeologists in the 1970s. The Ozette Loop Trail weaves past 56 **petroglyphs** that depict various aspects of historic Makah life.

Much of the Olympic coastline remains undeveloped. Hikers can wander along the high-water mark or on primitive trails, some wood-planked and raised above the forest floor. Offshore reefs have taken many lives over the centuries since European exploration began, and two memorials to shipwreck victims are good destinations for intrepid hikers. Nine miles south of Ozette, the **Norwegian Memorial** remembers seamen who died in an early 20th-century shipwreck. Six miles farther south, and about three miles north of Rialto Beach opposite La Push, the **Chilean Memorial** marks the grave of 20 South American sailors who died in a 1920 wreck.

Return to Sekiu to continue your drive south down the coast. Twenty-seven miles south of Clallam Bay on Route 101 is **Forks**, with 3000 people the largest town between Port Angeles and Hoquiam. (It's also Washington's rainiest town, with well over 100 inches a year.) Steelhead fishing, river rafting and mushroom gathering are major activities here, but the most evident to visitors is the timber industry. Some days, in fact, there seem to be more log trucks on the roads than passenger cars. The **Forks Timber Museum** (Route 101 North; 206-374-9663) is filled with exhibits of old-time logging equipment and historical photos, as well as pioneer and Indian rooms.

On the coast 14 miles west of Forks is the 800-year-old Indian fishing village of **La Push**, center of the **Quileute Indian Reservation**. Sportfishing, camping and beach walking are popular year-round. An abandoned Coast Guard station and lighthouse here are used as a school for resident children.

A national park road eight miles west of Forks branches off the La Push Road and follows the north shore of the Quillayute River five miles to **Rialto Beach**, where spectacular piles of driftwood often accumulate. There are picnic areas and campgrounds here, and a trailhead for hikes north up the beach toward Cape Alava.

The **Hoh Indian Reservation** is 25 miles south of Forks, off Route 101. Of more interest to most visitors is the **Kalaloch Lodge** (206-962-2271), 35 miles south of Forks on Route 101. A major national park facility, it affords spectacular ocean views at the southernmost end of the park's coastal strip.

OLYMPIC COAST HOTELS

The main population center on the Olympic Coast, and the nearest to the Hoh Rain Forest, is the lumber town of Forks. Among several budget-priced bed and breakfasts here is the **River Inn on the Bogachiel** (★) (Route 3, Box 3858, Forks; 206-374-6526), an A-frame chalet on the banks of the Calawah River two-and-a-half miles from town. Two bedrooms share a bath and a sun deck. You can fish from the shore or relax in the hot tub while keeping your eyes open for elk, deer and river otter.

Forks also has a youth hostel: the **Rain Forest Hostel** (mile marker 169.3, Route 101 South, Forks; 206-374-2270). As with other lodgings of its ilk, it offers dorm bunks and community bathrooms and kitchen. Budget.

Sixteen miles west of Forks in the Quileute Indian Reservation, surrounded by the coastal strip of Olympic National Park is the **La Push Ocean Park Resort** (P.O. Box 67, La Push, WA 98350; 206-374-5267). The driftwood-speckled beach is just beyond the lodgings, which fall into three categories: cabins with fully supplied kitchenettes and fireplaces; older townhouse units with balconies overlooking the beach; and rustic A-frames with wood stoves (haul your own fuel from the woodshed) and toilets (showers are in a communal washroom). Budget to moderate.

North of Forks 31 miles, the hamlet of Sekiu flanks Route 112 on the protected shore of Clallam Bay, on the Strait of Juan de Fuca. The lone waterfront hotel here is **Van Riper's Resort** (Front and Rice streets, Sekiu; 206-963-2334). Family owned and operated, it's a cozy getaway spot. More than half the 11 rooms have great views of the boats on the picturesque strait. Budget.

The Makah Indians of Neah Bay, the continental United States' northwesternmost community and a salmon-fishing center in its own right, operate a handful of small cabin resorts. One of the few open year-round is

Morton's Resort (P.O. Box 136, Neah Bay, WA 98357; 206-645-2250). The property has five motel rooms and six cottages; the latter all have kitchens, and one has a fireplace. Budget.

Back in Olympic National Park, one of the most picturesque spots on the Washington coastline is the **Kalaloch Lodge** (Star Route 1, Box 1100, 35 miles south of Forks; 206-962-2271). Accommodations here include eight lodge units, ten motel units, 21 log cabins with kitchenettes (but no utensils provided) and a half-dozen duplexes atop the bluff. The lodge has a dining room and lounge overlooking the Pacific Ocean, as well as a general store, gas station and gift shop. It's open year-round. Moderate.

If you're planning a stay in the corner of Olympic National Park that includes beauteous Lake Quinault, consider the **Lake Quinault Lodge** (South Shore Road, Quinault; 206-288-2571)—especially if you can get a lakefront room in the historic cedar-shingled lodge itself. Constructed in the 1920s, the huge building arcs around the shoreline, a totem-pole design on its massive chimney facing the water. Antiques and wicker furniture adorn the sun porch, dining room and bar. There are nice rooms in a newer wing, but they lack the lodge's historic ambience. You can rent boats or hike year-round, or relax in the pool, sauna or jacuzzi. Moderate to deluxe.

OLYMPIC COAST RESTAURANTS

Sunsets from the **Kalaloch Lodge** (Star Route 1, Box 1100, 35 miles south of Forks; 206-962-2271), high on a bluff overlooking the ocean in the national park's coastal strip, can make even the most ordinary food taste good. Fortunately, the fresh salmon and oysters served here don't need the view for their rich flavor. A lounge adjoins the dining room. Moderate.

The antique-filled restaurant at the park's **Lake Quinault Lodge** (South Shore Road, Quinault; 206-288-2571) faces another gorgeous lake surrounded by lush cedar forests. As you've come to expect along this coast, the seafood is excellent. Prices are moderate; the lodge is open year-round.

Other than the national park lodges, pickings are slim in the restaurant department along this stretch of highway. A mile north of Forks, the **Smoke House Restaurant** (Route 101 at La Push Road; 206-374-6258) occupies a salmon cannery on the Calabash River, and its alder-smoked salmon is superb. You can also get generous portions of other seafood and meats, plus a salad bar, for a moderate tab.

OLYMPIC COAST SHOPPING

For authentic Northwest Indian crafts, you won't do better than the gift shop at the **Makah Museum, Cultural and Research Center** (P.O. Box 95, Neah Bay, WA 98357; 206-645-2711) on the Makah Indian Reservation near Cape Flattery at the end of Route 112.

OLYMPIC COAST BEACHES AND PARKS

Bogachiel State Park—Not far from the Hoh Rain Forest, this eternally damp park sits on the Bogachiel River, famous for its salmon and steelhead runs. Hiking and hunting in the adjacent forest are popular activities.

Facilities: Restrooms, showers, picnic areas; restaurants and groceries in Forks; information, 206-374-6356. *Fishing:* Excellent in the river during runs.

Camping: There are 34 standard sites, six RV hookups and two primitive sites.

Getting there: Located on Route 101 six miles south of Forks.

Ocean Shores-Pacific Beach

A six-mile-long, 6000-acre peninsula, Ocean Shores was a cattle ranch when a group of investors bought it for $1 million in 1960. A decade later, its assessed value had risen to $35 million. Today, it would be hard to put a dollar figure on this strip of condominium-style hotels and second homes, many of them on a series of canals. The main tourist beach destination on the Grays Harbor County coastline, it's located along Route 115 three miles south of its junction with Route 109.

Folks come to Ocean Shores for oceanside rest and recreation, not for sightseeing. One of the few "attractions" is the **Ocean Shores Environmental Interpretive Center** (Point Brown Avenue; 206-289-4617) four miles south of the town center near the Ocean Shores Marina. Open summers only, it has exhibits describing the peninsula's geological formation and human development.

The 22-mile strip of beach that parallels Routes 115 and 109 north to Moclips is an attraction in its own right. Beyond Moclips, however, the coastline gets more rugged. Eleven miles past Moclips, the **Quinault Indian National Tribal Headquarters** in the village of Taholah, on the Quinault Indian Reservation, offers guided fishing and rafting trips on reservation land and a variety of tribal gifts in a small shop.

OCEAN SHORES-PACIFIC BEACH HOTELS

The nearest ocean beach area to the Seattle-Tacoma metropolitan area, Ocean Shores' condominiums and motels are frequently booked solid during the summer and on holiday weekends, even though prices can be high. Other times, it can be downright quiet . . . and inexpensive.

Like almost every other lodging on this stretch of shoreline, **The Polynesian** (291 Ocean Shores Boulevard, Ocean Shores; 206-289-3361) is as close to the water as you can get—a good-mile trek across the dunes to the high-tide mark. The three-story building has 70 rooms from motel units to three-bedroom penthouse suites. It has an indoor pool and spa, an outdoor games area popular with families and a restaurant and lively lounge. Moderate to deluxe.

Across the street from the Polynesian is Ocean Shores' largest property, with 83 units, and one of its least expensive: the **Gitche Gumee Motel** (Ocean Shores Boulevard, Ocean Shores; 206-289-3323). Basic sleeper units are small, but kitchen units (many with fireplaces) are good-sized. Rooms have televisions and phones; everyone can use the sauna and indoor and outdoor pools. Moderate in summer, budget in winter.

North up the coast from frenetic Ocean Shores are numerous quiet resort communities and accommodations. At Ocean City, four miles north, the **Pacific Sands Motel** (★) (2687 Route 109, Ocean City; 206-289-3588) is one of the top economy choices on the coast. There are just nine units, but they're well-kept; seven have kitchens and three have fireplaces. The extensive grounds include a nice swimming pool, playground, picnic tables, RV hookups and direct beach access across a suspension bridge. Deluxe.

The **Iron Springs Resort** (P.O. Box 207, Copalis Beach, WA 98535; 206-276-4230) has 27 units in 21 cottages built up a wooded hill and around a handsome cove at the mouth of Iron Springs Creek. The beach here is popular for razor clamming, crabbing and surf fishing; the cottages are equally popular for their spaciousness and panoramic views. All have kitchens and fireplaces. There are an indoor pool, playground and gift shop. Moderate.

Ocean Crest Resort (Sunset Beach, Route 109, Moclips; 206-276-4465) may be the most memorable accommodation on this entire stretch of beach. It's built atop a bluff, so getting to the beach involves a 132-step descent down a staircase through a wooden ravine. But the views from the rooms' private balconies are remarkable, and all but the smallest rooms have fireplaces and refrigerators. The adjoining athletic club opens its pool, jacuzzi and weight room to all guests free of charge. Moderate to deluxe.

OCEAN SHORES-PACIFIC BEACH RESTAURANTS

The best time to visit the **Misfit Restaurant** at the Ocean Shores Golf Course (Canal Road at Albatross Street, Ocean Shores; 206-298-3376) is early evening, when you can look across the 18th green at the golfers finishing their rounds, then stay for the sunset. Any time is good for eating at this steak-and seafood-specialty restaurant; Dungeness crab fettuccine amid the understated nautical decor is a special treat. Deluxe.

The **Home Port Restaurant** (Point Brown Avenue opposite Shoal Street, Ocean Shores; 206-289-2600) is appointed like the private garden of a sea captain home from the waves. Moderately priced steaks, seafood and pasta dominate the menu, but travelers watching their pennies can come between 4 and 6 p.m. for ample "budget-stretcher" dinners.

Numerous Ocean Shores restaurants appeal to more casual budget diners. **Flipper's Fish Bar** (Chance a la Mer at Ocean Court; 206-289-4676) has excellent fish and chips. **Barnacle Bill's** (Holman Square, Point Brown Avenue; 206-289-0218) is the place for chowder. And the **Sand Castle Drive-in** (Point Brown Avenue north of Chance a la Mer; 206-289-2777) is the in-spot for hamburgers.

Yesterday's (Damon Road at Chickaminn Avenue, Oyhut; 206-289-8657), on the access road for those who plan to drive the beach at Ocean City State Park, is another local favorite. The restaurant serves traditional American favorites (with a salad bar) at budget prices, and its lounge—with a great sunset view—has live music four nights a week.

North up the coast, **The Lighthouse Restaurant** (Ocean Beach Road, Pacific Beach; 206-276-4190) has an extensive menu of steaks, seafoods and other American traditions, like liver and onions and the three-quarter-pound Lighthouse burger. Fish can be grilled, poached or fried; steaks are well trimmed. Dinners include a salad bar and a sunset view across a playground to the blue Pacific. Lunch is served summers only. Moderate.

For a gourmet continental dinner in spectacular surroundings, check out the **Ocean Crest Resort** (Route 109, Moclips; 206-276-4465). Attentive service and superb meals (with a focus on seafood and Northwest regional cuisine), amid an atmosphere of Northwest Indian tribal art, only add to the enjoyment of the main reason to dine here: the view from a bluff, through a wooded ravine, to Sunset Beach.

OCEAN SHORES-PACIFIC BEACH SHOPPING

The most interesting galleries in Grays Harbor County are, not surprisingly, in the beach communities. For a wide range of works by regional artists, including oil paintings, watercolors, ceramics and textile crafts, seek out **The Cove Gallery** (Route 109, Iron Springs, Pacific Beach; 206-276-4360) and **Gallery Marjuli** (Homeport Plaza, Point Brown Avenue, Ocean Shores; 206-289-2858).

OCEAN SHORES-PACIFIC BEACH NIGHTLIFE

In Ocean Shores, **The Polynesian Lounge** (291 Ocean Shores Boulevard; 206-289-3315) and the **Ocean Shores Inn** (707 Ocean Shores Boulevard; 206-289-2407) feature rock or country bands in summer, solo performers during the off-season.

OCEAN SHORES-PACIFIC BEACH
BEACHES AND PARKS

Pacific Beach State Park—Broad, flat, sandy North Beach, extending 22 miles from Moclips (just north of Pacific Beach) to the north jetty of Grays Harbor at Ocean Shores, is the *raison d'être*. Beachcombing, kite flying, jogging and (in season) surf fishing and razor clam digging are popular activities.

Facilities: Restrooms, picnic areas; restaurants and groceries in downtown Pacific Beach; information, 206-276-4297. *Fishing:* In the surf. *Swimming:* Not recommended because of undertow and riptide.

Camping: There are 138 sites.

Getting there: Located along Route 109 in Pacific Beach.

Ocean City State Park—Stretching for several miles along the Pacific coastline, this North Beach park offers a dozen access points. There are clamming and fishing (in season), horseback riding and surf kayaking in summer, kite flying when the wind blows, birdwatching especially during migratory periods, beachcombing year-round. This flat, sandy beach is the same broad expanse that stretches 27 miles north to Pacific Beach. You can drive on some sections of the beach!

Facilities: Restrooms, picnic areas; restaurants and groceries in Ocean Shores and Ocean City; information, 206-289-3553. *Fishing:* In the surf. *Swimming:* Beware of the riptides.

Camping: There are 178 sites, 29 with RV hookups.

Getting there: Located off Route 115 and Route 109 north of Ocean Shores; campground is two miles north of Ocean Shores off Route 115.

Grays Harbor Area

Industrial towns are often not places of tourist interest. The twin cities of **Aberdeen** and **Hoquiam**, on the northeastern shore of the broad Grays Harbor estuary, are an exception. A historic seaport, a rich bird life and numerous handsome mansions built by old timber money make it worthwhile to pause in this corner of Washington.

Aberdeen has about 16,500 people, Hoquiam around 9000, and the metropolitan area includes some 30,000. Wood-products industries provide the economic base; in fact, more trees are harvested in Grays Harbor County than in any other county in the United States. Boat building and fisheries, both more important in past decades, remain key businesses. For information, check with the **Grays Harbor Chamber of Commerce** (Duffy Street at Route 101, Aberdeen; 206-532-1924).

If you're coming down Route 101 from the north, it's wise to follow the signs to make your first stop at **Hoquiam's Castle** (515 Chenault Avenue, Hoquiam; 206-533-2005; admission). A stately, 20-room hillside mansion built in 1897 by a millionaire lumber baron, it has been fully restored with elegant antiques like Tiffany lamps, grandfather clocks and a 600-piece, cut-crystal chandelier. With its round turret and bright-red color, the house is unmistakable.

Also in Hoquiam is the **Polson Museum** (1611 Riverside Avenue at Route 101 West; 206-533-5862). Built in the early 1920s by a pioneer timber family, the 26-room home contains original furnishings. It is surrounded by native trees and the Burton Ross Memorial Rose Gardens.

A couple miles west of Hoquiam on Route 109, at Bowerman Basin on Grays Harbor, is the **Grays Harbor National Wildlife Refuge** (206-753-9467), one of four major staging areas for migratory shorebirds in North America. Although this basin represents just two percent of the intertidal habitat of the estuary, fully half the one million shorebirds that visit each spring make their stop here. It's the last place to be flooded at high tide and the first to have its mudflats exposed, giving the avians extra feeding time. The refuge has an information center and viewing sites; April and early May are the best times to visit.

A major attraction in neighboring Aberdeen, just four miles east of Hoquiam on Route 101, is the **Grays Harbor Historical Seaport** (813 East Heron Street; 206-532-8611; admission). Craftspersons at this working 18th-century shipyard have constructed a replica of the *Lady Washington*, the brigantine in which Captain Robert Gray sailed when he discovered Grays Harbor and the Columbia River in 1783, and they're working on its companion vessel, the *Columbia Rediviva*. There are informational and hands-on exhibits, and visitors can stay and watch the shipbuilders.

A few blocks west, the **Aberdeen Museum of History** (11 East 3rd Street; 206-533-1976) offers exhibits, dioramas and videos of regional history in a 1922 armory. Displays include several re-created turn-of-the-century buildings: a one-room school, a general store, a church, a blacksmith's shop and more.

Inland from Aberdeen, Route 12 aims directly east toward Olympia. Near Elma, 20 miles east, the **Satsop Nuclear Power Plant** (East Access Road, Elma; 206-482-4428, ext. 5052) offers public tours at 10 a.m. Fridays or by appointment on weekends. Visitors can see the reactor and turbine buildings and observe the control room. The plant is operated by the Washington Public Power Supply System (WPPSS), known as "Whoops!" to many Washingtonians.

Route 105 follows the south shore of Grays Harbor west from Aberdeen to the atmospheric fishing village of **Westport**, at the estuary's south head. Perhaps the most interesting of several small museums here is the **Westport**

Maritime Museum (2202 Westhaven Drive, Westport; 206-268-0078), housed in a Nantucket-style Coast Guard station commissioned in 1939 but decommissioned in the 1970s. Historic photos, artifacts and memorabilia help tell the story of a sailor's life. The museum also has exhibits of skeletons of marine mammals, including whales.

Other spots of interest in Westport are the **Westport Aquarium** (321 Harbor Street; 206-268-0471; admission), with tanks of fish and other ocean creatures; **Shellflair** (102 South Forest Street; 206-268-9087; admission), featuring displays of sea shells and crystallites; and **Shark World Museum** (207 North Montesano Street; 206-268-9012; admission), which strives to make the world more savvy about sharks.

GRAYS HARBOR AREA HOTELS

Like any regional center, the twin cities of Aberdeen and Hoquiam have a strip of lookalike motels along Route 101. Though it's hard to choose one above another, the **Olympic Inn Motel** (616 West Heron Street, Aberdeen; 206-533-4200) is notable for its modern, spacious rooms. Decor in the 55 units is simple but pleasant. Moderate.

There's considerable character at the **Lytle House Bed & Breakfast** (509 Chenault Street, Hoquiam; 206-533-2320), a three-story Victorian hillside mansion. Each of the seven guest rooms has a different theme, such as nautical (Harbor View room), fox hunting (Esquire) and bridal (Castle Run). Period antiques include clawfoot tubs in the shared bathrooms. Guests choose a full gourmet breakfast from a menu offered the previous night. Twice a month, the house hosts murder-mystery parties. Moderate.

Just southeast of Aberdeen, the **Cooney Mansion** (802 East 5th Street, Cosmopolis; 206-533-0602) is located in a secluded wooded area on a golf course with an adjoining tennis court and park. A National Historic Landmark built in 1908 by a lumber baron, its interior was designed to show off local woods. Now a bed and breakfast, it has nine bedrooms, five with private baths, as well as a jacuzzi, sauna, sun deck and exercise room. Moderate.

East of Grays Harbor in the county seat of Montesano is the **Abel House** (117 Fleet Street South; 206-249-6002). This stately 1908 home has five bedrooms with shared baths, a gameroom and reading room and an exquisite English garden. A full breakfast and afternoon tea are included with the room. Moderate.

Farther east—halfway from Montesano to Olympia, in fact, but still in Grays Harbor County—**The Old McCleary Hotel** (42 Summit Road, McCleary; 206-495-3678) maintains antique-laden, budget-priced rooms that seem to be especially popular with touring bicyclists.

In Westport, at the mouth of Grays Harbor, the largest motel is the **Château Westport** (710 Hancock Avenue; 206-268-9101). Many of the 110 units have balconies and fireplaces, and a third are efficiency studios with kitchenettes. The upper floors of the four-story property, easily identified by its gray mansard roof, have excellent ocean views. Dip into the indoor pool and jacuzzi. Moderate.

More atmospheric is the **Glenacres Inn** (222 North Montesano Street; 206-268-9391), which will celebrate its 100th anniversary in 1998. Appointments are still turn-of-the-century in style, and all 12 units—five spacious guest bedrooms, three deck rooms and four cottages (each of which sleep four to 12)—have private baths. Outdoor recreation on nine acres centers around a huge deck with a gazebo-covered hot tub. Moderate.

For serious budget-watchers, the **Westport Dorm Hotel** (1780 North Nyhus Street, Westport; 206-268-0949) has accommodations at Float 17 from March through September.

GRAYS HARBOR AREA RESTAURANTS

It's a comfort to know that Grays Harbor has more memorable restaurants than memorable accommodations. The best of the best is **The Levee Street** (709 Levee Street, Hoquiam; 206-532-1959), which extends over the Hoquiam River on pilings. Though it's just a block off Route 101, it has a nondescript entrance that's easy to miss. Inside, though, it's a real charmer, with fresh seafood, steaks and an excellent wine list. Dinner only, Tuesday to Saturday. Moderate to deluxe.

When Chef Pierre Gabelli moved to the Washington coast from his native Italy, it was only natural that he should open the **Parma Ristorante Italiano** (★) (116 West Heron Street, Aberdeen; 206-532-3166). Gourmet pastas like gnocchi, manicotti and tortelli d'Erbetta, as well as seafood fettuccines and a handful of outstanding meat dishes, are served for budget to moderate prices. Best of all are the homemade desserts.

Bridges Restaurant (112 North G Street, Aberdeen; 206-532-6563) is a handsome, garden-style restaurant with one dining room that's actually a greenhouse. As the size of its parking lot attests, it's very popular locally, for its lounge as well as its cuisine. Local seafood, steaks, chicken and pasta highlight the menu. Moderate.

For historic flavor, you needn't look further than **Billy's Bar and Grill** (322 East Heron Street, Aberdeen; 206-533-7144). Named for an early 20th-century ne'er-do-well notorious for mugging loggers and shanghaiing sailors, Billy's boasts an ornate century-old ceiling, huge antique bar and wall murals that are colorful if not downright bawdy. This is the place to settle back with a burger and a beer and soak up the past. Budget.

Elsewhere in the Grays Harbor Area, the **Hong Kong Restaurant** (211 East 1st Street, Cosmopolis; 206-533-7594) is surprisingly authentic for a town so far removed from China! It has chop suey and egg foo yung, yes, but it also has egg flower soup, moo goo gai pan and other tastes from the old country. Budget.

Out in Westport, whose resemblance to a New England fishing village may be coincidence, is **Constantin's** (320 East Dock Street; 206-268-0550), whose similarity to Greek restaurants in the Aegean is no accident. Cross-cultural delights include tender calamari in garlic sauce, eggplant moussaka casserole and lamb souvlaki. Dinner only. Moderate.

GRAYS HARBOR AREA SHOPPING

For a sampling of creations by regional artisans visit the **Pacific Center of the Arts and Crafts** (1767 Route 105, Grayland; 206-267-1351) which features pottery, original art, prints and locally made gift items.

GRAYS HARBOR AREA NIGHTLIFE

Folks in the Grays Harbor area show a predilection for **Sidney's** sports lounge (512 West Heron Avenue, Aberdeen; 206-533-6635), where rock bands play regularly; the Victorian bar at **Billy's Bar and Grill** (322 East Heron Avenue, Aberdeen; 206-533-7144); and the posh lounge at **Bridges Restaurant** (112 North G Street; 206-532-6563).

GRAYS HARBOR AREA BEACHES AND PARKS

Lake Sylvia State Park—Visitors can circumambulate this narrow, forest-enshrouded lake on a two-mile hiking and mountain-biking trail. Also here are a swimming beach, fishing and boat launch, with rentals available.

Facilities: Restrooms, picnic areas, lifeguards (in summer), groceries; restaurants in Montesano; information, 206-249-3621. *Fishing:* For trout, from boat or shore. *Swimming:* Good.

Camping: There are 35 sites.

Getting there: Located two miles north of Montesano off Route 12, via North 3rd Street.

Schafer State Park—Once a family park for employees of the Schafer Logging Company, this tranquil, 119-acre site on the East Fork of the Satsop River is still popular with families. Located in a heavily forested area, it's ideal for picnics, hikes and fishing.

Facilities: Restrooms, picnic areas; groceries and restaurants in Elma; information, 206-482-3852. *Fishing:* In the river. *Swimming:* There's a beach, but the water's cold.

Camping: There are 55 sites, six with hookups.

Getting there: Located on East Satsop Road 12 miles north of Elma, off Route 12 via Brady.

Wynoochee Dam and Lake—An Army Corps of Engineers project, this four-and-a-half-mile-long lake was created in 1972 by a water-supply and flood-control dam on the Wynoochee River. The visitors center has interpretive displays. A ten-mile trail winds around the lake, past a beach and designated swimming area. Trout fishing, waterskiing and wildlife watching are also popular.

Facilities: Restrooms, picnic areas; groceries and restaurants in Montesano; information, 206-764-3520. *Fishing:* From a boat or the shore. *Swimming:* Good but cold.

Camping: There are 46 sites and ten walk-ins at nearby Coho campground in the national forest; information, 206-877-5254.

Getting there: Located 37 miles north of Montesano on Forest Service Road 22, off Route 12.

Westhaven and Westport Light State Parks—Westhaven State Park, which occupies the southern headland at the mouth of Grays Harbor, is a great place for watching birds and wildlife, including harbor seals and whales during migratory periods. It's adjacent to Westport Light State Park, which surrounds a historic lighthouse that's warned coastal ships of the entrance to Grays Harbor since 1897.

Facilities: Picnic areas; groceries and restaurants in town; information, 206-268-0214. *Fishing:* From the shore or jetty.

Getting there: Both parks are located about one-half mile from downtown Westport; Westhaven on East Yearout Drive and Westport Light at the end of Ocean Avenue.

Twin Harbors State Park—The Washington coast's largest campground dominates this 168-acre park. It also includes the Shifting Sands Nature Trail with interpretive signs for dunes explorers. Beachcombing and clamming are popular activities on the broad, sandy beach.

Facilities: Restrooms, picnic areas; groceries and restaurants in Westport and Grayland; information, 206-268-9565. *Fishing:* In the surf or from a charter boat. *Swimming:* Not recommended because of riptides.

Camping: There are 332 sites, 49 with RV hookups.

Getting there: Located along Route 105, four miles south of Westport and four miles north of Grayland.

Grayland Beach State Park—Like other coastal beaches, this is broad and flat and ideal for clam digging, beachcombing and other seaside diversions. An interpretive self-guided trail leads through the dunes of the 402-acre park, one of the larger of the coastal reserves.

Facilities: Restrooms, picnic areas; groceries and restaurants in Grayland; information, 206-267-4301. *Fishing:* In surf. *Swimming:* Not recommended due to riptide.

Camping: There are 60 sites with full RV hookups.

Getting there: Located on Route 105, one mile south of Grayland.

Long Beach-Willapa Bay

The largest "unpopulated" estuary in the continental United States, this region's pristine condition makes it one of the world's best places for farming oysters. From Tokeland to Bay Center to Oysterville, tiny villages that derive their sole income from the shelled creatures display mountains of empty shells as evidence of their success. Begin your visit on Route 105 south from Westport, then head east along the northern shore of Willapa Bay.

Thirty-three miles from Westport, Route 105 rejoins Route 101 at Raymond. This town of 3000, and its smaller sister community of South Bend four miles west on Route 101, are lumber ports on the lower Willapa River.

You'll find murals—43 of them, to be exact—on walls from Ocean Shores to the Columbia River, Elma to Ilwaco. Chambers of commerce and other visitor information centers have guide pamphlets. But no mural is larger than the 85-foot-wide painting of an early logger on the **Dennis Company Building** (5th Street, Raymond). The company's outdoor display of old-time farm equipment is across the street. Raymond's other main point of tourist interest is the **Willapa Heritage Museum** (331 3rd Street; 206-942-5419), whose collection includes a 1928 Wurlitzer theater organ.

Attractions in South Bend include the **Pacific County Historical Society Museum** (1008 West Robert Bush Drive; 206-875-5224), with pioneer artifacts from the turn of the century; the 1911 **Pacific County Courthouse** (Memorial Drive off Route 101; 206-875-5224), noted for its art-glass dome and historic foyer wall paintings; and the **Coast Oyster Company** (1200 Robert Bush Drive; 206-875-5557), the largest oyster-processing plant in the United States, offering public tours with a day's advance notice.

The **Long Beach Peninsula**, reached via Route 101 from South Bend (43 miles), has had a significant flow of vacationing Northwest urbanites for over a century. But its economy is more strongly founded in fish processing and cranberry growing. Get information from the **Long Beach Peninsula Visitor Bureau** (Box 562, Route 103, Long Beach; 206-642-2400).

Route 103, which runs north-south up the 28-mile-long, two-mile-wide peninsula, is intersected by Route 101 at **Seaview**. The town of **Long Beach** is just a mile north of the junction. Its principal new attraction is a 2300-foot wooden boardwalk (South 10th to Bolstad streets), elevated 40 feet above the dunes, enabling folks to make an easy trek to the high-tide mark. The beach, incidentally, is open to driving on the hard upper sand, and to surf fishing, clamming, beachcombing, kite flying and picnicking everywhere.

Kite flying is a big thing on the Washington coast, so it's no accident that the **World Kite Museum and Hall of Fame** (3rd Street Northwest at Route 103; 206-642-4020) is in Long Beach. The museum has rotating exhibits of kites from around the world—Japanese, Chinese, Thai, etc.—with displays of stunt kites, military kites, advertising kites and more.

In October and early November, the cranberry harvest takes precedence over all else on the peninsula. Most fields are owned by the folks from Ocean Spray. The **Washington State University-Long Beach Research and Extension Unit** (Pioneer Road, Long Beach; 206-642-2031) offers free tours of the cranberry "bogs" during harvest, and other times by appointment.

North of Long Beach ten miles is **Ocean Park**, the commercial hub of the central and northern Long Beach Peninsula. Developed as a Methodist camp in 1883, it evolved into a small resort town. Older yet is **Oysterville**, another three miles north via the Peninsula Highway. Founded in 1854, this National Historic District boasts the oldest continuously operating post office in Washington (1858) and 17 other designated historic sites. Get a walking-tour pamphlet from the **Old Church** beside the Village Green on Territory Road.

South of Seaview just two miles on Route 103 is **Ilwaco**, spanning the isthmus between the Columbia River and the Pacific Ocean. Local history is featured at the impressive **Ilwaco Heritage Museum** (115 Southeast Lake Street; 206-642-3446; admission). A series of galleries depicts the development of southwestern Washington from early Indian culture to European voyages of discovery, from pioneer settlement to the early 20th century.

About eight miles southeast, a short distance before Route 101 crosses the Columbia River to Astoria, Oregon, **Fort Columbia State Park** (Route 101, Chinook; 206-665-5504) is a highly recommended stop for history buffs. Two buildings at the site are museums: the **Fort Columbia Interpretive Center**, exhibiting artifacts of early 20th-century military life in a former coastal artillery post, and the **DAR House**, which the Daughters of the American Revolution have restored to depict the everyday lifestyle of a military officer of the time.

LONG BEACH-WILLAPA BAY HOTELS

Possibly the most delightful accommodation anywhere on the Washington coast is **The Shelburne Country Inn** (Route 103 at 46th Place, Seaview; 206-642-2442). The oldest continually operating hotel in the state, it opened in 1896 and is still going strong. Sixteen guest rooms are furnished with Victorian antiques, fresh flowers and (yum!) chocolate truffles, and nearly all have private baths and decks. A hearty country breakfast is served in the morning. Moderate to deluxe.

Another one-of-a-kinder, but for very different reasons, is **The Historic Sou'wester Lodge** (★) (Beach Access Road, 38th Place, Seaview; 206-642-2542): It's a place much beloved by youth hostelers who, well, grew up. Proprietors Len and Miriam Atkins have intentionally kept the accommodation simple and weathered. They advertise it as a B&MYODB—"bed and make your own damn breakfast." Kitchen rights extend to the living room, including the fireplace and library. Sleeping options include rooms in the historic lodge, cedar-shingled housekeeping cabins, a dozen-or-so vintage TCH! TCH! mobile homes ("Trailer Classics Hodgepodge") and an area for RVs and tent campers. Budget to moderate.

Numerous beachfront cabin communities speckle the shoreline of the Long Beach Peninsula north from Ilwaco and Seaview. One of the best is the **Klipsan Beach Cottages** (Route 1, Box 359, Ocean Park; 206-665-4888). Each of the nine cottages, in a lovely wooded setting seven miles north of the town of Long Beach, has a kitchen and fireplace (with free firewood). There's no phone or television—but who needs it, with the ocean just out the door? Some two-bedroom units are available. Moderate.

Shakti Cottages (253rd Place and Park Street, Ocean Park; 206-665-4000) is a lesbian and gay resort just five minutes from the water. Ten rustic cabins all are fully equipped with kitchens and sleep up to four guests. The units are furnished with queen sized beds, older couches and feature eclectic decor. Budget to moderate.

Willapa Bay oyster lovers frequent the beds near the north end of the Long Beach Peninsula, and this is where they'll find the **Moby Dick Hotel** (★) (Sandridge and Bay avenues, Nahcotta; 206-665-4543). A ten-room bed-and-breakfast inn that first opened its doors in 1930, it maintains a country nautical atmosphere, with rambling grounds, its own vegetable garden and oyster farm, and a hot tub and sauna house. A fireplace and piano beckon on rainy days. Moderate.

The **Fort Columbia State Park Youth Hostel** (Route 101, Chinook; 206-777-8755) occupies the former Coast Artillery Infirmary. There are two dorms—a 13-bunk room for men, a five-bunk room for women—and a single family room. Guests share kitchen, bathroom and living facilities. Priced in the budget range.

LONG BEACH-WILLAPA BAY RESTAURANTS

For a unique dining experience, visit the **Blue Heron Inn** (★) (Bay Center Road, Bay Center; 206-875-9990), on an off-the-beaten-track peninsula that juts into Willapa Bay 12 miles south of South Bend. Oysters, of course, are a specialty at this café-tavern. The fish market here also sells fresh crab and smoked salmon. Budget.

Expensive, but worth it. Everything is exquisite in **The Shoalwater Restaurant** (Shelburne Inn, Route 103 at 46th Place, Seaview; 206-642-4142), one of Washington's most highly acclaimed country restaurants. From the smoked salmon rosettes to the mussel chowder, the grilled duck breast and quail to the veal and wild-mushroom fettuccine, and the creative preparations of the day's fresh catches, a deluxe meal here is one to savor. The turn-of-the-century ambience adds an element of comfort. Opposite the restaurant entrance is **The Heron & Beaver Pub**, with light meals produced by the same kitchen for moderate prices.

My Mom's Pie (Route 103 at South 12th Street, Long Beach; 206-642-2342) has great pies—from wild blackberry to chocolate almond to sour-cream raisin—but that's not the only reason to dine in this charming double-wide trailer. Soups, salads and sandwiches are served all day, and the chicken-almond pot pie is a mouth-watering delight. Lunch only. Priced in the budget range.

Kopa Wecoma (★) (1024 Bay Avenue, Ocean Park) is on the beach at Ocean Park: Turn left at the blinking light off Route 103. Though signs in the style of Burma Shave preview its existence, visitors still may not be prepared for the generous portions offered at this serendipitous beachfront diner. Come for the clam chowder, the seafood plates, the sandwiches. Open Friday to Monday only. Budget.

Mountains of oyster shells surround **The Ark Restaurant** (273rd Street and Sandridge Road, Nahcotta; 206-665-4133), located near the north end of the Long Beach Peninsula on oyster-rich Willapa Bay. In fact, the restaurant has its own oyster beds—as well as an herb and edible-flower garden and a busy bakery. Nearby are cranberry bogs and forests of wild mushrooms. All these go into the preparation of creative dishes like salmon Louise (with chanterelle mushrooms, lime and cilantro) and filet mignon with pinenuts and caramelized garlic. Dinner and Sunday brunch only; closed January and February. Moderate.

Dining at **The Sanctuary** (Route 101 and Hazel Street, Chinook; 206-777-8380) is a sacred ritual to some folks. And well it should be: The restaurant occupies the premises of the historic Methodist Episcopal Church of Chinook (1906-1978). Few renovations have been made to the building, although wine is taken much more often than during communion, and sundaes can sometimes be sinful. The varied menu includes Swedish meatballs and fish cakes, steaks and fresh seafood. Dinner only. Prices fall in the moderate range.

LONG BEACH-WILLAPA BAY SHOPPING

On the Long Beach Peninsula, there's wonderful bric-a-brac at **Marsh's Free Museum** (400 Pacific Avenue South, Long Beach; 206-642-2188), from the world's largest frying pan (so they say) to antique music boxes. Noted watercolorist Eric Wiegardt displays his work at the **Potrimpos Gallery** (Bay Avenue between Route 103 and Sandridge Road, Ocean Park; 206-665-5976).

The souvenir most typical of beach recreation here, perhaps, would be a colorful kite. Look for them at **Ocean Kites** (511 Pacific Avenue South, Long Beach; 206-642-2229).

LONG BEACH-WILLAPA BAY NIGHTLIFE

The Lightship Restaurant (Nendel's Edgewater Inn, 409 Southwest 10th Street, Long Beach; 206-642-3252) has the Long Beach Peninsula's only ocean-view restaurant from its fourth-story loft; come for a sunset drink. Things may be a bit livelier at the **Bent Rudder Pub** (1700 Pacific Avenue South, Long Beach; 206-642-8330), which often features live rock bands. Quiet beers are best quaffed at **The Heron & Beaver Pub** in the Shelburne Inn (Route 103 at 46th Place, Seaview; 206-642-4142).

LONG BEACH-WILLAPA BAY BEACHES AND PARKS

Leadbetter Point State Park—Shifting dunes and mudflats, ponds and marshes, grasslands and forests make this northern tip of the Long Beach Peninsula an ideal place for those who like to observe nature. As many as 100 species of migratory bird stop over here. Among them is the rare snowy plover, which nests in the sand; foot traffic is restricted from their nesting grounds from April to August. There are numerous hiking trails.

Facilities: Restrooms, picnic areas; groceries in Oysterville, restaurants at Nahcotta and farther south on peninsula; information, 206-484-3482. *Fishing:* In the surf. *Swimming:* Not recommended due to riptides and undertows.

Getting there: Located three miles north of Oysterville on Stackpole Road, via Route 103 and Sandridge Road.

Pacific Pines State Park—This day-use park offers beach access for appropriate activities, like beachcombing, kite flying, jogging, surf fishing and razor clam digging in season. You can drive on the uppermost sand, but be sure it's hard-packed; more than one car owner has needed a tow after getting bogged in the sand.

Facilities: Restrooms, picnic areas; restaurants and groceries in Ocean Park; information, 206-642-2400. *Fishing:* In the surf. *Swimming:* Not recommended due to riptide.

Getting there: Located on 274 Place off Park Avenue, one mile north of Ocean Park.

Loomis Lake State Park—Situated on a narrow, three-mile-long freshwater lake south of Klipsan Beach, this day-use park offers the swimming that's discouraged in the surf, as well as good fishing from shore.

Facilities: Restrooms, picnic areas; restaurants and groceries in Ocean Park; information, 206-642-2400. *Fishing:* Trout and panfish. *Swimming:* Good.

Getting there: Located on Park Road, via 199 Place off Route 103, four miles south of Ocean Park.

Fort Canby State Park—The point where the Columbia River meets the Pacific Ocean has been a crossroads of history for two centuries. The Lewis and Clark expedition arrived at this dramatic headland in 1805 after 18 months on the trail. Two 19th-century lighthouses—at North Head on the Pacific and at Cape Disappointment on a Columbia sandbar—have limited the number of shipwrecks to a mere 200 through 1991. The Fort was occupied from the Civil War through World War II. Today, the 1700-acre park contains the Lewis and Clark Interpretive Center (with exhibits and a multimedia program), numerous forest, beach and clifftop trails, boat launch, swimming beach and summer interpretive programs.

Facilities: Restrooms, picnic areas, groceries; restaurants in Ilwaco; information, 206-642-3078. *Fishing:* In the surf, from the jetty or from a boat. *Swimming:* Okay at Waikiki Beach (on the river); discouraged at Benson Beach (on the ocean).

Camping: There are 250 sites, 60 with RV hookups.

Getting there: Located two-and-a-half miles southwest of Ilwaco on Route 101.

The Sporting Life

FISHING

Lakes and rivers—and, of course, the sea—offer a plethora of opportunities to catch everything from rainbow trout to salmon and halibut.

The Strait of Juan de Fuca is one of the nation's great salmon grounds, with chinook, coho and other species running the waters through the summer months. Other species include halibut (up to 240 pounds), ling cod, true cod, red snapper and black bass. Port Townsend, Port Angeles, Sekiu-Clallam Bay and Neah Bay are the main ports for charter vessels. Operators include **Thunderbird Boathouse** (P.O. Box 787, Port Angeles, WA 98362; 206-457-3595), **Woodie's Charter Service** (P.O. Box 154, Clallam Bay, WA 98326; 206-963-2421) and **Blue Chip Charters** (P.O. Box 204, Neah Bay, WA 98357; 206-645-2374).

Farther down the coast, on the south side of Grays Harbor, the year-round fishing port of Westport matches deep-sea anglers with charter boats. Operators include **Deep Sea Charters** (Float 6, Westport; 206-268-9300) and **Neptune Charters** (Float 14, Westport; 206-268-0124).

At the mouth of the Columbia River, Ilwaco is another center for deep-sea fishing. Salmon and sturgeon are caught near the river mouth, while tuna, rockfish, cod and sole are in deeper waters. See **Hobo Charters** (P.O.

Box 303, Ilwaco, WA 98624; 206-642-2300) or **Tidewind Charters** (P.O. Box 206, Ilwaco, WA 98624; 206-642-2111).

Inland, Olympic National Park and Olympic National Forest have marvelous trout fishing in their lakes and streams. The rivers flowing from the mountains are busy from December through April with steelhead. Licensed guide service is offered in most river communities. Check with **Northwest Fishing Adventures** (P.O. Box 295, Beaver, WA 98305; 206-374-3154), **Hoh Chalet** (HC 80, Box 1886, Forks, WA 98331; 206-962-2131) or **Quinault Sport Fishing Guides** (P.O. Box 176, Taholah, WA 98587; 206-276-8211 or 276-4315).

Many folks prefer shellfishing—the pursuit of clams, oysters, mussels, scallops, clams and the like—to dropping a line into the briny. Dungeness Spit, north of Sequim, is the home of the renowned Dungeness crab. Willapa Bay is famous for its oysters. Littleneck, butter, horse and Manila hardshell clams can be dug from the beaches along with that Northwest oddity, the geoduck (say "gooey-duck"), whose huge foot cannot fit within its shell. Before harvesting shellfish, call the Red Tide Hotline (800-562-5632) to find out if the waters are healthy.

RIVER RAFTING AND KAYAKING

Three of the rivers falling from the Olympics, the north-flowing Elwha and the west-flowing Hoh and Queets, attract whitewater rafters. **Olympic Raft and Guide Service** (464 Route 101 West, Lake Crescent; 206-457-7011) is the major outfitter in the area. Kayakers can run the Elwha, Sol Duc, Dosewallips or Wynoochee with the **Olympic Kayak Company** (26469 Circle Place Northwest, Poulsbo; 206-697-6095). Port Townsend is a sea-kayaking center; call **Peninsula Kayak Tours** (Port Townsend; 206-732-4541) or **Sport Townsend** (P.O. Box 265, Port Townsend, WA 98368; 206-385-0667).

KITE FLYING

"Oh, go fly a kite!" It must seem absurd to some folks that kite flying has taken on serious adult proportions on Washington beaches. Thanks to benevolent ocean breezes, Ocean Shores and Long Beach have major kite festivals and competitions in the summer and fall and numerous kite shops to support the hobby. Learn more from **Ocean Shores Kites** (Ocean Shores Mall, Chance a la Mer, Ocean Shores; 206-289-4103) or the **Long Beach World Kite Museum and Hall of Fame** (Route 103 at 3rd Street, Long Beach; 206-642-4020).

WHALE WATCHING

Gray whales and humpbacks migrate down the Pacific Coast, from Alaskan to tropical waters, between March and May. Orcas, or killer whales,

are frequently seen in the waters of the Strait of Juan de Fuca. Many fishing
charter operators throughout the region convert to whale-watching cruises
at this time, and in Ocean Shores, specialized boat tours (800-562-0145),
with a naturalist aboard, are scheduled every Saturday and Sunday throughout the migration period. From Westport, there's a number of specialty
whale-cruise operators, including **Westport Whale Watch** (Float 6; 206-
268-9144) and **Whales Ahoy** (Float 8; 206-268-9150).

SKIING

The snow-covered Olympics offer many opportunities for cross-country skiers, and one for downhillers. The **Hurricane Ridge Ski Area**, 17
miles south of Port Angeles via Hurricane Ridge Road, has several miles
of cross-country trails starting from the Hurricane Ridge Lodge. Rentals
of downhill, cross-country and snowshoeing equipment are also available.
Contact Hurricane Ridge Winter Sports Club (336 East 8th Street, Port Angeles; 206-457-5559).

Additional information on cross-country skiing in the Olympics can
be obtained from **Olympic National Park** (600 East Park Avenue, Port Angeles; 206-452-9235).

HORSEBACK RIDING AND PACK TRIPS

For casual riding, one of your best bets is **Seahorse Ranch** (Mile 9,
Route 109, east of Hoquiam; 206-532-6791). There are numerous trails
around the 400-acre ranch and an indoor arena for rainy days. The Seahorse,
as well as **Bridges Horse Service** (Route 3, Box 1082, Hoquiam; 206-533-
2096), bring horses to rent near the Ocean Shores Inn for beach riding.

Pack trips into the Olympic National Park and Olympic National Forest
can be arranged by the **Lost Mountain Ranch** (P.O. Box 562, Sequim, WA
98382; 206-683-4331). And llama lovers will be delighted to accompany
an Andean pack animal into the Olympics, thanks to **Kit's Llamas** (P.O.
Box 116, Olalla, WA 98359; 206-857-5274) or **Watts a Llama? Leisure
Treks** (735 Peters Street, Raymond; 206-942-5239).

GOLF

Full 18-hole courses in the region include the **Chevy Chase Golf Club**
(7401 Cape George Road, Port Townsend; 206-385-0704), **Port Ludlow
Golf Course** (9483 Oak Bay Road, Port Ludlow; 206-437-2222), **Dungeness Golf & Country Club** (491 Woodcock Road, Sequim; 206-683-6344),
Sunland Golf and Country Club (109 Hilltop Drive, Sequim; 206-683-
6800), **Peninsula Golf Club** (105 Linberg Road, Port Angeles; 206-457-
6501), **Ocean Shores Golf Course** (Canal Road and Albatross Street,
Ocean Shores; 206-289-3357) and **Oaksridge Golf Course** (207 Elma-
Monte Road, Elma; 206-482-3511).

BICYCLING

Except along the southwestern shore areas, bicycling this part of Washington requires strength and stamina. There's spectacular beauty here, but there's also rain—lots of it—and challenging terrain.

One of the gentlest biking opportunities is the 14-mile **Ocean Shores Loop** from North Bay Park. Other recommended road tours in this region include the 85-mile **Upper Peninsula Tour** from Sequim to Neah Bay, the 55-mile trip down Route 101 from **Port Angeles to Forks**, the 69-mile **Aberdeen-Raymond-Westport** loop on Routes 101 and 105 and the 42-mile **Seaview-Naselle** loop in Pacific County.

BIKE RENTALS   You can rent bikes from **Port Cyclery** (215 Taylor Street, Port Townsend; 206-385-6470), **Sport Townsend** (P.O. Box 265, Port Townsend, WA 98368; 206-385-0667) or **Andy's Skate and Surf** (Shores Mall, Chance a la Mer, Ocean Shores; 206-289-4103)

HIKING

Olympic National Park and adjacent areas of Olympic National Forest are rich in backpacking opportunities. Most trails follow rivers into the high country, with its peaks and alpine lakes. Coastal areas of the Olympic Peninsula, as well, have hiking trails. Along the southwestern Washington coast there are few inland trails, but the long stretches of flat beach appeal to many walkers.

PORT TOWNSEND AREA TRAIL   **Mount Walker Trail** (2.5 miles) ascends the Olympics' easternmost peak (2804 feet) through a rhododendron forest. The view from the summit, across Hood Canal and the Kitsap Peninsula to Seattle and the Cascades, is unforgettable. The trailhead is one-fifth mile off Route 101 at Walker Pass, five miles south of Quilcene.

PORT ANGELES AREA TRAIL   **Dungeness Spit Trail** (5.5 miles) extends down the outside of the longest natural sandspit in the United States, and back the inside. The spit is a national wildlife refuge with a lighthouse at its seaward end. The trail begins and ends at the Dungeness Recreation Area.

OLYMPIC NATIONAL PARK TRAILS   **Elk Mountain Trail** (7.6 miles) leads from the Deer Park Campground to Obstruction Peak, following a 6500-foot ridgeline.

Enchanted Valley Trail (28.5 miles) starts at the Dosewallips Ranger Station on the park's eastern boundary, follows the Dosewallips River to its source in the Anderson Glacier, then goes down the East Fork of the Quinault to the Graves Creek Campground.

Seven Lakes Basin Loop (25 miles) has several trail options, starting and ending at Sol Duc Hot Springs.

Hoh River Trail (19 miles) wanders through North America's most famous rain forest from the Hoh Ranger Station, to Glacier Meadows, at the base of the Blue Glacier on 7965-foot Mount Olympus, the park's highest point.

Cape Alava Loop (9 miles) crosses from the Ozette Ranger Station to Cape Alava; follows the shoreline south to Sand Point, from which there is beach access to shipwreck memorials farther south; and returns northeast to the ranger station. Prehistoric petroglyphs and an ancient Indian village are en route.

GRAYS HARBOR AREA TRAIL   Wynoochee Lake Trail (10 miles) circles this manmade reservoir in Olympic National Forest north of Montesano.

SOUTHWEST COAST TRAILS   Shifting Sands Nature Trail (.5 mile) teaches visitors to Twin Harbors State Park, south of Westport, about plant and animal life in the seaside dunes.

Leadbetter Point Loop Trail (2.5 miles) weaves through the forests and dunes, and past the ponds, mudflats and marshes, of the wildlife sanctuary/state park at the northern tip of the Long Beach Peninsula. Accessible from Oysterville, it's of special interest to birdwatchers.

Willapa Bay National Wildlife Refuge (3.2 miles) has an interpretive trail through an important grove of old-growth red cedar, some as large as 11 feet wide and 150 feet tall, on Long Island.

Transportation

BY CAR

Route 101 is the main artery of the Olympic Peninsula and Washington coastal region, virtually encircling the entire land mass. Branching off Route 5 in Olympia, at the foot of Puget Sound, it runs north 84 to Discovery Bay, where **Route 20** turns off to Port Townsend; west through Port Angeles to Sappho; then zigzags to Astoria, Oregon, and points south. Remarkably, when you reach Aberdeen, 292 miles after you start traveling on 101, you're just 36 miles from where you started!

Traveling from Seattle, most Olympic Peninsula visitors take either the Seattle-Winslow ferry (to Route 305) or the Edmonds-Kingston ferry (to Route 104), joining 101 just south of Discovery Bay. From Tacoma, the practical route is Route 16 across the Narrows Bridge. From the north, the Keystone ferry to Port Townsend has its eastern terminus midway down lanky Whidbey Island, off Route 20. Northbound travelers can reach the area either through Astoria, on Route 101, or via several routes that branch off Route 5 north of Portland.

BY AIR

Fairchild International Airport, near Port Angeles, links the northern Olympic Peninsula with major cities throughout the United States and western Canada via Horizon Air Lines. Coastal Airways, a commuter carrier based out of Sequim, also serves Hoquiam's **Bowerman Field,** Seattle, Bremerton and the San Juan Islands.

BY BUS

Greyhound/Trailways Bus Lines offers service to a number of towns including Sequim (113 East Washington Avenue; 206-683-4343), Port Angeles (1315 East Front Street; 206-452-8311) and Hoquiam/Aberdeen (Wishkah and G streets).

BY BOAT

Washington State Ferries (206-464-6400, Seattle) serves the Olympic Peninsula directly from Whidbey Island to Port Townsend and indirectly across Puget Sound (via the Kitsap Peninsula) from Seattle and Edmonds. The **Black Ball Ferry** (206-457-4491) offers direct daily service between Port Angeles and Victoria, B.C., and **Victoria Rapid Transit** (206-452-8088) provides foot-passenger service mid-May through October. The **Victoria Clipper** (206-443-2560, Seattle) stops at Port Townsend en route daily from Seattle to Victoria via Friday Harbor in the San Juans. There's summer foot-passenger ferry service between Port Townsend and Friday Harbor. Some smaller cruise lines may make stops in Port Angeles.

CAR RENTALS

In Port Angeles, **Budget Rent A Car** can be found at the airport (206-457-8000) or in town (206-452-4270). Other agencies are **Birdwell Ford** (206-457-3333), **Dan Wilder Volkswagen** (206-452-9268) and **U-Save Auto Rental** (206-452-6822).

There are rental agents at the Hoquiam airport: **Budget Rent A Car** (206-532-6002) and **U-Save** (206-533-6655). In Aberdeen, you'll again find **U-Save** (206-533-4230). In Forks, there's **Birdwell Ford** (206-374-6556).

PUBLIC TRANSPORTATION

For local bus service in the northern Olympic Peninsula, including Port Angeles and Sequim, call **Clallam Transit** (206-452-4511) in Port Angeles. Port Townsend and eastern Jefferson County are served by **Jefferson Transit** (206-385-4777). The **Grays Harbor Transportation Authority** (206-532-2770) offers bus service to Aberdeen, Ocean Shores and the surrounding region.

Bus service between Raymond, Long Beach and Astoria, Oregon, is provided by the **Pacific Transit System** (206-642-9418).

CHAPTER FIVE

The Cascades
and Central Washington

Perhaps without even realizing it, many Americans have a burning image of this region. For it was here, in the Cascade Range, that Mt. St. Helens blew its top in 1980. But the area has a lot more going for it than one hyperactive mountaintop. Indeed, think of the Cascades and Central Washington as one wild place for anyone who loves the outdoors.

The Cascade Range contains some of the most beautiful mountain scenery in the United States, much of it preserved by two major national parks, several national recreation areas and numerous wilderness areas that make this a major sports haven. There are also glaciers galore; 318 are in the North Cascades National Park alone. Thousands of miles of trails and logging roads lace the Cascades, leading to mountaintop lookout towers, old gold mines, lakes, streams and gorgeous sights.

The hand of man has done little to alter the Cascades. Not until 1952 did a highway cross the state north of Route 2. And when the North Cascades Highway (Route 20) was completed, it was with the understanding that it would be closed during the heavy snows, usually from October until May. Thus, most of the Cascades are still wild and remote, seen and experienced by humans but not transformed by them.

The range, about 700 miles long, begins at the Fraser River in southern British Columbia and extends southward through Washington and Oregon and into California just beyond Lassen Peak. The most dominant feature of the Cascades is the 15 volcanoes. Washington lays claim to five, with Mt. Rainier the granddaddy at 14,410 feet. However, these elevations are not the norm. Most peaks are under 10,000 feet, and Harts Pass, the highest pass in the state, is only 6197 feet.

Although the range is not a comparatively high one, it served as an effective barrier to exploration and development until well into the 20th century. The pioneers who came over the Oregon Trail avoided it, choosing instead to go down the Columbia River to the Cowlitz River, travel up to present-day Toledo, then move overland to Puget Sound at Tumwater and Olympia.

Mining has always been part of the Cascades story. Although no major gold strikes have been found, several smaller ones have kept the interest alive, and there's probably never been a day since the mid-1870s when someone wasn't panning or sluicing in the mountains.

The range supports a wide variety of plants and wildlife because it has so many climatic zones. Naturalists have given names to eight distinct ones: Coastal Forest Zone, Silver Fir Zone, Sierran Mixed-Conifer Zone, Red Fir Zone, Subalpine Zone, Alpine Zone, Interior Fir Zone and Ponderosa Pine Zone. Each zone has its own community of plants, animals and birds.

Although most of the range is under the stewardship of the Forest Service, which by law has to practice multiple-use policies, most people think of the Cascades as their very own. It is used by mushroom hunters, hikers, runners, birdwatchers, anglers, hunters, photographers, painters, skiers, horse riders, loggers and miners. Whichever of these apply to you, enjoy.

North Cascades

Extending from the Canadian border south into the Mt. Baker-Snoqualmie National Forest, the North Cascades region has over 300 glaciers, valleys famous for their spring tulip fields and some of the best skiing in the Pacific Northwest. Backroads wind through old logging towns past mountain lakes to unspoiled wilderness areas. The North Cascades National Park forms the core of this realm that includes Rainy and Washington passes, two of the Cascades' grandest viewpoints.

Beginning at the northernmost approach, **Route 542** enters the Cascades from Bellingham, a pleasant, two-lane, blacktop highway that is shared by loggers, skiers, anglers and hikers. Much of the route runs through dense forest beside fast streams and with only rare glimpses of the surrounding mountains. The road deadends just beyond the Mt. Baker day-use lodge for skiers. In clear weather you will see 9127-foot **Mt. Shuksan**, one of the most beautiful peaks in the Cascades. It can't be seen from any other part of the range, but it probably appears on more calendars and postcards than its neighbor Mt. Baker or even Mt. Rainier.

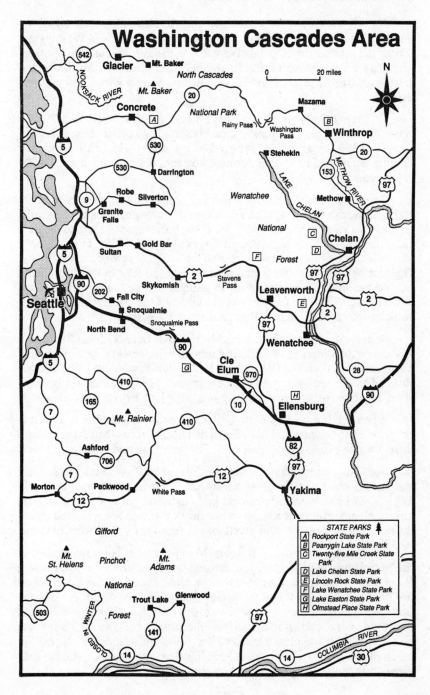

Washington Cascades Area

STATE PARKS 🌲
A Rockport State Park
B Pearrygin Lake State Park
C Twenty-five Mile Creek State Park
D Lake Chelan State Park
E Lincoln Rock State Park
F Lake Wenatchee State Park
G Lake Easton State Park
H Olmstead Place State Park

The Mt. Baker ski slopes usually open in November and run all the way into June, making it the longest ski season of any area in Washington. During the summer the mountain is popular with day hikers and backpackers who often hike over Austin Pass between Mt. Shuksan and Mt. Baker and down to Baker Lake, an artificial lake behind Seattle City Light's Lower Baker Dam.

Mt. Baker was named by George Vancouver on April 30, 1792, in honor of James Baker, a lieutenant on his ship. It was first climbed on August 17, 1868, by a party of four led by an experienced alpinist named Thomas Stratton. Listed as a dormant volcano, it last erupted some 6000 years ago.

Route 20, one of America's premier scenic routes, goes through the North Cascades National Park and along the way provides hiking trails, roadside parks, boat launches and one of the more unusual tours in the Cascades, the **Seattle City Light Skagit Tours** (206-684-3030). This four-hour tour tells how Seattle built three dams on the Skagit to produce its electricity. The tour begins at Diablo with a boat ride up the lake to the dam, then a ride up the side of a mountain on an antique Incline Stairway Lift to the powerhouse. After the tour, guests are taken to the cookhouse for an all-you-can-eat chicken dinner. Reservations are required.

Because the highway is enclosed by the Ross Lake National Recreation Area, new development is virtually nonexistent, and the small company towns of Newhalem and Diablo look frozen in the pre-World War II days. Ross Lake, created by the hydroelectric project, is a fjord-like lake between steep mountains that eventually crosses over into British Columbia.

When driving on Route 20, be forewarned: No gasoline is available between Marblemount and Mazama, a distance of more than 70 miles, and there are few places to buy groceries. Fill your tank and bring your lunch.

Ross Lake on the Skagit River was formed by Ross Dam. Diablo Dam was built a short distance downstream, creating the much-smaller Diablo Lake. Ross Lake is an international body of water because its backwaters cross the border into Canada, and when the timber was being cleared before the lake was formed, the work was done via a road in from British Columbia.

An alternate way to reach Route 20 is over what is locally known as the **Mountain Loop Highway**, a favorite weekend drive for years before Route 20 was completed across the mountains. The Mountain Loop begins in Granite Falls with Route 92, which goes along the South Fork of the Stillaguamish River past the one-store towns of Robe, Verlot and Silverton. The road is crooked and slow driving because it follows the river route closely—it is always closed in the winter. Sometimes landslides close it for much of the summer. Near the old mining town of Monte Cristo, the road turns north along the Sauk River and emerges in the logging town of Darrington. Here you can drive due north to catch Route 20 at Rockport or turn west on Route 530 and return to Route 5.

Route 20 plunges into the Cascades and goes over two passes—**Rainy Pass**, 4860 feet, and **Washington Pass**, 5477 feet—before descending into the Methow Valley. Stop at each viewpoint and turnout for stunning views of the region. One viewpoint above Ross Lake shows miles of the long, narrow lake, and another just beyond Washington Pass gives a grandstand view of the jagged mountains behind the pass.

The only way to visit the resort town of **Stehekin**, at the tip of Lake Chelan, is by boat, plane or hiking. Most visitors take the trip up the lake on the **Lady of the Lake**, the tour-mail-supply boat for Stehekin and points between. The schedule allows you three-and-a-half hours in Stehekin, and you can buy lunch either on the boat or at the Stehekin landing.

NORTH CASCADES HOTELS

The nearest lodging to Mt. Baker is the **Snowline Inn** (10433 Mt. Baker Highway, Glacier; 206-599-2788), a condominium complex with 45 units, about half with sleeping lofts. The pseudo-chalet, two-story building is set back in the trees away from the busy highway. The units with sleeping lofts can sleep up to four and have two double beds and a half-bath upstairs and a full bath with fold-out couch and bunk beds just inside the front door. The smaller units are also designed for up to four persons. All have completely equipped kitchens, and the loft units have microwaves. Moderate.

The **Glacier Creek Motel** (Box A, Glacier, WA 98244; 206-599-2991) earns its description of rustic. It is a motel with nine units and 12 blue-and-white cabins. The large lobby is a combination gift shop and espresso bar with a few café tables. The cabins are one room with bath, a kitchen, double bed and tired furniture. Heat is provided by an electric heater. The motel units are so small there's no room for a table. Budget to moderate.

Just west of Concrete, the **Cascade Mountain Inn** (3840 Pioneer Lane, Birdsview; 206-826-4333) has become very popular since opening in the mid-1980s. A true country inn, it was fashioned by owners Ingrid and Gerhard Meyer to look something like a barn. It has six rooms, all with private bath, each room furnished in the theme of a country in which the owners lived; the Philippines, Peru, the United States, Scotland and two from Germany. Large country breakfasts are served. The inn is open May 15 to October 15, plus the month of January because of the popularity of watching bald eagles along the nearby Skagit River. Moderate.

One of the larger lakeside resorts is **Baker Lake Resort** (P.O. Box 100, Concrete, WA 98237; 206-853-8325), 20 miles north of Concrete on Baker Lake Road. It is a mixture of RV sites and seven rustic cabins on the lake. The cabins have bathroom and showers, a refrigerator, dishes and cooking utensils, but guests must bring their own linen and towels. Boating and fishing are popular on the lake; boat rentals are available. Moderate.

Rustic reigns in remote Stehekin. *The* most outdoorsy is the **Stehekin Valley Ranch** (P.O. Box 36, Stehekin, WA 98852; 509-682-4677), owned and operated by the Courtneys, the major family in the valley. The ranch is nine miles from town, up the Stehekin River Valley. The accommodations are tent cabins with canvas-covered walls. Showers and toilets are in the main building. Guests are encouraged to bring their own sleeping bags and towels to save $5 per person. All meals are included and served in the dining room, which has split logs for tables and seats. Horseback rides, river float trips, scenic flights and day hikes are among the activities offered. Budget.

The fanciest Stehekin lodging is **Silver Bay Inn** (P.O. Box 43, Stehekin, WA 98852; 509-682-2212), at the head of the Stehekin River a short distance from the village. It has a large suite in the owners' home that includes a private bath and soaking tub, two decks and a breakfast that features Devonshire cream for your fresh fruit and scrambled eggs with cashews. Outside are two cabins that will sleep six and are complete with kitchens and dishwashers. Moderate to deluxe.

NORTH CASCADES RESTAURANTS

A popular place along the Mt. Baker Highway is **Milano's Market and Deli** (9990 Mt. Baker Highway, Glacier; 206-599-2863), a combination small restaurant and deli. With its café tables and black-and-white tile floor, it offers a hearty supply of soups, salads and homemade desserts. A good place to have a picnic lunch made up. If the weather is right the deck is open for outside dining. Moderate.

A mile east of Glacier, near the Snowline Inn, is a much larger restaurant with more of a rural flavor. **The Chandelier** (10458 Mt. Baker Highway; 206-599-2233) is built in the chalet style and divided into two sections with a large fireplace in the entrance hall. To the left is a large bar with the obligatory big-screen television set and wooden chairs and tables. The restaurant serves straightforward American food, large burgers, steaks, seafood, barbecued chicken, fresh strawberry pie and homemade cheese cakes. You can also have them make up box lunches for day trips. Moderate.

On the western edge of Concrete, **North Cascades Inn** (4284 Route 20; 206-853-8771) has established a local reputation for good, plain American food (steaks, chops, seafood) and delicious pie (made by a local woman especially for the restaurant). The exterior is decorated with farm and logging equipment, but the interior decor is softened a bit with antique furnishings and clothing. There's also a full service bar. Budget to moderate.

Keep in mind that there are no public restaurants in Stehekin. The only dining facilities are in the lodging places, and those are exclusively for guests.

NORTH CASCADES SHOPPING

In Concrete, stop in at **Fritzi's Quilts and Crafts Shoppe** (235 Main Street; 206-853-8932). She sells handmade quilts, potpourri and various other locally made products. If you're in town on Saturday during the summer months, hit the **Saturday Market** in the **North Cascades Visitor Center** (Route 20) for arts and crafts and baked goods.

NORTH CASCADES NIGHTLIFE

The Cascades isn't the place to go for nightlife. After a day traipsing around in the mountains, most people return to town tired and only want to eat and go to bed. Consequently, only the busiest areas even have live music.

Near Mt. Baker, the **Chandelier** (10458 Mt. Baker Highway; 206-599-2233) has live country and soft-rock music on weekends.

NORTH CASCADES BEACHES AND PARKS

Mt. Baker-Snoqualmie National Forest—This 1.7 million-acre forest begins at the Canadian border and goes south along the western slopes of the Cascades to Mt. Rainier National Park. It is dominated on the north by the inactive volcano, 10,778-foot Mt. Baker. Another inactive volcano, 10,568-foot Glacier Peak, lies in the middle of the forest. The Forest Service controls the land for the ski areas at Crystal Mountain, Mt. Baker and Snoqualmie Pass. Its best known wilderness area is Alpine Lakes Wilderness, but it also includes the Glacier Peak and Mt. Baker Wilderness areas.

Facilities: Picnic areas, restrooms and showers; restaurants and groceries in area towns; information, 206-775-9702. *Fishing:* Excellent for lake and rainbow trout in Baker Lake; other streams and lakes are equally good.

Camping: Permitted along the highways, trails and the Pacific Crest Trail, as well as at established campsites. Most of the 40-plus campgrounds are primitive with pit toilets and vary from walk-in to drive-in sites.

Getting there: Four east-west highways cross the national forest: Routes 90, 20, 2 and 410.

Rockport State Park—This park is essentially a large campground in a grove of old-growth Douglas fir. Most of the camping areas are shielded from one another by thick undergrowth. It is within easy walking distance of the Skagit River, which makes it popular with steelheaders.

Facilities: Picnic areas, restrooms and five miles of footpaths (one trail accommodates wheelchairs); restaurants and groceries a mile away in Rockport; information, 206-853-8461. *Fishing:* Excellent trout and steelhead fishing in the Skagit River.

Camping: There are 61 sites: 50 RV, eight tent and three primitive.

Getting there: Located on Route 20 one mile west of Rockport.

Howard Miller Steelhead County Park—One of the most popular parks on the Skagit River for anglers and travelers alike, it covers 93 acres and has extensive museum exhibits of a historic cabin, an old river ferry and dugout canoe. The clubhouse is a popular hangout for local anglers.

Facilities: Picnic areas, boat launch, volleyball court, playground, clubhouse, restrooms, showers and trailer dump; restaurants and groceries nearby; information, 206-853-8808. *Fishing:* Excellent steelheading.

Camping: There are 40 tent sites and 20 RV sites.

Getting there: Located in the middle of Rockport on Route 20.

North Cascades National Park—Covering 505,000 acres in the north-central part of the state, this park is divided into two units. The northern unit runs from the Canadian border to **Ross Lake National Recreation Area**. The southern unit continues on to the **Lake Chelan National Recreation Area**. Much of its eastern boundary is the summit of the Cascade Range, and the western boundary is the Mt. Baker-Snoqualmie National Forest. It is the most rugged and remote of the national parks in Washington and has the fewest roads. All visitor facilities and roads in the northern portion are inside the Ross Lake National Recreation Area. On the southern end, the Lake Chelan National Recreation Area covers the heavy-use area on the north end of the lake, including the city of Stehekin.

Facilities: Picnic areas, restrooms and nature walks; no restaurants or groceries stores; rangers sometimes lead nature walks from the Colonial Creek and Newhalem campgrounds; information, 509-682-2549. *Fishing:* Excellent for rainbow trout in Ross Lake, steelhead in the Skagit River downstream from Newhalem and rainbow and eastern brook trout in high lakes.

Camping: Permitted in summer only at Goodell Creek, Newhalem, Colonial Creek, Lone Fir and Early Winters campgrounds along Route 20.

Getting there: Only Route 20 goes through North Cascades National Park, and it is closed in winter, generally from mid-November to April.

Methow Valley

The scenery changes quickly and dramatically once you've crossed Washington Pass into the Methow Valley. Located along Route 20 between Mazama and Pateros, this region includes the tourist center of Chelan, gateway to one of the state's most popular lake-resort areas.

As you descend the east slope of the Cascades, the thick, fir forest gives way to smaller pine with almost no underbrush. The mountains become bare, and you can see for miles. And by the time you arrive in **Winthrop** you will wonder if you are in Colorado or Wyoming because the small town is all falsefronts, saloon doors, hitching rails and wooden porches.

Winthrop adopted the Wild West theme several years ago, and it revitalized the sawmill town and surrounding area to one of the state's most popular destinations. **The Shafer Museum** (one block up the hill off Route 20; 509-996-2712) is in the cabin built by town founder Guy Waring in 1897 and has exhibits from the valley's early days, including a stagecoach and antique automobiles.

There are several areas around Winthrop worth driving to, including 6197-foot **Harts Pass** (★) a short distance from town. This is the highest point to which you can drive in Washington and is only an hour's drive on a gravel Forest Service road. The views from the summit are spectacular.

Not long after driving south on Route 153, the last of the timbered mountains are left behind, and the Methow Valley flattens into a series of irrigated ranches with broad hayfields. The valley is gaining popularity with people from Puget Sound looking for more space, so houses are beginning to line the low hills on both sides.

When you reach the **Columbia River** at Pateros, the landscape is one of basaltic cliffs on both sides of the river. Instead of a fast-flowing river there is a chain of lakes behind dams all the way past Wenatchee. Route 97 hugs the west side of the Columbia, then swings away from the river to go through the resort town of Chelan, which sits at the end of **Lake Chelan**.

The lake is a remnant of the Ice Ages. Scoured out of the mountains by glaciers, it is one of the deepest lakes in the region, more than 1500 feet deep in at least one place, which places its bed at 400 feet below sea level. It is 55 miles long and narrow, and the mountains rising from its shores make it look like a Norwegian fjord.

Chelan is a small town that has been given over almost entirely to tourism. Woodin Avenue is the main drag and the lakefront is lined with resorts, but the small-town atmosphere is retained so a farmer can come to town and still buy a two-by-four or a cotter pin.

The **Lake Chelan Museum** (Woodin Avenue and Emerson Street; 509-682-5644) displays some Native American artifacts, early farming and orchard equipment. One room depicts a miner's cabin, and another shows a typical country kitchen. In addition to tourism, Chelan has some of the best **orchards** along the eastern slopes of the Cascades. If you take a drive northwest of town on Route 150 to Manson you will see thousands of acres of apple orchards climbing up the sun-baked hills from the lake. Every Wednesday the largest shipper in the area, **Blue Chelan** (100 Route 150; 509-682-4541), offers tours through their facility.

METHOW VALLEY HOTELS

If you want to get up close and personal with the North Cascades, head for the **Early Winters Cabins** (Mazama; 509-996-2355). The six cabins sit across the highway from the Forest Service/National Park Service information center at the foot of the mountains. Small and widely spaced apart, the cabins are heated with fireplaces; large stacks of firewood with chopblock and axes are outside each one. Electric heaters warm the bathrooms. All cooking utensils are provided for the woodstove cooking. Hiking and cross-country skiing are right outside the door. Budget to moderate.

The most elaborate place in the Methow Valley, and one of the best resorts in the Northwest, is **Sun Mountain Lodge** (P.O. Box 1000, Winthrop, WA 98862; 509-996-2211). Built at the 5000-foot level atop a small mountain, this low-rise, stone-and-timber resort gives a 360-degree view of the Cascades, Pasayten Wilderness, Okanogan Highlands and Methow Valley. The 86 units are spread over two buildings atop the mountain and down the road in eight rustic, cozy cabins. The resort has just about everything: several miles of hiking trails that become cross-country ski trails in the winter, pool, two hot tubs, exercise room, sauna, the largest string of saddle-and-pack horses in the state, mountain-bike rentals, canoe and sailing on the lake, heli-skiing and tennis. It also has a great restaurant. Rooms feature bentwood furniture, a fireplace (only the suites have real-wood fireplaces), coffee, the thickest and softest towels you can hope for and no television. Deluxe to ultra-deluxe.

Right in the heart of Western-themed Winthrop you'll find the **Trails End Motel** (P.O. Box 189, Winthrop, WA 98862; 509-996-2303) with its tall falsefront and wooden porch. The 12 units are simply furnished, and big windows look down onto Main Street. In season, the area's oldest irrigation canal runs behind the motel. A bookstore anchors one end of the building. Budget.

On the south edge of Winthrop is the **Early American Virginian Motel and Restaurant** (808 North Cascades Highway; 509-996-2535). Located on the high bank of the Methow River, the riverfront rooms in this 39-unit motel and seven cabins have balconies. Cedar was used extensively, and most units retain the pleasant aroma. Cabins are a bit more expensive, but several have fireplaces and room enough for six. Kitchens are large and well equipped; all have microwaves. Moderate.

The oldest and most reliable resort in Chelan is **Campbell's** (104 West Woodin Avenue; 509-682-2561), which has been in business since 1901. With 148 rooms it is still growing along the lakeshore in the heart of town. It has three heated pools, an outdoor jacuzzi, good beach and boat moorage. The rooms range from standard with queen-sized beds to larger rooms with kitchenettes and two queen beds, decorated in softer pastels. Moderate to deluxe in price.

One of the most complete resorts inside the Chelan city limits is **Darnell's Resort Motel** (901 Spader Road; 509-682-2015), a few blocks southwest of the city center on Route 150. It has a heated pool and hot tub, sauna and fitness center, putting greens, lighted tennis courts, swimming beach, boats and bicycle rentals, waterskiing, volleyball, badminton and conference rooms. The resort is divided into two three-story buildings. All rooms have peeled logs and exposed wood and come with balconies and a view of the lake. All units are called suites because they have separate bedrooms; some have two bedrooms, and the larger units have sleeping lofts. The penthouse suites have two fireplaces and private jacuzzi. Deluxe to ultra-deluxe in price.

Another bed and breakfast is **Mary Kay's Romantic Whaley Mansion** (415 3rd Street, Chelan; 509-682-5735). This white, frame house trimmed in pink has six rooms decorated with antiques from the family collection. Bamboo bird cages have singing canaries inside; a footstool has antlers for legs; ribbons and garlands of artificial flowers are everywhere. The guest rooms, on the second and third floors, are decorated with flowered wallpaper and have white-iron-and-brass beds and private baths. In addition to a hearty breakfast that includes champagne-dipped chocolates, Mary Kay will sing with the player piano accompanying her. Gay-friendly. Moderate.

On the eastern edge of Chelan is the clean and comfortable **Apple Inn Motel** (1002 East Woodin Avenue; 509-682-4044) with white, stucco walls and black trim of wood. The 41 rooms are decorated in knotty pine and are small and clean; some have kitchenettes. The outdoor pool is heated, and a hot tub is open year-round. Budget to moderate.

METHOW VALLEY RESTAURANTS

The newest restaurant to get statewide attention is the **Eagle's Nest** (Sun Mountain Lodge, Patterson Lake Road, Winthrop; 509-996-2211). The room is cantilevered with views down into the Methow Valley and Winthrop 5000 feet below. All seats have a view. The food is wonderful. The chef, Jack Hanes, spent some time in Arizona so he brought some Southwest-flavored dishes with him, including breaded cactus sautéed in olive oil and stuffed with black beans. Other dishes include a wild-game sampler (venison *foie gras*, rabbit sausage, broiled quail in raspberry sauce) steaks and seafood. Deluxe to ultra-deluxe.

One of Winthrop's most trendy restaurants is the oddly named **Duck Brand Cantina** (248 Riverside Avenue; 509-996-2192) in the hotel of the same name. The menu reflects an effort to please several palates, including Mexican, American, Continental and vegetarian. The restaurant is divided into three areas; a café with naugahyde booths, a dining room with several old, oak tables and hanging greenery, and a deck overlooking Winthrop's sole street. Moderate.

Another moderately priced establishment is **Virginian Restaurant** (Virginian Hotel, 816 North Cascades Highway; 509-996-2536), decorated in pure Early American with lots of red on the walls and chairs, bottles of herbs and spices, potted plants and baskets. The menu is strictly American:

steak, prawns, chicken and pork. Off the entrance is the Bicycle Bar with a gas-powered fireplace and casual seating.

Although **Campbell's Lodge** (401 East Woodin Avenue, Chelan; 509-682-2561) is so large that it overwhelms some people, it is hard to find a better place in the area for a good meal. The large room seats about 80 and is pleasantly decorated in Early American furnishings and maroon walls with an eclectic collection of prints, documents and paintings. The menu is large: prime rib, medallions of pork, broiled leg of lamb, chicken coronado, prawns provençal and a variety of pasta. Deluxe.

A few doors down from Campbell's on the lakefront is **River Park Dining** (114 East Woodin Avenue; 509-682-5626). It has two floors—a sun room on the top floor and an enclosed patio on the lower—and specializes in lunches of sandwiches (some are purely vegetarian), soups and salads. Dinner offers a series of specials throughout the week, salmon, prime rib and chicken among them. Budget to moderate.

METHOW VALLEY SHOPPING

Art is big, and often very good in Winthrop, especially in the **Riverside Gallery** (114 Riverside Avenue; 509-996-2166) where you will find paintings, sculpture and photographs. Other artworks, some by nationally known artists such as Richard Beyer, are usually on exhibit in the public rooms at **Sun Mountain Lodge** (Patterson Lake Road; 509-996-2211). For photographs by the area's best-known photographer, Bob Spiwak, try **Winthrop Mountain Sports** (133 South Route 20; 509-996-2886).

Art is also a growth industry in the Chelan area. Beyer and Rod Weagant exhibit at the **Manson Gallery** (Washington and Ford streets, Manson; 509-687-3959). It is open weekends during the summer and by appointment. Another is the **Signature Gallery** (114 East Woodin Avenue, Chelan; 509-682-2423), selling handmade furnishings and prints, weavings, pottery and jewelry.

However, apple is king in Chelan and the **Harvest Tree** (109 East Woodin Avenue; 509-682-3618) is a mail-order store for several choices of packages of apples and other food items. Their competition is **Ellen's Happy Apples** (7794 Entiat River Road, Entiat; 509-784-1815), just down the road a piece from Chelan. Ellen ships apples in a variety of wooden boxes.

METHOW VALLEY NIGHTLIFE

In Winthrop the **Winthrop Palace** (149 Riverside Avenue; 509-996-2245) offers live rock and country music most nights during the summer (weekends only during the winter).

Chelan has a few more choices, nearly all featuring live disco, rock and country music and dancing during the summer months. **Uncle Bub's**

(502 East Woodin Avenue; 509-682-2013) has live disco music on weekends and a deejay from Tuesday through Thursday. **Chelanigans** (Woodin Avenue and Sanders Street; 509-682-5137) features live rock and country music Wednesday through Saturday, summers only.

METHOW VALLEY BEACHES AND PARKS

Pearrygin Lake State Park—This is a popular park for travelers in RVs because it is close to Winthrop and has a sandy beach on a small lake surrounded by mountains. It is also a hotspot for boaters, anglers and snowmobilers during the winter, although the park is closed from December until April.

Facilities: Picnic areas, restrooms and showers; restaurants and groceries in Winthrop; information, 509-996-2370. *Swimming:* Permitted but no lifeguard. *Fishing:* Permitted.

Camping: There are 57 RV hookup sites and 29 tent sites.

Getting there: Located five miles north of Winthrop on Route 20.

Lake Chelan State Park—This is a favorite park for Puget Sound youths yearning for sunshine, and in July and August the beach looks more like California than Washington with its broad, sandy beach and play area. Because it has docks and launching areas for skiers, it is equally popular with power boaters and waterskiers.

Facilities: Picnic tables, restrooms, showers and boat-launch facility; information and campsite reservations, 509-687-3710. *Swimming:* Great, has lifeguards. *Fishing:* In Lake Chelan away from watersports.

Camping: By reservation; 127 tent sites and 17 RV hookup sites.

Getting there: Nine miles west of Chelan on Route 150.

Twenty-Five Mile Creek State Park—More remote than Lake Chelan State Park but popular with those more interested in mountain scenery than body scenery, it is quiet, with the Chelan Mountains behind and the jagged peaks of the Sawtooth Wilderness across the lake. The small beach is mostly for wading.

Facilities: Picnic areas, restrooms, showers and playground; concession offers snacks, groceries and fishing supplies; information, 509-687-3610. *Fishing:* In Lake Chelan.

Camping: There are 52 tent sites and 33 RV hookups.

Getting there: It's 18 miles west of Chelan on 25-Mile Creek Road.

Lincoln Rock State Park—Named for a rock outcropping that resembles Abraham Lincoln's profile, this is a heavily used state park in the Columbia River canyon a short distance north of Wenatchee. In addition to swimming and boating, park users may also take tours of the Rocky Reach

Dam a mile away. Several species of wildlife also reside in the park, including rabbits, deer, beaver, nighthawks and swallows.

Facilities: Picnic shelters, restrooms, showers, volleyball courts, playfield and play equipment for children; information 509-884-8702. *Fishing:* In the Columbia River.

Camping: There are 27 tent sites and 33 RV hookup sites.

Getting there: It's six miles north of East Wenatchee on Route 2.

Wenatchee Area

Famous for its apple orchards, the sunny Wenatchee Area is located in the heart of Washington. Popular with rafters and gold panners, this region is also home to one of the state's most picturesque gardens.

You have a choice of two highways when leaving Chelan: You can continue along Route 97, which cuts through the Cascade foothills back to the Columbia River and south to Wenatchee, or cross the Columbia at Chelan Falls, hardly more than a junction, and follow the lesser-used Route 151 south through the orchard town of Orando to East Wenatchee. Stop at **Rocky Reach Dam**, 28 miles south of Chelan, to visit the Fish Viewing Room where declining numbers of migratory salmon and steelhead swim past the windows. The dam also has two small museums, one showing the natural and human history of the Columbia River, complete with a handcarved Native American canoe, parts of steamboats and orchard equipment. The Gallery of Electricity also has hands-on exhibits that let you create electricity.

Wenatchee is the largest town in this region and directed more toward orchards than tourists, although you will certainly feel welcome. On the northern edge of town, overlooking the Columbia River, Wenatchee and Rocky Reach Dam, is **Ohme Gardens** (3327 Ohme Road; 509-662-5785). You'll find nine acres of alpine gardens built by an orchardist on the steep, rocky outcroppings at the edge of his property.

Downtown, the **North Central Washington Museum** (127 South Mission Street; 509-664-5989) has several permanent exhibits including a 1919 Wurlitzer theater pipe organ and an apple-packing shed featuring an apple wiper, sizing machine and a 1924 orchard truck. On the western edge of town is the **Washington Apple Commission Visitor Center** (2900 Euclid Avenue; 509-663-9600) which has another museum exhibit, but this one offers apple tasting; samples of different varieties of apples are given. The gift shop sells sweatshirts and other items with the commission message.

Ten miles west via Routes 2 and 97, **Cashmere**, so-named because it reminded a pioneer of Kashmir, India, has an Early American theme to its downtown buildings. The **Chelan County Historical Museum and Pio-**

neer Village (Big Rock Place and Cottage Avenue; 509-782-3230) has more than two dozen original buildings from Chelan and Douglas counties assembled to re-create a pioneer village, including a blacksmith shop, school, gold mine and hotel.

Liberty Orchards (117–123 Mission Street; 509-782-2191) offers 15-minute tours of its candy factory with samples of its product—Aplets, Cotlets and Grapelets, fruit-and-nut confections sprinkled with powdered sugar.

From Cashmere, Routes 2 and 97 follow the swift Wenatchee River into the Cascades. Shortly before reaching Leavenworth, Route 97 turns south toward the Route 90 Corridor towns of Cle Elum and Ellensburg by going over 4101-foot **Swauk Pass**. An alternative route, in the summer only, is to follow the **Old Blewett Pass Highway**, which has been preserved by the Wenatchee National Forest. The old highway is a series of switchbacks with sweeping views of the Cascades. No services are available until Cle Elum and Ellensburg, other than a small grocery store at **Liberty**, a gold-mining town just off the highway that is making a comeback as people move into its modest cabins along a single street.

WENATCHEE AREA HOTELS

Most hotels in Wenatchee are spotted along North Wenatchee Avenue. The newest and tallest is the **WestCoast Wenatchee Center** (201 North Wenatchee Avenue; 509-662-1234), at nine stories one of the tallest buildings along the eastern edge of the Cascades. The 148 rooms are larger than at most other hotels in town and suites have double sofas, potted plants and honor bars. A large lobby is lighted by a row of angled skylights. The hotel has a restaurant, an indoor-outdoor pool and a fitness center. Moderate.

For a budget-priced place, try the **Orchard Inn** (1401 North Miller Street; 509-662-3443). It has 103 rooms on two floors decorated with subtly flowered bedspreads, unobtrusive furniture and wallhangings. A heated pool and spa, and conference room round out the package.

If you want to be close to Routes 2 and 97, the best place is across the Columbia River in the **Rivers Inn** (580 Valley Mall Parkway, East Wenatchee; 509-884-1474). With 55 units on two floors that surround the heated pool, it is unpretentious but has basic, comfortable rooms with cable television, and there's always coffee in the office (after 7 a.m. free rolls are available). Moderate.

The **Cashmere Country Inn** (5801 Pioneer Avenue; 509-782-4212) is putting the town of Cashmere on the map. Owners Dale and Patti Swanson are unofficial ambassadors for this town, having remodeled an old farmhouse into a four-room inn that follows the Early American theme of Cashmere. Two rooms have shared baths. An area also has been set aside for guests' lounging. Breakfasts are imaginative with several kinds of fruit, crêpes and other lighter-than-air fare. Moderate.

More impersonal is the **Village Inn Motel** (229th Cottage Avenue, Cashmere; 509-782-3522) in the heart of town. The white-and-green motel has 21 units, six with refrigerators. Clean, quiet and reasonably priced. Budget to moderate.

WENATCHEE AREA RESTAURANTS

A top-notch steakhouse is **The Windmill** (1501 North Wenatchee Avenue; 509-663-3478). It is down to earth with waitresses who have been there for years. A blackboard keeps a running total of the number of steaks sold there since 1982, when the present owners took over. Seafood and pork chops also are offered, and fresh-baked pies round out the meals. Moderate.

One of Wenatchee's apple-pioneer homes has become a popular restaurant. The owners of the **John Horan House** (2 Horan Road; 509-663-0018) have turned three upstairs bedrooms into rooms for private parties, and the downstairs dining room has a fireplace that is welcome on chilly evenings. The fixed-price menu has dishes that range from roast pork to cassoulet and pasta dishes. Moderate.

As a reflection of Central Washington's growing Hispanic population, **Tequila's** (800 North Wenatchee Avenue; 509-662-7239) is owned by former residents of Mexico. The refried beans are homemade, and the salsa is as tangy as you'll get in Guadalajara. Budget.

If you're staying across the river in East Wenatchee, the best stop for a straightforward American menu with nice surroundings and a view of the river is **Rivers-Haven** (560 Valley Mall Parkway; 509-884-0988). The room is tiered so that all tables have the same view, and the lights are kept low. Expect steaks, shrimp and prawns in generous helpings. Deluxe.

WENATCHEE AREA SHOPPING

In Wenatchee, **Victorian Village** (611 South Mission Street) is a small mall constructed in the best of the Victorian Carpenter Gothic style—round towers, falsefronts and steeples. You will find fabrics, antiques and, interestingly for a Victorian theme, a Mexican restaurant. If you like stores with an eclectic attitude, try **Wells & Wade Hardware** (201 15th Avenue South; 509-662-7173). It stocks everything "from fine china to hardware." And if need a fix for an urban-sized mall, the **Valley Mall** (511 Valley Mall Parkway, East Wenatchee) has 47 stores, making it the largest shopping center you'll encounter in the shadow of the Cascades.

WENATCHEE AREA NIGHTLIFE

Although Wenatchee is the largest town along the Cascades, it doesn't have a wider choice than its smaller neighbors. The Chieftain's **Pow Wow**

Room (1005 North Wenatchee Avenue; 509-663-8141) features live Top-40 and country-and-western dance music Tuesday through Saturday.

WENATCHEE AREA BEACHES AND PARKS

Wenatchee National Forest—At 2.1 million acres, Wenatchee is one of the largest national forests in the United States. It encompasses seven wilderness areas, hundreds of lakes, downhill-ski areas and 2500 miles of trails for hiking, riding and biking (including the Pacific Crest National Scenic Trail). It also joins two of the state's three national parks, North Cascades and Mt. Rainier.

Facilities: Picnic areas, restrooms and showers; restaurants and groceries in towns nearby; information, 509-662-4335. *Fishing:* Salmon, steelhead, searun cutthroat trout, Dolly Varden, bass, crappie, walleye and sturgeon are among the fish found in streams and lakes.

Camping: There are more than 60 campgrounds.

Getting there: Crossed by Routes 20, 2 and 90.

Leavenworth Area

Think Bavarian! That is the order of the day when visiting **Leavenworth,** one of the major tourist spots in the Cascades. Almost everything here—architecture, hotels, restaurants, annual events—is centered around that theme. Mountains are on three sides, and a river rushes through town. During most of the summer, free concerts and dancing exhibitions are given in the City Park, and outdoor art exhibits are held on weekends.

Just west of Leavenworth, Route 2 enters **Tumwater Canyon,** which follows the Wenatchee River some 20 miles. It is marked by sheer canyon walls, plunging river rapids and deciduous trees along the riverbank that turn into brilliant colors each autumn.

Route 2 continues over **Stevens Pass,** a popular ski area and where the **Pacific Crest National Scenic Trail** (see "Hiking" below) crosses the highway. Soon after crossing the summit and passing Skykomish, the **Sky-komish River** parallels the highway. This is one of Western Washington's most popular whitewater rivers. Most trips originate in the small, alpine village of **Index,** a short distance off the highway. The sheer-faced, 5979-foot **Mt. Index** looms behind the town. From there, the river rumbles down past the small towns of **Gold Bar** and **Sultan,** then flattens out onto the Puget Sound lowlands.

LEAVENWORTH AREA HOTELS

If you like cuckoo clocks, fancy woodwork, beer steins and alpenhorns, you'll love staying in Leavenworth. One of the most pleasant spots is the **Pension Anna** (926 Commercial Street; 509-548-6273). It has 14 rooms with furniture and decor imported from Austria and has been decorated in the theme of a farmhouse. Heavy, wooden bed frames and cupboards are used throughout. Two suites come with fireplace and jacuzzi, and all rooms have private baths. Breakfast is included. Prices are in the moderate to deluxe range.

A Bavarian wood carver was imported to fashion the rails and ceiling beams of the **Enzian Motor Inn** (590 Route 2; 509-548-5269), and the entire 104-room motel with its turrets and chalet-styled roofs shows similar touches. The four suites have king-sized beds, spas and fireplaces. It has indoor and outdoor pools and a year-round hot tub. During the winter, free cross-country ski equipment is available to guests. The complimentary Continental breakfast is served in the big solarium on the fourth floor. Moderate to ultra-deluxe.

For a change of pace, try renting one of the **Holiday Townhouses** (P.O. Box 254, Leavenworth, WA 98826; 509-548-6173) next door to the Enzian Motor Inn. The ten townhouses are divided into one- and two-bedroom units that sleep six and eight respectively. They have cathedral ceilings with sleeping lofts, and full kitchen with all appliances. Deluxe.

More and more bed and breakfasts and inns are opening outside town. One is **Run of the River** (9308 East Leavenworth Road; 509-548-7171), a mile out on the Icicle River. The building is made of logs and has cathedral ceilings with pine walls and handmade log furniture. The four rooms come with private baths, cable television and plush, terrycloth robes. Each room also has its own deck and woodstove. Stay here, kick back and just contemplate the beautiful setting. Breakfasts are country-style. (For the health-conscious, this inn is for non-smokers only.) Moderate.

Skykomish is the closest town to Stevens Pass and where some skiers spend the night. Two inexpensive hotels are in the tiny downtown area. **Cascadia Hotel and Café** (P.O. Box 93, Skykomish, WA 98288; 206-677-2390), directly across the street from the old depot, is a reminder of when passenger trains stopped there. The rooms are bare-bones in amenities but clean. All ten rooms share baths. (A few permanent residents live there.) Prices are budget.

Further down the mountain you'll find the **Dutch Cup Motel** (918 Main Street, Sultan; 206-793-2215), which is popular with skiers (they offer ski packages that include lift tickets, two meals nearby in the Dutch Cup Restaurant and lodging). The two-story motel has 20 units with queen-sized beds and cable television. Budget.

LEAVENWORTH AREA RESTAURANTS

Reiner's Gasthaus (829 Front Street; 509-548-5111) is one of the best restaurants in Leavenworth for such delights as potato pancakes, homemade egg dumplings, pan-fried veal and beef goulash along with a variety of steaks and pork tenderloin. Moderate.

Want Italian? Try **Viscounti's Italian Restaurant** (217 8th Street; 509-782-0204). Both Southern and Northern Italian dishes are offered in a family-friendly atmosphere. Moderate.

The first place to eat after coming down off Stevens Pass is the **Sky Chalet** (Route 2, Skykomish; 206-677-2223), a large restaurant with a choice of buffet line or menu service. It has large booths with high backs and open tables and serves country breakfasts all day. Lunch specials might be swedish meatballs or chicken-fried steak. The dinner menu is unembellished—steaks, pork chops, chicken and salmon in season. Moderate.

In Index, the best place to eat is in the **Bush House Country Inn** (300 5th Street; 206-793-2312). Here, in the century-old hotel dining room you will find a big, stone fireplace and generous portions of dishes such as aged beef, fresh fish, chicken, fruits and vegetables—all at budget prices. The Sunday brunches include omelets, homemade pastries, biscuits and gravy and fresh fruit.

The Dutch Cup Restaurant (927 Main Street, Sultan; 206-793-1864) is one of the most popular restaurants on the Stevens Pass route. It opens at 5 a.m. to catch the ski crowd as they head up the highway and stays open until 2 a.m. to get them on the way home. The menu includes country breakfasts, burgers, soups and sandwiches for lunch, steaks and chicken and weekend specials for dinner. Moderate.

LEAVENWORTH AREA SHOPPING

Leavenworth has the best selection of specialty shops in the Cascades; about 100 are crammed into a two-block area. **A Different Drummer** (725 Front Street; 509-548-5320) sells international greeting cards, other paper supplies and children's books. **The Clock Shop** (721 Front Street; 509-548-7725) has a large collection of antique and contemporary timepieces. It is an interesting place on the hour, quarter and half hour when the cuckoos perform a veritable symphony. **Gingerbread Cottage** (220 9th Street; 509-548-5718) is a delight for children and parents alike with all the cookies and gingerbread houses. It also sells tole, gifts, paints and other art supplies. **Village Book and Music** (215 9th Street; 509-548-5911) has a good selection of Northwest books and artwork and a wide selection of European tapes—handbell music and that sort of thing.

In Startup you will find the **Swing King and Gift Shop** (36606 Route 2; 206-793-1145), which sells only products handmade by local craftspeo-

ple, at least five of whom are in their 80s. In addition to smaller items—
sweaters, dolls and hats—the shop sells picnic tables and yard furniture.

LEAVENWORTH AREA NIGHTLIFE

Leavenworth has almost no nighttime entertainment; its movie theater
collapsed beneath a heavy snowfall several years ago and hasn't been replaced, and only one or two places offer live music after dark. One is the
Tumwater Inn (219 9th Street; 509-548-4232), which has a guitarist and
singer playing music of the '60s and '70s.

LEAVENWORTH AREA BEACHES AND PARKS

Lake Wenatchee State Park—The lake is tucked away near Stevens
Pass and is popular in summer for canoeing, kayaking, sailing, swimming
and fishing and in the winter for cross-country skiing and snowmobiling.
The secluded, wooded campsites are great.

Facilities: Picnic areas, restrooms, showers, rental boats, horses and
evening interpretive programs; information, 509-763-3101. *Fishing:* Good.

Camping: There are 197 tent sites.

Getting there: Sixteen miles north of Leavenworth and four miles off
Route 2 on Route 207.

Route 90 Corridor

This pristine area remains one of America's scenic icons. From snow-
capped peaks to dramatic waterfalls, the corridor is one of the Northwest's
hidden treasures. It extends from Snoqualmie across the Cascades to Ellensburg and the Kittitas Valley. Fasten your seat belts for a breathtaking ride
past volcanic peaks, fir forests and rivers where you're likely to land
tonight's dinner.

The Cascades begin rising only a half-hour's drive east of Seattle. The
town of **Snoqualmie** has an ornate, old railroad depot that is home to the
Puget Sound and Snoqualmie Valley Railroad (P.O. Box 459, Snoqualmie, WA 98065; 206-888-3030), which makes a ten-mile trip through the
Snoqualmie Valley on weekends and runs a special Christmas train. Nearby
is **Snoqualmie Falls**, a thundering cataract with a small park, observation
platform and trails leading to the river below the 268-foot falls.

The town of **North Bend** has adopted an alpine theme for its downtown
buildings, but it hasn't caught on with the vigor of Winthrop and Leaven-

Snow Bound

It's all downhill from here: Yes, friends, we are going to take you skiing. Whether you are into slopes or cross-country, the best ski areas in Washington are stretched along the Cascades from Mt. Baker to Mt. Rainier.

Beginning at the northernmost ski area and working south toward the Columbia River, **Mt. Baker** (206-734-6771) is 56 miles east of Bellingham on Route 542 and has an elevation range from 3500 to 5040 feet. The state's only helicopter skiing is **North Cascade Heli-Hiking** (509-996-3272), which operates out of Mazama.

Some skiers prefer **Stevens Pass** (206-973-2244), located on Route 2 about 80 miles east of Everett, because it at times has more powdery snow than spots at the summit of Snoqualmie Pass. One of the smaller ski areas is **Echo Valley** (509-684-4002), which sits ten miles northwest of Chelan on a dirt road off Route 150 and has elevations of 3000 to 3500 feet. Another small one is **Leavenworth Ski Hill** (509-548-5115) a mile north of Leavenworth with a 400-foot vertical drop.

Probably the best powder snow at a large ski area is at **Mission Ridge** (509-663-7631) 13 miles southwest of Wenatchee on Squilchuck Creek Road. But the largest operation of all is at Snoqualmie Pass 47 miles east of Seattle. Four major ski areas are to be found in a space of two miles: **Alpental** (206-434-6112), **Ski Acres** (206-434-6671), **Snoqualmie** (206-434-6161) and **Hyak** (206-434-7600). The average summit elevation is 5400 feet and base is 3000 feet. For information on snow conditions, call 206-976-7623.

Way up in the sky is **Crystal Mountain** (206-663-2265). Forty miles east of Enumclaw just off Route 410 and in the shadow of Mt. Rainier, the summit has an elevation of 7000 feet. Crystal has 32 major runs and 1000 acres of back country for cross-country skiing. In the same general area, **White Pass** (509-453-8731) is 20 miles east of Packwood on Route 12 southeast of Mt. Rainier.

Cross-country skiing is particularly popular on the eastern slopes of the mountains. Some of the best is in the Methow Valley where 90 miles of trails are marked, the majority of which are groomed. The **Methow Valley Ski Touring Association** (P.O. Box 147, Winthrop, WA 98862; 800-422-3048) has a hotline for ski-touring information and a brochure showing the major trails.

Two ski centers are near Chelan: **Echo Valley** (509-682-4002) has both cross-country and downhill skiing, and **Bear Mountain Ranch** (Route 1, P.O. Box 63B, Chelan, WA 98816; 509-682-5444), five miles downlake from Chelan, has 33 miles of groomed trails. The Leavenworth Area maintains several ski trails, including the Icicle River Trail, seven miles; and Ski Hill, three miles.

worth. Fans of the television show "Twin Peaks" will recognize Mt. Si, which looms behind town, from the show's opening credits.

The summit of **Snoqualmie Pass** has four major ski areas, for both downhill and cross-country, and a Forest Service combination museum and information center where you can pick up brochures and outdoor-recreation information. The small collection of artifacts relate to pioneers of the pass and antique ski equipment.

In **Cle Elum**, an Indian name meaning "swift water," you will find the unusual **Cle Elum Historical Telephone Museum** (221 East 1st Street; 509-674-5958) where old telephones, switchboards and other equipment from the area are displayed. At the foot of 4th Street is the access point for the 25-mile-long **Iron Horse State Park**, a section of the former railroad right of way with the rails and ties removed and the roadbed smoothed over for walking, jogging and cross-country skiing. It is part of the **John Wayne Pioneer Trail** that will eventually run the width of the state.

Three miles away is the tiny town of **Roslyn**, which is being used as the set for television's "Northern Exposure." It was formerly a coal-mining town with a large population of Italians, Croats, Slavs and Austrian immigrants who worked in the mines. There are separate cemeteries—23 in fact—for these nationalities.

As you drive through the Kittitas Valley to Ellensburg, notice that the prevailing wind off the Cascades gives trees a permanent lean toward the east. When you reach Ellensburg, you are out of the Cascades and entering the arid climate that characterizes most of the eastern side of Washington. **Ellensburg** is perhaps best known for its rodeo each Labor Day weekend, and in keeping with the Western legacy, the Western Art Association has its headquarters there and holds an annual show and sale each fall. The **Clymer Museum Gallery** (416 North Pearl Street; 509-962-6416) displays work by the famous Western artist who lived in Ellensburg. The **Kittitas County Historical Museum** (East 3rd Avenue and Pine Street; 509-925-3778) displays Native American artifacts and pioneer tools and has an extensive photograph collection. Three miles east of town is the **Olmstead Place State Park** (Route 5; 509-925-1943), a working farm that uses pioneer horse-drawn equipment. The 217-acre farm and all its buildings were deeded to the state.

ROUTE 90 CORRIDOR HOTELS

"Twin Peaks" aficionados will recognize the **Salish Lodge at Snoqualmie Falls** (P.O. Box 1109, Snoqualmie, WA 98065; 206-888-2556). But it deserves better than the way it was shown in the spooky opening credits. The Salish perches on the cliff overlooking the spectacular falls, one of the more dramatic settings for a hotel and restaurant in the Northwest. The 91 rooms are decorated in an upscale-country motif with down comforters,

wicker furniture and woodburning fireplaces. Only a few rooms have views
of the falls, but the interiors are so well done that most visitors console themselves by watching the falls from the lounge. Deluxe.

A less pricey place to stay is the **Edgewick Inn** (14600 468th Avenue
Southeast, North Bend; 206-888-9000). It is a straightforward motel with
44 clean and quiet units three miles east of town. Check into one of the
"star rooms," decorated with fluorescent paint to make it look as though
you're drifting off in a galaxy. Budget.

About the only place to stay at Snoqualmie Summit is the **Best Western
Summit Inn** (P.O. Box 163, Snoqualmie Pass, WA 99607; 206-434-6300).
Outfitted for skiers, its 81 rooms come with king- or queen-sized beds, and
it has a complimentary ski-storage area and coin-operated laundry. The
lobby is large and is stocked with comfortable sofas and wing-back chairs
set around the native-stone fireplace. Moderate.

A former railroad boarding house, **The Moore House** (526 Marie
Street, South Cle Elum; 509-674-5939) has been converted into one of the
state's best inns. The 11 rooms, half with shared baths, are named for former
roomers. All are decorated in turn-of-the-century antiques—with an emphasis, not surprisingly, on railroad trinkets and tools. There's even a remodeled
caboose sporting a queen-sized bed, refrigerator and sun deck. The Moore
House is adjacent to the Iron Horse Trail State Park, where cross-country
skiing, bicycling and walking are popular. Moderate.

Although this is supposedly the state's oldest dude ranch, it is one of
those places that keeps being "discovered." **Hidden Valley Guest Ranch**
(★) (HC 61 P.O. Box 2060, Cle Elum, WA 98922; 509-857-2322) is 11
miles from Cle Elum nestled at the edge of a broad valley and at the base
of low mountains. In addition to the main building, where guests gather
for trail rides, hikes and the community meals, the ranch has nine cabins
that haven't had all the rustic removed, so don't expect sound- or cold-
proofing. However, the fireplaces are great for taking off the chill. Each
cabin has a kitchen, but all meals, and they are very large meals, are eaten
in the buffet-style dining room. Two-night minimum stay; moderate to deluxe.

For more impersonal lodgings, the **TimberLodge Motel** (301 West 1st
Street, Cle Elum; 509-674-5966), on the western edge of town, has 29 bright,
clean rooms far enough off the street to deaden the noise of the busy main
drag. Amenities include an exercise room and adjoining restaurant. Budget.

Murphy's Country Bed and Breakfast (Robinson Canyon Road;
509-925-7986) two miles southwest of Ellensburg has two rooms in a ranch
home built in 1915. It has a broad porch made of local stone with views
across the valley. The large guest rooms have wood-beamed ceilings and
antique furnishings. The rooms share one-and-a-half baths, and a full country breakfast is served. For an additional $15, guests traveling with horses
may keep them in a pasture and corral. Moderate.

ROUTE 90 CORRIDOR RESTAURANTS

Salish Lodge at Snoqualmie Falls (37807 Southeast Fall City Road; 206-888-2556), offers spectacular views over the falls and canyon below, and the food is first rate. The menu leans toward what has become known as Northwest cuisine; lots of seafood, fresh fruits and vegetables, waterfowl, a lengthy wine list and dessert list almost as long. Deluxe to ultra-deluxe.

Nearby in Fall City is **The Herbfarm** (32804 Issaquah-Fall City Road, Fall City; 206-784-2222). What began as a roadside stand selling herbs has grown into one of the region's most unusual and successful restaurants. Be warned: It may take months to get a dinner reservation. The menu changes constantly because it is built around seasonal herbs. Each meal takes at least two hours because they begin with a tour of the herb gardens, then during the meal the owners go from table to table discussing herbs with the patrons and explaining how they were used in the dishes. Ultra-deluxe.

Cle Elum is better known for its inns and small hotels, but it has at least one good restaurant, **Mama Vallone's Steak House and Inn** (302 West 1st Street; 509-674-5174). You probably won't find a friendlier hostess than Lexi Vallone, who treats customers like long-lost members of an extended Italian family. Tables are placed in most of the downstairs rooms, and you never have to wait for someone to replenish your water or bring more bread. A specialty is *bagna cauda*, a fondue-style mixture of olive oil, anchovy and garlic served with dipping strips of steak or seafood. Moderate.

You can order patty melts (if you must) in one of three or four truck stops at the Ellensburg cloverleaf, but for lighter fare that won't add so many calories, try **Giovanni's on Pearl** (402 North Pearl Street; 509-962-2260). Owner John Herbert, from the Isle of Jersey, has a menu of lamb, fish, chicken and other light entrées. A nice touch is the candlelight and flowers on each table. Moderate to deluxe.

A short walk away is **The Valley Café** (105 West 3rd Street; 509-925-3050). Food is American with a dash of Mexican dishes. Fish (frequently salmon) and chicken dominate the dinner menu. Moderate.

ROUTE 90 CORRIDOR SHOPPING

Very few wineries have opened thus far in the Cascades, so when one does exist, it is an event. **Snoqualmie Winery** (1000 Winery Road, Snoqualmie; (206-888-4000) produces seven varieties of wine, from riesling to merlot, and is open for tours and tasting daily.

Antique hunters will enjoy **Ellensburg**, which has at least half a dozen antique stores in a three-block area, including a mall. **Anchor in Time** (310 North Main Street; 509-925-7067) has antiques and Western artifacts, and espresso. The **Showplace Antique Mall** (103 East 3rd Street; 509-962-9331) is a restored art deco theater with up to 40 antique dealers displaying at a time.

ROUTE 90 CORRIDOR NIGHTLIFE

Cle Elum has almost nothing in nightlife other than taverns with juke boxes, although occasionally **Moore House** guests will bring their own instruments for a sing-along. In Ellensburg between the rodeos there is little entertainment, but the **Ellensburg Inn** (1700 Canyon Road; 509-925-9801) has a disco and **The Mint Tavern** (111 West 3rd Street; 509-925-1300) features live country music and dancing Wednesday through Saturday.

ROUTE 90 CORRIDOR BEACHES AND PARKS

Lake Easton State Park—On Route 5 and near Snoqualmie Pass, this lakeside park with forested trails is used as a base for skiers and snowmobilers in winter, as a lunch stop for travelers, and for hiking, swimming and fishing in the summer.

Facilities: Picnic areas, swimming beach and restrooms; information, 509-656-2230. *Fishing:* The lake is stocked with trout.

Camping: There are 91 tent sites and 45 RV hookups.

Getting there: Located on Route 90 a mile west of Easton.

Mt. Rainier Area

It is always a dramatic moment when Mt. Rainier suddenly appears ahead of you (in the Northwest it is often called just The Mountain). You could spend weeks in this area and only sample a small portion of its recreational possibilities. Whether you approach from the east or the west, the forest gets thicker and thicker and the roadside rivers get swifter and swifter. The national park is almost surrounded with national forest wilderness areas as buffer zones against clear-cut logging. Located southeast of Seattle, this peak is adjacent to the aptly named town of Paradise.

If you arrive via Route 706 you will have to go through Elbe, which has the **Mt. Rainier Scenic Railroad** (P.O. Box 921, Elbe, WA 98330; 206-569-2588), a steam-powered train that makes a 14-mile trip through the forest and across high bridges to Mineral Lake. It runs daily in the summer, on Saturdays and Sundays the rest of the year, and on special holidays.

Once inside the park you may be almost overwhelmed by the scenery. The mountain is so monstrous (14,410 feet) that it makes everything around it seem trivial. Mt. Rainier has numerous visitor centers and interpretive exhibits along winding roads.

In **Paradise,** head to the **Henry M. Jackson Visitor Center,** which has several exhibits and audiovisual shows. Paradise is one of the most beautiful places in the park, and the visitors' center one of the busiest. It has a snack bar and gift shop. The **Longmire Museum** emphasizes the natural history of the park with rock, flora and fauna exhibits. It is also an information center for hikers, and you can rent cross-country skis. The **Ohanapecosh Visitor Center** down in the southeast corner near a grove of giant, ancient cedar trees, has history and nature exhibits. The **Sunrise Visitor Center** has geological displays and at 6400 feet is the closest you can drive to the peak. Several trails fan out from the center for day hikes.

Nearby, at the intersection of Routes 410 and 12 east of the mountain, you can watch elk and bighorn sheep being fed by game officials during the middle of winter at the **Oak Creek Wildlife Recreation Area.**

MT. RAINIER AREA HOTELS

Two inns are inside Mt. Rainier National Park, and several other places to stay are around the park in Ashford, Packwood, Elbe, Crystal Mountain, Morton and the White Pass area.

The most popular is **Paradise Inn** (P.O. Box 108, Ashford, WA 98304; 206-569-2275). In the middle of the park, this inn has 125 rooms and a lobby that boasts exposed beams, peeled-log posts, wooden furniture, Indian-made rugs and two huge fireplaces. The views are grand, but the rooms are ordinary, and most of the bathrooms are museum pieces. Open May to October. Moderate.

The other in-park hotel is the **National Park Inn** (P.O. Box 108, Ashford; 206-569-2411) six miles from the Nisqually entrance. Offering much of the rustic charm of the Paradise Inn, it is much smaller with only 25 rooms, and only half have private baths. Some rooms have views of the mountain. In keeping with the rustic theme, there are no telephones or televisions. The lobby has an enormous, stone fireplace. Moderate.

Equally popular with lovers of old inns is **Alexander's Country Inn** (37515 Route 706 East, Ashford; 206-569-2300). This inn was built in 1912 as a small hotel designed to look like a manor with turret rooms and grand entrance hall. It retains the Old World look while adding modern conveniences such as a hot tub, sauna and heated pool. Moderate.

In Packwood on the southern flank of the national park is the **Cowlitz River Lodge** (13069 Route 12; 206-494-4444). It is notable for clean, brightly decorated rooms and views of the mountains, although not "The Mountain." It is set back from the busy Route 12 far enough for the logging trucks to be a distant hum rather than an immediate roar. Moderate.

On the northeast boundary of the park is **Crystal Mountain Resort** (P.O. Box 1, Crystal Mountain, WA 98597; 206-663-2558), a year-around resort that is best known for its skiing. Visitors can choose from a number of places to stay, ranging from condominiums to inexpensive motels. Don't expect much charm because skiing, not hotel amenities, is the focus. Typical is **Silver Skis Chalet Condominiums**, which has a cluster of one- and two-bedroom units, some with fireplaces and views. All have kitchens and cable television. They are decorated in the traditional rental-condo manner of plastic furniture and durable fabrics. Can sleep up to four persons. Deluxe.

A bit further east toward Yakima is the White Pass ski area with **The Village Inn Condominiums** (P.O. Box 3039, White Pass, WA 98937; call long-distance operator and ask for White Pass toll station number 2). The complex has 45 rental units designed for large groups, up to eight in many units, and they have a bit of variation in decor since all are privately owned. Some have fireplaces and sleeping lofts. Moderate.

MT. RAINIER AREA RESTAURANTS

Good restaurants are hard to find around Mt. Rainier. Two of the best are in Ashford:

Wild Berry Restaurant (37720 Route 706 East; 206-569-2628) is a mile outside the park, and all items on the menu will be packed to-go on request, including breakfast. As the name suggests, it tends toward ferns and granola (the owners call it "mountain yuppie") but the food is imaginative—quiche, yogurt, crêpes, wild blackberry pie—and budget-priced.

Nearby is the more traditional **Alexander's Country Inn** (37515 Route 706 East; 206-569-7615) serving lunch and dinner. The dining room has windows looking out across the patio—where you can eat in good weather—into the forest. Trout is a favorite, along with seafood, and all the breads and desserts are homemade. Moderate. Open weekends only in the winter.

One of the most popular restaurants between Mt. Rainier and Mt. St. Helens is **Peters Inn** (13051 Route 12, Packwood; 206-494-4000), a large, old-fashioned place where they serve burgers, steaks, veal and some seafood and have a large salad bar. Pies and cinnamon rolls are made locally. Budget.

MT. RAINIER AREA NIGHTLIFE

Nightlife is meager. Try **Crystal Mountain Resort,** which has an occasional small group in spite of skiers' notorious reputation for going to bed early.

MT. RAINIER AREA BEACHES AND PARKS

Mt. Rainier National Park—The most heavily used national park in Washington, Mt. Rainier is everybody's favorite because the mountain can be approached from so many directions and the area around it is glorious no matter the time of year. It is the tallest mountain in the Northwest and has more glaciers—26—than any other mountain in the contiguous 48 states. The mountain is climbed by groups under the leadership of Rainier

Mountaineering, a concessionaire. The lower elevations are notable for the vast meadows that are covered with wildflowers from late June until August and have dramatic fall colors in September and October. Numerous trails lead day hikers to viewpoints, and backpackers can explore the lower elevations on a permit system. It is open year-round with special areas set aside for wintersports at Paradise.

Facilities: Picnic areas, restrooms, four information centers and museums and self-guided nature trails; information, 206-569-2211. *Fishing:* Permitted without a state license. Check with a ranger for regulations.

Camping: There are five car campgrounds, a few walk-in sites and overnight hike-in backcountry areas by reservation.

Getting there: Entrances are on Route 165 on the northwest, Route 410 on the northeast, Route 706 on the southwest and Route 123 on the southeast.

Mt. St. Helens Area

There are few certitudes in travel writing, but here's one: Don't miss Mt. St. Helens. At the southern end of the Washington Cascades an hour north of Portland, this peak might best be described as a cross between a geology lesson and a bombing range. East of this landmark is Gifford Pinchot National Forest and Mt. Adams Wilderness, the heart of a popular recreation area ideal for rafting and fishing.

On May 18, 1980, Mt. St. Helens, dormant for 123 years, blew some 1300 feet off its top and killed 59 persons, causing one of the largest natural disasters in recorded North American history.

Today, access to the volcano remains limited because the blast and resulting mudslides and floods erased the roads that formerly entered the area. The road from Route 5 is being rebuilt at this writing.

A major sightseeing destination, **Mt. St. Helens National Volcanic Visitor Center**, is on Route 504 at Silver Lake, five miles east of Route 5. The center is elaborate and includes a walk-in model of the inside of the volcano. A 22-minute film on the eruption plays almost continuously, and an equally dramatic nine-minute slide show runs every 30 minutes.

Windy Ridge is the closest you can get to the volcano, and it is reached by driving south from Randle on a series of Forest Service roads. Hourly talks are given by rangers in the amphitheater there. **Meta Lake Walk** is on the way to Windy Ridge, and rangers tell how people survived the blast. A 30-minute talk is given in **Ape Cave** on the southern end of the monument. It includes a walk into the 1900-year-old lava tube that got its name from a reputed confrontation between some miners and what they believed were the legendary, ape-like creatures known as Sasquatches by Northwest Indians.

East of Mt. St. Helens, continue south through **Gifford Pinchot National Forest** on paved logging roads that are better maintained than many state or county roads. First, buy a copy of the national forest map at the visitors' center or from a ranger station. You can drive to the edge of **Indian Heaven Wilderness Area** and hike through peaceful meadows and acres of huckleberry bushes, or continue east to the edge of **Mt. Adams Wilderness** with views of that mountain reflected in lakes. This whole area is known for wild huckleberries, and there are two seasons for them; in the higher elevations they ripen in July and into August, then a week or two later the lower-elevation berries ripen.

The logging roads will eventually take you to **Trout Lake**, a small town close to a lake of the same name that reflects Mt. Adams in clear weather. Here you'll find all services and a Forest Service Ranger Station. Just west of town is a vast lava flow called the Big Lava Bed and a lava tube called Ice Cave, which is chilly all through the summer. Both are reached on Forest Service roads.

From Trout Lake, drive east 16 miles to the small cowboy town of **Glenwood** (★). There's not much more than a country tavern and post office to the town, but in the Shade Tree Inn tavern you can get directions to some of the more unusual sights in the area, such as a group of quartz crystals more than 200 feet in diameter and what is locally called "volcano pits," a series of small craters left behind by cinder cones.

From Glenwood, take the Glenwood-Goldendale Road to the junction with Route 142 and drive back southwest to Klickitat and the Columbia Gorge at Lyle. This takes you through the deep, winding **Klickitat River Canyon** with views of the river, a steelheaders' favorite. Mt. Adams often frames the scene.

MT. ST. HELENS AREA HOTELS

The **Seasons Motel** (200 Westlake Avenue, Morton; 206-496-6835), about halfway between Mt. Rainier and Mt. St. Helens, has 50 rooms in a slate-blue, two-story, frame building at the intersection of Routes 12 and 7. All beds in this moderately priced establishment are queen sized, and the clean, odor-free rooms have flowered drapes and bedspreads.

Mio Amore Pensione (P.O. Box 208, Trout Lake, WA 98672; 509-395-2264) is in a renovated 1904 farmhouse on the southern edge of Trout Lake, the closest town to Mt. Adams. Each of the three rooms in the main building has a theme—wine, gardening and Venus (love)—so the latter is used for the honeymoon suite and has its own bathroom and views of Mt. Adams. There is a fourth room in a converted ice house. Mio Amore has a fine restaurant; breakfasts are enormous with several choices of pastries, fruits, eggs and meats. Moderate to ultra-deluxe.

Also on the southern edge of Mt. Adams is the more outdoor-oriented **Flying L Ranch** (25 Flying L Lane, Glenwood; 509-364-3488). Originally a working ranch, since 1960 the Flying L has been a guest ranch but without horses. Hiking is popular here as are photography and fishing in the nearby Klickitat River. Bikes can be rented to get around the mostly flat roads in the area. In the winter, cross-country skiing and snowshoeing are offered. The main lodge has six rooms, most with shared bath; a two-story guest house has five rooms with private baths, and two separate cabins sleep two each. Breakfasts are provided and served in the cookhouse. The main lodge has a large common kitchen where guests can prepare their own lunches and dinners. Budget to moderate.

MT. ST. HELENS AREA RESTAURANTS

On the south edge of Trout Lake is **Mio Amore Pensione** (P.O. Box 208, Trout Lake, WA 98672; 509-395-2264), one of the more remote first-rate restaurants in the Cascades. This farmhouse, which also offers lodging under the same name, is owned by Tom and Jill Westbrook. The husband half of the team is an accomplished chef who learned his craft in Italy, and has simplified the operation by offering only one entrée; the first person to call for a reservation establishes the choice for the evening. The choices are usually chicken, veal and beef. Most dinners begin in the living room with drinks and often end there with Jill Westbrook's specialties: She makes the desserts and is an accomplished guitarist and songwriter. Deluxe.

MT. ST. HELENS AREA BEACHES AND PARKS

Mt. St. Helens National Volcanic Monument—The monument covers 110,000 acres and was created to preserve and interpret the area that was devastated by the eruption. Interpretive centers and overlooks show the destroyed Spirit Lake, vast mud flows and the forests that were flattened by the blast. Access to the monument is limited to a few Forest Service and county roads, most of which are closed in the winter. Guided tours are provided by several operators departing from Seattle, Olympia and Vancouver. Scenic flights in planes and helicopters operate out of area airports.

Facilities: Interpretive centers, picnic areas, scenic overlooks and self-guided nature walks; restaurants and groceries available in nearby towns; information, 206-247-5473. *Fishing:* Excellent for bass and trout in Silver Lake; good for trout in lakes behind dams on Lewis River, south of the monument.

Getting there: From the north, Forest Service roads branch off Route 12 at Randle. From the west, Route 504 from Route 5 leads five miles to the Mt. St. Helens National Volcanic Visitor Center on the shores of Silver Lake, and Route 503 leads up the Lewis River to the monument headquarters at Amboy and the southern flank of the monument.

Gifford Pinchot National Forest—This 1.3 million-acre forest covers most of the southern Cascades to the Columbia River, marked by the Mt. St. Helens National Monument on the west and Mt. Adams on the east. Enclosing seven wilderness areas, most of its forest roads have been paved and are used almost equally by logging trucks and recreationists. Of particular interest are the **Big Lava Beds**, 14 miles west of Trout Lake, where unusual formations of basalt are found, and the **Ice Cave**, six miles southwest of Trout Lake, a lava tube where ice remains until late summer.

Facilities: Picnic areas and restrooms; restaurants and groceries in nearby towns; information, 206-750-5000. *Fishing:* Excellent in lakes, which are stocked frequently, and in all rivers flowing out of the forest.

Camping: There are over 50 campgrounds.

Getting there: This is the most remote of the national forests and is traversed only by Route 12.

The Sporting Life

SPORTFISHING

Winter steelhead, Dolly Varden, rainbow trout, eastern brook trout, walleye, sturgeon, catfish, bass, perch and crappie all can be caught in the interior and along the flanks of the Cascade Range. Fishing is typically done from the water banks or on private boats, but most resorts on lakes and rivers have boats and fishing tackle for rent.

The rivers that drain into Puget Sound—particularly the Nooksack, Skagit, Skykomish and Snohomish—have steelhead and sea-run cutthroat trout. A few professional guides work on the Skagit where winter steelheading is very popular. Two are **Fred Hunger** (206-826-3646) and **John Bates** (206-856-5817).

The other Cascade rivers, such as the Methow, Wenatchee, Yakima, Snake and Klickitat, drain into the Columbia River. All have good trout, walleye and steelhead fishing. The Klickitat River has a good summer steelhead run as does the Columbia.

Fewer and fewer salmon can be caught upstream from Bonneville Dam, the first of 14 dams on the river, as their numbers continue to dwindle. **Wenatchee River Outfitters** (18485 Route 209, Leavenworth; 509-925-1166) leads fishing trips on the Yakima and Wenatchee rivers for steelhead and rainbow trout.

GOLF

Nearly every community in the foothills has a golf course. Around Mt. Baker you'll find the **Peaceful Valley Country Club** (8225 Kendall Road, Maple Falls; 206-599-2416).

Along the eastern slopes of the North Cascades in the Methow Valley you can play at the **Bear Creek Golf Course** (Route 1, P.O. Box 275, Winthrop, WA 98862; 509-996-2284) or **Lake Chelan Golf Course** (1501 Golf Course Road, Chelan; 509-682-5421). Wenatchee has two courses nearby: the **Three Lakes Golf Course** (2695 Golf Drive; 509-884-7105) and **Wenatchee Golf and Country Club** (1600 Country Club Drive; 509-884-7105).

In the Leavenworth Area tee off at the **Kahler Glen Golf Course and Condominiums** (20890 Kahler Drive, Leavenworth; 509-763-3785) or **Leavenworth Golf Club** (9101 Icicle Road; 509-548-7267).

Among the Route 90 Corridor links are the **Mt. Si Golf Course** (Snoqualmie; 206-888-1541), **Cascade Golf Club** (Cedar Falls Road, North Bend; 206-888-0227), **Sun Country Golf Course** (East Nelson Siding Road, Cle Elum; 509-674-2226) and **Ellensburg Golf Club** (Route 1, Ellensburg; 509-962-2984).

RIVER RAFTING

On the Skagit, **Downstream River Runners** (12112 Northeast 195th Street, Bothell; 206-483-0335) runs whitewater trips as well as tours to watch bald eagles and osprey. Another outfit operating on the Skagit River and delta is **Mountain Shadow Tours** (2300 Market Street, Mt. Vernon; 206-428-4709), which leads scenic and naturalist tours. **Four Seasons Outfitters and Guide Service** (314 East Johnson Street, Chelan; 509-682-5032) leads a variety of trips on the Methow, Stehekin, Nooksack, Tieton and Skykomish rivers. **River Masters Guide Service** (13901 119th Street, Brush Prairie; 206-256-4328) operates year-around on the Kalama, Lewis, Washougal and Klickitat rivers. **Silver Star Outfitters** (P.O. Box 458, Winthrop, WA 98862; 509-996-2070) leads trips on the Methow and Wenatchee rivers. **Orion River Expeditions** (1516 11th Avenue, Seattle; 206-322-9130) operates trips on most of the rivers in Washington, including baldeagle viewing trips on the Skagit.

HORSEBACK RIDING AND PACK TRIPS

Cascade Corrals (P.O. Box 67, Stehekin, WA 98852; 509-682-4677) operates in Glacier Peak Wilderness, Lake Chelan Sawtooth Wilderness and North Cascades National Park. **Paysaten and Sawtooth Wilderness: Sun Mountain Lodge** (P.O. Box 1000, Winthrop, WA 98862; 509-966-2211) has the largest stable of riding horses in the Cascades, available for hourly rides or overnight pack trips. **Icicle Outfitters and Guides** (P.O. Box 322, Leavenworth, WA 98826; 509-784-1145) offers hourly guided rides, day trips and summer pack trips. **Eagle Creek Ranch** (P.O. Box 719, Leavenworth, WA 98826; 509-548-7798) runs trips into the Alpine Lakes, Glacier Lakes and Henry M. Jackson Wilderness areas. **Longhorn Cattle Co. 1870s Cattle Drives** (P.O. Box 573, Ellensburg, WA 98926; 509-925-5811) offers four cattle drives a year lasting from four to six days. **Crystal Mountain Corral** (Crystal Mountain; 206-663-2589) offers hourly rides, day rides and longer trips in the Norse Peak Wilderness.

BICYCLING

The popularity of bicycling is growing in the Cascades, and one of the most popular trips is from Route 5 over Route 20 across the North Cascades. Although the highway has only two lanes, the shoulders are wide enough for biking in safety.

Several loop routes have been established along the eastern slopes of the Cascades. The **Leavenworth-Lake Wenatchee loop** is 50 miles and goes from Leavenworth along Route 209 north to Route 207 at Lake Wenatchee State Park and south to Route 2 and back to Leavenworth.

The **Wenatchee-Chelan loop** is 90 miles along the Columbia River and Lake Entiat. It goes north on Route 2 from East Wenatchee, then north on Route 151 to Chelan Station, across the Columbia River, then south on Route 97 to Wenatchee again.

BIKE RENTALS   The pickings here are pretty slim because the area is so remote, so it's best to bring along your own bicycles. If you want to try for rentals, check out resorts and any bike shops in towns along the way.

HIKING

The Cascades are a backpacker's paradise laced with thousands of miles of maintained trails.

NORTH CASCADES TRAILS   The **Pacific Crest National Scenic Trail** (480 miles) has its northern terminus in Washington. It is a hard hike in many places but can be broken into easier chunks, such as from Stevens Pass to Snoqualmie Pass. Contact the Forest Service Information Center (1022 1st Avenue, Seattle, WA 98104; 206-442-0170) for further details.

Coleman Glacier (6 miles round trip) is a popular hike that begins in the parking lot of Mt. Baker Lodge and goes through thick forest to timberline and beyond to the edge of Coleman Glacier slowly grinding its way down Mt. Baker.

In the Baker Lake area, try the hike up **Desolation Peak** (9 miles) to the lookout tower where the Beat Generation writer Jack Kerouac spent a summer. The views of the surrounding mountains and Ross Lake are spectacular.

Perhaps the most historic route in the North Cascades is **Cascade Pass Trail** (7 miles), the Native Americans' route across the mountains for centuries. It is also a route from Marblemount to Stehekin, if you want to really make a trip of it.

All along **Route 20** are signs denoting trailheads, and all are worth exploring. They tell the destination of the trail and the distance.

For a long trip—allow three or four days—**Image Lake** (32 miles) is considered one of the most beautiful in the Central Cascades. The lake mirrors Glacier Peak, the most remote and inaccessible of the Washington volcanoes.

METHOW VALLEY TRAILS   Setting Sun Mountain (6 miles) is a brisk walk from the Methow River Valley near Mazama to a high point of 7200 feet and a panoramic view across the valley.

LEAVENWORTH AREA TRAILS   Icicle Creek (1 mile) is an interpretive loop trail a short distance west of Leavenworth.

Enchantment Lakes (13 miles) is Washington's most beloved backpacking trip because the lakes are so other worldly. They are approached from Icicle Creek near Leavenworth. The hike is a hard one, and permits must be obtained through the Wenatchee National Forest.

ROUTE 90 CORRIDOR TRAILS   Iron Horse State Park (113 miles) is a former railroad right-of-way that is used by hikers, horse riders, cross-country skiers and bicyclists. No motorized vehicles are allowed here, which goes from North Bend over Snoqualmie Pass to Vantage.

MT. RAINIER AREA TRAILS   Naches Wagon Trail (10 miles), east of Yakima, is a good historical hike because this was one route pioneers used on their way to Puget Sound. They left behind blazed trees and other evidence of crude road building.

Wonderland Trail (94 miles) goes entirely around Mt. Rainier and can be made in stages ranging from the 6.5-mile section between Longmire and Paradise to the 39-mile section from Carbon River to Longmire.

Northern Loop Trail (17 miles) runs through the wilderness with frequent views of the mountain between Carbon River to Sunrise.

MT. ST. HELENS AREA TRAILS   Klickitat Trail (16 miles one-way) takes you through a remote part of the Gifford Pinchot National Forest and is believed to be part of a Native American trail network.

Conboy Wildlife Refuge Trail (3 miles) wends through the refuge just south of Glenwood with interpretive signs showing you nesting sites, migratory patterns and discussions on the ecology of the lava and desert area.

Indian Heaven (10 miles) is a beautiful section of the **Pacific Crest National Scenic Trail** that people return to again and again. It is near Trout Lake and goes past numerous lakes reflecting the surrounding mountains.

Transportation

BY CAR

Route 542 travels east from Bellingham through Glacier to deadend at Mt. Baker Lodge. **Route 20**, also known as the North Cascades Highway, is one of the state's most popular highways and goes east from Route 5 at Burlington to the Methow Valley. **Route 2**, one of the last intercontinental, two-lane, blacktop highways, runs from Everett to Maine and is called the Stevens Pass Highway in Washington. From Seattle, **Route 90** goes over Snoqualmie Pass to Cle Elum and Ellensburg.

BY AIR

Only one airport, **Pangborn Field** in Wenatchee, serves this large area, and only two carriers offer scheduled service: Horizon Air and United Express. The roadless Lake Chelan area is served by Chelan Airways, which makes scheduled and charter flights between Chelan and Stehekin.

BY BUS

Greyhound/Trailways Bus Lines offers service to Leavenworth (1408 Route 2, in the Kountry Kitchen Restaurant; 509-548-7414) and Wenatchee (301 1st Street; 509-662-2183) with stops in Cashmere and Peshastin. **Link Transit** (509-662-1155) serves Cashmere, Chelan, Dryden, East Wenatchee, Entiat, Leavenworth, Malaga, Manson, Monitor, Peshastin and Wenatchee. **Empire Lines** (509-624-4116) goes to Chelan, Entiat, Pateros and Wenatchee.

BY TRAIN

Amtrak (800-872-7245) travels from Seattle, Portland and Spokane to Wenatchee via the "Empire Builder."

BY BOAT

The **Lady of the Lake** (P.O. Box 186, Chelan, WA 98816; 509-682-2224) provides daily transportation in summer between Chelan, Manson, Fields Point, Prince Creek, Lucerne, Moore and Stehekin. Service drops to Sunday, Monday, Wednesday and Friday in the winter.

CAR RENTALS

At the Wenatchee airport is **Budget Rent A Car** (509-663-2636). In downtown Wenatchee are **Hertz Rent A Car** (509-662-6134) and **U-Save Auto Rental** (509-663-0587). Ellensburg has **Budget Rent A Car** (509-925-1455) and **Kelleher Motors** (509-925-1408).

CHAPTER SIX

East of the Cascades

If state boundaries were determined by similar geography, customs and attitude, Washington and Oregon as we know them would simply not exist. Instead, they'd be split into two more states using the crest of the Cascades as the dividing line or would run vertically from California on the south to Canada on the north with one state taking either side of the mountain range.

Well, who ever said life was perfect? So what we have are two states whose eastern and western halves bear almost no resemblance to each other. From the Cascades west, the land is damp, the forests thick and the climate temperate. The eastern side of the range is almost exactly the opposite: Very little rain falls and most crops are irrigated by water from the Columbia Basin Project created by Grand Coulee Dam, or by water from deep wells. Here, the winters are cold and the summers are hot.

Even the people are as different as east and west. While those in the western halves tend to be liberal and innovative, the eastern residents are more conservative and content with the status quo. And since we're in a status-quo frame of mind now, we take you through Eastern Washington and Oregon in this chapter. Other chapters look at the western sides of the states. So buckle up!

You may think of Washington as a rainy place, but without Grand Coulee Dam and the string of smaller dams that came along later to turn the Columbia and Snake rivers into a series of lakes, Eastern Washington would be barren. Instead, in this part of the state one of the most common scenes is an irrigation sprinkler going about its business of turning the sand into a rich soil that grows wheat, wine grapes, fruit, soybeans, barley, oats, rape, grass seed, corn, alfalfa, potatoes, peas and a host of other crops.

211

In contrast, only bits and pieces of Eastern Oregon are irrigated because it has not been blessed with any large rivers other than the Snake. It remains mostly arid, the northern reaches of the Great American Desert that runs north from Mexico through Arizona, California and Nevada. It is land more suitable for cattle grazing than growing crops, although in some valleys ranchers have drilled wells or dammed small streams to enable them to irrigate meadows. This kind of open and sparsely populated countryside doesn't appeal to all travelers, so you tend to see more recreational vehicles and truck stops than hotels and restaurants.

If urban amenities such as hotels, finer restaurants, theater and shopping centers are what you're after, head to Washington's larger cities—Spokane, Walla Walla, the Tri-Cities and Yakima—and to Pendleton in Eastern Oregon. Elsewhere you'll find RV parks and inexpensive but clean motels. On the lakes and streams are rustic resorts, some with log cabins.

Away from the cities, hunting and fishing abound. Deer, elk and an occasional black bear are popular quarry, as are waterfowl, pheasant, grouse and quail. Don't be startled while driving along a mountain road during hunting season if you spot someone in camouflage clothing carrying a rifle emerge from the forest. In the high desert of Eastern Oregon you'll sometimes see antelope and wild horses, usually in the distance since they justifiably avoid human encounters. Many streams and lakes are stocked regularly with trout, and a few sturgeon are still caught in the Snake and Columbia rivers.

Some of the most interesting geology in North America is found in this region due to its tortured creation by volcanoes, lava flows through vast fissures and floods gigantic beyond imagining. Throughout the two states' eastern sides you will find vivid reminders of this creation process. In Oregon it is shown by hundreds if not thousands of dead volcanoes and cinder cones, lava flows that have not yet been covered by wind-blown soil, brilliantly colored volcanic ash deposits, and sheer canyons whose basalt walls were created by these lava flows. In Washington it is the dramatic Coulee Country along the Columbia River and the beautiful Palouse Country with its steep, rolling hills.

The forests are mainly pine with very little underbrush. Along some parts of the eastern slope of the Cascades you will find larch, the only species of coniferous trees that are deciduous. They are brilliantly colored in the fall and stand out as vividly as sumac and maples in the dark-green forest.

One stretch of landscape of unusual origin is the Channeled Scablands south and west of Spokane, which was created by floods from a lake formed at the end of the Ice Age in the valley around Missoula, Montana.

In Oregon you will find the painted hills of the John Day Fossil Beds National Monument, the dramatic canyons of the Owyhee River and the vast Alvord Desert, barren of vegetation and flat as an airport. In both states east of the mountains is another treasure: peace and quiet. There are lonesome roads undulating off into the distance, small rivers stocked with trout, open pine forests, vast lakes made by man, working cowboys and mornings so tranquil you can hear a door slam.

As with elsewhere in America, the general rule is the smaller the town the friendlier the people, so don't be surprised if folks stop to talk about

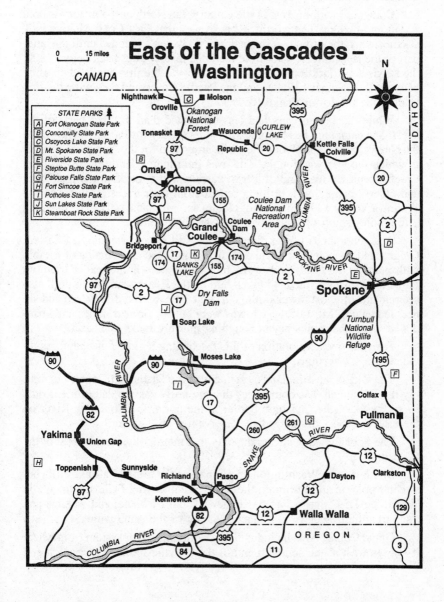

East of the Cascades – Washington

0 — 15 miles

CANADA

N

IDAHO

STATE PARKS 🌲
A Fort Okanogan State Park
B Conconully State Park
C Osoyoos Lake State Park
D Mt. Spokane State Park
E Riverside State Park
F Steptoe Butte State Park
G Palouse Falls State Park
H Fort Simcoe State Park
I Potholes State Park
J Sun Lakes State Park
K Steamboat Rock State Park

Nighthawk ■ C ■ Molson
Oroville ■
Okanogan National Forest
Tonasket ■ Wauconda ■ CURLEW LAKE
97 Republic 20 Kettle Falls ■ Colville
B
Omak ■ 395 20

Okanogan ■ 155 Coulee Dam National Recreation Area COLUMBIA RIVER 395 2 D

A Coulee Dam
Grand Coulee ■ SPOKANE RIVER E
Bridgeport ■ 17 K 174 155 174
97 BANKS LAKE 2 Spokane ■
2 17 Dry Falls Dam
J Turnbull National Wildlife Refuge
■ Soap Lake 90

90 90 ■ Moses Lake 195 F
I
17 395 Colfax ■
82 Pullman ■
Yakima ■ 260 261 G RIVER
■ Union Gap COLUMBIA RIVER SNAKE 12
H Toppenish ■ Sunnyside ■ 12 Clarkston ■
97 Richland ■ Pasco ■ ■ Dayton 12 129
Kennewick ■ 82 12 ■ Walla Walla
COLUMBIA RIVER 395 OREGON
84 11 3

anything or nothing in particular. Also, nearly everything is less expensive than along the coast.

Traveling these remote areas you will have a continual sense of discovery as you visit places barely large enough to get themselves onto state maps. And you will find small towns that don't bother opening tourist bureaus but have a clean motel, a good café, friendly people to talk to and a small city park for your picnic.

Compared with the rest of the country, the Northwest's history is both recent and benign. The Northwest is so new that East Coast visitors look askance when they find that the major cities weren't founded until the latter part of the last century. Very little recorded history goes back before 1800; the Lewis and Clark Expedition of 1804-06 was the first overland crossing between the original 13 states and the Pacific Coast, and they were the first to describe the lower Snake River.

While the Indian wars had less bloodshed than in other parts of the West, one campaign has become almost legendary for the skill with which the Nez Perce Indians eluded the white army, and for the "humane" manner in which the war was fought. This was the running battle of 1877, when Chief Joseph led his band of a few warriors and a lot of women, children and elderly people on a brilliant retreat from their ancestral home in the Wallowa Valley 1400 miles across Idaho and Montana, only to be captured a few miles south of their goal, the Canadian border.

A few remnants of the pioneer years still remain standing in Eastern Oregon and Washington. Here and there you'll see the remains of a cabin with perhaps the tall tripod of a windmill where a homesteader tried but failed to "prove up" the land given him by the Homestead Act. You'll also see remains of ghost towns (although some have been rediscovered and are peopled again). Most of these towns were built at or near mines and abandoned when the mines began coughing up only rocks and sand.

For your own exploration of this fascinating region, this chapter is divided into six sections:

The Okanogan Highlands, often called the Okanogan Country or simply the Okanogan, has boundaries that are fairly easy to determine: Route 97 to the west, the Canadian border to the north, the Columbia River on the east and the Colville Indian Reservation on the south.

The Spokane Area covers the only true metropolitan center east of the Cascades.

Southeastern Washington encompasses the famed Palouse Hills between Spokane and Pullman; the Snake River town of Clarkston; Walla Walla; the Tri-Cities of Pasco, Kennewick and Richland; and Yakima and the agricultural and wine-producing valley of the same name.

Grand Coulee Area includes all the Columbia River system from where it swings west at the southern end of the Colville Indian Reservation and follows past Grand Coulee Dam south to the Vantage-Wanapum Dam area, where the Columbia enters the Hanford Nuclear Reservation.

Northeastern Oregon covers the Pendleton and La Grande areas, the Blue Mountains, the beautiful Enterprise and Joseph area on the edge of the Eagle Cap Wilderness, and across the Wallowa Mountains to the few entrances to Hells Canyon on the Snake River. The centerpiece of this region is the Wallowas, a broad valley in the Enterprise and Joseph area where Wallowa Lake, one of the most beautiful in America, reflects the mountains of the Eagle Cap Wilderness.

Southeastern Oregon is the largest area covered and the least populated. It includes the cowboy country of the vast high desert that occupies most of the region, the lava wasteland near La Pine and the multicolored John Day Fossil Beds National Monument.

Okanogan Highlands

One of the pleasures of touring the Okanogan Country is simply driving down country roads to see where they lead. A number of ghost towns, some no more than a decaying log cabin today, dot the map.

Most visitors enter the Okanogan Country from Route 97, the north-south corridor that runs up the Columbia River Valley to Bridgeport, then follows the Okanogan River Valley north toward Canada. This is desert-like country with irrigated orchards on either side of the highway and open range climbing back up the mountains. First, contact the **State Information Center** (P.O. Box 2087, Omak, WA 98841; 509-826-1880) for brochures and maps.

The **Okanogan County Historical Museum** (502-422-4272), also headquarters for the county historical society, is on Okanogan's Main Street and has a collection of Indian artifacts, pioneer farm and ranch implements and historical photos. This is also a good place to start all your travels because members of the volunteer staff have lived in the region for many years and know where everything is, including skeletons in the county's closets.

One of the most interesting drives is to **Molson** (★), a ghost town 12 miles northeast of Tonasket off Route 97 near the Canadian border; follow the highway signs in downtown Tonasket. Molson was founded when a nearby mine was attracting hundreds of prospectors and workers. Due to a land-claim mix-up, a farmer took over the whole town, so a new one had to be built and it was named New Molson. The two towns, less than a mile apart, fought over everything except education for their children. They built a school halfway between the towns, and it became **Center Molson**. Today

Old Molson is an outdoor museum, and the Center Molson school building is a museum.

Another popular drive is to **Nighthawk,** just west of Oroville, which was a ghost town until recently. The paved county road, which heads west from Route 97 near the Canadian border, curves along the Similkmeen River Valley, then swings south into a valley between the mountains of the Pasayten Wilderness of the North Cascades National Park and a series of steep ridges to the east. This area is dotted with old mines, some still worked from time to time, but most of the land along the valley floor and stretching up the hillsides a few hundred feet has been turned into orchards and vineyards. Nighthawk is far from being a ghost town now, as is **Loomis,** the other mining town farther south on this loop drive. The highway passes Palmer Lake and Spectacle Lake, both of which have public beaches, before rejoining Route 97.

Route 20 is one of Washington's best highways for leisurely rural driving, especially as it traverses the Okanogan Country on its way to the Idaho border. It comes in from the Cascades to Omak-Okanogan, joins Route 97 north to Tonasket, swings east across the heart of the highlands through Wauconda and Republic, crosses the Columbia River at Kettle Falls and continues on to Kettle Falls and Tiger, where it follows the Pend Oreille River south to the Idaho border at Newport. There it disappears. The highway follows the path of least resistance along valleys beside streams where ranches amble off across the rolling hills to disappear in pine forests.

Republic was created by a gold rush in the late 1890s, and two gold mines still operate a short distance outside town. The **Echo Bay mine** (509-775-3373) offers tours to groups. Also, the **Stonerose Interpretive Center** (★) (509-775-2295) lets visitors dig for fossils on a hillside on the edge of town. The site is named for an extinct rose fossil found there.

Several buildings comprise the **Keller Historical Park** in Colville (700 North Wynne Street; 509-684-5968). Sponsored by the Stevens County Historical Society, the complex has a museum in a new building, a fire lookout tower, Colville's first schoolhouse, a trapper's cabin and the home of the pioneer Keller family.

Another historical site is the **St. Paul's Mission,** 12 miles north of Colville where Route 395 crosses the Columbia River. It was built as a chapel for Native Americans in 1845 and operated until the 1870s. A modest museum is also here.

OKANOGAN HIGHLANDS HOTELS

The most modern motel in Okanogan is the **Cedars Inn** (Route 97 and Route 20, Okanogan; 509-422-6431). It has 78 rooms, an unpretentious dining room and heated pool. Another moderately priced Okanogan motel is the **Ponderosa Motor Lodge** downtown (996 2nd Avenue; 509-826-9971), an older but clean two-story motel of basic design with a pool but no restaurant on the premises.

The **U and I Motel** 838 2nd Avenue; 509-422-2920) has small "cabinettes" with rustic paneling and basic kitchens. They come equipped with deck chairs, so you can sit and look across a lawn and flower garden to the Okanogan River. Budget.

In Omak are several small, budget-priced motels including the **Travel Inn** (122 North Main Street; 509-826-0400) and **Leisure Village Motel** (630 Okoma Drive; 509-826-4442).

Several small resorts are scattered along lakes in the area. Among them are **Bonaparte Lake Resort** (695 Bonaparte Road, Tonasket; 509-486-2828). This resort, 26 miles from both Republic and Tonasket, has ten airy and clean log cabins along the lake shore. Only one—called, of all things, the Penthouse—has bathroom, bedding, towels and kitchen supplies. There are a public shower and bathroom. Budget.

One of the few bed and breakfasts is the **Orchard Country Inn** (1st Street and Antwine Avenue, Tonasket; 509-486-1923), also listed as an America Youth Hostel. The house was built in 1917 as a seven-bedroom guest house by the owner of an orchard, and its large, airy rooms have period furniture. It has two bed-and-breakfast rooms upstairs and 16 beds in the basement hostel, and guests in both categories mingle freely. Bed-and-breakfast rates are budget, and the hostel rates are, of course, much lower.

OKANOGAN HIGHLANDS RESTAURANTS

Basic, standard fare is pretty much the order of the day here. For starters, there is the **Cedars Inn Restaurant and Lounge** (Appleway Avenue and Route 97, Okanogan; 509-422-6431), which serves adequate, straightforward lunches and dinners and farmer-sized breakfasts. Moderate.

For some local color and reasonable prices, try the **Gibson Girls' Stockyard Café** (Okanogan Livestock Market). This is a place where you can have breakfast and your choice of daily specials, ranging from hot-beef sandwiches to meat loaf at lunch while listening to the auctioneer selling horses and cattle. Budget.

The choices are fewer in Omak, but one café that rates high is the **Breadline Café** (102 South Ash Street; 509-826-5836) where the menu features big sandwiches on whole-grain breads and is perhaps the only place in the twin towns where you can ask for bean sprouts and get them. Antique decor. Moderate.

Oroville has a few places, including the **Whistle Stop Restaurant** (1918 North Main Street; 509-476-2515). It is decorated with railroad memorabilia in keeping with the town's emphasis on antique stores. Moderate.

In Tonasket you can dine, dance and gamble in the **Villa Fare** (21 West 6th Street; 509-486-4127). Breakfasts—those big ones laborers eat—are served all day. The drinking and gambling are done in the Bullpen Lounge. Moderate.

One of the more interesting places to stop for a snack or down-home American meal is **Wauconda** (Route 20, Wauconda; 509-486-2322), the one-store town on Route 20 east of Tonasket. A lunch counter to the left of the door is crammed between the cash register and a smaller dining room with a few booths overlooking a valley and low mountains beyond. The food is uncomplicated and hearty, and the portions are generous, especially the prime rib that is the house special on Friday and Saturday. Moderate.

Up north toward Canada, the **Roadhouse Restaurant** (half-mile south of Colville on Route 397; 509-684-3021) is in an old farmhouse overlooking the Colville River Valley. The cooking is Southern style—fried chicken is a favorite—from natural ingredients, many grown in the area. The owners also sell many of the products they serve: apple-pear preserves, their own barbecue sauce adapted from a Southern Methodist cookbook, peach preserves, a ranch dressing made from locally grown chives and a chili sauce dating to before the Civil War. Moderate.

OKANOGAN HIGHLANDS SHOPPING

Antiques of all ages are the biggest thing going in **Oroville**, and in keeping with the theme, some of the town's storefronts have been decorated with falsefronts. One of the largest antique and arts-and-crafts stores is the **Country Harvest General Store** (509-476-3118) one-half mile east of town on the Molson-Chesaw Road. In addition to antiques it stocks pottery, paintings, crafts and toys made locally.

In Chesaw, a town of some 30 souls a few miles east of Molson that is making a comeback from ghost-town status, the **Country Gift Shop** specializes in the work of "artisans of rural Washington."

In Coulee Dam, the **Colville Confederated Tribe Museum, Gallery and Gift Shop** (516 Birch Street; 509-633-0751) sells local beadwork and other artwork by tribal members.

OKANOGAN HIGHLANDS NIGHTLIFE

Most nightlife in this cowboy and fruit-picking area is limited to taverns, a few of which have live bands on weekends and during the Omak Stampede, the rodeo held each July. In Omak, you can dance off your dinner in **Lucky Jo's Restaurant and Lounge** (110 South Ash Street; 509-826-2704), which has live music and dancing on Thursday, Friday and Saturday nights after 9 p.m. Cover.

OKANOGAN HIGHLANDS BEACHES AND PARKS

Conconully State Park—Strung along the edge of the town of the same name, this site is popular with boaters, swimmers, families and anglers. For hikers, there is a nature trail.

Facilities: Picnic areas, wading pool; information, 509-826-7408.

Camping: There are 81 sites: 65 standard sites, 10 with water hookup and six primitive sites with pit toilets.

Getting there: Located 22 miles northwest of Omak on Conconully-Okanogan Highway.

Fort Okanogan—This is primarily an interpretive park set above the junction of the Okanogan and Columbia rivers with a visitor center on the bluff overlooking the original site, now under the waters of Wells Dam backwaters. The center tells the history of Fort Okanogan, an important part of the nation's fur trade.

Facilities: Picnic sites and a sheltered kitchen area; information, 509-689-2798 or 509-923-2473.

Getting there: Located at junction of Routes 97 and 7 between Brewster and Bridgeport.

Osoyoos State Park—This lakeshore park is one mile north of Oroville and stretches along the southern end of Osoyoos Lake. It has some of the few trees in the area for shade while picnicking and camping and is the most popular state park in the area. It is heavily used by Canadians and Americans alike since it is almost on the Canadian border. For nature-lovers, the lake is a prime nesting area for Canadian geese.

Facilities: Picnic areas; information, 509-476-3321. *Fishing:* Year-round for trout and spiny-ray.

Camping: There are 86 sites.

Getting there: Located on the northern end of Oroville on Route 97.

Curlew Lake State Park—This 128-acre setting is on the southeastern shore of a lake in a pine forest with several islands. Remnants of homesteaders' cabins can be seen near the park, and a large variety of animals, including chipmunks, squirrels and deer, lives in the area. Several species of birds also can be seen. The park is surrounded by Colville National Forest.

Facilities: Picnic area, restrooms and boat launch; restaurants and groceries in nearby resorts. *Fishing:* Good.

Camping: There are 64 standard sites and 18 with RV hookups.

Getting there: Located ten miles north of Republic on Route 21.

Spokane Area

The northeastern corner of Washington is an area of pine forests, sparkling lakes, sprawling wheat farms and urban pleasures in a rural setting. Spokane is where the Midas-rich miners from Idaho came to live in the late 19th century, so the city has an abundance of historic homes, museums, bed and breakfasts and inns and one of the most beautiful city park systems in the West.

The best way to become acquainted with Spokane is to take the self-guided "City Drive Tour" outlined in a brochure from the city that is available in all hotels and at the **Spokane Convention and Visitors Bureau** (West 926 Sprague Avenue; 509-624-1341). Another useful brochure is the self-guided tour of historic architectural in downtown Spokane. The "City Drive Tour" takes you along Cliff Drive where many of the finest old homes stand and through **Manito Park** (Stevens Street and 5th Avenue), one of the city's largest parks. Manito Park includes the Japanese Garden built by Spokane's sister city in Japan and the **Duncan Formal Gardens**, whose lush scenery looks like something out of a movie set in 18th-century Europe.

The tour continues past **St. Stephen's Episcopal Church** (57th Avenue and Hatch Road) and **Comstock Park** (High Drive Parkway and 29th Avenue), which has a large, public swimming pool and picnic area. It continues on to the **Cheney Cowles Memorial Museum** (West 2316 1st Avenue) with its major collection of regional history and fine art. Next is **Finch Arboretum**, on Sunset Boulevard, which features an extensive collection of trees from all over the world. From there the tour leads you back to the downtown area.

The city is most proud of its **Riverfront Park** (509-456-5512) located in the heart of downtown and known for the natural beauty of its waterfall and island. It has the restored 1909 Looff Carrousel, a gondola skyride over Spokane Falls, various other rides, food concessions and the 70mm IMAX Theater. It also has footpaths, natural amphitheaters, lawns and hills and always the roar of the waterfall for a backdrop.

A close second in local pride is the **Museum of Native American Cultures** (East 200 Cataldo Street; 509-326-4550). Its exhibits range from Alaska south through all the Northwest tribal groups, plus a good collection of paintings and sculpture.

Another must see is the **Spokane County Courthouse** across the river from downtown on Broadway just off Monroe Avenue. It resembles the 16th-century Château de Chambord and Château d'Azay Le Rideau. Oddly enough, it was designed in the 1890s by a young man whose only formal training in architecture came from a correspondence course. It is a magnificent conglomeration of towers and turrets, sculpture, iron and brickwork in the manner of French Renaissance.

Spokane has several wineries with sales and tasting rooms. **Steven Thomas Livingstone Winery** (East 14 Mission Street; 509-328-5069) is near the downtown area with a tasting room decorated with Victorian furnishings. **Worden Winery** (West 7217 45th Avenue; 509-455-7835) is one of the largest in the area with a capacity of 50,000 gallons. **Arbor Crest Wine Cellars** (North 4705 Fruithill Road; 509-927-9894) is in a building designated as a National Historic Site on a bluff overlooking the Spokane River. **Latah Creek Wine Cellars** (East 13030 Indiana Avenue; 509-926-0164) has a Spanish-style building with a large courtyard and a tasting room decorated with oak.

SPOKANE AREA HOTELS

Spokane has some pleasant hotels that don't carry big-city rates like those found in Seattle and Portland. You won't find deluxe or luxury accommodations here, but down-home hospitality by all the hotel staffs more than makes up for it.

Two of the largest offer perhaps the best rooms and service. The **West Coast Ridpath** (West 515 Sprague Avenue; 609-838-6122) is an old establishment downtown divided into two buildings across the street from each other with a second-story skywalk connecting them. The second building has the larger rooms, and all look inside to the courtyard and large swimming pool. The lobby is small, but the staff is cheerful, and the concierge desk goes to great lengths to help you. There are two restaurants. Moderate.

The **Sheraton Spokane Hotel** (322 North Spokane Falls Court; 509-455-9600) was built for Spokane's 1974 World's Fair and has the best location, right along the Spokane River and on the Riverfront Park. The lobby is impressive, and most rooms have good views of the river, park and downtown. It also has a covered pool. Moderate.

The **Quality Inn-Spokane House** (West 4212 Sunset Boulevard; 509-838-1471) is a favorite of many who visit Spokane frequently. Built on a hill west of town, it is roughly halfway between the airport and downtown, is quiet and affords good views of the city's growing skyline. Budget.

A newer downtown establishment is **Cavanaugh's Inn at the Park** (West 303 North River Drive; 509-326-8000). It has 186 rooms and is across North River Drive from the Riverfront Park. Unfortunately, it is just far enough away from the river to lose some of the waterfront charm. The inn is walking distance from downtown, and some of the rooms have private decks. Moderate.

Fotheringham House (West 2128 2nd Avenue; 509-838-4363) is Spokane's best bed and breakfast, and, for that matter, one of the best in the state. Fotheringham House is in the Brown's Addition, Spokane's equivalent of San Francisco's Nob Hill, where many of the mining barons built their homes. There are four guest rooms with Victorian furnishings in keeping with the architecture. Moderate.

A mile east of Kettle Falls on Route 395 is **My Parent's Estate Bed and Breakfast** (P.O. Box 725, Kettle Falls, WA 99141; 509-738-6220), one of the first bed and breakfasts in this part of the state. It formerly was a Catholic mission with a convent added later, then a boys' school. It offers three rooms with baths, queen-sized beds and central air conditioning. Each room is named for its period decor and furnishings: Queen Anne Lace, English Cottage room and French Country room. Included on the 47 acres are a gazebo, gymnasium, pond and a trail to the Colville River. Moderate.

SPOKANE AREA RESTAURANTS

Spokane's most popular Asian cuisine comes from the two **Mustard Seed Oriental Cafés** (West 245 Spokane Falls Boulevard, 509-547-2689; and East 9806 Sprague Avenue; 509-924-3194). The menu offers specialties from several provinces in China as well as Japanese and American dishes. The downtown location is open, airy and the service brisk and friendly. Priced in the moderate range.

The most striking restaurant in town is **Patsy Clark's** (West 2208 2nd Avenue; 509-838-8300). It is in the mansion designed for a millionaire miner and has marble from Italy, wood carvings from England and an enormous, stained-glass window from Tiffany's. Meals are served in several rooms, and during good weather you can have drinks served on the second-story veranda. The restaurant maintains a high standard for steaks, seafood, duckling, lamb and veal. Ultra-deluxe.

Fort Spokane Brewery (West 401 Spokane Falls Boulevard; 509-838-3809) is Spokane's only micro-brewery, and pub food is served daily. Moderate in price.

SPOKANE AREA SHOPPING

The Skywalk in the downtown core, a series of weatherproof bridges that connects 15 blocks on the second level, makes downtown shopping pleasant the year around. It leads to the major downtown department stores such as **Nordstrom's** (Post Street and Main Avenue; 509-455-6111), **Frederick & Nelson** (Post Street and Riverside Avenue; 509-838-3311), **Bon Marche** (Main Avenue and Wall Street; 509-747-5111), several specialty shops, restaurants and art galleries.

With more and more Canadians driving just over a hundred miles to Spokane where nearly all goods are less expensive, the city has had a surge of discount stores, from national chain stores to the West Coast warehouse stores. Shopping centers have sprung up on the north and northeast edges of town. Covered shopping areas include **Northtown Mall** (Division Street and Wellesley Avenue), **Franklin Park Mall** (Division Street and Rowan Avenue) and **University City** (Sprague Avenue and University Street).

The **Flour Mill** (West 621 Mallon Street; 509-838-7970) is one of the more charming places to shop. It was built as a flour mill but was turned into a specialty shopping center in 1974 with more than 20 shops, including bookstores, clothing and gift stores and cafés and restaurants.

Fresh vegetables, fruit and berries are one of the Spokane area's best buys. The **Green Bluff Growers** (East Green Bluff Road, Colbert; 509-238-4709), a marketing cooperative, publishes a map each year with directions to its member orchards, vegetable farms and Christmas-tree farms.

SPOKANE AREA NIGHTLIFE

You'll find live jazz and Top-40 music and dancing at **Ankeny's** on the top floor of the Ridpath Hotel (West 515 Sprague Avenue; 509-838-2711) Monday through Saturday.

The **Park Place Lounge** (Cavanaugh's Inn at the Park, West 303 North River Drive; 509-326-8000) has live music from the 1960s to the 1980s every night. Cover.

J's Lounge (Sheraton Hotel, North 322 Spokane Falls Court; 509-455-9600) has Top-40 music every night. Cover.

For a lively spot, try **Papagayo's Cantina** (North 4111 Division Street; 509-483-8346), which turns on the music videos every night.

JS PUMPS!! (415 North Monroe Street, Spokane; 503-325-9084) is a gay and lesbian dance bar featuring disco in a warehouse setting. Located on the north side of town, the club's hot dancefloor is cooled by casablanca fans. Decorated with posters, the club features drag shows and a Tuesday night talent search.

The **Spokane Symphony Orchestra** (West 601 Riverside Drive; 509-624-1200) performs a number of times throughout the year, including outdoor concerts in Riverfront Park during the summer months.

The **Spokane Civic Theater** (North 1020 Howard Street; 509-325-1413) presents musicals, dramas and comedies in the Civic Theater throughout the year.

SPOKANE AREA BEACHES AND PARKS

Riverside State Park—On the edge of Spokane, this 7655-acre park includes nearly eight miles of Spokane River shoreline, odd basaltic formations in the river and Indian paintings on rocks. It houses the Spokane House interpretive center, which tells the history of Spokane.

Facilities: Picnic areas with shelters, restrooms, hot showers and horse trails and wheelchair accessible; information, 509-456-3964. *Fishing:* Rainbow trout. *Swimming:* In the Spokane River.

Camping: There are 101 standard sites.

Getting there: Located six miles northwest of Spokane at junction of Route 291, Gun Club Road and Aubrey L. White Parkway.

Mount Spokane State Park—This 5881-foot mountain is used as much or more in the winter as summer, but warm-weather visitors will find its views spectacular; Idaho, Montana, Canada and much of Washington can be seen from the summit. It is especially pretty during the spring when its slopes are blanketed with flowers and in the fall when the fields are brown and the leaves have turned. For those into winter sports, there are downhill and cross-country skiing, snowmobiling and sledding.

Facilities: Picnic areas and restrooms; information, 509-456-4169.

Camping: There are 12 primitive sites.

Getting there: Located at the end of Route 206, 30 miles northeast of Spokane.

Turnbull National Wildlife Refuge—One of the most popular natural places for day trips in the Spokane area, the refuge was established primarily for waterfowl in 1937. It has several lakes and undisturbed wooded areas and a marked, self-guided auto-tour route. You will also find hiking and cross-country skiing trails as well as a photo blind.

Facilities: Restrooms; information, 509-235-4723.

Getting there: The refuge is four miles south of Cheney on Badger Lake Road.

Southeastern Washington

The drive from Spokane south into Oregon is one of unusual beauty, especially early or late in the day, or in the spring and fall. The entire region between the wooded hills around Spokane to the Blue Mountains is known as the Palouse Country. Here the barren hills are low but steep, and wheat is grown on nearly every acre. In fact, it is acknowledged as the best wheat-growing land in the world.

Proceeding south from Spokane along Route 195, you'll find that the two best places to view the Palouse Hills are **Steptoe Butte State Park** (see "Beaches and Parks" below) and Kamiak Butte in **Chief Kamiakim County Park**, which stands 3360 feet high with bird's-eye views of the Palouse Hills. The park has picnic areas, a hiking trail and, unlike Steptoe Butte, a fringe of trees on its crest and over 100 kinds of vegetation, including Douglas fir more common to the damp, coastal climate. Kamiak Butte is 18 miles east of Colfax and 15 miles north of Pullman just off Route 27.

The town of Pullman is almost entirely a product of Washington State University, although a few agricultural businesses operate on the edge of town. Continuing south from this campus town, Route 195 gains elevation through the small farming communities of Colton and Uniontown, then crosses over into the edge of Idaho just in time to disappear into Route 95 and then take a dizzying plunge down the steep Lewiston Hill, where you drop 2000 feet in a very short time over a twisting highway. The old highway with its hair-pin turns is still passable and is exciting driving if your brakes and nerves are in good condition.

Clarkston, Washington, and Lewiston, Idaho, are separated by the Snake River, which flows almost due north through Hells Canyon before taking a sudden westward turn where Idaho's Clearwater River enters in Lewiston. Most of the Snake River boat operators are headquartered in these two towns. For more information, contact the **Clarkston Chamber of Commerce** (731 5th Street; 509-758-7712).

The population has followed the Snake on its way west to join with the Columbia, but it is a tamed river now, a series of slackwater pools in deep canyons behind a series of dams: Lower Granite, Little Goose, Lower Monumental and Ice Harbor. The main highway doesn't follow the Snake River because of the deep canyon it carved, so from Clarkston you follow Route 12 west through the farming communities of Pomeroy and Dayton to Walla Walla, then on to the Tri-Cities area around Richland, where the Snake enters the Columbia River. Along the way is Dayton, an agricultural town with a large asparagus cannery. The town raised funds to preserve the beautiful **Dayton Depot** (Main Street; 509-382-4825), a classic Victorian building that had an upper floor for the station master's quarters.

Walla Walla looks much like a New England town that was packed up and moved to the rolling hills of Eastern Washington, weeping willows, oak and maple trees included. Best known for its colleges, Whitman and Walla Walla College, the town with a double name has many ivy-covered buildings, quiet streets lined with old, frame houses, enormous shade trees and, rather incongruously amid this Norman Rockwellian beauty, the state penitentiary. Contact the **Walla Walla Chamber of Commerce** (P.O. Box 644, Walla Walla, WA 99362; 509-525-0850).

At **Whitman Mission Historic Site** (509-524-2761) one of the Northwest's worst tragedies occurred because of a basic misunderstanding of Native American values by an American missionary, Marcus Whitman. He and his wife, Narcissa, founded a mission among the Cayuse Indians in 1836 to convert the Indians to Christianity. As traffic increased on the Oregon Trail, the mission became an important stop for the weary travelers. Eleven years later the Indians felt betrayed by Whitman because his religion hadn't protected them from a measles epidemic that killed half the tribe. On No-

(Text continued on page 228.)

Washington Wine

For a long time, Washington's liquor laws were so restrictive that it was illegal to bring wine into the state; you had to buy it from the state-run stores. The best Washington wine in those days was made by an Italian immigrant, Angelo Pelligrini, who taught Shakespeare at the University of Washington and made wine in his basement—illegally.

That has changed completely. Some 70 wineries are spread across the state, most in Eastern Washington, and many of those in the Puget Sound region own vineyards in Eastern Washington or buy their grapes there. The soil and climate are excellent for wine grapes, and the **Washington Wine Commission** (P.O. Box 61217, Seattle, WA 98121; 206-728-2252) likes to remind us that Eastern Washington is on the same latitude as some of France's great winegrowing regions. The wine commission publishes a free annual guide to wineries.

Washington has three viticultural regions: Columbia Valley, which extends southward from the Okanogan Country into Oregon and east to Idaho; Yakima Valley, which runs from the foothills of the Cascades east to the Kiona Hills near Richland and is bisected by Interstate 82, making it the most convenient for visits; and the Walla Walla Valley region, which straddles the Oregon-Washington border, taking in some vineyards in the Milton-Freewater area.

In keeping with the French adage that the best grape vines "like to be in sight of the water but don't want to get their feet wet," some of the best vineyards in Eastern Washington are on south-facing slopes above the Columbia, Yakima and Snake rivers where they get as much as 16 hours of sunlight a day and fresh irrigation water on well-drained soil. As with all wine-producing areas, many wineries have been built in palatial settings.

One of the most dramatic is the **Columbia Crest Winery** (Paterson; 509-875-2061). Built on a hillside overlooking the Columbia River, it produces more than a million gallons of wine annually and has a reflecting pool, fountain and courtyard, a luxurious lobby and tasting-and-sales room.

Running a close second is the eastern branch of **Château Ste. Michelle** (205 West 5th Street, Grandview; 509-882-3928). This is the state's oldest continuously operating winery and is the red-wine facility for the large winery best known for its Woodinville palace.

Champs de Brionne (98 Road W Northwest, Quincy; 509-785-6685) is built into the jagged cliffs overlooking the Columbia just above Vantage, a site chosen for growing pinot noir. During the summer, concerts by international stars are given in the natural amphitheater on the property.

A wine that keeps gaining new fans is the **Covey Run** label (1500 Vintage Road, Zillah; 509-829-6235). The tasting room stands on a hill overlooking the winery's hundreds of acres of grapes.

The quirky **L'Ecole No. 41** (41 Lowden School Road, Lowden; 509-525-0940) got its name from the retired schoolhouse in which it was built near Walla Walla. The owners are known for their sense of humor; they named their first chenin blanc "Walla Voila!" (pronounced Walla Valla). It is open on special occasions and has an open house the weekend after Labor Day.

Wine is only one of several agricultural products produced by Hogue Ranches. But the **Hogue Cellars** (Wine Country Road, Prosser; 509-786-4557) red wines have been getting much more attention than their asparagus.

Hunter Hill Vineyards (2752 West McMannaman Road, Othello; 509-346-2607) is named for the well-known bird-hunting area around the nearby Potholes Reservoir. The tasting room is in the original farmhouse, which gives a feeling of a country home to visitors who come by to taste.

The most homey of the wineries is probably **Kiona Vineyards** (Sunset Road, Benton City; 509-588-6716). It is a two-family operation with the tasting room, winery and the Kiona Vineyard at the home of John and Ann Williams, and the tank-aging facilities at the home of Jim and Pat Holmes. The winery was one of the originals to produce lemberger.

One of the largest is the **Langguth/Saddle Mountain Winery** (2340 Winery Road, Mattawa; 509-932-4943). It has the capacity for nearly a million gallons of wine. The red and white table wines are sold under the Saddle Mountain label, and rieslings under the Langguth label. Each July the winery sponsors a summer Weinfest and barbecue.

Pontin del Roza (McCreadie and Hinzerling roads, Prosser; 509-786-4449) came into being because the Pontin family's Italian heritage included a love of wine. They decided to add wine grapes to the crops they had been growing on their Prosser farm for two decades and produce both reds and white.

Cheers!

vember 29, 1847, the Indians killed both Whitmans and ten others and ransomed 50 to the Hudson's Bay Company. The site is seven miles west of Walla Walla on Route 125 and is administered by the National Park Service. There's a visitor center, memorial monument, millpond and walking paths to sites where various buildings stood. None of the original buildings remain.

The Columbia River runs free for about 60 miles through the Hanford Reservation, but when it swings through the Tri-Cities (Richland, Pasco and Kennewick) it is Lake Wallula, thanks to McNary Dam. Several city parks with picnic and boating facilities are along the river, such as **Columbia Park** in Kennewick.

The Tri-Cities are best known for the nuclear-power plant and research center in nearby Hanford. It was here that the components for the first atomic bombs were assembled. These three nuclear-related visitor centers tell the nuclear story. **Hanford Science Center** (Federal Building, on Jadwin Avenue near Lee Boulevard, Richland; 509-376-6374) is operated by Westinghouse for the Department of Energy and tells of the various sources of energy. **Fast Flux Test Facility Visitors Center** (11 miles north of Hanford on Stevens Drive near the Fast Flux Test Facility; 509-376-5101) explains how the sodium-cooled nuclear reactor works, along with other advanced-technology programs at Hanford. Still another nuclear facility for visitors is the **Washington Public Power System Plant 2 Visitor Center** (12 miles north of Richland off Stevens Drive; 509-372-5860), which offers a tour of the state's first commercial nuclear-power plant.

From the Tri-Cities the population follows the Yakima River, which flows into the Columbia at the Tri-Cities. The **Yakima Valley** is one of the state's richest in terms of agriculture; Yakima County ranks first nationally in the number of fruit trees, first in the production of apples, mint and hops and fourth in the value of all fruits grown. It is also the wine center of the state: Some 40 wineries have been built between Walla Walla and Yakima, and they have helped create a visitor industry that has encouraged the growth of country inns and bed and breakfasts. Brochures listing the wineries and locations are available in visitors' centers and many convenience stores, and once you're off Route 82, signs mark routes to the wineries.

Fort Simcoe State Park (end of Route 220, about 30 miles south of Yakima; 509-874-2372) is probably the best-preserved frontier army post in the West and was one of the few forts where no shots were fired in anger. It was used in the late 1850s during the conflict with the Indians. It has a museum and interpretive center. Five of the original buildings are still standing, including the commanding officer's home.

If you are a rail buff, take the **Spirit of Washington** (800-876-7245) that runs between Yakima and Ellensburg each weekend. You can also ride the rails on **Yakima Interurban Lines** (509-575-1700) that runs from 4th Avenue and Pine Street in downtown Yakima five miles to Selah on weekends and holidays.

Three important museums are in the Yakima Valley: The **Yakima Nation Cultural Center** (P.O. Box 151, Toppenish, WA 98948; 509-865-2800). Here, the history of the tribe is told in dioramas and writings by and about the tribe preserved in a large library. The center also has a large theater for films and concerts.

The **Central Washington Agricultural Museum** (102 West Ahtanum Street, Union Gap; 509-248-0432) has a large collection of early farm machinery.

The **Yakima Valley Museum** (2105 Tieton Drive, Yakima; 509-248-0747) has the most comprehensive collection of horse-drawn vehicles west of the Mississippi, an extensive collection of furniture and other belongings of the late Supreme Court Justice William O. Douglas and a fine pioneer photo collection.

South of the Yakima Valley on Route 97 overlooking the Columbia River is one of the most isolated museums in America. **Maryhill Museum of Art** (35 Maryhill Museum Drive; 509-773-3733; admission) still manages to attract some 80,000 visitors a year in spite of being ten miles from Goldendale, the nearest town. It was built during and after World War I and has many pieces of sculpture by Rodin as well as clothing, paintings and furniture from the Romanian royal collection.

An alternate route from Yakima down to the Columbia River is the **Mabton-Bickleton Road** (★), which heads south from the small town of Mabton through the even smaller Bickleton. An unincorporated town with a scattering of Victorian houses and falsefront store buildings, Bickleton's claim to fame is hundreds of houses for (are you ready for this?) bluebirds. Maintained by residents, the houses are on fence posts along the highway and country lanes and literally all over town. The one in front of the community church is a miniature copy of the church itself.

SOUTHEASTERN WASHINGTON HOTELS

It's difficult to find anything other than your basic, cookie-cutter motel in Southeast Washington, although Yakima shows some imagination.

Pullman has about half a dozen motels, none particularly distinguished, and all priced in the moderate range. The best view is the **Hilltop Motor Inn** (David Way and Colfax Avenue; 509-334-2555). The **Quality Inn** (Southeast 1050 Johnson Road; 509-332-0500) is near both the campus and the airport, and **Travelodge** (South 515 Grand Avenue; 800-255-3050) is on Pullman's busy, often noisy, main drag.

Walla Walla has about ten motels, most of them in the moderate range. One is **Whitman Motor Inn** (107 North 2nd Street; 509-525-2200), which also has some deluxe-priced rooms. A block away is the **Tapadera Budget Inn** (211 North 2nd Street; 509-529-2580), which offers a continental breakfast. Budget.

The Tri-Cities has several fair-sized motels, many with meeting rooms since the Hanford nuclear center is nearby. One of the largest is the **Quality Inn on Clover Island** (435 Clover Island; 509-586-0541) built on an island in the Columbia River. Every room has a view of the river, and the restaurant is open 24 hours a day. It has a pool, hot tub and sauna. Moderate.

Yakima does a lively convention business, and one of the best places to stay is next door to the convention center. The **Towne Plaza** (607 East Yakima Avenue; 509-248-5900) has 155 large, comfortable rooms with colorful furnishings and spacious bathrooms, two heated pools, dining room and coffee shop. Moderate.

On a hill overlooking Yakima, but only a few blocks from downtown, is the **Tudor Guest House** (3111 Tieton Drive; 509-452-8112), an English Tudor mansion. It has five guest rooms, two with shared baths, and a separate bridal suite. Other features are a sunken library with tile floors, oriental and carved carpets, period prints and carved-marble and tiled fireplaces. Full breakfast is served in a solarium room. Moderate.

SOUTHEASTERN WASHINGTON RESTAURANTS

In Pullman, the most popular place to eat is **The Seasons** (215 Southeast Paradise Street; 509-334-1410), on the hill near Washington State University. It is an elegant setting in a renovated house and has a menu that changes frequently. Salad dressings are made by the chef, as is most of the bread. Moderate.

The **Hilltop Steakhouse** (Davis Way; 509-334-2555) shares the steep hill with the Hilltop Motor Inn. It caters to the local trade with thick steaks, Sunday brunches and afternoon dinners. Moderate.

If you're good at what you do, so goes the saying, the world will beat a path to your door. This could be the slogan for **Petit Creek Restaurant** (725 East Dayton Street, Dayton; 509-382-2625). It has been in business since 1978 and has built a national reputation for excellent dishes in what is most accurately described as French country cuisine. Meat is the specialty—beef, lamb and pork. Most of the food is grown locally, some by the staff, and since some of the luxurious plants inside and around the outside are herbs, they will one day be in your food. Moderate.

If you're feeling nostalgic for New York delis, **Merchant's Ltd.** (21 East Main Street, Walla Walla; 509-525-0900) will help. It has a wide choice of foods and a sidewalk café ideal for Walla Walla's mostly sunny weather. Budget.

The **Cedars** (7 Clover Island, Kennewick; 509-582-2143) is one of the Tri-Cities' most striking restaurants. It is cantilevered over the Columbia River with boat-docking facilities. The specialties are steaks, seafood and prime rib. Moderate.

Emerald of Siam (1314 Jadwin Avenue, Richland; 509-946-9328) serves authentic Thai food in a former drug store that has a combination of French, Thai and American decor and menu. A buffet lunch is served on weekdays, or you may order from the menu. Budget.

Over the years, **Birchfield Manor** (2018 Birchfield Road, Yakima; 509-452-1960) has won more magazine awards than any restaurant outside the Puget Sound region. The owners restored an old farmhouse and filled it with antiques, then opened the restaurant where they serve fixed-price, multicourse dinners. Each consists of an appetizer, soup, salad, entrée and dessert. Local fruit and vegetables are used, and the entrée may be spring lamb or scampi stuffed with lobster mousse in a béarnaise sauce. Deluxe.

SOUTHEASTERN WASHINGTON SHOPPING

Walla Walla is perhaps best known outside the region for Walla Walla Sweets, the delicious onions that are raised only in this area. A number of produce firms sell them, and some will ship. They include **Amerifresh** (1137 North 13th Street, Walla Walla; 509-525-5922) and **Ed Ruzicka Farms** (Route 2, Walla Walla; 509-529-2089).

Yakima Valley Cheese Co. (Alexander Road just off Midvale Road at Exit 67 on Route 62, Sunnyside; 509-837-6005) specializes in gouda cheese. The company makes two sizes of rounds, an eight-to-ten pound and a 20-22 pound, but also sells wedges and various sizes.

The **Residential Fruit Stand** (South 3rd Street at Nob Hill, Yakima) is an institution where many locals go for their fruit, vegetables, berries and even Christmas trees.

Yesterday's Village and Farmer's Market (15 West Yakima Avenue; 509-457-4981) is a collection of shops in the former Fruit Exchange Building. Most of the interior has been left intact so you can see how fruit was cooled and processed, but the old building houses some 130 shops that sell antiques, glassware, jewelry and various kinds of food.

SOUTHEASTERN WASHINGTON NIGHTLIFE

Pullman is almost entirely a college town, so you'll find plenty of places that sell pizza, beer and wine. Live music is scarce, but if you're beyond college age you can have dinner, drinks and dancing at the **Oriental Restaurant and Ming Room Lounge** (South 300 Grand Avenue; 509-334-2413).

Walla Walla has several restaurants with dancefloors and a few with live entertainment. **Whitman Restaurant and Lounge** (107 North 2nd Street; 509-529-7276) has entertainment and dancing, as does the **Red Apple Restaurant and Lounge** (57 East Main Street; 509-525-5113).

Yakima has one of the widest selections of nightlife in Eastern Washington, ranging from cultural events to country-and-western taverns. **Grant's Brewery Pub** (32 North Front Street; 509-575-1900) serves British pub food and frequently has live music on weekends. The **Golden Kayland Chinese Restaurant** (40th Avenue and Summitview Street; 509-966-7696) has live music on weekends. In addition, it has frequent concerts sponsored by the Ladies' Musical Club and the **Yakima Symphony Orchestra** (509-248-1414).

Square dancing is very popular in the Yakima Valley, and numerous clubs welcome travelers to their dances. For information, the Friday *Yakima Herald-Republic* publishes a square dance column listing all the club news.

SOUTHEASTERN WASHINGTON BEACHES AND PARKS

Steptoe Butte State Park—This park consists of the butte and a picnic area at the base but has no amenities at all. The reason for the park's existence is the butte itself, which rises to an elevation of 3612 feet out of the rolling Palouse Hills with panoramic views that are popular with photographers. The butte is the top of a granite mountain that stands above the lava flows that covered all the other peaks. The word steptoe has entered the international geological vocabulary to represent any similar remnant of an earlier geological feature standing out from the newer feature.

Facilities: Picnic area at the foot of the butte. No water.

Getting there: It's 33 miles south of Spokane just off Route 195.

Fields Spring State Park—The 445-acre park is in forested land on the eastern slope of the Blue Mountains. It is just below Puffer Butte, a 4450-foot mountain that overlooks the Grand Ronde River Canyon. From its crest you can see parts of Washington, Oregon and Idaho. For hikers, there is a one-mile trail to the summit of Puffer Butte. Winter-sports enthusiasts will find cross-country skiing, snowshoeing and tubing.

Facilities: Restrooms and showers; information, 509-256-3332.

Camping: There are 20 standard sites.

Getting there: Located four-and-a-half miles south of Anatone on Route 129.

Fort Walla Walla Park—This collection of pioneer buildings is on a 208-acre former Army fort and cemetery containing victims from both sides of the first conflicts with the Indians. It also has 14 buildings, some authentic and others replicas, of pioneer homes, schools and public buildings. One of the largest collections of horse-drawn farm equipment in the Northwest is also owned by the museum. Admission. There are nature and bicycle trails.

Facilities: Picnic areas, restrooms, play equipment and volleyball courts; information, 509-527-3770.

Camping: There are 55 standard sites and 21 hookups.

Getting there: Located on southwest side of Walla Walla on Myra Road between Dalles Military Road and Rose Street.

Palouse Falls/Lyons Ferry State Park—The two-part, remote park is out in the rugged Channeled Scablands. One part consists of a pleasant, grassy area with boat ramps at the confluence of the Snake and Palouse rivers. About two miles up the Palouse River is the other part, a dramatic picnic area and viewpoint overlooking the thundering Palouse Falls.

Facilities: Picnic areas, restrooms and concession stand; information, 509-646-3252. *Swimming:* Permitted.

Camping: Palouse Falls has ten standard sites while Lyons Ferry has 52 sites.

Getting there: It's 36 miles southeast of Washtucna on Route 261.

McNarry National Wildlife Refuge—This is one of the major resting areas in the Pacific Flyway for migratory waterfowl, especially Canada geese, American widgeon, mallards, pintails and snow geese, teals and white pelicans. The population peaks in November, and the few summer migratory birds, such as the pelicans and long-billed curlews, arrive in the spring and summer. The refuge covers 3600 acres along the Snake River just before it enters the Columbia River at Pasco.

Facilities: Self-guided wildlife trail through the marsh and croplands; information, 503-922-3232. *Fishing:* Largemouth black bass, catfish and crappie. Hunting: Waterfowl and upland birds.

Getting there: Located southeast of Pasco just off Route 395 on the Snake River.

Grand Coulee Area

The centerpiece of the Grand Coulee Area, not surprisingly, is Grand Coulee Dam with its spectacular laser light shows during the summer months. The sheer mass of the dam is almost overwhelming and for decades was the largest concrete structure in the world.

Also of interest are the many lakes created by the dam that have become some of the Northwest's most popular recreation areas. The backwaters of the dam itself, named in honor of President Franklin D. Roosevelt, reach far north nearly to the Canadian border and east into the Spokane River system. For the irrigation project created by the dam in addition to hydroelectric power, a chain of lakes and some smaller dams were built to hold irrigation water for distribution south and east of the dam. These include Banks Lake and the Potholes Reservoir, known as the Winchester Wasteway. Don't be put off by the name because wasteway refers to the water that has been used for irrigation and has seeped along bedrock to emerge again ready for reuse. These lakes continue on south to the Crab Creek Valley before re-entering the Columbia River below Vantage.

This area is frequently confusing to visitors because of the similarity of place names. The towns of Coulee Dam and Grand Coulee are at the site of Grand Coulee Dam itself, and Coulee City is 30 miles away at the southern end of Banks Lake. In the same area are still two more small towns: Elmer City and Electric City.

Grand Coulee Dam (509-633-3074) was built in the 1930s and memorialized by the songs of Woody Guthrie. The area that became known as the Columbia Basin was so barren before the dam that locals liked to say you had to prime yourself to spit and that jackrabbits crossing the basin had to carry a canteen. The dam was the largest concrete pour in the world for many decades after its completion at the beginning of World War II. It stands 550 feet, as tall as a 46-story building, above bedrock and at 5223 feet is nearly a mile long. While its 12 million cubic yards of concrete may be difficult to imagine, the Bureau of Reclamation points out that this is enough to build a standard six-foot-wide sidewalk around the world at the Equator.

In addition to the 161-mile-long Roosevelt Lake used to power the hydroelectric system, the dam serves the dual purpose of irrigating more than 500,000 acres. Water is pumped 280 feet up the canyon wall to fill Banks Lake's reservoir, from where it is moved through canals and pipes to the farmland.

Visitors are welcome at the dam and can go on self-guided tours. One of the most popular events is the nightly **laser show**, a free, 40-minute demonstration that uses the spillway of the dam for its screen. It is shown from Memorial Day through September.

In Coulee Dam, the **Colville Confederated Tribe Museum, Gallery and Gift Shop** (516 Birch Street; 509-633-0751) charges an admission to the museum, which shows authentic village and fishing scenes, coins and metals dating from the 1800s and many ancient artifacts. The gift shop sells local beadwork and other artwork by tribal members.

The best way to appreciate the stark beauty of the Grand Coulee Area is to drive south from the dam on Route 155 along **Banks Lake**. The artificial lake is used for all watersports, and its color and character change dramatically with the time of day and weather.

At Coulee City you come to the **Dry Falls Dam**, which holds Banks Lake water and sends it on south into a system of canals. Pinto Ridge Road heads due south from Coulee City and passes **Summer Lake**, a favorite picnic spot. The falls are created by the irrigation water from Banks Lake.

The main route out of Coulee City is across Dry Falls Dam, then south on Route 17 past Dry Falls and Sun Lakes State Park, along a series of smaller lakes in the coulees—Park Lake, Blue Lake, Lake Lenore (where you can see the form of a small rhinoceros that was trapped in a prehistoric lava flow) and finally to Soap Lake.

Soap Lake was so named because the water forms foam, or "soap suds," along the shore when the wind blows. The water is rich in minerals—sodium, chloride, carbonate, sulphate, bicarbonate and several others—so it has attracted a number of motels that pump water for use in the rooms or into spas where people go to soak themselves seeking comfort from a variety of skin, muscle and bone afflictions.

South of Soap Lake the coulees flatten out, and the landscape away from the Columbia River becomes the gently rolling wheat-growing region. **Moses Lake** is the last town of any size connected with the Columbia Basin and is better known as a hub for farmers of the basin than as a tourist destination. The lake for which the town is named joins the Potholes Reservoir to the south.

GRAND COULEE AREA HOTELS

If you want a room with a view, there are two good places near the dam. The **Ponderosa Motel** (10 Lincoln Street, Coulee Dam; 509-633-2100) is right across the street from Grand Coulee Dam. Each room has a view of the spillway and the nightly laser light shows in the summer. The 20-year-old motel has 34 rooms on two floors. Two rooms have jacuzzis, and you pay for it. Moderate.

The other is **Coulee House Motel** (110 Roosevelt Way, Coulee Dam; 509-633-1101), which is up a steep hill and provides a top-notch view. It has clean, unremarkable rooms. Moderate.

Also in the moderate-price range, **Four Winds Guest House** (301 Lincoln Street, Coulee Dam; 509-633-3146) is a large, wood-frame Cape Cod bed and breakfast across the street from City Hall. It was built as a rooming house while the dam was being built in the 1930s. All rooms have furniture from that period, and all have wash basins. Two rooms have a shared bath; otherwise, the bathrooms are at the end of the hall.

Several budget-priced motels and resorts are along the shores of Banks Lake and Roosevelt Lake. One of the cleanest and least expensive is the **Lakeview II Motel & Spa** (HCR 1 Box 11, Coulee City, WA 99115; 509-632-5792) at the south end of Banks Lake half-a-mile off Route 2 at the intersection with Route 155. The motel has picnic tables, a whirlpool and a sauna. Some rooms have kitchens, and all have refrigerators.

In Soap Lake, **Notaris Lodge** (242 Main Street; 509-246-0462) is the best known and most modern motel in town. It also boasts an unusual decor in its rooms with names like the Bonnie Guitar room (the entertainer grew up in the area). Another room is called the Ben Snipes in honor of a pioneer cattleman and has cowboy gear for decoration. The accommodations are spacious and equipped with microwave ovens, refrigerators and breakfast nooks. Massages, whirlpool and mineral baths in Soap Lake water are available. Moderate.

Moses Lake is one of the most popular RV destinations in the central part of the state because several lakes are in the immediate vicinity, and hot, sunny weather is almost guaranteed. Several motels are also along the Route 90 corridor and the lake, including the **Best Western Landmark Inn** (3000 Marina Drive; 509-765-9211) which has 131 units right on Moses Lake. In addition to boating and waterskiing, right off the dock, the motel has tennis courts, a heated pool and sauna. Moderate.

The **Lakeshore Motel** (3206 West Lakeshore Drive; 509-765-9201) is also on the lake and has a marina with waterskiing available, and a heated pool. Nine housekeeping cabins are available. Budget to moderate.

GRAND COULEE AREA RESTAURANTS

The best-known eatery in this region is the **Wildlife Restaurant** (113 Midway Avenue, Coulee Dam; 509-633-1160). It has a bar with oak decor, big dining room with Spanish motif and a large menu with an emphasis on beef and seafood. Moderate.

In Grand Coulee, try the **Sage Inn** (415 Midway Avenue; 509-633-0550) for diner-style food: soups, sandwiches and pie. Budget.

Also in Grand Coulee, if you want Oriental food, **Siam Palace** (213 Main Street; 509-633-2921) will have it. Thai, Chinese and American dishes are served. Budget.

Moses Lake has the usual fast-food outlets and pancake houses and **The 4-B's Pantry** (3001 West Broadway; 509-765-8385), which caters to the family trade. Various sandwiches and highway dinner fare. Budget.

GRAND COULEE AREA NIGHTLIFE

Moses Lake (Route 17 out of Coulee City; 509-765-7888) has a series of free concerts, all beginning at 8 p.m. during May to September, in its 3000-seat outdoor amphitheater on the lakeshore. Nationally known musicians perform.

GRAND COULEE AREA BEACHES AND PARKS

Coulee Dam National Recreation Area—This area stretches 151 miles along the entire length of Roosevelt Lake, including parts of the Spokane and Kettle rivers. Due to the arid climate, the lake has miles and miles of sandy beaches and outcroppings of dramatic rocks. Only when you get close to the Spokane River do trees begin appearing along the shoreline.

It is a particular favorite for waterskiers. Sailing and windsurfing are also popular.

Facilities: Picnic areas and boat ramps; restaurants and groceries nearby; information, 509-633-9441. *Fishing:* More than 30 species, including walleye, rainbow trout, sturgeon, yellow perch and kokanee, the landlocked salmon. *Swimming:* Good.

Camping: There are 27 campgrounds with over 200 sites.

Getting there: Located 26 miles north of Coulee City on Route 155.

Steamboat Rock State Park—This is one of Washington's most popular state parks and thus is one of the dozen parks that requires camping-space reservations. The park is on the shores of Banks Lake at the foot of the butte by the same name. The ship-shaped butte rises 700 feet above the lake and has a good trail to the 640-acre flat top.

Facilities: Picnic tables, playground equipment, bathhouse and snack bar; information, 509-633-1304. *Swimming:* Good. *Fishing:* Good year-round; a popular place to ice fish.

Camping: There are 105 sites, the majority with RV hookups; make reservations by mail with reservation forms obtained from the State Parks Commission.

Getting there: It's 13 miles south of Grand Coulee on Route 155.

Sun Lakes State Park—On the floor of the coulee that was scoured out when the Columbia River's normal course was blocked by ice and debris at the end of the Ice Age. The river, three miles wide, flowed over nearby 400-foot-high Dry Falls, which was the original name of the state park but was changed because of the lakes and recreation. It is now home to boating, riding, hiking and golfing.

Facilities: Picnic areas; information, 509-632-5583. Included in the park is Camp Delaney, an environmental learning center with air-conditioned cabins; information, 206-586-6022.

Camping: There are 193 sites including 18 with RV hookups. Note: A private concessionaire (Sun Lakes Park Resort, HCRI Box 141, Coulee City, WA 98115; 509-632-5291) operates the park and rents cabins, the trailer park and hookups, a general store, the restaurant and soda-fountain, service station, heated swimming pool, boat rentals, riding stables, laundry and a nine-hole golf course.

Getting there: Located seven miles southwest of Grand Coulee on Route 17.

Potholes State Park—The Potholes Reservoir was created when water from the Columbia Basin Project seeped in to fill depressions around the coarse sand dunes in the area. Now the sand dunes stand above the water level and are used for campsites, bird blinds and picnic areas. The area supports a large population of waterfowl in addition to blue herons, white pelicans, sand-hill cranes, hawks and eagles. A lawn and shade trees, tables and stoves are beside the lake.

Facilities: Restrooms, showers and boat ramps. *Fishing:* Rainbow trout, bass, perch, crappie, bluegill and walleye. *Swimming:* Good.

Camping: There are 126 sites: 66 for tents, 60 with RV hookups.

Getting there: Located on O'Sullivan Dam Road 12 miles south of Moses Lake.

Ginkgo Petrified Forest State Park—More than 200 species of fossilized trees have been identified in this area of barren hillsides and lava flows, making it one of the largest fossil forests in the world. The park has an interpretive center overlooking the Columbia River with a wide selection of petrified wood. No camping, fishing or swimming are permitted at Ginkgo, but you can head four-and-a-half miles south on the Columbia River to the **Wanapum Recreation Area**. It also has hiking trails, and there is a one-mile interpretive trail at Ginkgo as well.

Facilities: Picnic areas and restrooms; information, 509-856-2700.

Getting there: Located on the edge of Vantage, a tiny town on Route 90 where it crosses the Columbia River.

Northeastern Oregon

Only in the late 1980s was the highway completely paved between the Wallowas and the Snake River Canyon. But now you can take one of the prettiest mountain drives in the Northwest by following Route 129 south from Clarkston in the southeastern corner of Washington through Anatone, then down into the Grande Ronde River Valley over probably the most crooked highway in the Northwest. Be sure your brakes (and fortitude) are in good condition.

At the Oregon-Washington border it changes to Route 3 and runs through ponderosa-pine forests and along high ridges until it enters the **Wallowa River Valley**, the famed Chief Joseph Country. This valley is postcard perfect with the jagged Wallowa Mountains providing a perfect backdrop to the broad valley with the lush farms and ranches, rail fences, ranch buildings and the small, winding Wallowa Rivers. Once you've seen it you'll understand why it is becoming a haven for artists and writers.

The twin towns of **Enterprise** and **Joseph** can be used as a base for exploratory trips around Wallowa Lake and backpacking into the Eagle Cap Wilderness. The **aerial tramway** that runs from Wallowa Lake to the 8200-foot summit of Mt. Howard is a popular way to spend part of a day. Another good day trip is the 30-mile drive from Joseph on a good road to Imnaha

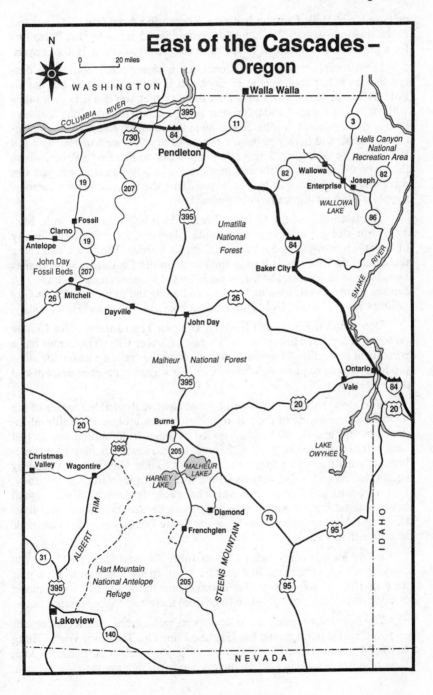

East of the Cascades – Oregon

N

0   20 miles

WASHINGTON

COLUMBIA RIVER

Walla Walla

395

11

3

730

84

Pendleton

Hells Canyon National Recreation Area

19

207

82

Wallowa

Joseph

82

Enterprise

WALLOWA LAKE

86

395

Fossil

Clarno

Antelope

19

Umatilla National Forest

John Day Fossil Beds

207

Baker City

26

Mitchell

Dayville

26

John Day

SNAKE RIVER

Malheur National Forest

395

Ontario

Vale

84

20

20

20

Burns

395

205

LAKE OWYHEE

Christmas Valley

Wagontire

MALHEUR LAKE

HARNEY LAKE

Diamond

78

95

ALBERT RIM

Frenchglen

31

Hart Mountain National Antelope Refuge

205

STEENS MOUNTAIN

95

IDAHO

395

Lakeview

140

NEVADA

on the edge of **Hells Canyon National Recreation Area** (see "Beaches and Parks" below). A gravel road takes you another 25 miles to **Hat Point** (★) for a grand view across one of the most rugged stretches of Hells Canyon.

From Joseph, newly paved Route 129 is under consideration for designation as a National Scenic Highway. It is well maintained but has so little traffic, even in the mid-summer months, that you can drive for miles without seeing anyone, and the Forest Service campgrounds along it always have good campsites. It joins Route 86 at the southern end of Wallowa National Forest, and here you have a choice of heading west to Halfway and Baker City or taking a sidetrip a few miles east to the Snake River, where the Oxbow Dam stands. By crossing the Snake River into Idaho, you can drive another 30 miles to Hells Canyon Dam, the last one before the most rugged stretch of the canyon is reached.

The last miles of the **Oregon Trail**, which began in St. Joseph, Missouri, run along the same general route taken by Route 84 from the city of Ontario northwest through Baker City, La Grande, Pendleton and along the Columbia River until hitting the rapids in the Cascades. Several sites have been set aside that show ruts made by the wagons along the trail. You can see them at Vail, west of Ontario, and along the route near Baker City in Burnt River Canyon, Gold Hill, Durkee, Pleasant Valley and Baker Valley.

Don't miss the **National Historic Oregon Trail Interpretive Center** on top of Flagstaff Hill on Route 86 east of Baker City. The center has a permanent collection of artifacts found along the trail, a theater for stage productions and outdoor exhibits showing a wagon-train encampment and mine operation.

You also can visit a number of **ghost towns**, all visible records of the boom-and-bust nature of the mining industry with broken windmills, abandoned shacks and fireplaces surrounded by ashes from burned houses that bear witness to failed homesteads. Some of these towns are making a comeback as Americans flee to greener pastures. Baker City is surrounded by such falsefronted old-timers as Greenhorn, Sumpter, Granite, Whitney, Bourne, Sparta and Cornucopia, which have colorful remains of the original towns and mining equipment standing among the summer homes that have taken root. Most of these towns are along Route 7 or on Forest Service roads leading off it.

Route 7 leads from Baker City to **John Day** and **Canyon City**, twin towns that look very much like the Old West. In fact, once or twice a year the main street of John Day is closed to vehicular traffic so that a local rancher can drive his cattle through town to or from their way to the summer range.

The best-known museum in these parts was a store owned for decades by two Chinese immigrants, Ing Hay and Lung On. The **Kam Wah Chung & Co. Museum** (503-575-0028), next to the city park in the center of John Day, began as a trading post on the military road that ran through the area.

Then the Chinese laborers in the mines bought the building for a community center, general store and an herbal doctor's office. The museum has thousands of artifacts related to the building's history and more than a thousand herbs, some from China and others from the immediate region.

The **John Day Fossil Beds National Monument** (503-575-0721) is a three-part preserve that attracts serious and amateur photographers from all over the world to capture the vivid colors of the volcanic-ash deposits and the fossils of plants and animals. **Sheep Rock,** five miles west of Dayville where Routes 26 and 19 intersect, has the main visitor center and the best fossil collection at the monument. **Painted Hills,** at the end of a three-mile paved access road northwest of Mitchell, is the best known because of the brilliantly colored ash deposits that range from rose to pink, gold and bronze. **Clarno** is on the John Day River 20 miles west of Fossil and 30 miles east of Shaniko on Route 218. It has a good collection of plant fossils. The monument has self-guided loop trails.

NORTHEASTERN OREGON HOTELS

In Pendleton, the best hotel is the **Red Lion Inn** (304 Southeast Nye Avenue; 503-276-6111), just off Route 84 on a hill overlooking the city. Rooms have picture windows and balconies overlooking the wheat fields rolling off to the north and west. It has a formal dining room with a window wall, coffee shop, pool, duck pond and gift shop. Moderate.

In the downtown area, the **Longhorn Motel** (411 Southwest Dorion Avenue; 503-276-6111) has most of the amenities, except a pool. Budget.

All but one of the hotels in the Enterprise-Joseph area are in the budget category. The lone exception is **Wallowa Lake Lodge** (Route 82, Joseph; 503-432-9821), an aging lodge on the lakeshore with adjoining cabins that have kitchenettes in some units. Moderate.

An alpine look was adopted by builders of the **Chandler's Bed, Bread and Trail Inn** (700 South Main Street, Joseph; 503-432-9765), which has five simply furnished rooms at the top of a log staircase. They share three baths and a kitchenette. Budget.

The **Wilderness Inn** (301 North Main Street, Enterprise; 503-426-4535); the **Melody Ranch Motel** (402 West North Street, Enterprise; 503-426-4022); and the **Ponderosa Motel** (102 Southeast Greenwood Street, Enterprise; 503-426-3186) are all basic motels: clean and uncomplicated by amenities such as pools and on-site restaurants. All are moderate.

Baker City has about ten motels, most offering the basic goodies of highway stopovers. The **Best Western Sunridge Inn** (One Sunridge Lane; 503-523-6444), just off Route 84, has 124 pine-paneled rooms and a pool. Priced in the moderate range.

The selection is thin in the area of John Day Fossil Beds National Monument. The town of John Day has four similar motels in the budget range. The **Best Western John Day Inn** (315 Main Street; 503-575-1700) has 36 units, and **Little Mac's Motel** (250 East Main Street; 503-575-1751) has 14. One small motel is in Mitchell, the town nearest the Painted Hills portion of the monument. The **Sky Hook Motel** (Route 26; 503-462-3569) has only six units. Budget.

NORTHEASTERN OREGON RESTAURANTS

Red meat is almost required eating in cowboy towns, but in Pendleton you can find a wider variety at **Rachael's Restaurant and Lounge** (233 Southeast 4th Street; 503-276-8500), a combination Native American art gallery, restaurant and cocktail lounge. The menu has beef (of course), but seafood items are also common, such as shrimp, bottom fish and clams. Moderate.

Good food is making inroads in the Wallowa Valley, and one of the first was **Val's Alpine Delicatessen** (Wallowa Lake State Park, Joseph; 503-432-5691). German-Hungarian dishes such as shish kebab and wienerschnitzel are served, but for the nonadventurous there is also plain, old American fare. The decor is German-Hungarian. Moderate.

The Anthony (1st Street and Washington Avenue, Baker City; 503-523-4475) is an unusual place—offbeat paintings, weird statues and busts of the famous—with a large menu of standard beef dishes and broiled and poached fish and chicken. Moderate.

NORTHEASTERN OREGON SHOPPING

Hamlet's Saddlery (30 Northeast Court Street; 503-276-2321) is a Pendleton institution where generations of folks have bought their saddles, clothes and various cowboy needs.

Baker City has become an antique mecca. You'll find items dating back to the pioneer years of the town, including oak furniture bought at estate sales, glass, rock collections, kitchen utensils and tools. **Baker City Collectibles** (2332 Broadway Street; 509-503-6077) handles mostly local furnishings. **Francis' Memory House Antiques** (2080 3rd Street; 503-523-6227) specializes in depression glass.

NORTHEASTERN OREGON NIGHTLIFE

Live music is hard to come by except on special occasions, such as rodeos and patriotic holidays. An exception is in Pendleton. **Crabby's Underground Saloon and Dance Hall** (220 Southwest 1st Street; 503-276-8118) has live country music by local talent five nights a week. It is in a basement beneath several small shops, and in addition to the music and dance-floor has darts, air ball and pool tables.

NORTHEASTERN OREGON BEACHES AND PARKS

Wallowa Lake State Park—On the southern end of the lake with large playground areas surrounded by trees, the park stretches from the lakeshore well back into the pine and spruce timber. Hiking trails are on the grounds.

Facilities: Day-use areas, boat dock and concessionaire; information, 503-238-4185. *Swimming:* Good. *Fishing:* Good rainbow trout fishing north of park.

Camping: There are 89 tent sites and 121 RV sites with hookups.

Getting there: Located at the southern end of Wallowa Lake on Route 82.

Hells Canyon National Recreation Area—This 652,000-acre monument protects the Snake River Gorge, a 20-mile-long canyon that has an average depth of 6000 feet, the deepest river gorge in the world. One of the most popular whitewater-rafting trips in the United States, it can be approached from deadend roads in Oregon and across the river in Idaho.

Facilities: Day-use picnic areas, scenic overlooks and restrooms; information, 503-426-4978. *Fishing:* Smallmouth bass and crappie are best.

Camping: There are 19 campgrounds with numerous sites.

Getting there: Located on Route 86 from Baker City through Halfway and Oxbow.

Southeastern Oregon

To travel in this part of the state you need a sturdy, reliable car, a cooler for cold drinks and snacks, and it might not be a bad idea to take along camping equipment because hotels/motels are few and far between. Harney County is the largest county in the United States, larger in fact than many Northeastern states, but this part of the country is really wide open. The three counties that make up the southeastern corner cover 28,450 square miles with a population of only 42,850. Harney is the largest at 10,228 square miles and has the smallest population, just under 8000. One town, Wagontire on Route 395, has a population that hovers around seven. Some say it depends on how many children are home for the holidays.

Few roads run through this area: Route 395 from California and Route 95 from Nevada are the main north-south corridors. Route 20 goes across the top from Idaho to the Cascades, and Route 140 runs across the bottom from northern Nevada through Lakeview to Klamath Falls. In Malheur

County you will find evidence of its diverse culture as Basque shepherds, Mexican cowboys, Japanese laborers and various Europeans came through and left their marks.

Oregon's longest lake, manmade **Lake Owyhee**, has miles of striking, desert topography along its shores. It is reached by taking Route 201 south from Nyassa to the small town of Owyhee, then a county road that deadends at the lake. Farther down in the desert where the Owyhee River still runs free is some of the state's best whitewater for river runners.

In Harney County are wildlife refuges around Malheur Lake and Steens Mountain. The only real population center is Burns. Crane, a dinky town southeast of Burns on Route 78, has the only high school in the county.

Sycan Marsh (P.O. Box 1267, Lakeview, OR 97630; 503-947-2691) is north of Lakeview off Route 31. It was purchased by the Nature Conservacy, which is using it as a research center for the effects of grazing on native grasses. Sycan Interpretive Center leads trips to the marsh with guests sleeping in tents and eating food cooked on a wood stove.

Northeast of Lakeview on Route 395 is **Abert Rim**, at 30 miles the largest exposed fault in North America. The massive fault juts up into the desert sky like a continuous cliff on the east side of Route 395, while on the west side of the highway is the talcum-white wasteland around **Lake Abert**.

Northwest of Lakeview just off Route 31 on county roads in Christmas Valley is **Crack in the Ground**, a 700-foot-deep crack caused by an earthquake. In the same area, **Fort Rock** is the remnant of a volcano crater and ocean shoreline that looks like one side of a destroyed fort. Indian sandals found there were carbon dated at 10,000 years.

About 25 miles northeast of Christmas Valley is **Lost Forest**, a 9000-acre, ponderosa-pine forest that has managed to survive in the middle of the harsh desert. The forest is surrounded by shifting sand dunes, which are popular with the all-terrain-vehicle set.

SOUTHEASTERN OREGON HOTELS

Down in the desert, Burns has four or five motels, including the **Best Western Ponderosa Motel** (577 West Monroe Street; 503-573-2047). It has 52 ordinary but clean rooms that don't smell of disinfectant, and a swimming pool. Budget.

There are only three places to stay in the area around Steens Mountain, Alvord Desert and Malheur and Harney lakes, so reservations are strongly recommended. All are closed between mid-November and April. A historic place is the **Frenchglen Hotel** (Frenchglen, OR 97736; 503-493-2825), a classic ranch house with screened porch built in 1916. Frenchglen has eight guest rooms decorated with rustic pine and patchwork quilts and has two shared baths. The managers serve a family-style dinner. Budget.

Hotel Diamond (★) (P.O. Box 10, Diamond, OR 97722; 503-493-1898) is 30 miles northeast of Frenchglen on a dirt road. It began as a log hotel, then was a ranch house, and now is a hotel again. It also serves as a general store and post office, so if you stay there you'll probably meet all the locals. It has five small, wallpapered rooms with shared baths. Meals are available. Budget.

Two miles north of Lakeview is **Hunter's Hot Springs Resort** (Route 395 North; 503-947-2127), which owns one of Oregon's two geysers. Named Old Perpetual, it shoots water and steam 60 feet into the air every 90 minutes. The resort has several thermal pools, and the hot water is reputed to have healing powers. The 36 units are simply decorated in what the owner calls country style. Budget.

SOUTHEASTERN OREGON RESTAURANTS

Almost everyone's favorite place to eat in Burns is the **Pine Room Café** (Monroe Street and Egan Avenue; 503-573-6631). The owners have been in business for three decades and have a secret recipe for potato-dumpling soup, cut all their own meat and make their own bread. Moderate.

SOUTHEASTERN OREGON BEACHES AND PARKS

Hart Mountain National Antelope Refuge—This 275,000-acre refuge 65 miles northeast of Lakeview protects a large population of antelope, bighorn sheep, mule deer, coyotes, a variety of smaller animals and a bird population. Hart Mountain, the centerpiece of the refuge, rises to 8065 feet and has deep gorges, ridges and cliffs on the west side. The east side climbs more gradually. For rockhounds, collections are limited to seven pounds per person.

Facilities: None; information, 503-947-3315. *Fishing:* Permitted in Rock and Guano creeks.

Camping: There are 12 primitive sites.

Getting there: Located 65 miles northwest of Lakeview on county roads off Routes 395 and 140.

Malheur National Wildlife Refuge—At 183,000 acres it is slightly smaller than the Hart Mountain refuge but covers an equally interesting and diverse wildlife population and geological features, including the almost-pure-white Alvord Desert. Malheur Lake is a major resting area for migratory birds on the Pacific Flyway.

Facilities: Malheur Field Station (503-493-2629) has dormitory and family housing and meals available; information, 509-493-2612.

Getting there: Located 26 miles south of Burns on Route 205, then 12 miles on Refuge Road.

The Sporting Life

GOLF

Golfers have a number of options, and with greens fees considerably lower than in urban areas. Try the **Okanogan Valley Golf Club** (Cherry Street off the Okanogan-Conconully Route between Omak and Okanogan; 509-826-9902) or **Oroville Golf Club** (Nighthawk Road, two miles west of Oroville; 509-476-2390), which has nine holes.

If you've seen San Francisco's Lincoln Park Municipal Golf Course with its view across the city skyline, Spokane's **Indian Canyon Golf Course** (West 4304 West Drive; 509-747-5353) will seem familiar. Set on a hillside that undulates downward toward Spokane, the 18-hole course is well known throughout the region.

The Tri-Cities area has seven courses, two of which are private clubs that honor reciprocal agreements. Courses include **Pasco Municipal Golf Course** (2535 North 20th Street, Pasco; 509-545-3440), **Canyon Lakes Golf Course** (3700 Canyon Lakes Drive, Kennewick; 509-582-3736) and **Sham-Na-Pum Golf Course** (72 George Washington Way, Richland; 509-946-2165).

The Yakima Valley has at least half a dozen including the **Suntides Golf Course** (22156 Pence Road, Yakima; 509-966-9065).

In the Grand Coulee Area are **Lakeview Golf and Country Club** (19th Street Northwest just off the Soap Lake-Ephrata Route south of Soap Lake; 509-246-1412) and **Banks Lake Golf Course** (two-and-a-half miles south of Grand Coulee on Route 155; 509-633-0163), with nine holes.

Courses are scarce in eastern Oregon simply because there aren't that many people around. A pleasant surprise is **Echo Hills Golf Course** (23 miles northwest of Pendleton, take the Echo exit off Route 84; 503-376-8244) with nine holes. Other nine-hole courses are **Baker Golf Course** (503-523-2358), **Pendleton Country Club** (503-278-1739) and **Mountain View Country Club** (503-575-0170) in John Day and **Alpine Meadows** (Enterprise; 503-426-3246). The **Kinzua Hills Golf Course** (ten miles east of Fossil; 503-763-2698) is Oregon's only six-hole approved course.

HORSEBACK RIDING

Most guest ranches and riding stables in both states are along the Cascade Range. The **Blue Mountain Outfitting** (Route 2, Box 54A, Asotin, WA 99402; 509-243-4774) offers fishing or scenic day trips in the Blue Mountains. West of Spokane the **Bar 41 Ranch** (HCR 11 Box 42, Wilbur, WA 99185; 509-647-5487) is for young people from 7 to 17 to "experience traditions of the Old West." Due north of Spokane in the Pend Oreille River

Valley, **Mountain Springs Guest Ranch** (P.O. Box 296, Ione, WA 99139; 509-442-3823) owns a herd of appaloosa horses and has a weekly range ride, overnight camping trips and daily lessons. In the **Hells Canyon National Recreation Area**, several outfitters are licensed to lead trips. For a list, contact the headquarters at P.O. Box 490, Enterprise, OR 97828; 503-426-3151.

SKIING

Downhill and cross-country skiing are both popular in this region, particularly the latter because there is so much open country and powdery snow. Cross-country trails are maintained at most downhill areas, but any country road, most golf courses and parks may be used by skiers.

Loup Loup (509-997-5334) between Okanogan and Twisp on Route 20 has a 1250-foot drop for downhill and a groomed area for cross-country skiers. **Sitzmark** (509-488-3323) 12 miles northeast of Tonasket is more modest with only a 650-foot drop. **Highland Park Snow Park** ten miles northeast of Tonasket has about seven miles of groomed trails. **Ski Bluewood** (509-382-2877) 22 miles southeast of Dayton at the end of a Forest Service road has cross-country skiing and ski school. **49 Degrees North** (509-924-5252) 16 miles west of Usk has four chairlifts on 1900 feet and night skiing.

BICYCLING

For the most part, automobile traffic is so sparse that bicyclists have little difficulty finding lonesome roads that are both challenging and beautiful. More and more cross-country bicyclists are seen along the smaller highways, especially Route 20 in Washington and the more remote highways in Oregon, such as Routes 3 and 86 through the Wallowa National Forest. Also in the cities you'll find some bicycle routes that double as hiking trails (see "Hiking" below).

The **Snake River Bikeway** runs six miles between Clarkston and Asotin along both the Clearwater and Snake rivers, and a 24-mile route from **Palouse** leads south on Route 27 to Clear Creek Road to Route 272 back to Palouse.

Routes have also been established along the Oregon Trail. One begins' at Oxbow in Hells Canyon and follows Route 86 westward to Halfway and **Baker City**, then on Route 7 to Sumpter and through the **John Day** area before crossing the Cascades.

BIKE RENTALS   Because of the remoteness of the trails here it's a good idea to bring your own gear. Otherwise, see if rentals are available at bicycle shops in cities and towns along your route.

HIKING

OKANOGAN HIGHLANDS TRAILS   Backpackers and day hikers alike enjoy this area because the weather is often clear and dry and the forest is more open than in the Cascades and Olympics. A number of established hiking trails are shown on Forest Service maps and in free brochures given out at the ranger station in Okanogan (509-826-3275).

A good walk for a family with small children is the 1.5-mile trail leading from Bonaparte Campground just north of the one-store town of Wauconda to the viewpoint overlooking the lake. Another easy one is the 7-mile loop **Big Tree Trail** from Lost Lake Campground, which is only a short distance north of Bonaparte. This one goes through a signed botanical area.

One of the most ambitious of the highlands trails is the **Kettle Crest Trail** (13 miles). The trek begins at the summit of Sherman Pass on Route 20 and winds southward past Sherman Peak and several other mountains. The trail is through mostly open terrain, and you'll have great views of the mountains and Columbia River Valley. Information: 509-775-3387.

SOUTHEASTERN WASHINGTON TRAILS   **Cowiche Canyon** (3 miles) starts five miles from Yakima. The trail is actually an old railroad bed that ran through the steep canyon. The canyon has unusual rock formations, and you can expect to see at least some wildlife.

Noel Pathway is a 4.6-mile trail inside the city limits of Yakima that follows the Yakima River. The pathway is used by bicyclists, too.

GRAND COULEE AREA TRAILS   A system of paths and trails connects the four towns clustered around Grand Coulee Dam. The Bureau of Reclamation built a paved route about 2 miles long called the **Community Trail**, which connects Coulee Dam and Grand Coulee. An informal system of unpaved paths connects these two towns to Elmer City and Electric City.

The newest is the walking-biking trail called the **Down River Trail** (6.5 miles). It runs north along the Columbia River from Grand Coulee, beginning in the Coulee Dam Shopping Center. It is accessible for wheelchairs.

Bunchgrass/Prairie Nature Trail (.5 mile loop) begins in the Spring Canyon Campground, which is three miles up Roosevelt Lake by water and two miles from Grand Coulee. The trail starts in the campground, and self-guided booklets are at the trailhead. It goes through one of the few remaining bunchgrass environments here. Information: 509-633-9441.

NORTHEASTERN OREGON TRAILS   The **Eagle Cap Wilderness** can be entered south of Enterprise and Joseph or from Lostine and has about a dozen major routes. One popular hike is from Wallowa Lake State Park 7.5 miles to Ice Lake. It is heavily used during the summer months.

The **Hells Canyon National Recreation Area** straddles the Snake River offering some of the most rugged landscape in the canyon. About a dozen trails have been established, rated from easy to difficult. The **Western Rim Trail** (34 miles) gives great views of the canyon and has the advantage of going from the end of one Forest Service road to another one. **HC Reservoir Trail** (4.8 miles) runs along the river between Copper Creek and Leep Creek.

Transportation

BY CAR

Eastern Washington and Oregon are served by a network of good roads that range from interstates to logging roads that have been paved by the Forest Service. **Route 97** serves as the north-south dividing line between the Cascade Mountains and the arid, rolling hills that undulate to the eastern boundaries of the states.

Route 90 runs through the center of the Washington, from Spokane southwest through Moses Lake, George and across the Columbia River at Vantage where the highway turns almost due west for its final run to Puget Sound.

Route 82 begins near Hermiston, Oregon, crosses the Columbia River to the Tri-Cities (Richland, Kennewick and Pasco) and runs on up the Yakima Valley to join Route 90 at Ellensburg. **Route 84** runs almost the entire length of the Columbia Gorge in Oregon before swinging southeast at Hermiston and connecting Pendleton, La Grande and Baker City with Ontario on the Idaho border.

Other major highways are **Route 395**, which runs through the center of the states from Lakeview, Oregon into Washington at the Tri-Cities to Ritzville. There it disappears into Route 90 at Ritzville only to emerge again at Spokane, where it continues north into British Columbia. Smaller but important highways include **Route 12**, which runs between Clarkston and Walla Walla, and **Route 195**, which runs between Pullman and Spokane.

Perhaps the most beautiful of all the highways in Washington is **Route 20**, which runs from Whidbey Island over the North Cascades, through the Methow Valley, then straight through the Okanogan Highlands to Kettle Falls, where it merges with Route 395. Oregon's **Route 26** is another lovely drive. It runs from Seaside over the Coast Range to Portland, then over the Cascades at Mt. Hood into the desert at Prineville and through the John Day Fossil Beds National Monument.

Certainly the loneliest major highway in the Northwest is **Route 95**, which comes up from McDermitt, Nevada, to cross the Oregon desert for nearly 150 miles before arriving at the first town, Burns.

BY AIR

Spokane International Airport is by far the busiest in Eastern Washington with five airlines serving the area: Alaska Airlines, Continental Airlines, Delta Airlines, Horizon Air and United Express.

Taxis and a shuttle service offer transportation from the Spokane airport downtown. Major taxi companies are **Inland Taxi** (509-326-8294), **Rainbow Enterprises** (509-327-4220) and **Spokane Cab** (509-489-1800). **Shields Industries** (509-535-6979) has a shuttle service from your door to the airport by appointment.

Other airports with scheduled service in Washington are **Clarkston, Moses Lake, Pullman, Wenatchee, Yakima, Tri-Cities** and **Walla Walla.** All these smaller cities are served by Horizon Air and United Express. In addition, Delta Air Lines serves Walla Walla and Pasco; Alaska Airlines and American Airlines serve Walla Walla.

The only Oregon city in this region with scheduled air service is **Pendleton**, served by Horizon Air.

BY BUS

Three bus lines operate throughout the region. From the Spokane terminal at West Sprague Avenue and South Jefferson Street are **Empire Lines** (509-624-4116), **Greyhound/Trailways Bus Lines** (509-624-5251) and **Northwestern Stage Lines** (509-838-4029). Greyhound and Empire also serve Yakima at the depot at 602 East Yakima Avenue.

Eastern Oregon is served primarily by **Greyhound** (320 Southwest Court, Pendleton; 503-276-1551).

BY TRAIN

Washington is one of the few states to have two **Amtrak** (800-872-7245) routes. Both start in Spokane. The first route runs from Spokane due west with stops in Wenatchee, Monroe, Everett and Edmonds before arriving in Seattle. The other route runs southwest from Spokane to the Columbia River Gorge with stops in Ritzville, the Tri-Cities and ultimately goes to Portland, Oregon.

In Oregon, Amtrak follows the same route pioneers took coming into Oregon, from Ontario to Baker City, La Grande, Pendleton and Hermiston before going down the Columbia Gorge to Portland.

CAR RENTALS

Rental agencies in Spokane include **Allstar Car Rentals** (509-747-8015), **Budget Rent A Car** (509-624-2255), **National Car Rental** (509-624-8995), **Thrifty Car Rental** (509-924-9111) and **U-Save Auto Rental** (509-455-8018).

Agencies in the Tri-Cities include **Budget Rent A Car** (509-547-6902), **Avis Rent A Car** (509-547-6971), **Hertz Rent A Car** (509-547-0111), **National Car Rental Systems** (509-545-9266) and **U-Save Auto Rental** (509-547-8326). Walla Walla and Moses Lake are served by **Budget Rent A Car** (Walla Walla; 509-525-8811, and Moses Lake; 509-765-6630). The lone agency at the Pendleton airport is **Hertz Rent A Car** (503-276-3183). Other, smaller airports served by scheduled airlines will have rental cars available, often by a local automobile dealer.

PUBLIC TRANSPORTATION

The Tri-Cities area (Pasco, Kennewick and Richland) has **Ben Franklin Transit** (509-735-5100). **Valley Transit** (509-525-6535) serves Walla Walla and College Place, and Prosser has its own **Rural Transit** (509-786-1707). **Basin Bus** (509-349-2971) serves a few Washington communities. Pullman has **Pullman Transit** (509-332-6535). Yakima has **Yakima Transit** (509-575-6175), which during the summer also runs a free shuttle service using cable-car-style buses that runs through the downtown business district.

CHAPTER SEVEN

Portland and
the Columbia River Gorge

But for the flip of a coin, Portland could have been called Boston. Our story begins with two pioneers, Asa Lovejoy of Massachusetts and Francis Pettygrove of Maine, hitting the Oregon Trail in search of the American dream. It was Lovejoy who found the perfect site for the new settlement on a fall 1843 canoe journey up the Willamette River from Fort Vancouver to Oregon City. His native guides called this wooded resting spot "The Clearing." Lovejoy, working on the safe assumption that the federal government would soon be handing out free 640-acre plots to settlers such as himself, had something bigger in mind.

Eager to start a new town, Lovejoy sprung for the 25-cent filing fee and soon found himself partners with Pettygrove at "The Clearing." Lovejoy wanted to call the new town Boston, but Pettygrove preferred to appropriate the name of Maine's Portland. True gentlemen, they settled the matter at Oregon City's Francis Ermatinger House with a coin toss.

Pettygrove won, but it was years before Portland began to rival Oregon City, the emigrant hub at the end of the overland trail. Even today, with a metropolitan population of more than 1.5 million, many visitors wonder how this city emerged as Oregon's centerpiece. Unlike the largest cities of the Pacific Northwest or California, it is not located on a major coast or sound. Although it is midway between the equator and the North Pole, Portland is not central to the geography of its own state. Yet from the arts and winter recreation to architecture and vineyards, this city is an admirable metropolis, one that merits inclusion on any Northwest itinerary.

253

The community has a rich cultural life, is blessed with some of the prettiest urban streets in the Northwest, is a veritable haven for antique lovers, runners, cyclists and garden aficionados and has an impressive array of jazz clubs, bistros, off-beat museums and a popular National Basketball Association franchise. And yet the legacy of "The Clearing" is very much intact as the city remains intimately connected to the great outdoors. Near the entrance to the fabled Columbia River gorge, Portland is just 65 miles from the nearest glacier and 110 miles from the ocean. Riverfront greenspace, the 5000-acre Forest Park and the wonderful wetlands of Sauvie Island all demonstrate why this city has been named "best" on the Green Index, a study of pollution, public health and environmental policy.

When the weather turns very wet, as it does in the winter months, residents head for the powder-packed slopes of Mt. Hood or start gearing up for a bit of steelheading on the nearby coastal rivers. Winter is also the heart of the cultural season, enjoyed at the Performing Arts Center and dozens of other venues around town.

Portland's emergence as a major city owes much to emigrant New England ship captains who decided, in the mid-19th century, that the town's deep riverfront harbor was preferable to the shallows of Oregon City. Easy ocean access via the Columbia made the new port an easy link to the emerging agrarian economy of the Willamette Valley, as well as the region's up-and-coming lumber mills. Like San Francisco, Portland flourished as an international shipping hub and as a gateway for the 1852 gold rush that began in the Jacksonville region.

As the Northwest's leading port and economic center, the town soon attracted the state's new gentry, the lumber barons, shipping titans, traders, mercantilists and agribusiness pioneers. They drew heavily on the architectural legacy of the Northeast and Europe, throwing up Cape Cod-style homes, Victorian mansions, villas and French Renaissance-style mini-châteaus complete with Italian marble and virgin-redwood interiors.

A city that started out in life as a kind of New England-style village crafted out of native fir was made over with brick office blocks sporting cast-iron facades. Florentine, Italianate, Gothic, even Baroque architecture began to emerge along the main drags. City fathers worked hard to upgrade the town's agrarian image, often with mixed results.

To unify the community, planners added a 25-block-long promenade through the heart of town. Lined with churches, office blocks, apartments and homes, these "Park Blocks" offered a grassy median ideal for contemplating the passing scene. Like a Parisian boulevard, this was the place where one might come for the hour and stay for the day. Brass water fountains, left on 24 hours a day, brought the pure waters of the Cascades to street level.

While the city's New England quality made Bostonians feel right at home, Portland also attracted a significant Chinese community that labored

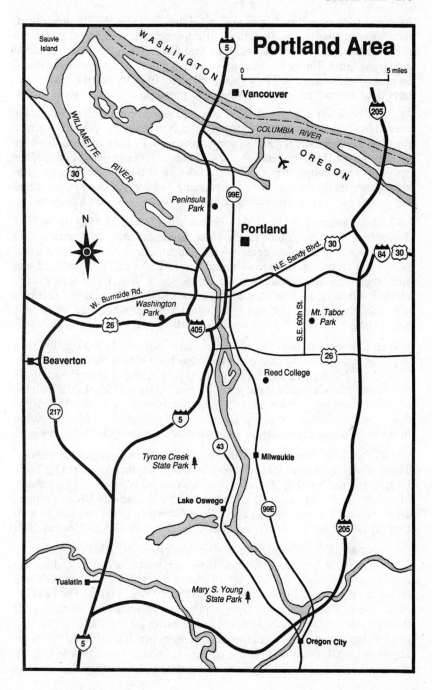

Portland Area

Sauvie
Island

WASHINGTON

5

0   5 miles

■ Vancouver

205

COLUMBIA RIVER

OREGON

WILLAMETTE

30

RIVER

Peninsula
Park

99E

Portland

30

84 30

N.E. Sandy Blvd.

N

S.E. 60th St.

Mt. Tabor
Park

W. Burnside Rd.

Washington
Park

26

405

26

Beaverton

Reed College

217

5

43

Tyrone Creek
State Park

Milwaukie

Lake Oswego

99E

205

Tualatin

Mary S. Young
State Park

5

Oregon City

long and hard on railroad lines and in salmon factories. Badly persecuted, they were just one of many victims of intolerance in this city that became a Ku Klux Klan center. Blacks, Jews and Catholics were also victimized at various times. But as Portland grew, this deplorable bigotry was replaced by a new egalitarianism. The city's intellectual life flourished thanks to the arrival of several major universities and prestigious liberal arts colleges.

As Portland modernized, it became a manufacturing center famous for everything from swimsuits to footwear. But as the city flourished as a center for high-tech industry, it did not forget its roots. Visitors eager to discover the Northwest flock here and to the Columbia Gorge in pursuit of outdoor activities from windsurfing to birding. An ideal home base, this city has also drawn many famous artists, musicians and writers from larger, more congested and expensive communities like New York and Los Angeles.

Although much of Portland's best is within easy walking distance of downtown, the city's outer reaches also invite leisurely exploration. The touchstones of great urban centers—science museums, zoos, children's museums and craft centers—are all found here. Amid its 50 museums, 23 theater companies and countless other ameneties, Portland also offers many pleasant surprises such as a strong used-book-seller community, America's only advertising museum, the sole extinct volcano within the limits of a continental U.S. city and the world's smallest park.

At a time when many major American urban centers are fighting hard to preserve their quality of life, Portland has been named the "Most Livable U.S. City" by the U.S. conference of mayors. Careful restoration of the downtown core and historic old town, a beautiful riverfront area and thriving nightlife make this town a winner. Neighborhoods such as Nob Hill, Hawthorne and Sellwood all invite leisurely exploration. And when it comes to parks you can choose from more than 80 spanning 37,000 acres.

In this chapter we have divided the city into three geographic regions. The Central Portland region encompasses downtown, the Skidmore Old Town District and the Yamhill Historic District. Portland West covers the balance of the city and metropolitan region west of the Willamette River. Portland East includes the metro area east of the Willamette River including Lloyd Center, Burnside, Sellwood and southerly destinations like Oregon City.

Because of its proximity to Portland, we have included the Columbia Gorge region in this chapter. Even if you only have a couple of hours to cruise up to Multnomah Falls, by all means go. The Gorge extends about 60 miles east to Hood River and White Salmon, Washington. The final leg of the journey west for many Oregon pioneers, imagine how it felt to glide through this verdant, waterfall-lined canyon after 2000 miles of hardscrabble, blazing desert and treacherous mountain passes. This fir-clad valley really was valhalla, the light at the end of the tunnel some people call the American dream. We think you'll enjoy it as much as they did.

Central Portland

The urban renaissance is clearly a success in Portland. A walkable city with perpetually flowing drinking fountains, this riverfront town is a place where commerce, history, classic architecture and the arts flourish side by side. Even when the weather is foul, Portland is an inviting place. A good place to orient yourself is the **Portland/Oregon Visitors Association** (Front and Salmon streets; 503-275-9750). Here you can pick up helpful maps and brochures.

Walk west on Main Street to Justice Center and the **Portland Police Historical Museum** (Room 1682, 1111 Southwest 2nd Avenue; 503-796-3019). After learning about the history of local law enforcement, continue west on Main Street to the **Portland Building** (1120 Southwest 5th Avenue; 503-823-4000), a postmodernist office landmark opened in 1982. Designed by Michael Gross, this whimsical skyscraper represents the Northwest with a Native American motif making extensive use of turquoise and earth tones. On the roof is **Portlandia**, the world's second-largest hammered-bronze sculpture. On the Portland building's second floor is the **Metropolitan Center For Public Art (★)** (1120 Southwest 5th Avenue; 503-796-5111). Here you'll find Portlandia molds and renderings of the building. A special exhibit and walking-tour map focus on public art across the city.

Continue west on Madison Street to South Park and turn left to the **Oregon Historical Center** (1230 Southwest Park Avenue; 503-222-1741). Home of the Oregon Historical Society, this is the place to learn the story of the region's Native Americans, the arrival of the Europeans and the westward migration. You'll find an Indian tepee, sea chests from early voyages to the region and artifacts documenting the political and social evolution of the West. A vast repository of Western Americana with nearly 22 million manuscripts, the Historical Society has a wonderful research library. Handsome *trompe l'oeil* murals featuring Lewis and Clark and their Indian guide, Sacagawea, grace the building's exterior.

Adjacent to the Oregon Historical Society is the **First Congregational Church** (1126 Southwest Park Avenue; 503-228-7219). This gothic landmark shaded by elms is at its best in the fall. We think this is one of the prettiest corners in Portland.

Directly across the street is the **Portland Art Museum** (1219 Southwest Park Avenue; 503-226-2811; admission), known for its collection of Asian art as well as 20th-century American and European sculpture. The Rasmussen Collection of Northwest Coastal Indian art and artifacts showcases excellent tribal masks and wood sculptures of mythical monsters who liked to dine on tourists, er humans. The pre-Columbian pieces, box drums, Potlatch dishes and cones are all notable. Don't miss the skylit sculpture courtyard.

Head west to 11th Avenue and then turn south to **Old Church** (1422 Southwest 11th Avenue; 503-222-2031). Since 1833 this Gothic classic has been a Portland landmark. Noon organ concerts are held Wednesdays.

Return to Park Avenue and continue north to Yamhill Street and turn right. Walk two more blocks to **Pioneer Courthouse Square** (Yamhill and Morrison streets; 503-223-1613), a popular Portland gathering point. A waterfall and 64,000 red bricks inscribed with the names of local residents who donated money for the square's construction are all here. Named for adjacent **Pioneer Courthouse**, the oldest public building in Oregon, which you may want to explore, the square offers a variety of special events including concerts and, at Christmas time, a skating rink. Since it's 25 feet high, you won't miss the square's unusual weather machine.

Continue walking east on Yamhill past the 19th-century Victorian Italianates and the shops of **Yamhill Marketplace** (110 Southwest Yamhill Street; 503-224-6705) to **Tom McCall Waterfront Park** (Front Avenue). Go south past **Mill Ends Park** located in the median at Southwest Front Avenue and Taylor Street. Just two feet wide, this is the smallest park in the world. Continue south to **Salmon Street Springs Fountain** (Salmon Street at Front Avenue) and **River Place** (Harbor Way), a popular shopping, hotel, restaurant and nightclub complex on the water. Then return north to the **Oregon Maritime Museum** (113 Southwest Front Avenue; 503-224-7724; admission). Here's your chance to learn northwestern maritime history and see models of early ships, historical photographs and interpretive displays.

To fully enjoy the Portland waterfront consider boarding an excursion boat; the following companies depart from Riverplace Marina at 1510 Southwest Harbor Way behind the Riverplace Alexis. **Sternwheeler Rose** (503-286-7673) offers scenic Willamette River cruises. For a dramatic trip on the Willamette and Columbia rivers, board the **Sternwheeler Columbia Gorge** (503-223-3928). **Rose City Riverboat Cruises/Yachts-O-Fun Cruises** (503-289-6665) offers harbor, brunch, dinner and evening trips.

Now go north to Skidmore Fountain. Your gateway to the Skidmore Historic District, the fountain area is the site of **Portland Saturday Market** (between Southwest Front and 1st avenues at the west end of the Burnside Bridge; 503-222-6072), held on weekends from March through Christmas. Akeny Park and the district beneath the Burnside Bridge is a great place to shop for arts and crafts, sample savory specialties served up by vendors and enjoy performances by musicians, street performers and clowns.

The **Skidmore/Old Town** area is a good example of adaptive reuse. Historic commercial buildings and warehouses have been reborn as trendy shops, galleries, restaurants and nightclubs. This area is also the home of the **American Advertising Museum** (9 Northwest 2nd Avenue; 503-226-0000; admission). A tribute to our hidden persuaders, this museum has a sensational collection of Madison Avenue artifacts and icons, mementos and memorabilia. The video collection featuring classic campaigns for products like the VW Bug and Sony is an absolute must.

Next, head north through **Chinatown** on 4th Avenue. At Glisan Street head west to 6th Avenue. Then walk north to **Union Station**, Portland's Richardsonian Romanesque Amtrak Station (800 Northwest 6th Avenue; 503-273-4865). Return south on 4th Avenue through the Chinatown gate to Burnside Street and walk west to 11th Avenue where you'll find the **Blitz-Weinhard Brewing Company** (1133 West Burnside Street; 503-222-4351). A free guided tour offers a chance to learn the brewer's art from one of the state's oldest beer makers. Following your visit enjoy a complimentary draft in the Hospitality Room.

Finally, we believe everyone should take time out to visit the 24-hour **Church of Elvis (★)** (219 Southwest Ankeny Street; 503-226-3671). Just walk down Burnside Street toward the river, turn right at 5th Avenue and left on Ankeny to reach this theological automat, also known as the world's first around-the-clock, coin-operated art gallery. The ultimate storefront parish fuses religion, rock and metaphysics in a multimedia-window presentation likely to keep you plunking quarter after quarter into the church's coin slot. Yes, it's cash up front to get the IBM-compatible ministerial computer rolling and set up your direct line to Graceland. Because there are no pews, much less a sanctuary, you're forced to stand outside, communicating with the interactive monitor behind the store window. By pushing multiple-choice buttons on the doorframe, you can respond directly to the computer screen's questions about Elvis, God, life, death and so forth. For a few extra quarters the church will issue wedding and divorce certificates. Unfortunately there isn't much to see inside the church—just a gift shop. Remember, every donation makes you a saint in the Church of Elvis.

CENTRAL PORTLAND HOTELS

From its paneled lounge to a collection of 250 film classics on tape, **The Heathman** (Southwest Broadway at Salmon Street; 503-241-4100) exemplifies Portland's charm. A library featuring signed copies of books by authors who have spent the night and 150 spacious rooms and suites appointed with contemporary art are some of the lures. Contemporary furniture, king beds, mirrored and marble baths make this refurbished landmark a good bet. Jazz is performed nightly on the lounge Steinway, and a popular café supplements the main dining room. How far does the Heathman go to make its guests happy? When Luciano Pavarotti wanted to sleep in after a late arrival, manager Mary Armistad asked a contractor across the street to postpone the start of noisy construction from 7 a.m. to 10 a.m. They agreed and the tenor slept soundly. Deluxe to ultra-deluxe.

A grand hotel and a registered historic landmark, **The Benson** (309 Southwest Broadway; 503-228-2000) offers casual fireside elegance in the lobby and 290 spacious rooms with understated grey decor, oak furniture, armoires and Early American prints. Like a good English club, the walnut-paneled lobby court features easy chairs, comfortable sofas and a mirrored bar. Marbled halls, chandeliers, brass fixtures, a grand staircase and grandfather clock add an elegant touch. The stamped-tin ceiling, a common architectural feature in the late 19th and early 20th century, is one of the finest we've seen. Deluxe to ultra-deluxe.

A good value in the moderate-price range, the **Imperial Hotel** (400 Southwest Broadway; 503-228-7221) has been busy renovating its 168 rooms. Paneling, floral-patterned spreads, small sitting areas and modern prints have brightened up this venerable establishment. Convenient to popular shops, cafés and clubs, the Imperial also has a full lounge and restaurant.

Boutique hotels are one of the fastest-growing trends in the lodging industry and now Portland has one of its own, **Hotel Vintage Plaza** (422 Southwest Broadway; 503-228-12121). A remake of the historic Wells Building, this deluxe-to-ultra-deluxe-priced hotel features a ten-story atrium. Each of the 107 guest rooms and spacious suites is named for a local winery. Rooms with blue or gold color schemes come with cherrywood armoires, neoclassical furniture, columned headboards, black-granite night stands and Empire-style column bedside lamps. Sampling the wine your room is named for is easily done at the complimentary tasting held each evening in front of the wood-burning fireplace in the lobby.

An excellent value, the moderate-to-deluxe-priced **Riverside Inn** (50 Southwest Morrison Street; 503-221-0711) is the place to enjoy views of boat traffic on the Willamette. Brass beds, wicker furniture, impressionist prints and contemporary posters brighten the rooms. Enjoy the sunset from the comfort of your deck. The 137-room inn is walking distance from Portland's business and shopping district. There are also a café and bar.

Enjoying one of the best locations in town, **River Place Alexis** (1510 Southwest Harbor Way; 503-228-3233) offers 74 rooms and suites, many with views of the Willamette. In the midst of the Esplanade area featuring bookstores, antique shops and restaurants, this establishment is a short walk from the downtown business district. Wingback chairs, teak tables, writing desks, fireplaces and pastel decor make the rooms inviting. A health club, whirlpool baths and indoor track are all available. Prices are in the deluxe to ultra-deluxe range.

For budget-to-moderate-priced rooms and suites head for the **Mallory Hotel** (729 Southwest 15th Avenue; 503-223-6311). This 143-unit establishment has a mirrored lobby, leaded skylights, a chandelier and grandfather clock. The eclectic rooms come with floral-print spreads, oak furniture, contemporary couches and, in some cases, small chandeliers. Also here is a classy dining room with marble pillars supporting the embossed-gold-leaf ceiling.

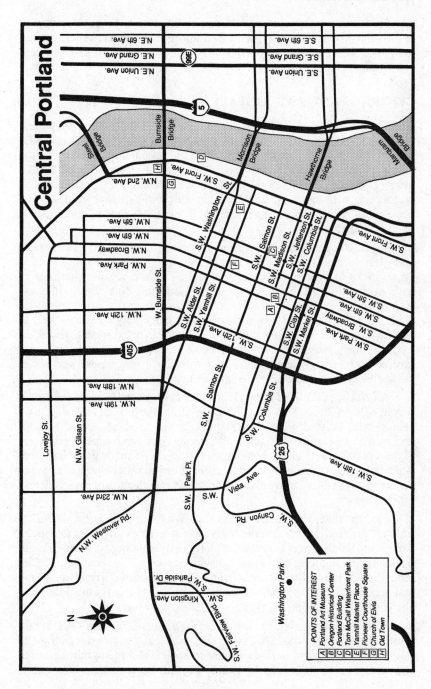

Central Portland

POINTS OF INTEREST
- A Portland Art Museum
- B Oregon Historical Center
- C Portland Building
- D Tom McCall Waterfront Park
- E Yamhill Market Place
- F Pioneer Courthouse Square
- G Church of Elvis
- H Old Town

Washington Park

Portland also has many small bed and breakfasts. To book a room in or near the city contact **Northwest Bed and Breakfast Travel Unlimited** (610 Southwest Broadway; 503-243-7616). They handle over 350 inspected establishments and cover other parts of the state.

CENTRAL PORTLAND RESTAURANTS

The brick pizza oven, trattoria ambience, dark wood booths and gleaming bar make **Pazzo Ristorante** (627 Southwest Washington Street; 503-228-1515) a welcome addition to the Portland restaurant scene. Dip a little of the fresh-baked bread in the special-press extra virgin olive oil, hoist a glass of the red and survey the Mediterranean menu. Pizza, grilled ribeye on foccacia with onions, creamy polenta with rosemary and parmesan and pasta tubes with lamb sausage, red chard, marinara and ricotta are some of the popular entrées. Deluxe.

A veritable designer showcase with Asian, art deco, nautical and brass-and-glass furnishings, **Atwater's** (111 Southwest 5th Avenue; 503-275-3600) looks like an exclusive private club. That's precisely what it is by day. At night the public is welcome to dine in this 30th-floor restaurant. Appetizers prepared in the display kitchen include terrine of pheasant and duck with filberts, dried sweet cherries and blackberry catsup as well as terrific butternut squash gnocchis with walnut sauce and fresh herbs. After a bowl of the lobster bisque try the grilled ahi, sautéed salmon or fresh pasta layered with turkey, ricotta cheese, acorn squash, sweet anise and home-made turkey sausage. Deluxe to ultra-deluxe.

A favorite in Portland is the **Heathman Restaurant** (Southwest Broadway at Salmon Street, Portland; 503-241-4100). The broiled filet of chinook salmon with sautéed green apples and sage beurre blanc, seared scallops and *magret of mouillard*, duck with poached pears and muscat reduction glaze, are just a few of the popular specialties. This spacious dining room and adjacent brass and marble bar is a great place to watch the passing scene on Broadway. The walls are graced with a classy collection of contemporary art. Deluxe.

Pass the retsina and toast **Alexis** (215 West Burnside Street; 503-224-8577). This family-style taverna brings the Aegean to the Columbia in the time-honored manner. Bouzouki music, belly dancing on the weekend, wallhangings and long tables upstairs with checkered blue-and-white tablecloths add to the ambience. Lamb souvlaki, moussaka, charbroiled shrimp and vegetarian specialties are all on the menu. Be sure to try the dolma and share an order of hummus and homemade pita. Moderate.

A memorable dining room is **Jake's Famous Crawfish** (401 Southwest 12th Avenue; 503-226-1419). This mahogany-paneled, century-old landmark has a grand bar, big tables and a seafood menu that seems to stretch from here to Seattle. Inevitably packed, the restaurant offers good chowder, smoked and fresh salmon, halibut, oysters and a good bouillabaisse. Despite the crowds, service is excellent. Moderate to deluxe.

B. Moloch Heathman Bakery and Pub (901 Southwest Salmon Street; 503-227-5700) is an ideal downtown stop for a light lunch or dinner, snacks, coffee or a drink at the bar supplied on the premises by the Widmer microbrewery, one of several found in the Portland area. Exposed concrete columns, oak floors and tables, silkscreen prints and casablanca fans give the place the ambience of a college student union. Order an individual pizza, smoked-chicken gazpacho salad or herb roast beef and potted cheddar on dark rye. Budget to moderate.

A vast menu offering Asian, Cajun, Italian and Oregon cuisine, **Harbor Side** (0309 Southwest Montgomery Street; 503-220-1865) is a kind of culinary United Nations. Window tables on the river or one of the paneled booths on the upper levels provide great views of the harbor traffic. Excellent seafood salads, pasta dishes, stir frys, steaks, hamburgers and pizza are served at moderate prices.

A display kitchen, stained-glass ceiling, oak tables and booths make **Opus Too Bar and Restaurant** (33 Northwest 2nd Avenue; 503-222-6077) one of the city's more stylish restaurants. The menu features mesquite-broiled seafood, steaks, sausages, chicken and a wide variety of fettucine dishes. Other highlights include Greek salads, pan-fried oysters, garlic prawns and a chocolate decadence cake that lives up to its name. After dinner enjoy recorded or live jazz in the lounge. Moderate to deluxe.

Obi (101 Northwest 2nd Avenue; 503-226-3826) is the place for sushi, *yaki soba*, seafood tempura, beef *shaabu shaabu*, vinegar lemon chicken, salmon teriyaki and dozens of other Japanese specialties. The dark dining room has modest plastic tables and displays silk-screen art, water colors and traditional costumes. Moderate.

Couch Street Fish House (105 Northwest 3rd Avenue; 503-223-6173) is an elegant Old Town restaurant located in a skylit brick storefront graced with historic photos and seascapes. Liveried waiters and comfortable booths and tables make the restaurant a good choice for a big night out. Seafood fettuccine, Pacific oysters, filet of cod with white wine caper sauce and crab legs toscana are a few of the specialties. Moderate to deluxe.

The setting alone justifies a trip to **Old Town Pizza Company** (226 Northwest Davis Street; 503-222-9999). A landmark commercial building with stained glass, wicker furniture, enough antiques to furnish a store and old root beer advertising signs make this two-level establishment a genuine period piece. More than two dozen ingredients from goat cheese to bay shrimp give you plenty of options. Foccacia, antipasta and salads are also available. Budget.

From the flocked foil wallpaper to the big red chairs, **Wilf's In Union Station** (800 Northwest 6th Avenue; 503-223-0070) is one of the most elaborate dining rooms in Portland. The Victorian setting along the tracks is a great place to enjoy roast duckling, pepper steak, scampi flambé, halibut meunière and, for dessert, baked Alaska or crêpes Suzette. Deluxe.

CENTRAL PORTLAND SHOPPING

The **Oregon Historical Society Bookstore** (1230 Southwest Park Avenue; 503-222-1741) has an outstanding collection of local and regional history titles. From Native American culture to walking-tours of Portland, this admirable shop is definitely worth a look. Souvenir books, guides and children's literature are all found in abundance.

Don't walk, run to **Nike Town** (930 Southwest 6th Avenue; 503-221-6453). From John McEnroe's tennis racket to statues of Michael Jordan, this store is a monument to conditioning. Two floors of museum-like galleries hawk the Nike line moved about the store on a network of conveyors.

Classic newsstands are hard to find these days. Fortunately century-old **Rich's Cigars** (801 Southwest Alder Street; 503-228-1700) continues this grand tradition. Browse for your favorite magazine or out-of-town newspaper in this beautiful, wood-paneled shop.

Bigger than many libraries, **Powell's City of Books** (1005 West Burnside Street; 503-228-4651) is only one of Portland's many fine bookstores. What makes it unique is its size. With over a million new and used titles, this goliath encourages customers to pick up a large map indexed into hundreds of categories ranging from abortion to Zen. Somewhere in between you're likely to find the title you want. Along the way, stop by the Anne Hughes Coffee Room for a break and a leisurely read. Powell's also has a **travel bookstore** (701 Southwest 6th Avenue; 503-228-1108). Both stores wheelchair accessible.

Several major malls are in the downtown area. They include **The Galleria**, a fine example of adaptive reuse that has transformed a historic building into a three-story retail center. **Pioneer Place** (Southwest 5th Avenue and Morrison Street; 503-228-5800) also offers 80 stores spread across a three-block area.

One of the region's best-known apparel makers offers its line at **The Portland Pendleton Shop** (900 Southwest 5th Avenue; 503-242-0037). Skirts, shirts, slacks, jackets and blankets are all sold at this popular shop. While the company built its reputation on woolens, it also sells excellent apparel in silk, rayon and other fabrics.

Elizabeth Leach Gallery (207 Southwest Pine Street; 503-224-0521) features regional and national painters, sculptors, photographers and print makers.

Oregon Mountain Community (60 Northwest Davis Street; 503-227-1038) is the ultimate shop for recreational equipment and supplies. In addition to a full line of outdoor wear, this retailer offers fishing, skiing, cycling, hiking and climbing gear.

An excellent place to find arts and crafts is **Portland Saturday Market** (108 West Burnside Street; 503-222-6072). More than 300 artisans offer glass, jewelry, gyroscopes, wool hats, sweaters, furniture, rugs, music boxes, folk and fine art. There's also live entertainment.

The **Attic Gallery** (206 Southwest 1st Avenue; 503-228-7830) features paintings, sculpture, prints and ceramics by major Northwest artists.

CENTRAL PORTLAND NIGHTLIFE

The city's cultural hub is the **Portland Center For The Performing Arts** (1111 Southwest Broadway; 503-248-4496). Included are the Arlene Schnitzer Concert Hall and the Intermediate and Winningstad theaters. This complex is home of the **Oregon Symphony Orchestra** (503-248-4496) and **Oregon Shakespeare Festival-Portland** (503-274-6588).

Portland Repertory Theater (25 Southwest Salmon Street; 503-224-4491) offers both contemporary and modern drama. A professional equity company, The Rep frequently sells out. **Artists Repertory Theater** (1111 Southwest 10th Avenue; 503-242-9043) is the place for off-broadway performances. Children's classics are the focus of **The New Rose Theater** (904 Southwest Main Street; 503-222-2495).

Both the **Oregon Ballet Theater** (503-227-6867) and **Portland Opera** (503-241-1802) perform at the Civic Auditorium (222 Southwest Clay Street).

For jazz piano, visit the **Heathman Lobby Lounge** (Southwest Broadway at Salmon Street; 503-241-4100) where performers like Dave Firshberg play jazz on the Steinway.

Enjoy a drink as the pianist performs pop and jazz at **The Benson Hotel's Lobby Lounge** (309 Southwest Broadway; 503-228-2000). This elegant setting includes plush sofas and wing chairs and walnut paneling. The lounge is a great place to impress your friends—or yourself.

In the heart of downtown Portland, **Dakota** (239 Southwest Broadway; 503-241-4151) offers big-band music, rock, fusion and soul. This utilitarian, track-lit café is ideal for dancing. Cover.

Brasserie Montmartre (626 Southwest Park Avenue; 503-224-5552) is another good jazz venue. This art-deco establishment, where patrons are encouraged to draw on their paper placemats, even has a strolling magician. Contemporary paintings, comfortable banquettes, chandeliers and a checkered black-and-white floor all add to the charm of this café.

The **Oregon Art Institute's Museum After Hours** program (1219 Southwest Park Avenue; 503-226-2811; admission) is a great place to be on Wednesday evenings in the winter months. Take a seat or explore the collection while the halls resonate to jazz or blues. Wine is served.

One of the best places in town is **Jazz de Opus** (33 Northwest 2nd Avenue; 503-222-6077). This low-slung lounge adjacent to a popular restaurant offers a full bar. Both recorded and live music are offered.

For cabaret there's nothing in Portland quite like **Darcelle XV** (208 Northwest 3rd Avenue; 503-222-5338). Female impersonators perform nightly in this small theater where dinner is also available. Cover.

For rhythm and blues, rock, jazz, folk and pop in a faux tropical setting head on down to **Key Largo** (31 Northwest 1st Avenue; 503-223-9919). This red-brick commercial building with an exposed beam ceiling, casablanca fans, wicker furniture and hanging plants is at its best in the summer. Then you can head out back to party on the patio. Dinner and munchies are served. Cover.

The Last Laugh (426 Northwest 6th Avenue; 503-295-2844) is the place to enjoy local and national comedy acts. Be sure to get a seat up close. Special dinner/show packages are offered. Cover.

A drag showbar at **Embers** (110 Northwest Broadway; 503-222-3082) features open-mike standup comedy nightly. In the rear of this brick building is **On The Avenue**, home of Portland's largest gay dancefloor. With neon-lit walls, three bars and deejay music, this room is always jumping. Capacity is limited to 500.

Get the jump on the holidays at the **X-Ray Café** (214 West Burnside Street; 503-721-0115), where they decorate for Christmas at Halloween time and celebrate Valentine's Day in December. Filled with stuffed animals, black-velvet paintings and David Cassidy pictures, the X-Ray offers pop and country music, meditation, yoga classes, poetry readings, story telling and square dancing in an alcohol- and drug-free environment. You never know what you might find at this eclectic spot that is always planning offbeat events like Tupperware demonstrations and lectures by an encyclopedia salesman. Cover.

Men, it pays to wear your high heels to **Silverado** (1217 Southwest Stark Street; 503-224-4493) on Monday nights. From 9 p.m. to closing you'll get two well drinks for the price of one. With male strippers four nights a week, neon bar signs and a swinging dancefloor, this club has plenty of action. Deejay music, a long bar and dining room featuring brunch on Saturday and Sunday make Silverado popular with the gay community.

Looking for Mr. or Ms. Right? Then come on down to **Shanghai** (0309 Southwest Montgomery Street; 503-220-1865). Live dance bands set the beat for this jam-packed club. Take a table or booth by the second-story window and survey the queue waiting below outside. While checking out the possibilities on the Willamette Esplanade, order a round of drinks and watch the Portland mating ritual. Cover.

Portland East

Just across the Willamette are some of Portland's most inviting neighborhoods. Home of the city's convention center, several popular shopping districts, antique centers and major museums, Portland East also features a rare heirloom, the classic old-time amusement park. This region, which includes such towns as Oregon City, also features several major parks and wildlife areas, as well as a rare religious retreat.

Cross the Willamette via MAX lightrail and disembark at the beautiful **Oregon Convention Center** (777 Northeast Martin Luther King Jr. Boulevard; 503-235-7575) plaza landscaped with terraced planters. Stroll over for a look at the 490,000-square-foot center crowned by a matching pair of glass-and-steel spires soaring 250 feet above the hall. The center's interior features art, dragon boats, a bronze pendulum and inspirational quotes about the state. Everywhere you go, even in the restrooms, you'll find talented artists and craftspeople have left their decorative touch.

A mile south of the convention center, the **Oregon Museum of Science and Industry** (1701 Southeast Water Avenue; 503-222-2828; admission) is opening a 240,000-square-foot science education center in the fall of 1992. Six exhibition halls offer displays on space, physical, earth, life and information sciences. Also here will be an Omnimax motion picture theater, an outdoor science park and esplanade. Special exhibits will focus on biotechnology, engineering for kids, communications and chemistry.

Lloyd Center, one MAX stop beyond the convention center, is a pioneer American shopping mall. In the neighborhood is **Carousel Courtyard** (between 7th and 9th avenues on Northeast Holladay Street; 503-230-0400), a lovely garden built around an 1895 merry-go-round. Concerts, special events, vendors and a gazebo make this a popular spot for families. Adjacent to the courtyard is the **International Museum of Carousel Art** (710 Northeast Holladay Street; 503-235-2252; admission). Besides seeing historic artifacts you'll likely spot artisans restoring the wooden menagerie that makes the merry-go-round experience such a joy. On weekends there's also children's theater.

Nearby is the **Cowboy Museum** (729 Northeast Oregon Street, Suite 190; 503-731-3333). Built in the belief that "anything worth doing can be done from the back of a horse," this small collection covers subjects ranging from the Oregon Trail to buckaroo music. Along the way audio-animatronic narrators offer insights on cowpunching, and you can check out exhibits on the cattle and ranching industries, as well as a swell saddle collection.

To the south are two popular Portland shopping districts. **Hawthorne Boulevard** from 30th to 40th avenues has become one of the city's more intriguing commercial districts. A great place to browse, shop and eat, this district is known for its used bookstores and offbeat boutiques. Another pop-
(Text continued on page 270.)

Oregon City—The Trail's End

Wagons, ho!

So you missed out on the 19th-century move west? (Well, at least we weren't around then.) Come 1993, you'll be able to do the next-best thing as cities across the United States celebrate the 150th anniversary of the route that launched America's greatest mass migration. Wagon trains will roll out of Independence, Missouri, wagon ruts will be examined in Scottsbluff, Nebraska, and Wyoming's South Pass will attract music, dramas and homecomings. But when it comes to curtain calls, all eyes will be on Oregon City. Just a half hour south of Portland, this community built along the 40-foot high Willamette River waterfalls is one of the best places in the Pacific Northwest to understand and appreciate manifest destiny. For this was the destination that launched the migration of over 300,000 Americans to a blank slate known as the promised land.

The center of human endeavor for more than 3000 years, the Willamette Falls was an important place long before the first white emigrants arrived. But once they did show up, things moved quickly. In 1818, just five years after the British took control of the Northwest region from the Astorians, the Americans and British agreed to jointly occupy Oregon Country. In 1829, Dr. John McLoughlin, the shrewd operator of the Hudson's Bay Company base at Fort Vancouver, built three homes at the Willamette Falls. Although the Native Americans responded by burning these buildings, McLoughlin forged ahead with a new sawmill and flour mill.

American settlers began trickling in, and by 1841 the first wagon trains started to arrive. Pouring in by boat and by land, the pioneers soon spread across the Willamette Valley in search of farmsteads. Thankfully, you don't have to retrace the entire trail to learn of this riveting history. Just head to Oregon City's museums, homes, farms and cemeteries.

The place to begin your visit is the **National End of the Oregon Trail Interpretive Center** (500 Washington Street; 503-657-9336; admission). Exhibits here offer background on the pioneer journey and display notable artifacts, photographs and maps. You'll gain a helpful perspective on Native American,

missionaries and emigrant history. You can also pick up helpful walking and driving tour guides to the community.

Among the major highlights are the **McLoughlin House** (713 Center Street; 503-656-5146; admission), where the Hudson's Bay Company leader and "Father of Oregon" retired. Although his employer was British, McLoughlin generously aided the new settlers and helped lay the groundwork for Americanization. Regular tours show off this home that was a social hub in pioneer days. Highlights include a Chilkoot Indian ceremonial robe, banjoshaped clock and Hudson's Bay Company sideboard. The adjacent Jagger house features quilts, wicker furniture, a doll collection and Victorian furniture. Incidentally, you can learn the rest of the McLoughlin story by visiting Fort Vancouver across the Columbia River from Portland (see "Columbia River and the Gorge" for more information).

Also of special interest is the **Frances Ermatinger House** (6th and John Adams streets; admission). This federal-style residence and the **Stevens Crawford House** (603 6th Street; 503-655-2866; admission) both showcase antiques and memorabilia. The latter home, headquarters of the local historical society, has an extensive collection of Native American artifacts and, surprise, the flag raised at Bunker Hill. Well worth your time is the **Rose Farm** (536 Holmes Lane), one of the state's oldest residences. The first territorial governor was inaugurated at this home surrounded by rose plantings. A two-tiered piazza and second-story ballroom are highlights of the recently restored residence now on the National Register of Historic Places.

As part of the 150th-anniversary celebration, Oregon City is promoting the **Trails End Interpretive Center** (High Street). This cultural heritage park is being designed to offer a panoramic view of Oregon emigration. An initial wing provides a convenient overview. Also of special interest is the **Oregon City Municipal Elevator** (7th and Main streets; admission). Founded in 1916, this water-driven ride was designed to make it easy for residents to journey from the riverfront to the upper part of town. One of only four municipal elevators in the world, the 90-foot ride is a great way to enjoy views of Willamette Falls, particularly at sunset.

ular neighborhood is **Sellwood**, an antique center extending along 13th Avenue from Clatsop to Maleden streets.

While cities across the land have scrapped these period pieces, Portland has held on to the **Oaks Amusement Park** (foot of Southeast Spokane Street; 503-236-5722). In addition to vintage thrill rides, you can enjoy roller skating to the strains of a Wurlitzer organ. This pretty park is part of the **Oaks Bottom Wildlife Sanctuary**, a major Portland marsh habitat.

One of the nation's premier liberal arts institutions, **Reed College** (3203 Southeast Woodstock Boulevard; 503-771-1112) has a forested, 98-acre campus cloaked in ivy. Reed's gothic buildings and old dorms are close to Crystal Springs Rhododendron Garden at 28th Avenue and Woodstock Boulevard (see "Beaches and Parks" for more information).

No visit to the city's east side is complete without a stop at **The Grotto** (Northeast 85th Avenue and Sandy Boulevard; 503-254-7371). Near the Portland airport, this 62-acre Catholic sanctuary and garden is a peaceful refuge that seems to have as much in common with a Zen retreat as it does with the Vatican. Beautiful ponds and shrines, paths leading through flower gardens and great views of the mountains and the Columbia River make the Grotto a local favorite.

PORTLAND EAST HOTELS

An exceptional value, **The John Palmer House** (4314 North Mississippi Avenue, Portland; 503-284-5893) is a circa 1890 Victorian that takes the bed-and-breakfast experience to the limit. Lace and chintz, a panoply of throw pillows on the canopied beds, oak headboards, stained glass and gingerbread detailing galore are all here. The good news is you can take advantage of the budget-priced cottage rooms, the moderate-priced Beethoven or Schuman suites or go for the deluxe-priced Debussy suite. All come with a full breakfast. Carriage rides, baskets of fruits or flowers, a private maid or butler, gourmet meals, massage service, gardenias on the pillows and serenades from the veranda can all be arranged for a reasonable fee.

Hail to the Chief! **Portland's White House** (★) (1914 Northeast 22nd Avenue; 503-287-7131) strongly resembles the other White House in Washington, D.C. The stately Greek columns, circular driveway, crystal chandeliers and French windows would all make the First Family feel right at home. The difference here is that you don't have to stand in line for a tour, and there's no Secret Service agents to hustle you along. Originally built as a lumber baron's summer home, this White House features handpainted murals of garden scenes and oak-inlaid floors. Canopy and brass beds, clawfoot tubs, leaded glass and wicker furniture adorn the six rooms. Moderate to deluxe.

Well located in the popular Hawthorne neighborhood, **Portland American Youth Hostel** (3031 Southeast Hawthorne Boulevard; 503-236-3380) offers dorm accommodations for men and women, as well as a mixed sleeping porch during the summer months. This older home also has a self-serve kitchen. Guests are asked to do easy chores that take just a few minutes. Check-in begins at 5 p.m. There's an 11 p.m. curfew weeknights and midnight curfew weekends. Budget.

Jagger House (512 6th Street, Oregon City; 503-657-7820) offers three rooms in a historic 19th-century home. Thirty minutes from downtown Portland, this bed and breakfast offers comfortable accommodations with queen-size iron beds, pine furnishings, quilts, lace and chintz accents and an unusual stenciled floor. Ideally located for walking tours of historic Oregon City, this vernacular-style home also lends bikes to those who want to pedal through the past. Moderate.

The largest bed-and-breakfast room we found in Oregon was at the **Inn of the Oregon Trail** (★) (416 South McLoughlin Boulevard, Oregon City; 503-656-2089). Roomy enough for a brass bed, full office desk, fireplace and sitting area, this is just one of three comfortable units at this country casual inn. The crocheted bedspreads, deep-blue quilts, oak furniture, armoires and river views make the inn a good base for touring Oregon City's historic treasures. Breakfasts are exceptional. Budget to moderate.

Shilo Inn Portland Airport Suites Hotel (11707 Northeast Airport Way; 503-252-7500) offers 144 two-room suites. Perfect for business meetings, the contemporary units feature modern prints, etched-glass partitions and floral-print spreads. With a phone and a remote control television in the bathroom, this is one place you'll never be out of touch. Each suite has two phone lines, four phones, three televisions, a microwave, refrigerator and wet bar. Also here are an indoor pool, spa, sauna, steam room and fitness center. A business center, hospitality center and meeting rooms prove you can take your office with you. Deluxe.

PORTLAND EAST RESTAURANTS

One of the Portland's better breakfasts is found at **Tabor Hill Café** (3766 Southeast Hawthorne Boulevard; 503-230-1231). This small, red-brick establishment with eclectic decor features modern art, a grey tile floor and red tables. The apple-walnut pancake (that's singular, not plural) is large enough to blanket your entire plate. Other choices include chicken omelettes, bran muffins and a fresh fruit cup. Lunch specialties include turkey breast, avocado-and-bacon sandwich, burgers, marinated chicken breast, blackened-snapper salad and Mexican dishes. Budget to moderate.

It's not easy to find a four-course kosher Sunday brunch these days, but we did it at **Bread and Ink** (3610 Southeast Hawthorne Boulevard; 503-239-4756). The coffee is strong, the lox are beautiful and the children kept content with crayons and paper. In addition to bagels and cream cheese, borscht, challah and a variety of omelettes, you'll enjoy the family-style atmosphere. Set in an elegant commercial building adorned with terra cotta, this weekly happening is a Portland original.

Located in the Sellwood district known for its antique stores, **Papa Haydn** (5829 Southeast Milwaukie Avenue; 503-232-9440) is a yummy storefront café where fans twirl from the ceilings, watercolors grace the beige walls and bentwood furniture accommodates guests who don't come to count calories. This is the place to begin the day with brie omelette, frittata de merida or apple brioche french toast. Dinner entrées include scallops genovese, shrimp curry, pepper and garlic prawns and Thai salmon salad. An extensive wine list and espresso drinks are found here along with one of the longest dessert menus in the Pacific Northwest. Moderate.

North of Oregon City, **Nonna Emilia** (★) (16691 Southeast McLoughlin Boulevard, Milwaukie; 503-786-1004) is the place to go for thick-crust pizza. In addition to familiar toppings like pepperoni, canadian bacon and sausage, you can order a taco version or a special "love your heart" version made with vegetarian toppings. Generous pasta entrées like manicotti, lasagna and canneloni are also on the menu. Italian arias add a graceful note to the spacious dining room. Moderate.

PORTLAND EAST SHOPPING

A favored used-bookstore in Portland is **David Morrison Books** (1420 Southeast 37th Avenue; 503-233-5688). Situated in a warehouse just off Hawthorne Boulevard, this shop has a wonderful collection of offbeat classics, as well as used, rare and art books. Browse through the vintage collection of pulp novels and be sure to check out the classic government pamphlets, including military gems like "Psychological Experience of the 8th Air Force In Fallout." We couldn't resist buying "What To Do When The Russians Come," a 1984 Cold War classic forecasting the fate of America under communism. If you're looking for an unusual book, signed works by Richard Nixon, photography collections or titles on 20th-century design, be sure to stop by.

Death can be proud at **Murder by the Book** (3210 Southeast Hawthorne Boulevard; 503-232-9995). Mystery addicts will get their fix here and also become acquainted with many well-known Northwest authors.

Even if you hate Garfield, you'll be charmed by **The Cat's Meow** (3538 Southeast Hawthorne Boulevard; 503-231-1341). From shirts and cards to ceramics and lamps, everything sold here has a feline theme.

PORTLAND EAST NIGHTLIFE

The Moorish **Bagdhad Theater and Pub** (3702 Southeast Hawthorne Boulevard; 503-236-9234) has a fairy-tale decor with painted walls and a fountain in the lobby. Every other row of theater seating has been removed to accommodate tables where patrons can order food and drinks and enjoy second-run films. Customers under 21 are only welcome for the Sunday matinees.

Echo Theater (1515 Southeast 37th Avenue; 503-231-1232) is the home of **Do Jump Movement Theater.** Shows include acrobatic and highwire acts. Visiting dance troupes also perform here.

Parchman Farm (1204 Southeast Clay Street; 503-235-7831), offers some of Portland's finest jazz in an intimate setting. Etched glass, wood detailing, a full bar and a good dinner menu make this jazz club and restaurant an excellent spot for a night on the town.

One of the city's finest classical programs is **Chamber Music Northwest** (Reed College, Southeast Woodstock Boulevard; 503-223-3202). Nationally known groups perform in a beautiful setting.

The East Side (3701 Southeast Division Street; 503-236-8689) features country-and-western dancing in the back-bar area and Caribbean cuisine in the dining room. Catering to a gay clientele, this 9000-square-foot club located in a former milk plant has a western interior featuring roughsawn wood booths and a long bar.

PORTLAND EAST BEACHES AND PARKS

Kelley Point Park (★)—At the confluence of the Willamette and Columbia rivers, this forested site is popular for swimming, biking and hiking. The park, largely undeveloped, is busy during the summer months but wide open the rest of the year.

Facilities: Restrooms. *Fishing:* Good. *Swimming:* Good.

Getting there: Located in northernmost Portland at the west end of Suttle Road off Northeast Marine Drive.

Peninsula Park—This 16-acre park features beautiful sunken rose gardens highlighted with fountains and a charming gazebo. Extensive recreational facilities and a small pond make Peninsula popular with families.

Facilities: Picnic tables, basketball court, horseshoe pits, swimming pool, soccer field, tennis courts and restrooms and wheelchair accessible.

Getting there: It's located at North Albina Street and Portland Boulevard.

Powell Butte Park—This rustic, 569-acre park centers around a 630-foot high volcanic mound that offers great views of the city and the Cascades. If you can, circle this volcanic butte via a two-mile loop route at day's end and take advantage of the sunset.

Facilities: None.

Getting there: It's at Southeast 140th Avenue and Holgate Street.

Laurelhurst Park—Bordered by rhododendron, a pretty lake is the heart of this 34-acre park in a historic residential district. Along the way you're likely to spot geese, ducks, swans and turtles. Forested with fir and oak, the park also features glens, gardens and contemporary sculpture.

Facilities: Restrooms, barbecue pits, picnic tables, playground, tennis courts and wheelchair accessible.

Getting there: Located on Southeast 39th Avenue and Stark Street.

Mt. Tabor Park—The only extinct volcano within the limits of an American city, Mt. Tabor was uncovered during excavations in 1912. While the cinder cone is the park's star attraction, it also offers an extensive network of trails for hiking, jogging and hiking. This forested setting affords great views of the city. Come for an hour, spend the day.

Facilities: Picnic tables, restrooms, horseshoe pits, playground and tennis courts and wheelchair accessible.

Getting there: It's at Southeast Salmon Street and 60th Avenue.

Leach Botanical Park—This nine-acre garden features 1500 flowers and plants, including many native species, and is laced by a small creek. You can explore the grounds of this one-time estate on your own or via a guided tour.

Facilities: Manor house, restrooms and self-guiding brochures; information, 503-761-9503.

Getting there: Located at 6704 Southeast 122nd Avenue.

Crystal Springs Rhododendron Garden—Five acres of flora and fauna, this park is at its best in May. The colorful panorama of more than 2000 rhododendron and azalea is enhanced by a waterfall and two bridges spanning a creek that flows into Crystal Lake. Ducks and other waterfowl are found year-around at this refuge near Reed College.

Facilities: Restrooms, wheelchair accessible; information, 503-796-5193.

Getting there: Located at Southeast 28th Avenue and Woodstock Boulevard.

Clackamette Park—A haven for ducks and geese, Clackamette's 22 acres border the Willamette River in the Oregon City area. It's also a great spot to see blue herons nesting on Goat Island.

Facilities: None.

Getting there: Take exit 9 from Route 205 toward Oregon City and Gladstone. Go west on Clackamette two-tenths of a mile.

Portland West

From vineyards to Japanese gardens, Portland's west side has many of the city's best parks, major museums and wildlife preserves. Just half an hour from downtown, you can enjoy wilderness areas or cycle along placid sloughs. Glamorous Victorians and the city's fabled Pittock Mansion add to the fun.

One of the trendiest areas in Portland is **Nob Hill**. At the Portland/Oregon Visitors Association downtown pick up the walking guide to this district focused around Northwest 23rd Avenue, north of Burnside Street. Home of many of the city's finest restaurants, bookstores and antique and art shops, Nob Hill also has noteworthy turn-of-the-century Victorian and Georgian homes, as well as churches and commercial buildings. Among them are the **Charles F. Adams House** (2363 Northwest Flanders Street) and the **Ayer-Shea House** (1809 Northwest Johnson Street).

This tree-lined district is also convenient to **Washington Park** (Southwest Park Place and Vista Avenue; 503-796-5274), a 332-acre refuge created by the Olmstead brothers, the same landscape architects who gave the world Central Park in New York and Golden Gate Park in San Francisco. Home to several major museums, gardens and the zoo, this park is one of Portland's most worthy destinations.

Begin your visit at the **International Rose Test Garden** (400 Southwest Kingston Avenue; 503-248-4302). Consisting of three terraces, this four-and-a-half-acre gem has over 8000 bushes, enough to make this park a true mecca for rose aficionados worldwide. In addition to the test area, visitors are welcome to see the Royal Rosarians and Gold Award Garden. When the roses are in bloom, it's hard to find a better vantage point for the city below.

Directly west of the Rose Garden is the **Japanese Garden** (611 Southwest Kingston Street; 503-223-4070; admission). Five traditional gardens spread across seven acres make this tranquil spot a great place for a quiet walk. The Flat Garden is reminiscent of Kyoto's Zen shrines. The Sand and Stone Garden is a simple geometric arrangement of sea and stone. The Tea Garden features a Japanese tea house, while the Natural Garden has a fine miniature arrangement. Don't miss the Strolling Pond Garden with its waterfalls, pools and beautiful wooden bridge. There's also a pavilion overlooking Mt. Hood, Oregon's answer to Mt. Fuji.

Follow Kingston Street until you see signs leading to 61-acre **Metro Washington Park Zoo** (4001 Southwest Canyon Road; 503-226-7627; admission). Also accessible by a steam train from the International Rose Test and Japanese Garden, the zoo features an African Rain Forest as well as a savannah roamed by giraffes, zebras, rhinos, impalas and hippos. Also of special interest are the zoo's Peruvian penguins, Arctic polar bears and orangutans. The staff is proud of the fact that it has one of the world's most successful elephant-breeding programs. You'll also find an extensive collection of Pacific Northwest animals, including beavers and otters.

Nearby is the **World Forestry Center** (4033 Southwest Canyon Road; 503-228-1367; admission). Here's your chance to learn tree nomenclature, logging history and the story of monumental fires like the Tillamook burn. Outside you'll see antique logging equipment. Kids will enjoy a chat with the 70-foot talking tree. While this center has a pro-logging slant, it does offer a useful perspective on the state's lumber industry.

One way to tell the trees from the forest is to visit the 175-acre **Hoyt Arboretum** (4000 Southwest Fairview Boulevard; 503-823-3654). You'll have a chance to see over 700 varieties of shrubs and trees, including the nation's largest collection of conifers.

North of Washington Park is a favorite Oregon house tour, **Pittock Mansion** (3229 Northwest Pittock Drive; 503-823-3624; admission). Built by Oregonian publisher Henry Pittock and his wife Georgiana, this 16,000-square-foot, château-style residence features an Edwardian dining room, a French Renaissance drawing room, Turkish smoking room and Jacobean library. Chandeliers, Italian marquetry, friezes on the doorways, a carved-stone fireplace and bronze grillwork make this 1914 home a treasure. The finest craftspeople of the day used native Northwest materials to make this house Portland's early 20th-century masterpiece. The 46-acre estate, landscaped with roses, azaleas, rhododendrons and cherry trees, has a great view of the city and the mountains. Be sure to stop for lunch or tea at the **Gate Lodge** (503-823-3627).

In nearby Forest Park you'll want to visit the **Portland Audubon Society Sanctuary and Wildlife Restoration Center** (5151 Northwest Cornell Road; 503-292-6855). At this rehabilitation facility you'll see barn and screech-owls and red-tailed hawks.

To fully experience the country's biggest wilderness park, continue on Skyline Boulevard along the Tualatin Mountains. Overlooking the Willamette River, Forest Park extends west for eight miles. Turn right at Germantown Road and drive north through Forest Park's woodlands to Route 30. Continue west to the Sauvie Island Bridge. Cross the bridge and proceed one mile to **James F. Bybee House and Howell Territorial Park** (Howell Park Road; 503-621-3344). Open only during the summer, the Bybee House is a restored 19th-century Classical Revival reflecting the island's culture and development during the 1855–1885 period. On the grounds is the **Agricultural Museum** displaying pioneer equipment, shops and hands-on exhibits. In addition you'll want to explore the **Pioneer Orchard** containing 115 varieties of apple trees as well as pears, plums and vineyards.

Another attraction in West Portland is the **Children's Museum** (3037 Southwest 2nd Avenue; 503-823-2227; admission). A must for families with small children, this brick home has the ultimate pediatric medical suite. Kids can put their patients through the low-rise examining room, a surgery suite and recovery room at their leisure. The pint-sized grocery has a barcode scanner and there's also a maritime model complete with drawbridges.

Washington County west of Portland has a number of excellent wineries. **Oak Knoll Winery** (29700 Southwest Burkhalter Road, Hillsboro; 503-648-8198) is known for pinot noirs and chardonnays. This small vineyard has a rustic, wood-paneled room with a redwood-slab bar and a charming picnic area. You can also picnic under the cherry trees at **Tualatin Vineyards** (10850 Northwest Seavey Road, Forest Grove; 503-357-5005), which offers estate-bottled chardonnays, rieslings, gewürztraminer and pinot noirs. **Laurel Ridge Winery** (46350 Northwest David Hill Road, Forest Grove; 503-359-5436) is on 143 acres of rolling terrain. Set on a hillside with commanding views of Forest Grove and the agricultural valley below, Laurel Ridge features sparkling wines and sauvignon blanc.

Traveling south, the **Willamette Shore Trolley** (333 South State Street, Lake Oswego; 503-222-2226) offers a 90-minute, 13-mile scenic trip along the Willamette River. Your trip aboard a vintage trolley runs along a section of the Jefferson Street Line built in the late 19th century.

Railfans may want to head out to **Trolley Park and Museum** (Glenwood; 503-357-3574). Here you'll see a vintage collection of inter-urban streetcars, trolleys and double-decker buses.

PORTLAND WEST HOTELS

Cypress Inn (809 Southwest King Street; 503-226-6288) offers moderate-priced contemporary rooms. Within walking distance of the popular shops and restaurants in the Nob Hill district, this five-story motel building is tucked into a residential neighborhood. Nondescript from the outside, the inn has attractive carpeted rooms with potted plants, posturepedic beds, desks and contemporary decor. Kitchenettes are available in the suites. The upper-story rooms have great views of downtown Portland.

Located in the handsome King's Hill district near Nob Hill, **Mumford Manor** (1130 Southwest King Street; 503-243-2443) is one of the city's showplaces. Deluxe-priced rooms and suites offer bay-window views of Mt. Hood. Other room amenities are fireplaces, antiques and claw-foot tubs. Public areas include a library, garden porch and a formal dining room where you'll enjoy a full breakfast. The south lawn is a perfect place to play that all-American sport of croquet.

A renovated English Tudor, **Heron Haus** (2545 Northwest Westover Road; 503-274-1846) offers a pleasant view of the city, the Cascades and Mt. St. Helens. A blend of country casual and contemporary furniture, the oak-parquet flooring, mahogany library, sun room and swimming pool make the establishment a delight. Fireplaces, quilts and wicker furniture add to the comfort of the five spacious rooms. After enjoying continental breakfast stroll down to the popular Nob Hill shops and boutiques. Deluxe.

With 260 rooms and suites, **The Greenwood Inn** (10700 Southwest Allen Boulevard, Beaverton; 503-643-7444) is a good bet for families or visitors planning long stays. Surrounded by verdant courtyards, the lower-priced rooms have murphy beds, full kitchens, twig rockers, berber carpets and sitting areas. Suites feature fireplaces and decks. An atrium restaurant and lounge, pool, jacuzzi, exercise room and sauna are on the premises. Ask for a room away from the highway. Moderate to deluxe.

At **The Yankee Tinker Bed and Breakfast** (★) (5460 Southwest 183rd Avenue, Beaverton; 503-649-0932) three New England-style guest rooms feature handcrafted quilts, antiques, flowers and wallhangings. Blueberry pancakes, muffins, peaches-and-cream french toast and herbed omelettes are on the breakfast menu. Special diets can be accommodated. Ten miles west of Portland, the inn is in the heart of Washington County's wine country and close to farmer's markets. Budget to moderate.

Pepper Tree Motor Inn (10720 Southwest Allen Boulevard, Beaverton; 503-641-7477) offers fully carpeted rooms with king- and queen-sized beds, sitting areas and small refrigerators. A pool and jacuzzi, weight room, rental movies and wheelchair accessible accommodations are all available. To avoid highway noise ask for rooms on the east side. Budget to moderate.

Located southwest of Portland off Route 5, the **Sweetbrier Inn** (★) (7124 Southwest Nyberg Road, Tulatin; 503-692-5800) offers nicely appointed contemporary rooms in a park-like stand of fir. Kings and queens, wicker furniture, comfortable sitting areas, a garden pool, children's play area and nearby jogging track make this establishment a winner. A restaurant and lounge are here, too. Moderate to deluxe.

PORTLAND WEST RESTAURANTS

With all the fresh seafood landing in Portland it's no surprise that sushi has become a big hit. Some of the best is served up at **Ginza** (730 Northwest 21st Avenue; 503-223-7881), a traditional Japanese establishment with paper-screen-divided booths and a traditional dining area where guests can dine seated on tatami mats. A long list of sushi favorites includes the tekka roll, California roll and salmon skin roll. The no-MSG menu includes beef teriyaki, deep-fried pork loin, sukiyaki and salt-broiled salmon. Moderate.

You say you were lusting for grilled poussin basted with a Moroccan sauce of honey, cumin and cinnamon, served with couscous and sautéed spicy zucchini? Then follow the crowds to **Zefiro Restaurant and Bar** (500 Northwest 21st Avenue; 503-226-3394), a high-tech makeover of a historic Nob Hill brick commercial building. From the copper tables in the bar area to the black and rattan furniture in the oak-floored dining area, this establishment is one of Portland's hottest bistros. The menu is filled with imaginative entrées like saffron risotto with prawns, roasted red peppers and *gremolata* and grilled Chinook salmon. Deluxe.

Café des Amis (1987 Northwest Kearney Street; 503-295-6487) is a cheery neighborhood restaurant furnished with oak furniture, antique breakfronts and sideboards. In the heart of Nob Hill, this deluxe-tabbed establishment offers entrées like grilled poussin with "40 cloves of garlic," filet of beef with a port garlic sauce, french market stew, lamb tenderloin with sauce béarnaise and sautéed chicken livers with grapes, cream and cognac. There's an excellent wine list, and the french rolls are great. Highly recommended.

Skip **Rose's Restaurant** (315 Northwest 23rd Avenue; 503-227-5181) and you're passing up one of Portland's unique dining experiences. The menu is big on deli fare: corned-beef sandwiches, matzo ball soup and blintzes. But what makes Rose's special are the gigantic pastries. Larger-than-life donuts, six layer cakes, gargantuan cinnamon rolls and mind-boggling tortes all qualify for the record books. Take the kids. Moderate.

Start the day at **Jamie's** (8383 Northwest 23rd Avenue; 503-248-6784), a classy Nob Hill diner with booth and counter seating, music from the juke box and a checkerboard floor. Buttermilk pancakes, french toast made with thick ranch bread, muffins, fresh fruit or orange juice are a great way to begin your day. You can also build your own omelette from a list of ten ingredients. Budget.

Located in a rustic home, **L'Auberge** (2601 Northwest Vaughn Street; 503-223-3302) is one of Portland's best French restaurants. Dine in front of the fireplace or, in the warm months, on the deck. Wicker furniture, antiques and impressionist prints grace this four-level restaurant. Specialties include steamed mussels, New York steaks, rack of lamb, veal, salmon, sturgeon and scallops. There's also a popular bar menu with lighter fare such as hamburgers made with gruyère cheese served on onion buns. Deluxe.

Yes, there is a free lunch or dinner at **Sayler's Old Country Kitchen** (★) (4655 Southwest Griffith Drive, Beaverton; 503-644-1492). All you have to do is eat one of the 72-ounce top-sirloin steaks along with a salad, slice of french bread, ten fries or a baked potato, two carrot sticks, two celery sticks, two olives, a beverage and ice cream (any flavor)—and the house will pick up the tab. Of course you only get one hour to finish. Over 500 customers have won the bet (not to appear sexist, but just 11 of them were women). Interestingly enough, the typical winner tends to have a slender build. If you're not that hungry try the tenderloin, prime rib, chicken, scallops, prawns or halibut steaks. Moderate.

High-tech Mex design is the hallmark of **Macheezmo Mouse** (10719 Southwest Beaverton-Hillsdale Highway; 503-646-6000) where the burritos, tacos, salads and other entrées are all listed with their calorie content. There's no deep frying here, and many of the entrées come with brown rice and black beans. The checkered-tile floor, counters and tables attract a budget-minded crowd that's become dependent on this quality fast food.

PORTLAND WEST SHOPPING

For that country casual look in wool or cashmere head for **Norm Thompson** (1805 Northwest Thurman Street; 503-221-0764). Enjoy a glass of Oregon wine as you check out the men's and women's apparel and gifts.

If you're looking for elegant lingerie for the man or woman in your life make a beeline for **Show and Tell** (602 Northwest 23rd Avenue; 503-224-0222). Underwear, outerwear and those special lacy gifts certain to generate a big laugh at a party (what kind of parties do you go to anyway?) are all here.

A good bet for the advanced or the eclectic print collector is the **Jamison/Thomas Gallery** (1313 Northwest Glisan Street; 503-222-0063). Both West Coast and nationally known artists are represented.

Pulliam/Nugent Gallery (522 Northwest 12th Avenue; 503-228-6665) specializes in contemporary Northwest art as well as work from other regions. Occasional exhibits feature work by folk artists.

Another excellent place to look for fine contemporary Northwest art is the **Laura Russo Gallery** (805 Northwest 21st Avenue; 503-226-2754). Paintings, original prints, drawings, watercolors and sculptures in a variety of media are all shown here.

We were impressed by the breadth of the offerings at **Contemporary Crafts Gallery** (3934 Southwest Corbett Avenue; 503-223-2654), a cooperative shop showcasing everything from ceramic pins and medallions to metal sculpture. Beautiful contemporary paintings along with fiber art, wood sculpture and pottery make this eclectic gallery a great place to shop for a gift.

Scholls Ferry Farm (Scholls; 503-644-3233) is a good place to pick up a gift everyone at home will appreciate—nicely packaged Oregon filberts. Call ahead for a tour and enjoy fresh cider from the apple orchard.

PORTLAND WEST NIGHTLIFE

Classical-music buffs will enjoy the **Portland Baroque Orchestra** (Trinity Episcopal Church, 147 Northwest 19th Avenue; 503-224-7908). Make it a point to hear this group if they're performing during your visit.

Dandelion Pub (31 Northwest 23rd Place; 503-223-0099) is the place to go for rhythm and blues in a tavern atmosphere. Located in the Nob Hill area, this L-shaped pub has wood-paneled walls featuring photos of many of the popular local and national acts that have headlined here. There also are a full dinner menu, booth seating and a cozy dancefloor. Cover.

Mission Theater (1624 Northwest Glisan Street; 503-223-4527) is a historic movie theater that now doubles as a pub with seating at tables and couches where you can dine and watch second-run films. There's also traditional theater seating on the balcony level.

The "in" crowd heads for **Oswego Point River Café** (320 Foothill Road, Lake Oswego; 503-697-8818), a paneled sports bar and nightclub where you may find Trailblazer stars enjoying themselves at the big booths with brass tables or out on the dancefloor. A disc jockey plays Top-40 and classic hits. A big deck offers great views of the Willamette River.

PORTLAND WEST BEACHES AND PARKS

MacCleay Park—This undeveloped eight-acre park offers several excellent trails, a pond, creek and viewing windows overlooking a bird-feeding area. In addition, it provides great views of the city and Mt. St. Helens. There's a good chance you'll spot deer and other wildlife on your walk. You may want to visit the park's wildlife care center.

Facilities: Restrooms, playground. The Portland Audubon Society's headquarters and bookstore is within the park.

Getting there: Take Lovejoy Street west to Northwest Cornell Road and continue to the park.

Council Crest Park—Atop a Tualatin Mountain peak, this forested 42-acre park is a great way to see the Cascades and the Coast Range. Make your way through stands of fir and maple via Marquam Hill Trail. A sculptured fountain of a mother and child, stolen in 1990, has been replaced.

Facilities: Picnic tables, restrooms.

Getting there: Located on Southwest Council Crest Drive near Fairmount Boulevard.

Sauvie Island Wildlife Area (★)—A special favorite, this 12,000-acre haven ten miles west of Portland is an ideal place to spot great blue heron, bald eagles, sandhill cranes and 250 other bird species. Featuring a sandy beach on the Columbia, the refuge is also home to 37 mammal species including black-tailed deer. The island trails which lead through orchards and gardens are ideal for leisurely exploration on foot or by bike. Small craft explore the sloughs while ocean-going freighters cruise by on the Columbia.

Facilities: Picnic tables, restrooms, boat ramps, bird observation platforms and museum; information, 503-229-5400. *Swimming:* Good. *Fishing:* Try for catfish, perch and crappie from slough and pond banks.

Getting there: Take Route 30 west from Portland toward Astoria. Four miles past St. John's Bridge take the Sauvie Bridge turnoff to the Island.

The Garden of the Bishop's Close (★)—For more than 75 years this refuge has been a favorite of Portland's garden societies. And why not? A terraced 13-acre estate overlooking the Willamette River and Elk Rock Island, the garden is also home to the Episcopal Diocese of Oregon's main office. Formal gardens and native plants, including dozens of magnolia varieties, make this a spot for Zen-like contemplation. Also here are lily ponds, a rock garden and a small spring.

Facilities: Restrooms; information, 503-636-5613.

Getting there: Located at 11800 Southwest Military Lane.

Tryon Creek State Park—Set in a shallow, steep-walled canyon, this 630-acre suburban park is a wonderful place for hiking, biking and horseback riding. Tryon is forested with fir, alder and maple and also has a grassy meadow and marsh. A favorite spot is the park's south end where Tryon Creek flows into the Willamette River. Look for beaver and pileated woodpeckers. There's a trillium festival in the spring.

Facilities: Observation area, nature house and wheelchair accessible.

Getting there: Located six miles southwest of downtown Portland. Take Terwilliger exit off Route 5 and follow signs to the park.

Mary S. Young State Park—A popular day-use area forested in fir, maple, cottonwood and oak, the park sits on the Willamette River. With 133 acres, this leisurely spot is ideal for fishing, riding or walking.

Facilities: Restrooms and picnic tables and wheelchair accessible. *Fishing:* Good.

Getting there: Located nine miles south of Portland on Route 43.

Columbia River and the Gorge

Every visitor to Portland owes it to themselves to see the Columbia River and the Gorge. The spectacular scenery includes one of the Northwest's most important historical sites, Fort Vancouver. Heaven for waterfall lovers, windsurfers, hikers and history buffs, this is the ultimate Portland day trip. Of course, if you love it as much as we did, you'll probably want to spend the night.

Although it's only half an hour from downtown Portland, many visitors to the region miss **Fort Vancouver** (East Evergreen Boulevard, Vancouver, WA; 206-696-7655). What a pity. Located in 300-acre Central Park, across the Columbia River from Portland, this National Historic Site is a cornerstone of Pacific Northwest history. Organized by the Hudson's Bay Company in 1825, the fort was a British fur-trading post and focal point for the commercial development of a region extending from British Columbia to Oregon and from Montana west to the Hawaiian Islands.

Five major buildings have been reconstructed on their original fort locations since 1966. Collectively they give a feel for life prior to the arrival of the first white settlers. On your tour you'll see the re-created home of **Dr. John McLoughlin,** the chief factor who befriended American settlers and is remembered as the "Father of Oregon." The phenomenal ability of the British to instantly gentrify the wilderness is reflected in the fine china, copper kettles and elegant furniture of this white clapboard home with a spacious veranda. You may be surprised to learn, as we were, that the male officers dined without their wives.

Also worth a visit are the **Blacksmith's Shop, Bakery, Kitchen, Stockade** and **Bastion.** At the **Indian Trade Shop and Dispensary** you'll learn how Native Americans bartered skillfully with the British. Because most of the trade items were imported, there was a two-year hiatus between ordering goods and receiving them.

On nearby **Officer's Row,** you'll see 21 grand homes built for American Army leaders who served here during the latter half of the 19th and the early 20th centuries. These charming Victorians are the focus of a mixed-use rehabilitation program combining interpretive and commercial use. Among these residences are the **Grant House** and the **George C. Marshall House,** an imposing Queen Anne. Both are open for tours (206-693-3103). Also at the fort are the **Vancouver Barracks,** the first military post opened in the Oregon territory.

Next to Fort Vancouver is **Pearson Air Museum (★)** (1105 East 5th Street, Vancouver, WA; 206-694-7026; admission). Opened in 1905, this is the oldest operating airfield in the United States. Exhibits feature a display on the world's first nonstop transpolar flight (Moscow to Vancouver) in 1937. The Soviet aviators were greeted by General George Marshall, who hosted them at his residence. The airpark exhibit features flyable vintage aircraft.

To see more of Vancouver stop by the **Vancouver/Clark County Visitors and Convention Bureau** (404 East 15th Street; 206-693-1313) and pick up the handy heritage tour brochure.

Returning to the Oregon side of the river take Route 84 east up the Gorge to the **Historic Columbia River Highway.** Beginning east of Troutdale (exit 17), this road ascends the bluff above the river to **Crown Point/Vista House** (Corbett; 503-695-2240), a must-see viewpoint. Descending east toward the Gorge you'll find yourself in one of the loveliest regions in the Northwest. With more than 70 waterfalls in the area, it's easy to have one to yourself.

Among the highlights are **LaTourell Falls, Bridal Veil Falls** and **Coopey Falls.** Perhaps the most popular destination is the **Multnomah Falls** area. Highlights include **Mist Falls, Wahkeena Falls, Necktie Falls, Fairy Falls** and, of course, the Gorge's majestic **Multnomah Falls.** Near the base of Lower Multnomah Falls is a visitor center.

The taming of the Columbia River to provide low-cost power is one of the most controversial stories in the evolution of this region. You'll get the pro side of the picture at **Bonneville Lock and Dam** (Cascade Locks; 503-374-8820) which is reached by taking exit 40 off Route 84. At the **Bradford Island Visitor Center** extensive interpretive displays provide an overview of the dam operation and history. You can also learn how the dam operates, see the fish ladders and visit the **Fort Cascades National Historic Site** on the Washington shore. To get there, cross the Columbia River on the **Bridge of the Gods**, named for a natural bridge famous in Indian legend and head west three miles on Route 14. The 59-acre historic site includes part of the old Portage Railroad, a onetime Chinook Indian village and an old military fort.

Retrace your route across the Bridge of the Gods to the Oregon side and stop at the **Cascade Locks Museum** (Marine Park, Cascade Locks; 503-374-8535) to see exhibits on Native Americans, the first Columbia River locks, the portage road, logging and fishwheels. Water powered, these rotating devices scooped so many salmon from the river that they were banned by the state in 1926. On the Washington side of the bridge is Stevenson, site of the new 15,000-square-foot **Columbia Gorge Interpretive Center** (150 Northwest Loop Road; 503-427-8211).

Farther east on Route 14 is **Carson Hot Mineral Springs Resort (★)** (Carson; 509-427-8292). On the Wind River, this resort is known for its mineral baths, massages, beautiful hiking trails and fishing and includes a hotel, rustic cabins and restaurant. From here you can drive east along Route 14 to Route 141, which leads north along the White Salmon River valley to Trout Lake. Then return to Route 14 and the town of White Salmon. Your next stop should be the **Hood River**, which has become a windsurfing capital thanks to the strong breezes here. Stop at the **Hood River County Visitors Center** (Port Marina Park; 503-386-2000) for information on this scenic hub. At the same location is the **Hood River County Historical Museum** (503-386-6772), featuring exhibits on Native American culture, the westward migration, pioneer farming, logging and the Columbia River. Also found here is an extensive collection of period furniture and early 20th-century artifacts.

One of the prettiest drives in the region is the 20-mile trip from Hood River to **Lost Lake (★)**. Take Route 281 south to Dee and then follow the signs west to this beautiful mountain lake where motorized boats are banned. Do keep an eye out for logging trucks en route.

We also recommend the **Mt. Hood Railroad** (101 Railroad Avenue, Hood River; 503-386-3556). This scenic excursion train links the gorge with Mt. Hood along a route pioneered in 1906. The trip climbs up the Hood River Valley through steep canyons, orchards and forests. You'll enjoy great views of the Cascades from the restored coaches on 17- or 44-mile roundtrips. Special fall foliage trips are well worth your while.

Although many visitors miss it, we strongly recommend a visit to **The Dalles**. The end of the Oregon Trail, where emigrants boarded vessels to float down the Columbia (the Barlow Trail later made it possible to complete the overland journey), this city has an excellent old-town walking tour. Pick up a copy of the route map at **The Dalles Convention and Visitors Bureau** (901 East 2nd Street; 503-296-6616). Highlights on this walk include one of the state's oldest bookstores, **Klindt's** (315 East 2nd Street), and the circa 1863 **Waldron Brothers Drugstore** nearby. If you're traveling with children don't miss **Wonder Works A Children's Museum** (419 East 2nd Street; 503-296-2444). A storefront gem, this volunteer organization has toy squad cars, a camping set-up, puppeteer area, crafts, kids' books, medical center and pint-sized office. The young folk will love it.

Our favorite stop in town is the **Fort Dalles Museum** (15th and Garrison streets; 503-296-4547). Only one fort building, the Surgeon's Quarters, remains today. But the museum does preserve an excellent collection of pioneer artifacts, rifles, quilts and historic photographs. Much of the memorabilia focuses on the lives of early settlers.

During your visit you'll want to see **The Dalles Dam**. Take Route 30 east to Route 197 north. Cross the freeway to Northeast Frontage Road and follow signs to the dam. Perhaps the saddest part of this story, the downside of that pro-dam story you saw at the Bonneville visitor center, focuses on the demise of the region's best-known Native American fishing grounds. Wherever you go along this part of the Columbia River, in coffeeshops and hotel lobbies, phone company offices and visitors' centers, you're likely to see classic photographs of Indians dipping their nets into the river at heavenly Celilo Falls. To get the full picture leaf through the scrapbook of Celilo Falls fishing pictures at the Fort Dalles Museum.

If you continue on Route 84 east of The Dalles for 18 miles you'll come to a small **Celilo Falls Marker** (★), which indicates where these bounteous fishing waters prospered before being destroyed by the dam in the late 1950s.

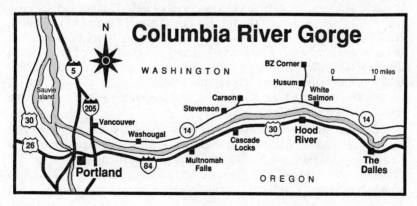

COLUMBIA RIVER AND THE GORGE HOTELS

The **Columbia Gorge Hotel** (400 Westcliff Drive, Hood River; 503-386-5566) is a 42-room landmark where strains of Bach waft through the halls, sculptured carpets highlight the public areas and the fireplace is always roaring. This Mediterranean-style hotel tucks guests in to wicker, brass, canopy or hand-carved antique beds. The dining room, home of a popular four-course farm breakfast, offers splendid riverfront dining. Relax in the Valentino Lounge or take a walk through the manicured gardens and enjoy the views of Mt. Hood. Ultra-deluxe.

The chandeliered **Hood River Hotel** (102 Oak Street, Hood River; 503-386-1900) is a gem. Forty rooms and suites offer a wide range of accommodations in this restored brick landmark. Brightly painted rooms are appointed with oak furniture, four-poster beds, casablanca fans, wing chairs and antiques. Some offer views of the Columbia River. Comfortable sitting areas, a lounge offering jazz music and a cheery café are all part of the charm. Kitchenettes suites are available. Moderate to deluxe.

Beautifully located overlooking the Columbia River Gorge, **Vagabond Lodge** (★) (4070 Westcliff Drive, Hood River; 503-386-2992) offers spacious, carpeted rooms—some opening right on to the riverfront. All feature contemporary furniture, doubles or queens and a secluded garden setting. For the budget-to-moderate price it's hard to beat this motel west of town.

If you crave country living, incomparable views of the Mt. Hood region and horseback riding, we know just the place. It's called **Fir Mountain Ranch** (★) (4051 Fir Mountain Road; 503-354-2753). Hidden on a secluded ridge 20 minutes south of the Hood River, this lodge-style home offers cozy, countrified lodgings, trail rides and easy access to both the Hood River Valley and Mt. Hood itself. A great escape, this isolated bed and breakfast is a great place for families. Deluxe.

One of the frustrating facts of life on the road is the Sunday brunch. If you crave broccoli quiche, italian sausage and eggs, artichoke frittata, baklava, date tarts, fresh fruit and a dozen other treats, Monday to Saturday just won't do. Fortunately, the **Inn Of The White Salmon** (★) (172 West Jewett Boulevard, White Salmon; 509-493-2335) has solved this problem in an imaginative way. This lovely bed and breakfast offers brunch seven days a week. All you need do is check in to one of the inn's countrified rooms featuring brass beds and antiques, and this splendid feast is yours. Across the Columbia from Hood River, this moderate-to-deluxe-priced inn also features a comfortable lounge.

Offering whitewater access to the White Salmon River, **Orchard Hill Inn** (★) (Husum; 206-493-3024) is the place for cozy country lodging at budget-to-moderate prices. Wicker, antiques, quilted bedspreads, oak floors, kerosene lamps and a fireplace will make you feel right at home in your gabled room. You'll enjoy a full breakfast, be welcome to explore the apple and pear orchards, play volleyball and soak in the whirlpool. Near White Salmon and Hood River, this secluded setting offers great views of Mt. Adams and features its very own beer garden.

Williams House Inn (★) (608 West 6th Street, The Dalles; 503-296-2889) is a picturesque Victorian on a wooded hilltop. Adjacent to an arboretum and a creek, the home is furnished with Georgian and Victorian antiques as well as Chinese art. Upstairs rooms in the moderate-price range feature canopied beds, a chaise lounge and writing desk. From your balcony you'll enjoy a great view of the Columbia River Gorge and the Klickitat Hills. The three-room main floor suite is a best buy in the moderate-to-deluxe range.

For contemporary motel accommodations try the **Tillicum Inn** (2114 West 6th Street, The Dalles; 503-298-5161). The fully carpeted rooms offer queen beds featuring pink spreads with seashell designs and oak tables. There's a pool on the premises as well as Cousins, the only restaurant we know featuring a John Deere tractor in the middle of the dining room. Moderate.

COLUMBIA RIVER AND THE GORGE RESTAURANTS

After a visit to Multnomah Falls it makes sense to dine at **Multnomah Falls Lodge** (Bridalveil, exit 31 off Route 84; 503-695-2376). The smoked-salmon-and cheese platter, stew served in a hollowed-out loaf of french bread, and generous salads are all recommended. The beautiful lodge building with a big stone fireplace, scenic paintings of the surroundings and lovely views will add to your enjoyment of the Gorge. Moderate.

Tucked away in the woods, **Stonehedge Inn** (★) (3405 Cascade Drive, Hood River; 503-386-3940) is an antique-filled home offering country dining at its finest. Set in a beautiful garden, this paneled restaurant has a tiny mahogany bar and a roaring fireplace. Entrées include scallop sauté, veal chanterelle, jumbo prawns and filet of salmon. Light entrées such as a seafood platter, are also recommended. Moderate to deluxe.

Hood River Hotel Café (102 Oak Street, Hood River; 503-386-6090) has pleasant indoor and sidewalk seating in the center of this resort town. The heart of the dining room is a handcrafted bar with an etched glass mirror. Moderate-priced entrées include filet of salmon, spaghetti bolognese and lamb chops. For a light meal try nachos Italiano and the pesto rotini antipasto salad.

An elegant dining room overlooking the Gorge, **Columbia River Court** (4000 Westcliff Drive, Hood River; 503-386-5566) is a romantic place to dine on specialties like roast pheasant on a bed of wild rice, fresh Oregon salmon, rack of northwest lamb or medallions of fallow venison. Done in an Early American design with oak furniture and candlelit tables, this establishment is well known for its lavish farm breakfast. Deluxe.

An A-frame tucked away in an industrial area, **Ole's Supper Club** (★) (2620 West 2nd Street, The Dalles; 503-296-6708) proves that location isn't everything in the restaurant business. The candlelit dining room with oak tables and floors, red plastic chairs, casablanca fans and western paintings is jammed with locals who swear by the prime rib, baked ham lorraine and Pacific salmon fresh from the nearby Columbia. Dinners, complete with fresh-baked bread, vegetables, salad and soup include chicken piccata, fettucine with fresh scallops and sautéed scampi. Moderate.

To the people at **Johnny's Café** (408 East 2nd Street, The Dalles; 503-296-4565) cordon bleu sounds like something you use to tint your fireplace. This temple of American cuisine has made few concessions to the trends of the '90s. Lit with fluorescent bulbs, furnished in formica and vinyl and kept in sync with Top-40 tunes from the jukebox, this eatery is big on macaroni and cheese. For decades, locals have been coming here to feast on broasted chicken, salmon steak, fish and chips, liver and onions, pies and puddings. Here's home cooking to write home about. Budget.

About 20 minutes north of the Gorge, and well worth the trip, is one of the region's most intriguing restaurants, **The Logs** (★) (Route 1, BZ Corners, WA; 509-493-1401). You'll be impressed by the fried chicken, hickory-smoked ribs, giant fries and fresh fruit pies served in this log-cabin setting. The battered and deep-fried chicken gizzards and beer dogs are a big hit with the regular clientele that includes locals, rafters, skiers and devotees of the peppermint fudge ice cream pie. In business for six decades, this is the place where city slickers will come face to face with their first jackalope, safely mounted on the wall. Budget to moderate.

A small café with tile floors and cane furniture, **Tyrone's Patisserie** (106 Evergreen Boulevard, Vancouver; 206-699-1212) is well known for 20 varieties of cheesecake, as well as chocolate fudge cake and napoleons. Settle in at one of the small tables or window-counter seats and enjoy breakfast specialties including croissants with ham or bacon, cheese and eggs, pastries, cinnamon rolls and muffins. For lunch try house specialties like beef pot pie, quiche or ratatouille. French onion soup and chicken salad made with walnuts, celery, scallions, sour cream and crème fraîche are also on the menu along with espresso and italian sodas. No dinner. Budget.

With a name like **Hidden House** (★) (100 West 13th Street, Vancouver; 206-696-2847) the star is automatic. This structure and the adjacent residence (now a retail business) at 110 West 13th Street were built by Lowell M. Hidden and his son Foster. Much of Vancouver was built with Hidden bricks from the family factory, still in operation today. Once the home of Clark College, this handsome, red-brick Victorian offers dining upstairs and down. Antiques are an integral part of the decor that includes three fireplaces, the original stained glass, ash and black-walnut woodwork and a covered veranda ideal for outside dining. The menu features steaks, seafood, chicken Kiev and veal dishes served with homemade poppyseed bread. Northwest wines are featured. Moderate to deluxe.

COLUMBIA RIVER AND THE GORGE SHOPPING

Fort Vancouver Gift Shop (East Evergreen Boulevard, Vancouver; 206-696-7655) is the place to go for books and pamphlets on Pacific Northwest history. Souvenir maps will add to your appreciation of the region's heritage. We recommend picking up a copy of the *Fort Vancouver National Historic Site Handbook 113*.

Aviation buffs will want to stop by the gift shop at **Pearson Air Museum** (1105 East 5th Street, Vancouver; 206-694-7026). The shop has a good collection of memorabilia and souvenirs for adults and juniors alike.

Pendleton Woolen Mills and Outlet Store (#2 17th Street, Washougal; 206-835-2131) offers big savings on irregulars. Tours of the mill, in operation since 1912, are available, but call first for schedule information.

A good place to select a fine Oregon white or red is **The Wine Sellers** (524 State Street, Hood River; 503-386-4647). Also here are fresh french bread, Oregon cheese and souvenirs.

Fruit makes a great present for the folks back home. **Rasmussen Farms** (3020 Thomsen Road off Route 35 south of Hood River; 503-386-4622) is a good place to buy Hood River apples, Comice pears and cherries. They can all be shipped as gift packs.

Columbia Arts Association (207 2nd Street, Hood River; 503-386-4512) represents 150 artists, primarily from the Columbia Gorge region. Featured are the works of photographers, printmakers, potters, glassblowers, weavers and painters.

The Dalles Art Center/Oregon Trail Art Gallery (220 East 4th Street, The Dalles; 503-296-4759), located in the historic Carnegie Library, exhibits work by local and regional artists. Much of this fine art is available for purchase. Both galleries showcase pottery, jewelry, paintings, beadwork, calligraphy, wearable art and baskets.

COLUMBIA RIVER AND THE GORGE NIGHTLIFE

On weekends a disk jockey plays dancable oldies in the **Stationhouse Lounge** (900 West 7th Street, Vancouver; 206-695-3374). Filled with railroad memorabilia and movie posters, the lounge offers booth and table seating. With 29 trains a day passing the premises, rail fans are guaranteed plenty of action. There's a full bar on the premises.

The **Power Station** (2126 Southwest Halsey Street, Troutdale; 503-669-8610) is a theater and pub located in the former Multnomuh County poor farm. The theater, which presents movies and occasional special events, is within the farm's former boiler room. The pub serves a full menu and is in the converted laundry building. Also on the premises is the Edgefield Brewery and Winery.

WhiteCap Brew Pub (506 Columbia Street, Hood River; 503-386-2247) offers live entertainment weekends. Big-screen television satisfies the needs of discriminating sports fans. While here you'll enjoy fine views of the Columbia.

COLUMBIA RIVER AND THE GORGE
BEACHES AND PARKS

Rooster Rock State Park—Offering more than three miles of sandy Columbia River frontage, this 872-acre park is near the Gorge's west end. The rock, named for a towering promontory, is adjacent to a camping site chosen by Lewis and Clark in 1805. Popular for swimming and windsurfing, Rooster Rock also has excellent hiking trails, a small lake and forested bluff.

Facilities: Picnic tables, restrooms and boat basin and wheelchair accessible; information, 503-695-2261. *Fishing:* Good for salmon. *Swimming:* Good. *Windsurfing:* Good.

Getting there: Located 22 miles east of Portland on Route 84.

Viento State Park—Originally a rest stop on the old Columbia River Highway, this 247-acre park includes a riverfront and Viento Creek forest section. Great views of the Columbia River make this a popular camping facility. It can get very windy.

Facilities: Picnic tables, showers, restrooms.

Camping: There are 17 tent sites and 58 RV hookups.

Getting there: Located on Route 84, eight miles west of Hood River.

Ainsworth State Park—Ranking high among the treasures of the Columbia River Scenic Highway is this 156-acre refuge. Near the bottom of St. Peter's Dome, the forested park has a beautiful hiking trail that connects with a network extending throughout the region. A serene getaway, the only sound of civilization you're likely to hear is from passing trains.

Facilities: Picnic tables, showers, restrooms.

Camping: There are 45 sites with full hookups.

Getting there: Located on Route 30, the Columbia Scenic Highway, 37 miles east of Portland.

Northwestern Lake Park (★)—A little Washington gem on the White Salmon River north of the Columbia. This is a great destination for a day trip where you can swim, fish, hike or just loaf. There are also summer cabins nearby for those who want to stay longer.

Facilities: Picnic tables, boat launch, cabins; restaurants and groceries in Husum or BZ Corners. *Swimming:* Good. *Fishing:* Excellent.

Getting there: Head west from White Salmon on Route 14 to Route 141. Continue north five miles to the park.

Memaloose State Park—The park is named for an offshore Columbia River island that was a Native American burial ground. This 336-acre site is located on the old Columbia River Highway. It spreads out along a two-mile stretch of riverfront and is forested with pine, oak and fir. Much of the park is steep and rocky. It can also be very windy. In case you were wondering, "Memaloose" is a Chinook word linked to the sacred burial ritual.

Facilities: Showers and restrooms and wheelchair accessible.

Camping: There are 67 tent sites and 43 RV hookups.

Getting there: Located off Route 84, 11 miles west of The Dalles. Westbound access only.

The Sporting Life

ROLLER SKATING AND ICE SKATING

Roller skate to the strains of the mighty Wurlitzer at the **Oaks Amusement Park** (205 Southeast Spokane Street; 503-236-5722), a grand Portland tradition on the east bank of the Willamette. A more contemporary setting is **Skateworld** (4935 Southeast Witch Hazel Road, Portland; 503-640-1333).

For ice skating head indoors to the **Clackamas Town Center** (12000 Southeast 82nd Street, Portland; 503-653-6911) rink. In December skate outdoors on a holiday rink created at Pioneer Courthouse Square, 6th Avenue and Morrison Street.

WINDSURFING

One of the world's best windsurfing areas, the Columbia Gorge is a great place to learn this exciting sport. **Rhonda Smith Windsurfing Center** (Port Marina Park, Hood River; 503-386-9463) is the place to go for equipment rentals, lessons, kids camps and racing lessons. **Gorge Windsurfing** (319 East 2nd Street, The Dalles; 503-298-8796) offers sailboard equipment and instructions. Lessons, rentals and demo equipment are all arranged at The Dalles Riverfront Park.

FISHING

Salmon, steelhead, walleye and sturgeon fishing are all convenient to the Portland/Columbia River area. **Page's Fish-A-Way Guide Service** (14321 Southeast Bush Street, Portland; 503-760-3373), **Portland Fishing Adventures** (17870 Davis Drive, Portland; 503-668-8541), **Northwest**

Fishing and Fun Guide Service (2480 Northwest 111th Avenue, Portland; 503-626-3885) and **Green's Fish On Charter Service** (1206 West 2nd Street, The Dalles; 503-296-4652) can help you land the big ones.

RIVER RAFTING

The White Salmon River north of the Columbia is a popular rafting spot. Both **Phil Zoller's Guide Service** (1244 Route 141, White Salmon; 503-493-2641) and **White Water Adventure** (38 Northwestern Lake, White Salmon; 503-493-3121) offer trips here. In addition, **River Drifters Whitewater Tours** (13570 Northwest Lakeview Drive, Portland; 503-645-6264) rafts a variety of rivers convenient to the Portland area.

GOLF

You are never far from the links in the Portland area. Possibilities include **Eastmoreland Golf Course** (2425 Southeast Bybee Boulevard, Portland; 503-775-2900), **Glendoveer Golf Course** (14015 Northeast Glisan Street, Portland; 503-253-7507), **Meriwether National Golf Club** (5200 Southwest Rood Bridge Road, Hillsboro; 503-648-4143), **King City Golf Club** (15355 Southwest Royalty Parkway, Tigard; 503-639-7986) and **The Cedars Golf Club** (15001 Northeast 181st Street, Brush Prairie; 206-285-7548). In Hood River, try the **Hood River Golf and Country Club** (1850 Country Club Road; 503-386-2272). In Carson, Washington, head for the **Hot Springs Golf Course** (Hot Springs Avenue and St. Martins Road; 503-427-5150).

TENNIS

The Portland/Oregon Visitors Association can provide a complete list of more than three dozen public courts. Among the numerous private clubs are **Portland Tennis Center** (324 Northeast 12th Street; 503-233-5959) and **Western Athletic Club** (8785 Southwest Beaverton-Hillsdale Highway; 503-297-3723).

BICYCLING

A city seemingly made for cyclists, Portland is blessed with easy terrain, challenging hills and, for those who want to get off-the-beaten track, splendid rural getaways.

A good place to start is Oregon City where you can begin the 15-mile trip to Portland by taking Route 9 north to River Road and then pick up McLoughlin Avenue and 17th Avenue to the Sellwood Bridge. After crossing the Willamette continue along Spokane north to downtown.

West of downtown, Burnside Street leads up to Skyline Boulevard where you can make the challenging 15-mile trip to Germantown Road and then loop back into town via Route 30.

Another popular route parallels Route 10 west of town to Route 210 and Beaverton. This ten-mile trip can be extended west into wine country.

A favorite cycling getaway in the area is Sauvie Island located ten miles west of Portland. Light traffic makes it a pleasure to peddle through this wildlife sanctuary. Or take a short spin out Reeder Road to the Columbia River and then loop back along Gillihan Road and Sauvie Island Road.

The Columbia River Gorge along Route 84 is prime cycling territory. Any portion of the 62-mile route between Portland and Hood River is worth your time. You can also turn this into an ambitious 158-mile loop around Mt. Hood by returning to Portland on Routes 35 and 26.

Portland's **Metropolitan Service District** (200 Southwest 1st Avenue; 503-221-1646) offers a convenient route guide, *From Here To There By Bike*. You'll find it at their office as well as the local bike shops. **Portland United Mt. Pedalers** (2148 Northeast Schuyler Street; 503-288-9627) and Club Vivo (35 Northwest 3rd Avenue; 503-227-3526) can also help get you rolling.

BIKE RENTALS   Rentals are available in Portland at **Agape Cycle and Sports** (2610 Southeast Clinton Street; 503-230-0317) and **Glacier's Edge** (8775 Southwest Canyon Lane; 503-297-4747). In Beaverton, try **Tailwind Outfitters** (Canyon Road at 117th Avenue; 503-641-2580). In Hood River, try **Discover Bicycles** (1020 Wasco Street; 503-386-4820). In The Dalles rent from **Life Cycles** (122 2nd Street; 503-296-9588).

HIKING

A hiker's paradise, the Portland region has beautiful riverfront walks, urban trails and wilderness loops perfect for a brief interlude or an all-day excursion. Trail information is available from the **Bureau of Parks and Recreation** (1120 Southwest 5th Avenue; 503-796-5193) or from the Portland/Oregon Visitors Association.

CENTRAL PORTLAND TRAILS   Named for a former governor, **Tom McCall Waterfront Park** offers a 2-mile-long path along the Willamette River. This is an ideal way to get an overview of the downtown area.

PORTLAND EAST TRAILS   You don't have to go all the way to Mt. St. Helens to hike a volcano. Just take the **Mt. Tabor Perimeter Loop** (2.7 miles). Your hike on Southeast 60th Avenue, Southeast Yamhill Street, Southeast 72nd Avenue and Southeast Lincoln Street provides a pleasant overview of this landmark.

Another easy route is the loop circling **Powell Butte** (2 miles). You'll ascend the 630-foot summit for a Portland overview you won't soon forget.

PORTLAND WEST TRAILS   Sauvie Island is ideal for short or long strolls. One of our favorite walks is the hike from **Coon Point** along Steelman Road to **Willow Hole** (2 miles). Another good bet is the hike from Walton Beach along the Columbia to **Warrior Rock Lighthouse** (4 miles).

With more than 5000 acres, Forest Park offers over 50 miles of connecting trails. Many of the routes are spurs off **Wildwood Trail** (24 miles), the primary route traversing this vast urban refuge. Depending on your time and mood, hike as much of this trail as you want, connecting easily to other convenient routes. Your starting point for Wildwood is Hoyt Arboretum's Vietnam Memorial. If you're feeling more ambitious, try **Marquam Nature Trail** (5 miles) leading from Hines Park to Washington Park via Terwilliger Boulevard and Council Crest Park.

Two popular mile-long walks will add to your enjoyment of Hoyt Arboretum. The **Conifer Tour** leads through a forest thick with spruce, fir and redwood. Also well worth your time is the **Oak Tour**.

COLUMBIA RIVER AND THE GORGE TRAILS   **Latourell Falls Trail** (2 miles), on the Old Columbia Gorge Scenic Highway three miles east of Crown Point, is a moderately difficult walk leading along a streambed to the base of the upper falls. To extend this walk another mile take a loop trail beginning at the top of lower Latourell Falls and returning to the highway at Talbot Park.

Near the Bridalveil exit off Route 84 is **#415 Angels Rest Trail** (2 miles), an easy hike leading to an overlook. This route can be extended another 15 miles to Bonneville Dam by taking the **#400 Gorge Trail**.

Eagle Creek Campground at exit 40 on Route 84 is the jumpoff point for the easy hike to **Punch Bowl Falls** (.3 mile) or the far more challenging trip to **Wahtum Lake** (13 miles). The latter trail leads up through the Columbia Wilderness and is part of the Pacific Crest Trail.

On the Washington side of the river west of Bonneville Dam is the 1-mile trail leading to the top of **Beacon Rock**, an 800-foot monolith noted by Lewis and Clark. Ascended by a series of switchbacks guarded by railings, this trail offers great views of the Gorge.

Transportation

BY CAR

Most visitors to Portland arrive on one of three primary highways. **Route 5** bisects the city and provides access from the north via Vancouver, Washington. This same highway also is the main line from points south like the Willamette Valley and California. From points east, **Route 84** along the Columbia River is the preferred way into town. From the west, **Route 26** is a major highway into town. Secondary routes include **Route 30** from the west and **Route 99** from the south.

BY AIR

Portland International Airport is the major gateway. Located ten miles northeast of downtown, it is served by Air B.C., Alaska Airlines, American Airlines, America West Airlines, Continental Airlines, Delta Air Lines, Horizon Air, Northwest Airlines, Trans World Airlines and United Airlines. Limousines, vans and buses take visitors to downtown locations, including **Raz Tranz Airporter** (503-246-4676), **MoveOut Transportation Services** (503-936-1680) and **Prestige Limousine** (503-282-5009).

BY BUS

Greyhound/Trailways Bus Lines offers bus service to Portland from across the nation. The main downtown terminal is at 550 Northwest 6th Avenue (503-243-2323). **Raz Transportation Company** (503-246-3301) provides service from Portland to Seaside, Astoria and Tillamook. Tickets for these routes are available from Greyhound.

BY TRAIN

Amtrak (800 Northwest 6th Avenue; 800-872-7245 or 503-273-4865) provides service from Washington and California via the "Coast Starlight." The "Pioneer" serves eastern Oregon, Idaho, Utah and points east. There is also a northerly connection to Spokane and the "Empire Builder."

CAR RENTALS

At the airport try **Avis Rent A Car** (503-249-4950), **Budget Rent A Car** ((503-249-6500), **Dollar Rent A Car** (503-249-4972) or **Hertz Rent A Car** (503-249-8216). Cars are also available from **Agency Rent A Car** (503-224-2009), **American International Rent A Car** (503-255-7711), **Bee Rent A Car** (503-233-7368) and **Enterprise Rent A Car** (503-256-9598). For used-car rentals, try **Rent A Wreck** (503-231-1640).

PUBLIC TRANSPORTATION

Tri-Met Buses/MAX-Light Rail (503-233-3511) serve the Portland region. Buses blanket the city, while the MAX-Light Rail line extends east from downtown to the Lloyd Center and then on to Gresham. There is free bus service downtown in the "Fareless Square" region spanning 300 blocks. For detailed bus route information call 503-231-3199. Hood River is served by **Hood River County Transit** (503-386-4202).

TAXIS

Broadway Deluxe (503-227-1234), **Radio Cab** (503-227-1212) and **Yellow Cab** (503-227-1234) all provide convenient local service. In Hood River, call **Hood River Taxi and Transportation** (503-386-4202).

CHAPTER EIGHT

Oregon Coast

As you take in the wonders of the Oregon Coast, do it with respect for in a very real sense you are stepping into a paradise borrowed. In 1806, when Lewis and Clark arrived at the mouth of the Columbia River, only about 10,000 Native Americans in such coast tribes as the Tillamook and Yaquina called this home. With roughly three square miles per inhabitant, these tribes were undisputed masters of their realm. Rich in fishing, hunting and gathering grounds, the Native Americans traveled almost entirely by water, were intensely spiritual and had, for the most part, a modest and self-sufficient lifestyle. Working hard during the spring and summer months, they harvested enough from the sea and forests to kick back during the winter.

But their world began to change, indeed it was doomed, when distant entrepreneurs set sights on the region's vast resources. These men believed that the Northwest did not belong to its native populace but instead that it was destined to be claimed by a new master race of settlers thousands of miles away. Among them was John Jacob Astor, the richest man in America. Eager to monopolize the lucrative fur trade in the uncharted Northwest, he dispatched the ship *Tonquin* from New York in the fall of 1810. Then, in the spring of 1811, just about the time the *Tonquin* was sailing across the Columbia River Bar, a second overland group sponsored by Astor left St. Louis. They began by following the river route pioneered by Lewis and Clark but then forged a new trail across the Rockies, eventually reaching the Snake River where they were turned back by impenetrable rapids. By early 1812, when the party limped into Astoria, the little settlement created by men from the *Tonquin*, it was clear that their patron's great vision remained distant. For one thing, most of the *Tonquin* group had headed north to Vancouver Island where dictatorial captain Jonathan Thorn spurned the

Native Americans, triggering a massacre that destroyed almost everyone aboard. In a final insane act of revenge, a surviving crew member lured the Native Americans back on the ship, went below and lit the ship's magazine, killing everyone aboard.

In September 1812, not long after they received news of this tragedy, the Astorians left behind at the little Columbia River settlement were visited by a party from the rival North West Fur Company. These newcomers announced that a British warship was en route to seize Fort Astoria. To make matters worse, they announced that the British had just won the War of 1812. Cut off from the news that would have exposed this lie, the Astorians decided to sell off their pelts and the first American settlement west of the Mississippi for pennies on the dollars. Then they began the long journey home.

While the British took over the fur trade, manifest destiny brought the Americans back on the Oregon Trail. In 1846, Oregon Country was returned to the Americans and new settlers gradually returned to the coast. Astoria and other settlements along the coast emerged as fishing, farming and logging centers. The arrival of the railroads spawned the development of resort towns like Newport and Seaside. Boardwalks, modeled after those found on the East Coast, soon sprang up to serve the growing clientele.

The coast may have been the magnet, but it didn't take the new arrivals long to discover that the lofty headlands, picturesque estuaries, rocky points, sand dunes and tidepools were only part of the attraction. Back behind the coastal rhododendron fields were rivers that offered legendary steelheading. Sunny valleys forested with fir, pine and redwood were perfect for camping. Stands of weird carnivorous plants, plunging waterfalls, myrtle groves and pristine lakes were all part of the draw. And the Indians, decimated by white man's diseases, were subjugated by the new settlers and ultimately forced onto reservations.

Having pushed the natives conveniently out of the way, the pioneers soon began reaping nature's bounty from the coastal region. Coos Bay became a major wood-processing center, and commercial fishing dominated the economies of communities like Port Orford. Other towns, such as Tillamook, flourished in the dairy trade. And, of course, farming also began to emerge in the sunnier valleys east of the coast.

Today, thanks in part to a comprehensive network of state parks, the coast is equally appealing to motorists, bikers and hikers. While it's hard to improve on this landscape, mankind has done its best to complement nature's handiwork. From bed and breakfasts heavy on chintz and lace, to bargain oceanfront motels furnished from garage sales, accommodations serve every taste. Everywhere you turn another executive chef weary of big-city life seems to be opening a pasta joint or a pita stand. Theater, classical music, jazz, pottery and sculpture galleries have all found a home in towns ranging from North Bend to Cannon Beach. A major aquarium in Newport, a world-class maritime museum in Astoria, a printing museum in Coos Bay,

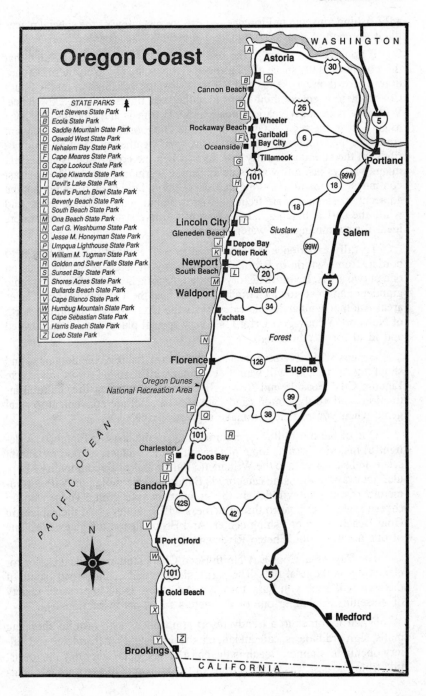

Oregon Coast

STATE PARKS
A Fort Stevens State Park
B Ecola State Park
C Saddle Mountain State Park
D Oswald West State Park
E Nehalem Bay State Park
F Cape Meares State Park
G Cape Lookout State Park
H Cape Kiwanda State Park
I Devil's Lake State Park
J Devil's Punch Bowl State Park
K Beverly Beach State Park
L South Beach State Park
M Ona Beach State Park
N Carl G. Washburne State Park
O Jesse M. Honeyman State Park
P Umpqua Lighthouse State Park
Q William M. Tugman State Park
R Golden and Silver Falls State Park
S Sunset Bay State Park
T Shores Acres State Park
U Bullards Beach State Park
V Cape Blanco State Park
W Humbug Mountain State Park
X Cape Sebastian State Park
Y Harris Beach State Park
Z Loeb State Park

WASHINGTON

Astoria
Cannon Beach
Wheeler
Rockaway Beach
Garibaldi
Oceanside
Bay City
Tillamook
Portland
Lincoln City
Gleneden Beach
Siuslaw
Salem
Depoe Bay
Otter Rock
Newport
South Beach
Waldport
National
Yachats
Forest
Florence
Oregon Dunes
National Recreation Area
Eugene
Charleston
Coos Bay
Bandon
Port Orford
Gold Beach
Medford
Brookings

PACIFIC OCEAN

N

CALIFORNIA

a fly-fishing museum in Florence—these are just a few of the special places likely to capture your attention.

If you must go down to the sea again, and you must, rest assured that this coast offers the space all of us need. True, some of the northern beaches draw a crowd on weekends and holidays. But traffic is lighter on the South Coast where beachcombing can be a lonely, at times solitary, experience. With vast national recreation areas, national forests and sloughs, it's easy to get lost in the region. Often foggy, the Oregon Coast is hit by frequent storms in the winter months. But this rugged weather is offset by mild periods, in the summer or early fall. Even when the coast itself is socked in, inland valleys just a few miles away can be warm and sunny. The contrast continues: Temperatures along the coast seldom fall below freezing, but the adjacent coastal peaks are frequently snowbound in the winter months. And while the surf is bracing, lakes adjacent to the coast offer warmer waters ideal for swimming and waterskiing.

To fully experience the coast, you're well advised to see it border to border, from Astoria to Brookings. But many travelers prefer to focus on one or two areas. If you're history minded, Astoria is a must. For pure scenic grandeur and small-town charm it's hard to beat the Tillamook/Three Capes area. Another winner in this category is the Otter Rock community north of Newport. Windy Port Orford is a very special place, scenic, uncrowded and ideal for steelheading.

Groups with diverse interests such as surf fishing, arcade games and shopping for folk art will want to consider well-rounded resort towns like Lincoln City, Seaside and Newport. They offer sporting life, cultural attractions and all the cotton candy you can eat. All are convenient to rural gems when you're ready to make a great escape.

One of the most alluring communities on the coast is Florence. A delightful historic district, some of Oregon's finest dunes, a good restaurant scene and easy access to the Willamette Valley make this community a popular getaway. In the same category is Bandon, a charming port with a commercial district that will delight the shoppers in your group. Those who are eager to take a jet boat to the wilderness will doubtless find themselves in Gold Beach, a major fishing center. And Brookings is the gateway to one of our favorites, the Chetco River country.

The Bay Area, Coos Bay/North Bend/Charleston, is an ideal choice for clamming on the tidal flats. The parks, sloughs and country roads south of the area will keep you busy for days. And there is an impressive variety of museums, including one of the state's finest art institutions.

When it comes to a trendy resort atmosphere with tasteful shopping malls, sign ordinances, café au lait, classical music, French cuisine and gallery openings, Cannon Beach is the coast's class act. Every day the tourist tide from the east washes in patrons of the arts and Oregon varietals. This town may set the record for merchant/punsters operating shops like "Sometimes a Great Lotion" and "Katz'ndoggers."

There are many other destinations that don't appear on any map. In fact, the best of the Oregon Coast may not be its incorporated cities or parklands. Think instead of rocky points home only to sea lions. Eddies so beautiful you don't care if you catch anything. Offshore haystacks that don't even have names. Dunes that form the perfect backdrop for a day of kite flying. Points that seem to have been created solely for the purpose of sunset watching.

All these possibilities may seem overwhelming. But we believe the following pages will put your mind at ease. An embarrassment of riches, the Oregon Coast is more byway than highway. As you explore the capes and coves, visit the sea-lion caves and sea-cut caverns, you're likely to make numerous finds of your own. Those hidden places we're always talking about will tempt you to linger for hours, maybe even days. And however long you stay, give pause to remember that another people once lived here.

North Coast

The North Coast is one of the most heavily traveled tourist routes in the Pacific Northwest. From June through early October, you can expect to have plenty of company. While most travelers hug the shoreline, some of the best sightseeing in this region is actually found a few miles inland. Less crowded and often sunnier, these hidden spots reward those willing to veer off Route 101.

A special tip for those who prefer to drive during off-peak times: Around 5 p.m. most of the logging trucks are berthed and the RVs are bedded down for the night. In the summer consider allocating a good part of your day for sightseeing. Then, at 5 p.m., when many of the museums and attractions close, take a couple of daylight hours to proceed to your next destination. Not only is the traffic lighter, the sunsets are remarkable. Plus, you'll be able to dine fashionably late.

Why not follow the path of Lewis and Clark by taking Route 30 west from Portland along the Columbia River to Astoria, the first American city established west of the Mississippi? About 20 miles east of town you can tune in **KMUN** (91.9 or 89.5 FM), one of the finest public-broadcasting stations in the Northwest. A kind of Radio Free Astoria, this listener-sponsored station features local kids reading their favorite fiction, opera buffs airing Bellini, bus drivers playing jazz and a nun who broadcasts local-history vignettes on Saturday and then heads out to hospitals and nursing homes to give away free radios she's picked up in thrift shops.

Set on a hillside overlooking the Columbia River, **Astoria** is one of the Pacific Northwest's most historic cities. Grand Victorians, steep streets and skies that belong to the gulls and shorebirds make this river town a must. As you enter Astoria, stop at the **Uppertown Fire Fighters Museum** (30th Street and Marine Drive; 503-325-2203; admission). The vintage collection includes a classic 1877 horse-drawn ladder wagon, antique motorized pumpers and fire-fighting memorabilia.

Continue west to the **Columbia River Maritime Museum** (1792 Marine Drive; 503-325-2333; admission). One of the nation's finest seafaring collections, this 24,000-square-foot building tells the story of the Northwest's mightiest river, discovered in 1792 by Captain Robert Gray and navigated by Lewis and Clark in 1805 on the final leg of their 4000-mile journey from St. Louis. One of the most treacherous spots on the West Coast, the turbulent Columbia River bar was a nautical graveyard claiming scores of ships. Besides documenting these disasters, the museum offers exhibits on Native American history, the Northwest fur trade, navigation and marine safety, fishing, canneries, whaling, sailing and steam and motor vessels. And that's not all. Docked outside is the *Columbia*, the last of numerous lightships that provided navigational aid along the Pacific Coast.

Continue west along Marine Drive to historic Astoria. Head to the **Greater Astoria Chamber of Commerce** (111 West Marine Drive; 503-325-6311) to pick up a helpful map and background. Among the many Astoria Victorians on the National Register of Historic Places is the **Flavel House** (441 Duane Street; 503-325-2563; admission), a Queen Anne with Italianate columns and Eastlake-style woodwork around the doors and windows. Featuring six fireplaces, a library, music parlor and three-story octagonal tower, this home is one of most visited residences on the Oregon Coast. For $2 you can pick up a walking-tour guide to Astoria's Victorian homes. Your admission ticket also pays for entrance to the **Heritage Museum** (16th and Exchange streets; 503-325-2203) where you'll see artifacts from the *Peter Iredale*, a ship wrecked in 1906. It remains visible off the beach at nearby Fort Stevens State Park. Other exhibits feature artifacts from local logging camps and a popular saloon called The Louvre.

You'll also want to visit **Fort Astoria** at 15th and Exchange streets. This small, blockhouse replica was home base for the Astorians when they settled here.

For a good overview follow the signs up 16th Street to **Coxcomb Hill**. Pictorial friezes wrapping around the 125-foot-high column cover the region's heritage from its Native American past to modern times. Unless you're prone to vertigo, climb the circular stairway to the top for a panoramic view of the Astoria region.

About five miles west of Astoria near Hammond is **Fort Stevens Historic Area and Military Museum** (Fort Stevens State Park; 503-861-2000). On June 21, 1942, the fort became the first American continental military installation shelled since the War of 1812. Seventeen shots fired by the Japanese hit the military installation. Fortunately none caused any damage. While visiting you can tour the fort in a two-and-a-half-ton Army truck or take an underground tour of Battery Mishler. Don't miss the wreck of the *Peter Iredale*, now a rusty skeleton easily reached by following signs inside the park.

Five miles south of Astoria off Route 101 is **Fort Clatsop National Memorial** (503-861-2471; admission). During the rainy winter of 1805-06, the 33-member Lewis and Clark party bivouacked here for three months before returning east. Named in honor of the Clatsop Indians, this reconstructed fort has an introductory slide presentation, interpretive displays and muzzleloading demonstrations put on by buckskin-clad rangers armed with flintlock rifles. Other guides show how Lewis and Clark's team built canoes, made candles, did woodworking and sewed hides.

Oregon's answer to Coney Island, the town of **Seaside** is the kind of place to visit when you long for saltwater taffy and game arcades, boardwalks and volleyball. Just head down Broadway to find the carnival atmosphere. By the time you reach the beach you'll feel a restless urge to start building sand castles. One of the most popular resorts on the coast, it is easy to visit with a little help from the **Seaside Chamber of Commerce** (7 North Roosevelt Drive; 503-738-6391).

Aided by a chamber brochure you'll be able to take the historic **walking tour** along the two-mile boardwalk known as the Prom. Along the way are Victorian-style homes, arts-and-crafts bungalows, Colonial revivals and English-style cottages. Another highlight is the Prom "Turnaround" marking the end of the Lewis and Clark Trail. At the south end is a reproduction of the cairn where the Lewis and Clark expedition boiled seawater during the winter of 1806 to make salt. More than three-and-a-half bushels were produced for the return trip.

Of special interest is the **Seaside Museum and Historical Society** (570 Necanicum Drive; 503-738-7065; admission), located in the old central school building. Inside are Clatsop Indian artifacts, turn-of-the-century photos of boardwalk hotels and bath houses and historic fire-fighting and logging equipment. Also here is the **Seaside Aquarium** (200 North Prom Drive; 503-738-6211; admission) where you can see seals, sea lions and other marine mammals.

Eighteen miles east of Seaside on Route 26 is **Camp 18 Logging Museum** (milepost 18, Route 26; 503-755-2476). Steam donkeys, cranes, train cabooses and other vintage equipment are among the exhibits. There's a restaurant on the premises.

Follow Route 26 east to Jewell Junction and continue north on Fishawk Falls Highway towards Jewell. Just north of town is the **Jewell Meadows Wildlife Area** (★), a good place to spot Roosevelt elk.

South of Seaside is **Tillamook Head Recreation Trail,** a six-mile route that extends to Cannon Beach's northern edge. Most of the route is within Ecola State Park. A highlight of this park is the tidepools of rocky Indian Beach. From the head you'll enjoy excellent views of the coast and the **Tillamook Rock lighthouse.**

Cannon Beach, one of the most popular villages on the North Coast, is an artists' colony and home of photogenic **Haystack Rock.** A marine and bird sanctuary, this is the place to explore tidepools and look for puffins. With its resorts and condos, boutiques and small malls, Cannon Beach (it's named for a cannon that drifted ashore after a shipwreck) can be a busy place. Gallery shows, the Stormy Weather Festival, sand-castle contests and concerts in the park add to the fun.

Twelve miles south of Cannon Beach, **Oswald West State Park** offers a series of beautiful viewpoints. Just south of the park is Neah-kah-nie Mountain, a promontory surrounded by a two-century-old Native American legend. Indian lore holds that a wrecked Spanish galleon carrying gold and beeswax washed up on the beach and the surviving crew members tucked the treasure into a hole dug at the base of the mountain. But treasure hunters, using everything from back hoes to bare hands, have failed to strike it rich here. **Manzanita,** a resort town at the foot of this famed peak, is a gem in its own right.

A lovely spot on the North Coast is **Nehalem Bay,** separated from the ocean by a sandspit. The historic Nehalem waterfront, a Native American community that was replaced by canneries, lumbering and dairy farms, is a popular antiquing center. Nearby **Wheeler,** on the Nehalem River, is a prime fishing spot with great views of the bay.

On your way into **Tillamook** you'll probably want to stop to sample the familiar orange cheddar at **Tillamook Cheese** (4175 North Route 101; 503-842-4481). A self-guided tour makes it easy to see the Pacific Northwest's largest cheese factory, Tillamook County Creamery, which produces 40 million pounds annually. Overhead walkways offer a birdseye view of the cheddaring process.

Next, stop by the **Tillamook Chamber of Commerce** (3705 North Route 101; 503-842-7525) to pick up helpful background on this area. Among the musts is **The Tillamook County Pioneer Museum** (2106 2nd Street; 503-842-4553; admission). Unlike many museums that display only a small portion of their holdings, this one is packed with 35,000 antiques, artifacts, dioramas, mounted animals, gems and gemstones. Highlights include Tillamook Indian basketry, pioneer implements, antique-clock section and fire-lookout cabin. This museum is a good place to learn about pioneer coastal life and natural history. You'll also learn that the giant hangars south of town berthed blimps that patrolled the West Coast for the Navy during World War II. Among the most recent additions to the military collection is a Scud fragment retrieved during the 1991 Operation Desert Storm.

Seven miles south of town via Route 101 take the turnoff to 266-foot-high **Munson Creek Falls** (★), easily reached via a half-mile trail. This horsetail falls is the highest in the Coast Range. The creek gorge is lovely.

West of Tillamook is one of the most picturesque drives on the Oregon Coast, 40-mile **Three Capes Loop**. As you follow Bay Ocean Road along the southern edge of Tillamook Bay you'll come to one of the region's most fascinating ghost towns, **Bay Ocean Park** (★). Designed to become a pre-casino Atlantic City of the West, this 1912 subdivision eventually grew to 59 homes. But between 1932 and 1949 the sea cut a half-mile swath across the spit, turning it into an island. Over the next 20 years the ocean eroded the Bay Ocean landscape and one by one homes were swept into the sea. Finally, in 1959, the last five remaining houses were moved. Today only a sign marks the site, which is also commemorated at the Tillamook County Pioneer Museum.

The Three Capes Loop continues past **Cape Meares Lake**, a haven for waterfowl and shorebirds, before continuing to **Cape Meares State Park**. While here you'll want to visit the Octopus Tree, a legendary Sitka spruce with six trunks extending horizontally for up to 30 feet before making a skyward turn. With just two more limbs this could have been the world's largest Hanukkah menorah. You can also take the short trail to the century-old Cape Meares lighthouse, surrounded by wild roses in the warm months.

Continue south to Oceanside and the **Three Arch Rocks Wildlife Refuge**, home of Oregon's largest seabird colony. Half a mile offshore, these islands harbor 75,000 common murres as well as tufted puffins, pigeon guillemots, storm-petrels, cormorants and gulls. Perched on the rocks below is a sea-lion colony.

At **Cape Lookout State Park**, nature trails and coast walks delight visitors. Dune buffs will enjoy visiting the **Sand Lake Recreation Area** seven miles south of Cape Lookout. **Pacific City**, at the bottom of the Three Capes Loop, is famous for its dory fleet launched into the surf from the Cape Kiwanda beach.

South of Neskowin, Cascade Head Road leads to the **Cascade Head Experimental Forest**. Cascade Head and Hart's Cove trails provide access to these headlands ideal for wildflower photography, whale watching and birdwatching.

NORTH COAST HOTELS

A Neo-Classical revival with fir wainscotting, leaded glass and rare, Pompeiian-red wall treatment in the living room, the **Rosebriar Inn Bed and Breakfast** (636 14th Street, Astoria; 503-325-7427) offers ten rooms in the convent addition. While some are spartan nun's quarters, others are nicely furnished with lace curtains, vintage rugs and plants. Moderate to deluxe in price.

East of town, the **Crest Motel** (5366 Leif Erickson Drive, Astoria; 503-325-3141) sits on a grassy hilltop overlooking the Columbia River. This trim and tidy establishment offers 40 modernized units with watercolor prints, writing desks, a jacuzzi and laundry facilities. There's fishing on the property. Try for one of the quieter rear rooms. Moderate.

Also on the Columbia River is **Bayshore Motor Inn** (555 Hamburg Street, Astoria; 503-325-2205). All 36 motel units have contemporary furniture and print bedspreads. There's also a comfortable lounge where a complimentary continental breakfast is served. Convenient to Astoria's historic district, this wheelchair-accessible lodge is an ideal spot to watch river traffic or fish. Moderate.

Hillcrest Inn (118 North Columbia Street, Seaside; 503-738-6273) offers 16 attractive, pine-shaded units in a quiet garden setting close to this resort town's beach, shops, restaurants and nightlife. Choose between budget studios and moderate-to-deluxe-priced one- and two-bedroom units with kitchens. Eclectic furniture ranges from fold-out sofas to wicker living-room sets. Some units offer fireplaces, decks and spas. Family groups will find this establishment a good value.

The moderately priced **Oceanfront Motel** (50 1st Avenue, Seaside; 503-738-5661) is an older, 35-unit brick motel offering two-room suites on the beach. Carpeted rooms have wooden bed frames, decks, refrigerators and picture windows ideal for sunset watching. Kitchenettes are available. The #13, a one-bedroom apartment, is a good bargain for the budget minded.

Right on the beach, the three-story **Seashore Resort Hotel** (60 North Prom Street, Seaside; 503-738-6368) offers spacious, moderate-to-deluxe-priced rooms with comfortable upholstered furniture, vanities, an enclosed pool, sauna and whirlpool. Within walking distance of Seaside's popular attractions, this hotel overlooks volleyball courts and the surf.

A mix of sleeping rooms and one- and two-bedroom units, the **McBee Court** (887 South Hemlock Street, Cannon Beach; 503-436-2569) is conveniently located on the south side of town. Some of the 11 units in this older, motel-style complex offer ocean views, kitchenettes and fireplaces. Several have been recently remodeled. Large groups may want to take the two-story coach house. Budget to moderate.

Eclectic is surely the word for **Ocean Locomotion Motel** (19130 Alder Avenue, Rockaway Beach; 503-355-2093) with eight moderate-to-deluxe-priced coastal units overlooking Twin Rocks. Modernized one-, two- and three-bedroom units offer kitchenettes and ocean views. Most have older furniture, but recently remodeled unit six has a contemporary look and qualifies as a best buy. Lawn furniture, barbecues, a fire pit, clam rakes and buckets make this family-oriented establishment appealing.

Large, carpeted accommodations in a charming, Salt Box-style home make **Pelican Perch Guest Suites** (112 East Cypress Street, Garibaldi; 503-

322-3633) an excellent choice. Brass beds, panoramic views and kitchenettes add to the charm of this bed and breakfast. A breakfast basket of cheese and fruit is at your door each morning. Convenient to fishing and an excursion railroad, this is one of our favorite inns on the coast. Moderate.

Set on a hill with commanding views of Nehalem Bay, the budget-to-moderate-priced motel rooms at **Wheeler Village Inn** (2nd and Gregory streets, Wheeler; 503-368-5734) are small, clean and brightly painted. All have carpets and kitchenettes. Pull up a chaise lounge and enjoy the sunsets.

A white, two-story lodge in a park setting, **View of the West** (294 Hall Street, Wheeler; 503-368-5766) (★) is one of the coast's authentic treasures. Ten beautifully furnished theme rooms, a great hillside setting, patio decks and flowers everywhere make this resort ideal for a honeymoon. Accommodations include an Early American room with a bent-willow frame bed and a Southwest room with a pine-lodgepole canopy bed as well as Indian arts and crafts. All rooms open onto porches with panoramic views of the North Coast. There's also a large deck with barbecue. Moderate.

On Nehalem Bay, **Wheeler Fishing Lodge** (580 Marine Street, Wheeler; 503-368-3474) offers refurbished, motel-style units and suites including some with decks and kitchens. Rooms range from Victorian style to art deco. All are carpeted. Convenient to fishing, clamming, sailboarding, hiking and birdwatching. Moderate.

The **Blue Haven Inn** (★) (3025 Gienger Road, Tillamook; 503-842-2265) is one of the few bed and breakfasts we know that has its own antique shop on the premises. You'll enjoy staying upstairs in one of the cozy rooms painted robin's-egg blue and appointed with a four-poster bed and plates featuring Scarlett O'Hara surrounded by half a dozen admiring beaux. The breakfasts are great. Moderate.

In the Tillamook region, cliffside **Sea Haven Inn** (★) (545 South Avenue Northwest, Oceanside; 503-842-3151) is a luxurious contemporary inn with seven moderate-to-deluxe-priced rooms and suites. Nautical decor, rose bedspreads, wicker furniture, small refrigerators and sitting areas make this bed and breakfast an excellent retreat. A comfortable lounge and deck offer panoramic views of the coast. With binoculars you may be able to spot sea lions or migrating whales.

On the Three Capes Scenic Loop, **Terrimore Motel** (5105 Crab Avenue, Netarts; 503-842-4623) offers 28 one- and two-bedroom cottages and kitchenettes. Located on the beach, these clean, modernized units are comfortably furnished with lofts, sitting areas and fireplaces. This inn is a quiet retreat ideal for fishing, whale watching and agate collecting.

NORTH COAST RESTAURANTS

For fish and chips you'll have a hard time beating the **Ship Inn** (1 2nd Street, Astoria; 503-325-0033). Huge portions of cod and halibut are served in the waterfront dining room along with chowder, generous salads and desserts. A full bar is one of the town's more popular gathering places. Nautical decor gives diners the feeling they are out on the bounding main. Moderate.

A great spot for river-watching, **Pier 11 Feedstore Restaurant and Lounge** (foot of 10th Street, Astoria; 503-325-0279) is the place to go for seafood, prime rib, crab legs, chicken Kiev and large salads. This renovated commercial building has picture windows offering a wonderful view of the Columbia River. Done in a seminautical style, the dining room offers seating at oak tables on bowback captain's chairs. Moderate.

The **House of Chan** (159 West Bond Street, Astoria; 503-325-7289) menu features Cantonese and Mandarin specialties in a large dining room with red booths and carpets, Asian art and vases. Dishes at this moderate-priced establishment include scallops with mushrooms, onions and vegetables sautéed in wine sauce, beef with orange flavor and pineapple *war shu* duck. You can also enjoy a drink in the Sampan Lounge.

One of the most beautiful dining rooms on the coast is found at **Café Uniontown** (218 West Marine Drive, Astoria; 503-325-8708). An elegant, paneled setting with a mirrored bar, pink tablecloths and marine view make this moderate-priced establishment a great place to enjoy tempura dishes, pesto shrimp, lamb milanese, cioppino, steaks and pasta dishes. Located under the bridge in the historic Uniontown district, this is also a good spot for a drink after a hard day of sightseeing.

Not every pizza parlor can boast a medieval-castle setting with a classic Wurlitzer "Bubbler" jukebox and deck seating overlooking a river that's home to gulls and ducks. But that's what awaits you at **Bonnie and Jerry's Pizza Palace** (2490 North Route 101, Seaside; 503-738-7763). This popular establishment with wood tables and booths features murals of jousting knights. The menu offers 32 kinds of pizza with traditional toppings as well as smoked oysters, shrimp and baby clams. Budget.

Pig N'Pancake (323 Broadway Street, Seaside; 503-738-7243) is the place to go for swedish pancakes, crêpe suzettes and strawberry waffles. This moderately priced establishment seats over 100 customers at booths and tables in a coffee-shop environment. Lunch and dinner entrées include patty melts, garden sandwiches, halibut and steaks.

Dooger's Seafood and Grill (505 Broadway Street, Seaside; 503-738-3773) serves specialties like bay scallops, crab legs, prawns, fish and chips, pasta dishes, burgers and steaks in a paneled dining room convenient to the city's popular attractions. The carpeted dining room features oak furniture and dessert specialties like marionberry cobbler. Moderate.

Dooley's West Texas Barbecue (upstairs in Ecola Square, Hemlock Street at West 1st Street, Cannon Beach; 503-436-1827) offers brisket, chicken breasts and ribs. All are prepared in the mesquite-fired smoker and served on tables with red-and-white-checkered table cloths. Styled like a ranch house, Dooley's also has pea salad, chili dogs, meat tamales, burgers, sandwiches, three-alarm chili and fruit cobblers. Moderate.

Start your day with omelettes or waffles at the **Lazy Susan** (126 North Hemlock Street, Cannon Beach; 503-436-2816), a cut above your average café. Or try their sandwiches, salads or soups for lunch. The paneled dining room with elegant bentwood furniture, bright-blue tablecloths and watercolor prints on the walls make this establishment a local favorite. Moderate.

Limited to take out and counter service, **Pizza a fetta** (231 North Hemlock Street, Cannon Beach; 503-436-0333) is a good choice for a slice or an entire pie. In addition to regular toppings you can order sun-dried tomatoes, artichoke hearts, pancetta ham or fruits. Cheeses include Monterey Jack, Oregon blue, French feta, fontina and Montrachet chèvre. Located in Village Center. Budget.

For elegant French dining try the **Bistro Restaurant and Bar** (263 North Hemlock Street, Cannon Beach; 503-436-2661). Set in a small house, this intimate dining room serves specialties like halibut with herbs and tomatoes, shrimp Dianne, veal scallopini, New York steak and steamed clams. Moderate to deluxe.

Many museums have cafés in the basement or out on the patio. But **Art Space** (★) (9120 5th Street, Bay City; 503-377-2787) is a rare find, a fine restaurant in an elegant gallery setting. You'll walk past contemporary paintings, prints, sculpture and jewelry by outstanding Northwest artists on the way to the white-walled dining area. At booths and tables, black-and-white-checkered tablecloths, ceiling fans and sunny bay windows add up to an inviting setting for specialties like oysters Italia, prawns marinara and lemon chicken. A pianist often performs on weekend evenings. Moderate.

It wasn't brie but the heavenly aroma of fresh cinnamon rolls baked with sherry, peach schnapps, raisins and walnuts that caught our attention at the **Blue Heron French Cheese Company** (2001 Blue Heron Drive, Tillamook; 503-842-8281). The rolls were a test batch produced hours before their appointed weekly serving time—Sunday morning. But we used our clout to buy a sample, and the memory lingers. Even if you can't visit on Sunday, the deli counter in the midst of this jam-packed shop is the place to go for pastrami and provolone, smoked turkey and creamy brie or roast beef with a tangy Cotswold cheese spread. Budget.

Set in a shingled Craftsman house, **La Casa Medello** (1160 North Route 101, Tillamook; 503-842-5768) is the place to try when you want south-of-the-border fare on the North Coast. The dark-wood interior featuring beautiful, built-in cabinetry and casablanca fans is brightened by floral arrangements and plants. You can dine family style at the big tables offering specialties like *chile rellenos*, spanish-rice salad, homemade tamales and generous burritos. If you're hungry try the La Casa Fajita Tostada with steak or chicken breast. Moderate.

Nautical decor, pink walls and valances, ocean views and an oak counter make **Roseanna's Oceanside Café** (1490 Pacific Street, Oceanside; 503-842-7351) an inviting place to enjoy Tillamook oysters, rock cod Vera Cruz, vegetable fettucine, burgers and pesto salmon. This board-and-batten building is packed on weekends with a loyal clientele that likes to toast those delicious moments when the sun finally burns through the fog. Moderate.

One of our favorite coastal short order joints is **Wee Willie Restaurant** (★) (6060 Whiskey Creek Road, Netarts; 503-842-6869). Locals and tourists flock to this carpeted, lodge-style building where the menu features burgers, long dogs, short dogs, chili dogs, B.L.T.s and seafood specialties like barbecue crab and cheese, grilled shrimp and cheese, oyster burgers, clam chowder and fresh shrimp salad. Picnic tables indoors and outside on the lawn attract a big beach crowd. Be sure to try the homemade pies or warm gingerbread for dessert. Budget.

NORTH COAST SHOPPING

Palo's Department Store (248 West Marine Drive, Astoria; 503-325-1952) is just the place to find woollen shirts, sweaters, jeans and casual menswear. Located beneath the bridge in the old Finnish Hall, this establishment is popular with the merchant marine, lumberjacks, farmers, teenagers and tourists in the midst of shopping-mall deprogramming. Located in Astoria's historic Uniontown district, this is not a place for quiche eaters.

Turn back the clock at **Persona Vintage Clothing** (100 10th Street, Astoria; 503-325-3837). Collectible and antique clothing and accessories for men, women and children span the 1900-to-1950 era. Also on hand are a large hat section, beaded bags, costume jewelry, linens and laces.

With more than a dozen varieties of saltwater taffy, as well as caramel apples and carmel corn, **Leonard's** (111 Broadway Street, Seaside; 503-738-3467) has been an Oregon Coast tradition for more than 60 years. Popular flavors include banana, licorice, molasses and cinnamon.

You made it all the way to Cannon Beach and discovered that your bathing suit is too big, last summer's T-shirt has faded and you're out of #15 sunblock. **The Beach House** (183 North Hemlock Street; 503-436-2401) is at your rescue with the latest in swimwear, T-shirts, running togs, and casual sportswear. If you can wear it near the water, they've got it.

Our idea of a coastal gallery is **Artspace** (★) (9120 5th Street, Garibaldi; 503-377-2782). Contemporary Northwest sculpture and painting, jewelry, arts and crafts are all found in this white showplace. There's a restaurant on the premises.

Rainy Day Books (2015 2nd Street, Tillamook; 503-842-7766) focuses on used titles and has an excellent section on the Pacific Northwest. This is also a good place to pick up inexpensive paperbacks that come in handy when you want to relax by the fireplace.

NORTH COAST NIGHTLIFE

The **Red Lion Inn** (400 Industry Street, Astoria; 503-325-7373) has live pop music and dancing nightly and is located on the waterfront.

Patriot, the resident band at **El Toucan** (311 Broadway Street, Seaside; 503-738-8417) offers classic rock and pop tunes from the '50s through the '80s along with a smattering of Top-40. Enjoy dancing, a full bar and table service.

In Cannon Beach, the **Bistro Restaurant and Bar** (263 North Hemlock Street; 503-436-2661) offers solo guitar weekends. Take a seat at the bar or order drinks and dessert at one of the adjacent tables. This romantic setting is the ideal way to wind up the evening.

For musicals and jazz piano, Broadway shows, revivals, comedies and melodramas check out the **Coaster Theater Playhouse** (108 North Hemlock Street, Cannon Beach; 503-436-1242).

NORTH COAST BEACHES AND PARKS

Fort Stevens State Park—This 3762-acre state park embraces a Civil War-era fort that defended the coast during World War II. The site of a rare coastal attack by a Japanese submarine in 1942, the park landscape includes shallow lakes, dunes, sand flats and a pine forest. Of special interest are the oceanfront remains of a wrecked British ship, the *Peter Iredale*. A museum and guided tours offer a valuable historical perspective on the region.

Facilities: Picnic tables, showers, restrooms and gift shop; restaurants and groceries in Hammond; information, 503-861-1671. *Swimming:* Permitted. *Fishing:* Fish the surf for perch. Excellent razor clamming.

Camping: There are 262 tent sites and 343 RV hookups.

Getting there: Take Pacific Drive west from Hammond.

Ecola State Park—Forested with Sitka spruce and western hemlock, this 1303-acre park includes Ecola Point and the steep shoreline leading to Tillamook Head. Named for the region's original inhabitants, the park has many important Indian landmarks at a prehistoric village site. You may see deer and elk during your visit.

Facilities: Picnic tables and restrooms and wheelchair accessible; restaurants and groceries in Cannon Beach; information, 503-436-2844. *Fishing:* Good for perch.

Getting there: It's two miles north of Cannon Beach off Route 101.

Saddle Mountain State Park—A 3283-foot twin peak is the heart of this natural heritage site that features unusual plants and flowers. The peak was originally called Swallahoost after a chief who, after being murdered, was said to have returned to life as an eagle. From the mountaintop you can see both the Columbia River's mouth and the Pacific Coast. Douglas fir, spruce, hemlock and alder shade the 2911-acre park.

Facilities: Picnic tables and restrooms; restaurants and groceries in Necanicum; information, 503-861-1671.

Camping: There are nine primitive sites.

Getting there: It's off Route 26, eight miles northeast of Necanicum.

Oswald West State Park—With four miles of Pacific shoreline, this 2474-acre park offers great views of Nehalem Bay. Douglas fir, spruce and western red cedar dominate the rain forest in this park bounded on the south by legendary Neah-kah-nie Mountain. You'll want to visit the picturesque creeks, coves and scenic Arch Cape.

Facilities: Picnic tables and restrooms; restaurants and groceries nearby in Manzanita; information, 503-368-5943. *Fishing:* Good at the beach for cod, perch and bass.

Camping: There are 36 primitive sites accessible by foot with wheel-barrows for walk-in campers.

Getting there: It's ten miles south of Cannon Beach off Route 101.

Nehalem Bay State Park—Encompassing a three-mile-long sandspit at Nehalem Bay's mouth, this 889-acre park is a popular recreational area. The open, windswept landscape is ideal for kite flying. Nehalem Bay park is also a favorite for horseback riding, cycling and walking.

Facilities: Picnic tables, restrooms, showers, boat ramp, bike trails and adjacent airport and wheelchair accessible; restaurants and groceries nearby in Manzanita; information, 503-368-5943. *Fishing:* Good around the jetty for rock bass, cod and perch.

Camping: There are 291 sites; includes hiker-biker camp.

Getting there: Located off Route 101, three miles south of Manzanita Junction.

Cape Meares State Park—Named for an 18th-century British naval officer and trader, this 94-acre park and adjacent wildlife refuge encompass memorable ocean headlands and a spruce-hemlock forest. While the historic lighthouse no longer shines, the cape remains a landmark for tourists who come to see the offshore national wildlife refuge and birds. Also here is the Octopus Tree, an exotic Sitka spruce that was once a meeting point for Tillamook Native American medicine men.

Facilities: Picnic tables and restrooms and wheelchair accessible; restaurants and groceries in Tillamook.

Getting there: Located off Route 101, ten miles west of Tillamook.

Cape Lookout State Park—With two miles of forested headlands, a rain forest, beaches and sand dunes on Netarts Bay, it's hard to resist this 2000-acre gem. Thanks to an extensive trail network, Cape Lookout is an excellent place to observe sea lions and shore birds. It is also one of the highlights of the Three Capes Loop.

Facilities: Picnic tables, restrooms and showers and wheelchair accessible; restaurants and groceries nearby; information, 503-842-4981. *Fishing:* Excellent crabbing in Netarts Bay.

Camping: There are 197 tent sites, 53 RV hookups; includes hiker-biker camp.

Getting there: Located off Route 101, 12 miles south of Tillamook.

Cape Kiwanda State Park—This 185-acre headland park has a beautiful, sheltered beach. On the road between Pacific City and Sand Lake, it has wave-sculptured sandstone cliffs, tidepools and dunes.

Facilities: Picnic tables and restrooms; wheelchair accessible; restaurants and groceries nearby in Pacific City. *Fishing:* Good shore fishing.

Getting there: It's off Route 101, one mile north of Pacific City.

Central Coast

Proceeding down the coast you'll appreciate an impressive state-park system protecting coastal beaches and bluffs, rivers and estuaries, wildlife refuges and forested promontories.

One of the largest communities on the coast, **Lincoln City** stretches along the shore for roughly ten miles. While the coastal sprawl may turn some visitors off, this region offers many fine parks, lakes, restaurants and great beaches. Stop by the **Visitor Information Center** (3939 Northwest Route 101; 503-994-8378) for helpful details on beachcombing, shopping for arts and crafts and recreational activities.

Many visitors flock to **Devil's Lake**, a popular watersports and fishing area. But few of them realize that **D River**, located at the lake's mouth, is reputedly the world's shortest, just under 500 feet at low tide. This is also a terrific place to fly a kite. A good bet at low tide are the tidepools at **Canyon Drive Park** on Southwest 11th Street. Just beyond the town's southern limits, Drift Creek Road leads to **Driftcreek Covered Bridge**.

When it's foggy on the coast, it makes sense to head inland where the sun is often shining. One way to do this is to take Route 229 inland along the Siletz River. Six miles beyond Kernville you'll come to **Medicine Rock** (★), a pioneer landmark. Indian legend held that presents left here would assure good fortune.

Rafters who don't want to be troubled by spotting a car at their put-out location may want to launch their craft at **Strome County Park** (★). Because the river doubles back on itself, it's easy to leave the river close to where you began.

Continue south to **Siletz**, named for one of the coast's better-known Native American tribes. In 1856, at the end of the Rogue River Wars, the American Army created the Siletz Indian Agency, which became home for 2000 Native Americans. Within a year, unspeakable conditions diminished their numbers to 600. The agency closed for good in 1925, and today the Siletz Indian Tribe gathers each August for its annual pow-wow featuring dancing and a salmon bake.

After continuing on to visit the popular antique shops at **Toledo**, return to Route 101 at **Newport**. A harbor town with an array of tourist attractions, Newport is a busy place, especially during the summer. Like Seaside, Newport is filled with souvenir shops, saltwater-taffy stores and enough T-shirt shops to outfit the city of Portland. But there are also fine museums, galleries and other sightseeing possibilities. Begin your visit to this popular vacation town with a stop at the **Greater Newport Chamber of Commerce** (555 Southwest Coast Highway, Newport; 503-265-9901)

A short walk from the Chamber is the **Lincoln County Historical Museum Complex** (579 Southwest 9th Street, Newport; 503-265-7509). At the Log Cabin Museum and adjacent Burrows House you'll see Siletz basketry, maritime memorabilia, farming, logging and pioneer displays, victrolas, patterned glass, period clothing and many historic photographs.

The most popular tourist area in Newport is **Bay Boulevard**, where canneries, restaurants, shops and attractions like **Undersea Gardens** (250 Southwest Bay Boulevard; 503-265-2206; admission) peacefully coexist. On **Yaquina Bay**, this waterfront extravaganza gives you a chance to look through windows at more than 5000 species including octopus, eel, salmon and starfish. Scuba divers perform for the crowds in this bayfront setting. You can also cruise the bay on the **Belle Of Newport** (425 East Olive Street; 503-265-2355; admission) a Mississippi-riverboat-style stern-wheeler offering excursions and dinner cruises.

The **Hatfield Marine Science Center** (2030 South Marine Science Drive, Newport; 503-867-0100) is the coast's premier aquarium with a quarter-mile-long, wheelchair-accessible estuary loop, archaeology and marine mammal exhibits. Tanks organized by geographic locale feature marine life from Yaquina Bay and Puget Sound. Others exhibits display kelp forest, sandy bottom and rocky intertidal-surge channels.

As you leave the Hatfield Center and head back up to the bridge you'll pass **El Fincho Rancho** (★) (2640 Southwest Adobe, Newport), a sculpture garden that deserves a place on the Oregon folk-art map. Wood sculptor Loran Finch has blanketed his yard and garden with ships masts, propellers, floats, fishnets, abalone shells and nicely carved figurines. The result is a kind of driftwood fantasia.

After crossing the bridge, follow the signs west to visit the **Yaquina Bay Lighthouse** in Yaquina Bay State Park. Continue north on Mark Street to **Nye Beach**. Newport's historic beach district is more than a century old, but many of the early-day hotels, cabins and beach houses survive. In this area you'll find the **Yaquina Art Association** (839 Northwest Beach Drive; 503-265-5133). This is a good place to familiarize yourself with paintings, handicrafts and photography by leading Northwest artists.

Drive north on Route 101 to **Agate Beach**, a great spot for rockhounds. Moonstones, jasper and tiger eyes are all found here. Continue north on Route 101 to the Otter Crest Loop. Begin by visiting **Devil's Punchbowl State Park**, near Otter Rock, named after a collapsed cavern flushed by high tides. There's a lovely beach here, and the tiny oceanfront hamlet of **Otter Rock** is a good place to shop for a picnic or mask art. Continue north past Cape Foulweather, named by Captain James Cook in 1778, to **Depoe Bay**, home of the smallest harbor in the world. This six-acre port is a fun place to explore on foot thanks to its seafood restaurants and shops.

While the harbor is the heart of this charming, seaside village, you may also want to head across Route 101 to the coast, one of the best whale-watching spots in Oregon. A location for the movie *One Flew Over the Cuckoo's Nest*, Depoe Bay is also famous for **Spouting Horn**, where the surf surges above the oceanfront cliffs in stormy weather. Also worth a visit is **Depoe Bay Aquarium and Shell Shop** (Route 101 at Bay Drive; 503-765-2259; admission), which has octopus, sea lions, harbor seals and a wide variety of bottom fish.

Return to Newport on Route 101 and continue south ten miles to **Seal Rock State Park**. This is a great place to watch the barking pinnipeds and hunt for agates.

Continue south on Route 101 to **Waldport** and **Alsea Bay**, one of the best clamming spots on the coast and easily accessed from numerous parks. The port town is a relatively peaceful alternative to the coast's tourist hubs. Pick up Route 34 east along the Alsea River for 9.5 miles to **Kozy Cove Marina** (★). You can rent a boat here and explore this tributary bounded by the Suislaw National Forest. A great fishing spot, this section of the Alsea can be a sunny alterative to the foggy coast. For a picturesque, albeit windy, drive, continue east 30 miles to the village of Alsea and follow the signs to **Alsea Falls** (★).

Return to Waldport and continue south to **Yachats**, a classy village with fine restaurants, inns and shops. This town is also home of the **Little Log Church** (3rd and Pontiac streets). Surrounded by a charming garden, this tiny house of worship has a handful of white pews for congregants warmed by a pioneer stove.

To the south is Cape Perpetua, discovered by Captain James Cook in 1778. The 2700-acre **Cape Perpetua Scenic Area** has miles of trails ideal for beachcombing, viewing deer and exploring tidepools. The **Cape Per-petua Visitors Center** (Route 101; 503-547-3289) is a good place to learn about the region's original inhabitants, the Alsi. Known for their woodworking, canoes and decorative, watertight basketry, the Alsi hunted in the Coastrange hills. A 19-mile auto-tour loop leads along Yachats River Road to Route 5590 and returns via Route 55. Interpretive signs provide a look at youthful, middle-aged and old-growth forests, a pastoral river valley and fabulous ocean panoramas. This road is not suitable for large RVs or vehicles towing trailers.

Two miles south of Cape Perpetua off Route 101 is **Strawberry Hill State Park**. The white blossoms of wild strawberries create a floral panorama in the spring months. This park is also a popular spot for seals that unwind on the shoreline's basalt rocks. The tidepools are a good place to find sea stars, anemone and bright-purple spin sea urchins. Down the road another two miles is the distinctive **Ziggurat** (95330 Route 101; 503-547-3925), a pyramid-shaped bed and breakfast.

Just beyond Heceta Head Lighthouse is pinniped heaven, **Sea Lion Caves** (91560 Route 101; 503-547-3111; admission). Ride the elevator down to the 12-story-high cave to see the resident stellar sea lions enjoying a life of leisure. The outside ledges are a rookery where these marine mammals breed and give birth in the spring and early summer. The bulls vigilantly protect their harem's territory. An overlook adjacent to the entrance is a great whale-watching spot.

As you continue on toward Florence, about four miles north of the city is **Darlingtonia Botanical Wayside,** a short path that takes you to see the bog where these serpent-shaped plants trap insects with a sticky substance and devour them. Nearby is **Indian Forest** (88493 Route 101; 503-997-3677; admission). Re-created Native American dwellings including tepees, hogans and wigwams are the prime attraction along with the resident deer and buffalo herds. To gain perspective on the region's Native American and pioneer history visit the **Siuslaw Pioneer Museum** (85294 Route 101; 503-997-7884), a former Lutheran Church.

In **Florence** the **Chamber of Commerce** (270 Route 101; 503-997-3128) will quickly orient you to this Siuslaw River community. Then with the help of a chamber walking-tour guide, explore Florence's historic old town. A small artists' colony with a gazebo park overlooking the Suislaw waterfront, Florence has a popular historic district centered around Bay Street. This is a good place to browse, sip an espresso or take in a film at the circa-1938 Harbor Theater, repainted in shocking pink. Anglers won't want to miss the **Fly Fishing Museum** (280 Nopal Street; 503-997-6102; admission) displaying angling prints and a vintage collection of flies from around the United States and 20 foreign countries.

Florence is also the northern gateway to **Oregon Dunes National Recreation Area**. Miles of sandy beaches and forested bluffs laced by streams

Let There Be Light

No matter where you are on the Oregon Coast, a powerful beacon may be sweeping the high seas and shoreline. From Tillamook to Port Orford, nine of these classic sentinels built since 1857 still stand. Five continue to operate as unmanned Coast Guard stations, and three inactive lighthouses are restored and open to the public.

One of the best, located at **Cape Meares**, five miles south of Tillamook Bay, is a dormant beam that was built in 1890. Special displays offer historical perspective on this beacon. Open during the summer months, the lighthouse is part of Cape Meares State Park off Route 101, ten miles west of Tillamook.

Also open to the public is **Yaquina Bay Lighthouse**, built in 1871. Authentically restored with 19th-century furniture, Yaquina Bay features an interpretive exhibit. It's off Route 101, just north of the Yaquina Bay Bridge.

Coquille River Lighthouse, dating to 1896, was the last lighthouse built on the Oregon Coast. Restored and open to the public, it serves as a public observatory with interpretive displays on the Coquille River region. The lighthouse is at the south end of Bullards Beach State Park, a mile north of Bandon.

While they are not open to the public, six other lighthouses attract visitors who come to admire the architecture of these whitewashed towers. **Tillamook Rock Lighthouse**, opened in 1881 and the state's only lighthouse that is actually offshore, was built of cut basalt and then ferried to the construction site by tender. Newport's **Yaquina Head Lighthouse**, four miles north of Yaquina Bay, was constructed in 1873. This automated light flashes every 20 seconds and is supplemented by a powerful radio beacon.

One of the most photographed spots on the coast is **Heceta Head Lighthouse** off Route 101, 13 miles north of Florence. At 4.5 million-candlepower, this is the brightest beacon on the Oregon Coast. Built in 1857, the **Umpqua River Lighthouse** was the coast's first. Destroyed in an 1861 flood, it was replaced in 1894. The 65-foot tower is adjacent to Umpqua River Lighthouse State Park off Route 101, six miles south of Reedsport.

The 1934 **Cape Arago Lighthouse** is on a rocky island at the Coos Bay entrance. The unmanned beacon has an automated white light, fog signal and beacon. It's next to Sunset Bay State Park off Route 101.

In service since 1870, **Cape Blanco Lighthouse** is the westernmost navigational beacon in the continental United States. It is also Oregon's oldest continuously operated light. This 300,000-candlepower light is near Cape Blanco State Park, nine miles north of Port Orford off Route 101.

flowing down from the mountains make this region a favorite Oregon vacation spot. Woodlands and freshwater lakes provide a nice contrast to the windswept beaches. Numerous parks offer access to the dunes. Among them is **Oregon Dunes Overlook**, ten miles south of Florence.

Near Reedsport on Route 38 about five miles east of Route 101 is **Dean Creek Elk Preserve**. The herd of Roosevelt elk makes a great photo opportunity. South of Reedsport is one of the most popular fishing ports in the dunes region, **Salmon Harbor** on Winchester Bay. The crabbing and rockfishing here are excellent.

CENTRAL COAST HOTELS

A deluxe-priced oceanfront resort, **The Inn at Spanish Head** (4009 South Route 101, Lincoln City; 503-996-2161), has 116 rooms and suites, most with kitchens. Furnished with wall-to-wall carpets, contemporary easy chairs, oak tables and nature prints, the units all feature decks. A pool, spa, recreation room and lounge add to the resort atmosphere.

Salishan Lodge (Route 101, Gleneden Beach; 503-764-2371) offers 205 deluxe-to-ultra-deluxe-priced units. In a forested setting above Siletz Bay, this lodge accommodates guests in two-story, hillside buildings. Units all feature stone fireplaces, balconies, contemporary prints and carports. Golf, tennis, a fitness center, library and art gallery are some of the amenities.

One of the best deals along the central coast is **Trollers Budget Motel** (355 Southwest Route 101, Depoe Bay; 503-765-2287). Set on an oceanfront bluff, this 12-unit establishment has clean, remodeled units with eclectic furniture, picture windows and kitchenettes. Picnic tables and benches ideal for watching the whales swim by in season add to the convenience of this budget establishment. One- and two-bedroom units in the moderate-price range are also available. The location is good for deep-sea fishing trips.

Modeled after a 19th-century New England-style inn, **Gracie's Landing** (235 Southeast Bay View Avenue, Depoe Bay; 503-765-2322) overlooks the nation's smallest harbor. Nautical decor, queen beds, Early American-style cherrywood furniture and comfortable sofas add to the charm of the inn's 13 rooms and suites. All the suites have decks overlooking this picturesque harbor; some feature jacuzzis. Deluxe.

Don't be surprised if you find a couple sitting on an oceanview bench outside **Alpine Chalets** (7045 Southwest Route 101, Otter Rock; 503-765-2572). They are probably coming back to remember a honeymoon spent at this oceanfront retreat adjacent to Otter Rock State Park. Blessed with its own private park and beach access, each one- and two-bedroom A-frame chalet has a large, paneled sitting area furnished with contemporary fold-out sofas. All ten units are fully carpeted and come with kitchenettes, patios and casablanca fans. Set on a wooded bluff, this moderate-priced resort is frequently chosen as a wedding site.

The Inn at Otter Crest (Otter Crest Loop off Route 101, Otter Rock; 503-765-2111) offers 125 studios, one- and two-bedroom suites with fireplaces, sofa beds, fully equipped kitchens, decks and a semiprivate cove where you can look for seals and, in season, migrating gray whales. Set in a fir forest, with duck ponds and wild rhododendron, the inn also sports tennis courts, a pool, sauna and miniature golf. Deluxe.

Considering our corporate identity it's not surprising we were attracted to the **Sylvia Beach Hotel** (267 Northwest Cliff Street, Newport; 503-265-5428). A honeymoon haven that had degenerated into a flophouse, this four-story establishment was renovated and renamed for the proprietor of Shakespeare and Co. and first publisher of James Joyce's *Ulysses*. Her Paris bookstore and coffee house was a home away from home for writers like Joyce, Ernest Hemingway, T. S. Eliot and Samuel Beckett. Twenty rooms, each themed after an author, now accommodate guests. Our favorites are the ornate Oscar Wilde room featuring garish Victorian wallpaper (while dying in a Paris hotel room his last words were: "Either this wallpaper goes or I do"), the Dr. Seuss room (*The Cat in the Hat* is front and center), the Mark Twain room (fireplace, deck, antique school seat) and the Emily Dickinson room (marble dresser, green carpet, beautiful antique desk). While he didn't get his own quarters, the basement Henry Miller Memorial Restrooms (*Tropic of Cancer* and *Tropic of Capricorn*) commemorate this man of letters. Incidentally, we'd love to see the owners add a James Joyce room in the years ahead. Moderate to deluxe.

The budget-priced **Summer Wind Motel** (728 North Coast Highway, Newport; 503-265-8076) offers fully carpeted rooms and kitchenettes with wood-frame beds, sofas, pine coffee tables and stall showers. One of many Route 101 strip motels serving the Newport crowd, it's set back from the highway, and the rear rooms are relatively quiet.

The **Cliff House** (1450 Southwest Adahi Street, Waldport; 503-563-2506) is a gay-friendly bed and breakfast on the ocean. It features a baby-grand piano, big fireplace in the living room and gazebo in the front yard. Convenient to eight miles of walking beach, the inn also offers a jacuzzi and an on-call masseuse. The five themed rooms have chandeliers, down comforters and wall-to-wall carpeting. Deluxe to ultra-deluxe.

Pine Beach Motel (1339 West Corona Court, Waldport; 503-563-2155) is a coast tradition—the kind of modest but cozy spot where families hole up for an entire vacation. Seven budget-priced rooms and moderate-priced family units with kitchenettes are a short walk from fishing, clamming and crabbing on the beach. Located south of town, the paneled units have older wood furniture and wall-to-wall carpeting. There's nothing elegant about these units, but they are an excellent value, and the beach is terrific.

Set in a sunny valley surrounded by the Siuslaw National Forest, a wild-life refuge and the Yachats River, **Serenity Bed and Breakfast** (★) (5985 Yachats River Road, Yachats; 503-547-3813) lives up to its name. Six miles from the coast, this resort is a verdant, country retreat ideal for hiking, biking or birding. While resting in the Alt Heidelberg room's oak-frame double bed imported from a German castle, you can listen to a vintage collection of Bavarian music. Or perhaps you'd prefer to try one of this ten-acre bed and breakfast's other rooms featuring canopied beds, French-provincial furniture and an Italian writing desk. Moderate to deluxe.

On a 40-foot cliff overlooking the Pacific six miles south of Yachats, **See Vue** (95590 Route 101; 503-547-3227) offers ten budget rooms. Each of the small units in this gay-friendly establishment is named and themed. All have plants and antiques.

Turn up the Vivaldi and step right in to the circa-1914 **Edwin K Bed and Breakfast** (1155 Bay Street, Florence; 503-997-8360) where rooms are named for the four seasons. As you might expect, Winter features a white Battenberg bedspread, while Fall has a brown quilt. Furnished with oak armoires, chandeliers and white carpets, this elegant home has a backyard waterfall and Suislaw River views. Deluxe.

On the Siuslaw River, the 40-unit **River House Motel** (1202 Bay Street, Florence; 503-997-3933) is a one block walk from the heart of this popular town's historic shopping district. Many of the moderate-priced units have decks overlooking the river traffic and drawbridge. Immaculate rooms feature oak furniture, queens and kings with floral-print bedspreads. A spa room overlooks the waterfront.

If you're interested in cetaceans, consider checking in to **Driftwood Shores** (88415 1st Avenue, Florence; 503-997-8263). An estimated 21,000 whales migrate south past this inn each winter and return northward in the spring. Overlooking Heceta Beach, the 136-unit establishment has rooms and kitchenette suites featuring nautical prints, stone fireplaces, picture windows, big closets, decks and contemporary furniture. Moderate to deluxe.

CENTRAL COAST RESTAURANTS

The Noodle (2185 Northwest Route 101, Lincoln City; 994-8800) is one of those Italian restaurant you might buzz right by were it not for a book like this one. Located at the north end of town, it is favored by locals who enjoy this cross between a trattoria and a yacht club. Take a seat on one of the deck chairs beneath a sailboat photo and order lasagna made with ricotta, cheddar and mozzarella cheese, blended with fresh chicken and chopped spinach. Or try the vegetarian linguini or pesto manicotti. Be sure to specify the red sauce. Garlic bread and ice cream come (not together!) with all dinners. Budget to moderate.

We wish there were more restaurants in the moderate-price range like **Kernville Steak and Seafood** (186 Siletz Highway, Lincoln City; 503-994-6200). Dine outdoors on the deck overlooking the Siletz River or indoors in the paneled dining room beneath a vaulted ceiling. White linen, captain's chairs, flamingo pictures and a touch of greenery set the scene. Known for its generous bacon-wrapped filet mignon, prime rib, steamers and scallops, the restaurant also has an excellent vegetarian menu, seafood pasta salad and smaller portions for those who don't arrive famished.

Salishan Lodge's **Sun Room** (Route 101, Gleneden Beach; 503-764-2371) lives up to its name, a bright, paneled dining room with cedar tables, windsor chairs and garden views. This lodge-style restaurant offers seafood specialties, natural veal stew, butter clams steamed in a broth of thyme, garlic and Weinhard's Ale, shrimp-salad pita sandwiches, oyster stew and chilled gazpacho. Moderate to deluxe. For deluxe-priced fare try **The Dining Room**, Salishan's romantic, tri-level, gourmet restaurant with one of the biggest wine lists on the coast. Specialties include lamb chops with garlic-roasted pepper butter, grilled Pacific halibut with shellfish sausage and a summer vegetable plate.

Chez Jeannette (7150 Old Route 101, Gleneden Beach; 503-764-3434) is French dining with an Oregon twist. Set in a shady grove, this pastoral, candlelit restaurant has a cozy fireplace, burgundy carpet and high-backed oak chairs. Reservations are a good idea at this establishment where you might start with smoked salmon served with a horseradish, sour-cream caper, dill-and-brandy sauce and then enjoy specialties like seafood ragoût, rack of lamb, rabbit and filet mignon. For lighter appetites there's a crab-and-shrimp salad. Dinner only. Deluxe.

If you've had it with minimalist nouvelle cuisine, head straight for the **Whale Cove Inn** (Route 101, two miles south of Depoe Bay; 503-765-2255). Half the customers leave with doggie bags, proof positive that few establishments offer more generous helpings of fresh salmon, cod or halibut. Also on the menu are vegetarian fettucine dishes, steamed clams, beef marsala, scallops poached in white-wine sauce and a towering shrimp Louie. The dining room is a blend of semicircular booths and plastic tables with a panoramic view of this first-rate whale-watching spot. Ask for a pair of binoculars. A primo choice for sunset dining. Moderate.

Tourists ask proprietors of the **Otter Rock Café** (★) (845 1st Street, Otter Rock; 503-765-2628) why they have named their heavenly marionberry coffee cake after the defrocked mayor of Washington, D.C. Actually, the marionberry is a popular Oregon fruit that has never been in politics. It is just one of the key attractions at this heavenly spot just down the block from Devil's Punchbowl. Also worth trying are the excellent Manhattan chowder, fresh roasted coffee, sandwiches and mint brownies. There's also a deck with table service. This is a good place to provision a picnic. Budget.

Shrimp cocktail with ale sauce, a pizza crust made with stout, bangers with beer mustard, oysters with ale sauce—do we detect a trend here? **The Bayfront Brewery and Public House** (748 Southwest Bay Boulevard, Newport; 503-265-2537) serves these specialties with its golden ales, stouts, lagers and gold-medal-winning Rogue Smoke in a wood-paneled lounge.

Tiffany-style lamps illuminate the booths, and the walls are decorated with classic advertising signs. An adjacent gameroom serves diners at picnic tables. Specialties include sandwiches and salads. Moderate.

For the ultimate waterfront-dining experience try **Kozy Kove Café** (★) (9464 Alsea Highway, nine miles east of Waldport; 503-528-3251). Built on a dock, this floating restaurant continues a century-old tradition in an open-beamed dining room with handcrafted tables and casablanca fans. Created with the true angler in mind, Kozy Kove has a 3-D Hummingbird Fish Finder displaying trout and salmon swimming beneath the restaurant. The menu features steamer clams, oysters, steaks, Mexican specialties and honey-stung chicken. Black swans, deer and otter are frequently visible from a restaurant that rises and falls with the tides. Moderate.

Gino's Seafood and Deli (808 Southwest Bay Boulevard, Newport; 503-265-2424) is a good choice for crab and deli sandwiches, chowder or fish and chips. You can dine al fresco on picnic tables. There's also a large fresh-fish counter if you're doing your own cooking. A good bet for picnic fare. Budget.

The Whale's Tale (452 Southwest Bay Boulevard, Newport; 503-265-8660) serves excellent breakfasts, vegetarian lasagna, cioppino, hamburgers, seafood poorboys and fish filets with mushrooms, lemon butter and wine. This dark-wood café has open-beam ceiling, plank tables and tiffany-style lamps. A canoe frame, harpoon, whale's vertebrae and tail suspended from the ceiling complete the decor. Moderate.

Canyon Way Restaurant and Bookstore (1216 Southwest Canyon Way, Newport; 503-265-8319) offers pasta dishes, quiche, cheese-board platter, *muffulettas*, grilled fish and chips and seafood salads in a contemporary setting. Choose between a cozy, bistro-style room adjoining the bar, a main room with wicker furniture and, best of all, a handsome, brick patio with booths and tables in a garden setting. Moderate to deluxe.

They don't have arches, a drive-through line or a mascot named Ronald. But Ken and Mary Ghormley do have one of the Central Coast's most loyal clientele. They've also proven once and for all that there's no truth to the adage "Never eat at a place called 'Mom's.'" An entire generation of young people in this community have been raised on the home cooking at **Mom's Kitchen** (★) (3734 South Coast Highway, South Beach; 503-867-4200). This hole-in-the-wall orange trailer just south of Newport's Yaquina Bay Bridge is the place to go for hamburgers, cheddar cheeseburgers and chili burgers consumed at one of the Ghormleys' picnic tables or in the comfort of your own car. No dinner. Budget.

If you're looking for a sushi bar try **Yuzen Japanese Cuisine** (10111 Northwest Route 101, Seal Rock; 503-563-4766). Set in a former rathskeller with leaded glass windows and tiffany-style lamps, the restaurant has been redecorated with red paper lanterns, paper screens and a new wooden sushi bar. The menu includes tempura, sukiyaki, katsu don, bento dinners, sashimi deluxe and, by reservation, *shabu shabu nabe*. Moderate.

While some restaurants may be advertising "fresh crab" just flown in from Anchorage, **La Serre** (2nd and Beach streets, Yachats; 503-547-3420) insists on truth in labeling. Only fresh local fish off the boat is served in the contemporary dining room with oak tables and chairs, gas-style lanterns, potted plants and polished-hardwood floors. A fireplace lounge and full bar also provide a relaxed setting for drinks or dinner. La Serre specializes in seafood like razor clams, scallops and bay oysters, an excellent shrimp creole, vegetarian entrées, chicken pot pies and steaks. Moderate to deluxe.

One of the better coffee shops on the coast is **Coffee Merchants Restaurant** (220 Route 101, Yachats; 503-547-3100). An elegant, carpeted dining room with blue booths, oak tables, bentwood chairs and counter service, the eatery is known for its pressure-smoked barbecue meats. Specialties include alderwood-smoked chicken, shrimp platter and halibut steak. Budget to moderate.

It's hard to resist a tea house on the brisk Oregon coast. Set in a Cape Cod-style house, the **Old English Tea Company** (239 Maple Street, Florence; 503-997-8890) features walls decorated with crockery and quilts, an intimate dining room and, for sunny days, garden decks. This is one of the few places on the coast where you can order up a ploughman's lunch, cornish pasty, shepherd's pie or welsh rarebit. Budget to moderate.

Lotus Sea Food Palace (1150 Bay Street, Florence; 503-997-7168) specializes in oriental seafood dishes like steamed crab, prawns with mild chili sauce and sautéed clams with black-bean sauce, as well as mongolian beef, moo shu pork, crispy duck and sweet-and-sour chicken. There's also an extensive Western menu here that includes steak, pork chops and seafood. The pink-carpeted dining room is landscaped with hanging and potted plants. Guests dine at oak tables overlooking the Siletz River.

CENTRAL COAST SHOPPING

Ocean Surf Shop (4933 Southwest Route 101, Lincoln City; 503-996-3957) offers a complete line of surfboards, boogie boards, skimboards, wet suits and, for the landlubber, skate boards. Rentals are available. There are also good beachwear and swimwear departments.

For watercolors, mixed media, monoprints, wood blocks and other art, visit the **Illustrated Gallery** (305 North Main Street, Toledo; 503-336-3025). Workshops are also offered here twice a week.

The Wood Gallery (818 Southwest Bay Boulevard, Newport; 503-265-6843) offers beautiful wooden sculptures, myrtlewood bowls, cherrywood cabinets and jewelry boxes. Also here are metal sculptures, Elk antler knives, leather goods, jewelry, ceramics, pottery and stained glass. Handmade children's toys, furniture and ceramic tables are all worth a look.

Oceanic Arts Center (444 Southwest Bay Boulevard, Newport; 503-265-5963) has innovative water sculptures as well as Oregon totem chains, pottery, weavings and decorative basketry.

Forget your kite? For stunt, quad line, box, delta, cellular, dragon and diamond kites try **Catch The Wind** (1250 Southwest Bay Street, Florence; 503-997-9500). A full line of accessories and free advice are also available from the resident experts.

The Bay Window (1312 Bay Street, Florence; 503-997-2002) will delight antiquarians in the market for old and rare prints, books and antiques. Classic maps, historic photographs and ad signs are found in this charming waterfront shop.

Located in a charming historic building, **Pacific Stamp Gallery** (705 Route 101, Bandon; 503-347-3087) is a great place to look for stamps from all over the world, particularly from the British Commonwealth.

CENTRAL COAST NIGHTLIFE

To enjoy pop, rock and jazz you can dance to, try the second-story lounge at **Salishan Lodge** (Route 101, Gleneden Beach; 503-764-2371). When you're tired of the dancefloor, take a table by the fireplace or at the bar. There's also a deck overlooking the golf course. Contemporary painting completes the decorating scheme.

The **Wardroom Lounge** at The Inn at Otter Crest's Flying Dutchman restaurant (Otter Crest Loop Road, Otter Rock; 503-765-2060) offers live music weekends.

The **Newport Performing Arts Center** (777 West Olive Street, Newport; 503-265-9231) presents a wide variety of concerts, dance programs and theatrical events in the Alice Silverman Theater and the Studio Theater. Both local groups and touring companies perform.

At the **Hotel Newport Casey's Restaurant** (3019 North Coast Highway, Newport; 503-265-9411) you'll enjoy listening to a pianist playing pop tunes each weekend. There's also blackjack nightly.

For rock-and-roll, dancing and low-stakes blackjack try **Pip Tide's Restaurant and Lounge** (836 Southwest Bay Boulevard, Newport; 503-265-7796). Across the street from the waterfront, Pip Tide's has a fireplace lounge with dark-wood booths and casablanca fans to beat the heat. There's also a gameroom upstairs.

The **Lotus Lounge** (1150 Bay Street, Florence; 503-997-7168) presents live music, dancing and light shows nightly. In addition to rock-and-roll bands performing at this nightplace, you can join the laser karaoke singalong craze. Just follow the bouncing ball on the television monitor, bellow into the microphone and you'll be serenading the crowd. A traditional, mounted moose head surveys the party atmosphere.

CENTRAL COAST BEACHES AND PARKS

Devil's Lake State Park—Is there really a devil in the deep, blue sea? That's what Indian legend says right here in Lincoln City. Find out for yourself by visiting this 109-acre spot offering day-use and overnight facilities. The camping area is protected with a shore-pine windbreak.

Facilities: Picnic tables, restrooms, boat launch and solar showers; restaurants and groceries nearby; information, 503-994-2002. *Swimming:* Good. *Fishing:* Go for the bass and trout.

Camping: There are 68 tent sites and 32 RV hookups in the West Devil's Lake section.

Getting there: The West Devil's Lake section is located at 1450 Northeast 6th Drive off Route 101. The day-use section is located two miles east of Route 101 on East Devil's Lake Road.

Devil's Punchbowl State Park—Don't miss this one. The forested, eight-acre park is named for a sea-washed cavern where breakers crash against the rocks with great special effects. Besides the thundering plumes, the adjacent beach has impressive tidepools.

Facilities: Picnic tables, barbecue pits and restrooms and wheelchair accessible; restaurants and groceries in adjacent Otter Rock.

Getting there: Located off Route 101, eight miles north of Newport.

Beverly Beach State Park—Numerous coastal creeks make ideal fishing, hiking and camping areas. Among them is Spencer Creek, part of this 130-acre refuge. The windswept beach is reached via a highway underpass.

Facilities: Picnic tables, restrooms and showers; restaurants and groceries nearby; information, 503-265-9278. *Fishing:* Some of Oregon's best surf fishing.

Camping: There are 279 sites and 53 RV hookups.

Getting there: Located seven miles north of Newport on Route 101.

South Beach State Park—South of Newport's Yaquina Bay Bridge, the 434-acre park includes a sandy beach and a forest with pine and spruce, Extremely popular in the summer months, the park includes rolling terrain and a portion of Yaquina Bay's south-jetty entrance.

Facilities: Picnic tables, restrooms and showers and wheelchair accessible; restaurants and groceries nearby; information, 503-867-4715. *Fishing:* Try for striped perch in the south jetty area.

Camping: There are 152 tent-only sites and 127 sites for tents or hookups; includes hiker-biker camp.

Getting there: Located on Route 101, two miles south of Newport.

Ona Beach State Park—Beaver Creek winds through this forested, parklike setting to the ocean. Picturesque bridges, broad lawns and an idyllic shoreline. Don't miss this 237-acre gem.

Facilities: Picnic tables and boat launch; restaurants and groceries nearby. *Swimming:* Good. *Fishing:* Good in the river for salmon or trout in season, and from the shore.

Getting there: Located on Route 101, eight miles south of Newport.

Carl G. Washburne State Park—A mile of sandy beach with excellent tidepools and forested, rolling terrain make this park yet another coastal gem. Elk are often sighted at 1089-acre Washburne Park. The south end of the park connects to Devil's Elbow State Park's Cape Creek drainage.

Facilities: Picnic tables, restrooms and showers; restaurants and groceries in Florence. *Fishing:* Excellent. Go for tuna, bass or snapper; several streams offer trout, salmon and steelhead. Clamming is also good.

Camping: There are 58 sites with hookups and 8 walk-in tent sites.

Getting there: Located on Route 101, 14 miles north of Florence.

Siuslaw National Forest—With two sections on the coast, this 835,376-acre region has more seacoast, 43 miles, than any other national forest in the United States. The terrain includes the Coast Range, Mt. Hebo and Mary's Peak. Oceanfront areas include the Cascade Head Scenic Area, Umpqua Spit wilderness and the Cape Perpetua Visitors Center. Hiking some of the forest's 103 miles of trails you may see deer, elk, otter, beaver, fox and bobcat. Northeast of Waldport, several trails lead into the old-growth forests of the Drift Creek wilderness areas. Incidentally, Siuslaw is taken from a Yakona Indian word meaning "far away waters."

Facilities: Picnic areas, restrooms and showers; restaurants and groceries in nearby towns; information, 503-750-7000. *Fishing:* Over 200 species including salmon, perch and trout in local streams and along the coast.

Camping: There are 45 sites.

Getting there: Route 101 passes through the Siuslaw in Tillamook, Lincoln and Lane counties.

Jesse M. Honeyman State Park—Richly endowed with 500-foot-high sand dunes, forested lakes, rhododendron and huckleberry. Bisected by Route 101, 522-acre Honeyman is ideal for watersports, dune walks and camping. As far as we know it has the only bathhouse on the National Register of Historic Places. A stone-and-log structure at Cleawox Lake, the unit now serves as a multipurpose building.

Facilities: Picnic tables, restrooms, showers, boat ramp, store and restaurant and wheelchair accessible; information, 503-997-3641. *Swimming:* Good. *Fishing:* Go for trout, perch, bullhead and bluegill.

Camping: There are 242 tent sites, 141 campgrounds with RV hookups; includes hiker-biker camp.

Getting there: Located three miles south of Florence on Route 101.

Umpqua Lighthouse State Park—South of Winchester Bay, this park offers beautiful sand dunes and a popular hiking trail. Forested with spruce, western hemlock and shore pine, the 450-acre park is at its peak when the rhododendron bloom. Great views of the Umpqua River are available from the highway. The lighthouse was built to signal the river's entrance.

Facilities: Picnic tables, restrooms, boat launch and showers and wheelchair accessible; restaurants and groceries in Reedsport; information, 503-271-4118. *Fishing:* Good.

Camping: There are 41 sites, 22 with hookups; laundromat.

Getting there: Located off Route 101, six miles south of Reedsport.

William M. Tugman State Park—This 560-acre park includes Eel Lake, cleaned of logging debris and turned into a popular recreational area. An excellent day-use area, Tugman is ideal for swimming and boating.

Facilities: Camping, restrooms, boat launch; wheelchair accessible; restaurants and groceries in Reedsport. *Swimming:* Good. *Fishing:* Good.

Camping: There are 115 sites; includes hiker-biker camp, showers and laundromat.

Getting there: On Route 101, eight miles south of Reedsport.

Golden and Silver Falls State Park (★)—A pair of 100-foot high waterfalls, old-growth forest including myrtlewood trees, and beautiful trails make this 157-acre park an excellent choice for a picnic.

Facilities: Picnic tables and restrooms. *Fishing:* Good.

Getting there: It's off Route 101, 24 miles northeast of Coos Bay.

South Coast

The quietest part of the Oregon coastline, this region offers miles of uncrowded beaches, beautiful dunes and excellent lakes for fishing or water-skiing. The smaller towns make an excellent base for the traveler who appreciates fine restaurants, museums, festivals and shopping.

A real sleeper, the **Coos Bay/North Bend/Charleston Bay area** is the coast's largest metropolitan area, a logging center, college town and fishing center. Historic residential districts, a grand harbor and towering piles of logs awaiting their turn to be sliced into lumber make this working-class town an intriguing place.

The **Chamber of Commerce** (50 East Central Avenue, Coos Bay; 503-269-0215) is the ideal place to orient yourself. One of our favorite galleries in the Pacific Northwest is the **Coos Art Museum** (235 Anderson Avenue, Coos Bay; 503-267-3901) where 20th-century American paintings and sculpture as well as prints and historic photographs form the heart of the collection. Special exhibits feature well-known local and regional artists.

Of special interest is the museum's **Prefontaine Memorial Room** (★), a touching collection honoring the life and times of Steve Prefontaine, the distance runner who died in a 1975 car accident at the age of 24. During his short life Prefontaine set 11 United States indoor and outdoor records including several that still stand. Every fall a running event commemorates the memory of this Coos Bay native. The art museum is just one of 22 landmarks on the town's self-guided tour of historic buildings. Easily followed with the help of a Chamber of Commerce brochure, this route includes Victorian homes, Greek Classic commercial buildings and the Myrtle Arms Apartments, a rare Oregon building done in the Mission/Pueblo style.

A landmark in Coos Bay is the **Marshfield Sun** (1049 Front Street; 503-756-6418). This museum preserves the Sun printing office with its antique handset presses, typecases, proof press and other tools of the trade. The building, with an oak floor and pot-bellied stove, is a delightful period piece. Second-story exhibits cover the history of printing.

Also worth a visit is the **Coos County Historical Society Museum** (1220 Sherman Avenue, North Bend; 503-756-6320) where you'll see Native American baskets, tools and dugout canoes. Pioneer logging and mining equipment and a homestead kitchen are found here along with a hands-on exhibit that gives you an opportunity to touch a variety of artifacts.

A popular recreational region, the Bay Area offers watersports and fishing at **Tenmile Lakes**. The **Charleston Boat Basin** is ideal for sportfishing, clamming, crabbing, birdwatching and boating. From Charleston continue south four miles to **Shore Acres State Park** (13030 Cape Arago Highway; 503-888-3732). Although the mansion of lumberman Louis Simpson burned down years ago, the grand, seven-acre botanical garden, including a 100-foot lily pond, is preserved. From here continue south to **Cape Arago State Park**, your best bet for local tidepools and seal watching.

Return toward Charleston and head south on Seven Devil's Road to **South Slough National Estuarine Sanctuary** (503-888-5558). An extension of the Coos Bay Estuary, this splendid nature sanctuary is a drowned river mouth where saltwater tides and freshwater streams create a rich estuarine environment. Even if you only have time to stop at the Interpretive Center don't miss **South Slough**. Easily explored on foot, thanks to a network of trails and wooden walkways, the estuaries, tideflats, salt marshes, open water and forest communities are a living ecology textbook. A major resting spot for birds like the great blue heron, the slough can also be navigated by canoe.

Back at Charleston and Coos Bay, pick up Route 42 south to **North Bank Road** (★) and drive west along the Coquille River. This pastoral route, one-lane at times, is the hidden Northwest of your dreams. You'll see farms, pastureland, orchards, towering stands of fir and a wide array of bird life. Tread lightly.

Bandon is one of those popular resort towns that seems to have everything. From myrtlewood and cranberry bogs to salmon bakes and dune lakes, it's hard to be bored in Bandon. Swing by the **Bandon Chamber of Commerce** (300 2nd Street; 503-347-9616) for brochures and information. The **Bandon Historical Society Museum** (West 1st Street; 503-347-2164), located in Old Town's historic Coast Guard Station, features exhibits on natural history, coastal and Coquille River maritime life, Coast Guard operations and Native American history.

Bandon's Old Town is an engaging neighborhood where you can shop for cranberry treats or pottery, book a Coquille River excursion on the **Sternwheeler Rose** (315 South 1st Street; 503-347-3942; admission) or visit one of the local art galleries. Also here is the **Bandon Driftwood Museum** (1st and Baltimore streets; 503-347-3719). In an old general store, the museum features driftwood sculptures well worth a look. Don't miss town highlights like **Tupper Rock**, a sacred Indian site returned to the Coquille Indian Tribe in 1990. South of town, **Beach Loop Road** leads past Bandon's scenic trio—Table Rock, Elephant Rock and legendary Face Rock. One of Oregon's most photographed coastlines, the offshore seastacks make an ideal backdrop at sunset.

The Bandon region is a major center for cranberry growing. The colorful bogs, where activity peaks in August, are fun to see. The Bandon Chamber of Commerce can direct you to the bogs where workers in waders corral the berries.

Continue south four miles to the **Professional Sports Hall of Fame** (Route 101 eight miles south of Bandon; 503-347-9131; admission). This collection contains 3200 baseball, basketball and football jerseys. Among them are Wilt Chamberlain's number 5 from his early days at Philadelphia (maybe his number should have been 20,000!), Steve Garvey's flannel Dodger jersey and the last jersey worn by Roy Campanella before his career-ending 1957 accident.

West Coast Game Park Safari (Route 101; 503-347-3106; admission), located a mile south of the hall of fame, gives visitors a chance to see more than 75 species including lions, tigers, snow leopards, bison, zebras and elk. On their walk through the park children can pet cubs, pups and kits in the company of attendants. Many endangered species are found at this wooded, 21-acre site.

Port Orford, first townsite on the Oregon Coast and westernmost town in the continental United States, is a major commercial and sportfishing center. Windsurfers flock to local Floras and Garrison lakes. Harbor seals and sea lions breed on the offshore rocks known as the "Thousand Island Coast." The Sixes and Elk rivers are popular salmon and steelhead fishing spots.

Five miles south of Port Orford is **Humbug Mountain State Park** (503-332-6774) where hiking trails offer majestic views of the South Coast.

Continue another six miles to the **Prehistoric Gardens** (36848 Route 101, Port Orford; 503-332-4463; admission). Filled with life-size replicas of dinosaurs and other extinct species, this touristy menagerie includes the parrot-beaked *Psittacosaurus*, an ancestral form of the horn-faced dinosaur.

At **Gold Beach**, a settlement at the mouth of the Rogue River, you'll find yourself on the edge of one of the coast's great wilderness areas. Here you can arrange an ocean-fishing trip or a jetboat ride up the wild and scenic Rogue River. Along the way you may see deer, bald eagle, bear or otter. Accessible only by water, some of the rustic Rogue lodges are perfect for an overnight getaway. It's also possible to drive along the Rogue to Agness. For more details check with the **Gold Beach Chamber of Commerce** (510 South Ellensburg Street; 503-247-7526).

Fifteen miles south of Gold Beach is Samuel H. Boardman State Park where you'll begin a ten-mile stretch that includes **Arch Rock Point, Natural Bridges Cove, House Rock** and **Rainbow Rock**. Many visitors and locals agree this is the prettiest stretch on the Oregon coastline.

Just when you thought it would never end, the Oregon Coast comes to a screeching halt. The end of the line is Brookings, the Chetco River port town that produces 75 percent of the Easter lilies grown in America. They are complemented by daffodils raised commercially in the area. **North Bank Chetco River Road** provides easy access to the fishing holes upstream. One of the most popular destinations is **Loeb State Park** ten miles east of Brookings. Redwood and myrtlewood groves are your reward. You can loop back to Brookings on South Bank Road. En route consider turning off on **Forest Service Road 4013** (★) and take the trail to the only continental United States location bombed by a Japanese pilot during World War II. The raider, who used a plane built aboard an offshore submarine, returned years later to give the city a samurai sword as a peace offering.

The **Brookings/Harbor Chamber of Commerce** (South Route 101; 503-469-3181) can provide additional information on visiting this region. Shortly before reaching the California line you'll see the Blake House, site of the **Chetco Valley Historical Society Museum** (15461 Museum Road, Brookings; 503-469-6651). The oldest standing house in the region, it features a turn-of-the-century kitchen, antique sewing machines, lincoln rocker, patchwork quilts dating back to 1844 and Indian artifacts. Once a trading post and way station, the old home is filled with period furniture. The world's largest Monterey Cypress is found here.

SOUTH COAST HOTELS

A 1911 Colonial-style house, **Coos Bay Manor** (955 South 5th Street, Coos Bay; 503-269-1224) has rooms themed in Victorian, Wild West and country-casual style. Also here are a Colonial room with twin-poster beds and a garden room furnished with rattan furniture. A rhododendron garden, redwoods and a delicious breakfast add to the fun. Moderate.

If you're eager to crab or clam, consider unpretentious **Captain John's Motel** (8061 Kingfisher Drive, Charleston; 503-888-4041). On the small boat basin, this budget-to-moderate-priced establishment is within walking distance of fishing and charter boats. Special facilities are available to cook and clean crabs. Forty-three rooms and kitchenettes are fully carpeted and feature contemporary motel furniture.

Sea Star Guest House (370 1st Street, Bandon; 503-347-9632) offers four modern, carpeted units with brass beds, quilts and harbor views. One block from Bandon's commercial district, the moderate-priced, two-story inn has a restaurant. In the same complex is the **Sea Star Youth Hostel** (375 2nd Street). You'll sleep in bunk beds and be asked to do minor chores in the morning. Budget.

You can hear the foghorn from the **Bandon Beach Motel** (1110 11th Street, Bandon; 503-347-4430) where many of the 28 units have balconies overlooking the ocean. Nautical decor, wood paneling and vanities make these rooms appealing. Pets are welcome. Moderate.

Native American legend tells us that Ewauna, the willful daughter of Chief Siskiyou, wandered too far out into the surf and was snatched up by Seatka, the evil spirit of the sea. Today, Bandon visitors learn that images of all the protagonists in this tragedy have been frozen in stone at Face Rock. That may be one of the reasons proprietors of **The Inn at Face Rock** (3225 Beach Loop Road, Bandon; 503-347-9441) caution guests to be wary of the local surf. Adjacent to a public golf course, this 55-unit resort offers large, ocean-view rooms. Wallhangings, comfortable sofas, fireplaces and decks make the king- and queen-bedded rooms appealing. Moderate.

Castaway-by-the-Sea Motel (545 West 5th Street, Port Orford; 503-332-4502) offers rooms and suites overlooking one of the South Coast's most picturesque, albeit windblown, beaches. Kitchenettes, glassed-in decks, contemporary upholstered furniture, wall-to-wall carpeting and easy access to fishing make this 14-unit motel a popular place. Moderate to deluxe.

Breathtaking views of the coast are found at **Home by the Sea** (★) (444 Jackson Street, Port Orford; 503-332-2855). Oak floors, myrtlewood beds with quilted spreads, leather easy chairs, oriental carpets and stained glass add to the charm of these moderate-priced units. Every room in this bed and breakfast comes with binoculars perfect for whale watching through the picture windows.

If you're an adventurer eager to go deep-sea fishing, raft the Rogue, go boating, cycling or hike the coastal mountains, consider **Jot's Resort** (94360 Waterfront Loop, Gold Beach; 503-247-6676). With 140 moderate-to-deluxe-priced units, Jot's offers attractive, contemporary rooms and suites with pink wall-to-wall carpet, oak furniture, vanities and decks featuring river views. Crabbing and clamming are great here. A full-service resort, the place is wheelchair accessible.

On the Rogue River, **Tu Tu Tun Lodge** (96550 North Bank Rogue Road, Gold Beach; 503-247-6664) can be a sunny alternative to the cloudy coast. Seven miles upriver from Gold Beach, this lodge offers 16 paneled rooms with wicker furniture, vanities, carpeting and decks or patios over-looking the water. The suites have kitchen facilities. Deluxe.

For a top-notch budget-priced hotel try the **Chetco Inn** (417 Fern Street, Brookings; 503-469-5347). This venerable, blue-shingled establishment is a charming period piece with wicker patio furniture, an antique-filled parlor and sun porch. Set on a hill overlooking the coast, the inn's rooms have been renovated without losing their charm. In the 44 units expect to find quilted bedspreads, lace curtains, clawfoot tubs, classic ad posters, ceiling fans and, in some cases, cooking facilities.

At **Best Western Beachfront Inn** (16008 Boat Basin Road, Brookings; 503-469-7779) 72 units, many with bay views and kitchenettes, offer a quiet resting place. Furnished with contemporary oak dressers and tables, the king- and queen-bedded units come with microwaves, refrigerators, sofas and decks. Suites offer jacuzzis. Moderate to deluxe.

A one-lane road takes you to **Chetco River Inn Bed and Breakfast** (★) (21202 High Prairie Road, 16 miles east of Brookings on the Chetco River; 503-469-2114). This deluxe-priced, solar-powered establishment on 40 wooded acres is an ideal retreat for fishing, swimming, hiking through myrtle groves or loafing on the riverbank. A contemporary home furnished with antiques, the inn has wicker furniture and brass beds, casablanca fans and, by advance request, dinner. The cooking is innovative, and portions are generous. Special discounts are offered for anglers who agree to catch and release their fish.

SOUTH COAST RESTAURANTS

To get a big laugh at **Portside Restaurant and Lounge** (Charleston Bay Boat Basin, Charleston; 503-888-5544) just ask if the fish is fresh. Their own boat delivers the daily catch. Grilled sole, deep-fried scallops, steamed clams, salmon and Coquille St. Jacques are among the specialties. Also rec-ommended is the cucumber boat, a salad with shrimp, crab, smoked salmon and served with cucumber dressing and garlic toast. The contemporary din-ing room features photos of the fishing industry. Moderate.

For *chile rellenos*, *chilaquiles*, chicken *mole* and *carne asada*, try **Playa Del Sol** (525 Newport Avenue, Coos Bay; 503-267-0325). Decorated with Spanish carvings, piñatas, sombreros and photographs of Mexico, this pop-ular, little restaurant has a small bar offering beer, wine and margaritas. Bud-get to moderate.

If you've been looking for Korean, Japanese or Szechuan dishes stop by **Kum-Yon's** (835 South Broadway, Coos Bay; 503-269-2662). *Bulgoki, ton katsu, yakitori,* mongolian beef, tempura *udon* and tofu dishes are just a few of the enticing specialties. Like the menu, the decor is pan-Asian with Japanese-shell plaques, Korean wedding decorations and Chinese fans accenting the brick dining room. Moderate.

Sea Star Bistro (370 1st Street, Bandon; 503-347-9632) offers fresh seafood, omelettes, sandwiches, soups and salads in a pleasant café setting. The pine-paneled dining room has an open-beam ceiling, bentwood furniture and paintings by local artists. A good choice for those who want to sample Oregon cuisine, complete with edible flowers. Moderate.

At **Andrea's Old Town Café** (160 Baltimore Street, Bandon; 503-347-3022) you can breakfast on fresh-baked cinnamon rolls and omelettes, return for pizza or burgers at lunch and then choose from specialties at dinner such as ginger-sherry crab legs, locally grown lamb, fresh seafood and creole dishes. An extensive wine list, fruit pies or cheesecake will round out your day at this traditional, oak-furnished café. Moderate.

With its ocean views, silk-screen prints, soft sculpture and hand-dyed fiber art, **Whale Cove Restaurant** (Route 101, Port Orford; 503-332-7575) boasts a romantic coastal setting. What about the food? Happily we can report that the grilled salmon is exemplary. So are other specialties like escargot pears William, the hot-duck salad, veal and calvados with roasted apples and crayfish Cajun. This deluxe-priced establishment also offers fixed-price dinners and excellent desserts. The adjacent **Pasta Gallery**, open weekends, is served by the same kitchen and phone number.

The Truculent Oyster (236 6th Street, Port Orford; 503-332-9641) is known for its seafood and steaks. The dimly lit, Western-style bar and knotty-pine-paneled dining room are done in nautical decor and feature antique advertising signs. Try the sautéed prawns, clam chowder, shrimp Louie, escargots and, of course, the fresh oysters. Moderate.

When the natives get restless for budget-priced logger breakfasts, fish and chips, burgers, clam chowder, shrimp cocktails or homemade chili they head for **Pelican Bay Seafoods** (16403 Lower Harbor Road, Brookings; 503-469-7971). This modest establishment seats customers at pine tables in the nautically themed dining room featuring fishing photos.

A culinary time warp on the coast, **O'Holleran's Restaurant and Lounge** (1210 Chetco Avenue, Brookings; 503-469-9907) serves middle-of-the-road entrées in a modest, yellow-hued dining room graced with Impressionist prints. You'll find few bells or whistles on the traditional menu featuring steaks, chicken Kiev, french dip sandwiches, frogs' legs, salmon and fried razor clams. While you can't get blackberry catsup on the side, the food is well prepared. Moderate.

You say Mexican food, we say **Rubio's** (1136 Chetco Avenue, Brookings; 503-469-4919). A bright red and yellow bungalow decorated with piñatas and casablanca fans, this budget-priced stop also offers picnic-table seating outside beneath patio umbrellas. An extensive menu features burrito asada, enchiladas verde, chicken fajitas and brunch specialties like *huevos rancheros*. Burgers and sandwiches are also available for yankee appetites. Budget to moderate.

SOUTH COAST SHOPPING

We were impressed by **The Museum Shop** at the Coos Bay Art Museum (235 Anderson Avenue, Coos Bay; 503-267-3901). Jewelry, glassware, pottery, sculptures, baskets, carvings, cards and a great poster of Babe Ruth watching one of his home runs blast off are some of the attractions.

For beaded earrings, silver and turquoise, dance regalia and other authentic Native American arts and crafts, visit **Klahowya** (947 South 1st Street, Coos Bay; 503-269-7349). They also carry Native American art originals, pottery and ceramics.

And now let's hear it for **Margaret Brinegar "The Bird Lady"** (6943 Beacon Street, Coos Bay; 503-888-3549). This folk artist, operating out of her garage, produces outstanding wind-powered whirlygigs perfect for your yard. You can choose between colorful lumberjacks, birds and many other colorful Rube Goldberg attractions.

Oregon Myrtlewood Factory (Route 101, six miles south of Bandon; 503-347-2500) is the place to see craftspeople creating dinnerware, vases, sculptures, clocks and other popular souvenirs. Free tours are offered.

Weaver Ellen Warring's beautiful baskets incorporate local driftwood. Her **Basket Studio** (736 Route 101, Port Orford; 503-332-0735) is a good place to browse and learn about this delicate art. It's also a Kalmiopsis Audubon Society Outlet.

If you're looking for smoked salmon, smoked albacore, crab or shrimp, head for **Bandon Fisheries** (250 Southwest 1st Street, Bandon; 503-347-4454). Tours give you a chance to see the seafood industry at work.

Jerry's Rogue River Museum and Gift Shop (Port of Gold Beach; 503-247-4571) offers a broad selection of locally made arts and crafts. There is also an extensive collection of artifacts, photos and natural-history exhibits on the Rogue River area.

For wall masks, magical creatures like dragons and wizards or Bisque pieces try **Dragon Stone Ceramics** (South Route 101 and Winchuck Road, Brookings; 503-469-9534). Handpainted gifts and Native American pieces are also available.

SOUTH COAST NIGHTLIFE

Playwrights American Conservatory Theater (226 South Broadway, Coos Bay; 503-269-2501) presents classical and contemporary drama and musical theater in an intimate, 90-seat auditorium.

We were impressed by the performances at **Timber Inn Lounge** (10001 North Bayshore Drive, Coos Bay; 503-267-4622). Live country, rhythm-and-blues and pop are all popular in this big, second-story room heavy on silver foil, lumberjack photos and Spuds McKenzie. The bartenders are cordial, and you can really jam on the spacious dancefloor.

For music and dancing weekends try the **Portside Lounge** (Charleston Boat Basin, Charleston; 503-888-5544). Bands and combos offer '60s and '70s hits, easy listening and jazz. You can enjoy the performers from the patio on warm nights. Great sunsets and harbor views.

Sawdust Theater (145 East 2nd Street, Coquille; 503-396-3947) presents summer melodramas in a Gay '90s setting. Performers drawn from the community give you a chance to boo villains and cheer heroes.

Crow's Nest Lounge and Wheelhouse (125 Chicago Avenue, Bandon; 503-347-9331) offers easy listening nightly during the summer. This pleasant, second-story establishment has a great waterfront view and a full bar serving munchies, fish and chips, steamers and oyster shooters.

Jot's Rod and Reel Restaurant (94360 Waterfront Loop, Gold Beach; 503-247-6676) offers pop, country-and-western, jazz and oldies ideal for dancing weekends. Bands, combos and soloists perform in the contemporary lounge which enjoys a Rogue River view.

When it's time for live country-and-western tunes head for the **Sea Horse Lounge** (Lower Harbor Road, Brookings; 503-469-5200). The bands play every weekend to a dimly lit room with café seating and a full bar. If you don't want to dance, head on over to the low-stakes blackjack tables and struggle against the odds.

SOUTH COAST BEACHES AND PARKS

Sunset Bay State Park—A splendid park on dramatic headlands, Sunset is forested with spruce and hemlock. Highlights include Big Creek, a popular fishing stream flowing into the bay. As the name implies, this is the place to be when the sun rises or sets.

Facilities: Picnic tables, restrooms and showers and wheelchair accessible; restaurants and groceries in Charleston or Coos Bay; information, 503-888-4902. *Swimming:* Good. *Fishing:* Excellent.

Camping: There are 138 sites, 29 with RV hookups; includes hiker-biker camp.

Getting there: It's off Route 101, 12 miles southwest of Coos Bay.

Shores Acres State Park—Let's skip the superlatives and get to the point: Visit Shore Acres. This 745-acre estate was once the site of a timber baron's mansion. Although the house burned down, the formal garden remains a showcase. Planted with azaleas, rhododendrons, irises, dahlias and roses, Shore Acres also offers trails on the forested bluffs.

Facilities: Picnic tables, restrooms, observation shelter and gift shop and wheelchair accessible; restaurants and groceries nearby.

Getting there: It's off Route 101, 13 miles southwest of Coos Bay.

Bullards Beach State Park—All good things come to an end, even the Coquille River. Fortunately, this 1289-acre park makes it possible to enjoy the tail end of the stream as it flows into the estuary and the Pacific opposite the city of Bandon. The Coquille River lighthouse is on the premises. A great recreation area, the park has fine dunes, beaches and forested lowlands. It's also ideal for crabbing and clamming.

Facilities: Picnic tables, restrooms, showers, boat ramp and wheelchair accessible; restaurants and groceries nearby in Bandon; information, 503-347-2209. *Fishing:* Good for steelhead, silver and chinook salmon.

Camping: There are 192 sites, 92 with RV hookups; includes hiker-biker and horse camps.

Getting there: Located off Route 101, two miles north of Bandon.

Cape Blanco State Park—Settled by an Irish dairy farmer, these dramatic, pastured headlands include the westernmost lighthouse in the continental United States. A windswept, 1880-acre retreat, Cape Blanco welcomes visitors to the Hughes House built by a pioneer family in 1898.

Facilities: Picnic tables, restrooms and showers and wheelchair accessible; restaurants and groceries in Port Orford; information, 503-332-6744. *Fishing:* Good.

Camping: Permitted, includes hiker-biker and horse camps. Open from April through October.

Getting there: It's nine miles north of Port Orford off Route 101.

Port Orford Heads State Wayside—You'll love this windblown and unforgettable 96-acre wayside. It encompasses the ocean bluff as well as Nellies Cove. The park protects marine gardens and prehistoric archaeological landmarks.

Facilities: Picnic tables and restrooms. *Fishing:* Permitted.

Getting there: Located off Route 101 at Port Orford.

Humbug Mountain State Park—A 1750-foot peak forested with fir, spruce, alder and cedar, Humbug is one of the coast's finest parks. Hiking trails, viewpoints, Brush Creek and ocean frontage make the 1842-acre sanctuary a great retreat. If you're feeling ambitious why not take the three-mile hike up the wildflower lined trail to the summit?

Facilities: Picnic tables, restrooms and showers and wheelchair accessible; restaurants and groceries in Port Orford; information, 503-332-6774. *Fishing:* Good at Brush Creek for salmon and steelhead.

Camping: There are 75 tent sites plus 70 with RV hookups; includes hiker-biker camp.

Getting there: The park is located off Route 101, six miles south of Port Orford.

Cape Sebastian State Park—This narrow park includes several miles of exceptional coastline. The centerpiece of the 1104-acre place is the cape, carpeted with wildflowers and rhododendron in the spring months. Views are magnificent. Old-growth Douglas fir and shore pine form a handsome backdrop.

Facilities: Hiking trails; restaurants and groceries in Gold Beach.

Getting there: It's located seven miles south of Gold Beach off of Route 101.

Harris Beach State Park—Named for a butte rising above the coast, this one-time sheep-and-cattle ranch is the southernmost state camping facility on the coast. The 172-acre park offers sandy beaches and great sunsets. Enjoy the shoreline punctuated with dramatic, surf-sculptured rocks.

Facilities: Picnic tables, restrooms and showers and wheelchair accessible; restaurants and groceries in Brookings; information, 503-469-2021. *Fishing:* Good for salmon and perch.

Camping: There are 151 sites, some with RV hookups; includes hiker-biker camp.

Getting there: Located at 1655 Route 101 in Brookings.

Loeb State Park (★)—On the Chetco River, this park can be a warm place when the coast is not. A one-mile trail leads to Loeb's redwood grove. There's also a Myrtle Grove here. A popular fishing region, particularly during the steelhead season, the Chetco is one of Oregon's special havens. With 320 acres, the park provides easy access to a prime stretch of this river canyon.

Facilities: Picnic tables, restrooms and showers and wheelchair accessible; restaurants and groceries in Brookings; information, 503-469-2021. *Fishing:* Great for salmon and steelhead.

Camping: There are 53 sites.

Getting there: Located ten miles northeast of Brookings along the Chetco River.

The Sporting Life

FISHING

Many companies provide deep-sea and river fishing trips for salmon, steelhead, perch or rockfish. Among the charter and party-boat operators are **Warrenton Deep Sea Inc.** (45 Northeast Harbor Street, Warrenton; 503-861-1233), **Garibaldi Charters** (606 South Commercial Street, Garibaldi; 503-322-0007), **Deep Sea Trollers** (Depoe Bay; 503-765-2248), **Newport Sportfishing** (1000 Southeast Bay Boulevard, Newport; 503-265-7558), **Bob's Sport Fishing** (7960 Kingfisher Drive, Charleston; 503-888-4241) and **Port Orford Charters** (94893 Elk River Road, Port Orford; 503-332-3140).

For guided river fishing trips try **Doug's Guide Service** (9185 North Echo Mountain Road, Lincoln City; 503-994-7781), **Merle's Guide Service** (28220 Hunter Creek Heights, Gold Beach; 503-247-2221) and in the Brookings area **Dick's Sporthaven Marina** (Route 101 and the Chetco River, Brookings Harbor; 503-469-3301).

HORSEBACK RIDING

Can there be a more picturesque place to ride than the Oregon Coast? Possibilities include **Track and Trail Rides** (Seaside; 503-738-6336), **Gearhart Stables** (Gun Club Road, Gearhart; 503-738-9757), **C&M Stables** (90421 Route 101, Florence; 503-997-7540), **Bandon Riding Stables** (Beach Loop Drive, Bandon; 503-347-3423) and **Indian Creek Trail Rides** (Jerry's Flat Road, Gold Beach; 503-247-7704).

BOATING

Rentals for crabbing and fishing on Newport Bay are available at **Embarcadero Marina** (100 Southeast Bay Boulevard, Newport; 503-265-5435). On the Alsea River, **Kozy Kove Marina** (9464 Alsea Highway, ten miles east of Waldport; 503-528-3251) also rents fishing boats. In Waldport try **McKinley's Marina** (Route 34; 503-563-4656). Near the Florence area try **Westlake Resort** (Westlake; 503-997-3722). **Tenmile Marine** (7th and Park streets, Lakeside; 503-759-3137) in the Coos Bay area rents canoes and boats. Another possibility is **Blue Heron Houseboat Rentals** (Tenmile Lake, Lakeside; 503-332-8585).

WHALE WATCHING

The Oregon Coast is prime whale-watching territory mid-December through mid-January and mid-March through mid-April. For whale-watching excursions **Dockside Charters** (next to the Coast Guard, Depoe Bay; 503-765-2545) offers one-hour trips. In Newport, the **Mark Hatfield Ma-**

rine Science Center (2000 South Marine Science Drive; 503-867-0100) operates major whale-watching programs with helpful lectures and informative brochures. The center's cetacean exhibits are also helpful. **Newport Tradewinds** (653 Southwest Bay Boulevard, Newport; 503-265-2101) also operates short whale-watching trips. **Charleston Charters** (5100 Cape Arago Highway, Charleston; 503-888-4846) recommends spring trips to see northerly migrations with new calves.

GOLF

For those who need to tee off, public courses include **Lakeside Golf and Racquet Club** (3245 Clubhouse Drive, Lincoln City; 503-994-8442), **Sailisan Golf Links** (Gleneden Beach; 503-764-3632), **Agate Beach Golf Course** (4100 North Coast Highway, Newport; 503-265-73310), **Crestview Hills Golf Course** (1680 Crestline Drive, Waldport; 503-563-3020), **Ocean Dunes Golf Links** (3345 Munsel Lake Road, Florence; 503-997-3232), **Sunset Bay Golf Course** (11001 Cape Arago Highway, Coos Bay; 503-888-9301), **Bandon by the Sea Face Rock Golf Club** (3235 Beach Loop Road, Bandon; 503-347-3818) and **Cedar Bend Golf Course** (34391 Squaw Valley Road, Gold Beach; 503-247-6911).

TENNIS

Time for tennis? Here are good possibilities: **Del Monte Park** (3rd Street and Goodspeed Place, Tillamook), **Lakeside Golf and Racquet Club** (3245 Clubhouse Drive, Lincoln City; 503-994-8442), **Salishan Lodge Tennis Club** (Gleneden Beach; 503-764-3633), **Mingus Park** (Commercial Street at 10th Street, Coos Bay), **Bandon High School** (11th and Franklin streets, Bandon), **Buffington Park** (14th and Arizona streets, Port Orford) and **Bud Cross Park** (Ransom Avenue at North 2nd Street, Brookings). Additional public courts are located at 2nd and Spruce streets in Cannon Beach, Northeast 4th and Benton streets in Newport and Snookum Drive and 35th Street in Florence.

BICYCLING

Route 101 is the state's most popular biking trail. Every year thousands of travelers do the coast, taking advantage of many side roads, hiker-bike camps and facilities that cater to the cycling crowd.

The 367-mile long **Oregon Coast Bike Route** is the jewel of the network. Although much of the trail parallels Route 101 as a shoulder bikeway, there are numerous sections that take in scenic and relatively quiet side roads. Most cyclists do the trip in six to eight days, a pace that takes into account the fact that the route rises and falls 16,000 feet along the way.

If you're planning a ride between April and November head south to take advantage of the prevailing Northwest winds. You'll also benefit from the fact that most of the bikeway improvements have been made on the south-bound shoulder. The State Department of Transportation (Room 200, Transportation Building, Salem, OR 97310; 503-378-3432) offers a free bike map.

You can also enjoy many other shorter routes along the coast. At **Fort Stevens** east of Astoria an easy, six-and-a-half-mile trail network makes it convenient to explore this Civil War-era landmark on the Columbia River.

The 83-mile **Seaside-Garibaldi Bike Tour** loops south along Route 101 and then takes Miami River Road back to Mohler where routes 53 and 26 lead back to your starting point. You can shorten the trip to 52 miles by returning north at Nehalem.

The 40-mile **Three Capes Loop** route from Tillamook to Cape Kiwanda at Pacific City is scenic, steep and spectacular. Another gentler approach to Cape Kiwanda is **Sandlake Road** off Route 101 south of Tillamook.

At Kernville, a pleasant alternative to Route 101 is **Route 229 (★)**. This road heads inland to the town of Siletz before hitting the Yaquina River at Toledo, whose art and antique galleries are worth a breather if you need one. Follow Yaquina Bay Road west along the river into Newport to complete this 50-mile loop.

Otter Crest Loop (★) off Route 101 south of Depoe Bay is a forested, four-mile gem that includes great views from the steep cliffs of Cape Foulweather. Be sure to follow 1st Street to Devil's Punchbowl and the village of Otter Rock.

From Newport an easy, 20-mile loop leads east along **Route 20** to Toledo. After exploring the town return to Newport on Yaquina Bay Road.

Newport's **Ocean View Drive** is an excellent, four-mile alternative to Route 101. This route leads past the Agate Beach area and takes you through the historic Nye Beach community, one of Newport's earliest resorts. You'll wind up at Yaquina Bay State Park, home of the community's signature lighthouse.

One of our favorite rides in Florence is **Rhododendron Drive** west from Route 101 to Spruce Point and then north to the Coast Guard Station. The round trip is eight miles. The ten-mile roundtrip from **Charleston to Cape Arago** includes Shore Acres Botanical Gardens. **Seven Devil's Road** in Charleston leads to South Slough National Estuarine Sanctuary on a scenic, 13-mile route that ends up at Route 101.

Bandon Bypass is a relatively easy trip that departs Route 101 at milepost 260.1 and follows Riverside Drive south through historic Old Town. It continues along Beach Loop Road before linking back up with the coast highway.

Off Route 101 north of Bandon, **North Bank Road (★)** winds for 16 miles along the Coquille River. This flat, scenic route is lightly trafficked, lush and unforgettable. Then head south on Route 42 to Coquille and pick up South Route 42 back to Bandon. The round trip is 52 miles.

BIKE RENTALS   To rent bikes along the coast try **Prom Bike Shop** (622 12th Avenue, Seaside; 503-738-8251), **Mike's Bike Shop** (248 North Spruce Street, Cannon Beach; 503-436-1266), **Gold Coast Cycle** (115 North 3rd Street, Rockaway Beach; 503-355-8018) and **Manzanita Fun Merchants** (1235 South Hemlock Street, Cannon Beach; 503-436-1880) and 186 Laneda Avenue, Manzanita; 503-368-6606).

HIKING

NORTH COAST TRAILS   **Fort Stevens State Park** has several easy trails including the 1.8-mile stroll from Battery Russell to the wreck of the *Peter Iredale*.

Saddle Mountain Trail (3 miles) ascends the highest mountain on the coastal range. A challenging climb offering great views. It's located off Route 26 near Necanicum.

Tillamook Head Trail (6 miles) begins south of Seaside and ascends to 1200 feet on the route to Ecola State Park's Indian Beach. This is believed to be the route followed by Lewis and Clark when they journeyed to Ecola Creek.

Inland from Tillamook on Route 6 is the moderate-to-difficult **King Mountain Trail** (★) (2 miles). This route takes you through the area of the famed Tillamook burn, a series of 1939, 1945 and 1951 fires that took out enough lumber to build over one million homes. While the area, now the Tillamook State Forest, is covered with younger timber, some evidence of the old burn can still be seen.

Neah-kah-nie Mountain Trail (1 mile) is a challenging climb that begins 2.6 miles south of Oswald West State Park's Short Sands parking area. Great views of the coast.

In the Siuslaw National Forest east of Pacific City, the **Pioneer Indian Trail** (★) (8 miles) is highly recommended. This moderately difficult trail runs from Itebo Lake to South Lake through a fir forest and a meadow that has a wide array of wildflowers in the summer.

CENTRAL COAST TRAILS   Otter Creek State Park has an easy, 1-mile hike along the beach to the base of the **Devil's Punchbowl**. This walk includes the Marine Gardens tidepool.

The .25-mile **Estuary Trail** at the Hatfield Marine Science Center (2030 South Marine Science Drive, Newport; 503-867-0100) is a great introduction to local marine life. This posted route is wheelchair accessible.

Captain Cook's Trail (.6 mile) leads from the Cape Perpetua visitors' center below Route 101 past Indian shell middens to coastal tidepools. At high tide you'll see the spouting horn across Cook's Chasm. Far more challenging is the **Cummins Creek Loop** (10 miles) up Cook's Ridge to Cummins Creek Trail and back down to the visitors' center. Enjoy the old-growth forests and meadows.

At the southern end of the Oregon Dunes National Recreation Area **Bluebill Trail** (1 mile), two-and-a-half miles off Route 101 near Horsefall Beach Road, offers a beautiful loop hike around Bluebill Lake. It includes an extensive boardwalk system.

SOUTH COAST TRAILS   The **Estuary Study Trail** at South Slough National Estuarine Reserve south of Coos Bay (2 miles) is one of the finest hikes on the Oregon Coast. Leading down through a coastal forest, you'll see a pioneer log landing, use a boardwalk to cross a skunk-cabbage bog and visit a salt marsh.

Shrader Old Growth Trail (★) (1 mile) off Jerry's Flat Road, east of Gold Beach, is a pleasant loop where you'll see rhododendron, cedar, streams and riparian areas. The marked route identifies coastal species along the way.

To really get away from it all hike the **Lower Rogue River Trail** (★) south from Agness (12.2 miles). You'll pass Indian landmarks, see picturesque bridges and spot wildlife as you hike this wild and scenic canyon.

Bandon to Fourmile Creek (8.5 miles) is one of the coast's most scenic walks. Begin at Bandon Harbor and head south past the Bandon Needles, dunes, ponds and lakes to the creek. Of course you can abbreviate this hike at any point. One easy possibility is to head south on Beach Loop Drive to the point where it swings east toward Route 101. Park here and take the short (.2 mile) walk through the woods and up over the dune to Bradley Lake, a good swimming hole.

Redwood Nature Trail (1 mile) north of Loeb State Park, ten miles east of Brookings, is a beautiful streamside walk leading past rhododendron, myrtlewood and towering redwoods.

Transportation

BY CAR

From Northern California or Washington the coast is easily reached via **Route 101**. Within Oregon many roads link the Portland and the Willamette Valley to resort destinations. **Routes 30** and **26** provide easy access to the North Coast communities of Astoria and Seaside, while **Route 6** connects with Tillamook. **Route 18** leads to Lincoln City, and **Routes 20** and **34** connect with the Central Coast region in the vicinity of Newport and Waldport. **Route 126** is the way to Florence. **Route 38** heads to Reedsport. To reach Bandon and the South Coast take **Route 42**.

BY AIR

Horizon Air flies to **North Bend Airport**, the only coast city with commercial air service. The Portland International Airport and Eugene Airport, described in other chapters, also provide gateways to the coast.

BY BUS

Greyhound/Trailways Bus Lines and **Raz Transportation Company** serve many coast destinations. Stations are found at Astoria (364 9th Street; 503-325-5641), Seaside (622 12th Street; 503-738-5121), Tillamook (604 Main Street; 503-842-6186), Lincoln City (316 Southeast Route 101; 503-994-8418), Newport (956 Southwest 10th Street; 503-265-2253), Waldport (Routes 101 and 34; 503-563-4711), Florence (478 Route 101; 503-997-8782), Coos Bay (275 North Broadway; 503-267-6517), Reedsport (2207 Winchester Street; 503-271-5223), Gold Beach (310 Colvin Street; 503-247-7710) and Brookings (601 Railroad Street; 503-469-3326).

CAR RENTALS

In Astoria try **Hertz Rent A Car** (503-325-7700). **Hertz Rent A Car** (503-756-4426) is at the North Bend Airport.

PUBLIC TRANSPORTATION

North Coast Transit operates service from Portland to Astoria (350 West Marine Drive; 503-738-7083) and Seaside (Broadway and Route 101; 503-738-7083). Local service is also provided by **Newport Area Transit** (924 Southwest 8th Street; 503-265-8088).

TAXIS

For service in Seaside try **Seaside Cab Co.** (503-738-5252). On the South Coast, **Yellow Cab** operates in Coos Bay/North Bend (503-267-3111), Bandon (503-347-9597) and Brookings (503-469-4800). Gold Beach is served by **American Transit Systems** (503-247-7716), while **Reedsport Cab** (503-271-5112) serves that community. In Coquille call **Valley Cab Co.** (503-396-5870).

CHAPTER NINE

Oregon Cascades

Some questions are impossible to answer. Here's one that came to mind while we traveled the highways and byways of the Oregon Cascades swimming in crystal-clear pools, basking at alpine resorts, fishing pristine streams, dining on fresh salmon and cooling off beneath the spray of yet another waterfall: Why isn't this heavenly space positively jammed with people who want to get away from it all?

Except for a handful of places such as Mt. Hood on a Saturday afternoon, Route 97 in the vicinity of Bend or Crater Lake's Rim Drive, it's often hard to find a crowd in this seemingly inexhaustible resort area. Sure there's a fair number of timber rigs out on major routes. And the no-vacancy sign does pop up a good deal at popular resorts during the summer and weekends. But who cares when you can head down the road half a mile and check into a glorious streamside campground where the tab is $4 a night and there's no extra charge for the nocturnal view of the Milky Way. The fact is that mile for mile, the Oregon Cascades offer some of the best wilderness and recreational opportunities in the Pacific Northwest.

To really get a feel for the area you need a week or longer. But even if you only have time to buzz up to Mt. Hood for an afternoon, this region is the best way we know to gain perspective on the volcanic history of the Pacific Northwest. A chain of peaks topped by 11,245-foot Mt. Hood, the Cascades have an average elevation of about 5000 feet. Heavily forested, these mountains are the headwaters for many important rivers such as the Rogue, the Umpqua and the McKenzie. Klamath Falls is the principal southern gateway to the region, and Bend and Redmond provide easy access from the east. Within the mountains are a number of charming towns and villages such as Sisters, McKenzie Bridge and Camp Sherman. While the summer months can be mild and sunny, winter snowfalls blanket the western slopes with 300 to 500 inches of snow.

For some perspective on the Cascades, take a look at the region's good-old days. Begin with the evolution of one of the Northwest's signature attractions, Crater Lake. Looking at this placid sea, it's hard to imagine what this region looked like 60 million years ago during the late-Cretaceous period. As Lowell Williams has written: "At that time the Coast Ranges of Oregon . . . were submerged and the waves of the Pacific lapped against the foothills of the Sierra Nevada and the Blue Mountains of Oregon. Where the Cascade peaks now rise in lofty grandeur, water teemed with shellfish . . . giant marine lizards swam in the seas, and winged reptiles sailed above in search of prey."

Later, in the Eocene and Oligocene periods, roughly 25 million to 60 million years ago, the Crater Lake region became a low plain. Throughout this period and the late Miocene, volcanoes erupted. Finally, about one million to two million years ago, in the last great Ice Age, the Cascades were formed. The largest of these peaks became 12,000-foot Mount Mazama. About 7000 years ago, this promontory literally blew its top, leaving behind the caldera that is now Crater Lake.

The Native Americans, who viewed this area as a sacred and treacherous place, went out of their way to avoid Crater Lake. It was only after the white man arrived in the 19th century that it became a tourist attraction and eventually a national park. Today the lake is considered a unique national treasure.

Because of their historic status on the Oregon Trail, the Cascades have also gained an important place in the history of the West. Landmarks in the Mt. Hood area tell the dramatic story of pioneers who blazed time-saving new routes to the promised land across this precipitous terrain. Of course, their arrival permanently altered Native American life. Inevitably, efforts to colonize the Indians, turn them into farmers and Christians, met with resistance. Native American leader Captain Jack led perhaps the most famous tribal rebellion against the miseries of reservation life in the 1872–73 Modoc War. This fighting raged in an area that is now part of the Lava Beds National Monument across the border in California. Captain Jack and his fellow renegades were ultimately hanged at Fort Klamath.

While logging became the Cascade's leading industry, tourism emerged in the late 19th century. Summer resorts, typically primitive cabins built at the water's edge, were popular with the fishing crowd. The later arrival of resort lodges like Timberline on the slopes of Mt. Hood drew a significant winter trade.

Thanks to dependable snowpack throughout the summer months, it is possible to spend the morning skiing on Mt. Hood and devote the afternoon

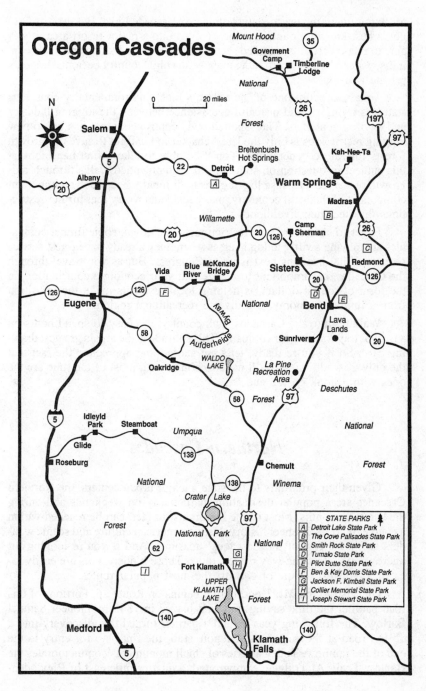

Oregon Cascades

N

0 _____ 20 miles

Mount Hood

Goverment Camp

Timberline Lodge

35

National

26

197

97

Salem

Breitenbush Hot Springs

Kah-Nee-Ta

22

Detroit

A

Albany

20

5

Warm Springs

Madras

B

26

Willamette

20

20

126

Camp Sherman

C

Redmond

Vida

Blue River

McKenzie Bridge

Sisters

20

126

Eugene

126

F

National

D

Bend

E

58

Byway

Aufderheide

Lava Lands

Sunriver

20

Oakridge

WALDO LAKE

La Pine Recreation Area

Deschutes

58

97

National

5

Idleyld Park

Steamboat

Umpqua

Glide

138

Roseburg

Chemult

Forest

National

138

Winema

Forest

Crater Lake

62

National

Park

97

National

I

Fort Klamath

G

H

UPPER KLAMATH LAKE

Forest

Medford

140

5

Klamath Falls

140

STATE PARKS
A Detroit Lake State Park
B The Cove Palisades State Park
C Smith Rock State Park
D Tumalo State Park
E Pilot Butte State Park
F Ben & Kay Dorris State Park
G Jackson F. Kimball State Park
H Collier Memorial State Park
I Joseph Stewart State Park

to swimming in the warm waters of nearby Cascade Lake. But even as Oregon's best-known mountain range evolved into a major resort area, it was able to retain carefully guarded secrets. Little-known fishing spots, obscure trails, waterfalls absent from the maps—this high country became Oregon's private treasure.

Today, Oregon, one of the nation's most environmentally conscious states, is trying to find peaceful coexistence between the logging industry and environmentalists. The "spotted owl" controversy that has led to new logging restrictions is only the latest chapter in the fight to save old-growth forests for future generations. You'll be able to take a first-hand look at this subject in question on some of our recommended walks through old-growth preserves. Because logging has traditionally been such an important component of the local economy, many residents worry that further restrictions threaten their livelihood.

Eager to cut before new restrictions come down, some timber companies are moving swiftly to log in areas where they already have forest-service permits. What happens next is up to Congress. But as you travel through the Cascades, it's important to realize that your economic contribution, in the form of tourist dollars, is helping local residents make the transition from a lumber economy to a diverse recreational region.

Walking into the Cascades back country, it's easy to spend hours on a road or trail looking for company. This solitude is the area's greatest drawing card. So if you're ready, let's get started and appreciate the fact that the only Cascade lines you'll have to bother with most of the time are the ones with a hook on the end.

Northern Cascades

Given their proximity to the state's major urban centers, the Northern Cascades are a popular destination, particularly on weekends and during the summer months. Most of the highlights, in fact, can be reached within a couple of hours. Pioneer history, Native American culture and scenic wonders are just a few of the Cascades' treasures. And if you're looking for uncrowded, out-of-the-way places, relax. Those hidden spots are easily located, often just a mile or two off the most popular routes.

Our visit to the **Mt. Hood** region begins on Route 26. Portions of this road parallel the time-saving trail first blazed in 1845 by pioneer Samuel Barlow. The following year he and a partner turned this discovery into a $5 toll road at the end of the Oregon Trail, the final tab for entry to the end of the rainbow. Today a series of small monuments commemorates the **Barlow Trail**. At Tollgate campground, a quarter-mile east of Rhododendron on the south side of Route 26, you'll want to visit a reproduction of the historic Barlow Tollgate. Continue five miles east of Rhododendron to the **Laurel Hill Chute** marker. You can take the short, steep hike to the infamous "chute" where wagon trains descended the perilous grade to Zigzag River Valley.

Two of the regions most popular fishing streams, the **Salmon River** and **Sandy River** are convenient to old-growth forests, waterfalls and hiking trails. The Sandy is also popular for swimming. Continuing east you'll reach Zigzag and **Lolo Pass Road**. This backcountry route on the west side of Mt. Hood leads to **Lost Lake** (★), a great escape.

After returning to Route 26, drive east to Government Camp and head uphill to Mt. Hood's **Timberline Lodge** (Timberline; 503-272-3311) one of the Northwest's most important arts-and-crafts architectural landmarks. Massive is the word for this skiing hub framed with giant timber beams and warmed by a six-sided fireplace. In warm weather you can hike the wildflower trails. Be sure to check out the lower-level display on the lodge's fascinating history and current restoration. Three miles east of Government Camp turn south on Route 2656 to picturesque **Trillium Lake**, a popular fishing, swimming and sailboat spot created by the damming of Mud Creek. This is an ideal place for a picnic and wildlife viewing.

Returning to Route 26, pick up Route 35 over Barlow Pass. East of the junction of these two highways you'll pass a stone cairn marking a **Pioneer Women's Grave**. It commemorates the heroism of all the women who bravely crossed the Oregon Trail. Continue another one-and-three-quarters miles to Forest Road 3530 and the **Barlow Road Sign**. Hand-carved by the Civilian Conservation Corps, this marker is a short walk from the wagon ruts left behind by the pioneers.

Half a century after the pioneers arrived, tourism began to put down roots on this Cascades Peak. Overnight guests were accommodated at **Cloud Cap Inn**. Located 10.5 miles north of Route 35, this turn-of-the-century building was the first structure built on Mt. Hood. Although it no longer accepts the public, the shingled inn is on the National Register of Historic Places. Today the inn serves as a base for a mountain-climbing-and-rescue organization and provides views of Mt. Hood's north side. Here you can pick up the brochure for the **Cloud Cap/Tilly Jane Historic District Auto Tour** (★). This hour-long route takes you through one of the region's original tourist centers. Along the way you'll see the wagon road that brought visitors to the hotel on a steep grade.

Return south to Route 26 and continue southeast to Warm Springs and **Kah-Nee-Ta** (503-553-1112), one of the Pacific Northwest's most intriguing Native American reservations. Near the lodge entrance an interpretive display offers background on the Confederated Tribes of Warm Springs. Indian dance performances are held on Sunday in the summer months. Saturday the traditional salmon bake is put on by tribal members who skewer

Columbia River salmon on cedar sticks and cook it over alderwood coals. The hot springs are highly recommended.

Richardson's Recreational Ranch (11 miles north of Madras on Route 97, at milepost 81 turn right and continue southeast three miles; 503-475-2680) could also be called the world's largest pick-and-pay thunder-egg farm. Formed as gas bubbles in rhyolite flows and filled with silicon, these colorful stones range from the size of a seed to 1760 pounds. You can pick up, chisel or dig your thunder eggs out of 12 beds spread across this 4000-acre rock ranch.

The 31-mile **Cove Palisades Tour Route** off Route 97 is the best way to reach the dramatic volcanic scenery and one of the Northwest's geologic anomalies. Begin by picking up a brochure detailing this excursion at the **Madras-Jefferson County Chamber of Commerce** (366 5th Street, Madras; 503-475-2350). Three major rivers, the Deschutes, Crooked and Metolius, have cut canyons through this Oregon plain and merged at Lake Billy Chinook behind **Cove Palisades State Park's** Round Butte Dam. Be sure to visit the observatory viewpoint and museum on the lake's Metolius River arm. In addition to memorable views of **Deschutes Canyon**, you'll have a chance to learn about local wildlife and Native American artifacts.

After completing this tour, return to Route 97. Continue south 12 miles to Terrebonne. Then head east three miles to **Smith Rock State Park**, a favorite of world-class rock climbers. Don't worry if you forgot to bring your spikes and pitons. You can still enjoy the Cascades scenery from your vantage point along the Crooked River Gorge.

NORTHERN CASCADES HOTELS

When it comes to architecture, history, location and ambience, few hotels in the Cascades match **Timberline Lodge** (Timberline; 503-272-3311). A veritable museum of Northwest arts and crafts, this 50-year-old lodge was built by the Works Progress Administration on the slopes of Mount Hood. Each of the 59 rooms have handwoven draperies, bedspreads and rugs featuring a different theme; there are iron-and-oak beds, writing desks, WPA watercolors and views of the valley and mountain. While the rooms are small, there is nothing modest about the public areas which feature a six-sided stone fireplace and banisters decorated with handcarved owls and beavers. Perfectly situated for skiing, hiking or climbing. Moderate to deluxe.

Huckleberry Inn (Government Camp; 503-272-3325) offers 16 accommodations in varying price ranges. Moderate-priced standard rooms sleep small groups, while deluxe rooms with spiral staircases leading up to sleeping lofts accommodate more. Budget dorm rooms are also available.

Fernwood at Alder Creek Bed and Breakfast (54850 East Route 26; 503-622-3570) is a historic log home in the Mt. Hood foothills. The two moderate rooms have wood stoves, antique furnishings, sitting rooms, oak rocking chairs, whirlpools and decks overlooking the creek and ponds. An early breakfast is served family style each morning. Moderate.

In the mid-1960s the federal government built the Dalles Dam on the Columbia River, submerging the ancestral fishing grounds of local Indians. The Confederated Tribes of Warm Springs used their compensation to pay for **Kah-Nee-Ta Resort** (Warm Springs; 503-553-1112). Located in the midst of the 600,000-acre reservation, this 139-room-and-cottage complex offers visitors a choice between a campground, tepee with a cement floor, hotel room or small cottages. The cottages, in the same price range as the moderate-to-deluxe hotel rooms, are a real value. The rooms have a slightly dated feel with brown, wall-to-wall carpets, vanity areas, easy chairs and decks. Set in a red-rock canyon about an hour southeast of Mt. Hood, this resort offers rafting, golfing, horseback riding, pools, fishing and tennis.

NORTHERN CASCADES RESTAURANTS

If you don't have a meal at the **Timberline Lodge Restaurant** (Timberline; 503-272-3311) you'll be missing one of the best dining rooms in the Pacific Northwest. Liveried waiters and waitresses preside over this arts-and-crafts establishment with a stone fireplace and views of Mt. Hood. On a frosty morning there's no better place to down *Birchermuesli* (nut cereal with fresh fruit) or apple oat cakes. Dinner entrées include rabbit, smoked salmon, prawns with ginger and vegetarian specialties. Moderate.

Convenient to the Timberline area is **Mt. Hood Brewing Company** (Route 26 at Government Camp Loop Road; 503-272-3724). Located in a three-story, stone-and-wood building, this restaurant features a fly-fishing motif with knotty-pine paneling, a red-quarry tile floor and a 43-foot-long copper bar. The family-style menu offers gourmet pizza, pasta, steaks, salads and hamburgers served on sourdough rolls. Moderate.

The informal **River Room** next to the recreation center at Kah-Nee-Ta (Warm Springs; 503-553-1112) features Indian wallhangings that blend nicely with the pink-and-turquoise decor. The menu features Indian fry bread, burgers, short cake and several dinner entrées. Service is friendly. Moderate. Two more upscale restaurants are found in the lodge. **The Pinto Grill** serves moderately priced entrées in a contemporary café-style dining room while the deluxe **Juniper Room** is the place to go for buffalo steak or prawns, halibut and steamed clams blended in a seafood pot.

NORTHERN CASCADES SHOPPING

Oregon Candy Farm (48620 Southeast Route 26, Sandy; 503-668-5066) is the place to shop for homemade, hand-dipped chocolates. Even the nutmeats are roasted in house. Part of the fun is watching the candy-making process through big windows.

For limited-edition prints, posters, books, cards and other high-country souvenirs visit the **Wy'East Store** (Timberline; 503-272-3311) adjacent to Timberline Lodge. A cross between a gift shop and a mountain outfitter, this is also a good place to find sportswear that will make you even more stylish on your way down the slopes.

When it comes to shopping for Native America arts and crafts, why not go to the source. At **Kah-Nee-Ta** both the Lodge and Village (Warm Springs; 503-553-1112) have gift shops offering beautiful basketry, handicrafts, blankets and jewelry. Many are made right on the reservation.

Richardson Recreational Ranch Gift Shop (11 miles north of Madras on Route 97, at milepost 81 turn right and continue southeast three miles; 503-475-2680) offers a wide variety of polished spheres as well as other rocks from around the world. Choose from agates, jasper, marble, petrified wood and novelty items.

NORTHERN CASCADES NIGHTLIFE

On weekends live bands play rock-and-roll, blues, folk or country-and-western at **Charlie's Mountain View** (Government Camp Loop off Route 26, Government Camp; 503-272-3333). This rustic mountain lodge offers booth and table seating. The walls and ceilings are appointed with old-time skis, boots, snowshoes, ski bibs and other high-country memorabilia.

At the **Appaloosa Lounge** at Kah-Nee-Ta (Warm Springs; 503-553-1112) you can dance to live bands in a disco setting. It's also fun to enjoy the music outside on the adjacent deck. When the stars are out this is a particularly romantic setting.

NORTHERN CASCADES BEACHES AND PARKS

Mt. Hood National Forest—This one-million-acre national forest is named for the 11,235-foot Cascades peak that dazzles newcomers and natives alike. Extending from the Columbia River Gorge south to the Willamette National Forest boundary, the popular resort region includes four major wilderness and roadless areas. Popular destinations include the Olallie scenic area known for its beautiful lakes and wildflowers and the Mt. Hood Loop, a 170-mile scenic drive circling Oregon's highest peak. Along the way you'll see mountain meadows, waterfalls, scenic streams, major ski areas and the magical Columbia River Gorge.

Facilities: Picnic tables, boat ramps, ski areas, horseback riding trails, visitors center and restrooms; information, 503-666-0700. *Fishing:* More than 4500 miles of rivers and streams and 167 lakes and reservoirs will delight anglers seeking trout, salmon or steelhead.

Camping: Permitted in 107 campgrounds.

Getting there: Access is by Routes 84, 30, 35, 224 and 26.

Cove Palisades State Park—Located at the junction of the Crooked, Deschutes and Metolius rivers, this 4129-acre park encompasses two arms of Lake Billy Chinook. The cove is set beneath towering palisades and located on benchland punctuated by volcanic cones. Rich in petroglyphs and Native American history, this region is a geological showcase.

Facilities: Picnic area, restrooms, marina, boat ramp, playground, nature trails and concessions; restaurants and groceries in Madras; information, 503-546-3412. *Swimming:* Good. *Fishing:* Excellent for smallmouth bass, trout and kokanee.

Camping: There are 272 sites, including 87 RV hookups.

Getting there: Located off Route 97, 15 miles southwest of Madras.

Central Cascades

One of Oregon's top recreational areas, the Central Cascades include some of the state's finest museums and interpretive centers. A year-around getaway for hiking, fishing, climbing and skiing, this area is also famous for its volcanic scenery, mountain lakes and rafting. Within the national forests are some of the West's leading wilderness areas and great opportunities for wildlife viewing. The region is an ideal family resort and also boasts one of the best scenic drives in the Northwest, the Cascades Loop Highway.

A good way to begin your visit is by heading west from Redmond 20 miles on Route 126 to **Sisters**. Gateway to some of the Cascades' most memorable scenery, this small town has a Wild West-style main street that delights tourists driving between the Willamette Valley and the Bend area. After pausing to shop, dine or provision, head west nine miles on Route 20 and then turn north to the **Metolius River Recreation Area**. For information on this area call the Metolious Recreation Association in the village of Camp Sherman (503-595-6117). Here you'll enjoy fly fishing, horseback riding, sign up for a river trip or, in winter, go cross-country skiing.

Nearby **Black Butte Ranch** (Route 20, eight miles west of Sisters; 503-595-6211) is a resort area named for a towering volcanic cone. To the west off Route 20, **Blue and Subtle Lakes** are resort destinations as well, with easy access to the scenic treasures of the Mt. Washington wilderness.

Continue west on Route 20 past Lost Lake to Route 22 and **Detroit Lake**, a recreational area ideal for waterskiing. This area is also home of the **Shady Cove Bridge** (★), an unusual three-span, wooden-truss structure. Handcut and hand-assembled using hundreds of small interlocking pieces, the bridge links French Creek Road with Little North Santiam drainage.

From Detroit Lakes take Route 46 northeast ten miles to **Breitenbush Hot Springs** (503-854-3314), a New Age resort with a director of marketing and efficient employees armed with cellular phones. Sweat lodges, hot-springs pools, steam saunas and massage therapy are all part of the fun. The artesian hot springs boast 30 minerals said to have curative powers. Before the arrival of the white man, Native Americans conducted rituals and ceremonies at this soothing spot.

Return to Route 22 and head east. When you reach Route 126 go west three miles to **Sawyer's Ice Cave** (★), a lengthy lava tube that served as a refrigerator for the pioneers. Another major volcanic landmark three miles southeast via Route 126 is **Clear Lake** (★), the source of the McKenzie River. Created when lava blocked a canyon, this lake lives up to its name in every respect.

Continue south on Route 126 to **Sahalie Falls**, a wheelchair-accessible landmark where the McKenzie pours over lava cliffs. A short drive south is **Koosah Falls**, which plunges more than 80 feet. In the fall this waterfall divides into several sections. Southeast on Route 126 another 17.6 miles is the hamlet of **McKenzie Bridge**, gateway to many scenic highlights of the Central Cascades. Continue west to the **Blue River Ranger Station** and pick up the **Aufderheide National Scenic Byway** (★) audio tape. You can also begin this 40-mile tour from the south end at the **Oakridge Ranger Station** on Route 58, three miles west of Oakridge. The same tape is available here.

Before returning north to the McKenzie Bridge area, take a look around the Oakridge area. We enjoyed visiting **Oakridge Pioneer Museum** (76433 Pine Street; 503-782-2666). Even if you're not into chainsaws—one of the Northwest's best collections is found here—you'll enjoy seeing the antique farm implements, grocery displays and vintage crockery.

Twenty miles east of Oakridge is pristine **Waldo Lake** (★) (Route 5897 north of Route 58). Clean enough to qualify as distilled water, the six-mile-long lake has astonishing visibility. Out on the water you can see down 100 feet to the bottom. While there are facilities here, the lake, one of Oregon's largest, also has wilderness on the west and north shores.

Heading north to the McKenzie Bridge area again, pick up Route 126 east to Route 242 (a narrow route not recommended for long motor homes) up McKenzie Pass to the **Dee Wright Observatory** where a half-mile paved trail leads through one of the Cascades' largest lava fields. From the observatory you can see 11 mountain peaks. Also worth a visit nearby is **Black Crater,** a volcanic summit close to North Sister Mountain.

Continue east to Sisters and pick up Route 20 east to **Bend**. One of Oregon's fastest-growing resort communities, this town has become a year-round recreational center. A sunny alternative to the damper parts of the state, Bend also has one of the Northwest's largest ski resorts, **Mt. Bachelor**.

As you drive into town be sure to stop at the **Bend Chamber of Commerce** (63085 North Route 97; 503-382-3221). Extensively decorated by

Oregon artists (even the restrooms feature artwork), this is the best place to orient yourself. In the center of Bend, **Drake Park** on Riverside Boulevard shouldn't be missed. On the Deschutes River, this urban sanctuary features picturesque **Mirror Pond** (★). Put out a blanket on the lawn, have a picnic, feed the ducks and study your own reflection.

Although strip development along Route 97 is changing Bend's small-town character, the past is well preserved at the **Deschutes Historical Center** (Idaho Street between Wall Street and Bond Street; 503-389-1813; admission). Located in the Richardsonian Romanesque Reid School building, the museum features exhibits on Native American history, early-day trappers and explorers, pioneer trails, the lumber industry and the tourist business.

South of Bend is the **High Desert Museum** (59800 South Route 97; 503-382-4754; admission). One of the finest collections in the Pacific Northwest, the indoor galleries are complemented by 20 acres of nature trails and outdoor exhibits including a high-desert stream and pond. Permanent exhibits include exploration and settlement, natural history and a walk-through hard-rock mine that authentically re-creates life underground. A nice display here is a dawn-to-dusk "walk through time" that showcases the past. Along the way you'll have a look at Native American history and the 19th-century heyday of the cowboy.

After seeing Native American exhibits, crafts and quilting displays, visitors head outdoors to view the river-otter pool, hand-feeding of native porcupines and a birds-of-prey show. Hands-on exhibits and demonstrations at the forestry-learning center, sheepherder's wagon and settler's cabin make the museum a major pioneer-history center.

Continue south on Route 97 to the **Lava Lands Visitor Center** (58201 Route 97; 503-593-2421). This small museum is one of Oregon's geologic showcases, the product of more than 500,000 years of volcanic eruptions. Part of the Deschutes National Forest, Lava Lands encompass numerous volcanic landmarks. At the visitor center you'll find interpretive exhibits, dioramas, slide talks and rangers who can suggest a variety of nature trails that lead through the lava flow.

Within this ten-square-mile lava flow are highlights like 6100 year-old **Lava Butte**, which changed the course of the Deschutes River. Reached by a paved road from the visitors center, it's necessary to hike the final quarter-mile to the summit and a 360-degree view of the Cascades and Lava Lands. Continue west six miles from the visitors center (follow the signs saying "Deschutes River Views") to reach **Benham Falls**, a popular picnic spot.

Much of the best sightseeing in Lava Lands is found on the east side of Route 97. Two worthy spots in this fascinating region are **Lava River Cave** and **Lava Cast Forest**. The former, a caved-in lava tube, is great for spelunkers. Flashlight in hand you can walk a mile down this eerie tunnel,

(Text continued on page 358.)

Gorges in the Mist

The land of falling waters, the Pacific Northwest is the place to go for plunging rivers. Thousands of waterfalls are found here, often convenient to major highways or trails. Reached via fern canyons, paths through old-growth forests and along pristine streams, waterfall hunting is great sport, even on a rainy day. And part of the fun is getting misted or sprayed by the raging waters.

In the Oregon Cascades, these falls are at their peak in late spring or early summer. But even if you come later in the summer or fall, there will still be plenty to see: deep, plunging streams, tiered falls that split into roaring ribbons before converging in swirling pools, horsetails that drop at a 90-degree angle while retaining contact with bedrock. And, of course, you can count on frequently spotting the distinctive waterfall that gives this region its name—the Cascades that drop down in a series of steps.

The Mt. Hood area offers some of the loveliest falls. Among the easiest to reach is **Yocum Falls**, on Route 26 seven miles east of Rhododendron. Here, Camp Creek drops several hundred feet. Continue east to Route 35 and the entrance to Mt. Hood Meadows ski area. You'll see a sign marking the .2 mile trail to **Umbrella Falls**. Although these falls drop only about 60 feet, the verdant setting and fields of wildflowers make this an excellent choice, especially for families with small children. In early summer the falls trail is reached via a hike through fields of wildflowers. Return to Route 35 and continue 1.4 miles east to **Switchback Falls**. At its peak, in the late spring, North Fork Iron Creeks drops 200 feet.

To the south, the McKenzie River has two highly recommended falls accessible via Route 126. Located five miles south of the Route 20 junction, the river drops 140 feet at **Sahalie Falls**. Continue south another .4 mile to **Koosah Falls**. A trail takes you down the river canyon to enjoy the view from a series of overlooks. Continue another 5.2 miles south to a road that heads to the McKenzie River Trailhead. After hiking upriver for two miles you'll discover that **Tamolitch Falls** have now run dry. Although the river has been diverted to a reservoir at this point, it remains a scenic spot. Thanks to local springs, the river begins anew at this location.

The Bend area is an excellent choice for waterfall lovers. **Tumalo Falls**, 15 miles west of town, is reached via Galveston Avenue and Route 1828. The falls drop nearly 100 feet in an area badly damaged by a fire 12 years ago. South of town, off Route 97, is **Paulina Creek Falls**. Located in Newberry Crater, this 100-foot drop is an easy walk from Paulina Creek Falls picnic ground.

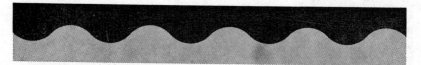

Century Drive, the beginning of the Cascade Lakes Highway west of Bend, provides easy access to **Lava Island Falls** on the Deschutes River. Take this road to Route 41 and drive south for .4 mile. Go left on Route 620 for .8 mile to reach the falls. If you take Route 41 south from Century Drive three miles and pick up Route 500 for .9 mile you'll reach **Dillon Falls**. Take Route 620 south about three miles from the intersection of Route 500 to see a 50-foot cataract called **Benham Falls**.

Off Cascade Lakes Highway, **Fall Creek Falls** is another fine choice. Take Century Drive 28 miles west of Bend to Route 46. Drive .2 mile on the road to Green Lakes Trail and then hike the last .3 mile to the falls.

In the Umpqua River Valley, Route 138 gets you to a number of beautiful falls. Among them is **Susan Creek Falls**, located via a trail seven and a half miles east of Idleyld Park. You'll hike one mile north of the highway to reach the falls. Drive Steamboat Road northeast from Steamboat 4.2 miles to reach **Steamboat Falls**. Located at a forest-service campground, this small waterfall is circumvented by fish that use an adjacent ladder. Near mile marker 42 about three miles southeast of Steamboat are **Jack Creek** and tiered **Jack Falls**. These three falls are particularly rewarding for photo buffs.

Also popular are **Toketee Falls**. To see this 90-foot drop, take Route 138 to the Toketee Lake turnoff. Continue north .3 mile to the trail leading west .6 mile to the falls. East of Toketee Lake is Lemolo Lake, a popular resort destination. From here Thorn Prairie Road leads to Lemolo Falls Road. Hike the Lemolo Falls Trail one mile west to this cataract.

Off Route 62, the main highway from Medford to Crater Lake, is one of the Cascades' grander waterfalls, 175-foot **Mill Creek Falls**. Accessible by Mill Creek Road, this scenic spot is an easy .3 mile hike from the Mill Creek Falls Scenic Area trailhead on the south side of Prospect. Also accessible on this hike are **Barr Creek Falls, Prospect Falls, Pearsoney Falls** and **Lower Red Blanket Falls**.

Within Crater Lake National Park, **Annie Falls** is off Route 62, 4.7 miles north of the park's southern entrance. Because this falls is located in an unstable canyon-rim area, visitors should approach it with extreme caution. Also in the park, close to Applegate Peak, is **Vidae Falls**.

To get a complete rundown on these watery delights, check with local park or ranger offices. Or pick up a copy of the definitive guide to this subject, *A Waterfall Lover's Guide to the Pacific Northwest* by Gregory A. Plumb (The Mountaineers). And remember to always exercise extreme caution in the vicinity of any waterfall. Children must remain at arm's length at all times!

Oregon's longest uncollapsed lava tube. The latter, explored via a mile-long trail, is a unique piece of Oregon scenery, a forest created out of lava. This unusual landscape was shaped when lava swept across a stand of pine 6000 years ago, creating casts of each tree.

The region's largest geologic feature is 500 square-mile **Newberry Volcano** created by eruption from more than 400 cinder cones. **Paulina and East lakes**, two popular resort areas, are found in the five-mile-wide **Newberry Caldera**. Also worth a visit is the crater's shiny, black obsidian flow.

West of Bend is **Mt. Bachelor**, central Oregon's premier ski area. Continue up the **Cascade Lakes Highway** to tour one the region's most idyllic resort regions. Todd, Sparks, Devils, Elk, Hosmer, Lava, Cultus and Davis lakes are a few of the popular spots for fishing, boating, swimming and camping. For those eager to head for the outback, there's easy access to high-country lakes, streams and creeks in the Three Sisters Wilderness.

Scenic highlights in this region include spots like **Devils Garden (★)**, a beautiful meadow where you can spot pictographs left behind by Warm Springs Indians. One piece of the **Devils Hill Flow** found in this area was flown to the moon by Apollo astronaut James Irwin.

CENTRAL CASCADES HOTELS

Located in a park setting, **4th Sister Lodge** (Route 20 at Route 126, Sisters; 503-549-6441) features a dozen budget-priced rooms and moderate-to-deluxe-priced suites with kitchens and fireplaces. An excellent choice for families or groups, these large units have contemporary furniture, separate vanities, wall-to-wall carpets, decks, washers and dryers. The lodge also has a swimming pool, sauna, spa and recreation room.

One look at the aging exterior of the **Silver Spur Motel** (514 West Cascade Street, Sisters; 503-549-6591) might prompt you to pass right by. But all ten rooms here have been freshly painted, paneled with knotty pine, appointed with new beds and, in one case, a fireplace. Budget.

When it comes to lodging, you really can get just about anything you want at **Black Butte Ranch** (Route 20, eight miles west of Sisters; 503-595-6211). This 1800-acre resort offers 100 moderately priced hotel rooms, deluxe condos, cabins and private homes. Chalet-style accommodations nestled in the pines have paneled walls and ceilings, decks, fireplaces and, in the condos, fully equipped kitchens. Choose between two golf courses, 16 miles of bike and jogging trails and 19 tennis courts. There's canoeing in a chain of spring-fed lakes, as well as skiing, hiking, fishing, boating, canoeing and horseback riding.

The **Metolius River Lodges** in Camp Sherman (five miles north of Route 20; 503-595-6290) are 12 duplexes, cabins and homes where you can fly fish off your deck. Located 18 miles northwest of Sisters, this wooded retreat is ideal for horseback riding, mountain biking, rafting, cross-country skiing and watersports. The wood-paneled units have braided rugs, fireplaces, barbecues and casual, '50s-style furniture. Moderate to deluxe.

A small lake created by a dammed stream is just one of the attractions at Camp Sherman's **Lake Creek Lodge** (Camp Sherman Road, four miles north of Route 20; 503-595-6331). Sixteen one-, two- or three-bedroom knotty-pine-paneled cabins feature Early American furniture, full kitchens, fireplaces and decks. On the Metolius River, this 60-acre resort has tennis courts, bike and hiking trails and serves meals family style. Special activities are offered for children. Deluxe.

Blue Lake Resort (13900 Blue Lake Drive, 20 miles west of Sisters off Route 20; 503-595-6671) offers 25 log cottages, townhouses and A-frame loft units, with full kitchens and porches. Just steps away from a crystal-clear lake and warm swimming hole, the resort offers motor, row and paddle boats, canoes, kayaks and fishing gear. This forested retreat is ideal for horseback riding, hiking and, in winter, nordic or alpine skiing.

Possibly the only resort in Oregon with a resident channel offering metaphysical counseling, **Breitenbush Hot Springs** (503-854-3314) has it all. About 12 miles northeast of Detroit in the western Cascades, this retreat provides everything from massage therapy to yoga. You can even learn how to run firewalking seminars for fun and profit here. Guests bring their own bedding and are housed in spartan, cedar-shake cabins paneled with fir. Geothermal heat and electricity from hydropower provide energy self-sufficiency. Guests can choose between hot tubs, *au natural* hot springs overlooking the river and mountains and a hot natural-steam sauna complete with a cold-water tub. Moderate prices include vegetarian meals.

Herbert Hoover, Sean Penn and Clark Gable have all stayed at the century-old **Log Cabin Inn** (56483 McKenzie Highway, McKenzie Bridge; 503-822-3432). A 19th-century stage stop, this three-story log building replaced the original building that burned down in a 1906 fire. Although the second-story bordello is now only a dim memory, many other traditions endure at the cedar-paneled dining room, bar and wrap-around porch. Eight rustic rooms and cottages with kitchenettes on this six-and-a-half-acre site all enjoy McKenzie River frontage. The units have eclectic furniture, fireplaces, braided rugs and decks. Moderate.

Nestled in a walnut orchard, the **McKenzie River Inn** (★) (49164 McKenzie Highway, Vida; 503-822-6260) provides three spacious, paneled rooms and a cottage on the water. Just steps from the river, this two-and-a-half-acre retreat has a library and piano in the main living room, peacock chairs and ceiling fans in the bedrooms and kitchen facilities in the cottage. Moderate.

Holiday Farm (54455 McKenzie River Drive, Blue River; 503-822-3715) offers spacious, knotty-pine-paneled cabins on the McKenzie River complete with fireplaces, decks and kitchenettes. The units make an ideal fishing retreat—you can cast for trout from your porch! This 90-acre resort has two private lakes and serves meals in a farmhouse that was once a stage stop. Deluxe.

On a lake created by a lava dam, **Clear Lake Resort** (19 miles northeast of McKenzie Bridge on Route 126; c/o Santiam Fish & Game Association, P.O. Box 550, Lebanon, OR 97355) offers four units with kitchens, baths and showers. Sixteen rustic cabins without bath facilities are also available. There are no electric outlets in these units, and generator-powered lights are shut off at 10 p.m. You must provide your own bedding. Cultus Lake is limited to row boats that can be rented at the resort. Moderate.

Located across from Drake Park, **Lara House Bed and Breakfast** (640 Northwest Congress Street, Bend; 503-388-4064) hosts guests in four big, carpeted rooms with easy chairs, antiques, colorful quilts and, in the bathrooms, claw-foot tubs. You can take your full breakfast on the sun porch. This 1910 Colonial also has a comfortable, paneled living room. Moderate.

The **Bend Riverside Motel** (1575 Northwest Hill Street, Bend; 503-389-2363) offers 193 budget rooms, moderately priced studios and deluxe suites with park or river views. The studios and suites have fireplaces, kitchen facilities, sauna, hot tub and tennis facilities. Convenient to downtown in a secluded setting.

The **Riverhouse** (3075 North Route 97; 503-389-3111) in Bend is one of over a dozen motels on the city's main drag. There are 208 moderately priced rooms featuring contemporary furniture, floral-print bedspreads and sitting areas. In the evening you can relax in front of the fireplace or have a drink on your deck overlooking the Deschutes River. Deluxe suites are also available with kitchen facilities. A nine-hole golf course, jogging trail, two pools and whirlpool make this a good place to relax.

In the same part of Bend are the budget-priced **Sportsman's Motel** (3705 Route 97 North; 503-382-2211) and the **Dunes Motel** (1515 Northeast 3rd Street; 503-382-6811).

Fifteen miles south of Bend on Route 97, at **Sunriver Lodge and Resort** (Sunriver; 503-593-1221), you can choose between 300 deluxe-priced rooms and suites featuring pine furniture, brass beds, fireplaces, wall-to-wall carpets and decks with views of the Cascades. Condos and homes are also available. All guests can take advantage of pools, saunas, tennis courts, racquetball, skiing and other facilities available at this 3300-acre resort.

In the wooded Cascades foothills, **The Inn Of the Seventh Mountain** (18575 Century Drive, Bend; 503-382-8711) is the only resort in Oregon with its own skating rink and waterslide. The 327 rooms, suites and apartments have queens and Murphy beds, knotty-pine paneling, fireplaces and contemporary prints. Convenient to Mt. Bachelor, the inn is ideally located for horseback riding, whitewater rafting and mountain biking. Moderate to deluxe.

Built around a circa-1924 lodge, 12-unit **Elk Lake Resort** (★) (Cascade Lakes Highway, 32 miles west of Bend; radio phone YP7-3954) is a forested retreat ideal for fishing, boating, swimming and loafing. The knotty-pine cabins, with lofts, kitchens and spacious decks, are near wilderness hiking, nordic skiing and horseback riding. This moderately priced retreat is accessible only by snowmobile or snowcat in the winter months.

CENTRAL CASCADES RESTAURANTS

In Sisters, **Ali's** (Town Square; 503-549-2547) offers a convenient solution for those who can't decide between a sandwich or a salad. Generous sandwiches served on an open-faced bagel or wrapped pita bread include curry chicken, dilly tuna, lemon-ginger chicken and Mexican chicken *olé*. A wide variety of vegetarian sandwiches and smoked-turkey sandwiches are offered as well as soups, bagels and coffee drinks like the mocha-mint espresso float. Budget.

One of the most popular pizza parlors in these parts is **Papandrea's** (325 East Hood Street, Sisters; 503-549-6081). The modest board-and-batten establishment offers indoor seating at tables covered with red-and-white-checkered tablecloths. Antique farm implements decorate the dining room. There's also patio service on picnic tables. All dough and sauces are homemade, and the tomatoes are fresh. Budget.

For deluxe-priced dining in a contemporary setting, consider the **Lodge Restaurant at Black Butte Ranch** (Route 20, eight miles west of Sisters; 503-595-1260). This split-level establishment has cathedral ceilings, picture windows and Early American furniture. While enjoying the panoramic Cascades view, you can order prime rib, roast duck, halibut filet or pasta with bay shrimp.

Located in a shingled lodge-style building adjacent to the Metolius River, **Kokanee Café** (★) (Camp Sherman; 503-595-6420) is recommended for seafood salads with fresh Dungeness crab, smoked pork chops, fresh salmon or steaks accompanied by soup and a garden salad with the house vinegarette. The desserts are exceptional. Worth a special trip. Moderate.

Whether you choose one of the porch lunches served al fresco or head in to the paneled dining room for supper, the historic **Log Cabin Inn** (★) (Route 126, McKenzie Bridge; 503-822-3432) offers fine dining in a traditional setting. Specialties include roast of wild boar, buffalo steak, quail, rainbow trout fresh from the McKenzie River, a bucket of fresh steamer clams and pioneer game stew. Moderate.

French restaurants are in short supply in the Cascades. One of the best is **Le Bistro** (1203 Northeast 3rd Street, Bend; 503-389-7274). The cheery, café-style dining room is decorated like a Hollywood set for a Parisian movie. Moderate-to-deluxe-priced entrées include pork loin *au citron*, rack of lamb, duck *a l'orange* and seafood Wellington.

A Bend tradition since 1936 and one of our Northwest favorites, **Pine Tavern** (foot of Northwest Oregon Street; 503-382-5581) has an enviable location overlooking Mirror Pond. Built around 200-year-old ponderosa pines, the restaurant prides itself on moderately priced, home-cooked dishes like steamed vegetables and fettucine, pork back ribs, fish and chips and Cobb salad. A special, heart-healthy menu features entrées such as halibut filet and herbed chicken. Seafood specials are offered each evening, and there's also a children's menu.

For some different fare, head for **Deschutes Brewery and Public House** (1044 Bond Street, Bend; 503-382-9242). This micro-brewery, known for its Cascade Golden Ale and Black Butte Porter, homemade root beer and ginger ale, offers a menu featuring items like pastrami reuben, buffalo wings and black-bean chili. Moderate.

Located in a chalet-style building behind a gasoline station, **Marcello's Italian Cuisine and Pizzeria** (★) (Beaver Drive and North Ponderosa Road, Sunriver; 503-593-8300) proves that location isn't everything. Locals pack this carpeted, brick dining room decorated with stained glass and hanging flower pots. Their reward is moderately priced pasta, veal and chicken specialties, as well as calzones, seafood and of course, a dozen varieties of pizza.

For deluxe-priced dining overlooking the Cascades, try **The Meadows** (Sunriver Lodge; 503-593-1221). You'll be seated on burgundy-colored chairs and served on white linen. Entrées include sautéed duck, crab cakes, wild-game ravioli, oysters and steaks. Also in the lodge is the moderately priced **Provision Company** (503-593-1221).

With picture windows and patio seating, **Poppy Seed Café** (Cascade Lakes Highway, west of Bend; 503-382-8711) offers moderate-priced dining at the Inn of the Seventh Mountain. Fettucini dishes, shrimp salads, steaks, burgers and sandwiches are all popular here.

If you're looking for a hearty breakfast or coffee-shop lunch fare, try the counter at the rustic **Elk Lake Resort** (★) (Cascade Lakes Highway, 32 miles west of Bend; radio phone YP7-3954). The knotty-pine-paneled dining area is a great place for bacon and eggs, blueberry pancakes or french toast. At lunch or dinner try the burgers, salads, sandwiches and, especially, the homemade pies. Although table service is available, we recommend taking a stool for the maximum waterfront view. Budget.

CENTRAL CASCADES SHOPPING

The Dromedary and Knotting Tree (140 West Cascade Street, Sisters; 503-549-8103) is a great place to browse. Jewelry, crafts, wallhangings, cotton afghans, pewter necklaces and tapestries are just a few of the possibilities at this eclectic shop.

If you're in the market for stained glass, wood sculpture, pottery or basketry, try the **Three Sisters Folk Art Center** (138 West Hood Street, Sisters; 503-549-9556).

You say it's hot out there and you left your bandanna back home? Those storm clouds are threatening and you forgot your rain jacket? About to head uphill on your 18 speed and your handlebars need adjustment? Then head to **Mountain Supply** (148 West Hood Street, Sisters; 503-549-3251). This hiking, biking and camping supply store also offers Patagonia shirts, topo maps, sunglasses and, for those who know when to quit, a hammock.

For Southwestern art and jewelry, leather handbags, gifts and accessories try **Coyote Creek Collective** (842 Northwest Wall Street, Bend; 503-389-3381). Also available are belts and leather goods.

Blue Spruce Pottery (★) (61021 South Route 97, Bend; 503-389-7745) offers a beautiful collection of ceramic vases, teapots, candlesticks, dishes, lamps, paintings, jewelry and decorative art.

The **High Desert Museum Store** (59800 South Route 97, Bend; 503-382-4754) is a great place to browse for Native American basketry, nature books, handmade jewelry, cards and photographs. The shop also offers bird feeders, mobiles, wildflower seeds and posters.

A good place to find Oregon dried fruits and nuts is **Sunfruits of Sunriver** (3078 North Route 97, Bend River Mall; 503-388-3232). Gift packs and baskets, including Oregon foods and wines, make nice things for the folks back home.

CENTRAL CASCADES NIGHTLIFE

The **Crooked River Dinner Train** (530 Southwest 6th Street, Redmond; 503-923-7626) operates a 38-mile-long desert run on Friday and Sunday nights in the summer months. Enjoy fine dining as you watch the sun set over the Cascades.

For rock bands head to the **River House** (3075 North Route 97, Bend; 503-389-3111). This contemporary lounge has a roomy dancefloor, full bar and spacious deck overlooking the Deschutes. In warm weather you can enjoy the music from the spacious deck.

Community Theatre of the Cascades (148 Northwest Greenwood, Bend; 503-389-0803) presents a variety of musicals and Broadway hits.

At Inn of the Seventh Mountain, **El Crab Catcher** (18575 Century Drive, west of Bend; 503-389-2722) has live music and dancing in the lounge.

CENTRAL CASCADES BEACHES AND PARKS

Detroit Lake State Park—This 104-acre park is a popular day-use and overnight facility on the shore of one of the busier Cascade Lakes. A forested spot on the north shore of Detroit Reservoir, the park is divided into two units. The smaller Mongold has lake frontage and picnic tables. To the east is the Lake Shore campground.

Facilities: Picnic area, restrooms and boat ramp; restaurants and groceries nearby in Detroit; information, 503-854-3346. *Swimming:* Good. *Fishing:* Go for the trout and kokanee salmon.

Camping: There are 311 sites including 107 full RV hookups.

Getting there: Located on Route 22, two miles west of Detroit.

Willamette National Forest—Roughly the size of New Jersey, this 1.6 million-acre region covers from 10,495-foot Mt. Jefferson to the Calapooya Mountains northeast of Roseburg. Diverse terrain ranges from volcanic moonscapes to wooded slopes and cascading rivers. One of the world's purest bodies of water, Waldo Lake is found here. More than 380,000 acres of wilderness encompass seven major Cascade peaks. Home to more than 300 species, including deer, cougar, grouse and Roosevelt elk, this forest also boasts more than 600 varieties of rhododendron. In the winter months, heavy snowfall traditionally blankets this popular nordic and alpine skiing area.

Facilities: Picnic tables, boat ramps, ski touring, interpretive centers and restrooms; information, 503-687-6521. *Fishing:* More than 1500 miles of rivers and streams, as well as 375 lakes, offer countless opportunities.

Camping: Permitted at over 80 campgrounds.

Getting there: Access is via Routes 22, 20, 126, 46, 242 and 58.

Ben and Kay Dorris State Park—A picturesque, 92-acre park blending river frontage with an old orchard that will tempt you to prolong your stay in Oregon. At the head of Martin Rapids, the park is shaded by Douglas fir and big-leaf maple that add color to the region in the fall months. While a mile of river frontage is the park's leading attraction, the "Rock House," an outcropping that provided shelter for pioneers traveling the historic wagon road, is also worth a visit.

Facilities: Picnic areas, restrooms and boat ramp. *Fishing:* One of Oregon's better places to catch trout.

Getting there: Located on Route 126, 31 miles east of Eugene.

Smith Rock State Park—Along steep Crooked River canyon, this day-use park is popular with climbers. They enjoy scaling striated Smith Rock, a formation rising several hundred feet above the tributary's north bank. Named for John Smith, a 19th-century pioneer, the park includes a forested bluff on the river's south bank.

Facilities: Picnic areas and restrooms. *Fishing:* Great for rainbows and smallmouth bass.

Getting there: Located on Northeast Crooked River Drive, east of Route 97, nine miles north of Redmond.

Tumalo State Park—Convenient to the Bend area in Deschutes River Canyon, it is forested with juniper, ponderosa pine, willow and poplar.

Named for "temolo," the Klamath Indian word for wild plum, the 329-acre park has handsome, basalt bluffs above the canyon.

Facilities: Picnic area, restrooms, playground and nature trails; restaurants and groceries in Bend; information, 503-388-6055. *Fishing:* Good for small trout.

Camping: There are 68 sites and 20 full RV hookups.

Getting there: Located six miles north of Bend on O. B. Riley Road off Route 20.

Drake Park—This verdant, 11-acre park is along the Deschutes River. Adjacent to downtown, it includes picturesque Mirror Pond.

Facilities: Picnic areas, playground (across the bridge at Harmon Park).

Getting there: Take Franklin Avenue west from Route 97 into downtown Bend where it becomes Riverside Boulevard. Continue west to the park.

Pilot Butte State Park—A cinder cone that served as a landmark for Oregon pioneers is the heart of this 100-acre urban park. Ascend to the top of this pine-covered butte to enjoy great views of the Cascades from Mt. St. Helens to the Three Sisters.

Facilities: None.

Getting there: Located on Greenwood Avenue in Bend, half-a-mile east of Route 20.

LaPine State Park (★)—This rolling Deschutes River Valley park is shaded by pine and old-growth forest. Expect to spot mule deer as you explore this uncrowded 2333-acre getaway. It's ideal for boating and a good base for visiting the surrounding volcanic landmarks including Newberry Crater, lava tubes and caves.

Facilities: Picnic areas, restrooms, showers and boating and wheelchair accessible; restaurants and groceries in Bend. *Fishing:* Fly cast for rainbow and brown trout.

Camping: There are 145 sites with hookups.

Getting there: Located east of Route 97 on LaPine State Park Road, 27 miles south of Bend.

Deschutes National Forest—Named for the popular river that descends the east slope of the Cascades, this 1.6 million-acre forest embraces Mt. Bachelor, the Three Sisters Wilderness, the Cascade Lakes region and Newberry National Volcanic Monument. Many popular resorts are found in the Deschutes forests, meadows and high country. Climbing from 2000 to 10,358 feet, the forest is dominated by ponderosa pine. Five wilderness areas are found in this forest known for its raftable rivers, spelunking and skiing. Bend is the most convenient jump-off point.

Facilities: Picnic tables, interpretive centers, marinas, ski areas, pack stations and restrooms; information, 503-388-2715. *Fishing:* More than 240 miles of streams and 158 lakes and reservoirs.

Camping: There are over 100 campgrounds throughout the national forest; call for details.

Getting there: Access via Routes 126, 242, 58, 97, 31, 20 and 46.

Southern Cascades

Blessed with several major wilderness areas, the Southern Cascades are also home of Oregon's only national park. A great region for viewing wildlife or birdwatching, this realm includes a real sleeper, the Klamath Lake area.

CRATER LAKE   One of the world's most famous mountain lakes, tucked inside the caldera of an exploded volcano, Crater Lake is known for its shimmering vistas and dark, cold depths. The best way to see this geologic wonder is to take **Rim Drive**, the 33-mile road circling Crater Lake. With more than 50 turnouts, it's the best way to enjoy an overview of this mountain-rimmed, deep-blue lake. Vertical lava flow patterns add to the majesty of the volcanic scenery.

While the crystal-clear waters are the prime attraction, the 2000-foot-high rim walls create an excellent cutaway view of the remains of Mt. Mazama. Allow at least five hours for this trip around the 20-square-mile, 2000-foot-deep lake. You'll want to begin your tour at the **Visitor Center** (503-594-2211) located across from **Rim Village**. A short walk below the crater rim is **Sinnott Memorial**. There's a small museum on this rock ledge, and rangers lead geology talks in the neighborhood. Continue clockwise around the lake to **Discovery Point** where explorer John Wesley Hillman became the first white man to spot this treasure in 1853. From here you'll want to go to major viewpoints. About three miles past Discovery Point is a turnout ideal for seeing one of the park's major volcanoes, **Union Peak**. Continue another seventh-tenths mile to **Wizard Island** overlook. It's named for the small Crater Lake island that is actually the top of a small volcano. For a panoramic view of the lake, ideal for photographs, pull off at **Steel Bay**. Rim Drive's highest viewpoint is **Cloudcap**. This is a great spot to see how part of Mt. Mazama was sliced away by the caldera's collapse. Also of special interest is **Pumice Castle**, an orange and pink landmark sculpted by the elements into a defensive formation.

The only access to the lakeshore is found at **Cleetwood Cove Trail**. This steep route takes you down to Cleetwood Boat Landing where you can tour the lake by boat (503-594-2511; admission). On this two-hour tour you'll be able to explore **Wizard Island**, a 700-foot-high cinder cone and see remnants of an older volcano called the **Phantom Ship**.

Although America's deepest (1932 feet) lake is the centerpiece of this national park, other attractions are well worth your time. Southeast of Rim Village you'll find **Steel Center**, an information office where you can see an 18-minute video on the lake as well as interpretive exhibits.

We also recommend visiting **The Pinnacles** area on the park's east side. Pumice and ash left behind by the Mt. Mazama collapse were gradually eroded by rain and snow. These formations evolved into rock pinnacles, further eroded by the elements into weird, hoodoo shapes. Today, hiking through these colorful canyons is one of the park's authentic pleasures.

Sixteen miles west of Crater Lake National Park in the vicinity of Union Creek is **Rogue River Gorge**. Here this mighty river is channeled into a beautiful, little canyon easily accessed on foot. It's a must for whitewater fans. In the same area, a mile west of Union Creek, is **Natural Bridge** where the Rogue flows into a lava tube for a short distance before reappearing. The bridge is well worth a visit and an easy walk.

KLAMATH LAKE REGION   While it is not in the mountains, its proximity to the high country makes it a favorite of travelers coming or going to them.

East of Crater Lake National Park is **Thunderbeast Park** (15 miles north of Chiloquin on Route 97; 503-783-2767) which features a dozen life-sized, prehistoric mammals including dinosaurs, horned rhinoceroses and saber-toothed tigers. In the gift shop you'll see bones of woolly mammoths.

One of the best ways to visit is via the **Upper Klamath Lake Tour Route**. Take Route 97 south to Chiloquin and then turn north on Route 62 to Fort Klamath. (If you're coming direct from Crater Lake simply take Route 62 south.) Several state parks, botanical areas, nature sites, canoe trails and waterfowl observation points make this trip a winner. Your first stop is **Fort Klamath Museum** (Sun Mountain Road, south of Fort Klamath; 503-381-2230). Built in 1863, this frontier post tells the story of the 1872–73 Modoc Indian War. Captain Jack and three other Native Americans executed after this uprising are buried here. Further south is the **Klamath Indian Tribal Museum** (Route 97, Chiloquin; 503-783-2218), distinguished by its basketry exhibits.

The centerpiece of your tour is **Upper Klamath Lake**. At roughly 64,000 acres, this is one of the state's largest lakes, extending nearly 25 miles to the town of Klamath Falls. The shallow waters here are prime fishing territory and a major wildlife refuge. One of the best birdwatching areas in the Pacific Northwest, these wetlands and marsh are also home to otter, beaver and muskrat.

In Klamath Falls, the **Baldwin Hotel** (31 Main Street; 503-883-4208; admission) has been restored to its turn-of-the-century heyday. A guided tour shows off the four-story building's architectural gems and historic memorabilia.

At the **Klamath County Museum** (1451 Main Street, Klamath Falls; 503-883-4208), flora and fauna and Native American and pioneer history are all on display. There's also a special exhibit on geothermal energy.

Also in the Klamath Falls area is the **Favell Museum of Western Art and Indian Artifacts** (125 West Main Street; 503-882-9996). The contemporary building features Native American art and artifacts, art of the West, taxidermy and a vast collection of miniature firearms. You won't have trouble finding arrowheads because more than 60,000 are on display.

SOUTHERN CASCADES HOTELS

For moderate-to-deluxe-priced cabins in a wooded setting, head for **Cultus Lake Resort** (50 miles southwest of Bend off Cascade Lakes Highway; radio phone YP7-3903). Twenty-three spacious, pine-paneled units with brick fireplaces, Western decor, alcove kitchens and drop-beam ceilings are set in a forest glen. The four-mile-long lake is great for sailing, fishing and kayaking. There's also a beach popular for sunbathing and swimming.

Zane Grey loved the north Umpqua River, and today a 31-mile stretch has been limited to "fly-fishing only." In the heart of the river region is **Steamboat Inn** (Route 138, 18 miles east of Idleyld Park; 503-463-3495). An eclectic mix of streamside cabins, hideaway cottages and river suites, the inn serves meals family style in the main lodge. Depending on your mood you can choose deluxe or ultra-deluxe accommodations done in Early American, Native American or contemporary motifs. Some of the two dozen units are pine paneled; others offer river views, mini-kitchens, fireplaces, hot tubs, quilted comforters and paintings by leading Northwest artists.

For budget-priced lodging in modernized one- and two-room units, check into **Singing Pines** (Route 97, Chemult; 503-365-9909) on the road from Bend to Crater Lake. A cut above your average strip motel, these eight units are clean and carpeted; some even have fireplaces. There's some highway noise but the price is worth it. Bar.

Because historic Crater Lake Lodge is closed for renovation until 1995, the only lodging in the national park is at **Mazama Village** (Route 62; 503-594-2511). Forty modern, moderately priced units are available from mid-May to late October. Board-and-batten exteriors, paneled interiors and wall-to-wall carpeting make these gray-toned accommodations rather appealing.

With 92 units, **Diamond Lake Resort** (Route 138, seven miles north of the Crater Lake entrance; 503-793-3333) is now the largest hostelry in the Crater Lake region. This complex includes 50 moderate-priced motel rooms, studios and 42 deluxe-priced cabins, all a short walk from the busy waterfront. Expect paneled, carpeted rooms with fireplaces, Franklin stoves and marine views. The studios and cabins come with kitchen facilities and, in some cases, private decks. The lake has a biking trail, boat rentals, birdwatching and hiking trails. While some find Diamond Lake too crowded for their tastes, it is convenient to many beautiful wilderness areas.

If you like the ambience of a historic inn but prefer the comfort of motel-style units, the **Prospect Historical Hotel and Motel** (★) (391 Mill Creek Road, Prospect; 503-560-3664) may be just the place. Located just a mile off Route 62, this white-frame establishment 20 miles from the west entrance to Crater Lake National Park has 14 cozy rooms with Early American furniture, quilts, watercolor prints and vanities. All are in the budget category, and some have kitchens. Or, if you prefer, choose one of the brass-bedded hotel rooms with floral-print wallpaper. These moderately tabbed bed and breakfast units also have quilt bedspreads, antiques and access to a pleasant front porch.

On the west side of Klamath Lake, **Crystal Creek Lodge** (★) (15 miles southeast of Fort Klamath; 503-381-2239) offers budget rooms convenient to birdwatching and fishing. With luck you may even spot a bald eagle. This remote lodge, known for its excellent restaurant, is halfway between Klamath Falls and Crater Lake. Paneled, second-story rooms feature king beds and wall-to-wall carpeting. An unusual getaway and exceptionally friendly service. Budget.

Motel-style units and moderate cabins convenient to Upper Klamath Lake's Pelican Bay are found at **Rocky Point Resort** (28121 Rocky Point Road, Klamath Falls; 503-356-2287). Set in a fir forest frequented by elk and deer, this waterfront resort is a good place to photograph bald eagles, osprey and white pelican colonies. The paneled rooms are clean and comfortable. Cabins offer kitchen facilities. Boat rentals, moorage, fishing tackle and guide service are all available on the premises. Budget.

For budget-priced lodging try the **Maverick Motel** (1220 Main Street, Klamath Falls; 503-882-4666). Forty-nine carpeted units are brightly painted and furnished with dark-wood furniture. There's a pool here. Among the many other motels in the downtown Klamath Falls area is **Molatore's Motor Inn** (100 Main Street; 503-882-4666). Moderate.

A moderately priced bed and breakfast, **Klamath Manor** (219 Pine Street, Klamath Falls; 503-883-5459) is a turn-of-the-century home with oak floors and staircases, french doors and a jacuzzi. Three rooms feature lace curtains, fresh flowers, brick fireplaces and poster beds. Afternoon tea and English or vegetarian breakfasts are served. Picnic lunches are available on request.

SOUTHERN CASCADES RESTAURANTS

With Native American decor, a menu featuring specialties like the buckaroo breakfast, and a parking lot filled with diesel rigs, station wagons and motorcycles, it's obvious that the **Wheel Café** (Route 97, Chemult; 503-365-2284) cultivates an eclectic clientele. Take a seat at the counter and order turkey, swiss cheese, bacon and tomato on a french roll, a chef's salad or plantation chicken. The peaches in the pie tasted like they had been picked the same morning. Budget.

For deluxe-priced dining, you'll have a hard time beating the **Steamboat Inn** (Route 138, 18 miles east of Idleyld Park; 503-463-3495). This establishment is famous for its fisherman's dinner. After enjoying aperitifs on the back porch, guests head inside to the lodge where dinner is served family style on gleaming wood tables illuminated by the glow of the fireplace. Appetizers are followed by salad, soup and homemade bread. Entrées include beef, fish, lamb or pork. Breakfasts here are also memorable. Don't miss the fruit rollups, an inn tradition.

For burgers, steak, chicken, fries, shakes and outstanding pies, head for the **Red Barn** (★) (Route 138, Glide; 503-496-0246) overlooking the Umpqua River. You can take a seat at the fir counter or settle in to one of the comfortable booths. Be sure to order the crispy bacon with your eggs at breakfast. Decorated with historic prints, the Red Barn also features a small gift shop. Budget.

Casual dining overlooking Crater Lake can be found at the **Watchman Deli Lounge** (Rim Village, Crater Lake; 503-549-2511). On the upper story of an A-frame lodge, this carpeted restaurant decorated with historic Oregon photos offers pizza, fresh salmon, chimichangas and salad. A modest establishment with moderate prices, the Watchman serves visitors while neighboring Crater Lake Lodge is being rebuilt.

An Early American setting makes the carpeted **Prospect Historical Hotel and Motel Restaurant** (★) (391 Mill Creek Road, Prospect; 503-560-3664) a comfortable dining spot. From the combination seafood plate to the prime rib, this establishment will challenge any dieter's willpower. Entrées like grilled ham steak and barbecued ribs come with soup, salad, vegetables, potatoes, dinner rolls, beverage and dessert. Although the ambience is elegant, prices are moderate.

It's not uncommon for Oregonians to drive 100 miles or more to enjoy a meal at **Crystal Creek Lodge** (★) (Westside Road, 15 miles southeast of Fort Klamath; 503-381-2239). This pine-paneled dining room with an exposed-beam ceiling and Franklin stove offers memorable home cooking. You'll be hard pressed to finish the a la carte portions of barbecue beef ribs, chicken kiev or New York steak. If you're famished, go for one of the deluxe-priced dinners with french fries, baked potato and mixed vegetables. Topped off with a slice of homemade pie, this is one of the Pacific Northwest's better bets.

With its beautiful setting overlooking Klamath Lake, rustic **Rocky Point Resort** (28121 Rocky Point Road, Klamath Falls; 503-356-2287) is known for its freshly caught seafood. At this lodge-style restaurant you'll also enjoy steaks, chicken, pies and cakes. Moderate.

When an Oregon restaurant boasts of its "San Francisco Bay Area at-mosphere" you know you're in for a real dining experience. **Alice's Saddle Rock Café** (1012 Main Street, Klamath Falls; 503-884-1444) is as unpre-tentious as the town it calls home. But the interior is a fine example of adap-tive reuse with handsome brick walls and modern art. Go for the steaks, pasta dishes, burgers or salads. Moderate.

Moderately priced **Classico Italian Ristorante** (404 Main Street, Klamath Falls; 503-883-6412) serves in a spacious, brick-walled dining room illuminated by Tiffany-style lamps and cooled by Casablanca-style fans. Diners seated in captain's chairs at glass tables can start on stuffed potato skins or deep-fried cauliflower, move on to minestrone and pasta or order a steak, stuffed sole or charbroiled-chicken salad.

Across the street from the Amtrak station, **Valliers** (15770 Oak Av-enue, Klamath Falls; 503-884-6121) is a good place for hearty breakfasts, sandwiches, steaks, liver and onions and homemade cinnamon rolls and pies. This coffee shop offers counter and table service. Budget.

SOUTHERN CASCADES SHOPPING

An excellent collection of Indian and Western art, limited-edition prints, squash-blossom jewelry and arrowheads is found at the **Favell Museum Gift Shop** (125 West Main Street, Klamath Falls; 503-882-9996). Exhibited in an attractive, two-story shop, this store features many one-of-a-kind pieces.

For knives, cutlery, beads and beading supplies, Native American ear-rings, buckskins and leather goods visit **Oregon Trail Outfitters** (5728 South 6th Street, Klamath Falls; 503-883-1369). This board-and-batten building is extremely popular with visitors searching for a piece of the Old West. The owners frequently help stage historic rendezvous. Participants clad in traditional buckskin costumes demonstrate muzzle loading, knife and tomahawk throwing, fire-starting with flint steel and cannon shoots.

SOUTHERN CASCADES NIGHTLIFE

Ross Ragland Theater (218 North 7th Street, Klamath Falls; 503-884-5483) is a performing center offering touring theater companies, country and western bands, jazz and blues, classical performers and locally produced musicals. The year-around calendar also includes special children's shows and, in the summer, locally produced musicals.

The Linkville Playhouse (201 Main Street, Klamath Falls; 503-884-6782) offers plays and musicals throughout the year. The local productions feature Broadway classics ranging from *The Crucible* to *Blithe Spirit*. The company is known for its comedies.

SOUTHERN CASCADES BEACHES AND PARKS

Jackson F. Kimball State Park (★)—The 19-acre Klamath County park is a scenic, forested spot on the headwaters of the Wood River. Ideal for those seeking a quiet getaway.

Facilities: Picnic area; restaurants and groceries nearby in Fort Klamath. *Fishing:* Good fly fishing for rainbow and brown trout.

Camping: There are six primitive sites.

Getting there: On Route 232, three miles north of Fort Klamath.

Joseph Stewart State Park—A lush lawn leads down to Lost Creek Lake, making this park on the road to Crater Lake particularly inviting on a warm day. With 910 acres, there's room to spare for day and overnight use. Take a seat on a blanket beneath one of the pine groves and watch the waterskiers slalom their way to happiness. Or toss in a line and wait for the big ones to nibble. With more than a mile of waterfront, this Rogue River Canyon park is a great place to take the kids.

Facilities: Picnic area, restrooms, marina, boat launch, bike and hiking trails and wheelchair accessible; information, 503-560-3334. *Swimming:* Permitted. *Fishing:* Excellent for bass, rainbow, brook or brown trout.

Camping: There are 201 sites, some with hookups.

Getting there: Located 35 miles north of Medford on Route 62.

Umpqua National Forest—Named for the Umpqua Indians, this forest spans almost a million acres and embraces three wilderness areas, numerous secluded waterfalls and high-country trails. Within the Umpqua are volcanic ridges, pine benches, alpine forests and meadows laced by snow-fed streams. Among the Umpqua landmarks are the world's tallest sugar pine, bedrock gorges and volcanic-rock arches. Major destinations include the scenic Umpqua River Canyon and Diamond, Lemolo and Toketee lakes. Also convenient to Crater Lake.

Facilities: Picnic tables, history programs, boat ramps, pack stations, skiing, bike and hiking trails and restrooms; information, 503-672-6601. *Fishing:* Hundreds of miles of streams and numerous lakes make this a great spot for angling.

Camping: There are 33 sites.

Getting there: Access by Routes 138, 227, 62 and 230.

Mill Pond Park (★)—With half a mile of frontage on Rock Creek, this serene campground is a beautiful getaway on the edge of the Umpqua National Forest near Idleyld Park. It has a picturesque swimming hole and towering, moss-covered trees and, is the small Oregon park at its finest.

Facilities: Picnic areas, playground, restrooms; groceries and restaurants in Idleyld Park. *Swimming:* Permitted.

Camping: There are 12 sites.

Getting there: From Idleyld Park take Route 138 east to Route 78 and head north three miles.

Crater Lake National Park—One of the unique geologic features of the Pacific Northwest, Crater Lake is irresistible. The 183,180-acre park offers hundreds of miles of hiking and cross-country skiing trails, a fascinating boat tour of this volcanic lake and opportunities for biking, fishing and backpacking.

Facilities: Picnic areas, restaurants, motel units and museums; information 503-594-2211. *Fishing:* Nothing to get excited about though there are rainbow, kokanee and brook trout around.

Camping: There are 198 sites at Mazama Campground and 16 tent sites at Lost Creek. Backcountry camping by permit. Closed in winter.

Getting there: On Route 62, 55 miles northwest of Klamath Falls.

Winema National Forest—Between Crater Lake National Park and Upper Klamath Lake, the national forest is famous for its fishing and waterfowl habitat. Although the forest elevation ranges from roughly 4100 to 9200 feet, much of the eastern portion of this semiarid region is high-plateau country. The Winema is forested with pine and fir and has several roadless places including the Mountain Lakes Wilderness Area. More than 200 bird species have been identified on this Pacific Flyway. In addition, elk, deer, bear, coyote, bobcat, beaver, otters and many other species live here.

Facilities: Picnic tables, skiing, rock hounding, hiking, ski touring, boat ramps and restrooms; information, 503-883-6714. *Fishing:* Forty lakes and rivers like the Sycan, Sprague and Williamson offer good opportunities to catch trout, salmon and mullet.

Camping: There are 11 campgrounds.

Getting there: Routes 97, 232 and 140 all provide easy access.

Collier Memorial State Park—Set in a ponderosa-pine forest at the junction of Spring Creek and Williamson River, this 655-acre park is an ideal place to spend the day or the night. The park is also a logging heritage site, filled with important mementos and lumberjack equipment.

Facilities: Picnic tables, restrooms, playground and museum; restaurants and groceries 30 miles south in Klamath Falls; information, 503-783-2471. *Fishing:* Good trout fishing in the streams.

Camping: There are 18 sites and 50 full hookups.

Getting there: From Klamath Falls go north 30 miles on Route 97.

The Sporting Life

FISHING

The Oregon Cascades are famous for rivers and lakes brimming with trout, salmon, bass and steelhead. Whether you bring your own boat, fish from shore or hire a guide to take you downriver in a classic McKenzie River drift boat, you won't go away disappointed.

Companies offering fishing charters include **Michael Gehrman** (6700 Cooper Spur Road, Mt. Hood; 503-352-6457), **Deschutes River Tours** (1921 Cherry Lane, Madras; 503-475-3550) and **Michael McLucas** (Oasis Café, Maupin; 503-395-2611).

Further south try the **Fly Fisher's Place** (230 Main Street, Sisters; 503-549-3474), **Mid Columbia Outfitters** (61345 Brosterhouse Road, Bend; 503-382-2254), **Rick Killingsworth** (721 Northwest Ogden Street, Bend; 503-389-0607), **Pat Schatz/Mickey Finn Guide Service** (Bend; 503-382-2787), **Sunriver Guides and Outfitters Ltd.** (Sunriver; 503-593-5057) or **Jim's Oregon Whitewater** (56324 McKenzie Highway, McKenzie Bridge; 503-822-6003).

North River Guide Service (Glide; 503-496-0309) offers trips on the Umpqua. In the Klamath Falls area call **Siens Guide Service** (1236 Shadow Lane, Klamath Falls; 503-883-2642).

GOLF

In the Northern Cascades region, the **Resort at the Mountain** (68010 East Fairway Avenue, Welches; 503-622-3101) offers a 27-hole course. **Kah-Nee-Ta Golf Course** (Warm Springs; 503-553-1112) is often a sunny alternative to socked-in western Oregon courses. **Black Butte Ranch** (Route 20, eight miles west of Sisters; 503-595-6689), **Seventh Mountain Golf Village** (five miles west of Bend on Century Drive; 503-382-4449) and **Mountain High Golf Course** (60650 China Hat Road, Bend; 503-382-1111) are other good possibilities. South of Bend you'll find **Sunriver Lodge and Resort**'s two 18-hole courses (Sunriver; 503-593-1221) and **Quail Run** (two miles west of entrance to Newberry National Monument; 503-536-1303).

Set above the McKenzie River Valley, the **Tokatee Golf Club** (★) (5947 McKenzie Highway, Blue River; 503-822-3220) is one of the most picturesque courses in the Pacific Northwest.

In the Southern Cascades, the **Circle Bar Golf Club** (Oakridge; 503-782-3541) and **Harbor Links Golf Course** (Harbor Isles Boulevard, Klamath Falls; 503-882-0663) are in the fore.

TENNIS

While some public courts are found at city parks and schools, many resorts like Black Butte limit their courts to guests. These courts are open to the public:

Kah-Nee-Ta Resort (Warm Springs; 503-553-1112) rents courts. The **Bend Metro Park and Recreation District** (503-389-7275) offers courts at Juniper Park, Franklin Avenue and Northwest 8th Street, Sylvan Park, Three Sisters Drive on the north side of Aubrey Butte and Summit Park at Summit and Promontory drives. **Sunriver Lodge and Resort** (Sunriver Junction at Route 97, 15 miles south of Bend; 503-593-1221) rents courts. In Sisters head for **Sisters Middle School** (Cascade and Camp Polk Road; 503-549-8521). In Klamath Falls, courts are available at **Moore Park** (Lakeshore Drive; 503-883-5391), **Hilyard Park** (Hilyard Avenue and Crest Street; 503-883-4696) and **Wiard Park** (Wiard Street at Hilyard Avenue; 503-882-3193).

SKIING

Skiing in July? It's possible in Oregon's endless winter. With one of the longest ski seasons in the West, the Cascades offer a ton of alpine and nordic opportunities.

In the Northern Cascades the best-known resorts are found on the slopes of Mt. Hood. They include the venerable **Timberline Resort** (Timberline; 503-272-3311) with six chairlifts serving open-bowl and tree-lined runs. Three lifts operate at night. From May to September the resort offers a summer season at the 8500-foot level.

Other resorts serving the same area are **Mt. Hood Skibowl** (503-272-3206) with day and night skiing on 61 trails and **Mt. Hood Meadows** (503-337-2222) with nine chairlifts serving 62 trails. This resort features a ski program for the physically challenged.

On Route 20's Santiam Pass west of Sisters, **Hoodoo Ski Bowl** (503-385-1048) is a good bet for families looking for alpine or nordic skiing. **Mt. Bachelor** (503-389-5900) west of Bend is Oregon's largest ski area, offering dry powder and a season extending to July. Nine chairs serve 6000 skiable acres. Mt. Bachelor also offers extensive, groomed nordic trails as does **Blue Lake Nordic Center** (west of Sisters; 503-595-6675). Nordic trail maps are available from the Bend Chamber of Commerce.

Crater Lake National Park has extensive nordic trails with views of the blue water beneath the snowcapped rim (503-594-2511). Diamond Lake Resort also has nordic trails as well as snowcat skiing on **Mount Bailey** (503-793-3333). The latter, limited to just a dozen people per day, transports skiers uphill to enjoy 3000 feet of deep-powder terrain.

HORSEBACK RIDING

Kah-Nee-Ta (Warm Springs; 503-553-1112) organizes guided trail rides across scenic, red-rock country. This is an excellent way to see one of the Northwest's largest Native American reservations.

A great way to explore the Central Cascades is to saddle up at **Black Butte Ranch** (Route 20, eight miles west of Sisters; 503-595-6211). Nearby **Blue Lake Resort** (13900 Blue Lake Drive, 20 miles west of Sisters off Route 20; 503-595-6671) also offers guided trail rides. **High Cascade Stables and Pack Station** (70775 Indian Ford Road, Sisters; 503-549-4972) operates two-hour rides, all-day wilderness rides and overnight pack trips in the Three Sisters, Mt. Jefferson or Mt. Washington wilderness areas.

At **Inn of the Seventh Mountain** (18575 Century Drive, Bend; 503-389-9458) Nova Stables leads a variety of intriguing trail rides up into the Cascades.

In the Southern Cascades, near Crater Lake, **Diamond Lake Resort** (503-793-3310) is the place to go for guided day rides.

RAFTING

Wonderful rafting opportunities await you here. **Jim's Oregon Whitewater** (56324 McKenzie Highway, McKenzie Bridge; 503-822-6003) leads day trips on the McKenzie River. **Rapid River Rafts** (60107 Cinder Butte Road, Bend; 503-382-1514) runs one-to-four-day whitewater packages on the McKenzie, Umpqua and Deschutes rivers. **Hunter Expeditions** (Route 97, Bend; 503-389-8370) and Sunriver Mall, Sunriver; 503-593-3113) specializes in half-day, full-day and overnight expeditions on the Deschutes.

BICYCLING

From easy town rides to mountain biking on rugged backcountry trails, the Oregon Cascades offer thousands of miles of scenic cycling.

Mountain-bike trails in the Zigzag Ranger District offer scenic views of the Mt. Hood region. Among the best is the 12-mile **Still Creek Road**. This rarely traveled route connects Trillium Lake with the town of Rhododendron. The ten-mile **Sherap Burn Road/Veda Lake** trail leads up to outstanding viewpoints.

In the Bend area take **West Newport Avenue** for a six-mile trip to Shevlin Park or follow **O. B. Riley Road** five miles to Tumalo State Park. Another possibility is to take the road east 23 miles from Route 97 to **Newberry Volcano**.

At Black Butte Ranch, 16 miles of bike paths include the **Lodge Loop** (five miles) and the scenic **Glaze Meadow Loop** (four miles).

A popular **Cascades Loop** trail begins in Bend, heads west on Century Drive to Mt. Bachelor and then continues on Cascades Lakes Highway to Route 58. Allow several days to enjoy these demanding 74 miles.

One of the most popular biking trails in the Southern Cascades is the 11-mile **Diamond Lake Bike Path**. This level route is ideal for the whole family. The route takes cyclists from Thielsen View Campground to Silent Creek. Complete the loop on the highway returning to Thielsen View. A two-mile section of this route is wheelchair accessible.

The ultimate biking experience at Crater Lake is **Rim Drive** offering the complete 33-mile overview of this volcanic landmark. Another excellent possibility is **Grayback Trail**, a scenic, unpaved route ideal for mountain bikes. In Klamath Falls, **Nevada Avenue** and **Lakeshore Drive** provide convenient bike-touring access to Upper Klamath Lake. This route continues west to Route 140 along the lake's west shore. **Kit Carson Way** also has a separated bike path.

For more information on biking in the Cascades region contact the **Bend Alpenglo Velo Club** (503-385-2655).

BIKE RENTALS   In Bend contact **High Cascade Descent** (333 Riverfront Street; 503-389-0562) or **Skjersaa's** (130 Southwest Century Drive; 503-382-2154). In Sunriver head for the **Chrome Pony** (1 West Mall; 503-593-2728).

HIKING

With hundreds of miles of trails, including many in wilderness areas, the Oregon Cascades are ideal for relaxed rambles or ambitious journeys. All are best tackled in the warmer seasons and not recommended in the winter months.

NORTHERN CASCADES TRAILS   **Zigzag Trail** (1 mile) takes you across the Hood River's east fork via a drawbridge (closed in winter). You'll continue up the canyon to Dog River Trail, which leads to a viewpoint overlooking Mt. Hood and the Upper Hood River Valley.

Tamanawas Falls Loop (5.5 miles) leads along the north bank of Mt. Hood National Forest's Cold Spring Creek. After hiking to scenic Tamanawas Falls you'll return to the trailhead via Elk Meadows Trail.

Also in Mt. Hood National Forest is **Castle Canyon Trail** (2 miles) climbing out of the Rhododendron area to rocky pinnacles. Views of the scenic Zigzag Valley are your reward.

Another relatively easy possibility is **Bonney Meadow Trail**, reached by taking Route 35 to Bennett Pass and then following Routes 3550 and 4891 to Bonney Meadows Campground. Take trail #473 east along the ridge (3.5 miles) to enjoy the views of Boulder and Little Boulder lakes. Return to the campground by turning right on trail #472.

CENTRAL CASCADES TRAILS   Located 33.4 miles west of Sisters off Route 20 is **Black Butte Trail** (2 miles) a steep route to the top of a volcanic cone.

About one mile further west on Route 20 is Blue Lake, where **Crater Rim Trail** (2.5 miles) offers an easy ramble around this scenic landmark.

In the Detroit Lake area you might want to try **Tumble Ridge Trail** (5.3 miles), which begins on Route 22. This demanding trek heads up through second-growth forest, past Dome and Needle rocks to Tumble Lake.

One of the newest hikes is the **Little North Santiam Trail** (★) (4.2 miles). Built along the Little North Santiam River, it crosses eight tributaries with stringer bridges. Fishing and swimming holes are easily reached from this trail leading through old-growth forests.

Return east on Route 20 and turn south on Route 126. Continue for eight miles to Robinson Lake Road and go east 4.4 miles to **Robinson Lake Trail** (★) (.3 mile). It's an easy, family hike leading to a pleasant hideaway.

In the McKenzie Bridge area the **Olallie Trail** (9.7 miles) is an all-day-hike offering memorable views of the Three Sisters, Mt. Washington, Mt. Jefferson and Bachelor Butte. Take this trail in the summer and fall. The trailhead is three miles from Horse Creek Road.

For an easier hike off McKenzie Pass Highway (Route 242) take the **Lava River Trail** (.5 mile). This interpretive trail beginning near the Dee Wright Trail leads through lava flows. Signs add to your understanding of this moonscape's volcanic past. Wheelchair accessible.

To the south the Willamette National Forest's Oakridge Ranger District offers many fine hikes including **Fisher Creek Trail** (2.5 miles). A great way to see a primitive-forest region, you'll get a closeup view of old-growth trees. The silence is deafening. The **Waldo Lake Trail** (21.8 miles) is a challenging route around this incredibly pure lake.

The **Lava River Cave Trail** (1.2 miles) is an easy, rather chilly trail through the state's largest lava tube. It's off Route 97 south of Bend near the High Desert Museum. Lanterns are available close to the parking lot.

Fourteen miles south of Bend off Route 97, **Lava Cast Forest Nature Trail** (.9 mile) takes you through one of the Pacific Northwest's weirdest landscape. You'll see tree molds created when molten lava destroyed a forest thousands of years ago.

SOUTHERN CASCADES TRAILS   Off Route 62, the road from Medford to Crater Lake, the **Upper Rogue River Trail** (6.5 miles) is an easy ramble. Begin at the Prospect Ranger Station and make your way through sugar pines, pausing along the way to cool off in the stream.

Toketee Lake Trail (.6 mile) runs parallel to this spot. Short spurs lead to the waterfront where you'll find otter, beaver and ducks complementing the scenery.

The **North Umpqua Trail** (77 miles) offers a wide variety of hiking opportunities. Crossing both the Boulder Creek and Mt. Thielsen wilderness areas, most of this route is easy to moderate. Spur trails lead to waterfalls, fishing spots and campgrounds. Among the North Umpqua's most popular segments are **Panther Trail** (5 miles) beginning at Steamboat and **Lemolo Trail** (6.3 miles) starting at Lemolo Lake.

Mt. Bailey Trail (5 miles) is a steep route west of Diamond Lake. Your reward for climbing 3000 feet is a panoramic view of Diamond Lake, Mt. Thielsen and the Southern Cascades.

Running 2570 miles from Canada to Mexico, the **Pacific Crest Scenic Trail** is western America's back door to the wilderness, the kind of place John Muir lived for. Scenic, uncrowded, larger than life, it's worth a special trip. You can pick up a 30-mile segment at the North Crater Trailhead, a mile east of the Crater Lake National Park Trailhead on Route 138. Hike as much of this section as you care to. You can exit via the Tipsoo, Howlock Mountain, North Umpqua or Mt. Thielsen trails.

CRATER LAKE NATIONAL PARK   **Watchman Peak Trail** (.8 mile) is a steep route up Watchman Peak. From the top you'll have a great view of Wizard Island.

It's ironic that most visitors to Crater Lake never actually reach the shore. Doing so requires a steep descent on **Cleetwood Cove Trail** (1 mile). This is the route that leads to boat tours of Wizard Island.

For a good workout try the **Mount Scott Trail** (2.5 miles). Along the way you'll spot many small animals and birds. The gnarled whitebark pines make a good photographic backdrop. On top you'll have a 360-degree view of the park.

To see the park's impressive pinnacles take **Godfrey Glen Trail** (★) (1 mile). This route leads through a hemlock and red-fir forest to Sand Creek Canyon.

East of Crater Lake Lodge, **Garfield Peak Trail** (1.7 miles) is a fairly steep route offering views of the lake. Look for eagles and hawks along the way.

A short walk in the park is **Castle Crest Wildflower Trail** (★) (.4 mile). This easy loop is the best way to sample Oregon wildflowers in mid-summer. An eden-like setting with small streams trickling down the hillside, the trail is one of Oregon's best-kept secrets.

Sevenmile Trail/Pacific Crest Trail (15 miles) west of Fort Klamath off Route 3334 is a great way to see the Sky Lakes Wilderness south of Crater Lake National Park. Sevenmile Trail hooks up with the Pacific Coast Trail for a 2.5-mile stretch and then cuts off to Seven Lakes Basin. You can also follow the Pacific Crest Trail to Devil's Pass and the steep ascent of Devil's Peak.

Transportation

BY CAR

The Oregon Cascades are a 50-to-100-mile-wide band extending almost the entire length of the state. They begin on the eastern edge of the Willamette Valley and Ashland-Rogue River area and extend to the high-desert region of central Oregon.

Route 26 travels east from Portland to the Mt. Hood area. You can also reach Mt. Hood by taking **Route 35** south from the Hood River area.

From Salem take **Route 22** east to the Detroit Lakes and Santiam Pass area. **Route 20** east of Albany leads to the same destination, while **Route 126** is Eugene's mainline east to the McKenzie Bridge and McKenzie Pass area. **Route 58** southeast of Eugene is convenient to the Deschutes National Forest, and **Route 138** takes you from Roseburg to the Umpqua River Canyon.

From Medford take **Route 62** northeast to Crater Lake. An alternate route to Crater Lake is **Route 97** north of Klamath Falls. This same highway also provides access to the Bend area and the Central Cascades. If you're coming from the east, Routes 20 and 26 are the most convenient ways to reach the mountains.

BY AIR

Redmond Airport, 16 miles north of Bend, is served by Horizon Airlines and United Express. **Klamath Falls Airport** is served by Horizon Airlines and American Eagle. **Portland International Airport**, **Eugene** and **Medford airports** are also convenient to the Cascades.

Call-A-Van (503-382-1687) provides limousine service from the Redmond Airport to Bend and Cascades destinations like Sunriver, Mt. Bachelor, Sisters and Black Butte Ranch. **Trans Central** (503-382-9371) provides airport and resort service as well as transportation to Amtrak in Chemult. Ground transportation is also provided by **Redmond Taxi** (503-923-8830). In Klamath Falls call **Klamath Kab** (503-882-7875).

Mt. Hood Express (503-250-4379) offers limousine van service from the Portland airport to the popular Northern Cascades recreation area.

BY TRAIN

Amtrak's "Coast Starlight" (800-872-7245) is a scenic and comfortable way to reach the Cascades. It serves stations in Klamath Falls, Chemult, Eugene, Salem, Albany and Portland, all convenient starting points for the mountain resorts.

BY BUS

Greyhound/Trailways Bus Lines has service to depots at Klamath Falls (1200 Klamath Avenue; 503-882-4616) and Bend (2045 Northeast Route 20; 503-382-2151) as well as stops at McKenzie Bridge, Sisters, Chemult (503-365-2284) and Government Camp (503-272-3325). **Oregon Bus Line** (800-452-2877) runs from Salem to Bend, with stops at Detroit, Black Butte Ranch and Sisters.

CAR RENTALS

Arriving passengers at the Redmond Airport are served by **Budget Rent A Car** (503-389-3031), **Hertz Rent A Car** (503-923-1411) and **National Car Rental** (503-548-8166).

Klamath Falls Airport is served by **Avis Rent A Car** (503-882-7232), **Budget Rent A Car** (503-885-5421) and **Hertz Rent A Car** (503-882-0220).

In Bend you can rent from **Budget Rent A Car** (503-389-3031), **Cheap Wheels Car Rental** (503-389-8893), **Hertz Rent A Car** (503-382-1711) and **Rent A Wreck** (503-385-3183).

PUBLIC TRANSPORTATION

Lane Transit District (503-687-5555) serves McKenzie Bridge. **Basin Transit Service** (503-883-2877) operates in the Klamath Falls area. In Bend local service is provided by **Transcentral** (503-382-0800).

CHAPTER TEN

The Heart of Oregon

Drivers in a hurry barrel down Oregon's 280-mile Route 5 corridor in about five hours. Incredibly, that's the way many people see the region that lies at the end of the fabled Oregon Trail. Tempted by free land or the prospect of finding gold, the pioneers risked everything to get here. Today a new generation, rushing to reach Crater Lake, Mt. Hood or the Oregon Coast, speeds through, never knowing what they've missed.

That's progress. Fortunately all it takes is a trip down a Route 5 offramp to get hooked on the Heart of Oregon, the 60-mile wide region that extends from Salem to the California border. With the freeway left behind in the rearview mirror, you may understand why residents say God spent six days creating the Earth and on the seventh he went to Oregon.

Framed by the Klamath and Coast ranges on the west and the Cascades on the east, this is the place to find peaceful covered bridges and exciting rafting runs, the nation's oldest Shakespeare festival and a legislature that has made Oregon America's most environmentally conscious state. Home to two major universities, the center of Oregon agriculture and some of its most historic towns, this region is also where you'll find many of Oregon's best-known writers, poets, artists and artisans.

Just an hour from the state's famous mountain and seaside resorts, the Willamette Valley and the Ashland-Rogue River areas are the primary destinations in the Heart of Oregon. Fields of wildflowers, small towns with falsefront stores and gabled homes, businesses with names like "Wild and Scenic Trailer Park," pies made with fresh-picked marionberries—this is the Oregon found in the postcard rack. Soda fountains with mirrored back-bars, jazz preservation societies, old river ferries, museums built out of railroad cars, music festivals and folk-art shrines—you'll find them all and even more here.

In many ways this region's heritage, touted by writers ranging from Washington Irving to Zane Grey, sums up the evolution of the West: Native Americans followed by British fur traders, American explorers, missionaries, pioneer settlers, gold miners and the merchants who served them. The 19th-century *nouveau riche* tapped the hardwood forests to create Victorian mansions. As the mines were played out, lumber and agriculture became king. Strategically located on the main stage and rail lines to California and Washington, this corridor also became the principal gateway to most of Oregon's cities, as well as its emerging mountain retreats and coastal beaches.

But the Heart of Oregon story also has a special dimension, one told at local museums and historic sites. The fatal impact of American expansion on the Native American culture began with the arrival of missionaries who preached Christianity but left behind diseases that decimated their converts. In 1843 the promise of free land triggered a stampede as "Oregon or bust" pioneers stampeded west. Many became farmers who prospered in the California trade after gold was discovered in 1848 at Sutter's Mill. Three years later, after gold was found closer to home near Jacksonville, many settlers put down their plows and made a beeline for the mines. A new boom brought instant prosperity to this sleepy town as millions in gold dust poured through banks on California Street and miners dazzled their brides with mansions shipped in piecemeal from Tennessee.

Not sharing in this windfall were Native Americans pushed from their ancestral lands by the settlers and miners. The Indians fought back in the Rogue River Wars between 1851 and 1856. But they were ultimately forced onto reservations, easing the path to statehood in 1859. Settled by Methodist missionaries in 1840, the capital of Salem was one of several towns that emerged as a regional supply center. Others included Eugene and Corvallis.

As the railroad improved access to this area, businessmen discovered there was more to sell in Oregon than gold, lumber, dairy products and bountiful crops. Visitors began to explore the fishing streams, caves and forests. Chautauqua tents brought intellectuals and entertainers to Ashland, as Jacksonville offered a different kind of nightlife that gave preachers something to denounce on their pulpits. When Zane Grey showed up to fish the Rogue and the Umpqua rivers, the entire country read about it in his articles. As the good word spread, more visitors began arriving to raft these and other rivers, to see the waterfalls and photograph the vernacular architecture.

Although it was a long way from Middle America, the tourists loved the region's Main Street look and unspoiled countryside. Culturally the region became a hub for social experiments and alternative lifestyles, happily exported by local celebrities like Ken Kesey, who took his famous traffic-stopping bus on a national tour with the "Merry Pranksters" in the 1960s.

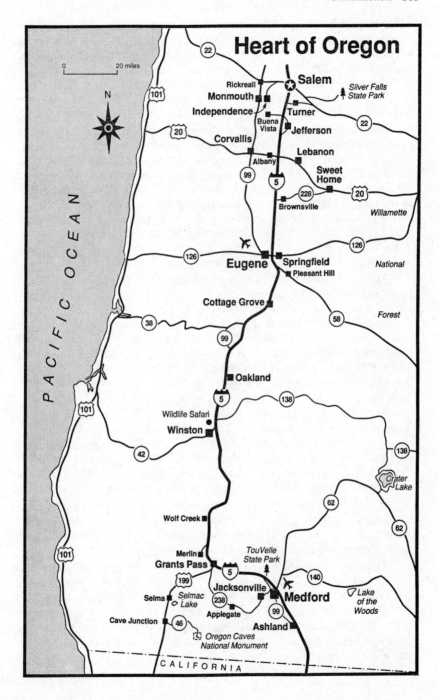

Heart of Oregon

0   20 miles

N

PACIFIC OCEAN

22

101

20

99

5

22

Rickreall
Monmouth
Independence
Buena Vista

Salem

Silver Falls
State Park

Turner
Jefferson

Corvallis

Albany

Lebanon

Sweet
Home

126

228

Brownsville

Willamette

126

Eugene

Springfield
Pleasant Hill

National

Cottage Grove

58

Forest

38

99

Oakland

5

138

Wildlife Safari
Winston

42

138

Crater
Lake

62

62

Wolf Creek

101

Merlin
Grants Pass

199

5

TouVelle
State Park

Jacksonville

238

140

Medford

Lake
of the
Woods

Selma

Selmac
Lake

99

Cave Junction

46

Applegate

Ashland

Oregon Caves
National Monument

CALIFORNIA

Although the Heart of Oregon can be overcast and wet during the winter months, summers tend to be sunny and hot, particularly in the Ashland-Rogue River area. While Route 5 is the mainline, Route 99 is a pleasant alternative. Because the Willamette Valley is flat, it's ideal terrain for cyclists. South of Eugene, the Klamath mountains frame picturesque valleys and towns like Medford, Ashland and Jacksonville. At the bottom of the state the Siskiyous form the backdrop to the California border.

Because this is the state's primary transportation corridor, it's convenient to scores of popular attractions. An hour from the beach or the Cascades, this is the kind of place where you can easily spend your days waterskiing or spelunking and your nights enjoying King Lear. Blessed with some of the finest resorts and restaurants in the Pacific Northwest, the Heart of Oregon is also a great place to go birdwatching thanks to several wildlife preserves found along the Willamette River. Here you're likely to spot great blue herons, red-tailed hawks, quails and woodpeckers. Deer, fox, opossums, coyotes and raccoons abound in the valley, while elk, bobcats, bear and flying squirrels are found in the southern mountains.

The region's highlands, which offer hundreds of miles of remote hiking trails, are pocketed by pristine lakes with resort lodges paneled in knotty pine. There's even downhill skiing on the highest peak here, 7000-foot Mt. Ashland. But there's little doubt that the signature attraction between Salem and Ashland is its river valleys. From the Willamette wetlands to the swimming holes of Applegate River, it's hard to beat the streamside life. Rushing down from the Cascades, roaring through Hellgate Canyon, flowing through restaurants at the Oregon Caves, these tributaries define every area and delight every visitor.

One of the most attractive features is the proximity to the wilderness. You are seldom more than 15 or 20 minutes from the countryside, and even the bigger towns, like Eugene and Salem, have major greenbelts within the city limits. The Salem region is the center of Oregon's wine country. While the state capitol is the primary attraction, many historic restorations and historic neighborhoods add to the charm of the central city.

Eugene's college-town status gives it the amenities you would expect in a larger community. Its central location makes the city an ideal base for visiting most of the state's popular destinations. And the city's Ecotopian fervor, shows what can happen when environmentalists take control.

Jacksonville, one of the state's most historic cities, is a delightful period piece, the kind of town where bed and breakfasts outnumber motels ten to one. The tree-lined streets, red-brick office blocks and historic bars make the town a favorite. Artists flock here and to Ashland, an Oregon mecca for the dramatic arts. Thoroughly gentrified, heavily booked and loaded with great restaurants, Ashland is the state's last temptation and a hard one to leave on the route south. No mere stepping stone to other parts of the state, the Heart of Oregon is an end in itself.

Salem Area

Although it is best known as Oregon's capital, Salem offers many other attractions that make it a desirable daytrip. A short drive from some of the state's best wineries, Salem is also close to several historic Willamette Valley ferries. Near the Willamette, the downtown area is alive with historic buildings, museums, churches, and a pioneer cemetery.

Most travelers from Portland drive down the Willamette Valley to Salem via Route 5. But a far more scenic approach is to exit Route 5 in southern Portland and pick up **Route 99 West** through Tigard. Here you can continue through Oregon's wine country on 99 West, head through McMinnville and then cut east to Salem at Rickreall. Even better, turn off Route 99 West at the historic town of Dayton and pick up **Route 221**, a beautiful backroad paralleling the Willamette River. Near Hopewell it's fun to cross the river on the historic Wheatland Ferry.

In Salem, you'll find **Mission Mill Village** (1313 Mill Street Southeast; 503-585-7012; admission), a historic restoration that turns back the clock to Oregon's pioneer days. Built around the 19th-century is the Thomas Kay Woolen Mill, a factory-turned-museum. Adjacent are the Jason Lee House, the oldest residence standing in the Pacific Northwest, and the John Boon House where you'll learn what family life was like in the mid-19th century. Also open for tours is the 1841 Methodist Parsonage. Enjoy a picnic here by the millstream. The **Salem Convention and Visitors Association** (503-581-4325) serves the public from an office in the Mission Mill complex.

Two blocks south in **Bush's Pasture Park** is the historic **Deepwood Estate** (1116 Mission Street Southeast; 503-363-1825; admission). With its stained glass windows, oak woodwork and solarium, this Queen Anne is a monument to turn-of-the-century craftsmanship. Of special interest are the formal gardens. A nature trail leads through the adjacent wildlife area.

Court-Chemeketa Residential Historic District (Court and Chemeketa streets; 503-588-6011) showcases 117 historic Queen Anne, Italianate, Gothic, Craftsman and Saltbox homes. On this mile long walk you'll see many of the fine homes built by the city's founders.

The **Oregon State Capitol** (Court Street; 503-378-4423) is a four-story Greek landmark featuring half a dozen bronze sculptures over the entrances. Built from Vermont marble, the state building is crowned by the 23-foot high gilded statue, "The Oregon Pioneer." Historic murals grace the interior walls. Be sure to take the walk to the top of the dome for a bird's-eye view of the valley. The surrounding Wilson Park has a pretty fountain and gazebo.

Across from the capitol, **Willamette University** (900 State Street; 503-370-6300) is the state's oldest institution of higher learning. On this shady campus you'll want to see the history exhibit at venerable Waller Hall, as well as Cone Chapel.

Mt. Angel Abbey (★) (East College Street, St. Benedict; 503-845-3030) is a century-old Benedictine monastic community 18 miles northeast of Salem. On tours, arranged by advance appointment, you'll visit the Romanesque church and retreat houses. A small museum focuses on the Russian Old Believer community, while another building has an unusual natural history collection. The beautiful library, designed by Alvar Aalto, features a display of rare handprinted books. Near the top of this 300-foot butte is the grotto of Our Lady of Lourdes. In July the retreat is home of the **Abbey Bach Festival**. Lodging is available.

In the spring don't miss **Schreiner's Iris Garden** (3625 Quinaby Road Northeast; 503-393-3232) five miles north of Salem. The 200-acre floral extravaganza is a photographer's dream. A display area is open to the public.

Take the kids to **Enchanted Forest** (8462 Enchanted Way Southeast, Turner; 503-363-3060; admission), located in a park setting seven miles south of Salem on Route 5. The dream of creator Roger Tofte, this family fun spot has fairytale attractions like a crooked house, Seven Dwarfs' cottage, an Alice in Wonderland rabbit hole, old lady's shoe slide and haunted house. Plays are performed in an outdoor theater. Open March through September.

From Independence follow the signs seven miles south to the historic **Buena Vista Ferry**, which carries a handful of cars and cyclists across the Willamette in the time-honored manner. No trip to Oregon is complete without a ride on one of these old-timers.

South of Albany, Route 34 leads east to the town of Lebanon. Continue east to Sweet Home and one of the Northwest's better pioneer museums. In a 19th-century wood frame church, the **East Linn Museum** (746 Long Street; 503-367-4580; admission) collection is big on logging equipment, antique dolls, quilts, butter churns, linotypes and saddles. There's also a full blacksmith shop here. The **Sweet Home Chamber of Commerce** (1575 Main Street; 503-367-6186) offers information on this Cascades gateway.

Just east of Sweet Home are **Foster Reservoir** and the adjacent **Green Peter Reservoir** (★) (Quartzville Road, ten miles east of Sweet Home). Perched in the foothills, the lakes, particularly Green Peter, offer the kind of mountain views you'd expect to find in Switzerland.

Brownsville, west of Sweet Home on Route 228, is one of the valley's most charming small towns. The **Linn County Historical Museum** (Park Avenue, east of Main Street; 503-466-3390; admission), in the Oregon and California Railroad depot, is flanked by box cars and a caboose. Native American, natural history, manufacturing and agricultural exhibits are on display. You can pick up a walking tour brochure here that guides you to other local museums like the century-old **Moyer House** (Main Street at Kirk Avenue). Built from lumber milled in John Moyer's own sash and door factory, this Italianate home features 12-foot ceilings. Landscapes are painted on the walls and window transoms.

Howard Taylor and his wife Faye devoted 20 years to create the folk art capital of central Oregon, the **Living Rock Studios** (★) (911 Bishop Way West, Brownsville; 503-466-5814; admission). Howard created this memorial to his pioneer ancestors with 800 tons of rock. The circular stone building is inlaid with pioneer wagon wheel rims, a Native American mortar and pestle, fool's gold, obsidian and coffee jars filled with lava specimens. A series of illuminated biblical pictures are displayed downstairs, while a circular staircase leads upstairs to a display of Taylor's carvings.

A popular Oregon college town located on the west side of the valley at the edge of the coast range, **Corvallis** is also the seat of Benton County. A prominent landmark here is the **Benton County Courthouse** (120 Northwest 4th Street; 503-757-6831). The building, dating to 1888 and still in use, has an impressive clock tower. Guided tours are available.

On the 500-acre Oregon State University campus in Corvallis (Campus Way; 503-737-0123) you'll find **Horner Museum** (26th and Washington streets; 503-754-2951). Located in the Gill Coliseum, this collection focuses on natural science, history and world culture. Also worth a visit are the OSU art department's **Fairbanks Gallery** (Fairbanks Hall; 503-737-4745) and **Guistina Gallery** (26th and Western Streets; 503-737-2402).For information on other local attractions contact the **Corvallis Convention and Visitors Bureau** (420 Northwest 2nd Street; 503-757-1544).

East of Corvallis on Route 20 is **Albany**, where you'll find over 300 Victorian homes. One of the best is the **Monteith House** (518 Southwest 2nd Street), a frame residence with period 19th-century furnishings. Dressed in Victorian costumes, docents offer intriguing guided tours. At the **Albany Regional Museum** (3rd and Ferry streets) are an old-time general store, barber shop and doctor's office. To arrange tours of either location contact the **Albany Visitors Association** (435 1st Avenue; 503-926-1517) where you can pick up a helpful walking-tour map.

Wineries are one of the true delights of the Salem area. Many are found along Route 99 West in the Willamette Valley north and west of the city. All the establishments mentioned below offer tours; call ahead to confirm visiting hours.

Rex Hill Vineyards (30835 North Route 99 West, Newberg; 503-538-0666) is a beautifully landscaped 25-acre winery with an inviting terraced picnic area. Furnished with antiques, the tasting room has a warming fire place. Try the pinot noir or the chardonnay.

One of Oregon's older vineyards, **Knudsen Erath Winery** (Worden Hill Road, Dundee; 503-538-3318) is set high above the Willamette Valley in the Dundee Hills. You can sample the winery's pinot noir, cabernet sauvignon and white riesling in a rustic, wood-paneled tasting room.

A relatively new player receiving high marks on the Oregon wine scene is **Argyle** (691 Route 99 West, Dundee; 503-538-8520). Located at a one-time hazelnut processing plant, this winery makes excellent sparkling wines and small quantities of still wine. The tasting room is an inviting farmhouse.

Among the most scenic vineyards in Oregon is **Sokol Blosser Winery** (5000 Sokol Blosser Lane, Dundee; 503-864-2282). Here you'll enjoy great views of the Willamette Valley, along with a pleasant picnic area and contemporary tasting room. The well-stocked tasting room—try the white riesling and chardonnay—features a full range of Northwest products including smoked salmon, fruit preserves, gourmet mustards, salad dressings and candies.

Yamhill Valley Vineyards (16250 Southwest Oldsville Road off Route 18, McMinnville; 503-843-3100) is located on a 300-acre estate in the coast range foothills. Specializing in Burgundian and Alsatian wines, Yamhill has an elegant tasting room set in an oak grove. The cathedral ceiling, stained-glass windows and balcony overlooking the vineyard add to the charm.

SALEM AREA HOTELS

State House Bed and Breakfast (2146 State Street, Salem; 503-588-1340), a refurbished 1920s craftsman on Mill Creek, has four contemporary furnished rooms and a pair of two-bedroom cottages ideal for families. Large rooms are appointed with brass fixtures, handmade toys and dolls. Take your breakfast , featuring homemade sausage, bacon and eggs, in the garden. You can feed the ducks and geese in the pond, relax in the spray of the waterfall or grab a tube and float down the creek. Moderate.

Convenient to Route 5, the **Mill Creek Inn Best Western** (3095 Ryan Drive Southeast, Salem; 503-585-3332) has 106 moderately priced units including junior suites with microwaves, refrigerators and wet bars. The large rooms have contemporary furniture and ample closet space.

The **Madison Inn Bed and Breakfast** (660 Southwest Madison Avenue, Corvallis; 503 757-1274), a Queen Anne across from Central Park's beautiful gardens and gazebo, is moderate only in price. Appointed with fine antiques, including an Edison Victrola and carousel animals, this three-story, bay-windowed home has seven large rooms. Guests tuck themselves in to brass beds beneath colorful quilts.

Riverbank Inn (101 Northwest Van Buren Boulevard, Corvallis; 503-752-9601) offers budget lodging just 50 yards from the Willamette River. Clean, air-conditioned rooms are comfortably furnished in modern decor. The price is right for this motel convenient to downtown.

The 15-unit **Porta Via Motel** (805 Long Street, Sweet Home; 503-367-5137) offers budget lodging in clean rooms with beige brick walls, dark carpet and contemporary furniture. A small pond and garden are located on the premises, which is a block away from the museums and shops of this gateway to some of the valley's best boating and fishing.

We visited **Historical Booth House Bed and Breakfast** (486 Park Street, Lebanon; 503-258-2954) on the day the whole town was out building the world's largest strawberry shortcake. This annual June event is only one of the reasons to stay at one of Oregon's Queen Annes. Bay-windowed rooms with fireplaces, marble-topped dressers, satin comforters and carved walnut bedframes make this historic home a treat. Full breakfast is served on the sun porch. Moderate.

SALEM AREA RESTAURANTS

Just when you're about ready to give up on McMinnville as another franchise landscape, the chain stores of Route 99 give way to the town's well-preserved downtown. Tucked away in a storefront is **Nick's Italian Café** (521 East 3rd Street; 503-434-4471) where the set menu features specialties like smoked salmon, homemade lasagna with pesto, mushrooms and Oregon filberts. Don't despair if you can't get a reservation because there's nearly always seating available at the counter. Deluxe.

When it's time for tea in McMinnville, the obvious choice is **Lavender's Blue** (★) (535 North Cowls Street; 503-472-4594). Two blocks north of downtown in a historic home, this antique-furnished salon brings the English tradition to the Northwest. High tea and light lunches are served on linen tablecloths. In addition to more than a dozen teas, you'll enjoy cucumber sandwiches, almond tea bread, ginger scones and hazelnut tortes. Moderate.

Although the ambiance and setting are deluxe, prices are moderate at the **Inn at Orchard Heights** (695 Orchard Heights Road Northwest, Salem; 503-378-178). Prime rib, fresh salmon, stuffed shrimp, pasta and chicken sautéed with seasonal fruits are a few of the entrées on the extensive menu. Indian artifacts, wallhangings, plants and pottery decorate the elegant, pine-paneled dining room. On warm days ask for patio seating.

There's no MSG at **Kwan's** (835 Commercial Street, Salem; 503-362-7711), a Korean establishment with seating for 400 at comfortable booths and large tables ideal for the whole family. Specialties like steamed salmon with black bean sauce, imperial fried rice and garlic chicken have won a loyal following. Entering this pagoda-style building, you'll find a 15-foot-tall redwood Buddha in the lobby. Moderate.

It's easy to find Margaritaville in the Willamette Valley. Just head for **La Casa Real** (698 12th Street, Salem; 503-588-0700). This adobe-style restaurant with tropical birds, piñatas hanging from the walls, a generous supply of hors d'oeuvres in the bar, is also, thanks to a children's menu, a good bet for families. Prawns sautéed with rice, onions, mushrooms, sour cream and cheese are a specialty. Moderate.

A good place to begin your day in Corvallis is **Café Croissant** (215 Southwest 5th Street; 503-752-5111). There are free refills on the cappuccino that goes well with the array of croissants, muffins (including cappuccino chip) and butter pecan buns baked on the premises. Budget. No dinner.

Michael's Landing (603 Northwest 2nd Street, Corvallis; 503-754-6141) offers rock shrimp fettucine, red snapper, a seafood salad and Monte Christo sandwiches in the restored Southern Pacific Station. One of the city's most popular restaurants, it has a great view of the Willamette. Moderate.

For steaks, lamb chops, prime rib, scallops or oysters try **The Gables** (1121 Northwest 9th Street, Corvallis; 503-752-3364). This moderate-to-deluxe establishment serves guests in a traditional dining room with oak furniture and a roaring fireplace. Portions are generous, and there's an extensive wine cellar.

Located in a strip shopping center, **Amador's Alley** (★) (870 North Main Street, Independence; 503-838-0178) is one of the most popular Mexican restaurants in the area. Huge portions of *huevos con chorizo*, chile colorado and enchiladas rancheros are served by waiters in guayaberos. Diners are seated at plastic tables and chairs in this budget-priced establishment. Arrive early or be prepared to wait.

Take one of the window booths at **The Point Restaurant and Lounge** (6000 Main Street, Sweet Home; 503-367-9606) and enjoy a perfect waterfront view. Fresh fish, steak, crab and cheese on an English muffin as well as generous salads are a few of the specialties at this eatery that includes a fresh-baked loaf of bread with every meal. Budget to moderate.

SALEM AREA SHOPPING

Mission Mill Village's warehouse complex (1313 Mill Street Southeast, Salem; 503-585-7012) has a dozen shops including the **Salem Audubon Society** (503-585-5689) offering birdfeeders and books on birds. Also here is **Grandma's Temptations** (503-585-8773) where you'll be able to purchase handcrafted dolls, country woodenware, needlepoint, handmade toys, jewelry and a good selection of Oregon regional travel and history books.

An excellent place to shop for Northwest arts and crafts—including pottery, sculpture, paintings, prints and quilts—is the **Bush Barn Art Center** (600 Mission Street Southeast, Salem; 503-581-2228).

The **Made in Jefferson Gallery** (3259 Jefferson-Scio Drive Southeast, Jefferson; 503-327-2543) features handcrafted furniture.

SALEM AREA NIGHTLIFE

The **Oregon Symphony Association** (1313 Mill Street Southeast, Salem; 503-364-0149) performs classical concerts, as well as a pops series.

Salem Folklore Community at Mission Mill Museum (1313 Mill Street Southeast; 503-585-7012) offers Friday evening folk performances.

For belly dancing, big band music, folk, reggae, rock or blue grass check out **Boon's Treasury** (888 Liberty Street Northeast, Salem; 503-399-9062). This circa 1860 two-story brick building has a small dancefloor. Artworks by local artists are frequently exhibited. Cover on weekends.

Pentacle Theater (324 52nd Avenue Northwest, Salem; 503-364-7121) is a well-established community theater offering several plays each season.

For live music in an eclectic off-campus setting ornamented with pink flamingos, try **Nearly Normal's** (109 Northwest 15th Street, Corvallis; 503-753-0791). Bands play rock music in a smoke-free environment.

SALEM AREA BEACHES AND PARKS

Willamette Mission State Park—Set in orchards and hop fields south of Wheatland landing, this 1686-acre Willamette River park is the site of an 1830s Methodist Mission. A monument commemorates these early settlers. In the midst of the park are the historic Wheatland Ferry landings. This shady spot is a delightful retreat on a warm day.

Facilities: Picnic tables, restrooms, bicycling and equestrian trails; groceries and restaurants in Salem. *Fishing:* Catch trout in the river.

Getting there: On Wheatland Ferry Road, 12 miles north of Salem.

Bush's Pasture Park—The Bush Collection of Old Garden Roses is one of the highlights in this 89-acre park south of the capitol. They were originally collected from pioneer homesteads to represent roses brought East on the Oregon Trail. Also here is the **Bush Conservatory**, the West's oldest greenhouse, natural wildflower gardens and the Gilbert House Children's Museum.

Facilities: Picnic area, restrooms and tours; restaurants and groceries nearby; information, 503-588-2410.

Getting there: Located at 600 Mission Street in Salem.

Silver Falls State Park—If you're addicted to waterfalls, look no further. Located in twin lava rock gorges created by Silver Creek's north and south forks, the 8300-acre park has ten waterfalls. Also here are bike and equestrian trails leading through an old-growth fir forest with towering maples and quaking Aspen ideal for fall color buffs. Double Falls, a 2.4-mile roundtrip hike from the highway, has the biggest drop, 178 feet, or 25 feet more than Niagara Falls.

Facilities: Picnic tables, restrooms, rustic group lodging, nature lodge, jogging trail and horse camp; information, 503-873-8681. *Fishing:* Good in the creek. *Swimming:* Good.

Camping: There are 53 RV hook-ups and 51 tent sites.

Getting there: Located 25 miles east of Salem on Highway 214.

Cascadia State Park—On the South Santiam River Canyon, this 253-acre park has a beautiful two-mile trail leading to a waterfall. Pump your own soda water from a spring. Largely forested with Douglas fir, the park also has an open meadow on the north river bank.

Facilities: Picnic tables, restrooms and handicapped accessible; information, 503-367-6021. *Fishing:* Salmon and trout in the river.

Camping: There are 26 primitive sites.

Getting there: Located on Route 20, 14 miles east of Sweet Home.

McDowell Creek Falls Park (★)—The forested glen is a perfect refuge. An easy hike across the creek and up through a fir forest takes you to a pair of scenic falls. On a weekday you may have this park to yourself.

Facilities: Picnic tables and restrooms; restaurants and groceries in Lebanon; information, 503-967-3917. *Fishing:* Try for trout in the creek.

Getting there: Twelve miles southeast of Lebanon via Berlin Road and McDowell Creek Drive.

Lewis Creek Park—On the north shore of Foster Lake, Lewis Creek Park is a good spot to enjoy water sports. There's a big swimming beach, and the park offers fine views of the Cascades. The park includes 20 acres of open space and 20 acres of brush and forest.

Facilities: Picnic tables, boat launch and waterskiing; restaurants and groceries in Sweet Home; information, 503-967-3917. *Fishing:* Troll for bass and trout in the lake.

Getting there: Four miles northeast of Sweet Home. Take Route 20 east to Foster Dam and turn left. At North River Road turn right to the park.

Whitcomb Creek County Park (★)—With its beautiful rain-forest terrain on the shores of ten-mile long Green Peter Reservoir, this 328-acre park in the foothills east of Sweet Home is a winner. It offers spectacular views of the Cascades. The park is forested with fir and deciduous trees.

Facilities: Picnic tables, hiking trails and restrooms; restaurants and groceries in Sweet Home; information, 503-967-3917. *Fishing:* Trout.

Camping: There are 37 sites.

Getting there: From Sweet Home take Route 20 east three miles to Green Peter Dam. Continue north nine miles to the park.

Eugene Area

College towns are often inviting and Eugene is no exception. Climb one of the town buttes and you'll find the city surrounded by rich farmland, inviting lakes and streams. With the Cascades and the McKenzie River Valley to the east and the Coast Mountains to the west, Eugene has an ideal location. The city, location for the film *Animal House*, offers sidewalk cafés, malled streets and upscale shops. The city is at its best in the fall when maples, black walnuts, chestnuts and cottonwood brighten the landscape. Pick up touring ideas at the **Eugene Convention and Visitors Bureau** (305 West 7th Avenue; 503-484-5307).

Stop by the **University of Oregon**'s (503-346-3111) 250-acre campus. Here you'll find an arboretum with over 2000 varieties of trees; weekday tours are offered from Oregon Hall (13th and Agate streets; 503-346-3014). Among the campus highlights is the **Museum of Natural History** (1680 East 15th Avenue; 503-346-3024; admission). This collection is a good way to orient yourself to the state's geology and anthropology. Permanent exhibits cover Oregon's fossil history, archaeology and Northwest Coast art.

Also recommended is the **Museum of Art** (University and Kincaid streets; 503-686-3027; admission). The colonnaded sculpture court and pool adjacent to the entrance is one of the campus's architectural highlights. The collection, one of the best in the state, features Northwest art and photography as well as international artworks.

Eugene is big on adaptive reuse of commercial buildings like the **5th Street Public Market** (296 East 5th Street; 503-484-0383), home to dozens of shops, 17 restaurants and a courtyard that's a popular venue for local musicians, artists and acrobats.

Nearby Springfield has preserved part of its agrarian past at the Willamalane Park and Recreation District's 250-acre **Dorris Ranch** (151 North 4th Street; 503-726-4335). Call ahead to arrange a tour of this living history farm where you'll learn how filberts are cultivated.

No trip to the Eugene area is complete without an excursion into the nearby countryside. You can head east on **Route 126** along the McKenzie River or southeast on **Route 58** to Lookout Point Reservoir, Oakridge and Salt Creek Falls. **Route 5** takes you south to Cottage Grove. Government Road leads east past Dorena Reservoir and several covered bridges to the historic **Bohemia Mining District**. This mountainous region was the scene of a mid-19th century gold rush that proved to be a bust. Today, tourists roam the district by car and four-wheel-drive vehicles to see lost mines, ghost towns like Bohemia City and covered bridges. Before setting out for this national forest area be sure to check with the Cottage Grove Ranger Station (503-942-5591). Because there are active mining claims in the area it is important not to trespass. The **Cottage Grove Historical Museum** (Birch and H streets; 503-942-3963) has a major exhibit on the Bohemia District.

The **Willamette Valley Loop** is a 195-mile adventure. It begins and ends in Eugene, looping through Corvallis, Salem and Albany. This backroad journey includes historical sites, museums, covered bridges, ferries, parks, gardens and wineries. A detailed brochure is available at the **Eugene-Springfield Convention and Visitors Bureau** (800-547-5445 outside Oregon and 800-452-3670 in Oregon).

The **Roseburg Visitors and Convention Bureau** (900 Southeast Douglas Street; 503-672-9731) offers a handy historical tour guide. Highlights include the **Roseburg Historic District** in the Mill Street/Pine Street Neighborhood. You'll find many modest cottages built in the late 19th century. **The Floed-Lane House** (544 Southeast Douglas Street; 503-459-1393) is a Classic Revival featuring a full-length two-tier veranda with half a dozen square columns supporting each level. It's open for tours on weekends. The **Douglas County Museum of History and Natural History** (Douglas County Fairgrounds, 1299 Southwest Medford Street; 503-440-4507) features Native American and pioneer artifacts, and a 19th century railroad depot.

Wildlife Safari (Safari Road, Winston; 503-679-6761; admission) is Oregon's drive-through adventure, a 600-acre park where over 550 animals and birds roam freely. Visitors motor past bactrian camels, hippopotamus, lions, and scores of other species. In addition to the self-paced driving tour, the Safari Village offers a petting zoo and newborn nursery. Elephant rides are also available.

EUGENE AREA HOTELS

The deluxe-priced **Valley River Inn** (1000 Valley River Way, Eugene; 503-687-0123) enjoys an enviable view of the Willamette River. Adjacent to the 140-store Valley River Center, this 257-room hotel features Indian rugs over the big lobby fireplace that faces a conversation pit. Large rooms, decorated with wicker and furniture and impressionist prints, open on to small patios. Bicycling and jogging paths are adjacent to the inn.

The 66-unit **Best Western Greentree Inn** (1759 Franklin Boulevard, Eugene; 503-485-2727) offers attractive, contemporary rooms with woven wallpaper, hanging lamps, rust-colored carpets, sitting areas and balconies, including some overlooking the Willamette. Most units have refrigerators. Adjacent to the University of Oregon campus, this establishment has a pool, jacuzzi and restaurant. Budget to moderate.

A budget-to-moderate inn ideal for families, **B&G's Bed and Breakfast** (711 West 11th Street, Eugene; 503-343-5739) offers a suite complete with kitchen, a skylit cottage or the simply furnished Shoji Room. Near the University of Oregon, this Dutch Colonial is one of the few bed and breakfasts that offers guests free use of a computer. The innkeeper frequently leads tours through Eugene's Rose Garden or along the Ridgeline Trail.

Lighten up at **Gile's Guest House Bed and Breakfast** (609 West Broadway, Eugene; 503-683-2674) where the windows and French doors have over 600 panes. The 1920s home is furnished in a California-casual style. Mauve, blue, white and beige walls, wicker furniture, fans, Tiffany-style lamps and four-poster beds accent the guest rooms. There are a library, sun porch and, when you're ill-disposed, a fainting couch. Moderate.

Bridging the Past

Oregon takes pride in the fact that it has more covered bridges—53—than any state west of the Mississippi. Most of these wooden spans are found in the Willamette Valley, although a handful are scattered along the coast, in the Cascades, the Ashland-Rogue River area and around Bend. Although some have been retired from active duty and now serve only pedestrians and cyclists, all these bridges are worth a special trip.

Originally the idea of covering a bridge was to protect its plank deck and trusses from the elements. But aesthetics eventually proved as important as engineering, and Oregon's beautiful hooded spans became one of the state's signature attractions.

Highly recommended is the Calapooia River's **Crawfordsville Bridge** east of Brownsville on Route 228. Clustered around the nearby agricultural communities of Crabtree and Scio are many other "kissing bridges" including **Shimanek, Larwood, Gilkey, Weedle, Bohemian Hall** and **Hannah**.

To the south, Lane County is home to 18 covered bridges, all listed on the National Register of Historic Places. The Lowell area, on Route 58 south of Eugene, has four of these spans including the **Lowell Bridge**, which crosses a river later flooded to create a lake. Other bridges are at **Pengra, Unity** and **Parvin**. A highlight in the Cottage Grove area is **Chamber's Bridge**, a rare covered railroad span. In the same region, south of Dorena Reservoir, is **Dorena Bridge**. With barbecue pits and tables, it's a pleasant place to picnic. Other covered bridges in the same area are found at **Mosby Creek, Currin, Stewart** and **Chambers**.

Douglas County has a number of fine spans including the **Roaring Camp Bridge** off Route 38 west of Drain. It still stands thanks to the dedicated volunteer efforts of three families living nearby. The **Rochester Bridge** west of Sutherlin on County Road 10A also has some history behind it. After county highway workers burned down a bridge in the late 1950s, residents feared the beloved Rochester Bridge nearby was destined for the same fate. Armed with shotguns, they kept an all-night vigil and saved the span.

Worth a special trip is **Weddle Bridge** in Sweet Home. In 1987, after 43 years of service, it was damaged but the county wisely decided to take the bridge apart piece by piece and put it in storage. A local forester raised $190,000 to reassemble the bridge, originally built in 1937 for $8500.

An indispensable guide to all these spans is *Roofs Over Rivers* (Oregon Sentinel Publishing) by Bill and Nick Cockrell. Another good resource is the **Covered Bridge Society of Oregon** (503-246-2953).

Tolly's Beckley House (★) (338 Southeast 2nd Street, Oakland; 503-459-3796) overlooks this historic town and surrounding countryside. The Classic Revival is furnished with armoires, braided rugs and wicker and pine furniture. The bright blue-and-white decor and comfortable sun porch make this a cheerful spot, even on a gray Oregon day. Moderate.

EUGENE AREA RESTAURANTS

In Eugene, **The River Room** (Valley River Inn, 1000 Valley River Way; 503-341-3462) offers deluxe-priced dining overlooking the Willamette. The emphasis is on Oregon cuisine featuring locally grown veal, lamb, lettuces, herbs, mushrooms and fruits. Seafood entrées include grilled fresh Chinook salmon, Dungeness crab sandwiches, fresh swordfish and cioppino. This contemporary dining room is complemented by a deck ideal for drinks before or after dinner.

Ambrosia (174 East Broadway, Eugene; 503-342-4141) offers Italian specialties in a red-brick building distinguished by leaded glass, a mirrored oak and mahogany backbar, Tiffany-style lamps and a tintype ceiling. Specialties include pizza and calzone made with a plum tomato sauce, pasta and entrées like grilled fresh lamb and fresh seafood. There are 325 vintages on the wine list, including 25 ports. Outdoor dining is available. Moderate.

For pasta dishes, fresh salmon, lamb, steaks and generous salads, the **Excelsior Café** (754 East 13th Street, Eugene; 503-342-6963) is a good choice. Located in a Victorian near the university, this pleasing restaurant also has an excellent Oregon wine list and offers a generous brunch on Sunday. Ask for a table in the greenhouse. Moderate.

Zenon Café (898 Pearl Street, Eugene; 503-343-3005), an elegant, yuppified establishment with knotty-pine paneling, marble tables, white tile and booths stained jet black, offers an eclectic menu featuring items like oysters Bienvielle, fettucini rustica and Tuscan roast rabbit. Moderate to deluxe.

Yen Jing (1775 West 6th Street, Eugene; 503-484-6496) offers a big Mandarin, Hunan and Szechuan menu that takes advantage of fresh Oregon seafood like abalone, shrimp and crab. Look no further for mu-shu pork, garlic chicken or spicy vegetable and tofu dishes. All entrées are served without MSG. Moderate.

Tolly's Soda Fountain (★) (115 South Locust Street, Oakland; 503-459-3796) is one of the most inviting lunch counters in the Pacific Northwest. Located in a brick building, Tolly's is an architectural landmark with a mirrored-back bar, varnished fir counters and stools, brass footrests and Tiffany lamps. Enjoy a soda, phosphate, milkshake or banana split. Also available are breakfast hash and eggs, as well as Reuben sandwiches, croissants, a Cobb salad, lasagna and fresh strawberry pie. Budget.

EUGENE AREA SHOPPING

The **5th Street Public Market** (296 East 5th Street, Eugene; 503-484-0383) has an impressive collection of shops and galleries. Among the best are **Eugene Leather Works** (503-345-1410) where you can buy handtooled checkbook holders. Also look at **Wildflower Stained Glass** (503-342-8330), **Limbo Graphics** (503-344-1844) and **Claytrade** (503-342-8686).

Dozens of other arts-and-crafts galleries are found in the Eugene area. **Opus 5 Gallery of Crafts** (136 East Broadway, Eugene; 503-484-1710) offers paintings, ceramics, handblown glass, metal works and jewelry by several noted Northwest artists. **Soaring Wings Gallery** (760 Willamette, Eugene; 503-683-8474) focuses on wildlife, Western outdoors and maritime art. **Ruby Chasm** (152 West 5th Street, Eugene; 503-344-4074) sells necklaces, shirts, ceramics and tribal art.

If you're searching for petroglyphs, shells, Native American art, Russian stone carvings, or Klickitat Indian baskets, head for the **University of Oregon Museum of Natural History Gift Shop** (1680 East 15th Avenue, Eugene; 503-346-3024).

Oyate Luta (602 Main Street, Springfield; 503-741-0322) sells handmade Native American arts and crafts including beaded items, silver and leather in contemporary and traditional styles.

EUGENE AREA NIGHTLIFE

Allann Brothers Bakery and Coffee House (152 West 5th Street, Eugene; 503-342-3378) presents a wide variety of performances including Zydeco, blues, reggae, salsa, jazz, folk and classical trios.

For jazz, try **Jo Federigo's Café & Bar** (259 5th Avenue, Eugene; 503-343-8488). An intimate cellar-setting with hanging plants, fans and modern art provides the background for some of the region's finest musicians.

The Valley River Inn's **River Room** (1000 Valley River Way, Eugene; 503-341-3462) provides live entertainment in a fireplace lounge setting. On warm nights the strains of rhythm and blues, rock and standards drift out to the big deck overlooking the Willamette.

The **Hult Center for the Performing Arts** (1 Eugene Center, Eugene; 503-687-5000) is the home of the summer Oregon Bach Festival, Eugene's symphony, opera and ballet, as well as visiting artists from around the world. Performances take place in Silva Hall or the smaller Soreng Theater.

Three theater companies perform in Eugene. The **University Theater** (Villard Hall; 503-346-4191) offers full-scale productions in the Robinson Theater and smaller plays in the Arena Theater. The **Very Little Theater** (2350 Hilyard Street; 503-344-7751) is considered one of the best community theaters in the area. The **Actors Cabaret/Mainstage Theater** (530 West

21st Street; 503-683-4368) showcases Broadway and off-Broadway comedies and musicals.

The Eugene Jazz Society (789 Calvin Street; 503-343-1101) presents a wide variety of dance programs. The **Traditional Jazz Society of Oregon** (36475 Star Road, Pleasant Hill; 503-746-0992) is dedicated to preserving this American tradition.

EUGENE AREA BEACHES AND PARKS

Brownsville Pioneer Park—The forested, ten-acre city park is a short walk from the center of a historic Willamette Valley community and is along the banks of the Calapooia River. Big playfields, shady glens and a spacious picnic area will add to your enjoyment.

Facilities: Picnic tables, restrooms; restaurants and groceries in downtown Brownsville; information, 503-466-5666.

Camping: Permitted, though there are no formal sites.

Getting there: Take Route 5 north from Eugene 22 miles to Route 228 and continue east four miles. An alternative scenic loop heads north from Springfield via Mohawk, Marcola and Crawfordsville.

Hendricks Park and Rhododendron Garden—A glorious springtime spot when over 3000 rhododendrons brighten the landscape. The 47-acre park is shaded by Oregon white oaks and maples. Owen Rose Garden, adjacent on the banks of the Willamette, features 30 rose varieties.

Facilities: Picnic tables, restrooms, trails and tours; information, 503-687-5334.

Getting there: Located at the east end of Summit Avenue in Eugene.

Ashland-Rogue River Area

If your vision of a good vacation is rafting by day and Shakespeare by night, look no further. One of the Northwest's most popular destinations, this region also features one of Oregon's most historic towns. Home of the largest concentration of bed and breakfasts in the Pacific Northwest, Ashland is also your gateway to backcountry famous for its hidden gems.

The wild and scenic Rogue River is one of the Northwest's signature attractions. It is also convenient to wilderness areas, mountain lakes, thundering waterfalls, marble caves and popular resort communities. A good place to orient yourself is the **Grants Pass Visitors and Convention Bureau** (6th and Midland streets; 503-476-5510.)

Wildlife Images (★) (11850 Lower River Road, Grants Pass; 503-476-2774; tours by appointment) is a fascinating animal rehabilitation center. Each year more than 150 injured animals are nursed back to health by a veterinary staff and volunteers. Among the creatures you can see being treated are owls, eagles, weasels, black bears and cougars. Highly recommended.

Pottsville Powerland (Pleasant Valley Road west of Monument Drive, Pleasant Valley) is the place to see a vintage collection of tractors, farm and logging equipment. It's five miles north of Grants Pass.

Although it's far from the core of Oregon's wine country, **Bridgeview Vineyards** (★) (4210 Holland Loop Road, Cave Junction; 503-592-4688) is attracting a loyal following. Set on 74 acres in the Illinois Valley, this European-style winery offers a tasting room at **The Oregon Wine Barrel** (24310 Redwood Highway, Kerby; 503-592-4698). Try the gewürztraminer, chardonnay or riesling.

The **Oregon Caves National Monument** (20000 Caves Highway, Cave Junction; 503-592-3400; admission) is the Pacific Northwest's grandest spelunking adventure. Fifty miles southwest of Grants Pass, it's reached by taking Route 199 to Cave Junction and then continuing east on Route 46. Now under restoration (construction workers diverted an underground river and left rubble behind during the 1930s), the cave has over three miles of passageways lined with stalagmites, flowstone, translucent draperies and cave coral. It is not recommended for those with respiratory or heart problems.

Southeast of Grants Pass is **Jacksonville**, a historic 19th-century mining town that has clung to its frontier tradition. The entire town is a National Historic Landmark with over 80 homes, stores and public buildings. Stop at the **Jacksonville Chamber of Commerce** (Oregon and C streets; 503-899-8118) to pick up a walking tour map of the town's tree-lined streets.

Along the way you'll want to stop at the **Jackson County Museum** (206 North 5th Street; 503-773-6536; admission). Exhibits feature gold-mining artifacts, quilts, railroad history and Takelma Indian handicrafts. Next door is the **Children's Museum**. Kids, take your parents to this former jail filled with "please touch" exhibits including a miniature kitchen and general store.

California Street, the heart of Jacksonville, is a step back in time. The graceful balustraded brick buildings have been lovingly restored. A good way to find out about the movers and shakers who made this town is to visit the **Jeremiah Nunan House** (635 North Oregon Street; 503-899-1890; admission). This circa 1892 Catalog House was shipped from Tennessee in 14 boxcars and assembled in Jacksonville for $7800. Touring this Queen Anne Colonial Revival, you'll learn about the tragic life of Jeremiah Nunan, a wealthy merchant who gave his wife the house as a Christmas present.

Also worth a visit is the gothic **C. C. Beekman House** (California Street east of Beekman Square; 503-773-6536; admission). The living history tour re-creates the lifestyle of the rich and famous, circa 1876.Along the way you see banker Beekman's carved oak bedframe, overstuffed furniture, lap desk and summer kitchen. Nearby at California and Third streets, visit the Beekman Bank, one of the first buildings restored in Jacksonville.

Route 238 southwest of Jacksonville leads to the picturesque **Applegate Valley**, a two-mile-wide, 50-mile-long canyon with memorable views and few tourists. After reaching the town of Applegate you can continue south on Applegate Road to the foot of the Siskiyous. Alternatively, Little Applegate and Anderson Creek Roads loop back to Route 99.

One of the most popular attractions in the Medford area is **Harry and David's Original Country Store** (2836 South Pacific Highway; 503-776-2277), famous for its fruit and gift packs shipped nationwide. The store features a fruit stand, gourmet pantry, gift shop, restaurant and deli. Tours of the Medford packing house depart from the gift store.

Medford Visitors and Convention Bureau (304 South Central Avenue; 503-772-5194) is an excellent source of information on southern Oregon. The nearby **Southern Oregon Historical Society's Historical Center** (106 North Central Avenue; 503-773-6536) has an extensive collection of artifacts featuring textiles, furniture, shawls, saddles, agricultural tools and Peter Britt's buggy.

Ten miles north of Medford off Route 62, **Butte Creek Mill** (★) (402 Royal Avenue North, Eagle Point; 503-826-3531) has been producing stone ground products since 1872. On your visit you'll see the miller grinding wheat, rye and corn on giant white stones quarried in France, assembled in Illinois shipped around the Horn to California and finally brought over the Siskiyous by wagon.

Next door to the mill is the **Oregon General Store Museum**. Set up as an 1890s shop, this fascinating collection features over-the-counter medicines. hardware, toys, clothing, tobacco tins, Coca-Cola signs and a wide variety of unusual memorabilia. The delightful period piece is open only on Saturdays in the summer months.

While **Ashland** is best known for the Oregon Shakespeare Festival, the play is not the only thing here. From shopping to restaurants to biking, this city offers plenty of diversions. Home to more bed and breakfasts than any city in the state, Ashland has strict zoning controls that protect the historic architectural landscape. The town is heavily booked during the Shakespeare season when street vendors are out in force selling espresso.

To explore the possibilities stop by the **Ashland Chamber of Commerce** (110 East Main Street; 503-482-3486). A good place to begin your visit is the downtown plaza and verdant Lithia Park. Next door is the **Shakespeare Festival complex** (15 South Pioneer Street; 503-482-4331) and the fascinating **Backstage Tour** (admission). This excellent behind-the-scenes program is a helpful introduction to stagecraft. Members of the theater company guide you through the making of a play on this comprehensive two-hour look at the dramatic arts. Also worth a visit is the festival's **Exhibit Center** where you can see, and try on, costumes and props.

Most people come to Ashland for the plays, but the mountain lakes east of town are a tempting day trip. Take Route 5 north and pick up Route 140 east to Dead Indian Road. Turn south to the first and most picturesque of these retreats, **Lake of the Woods**, an ideal place for a picnic, swimming or sunbathing. Continue southeast to **Howard Prairie Reservoir** and **Hyatt Reservoir**, both popular for water sports and fishing. Return to Dead Indian Road for the cliffhanging descent back into Ashland, an entrance that rivals anything you're likely to see on the Elizabethan stage.

ASHLAND-ROGUE RIVER AREA HOTELS

Wolf Creek Tavern (100 Railroad Avenue, Wolf Creek; 503-866-2474) is an 1850s stage stop now operated as a state historic property. Handsomely restored and run by a staff in 19th century-style attire, the tavern offers eight moderate-priced rooms with private baths. You'll find antiques and brass beds in the medium-sized rooms decorated with historic photos. You can also see the room where Jack London stayed on his visit.

Eight miles west of Merlin on the Rogue River, the **Riverbanks Inn** (★) (8401 Riverbanks Road; 503-479-1118) is a kind of bed and breakfast theme park. In the main house choose between the Casablanca and Jean Harlow rooms or check in to the Caribbean Dream Suite. For a more spartan experience try the Zen Cabin. Family groups can hole up in the River Cottage or the Riverlodge House. Other amenities at this deluxe, seven-acre resort include a duck pond, pear orchard, ping-pong terrace, therapeutic massage and a Steinway grand for singalongs.

A glorious view of the Coastal Mountain range is just one of the pluses at the deluxe-priced **Paradise Ranch Inn** (7000-D Monument Drive, Grants Pass; 503-479-4333). Whether you arrive by plane on the ranch's runway or come by car, expect a great escape at this Rogue Valley resort. One of 18 motel-style rooms, with Early American furniture and pond views, will be your base. A house is also available for families. You can photograph swans on the pond, fish for trout at three-acre Paradise Lake, golf or enjoy tennis, hiking, biking and rafting. Horse-drawn carriage rides are a treat.

The moderate-priced **Riverside Inn** (971 6th Street, Grants Pass; 503-476-6873) is the largest motel in town with an enviable location on the Rogue River across from Riverside Park. This 175-unit inn's large rooms and kitchenette suites are furnished with comfortable sofas and easy chairs. Most rooms have private balconies overlooking the river. In some cases you can pick blackberries from your deck. A Rogue jet-boat dock is next door, and there is some highway noise from the bridge traffic.

The **Oregon Caves Château** (20000 Caves Highway, Cave Junction; 503-592-3400), in a wooded glen surrounded by waterfalls, is an ideal place to spend the night after a visit to the Oregon Caves National Monument. Faced with cedar shakes, this national historic landmark has two big marble fireplaces framed with fir timbers in the lobby. Moderate-sized rooms with pine furnishings and floral print bedspreads offer forest and pond views in this serene setting. Open June through September. Moderate.

The historic red-brick **Jacksonville Inn** (175 East California Street, Jacksonville; 503-899-1900) offers nicely restored rooms with oak frame beds, down comforters, wall-to-wall carpets, antiques, gas-style lamps and floral print wallpaper. Moderate.

The **Stage Lodge** (830 North 5th Street, Jacksonville; 503-899-3953), a faux-Victorian motel, offers moderately priced rooms with cherrywood furniture, armoires, ceiling fans and wall-to-wall carpets. Suites include wet bars, microwaves and spas. There's some highway noise in the front units.

Convenient to downtown Jacksonville, the **McCully House Inn** (240 East California Street; 503-899-1942) is a charming 19th-century home where a grandfather clock sounds the hour and guests sip wine around the fireplace. This immaculate, white house has hardwood floors, painted friezes on the walls and rooms big on lace, walnut furniture and clawfoot tubs. Moderate to deluxe.

Take a 125-year-old country estate, complete with a three-story barn, historic farm implements, add a redwood deck, flower garden, orchard and angora rabbits and what do you get? **Under the Greenwood Tree Bed and Breakfast Farm** (★) (3045 Bellinger Lane, Medford; 503-776-0000). Overfurnished with Persian rugs, Chippendale and chintz, this is the place for travelers who want to wind down with high tea or sherry and pluck a truffle off their pillow before turning in on a brass bed. Moderate to deluxe.

Reached via a redwood staircase, the budget-to-moderate **Columbia Hotel** (262½ East Main Street, Ashland; 503-482-3726) is a comfortable European-style inn. Rooms are furnished with brass beds, floral-print drapes, fans and wall-to-wall carpet. Some offer views of the surrounding mountains.

Devotees of Craftsman-style architecture will enjoy the **Redwing Bed and Breakfast** (115 North Main Street, Ashland; 503-482-1807). Gleaming fir woodwork, original lighting fixtures and swing music, played on the baby grand by the owner are a few of the pluses. Queen beds, wicker furniture, antiques, and country quilts make the rooms inviting. Moderate.

The **Queen Anne Bed and Breakfast** (125 North Main Street, Ashland; 503-482-0220) has fine views of the Cascades and the Coast Range. In the library you can choose from the Bard's complete works. A beautiful English garden behind the inn is a great place to read the play you're about to see at the Shakespeare festival. The room and suite feature queen beds (naturally), bay windows, handmade quilts and clawfoot tubs. Moderate.

The **Fox House Inn** (269 B Street, Ashland; 503-488-1055) is a restored early Victorian with dark wood wainscotting, stained-glass windows and oriental rugs. Choose between a room or suite with a queen canopied bed, ceiling windows and a clawfoot tub. The upstairs suite has floor-to-ceiling windows while the downstairs room opens onto a flower garden. Deluxe.

One block from the Shakespeare festival, **Will's Reste** (298 Hargadine Street; 503-482-4394) is an inviting Anne Hathaway cottage. Shaker furniture and original artworks add to the pleasure of staying at the inn's two rooms. There's also a cottage with kitchen facilities. You'll enjoy the deck with its views of the Siskiyou and Cascade ranges. Continental breakfast is served at this gay-friendly establishment. Moderate.

Cedarwood Inn of Ashland (1801 Siskiyou Boulevard; 503-488-2000) is one of several modern motels found south of downtown. Choose between moderately priced wood-paneled rooms with queens and deluxe courtyard suites offering kitchens and decks. All 64 rooms have contemporary oak furniture. Pools, saunas and barbecue facilities are available.

ASHLAND-ROGUE RIVER AREA RESTAURANTS

The shortest stack of pancakes in Oregon is served at **Buzz's Wheel Inn** (450 Merlin Road, Merlin; 503 479-7157). You only get one flapjack, but don't worry about leaving hungry. It fills your entire plate. The kind of place where the restrooms are labeled "Does" and "Bucks," this coffee shop is just the place for omelettes, milkshakes, turkey sandwiches and patty melts. A seat at Buzz's counter is a sure way to meet the locals. Budget.

For dining in a glorious country setting consider **Paradise Ranch Inn** (7000 Monument Drive, Grants Pass; 503-479-4333). Dinner specialties include roasted duck served with Swedish lingonberry sauce, fresh salmon filet, and homemade cheese tortellini. There's also a Sunday brunch where you can enjoy petite steak and eggs, ham and apricot crêpes and french toast with Grand Marnier and ginger syrup. Deluxe.

Just when you thought country cooking was limited to chili and chicken fried steak, **The House of Thai Kitchen** (328 Oregon Cave Highway, Cave Junction; 503-592-4362) brings a taste of the East to the Wild West. The budget-priced menu features entrées such as Thai beef salad, barbecued red pork with yellow noodles, and chicken in ginger sauce. There is nothing fancy about the dining room, with its Bangkok photos and strings of Christmas lights that twinkle year-round. But the food is a welcome change.

Traversed by a stream, the **Oregon Caves Château Restaurant** (503-592-3400) offers steaks, seafood and deli sandwiches. Downstairs is one of America's largest soda fountains. Scores of patrons seated on red stools at three counters enjoy malts, sodas, sundaes, omelettes, french toast, salads and burgers. Don't miss this knotty-pine paneled classic. Moderate.

The **Jacksonville Inn** (175 East California Street, Jacksonville; 503-899-1900) serves dinner in the restored 19th-century Ryan and Morgan general store building. The low-light, brick-walled dining room with red carpets and tablecloths creates a great setting for vast, seven-course dinners or a la carte specialties. A large menu features Oregon cuisine including razor clams, scallops, veal scallopini, prime rib and vegetarian dishes. The wine list is endless. Moderate to deluxe.

For patio dining it's hard to beat the **McCully House Inn** (240 East California Street, Jacksonville; 503-899-1942). Entrées served outside or in the lovely dining room include pecan chicken with brandy sauce, grilled leg of lamb and roast cornish game hen with braised red cabbage. You'll find Oregon wildflowers on every table. Moderate to deluxe.

Phoenix-like, the moderately priced **Bella Union** (170 West California Street; 503-899-1770) has risen from the ashes of one of Jacksonville's best loved 19th-century saloons. Like its predecessor, this establishment is an important social center. The menu features pizza, steak, pasta, and sandwiches. You have your choice of several noisy dining rooms or the more serene patio out back.

On a warm evening, the garden patio at The **Winchester Country Inn** (35 South 2nd Street, Ashland; 503-488-1115) is an ideal place to enjoy an Eastern European sausage plate, ocean garden prawns, lamb du jour or polenta aubergine. This opulent Victorian, surrounded by a colorful garden, also has gazebo seating and a dining room with wicker furniture. Deluxe.

Whether you choose a seat at the counter or one of the glass-paneled booths, you'll find **Geppetto's** (345 East Main Street, Ashland; 503-482-1138) a comfortable place to enjoy Italian and Ashland cuisine like linguini carbonara, five-spice chicken, polenta, and snapper. The decor is country casual. Be sure to try the fresh fruit pies. Moderate.

Looking for Asian cuisine served at a creekside setting? Consider **Thai Pepper** (84 North Main Street, Ashland; 503-482-8058). Step into the romantic, gray-walled dining room, take a seat on the wicker furniture and order such dishes as green chicken curry, yellow shrimp curry and crispy fish served with cold Singha beer. But your best bet, especially on a warm evening, is a seat on the shady patio next to the creek. Moderate.

A French bistro with stained-glass windows and dark wood booths illuminated by Tiffany-style lamps, **Châteaulin Restaurant** (50 East Main Street, Ashland; 503-482-2264) offers such dishes as veal and pork sausage with Dijon mustard, rotini noodles with smoked salmon, and gulf shrimp. In addition to deluxe-priced dinners, the café menu offers dishes such as fresh fettucine with cream mushroom sauce and sliced boneless Oregon chicken at moderate prices.

Alex's Plaza Restaurant (35 North Main Street, Ashland; 503-482-8818) has a good house pizza topped with pesto, pine nuts and cheese. Also on the menu are a New York steak with a Tulelake horseradish béarnaise, smoked salmon and a mixed grill featuring breaded cajun sausage and buffalo wings. Located in the first brick building built following the disastrous

1879 downtown fire, this second-story dining room still has its original fir floors. It's flanked by patios. Moderate to deluxe.

For Mediterranean, Italian or vegetarian fare in a creekside setting it's hard to beat **Greenleaf Restaurant** (49 North Main Street, Ashland; 503-482-2808). Budget to moderate specialties include breakfast dishes like tofu scrambles and sausage or mushroom frittatas. For lunch or dinner try pasta primavera, fruit salad or red snapper. An excellent choice for to-go fare.

Brother's Restaurant and Delicatessen (95 North Main Street, Ashland; 503-482-9671) offers a vast kosher and vegetarian menu including shrimp omelettes, *huevos rancheros*, bagels and lox, corned beef and cabbage and a Greek salad. The carpeted, wood-paneled dining room with balcony seating puts Brother's a cut above your average deli. Budget.

ASHLAND-ROGUE RIVER AREA SHOPPING

Stop, look and listen. **Walker's Antique Radio** (300 Merlin Road, Merlin; 503-476-1259) sells early oak and mahogany consoles, spiffy catalin plastic sets, classic "tombstone" table models, as well as novelty and short-wave radios.

Windy River Farms (★) (348 Hussey Lane, Grants Pass; 503-476-8979) has culinary and medicinal herbs, organic teas, honeys, dried fruits and vegetables. The farm is located 15 miles northwest of Grants Pass.

A good place to search for circus items, country kitchenware, jewelry, country quilts, rare books and Western memorabilia is **Turner House Antiques** (120 North 5th Street, Jacksonville; 503-899-1936).

Tudor Guild Gift Shop (15 South Pioneer Street, Ashland; 503-482-0940), adjacent to the Elizabethan Theater, sells all the Bard's works, brass rubbings, costumes, jewelry, and pull toys with a dramatic flair.

The Northwest Nature Shop (154 Oak Street, Ashland; 503-482-3241) is a wonderful place to shop for bird houses, minerals, wind chimes, hiking maps, nature and travel books. In a Craftsman-style house near downtown, this shop has a good selection of nature-oriented children's games.

For locally made products **The Oregon Store** (33 North Main Street, Ashland; 503-482-5453) is a good bet. You can sample smoked salmon, Oregon wines, cheeses and truffles. Scores of other local products such as wooden toys and handicrafts are also offered here.

ASHLAND-ROGUE RIVER AREA NIGHTLIFE

The **Blue Heron Dinner Theater** (330 Merlin Road, Merlin; 503-479-6604) is known for its melodramas performed by the heroes and villains of Col. Edwards Traveling Troupe.

The **River Room** lounge at the Riverside Inn (971 6th Street, Grants Pass; 503-479-2052) offers live music and dancing overlooking the Rogue River. You can also enjoy music and drinks outdoors on the deck.

Britt Festivals (Britt Pavilion, Jacksonville; 503-773-6077) offers classical, jazz, folk, theater and dance performances from late June through September. Headliners such as the Duke Ellington Orchestra, Preservation Hall Jazz Band and Fats Domino make this event a worthy companion to the nearby Oregon Shakespeare Festival. An outdoor theater, choose between lawn and reserved seating in the natural setting of the historic Britt estate.

The **Oregon Shakespeare Festival** (15 South Pioneer Street, Ashland; 503-482-4331) is the nation's oldest annual Shakespeare celebration, attracting more than 100,000 people each season. The most popular venue is the **Elizabethan Theater**, which stages plays during summer. The indoor **Angus Bower Theater** also presents Shakespearian performances, as well as classics by Shaw and Wilder. Contemporary works are performed at the festival's **Bower Theater** and experimental works are offered at the **Black Swan Theater**. The program runs from mid-February through late October. Advance reservations are mandatory during the peak season. Around 7 p.m. the Renaissance Musicians and Dancers offer free half-hour performances in the Oregon Shakespeare plaza.

The **Oregon Cabaret Theatre** (1st and Hargadine streets, Ashland; 503-488-2902) offers offbeat mysteries, musicals based on the Elvis legend and comedies in a theater featuring stained-glass windows, wooden balustrades and a crystal chandelier from an old movie palace. The **Actor's Theater of Ashland** (295 East Main Street; 503-482-9659) is an off-Broadway style community theater group performing in downtown Ashland and the nearby Minshall Theater in Talent.

The lounge at the **Mark Antony Hotel** (212 East Main Street, Ashland; 503-482-1721) offers live music and dancing in an elegant setting. There's also a lobby piano bar.

For live music and dancing weekends, try the **Rogue Brewery and Publichouse** (31 South Water Street, Ashland; 503-488-5061) beneath an art gallery with a deck overlooking Lithia Creek. Groups offer rock, jazz and blues.

ASHLAND-ROGUE RIVER BEACHES AND PARKS

Valley of the Rogue State Park—This 316-acre park on the Rogue River is convenient to the Grants Pass Area. Near the interstate, it's central to many rafting operators. The grassy, mile-long riverfront park is shaded by madrone, black locust and oak.

Facilities: Picnic areas, restrooms, boating and handicapped access; restaurants and groceries in Grants Pass; information, 503-582-1118. *Fishing:* Trout and steelhead are caught in the Rogue River.

Camping: There are 21 tent sites, 55 sites with electricity and water and 97 RV hookups; showers and laundry facilities.

Getting there: Located off Route 5, 12 miles east of Grants Pass.

Ben Hur Lampman State Park—On the south bank of the Rogue River opposite Gold Hill, the 23-acre day-use park is named for the late Ben Hur Lampman, a popular Oregon newspaper editor, fisherman and poet laureate.

Facilities: Picnic tables and restrooms; restaurants and groceries are in Grants Pass. *Swimming:* Permitted. *Fishing:* Trout and steelhead in the Rogue River.

Getting there: Located off Route 5, 16 miles east of Grants Pass.

TouVelle State Park—The 54-acre day-use facility is adjacent to Table Rock, an 1890-acre biologic, geologic and historic preserve forested with Pacific madrone, white oak and ponderosa pine.

Facilities: Picnic tables, restrooms, boat launch and wildlife viewing; restaurants and groceries are in Medford. *Swimming:* Good. *Fishing:* Salmon and trout in the Rogue.

Getting there: Take Route 62 nine miles north of Medford to Table Rock Road.

Rogue Elk Park—The mile-long park on the Rogue includes a warm creek ideal for swimming, and the kids can swing out into the river Tarzan-style on a rope hanging from an oak limb. Shade trees make this park a good choice on warm days. An ideal stopover en route to Crater Lake.

Facilities: Picnic tables, boat ramp, restrooms, showers and hiking trail; there's a restaurant across the street; information, 503-776-7001. *Fishing:* Steelhead and trout are caught in the Rogue. *Swimming:* Excellent.

Camping: There are 36 tent sites and 25 RV hookups.

Getting there: It's eight miles north of Shady Cove on Route 62.

Indian Mary Park (★)—This half-mile long park on the Rogue River west of Merlin is another ideal retreat for the entire family. Kids can play on the sandy beach or enjoy themselves at the playground. If you're towing a boat or raft you can launch it here.

Facilities: Picnic areas, restrooms, playgrounds and baseball field; restaurants and groceries are eight miles away in Merlin; information, 503-474-5285. *Fishing:* Good from the beach. *Swimming:* Good.

Camping: There are 90 sites, 35 of which are full RV hookups.

Getting there: From Grants Pass take Route 5 north to the Merlin exit. Continue west eight miles on Merlin-Galice Road.

Lake Selmac—A large Illinois Valley lake convenient to the Grants Pass area, this is popular summer resort. The 160-acre lake near Selma is a good choice for waterskiing, fishing, canoeing and sailing. The waters here tend to be warmer than the nearby rivers.

Facilities: Picnic tables, boat ramp and restrooms; restaurants and groceries are in Selma; information, 503-474-5285. *Fishing:* Good for trout, bass or crappie.

Camping: There are 90 sites (38 are full RV hookups) at Lake Selmac Campground.

Getting there: It's located 2.3 miles east of Selma via Upper Deer Creek Road.

Illinois River State Park—The largely undeveloped 511-acre day-use park at the junction of the east and west forks of the Illinois River is a secluded spot perfect for birdlife and wildlife viewing.

Facilities: Picnic tables, restrooms and hiking trails; restaurants and groceries nearby in Cave Junction; information 503-592-2166. *Fishing:* Try for trout and steelhead in the river. *Swimming:* Good.

Camping: Permitted in nearby U.S. Forest Service campgrounds in the Illinois Valley. Among them are Grayback and Cave Creek campgrounds, 12 and 17 miles, respectively, east of Cave Junction on Oregon Caves Highway. Grayback has 35 sites and Cave Creek, 18 sites.

Getting there: On Route 199, one mile south of Cave Junction.

Lithia Park—Ashland's 100-acre urban forest was designed by John McLaren, the creator of Golden Gate Park in San Francisco. A beautiful place to walk or jog, the park is a botanical garden with towering maples, black oaks, sycamore, sequoia, bamboo, European Beech, flowering Catalpa and the Chinese Tree of Heaven. Also here are a Japanese garden, rose garden and two duck ponds.

Facilities: Picnic tables, playground, tennis court, band shell, fountain and restrooms.

Getting there: On the south side of the Ashland Plaza in Ashland.

Cantrall-Buckley Park (★)—Just eight miles southwest of Jacksonville on a wooded hillside above the Applegate Valley, Cantrall-Buckley extends half a mile along the inviting Applegate River and offers beautiful views of this farming region.

Facilities: Picnic area, showers, restrooms, interpretive display and hiking trails; restaurant and groceries in Jacksonville; information, 503-776-7001. *Fishing:* Trout are caught in the river.

Camping: There are 40 sites; pit toilets.

Getting there: Take Route 238 eight miles southwest from Jackson and turn right on Hamilton Road.

The Sporting Life

FISHING AND BOATING

The Rogue, Umpqua and McKenzie rivers are all popular for salmon and steelhead fishing. For instruction in fishing and boat handling contact **The Executive Launch** (Salem; 503-581-1256). McKenzie River cutthroat trout fishing trips are arranged by **Bill Kremers and Butch Wicks** (29606 Northeast Pheasant Street, Corvallis; 503-754-6411). For fishing gear rentals and helpful advice, contact **Specialty Tackle Shop** (Medford; 503-772-7375). Both **Rogue Wilderness Inc.** (325 Galice Road, Merlin; 800-336-1647) and **River Trips Unlimited** (4140 Dry Creek Road, Medford; 503-779-3798) offer completely outfitted fishing trips.

You can rent fishing boats at **Wilderness Water Ways** (625 Northwest Starker, Corvallis; 503-758-3150), **Baker Bay Park** (Dorena Reservoir; 503-942-7669), **Lake Selmac RV Resort** (2700 Lakeshore Drive, Selma; 503-597-4989), **Howard Prairie Resort** (503-482-1979) and **Lake of the Woods Resort** (503-949-8300).

RAFTING

McKenzie River whitewater is ideal for rafting. You'll see why on a scenic day or overnight trip with such companies as **Bob Spencer's McKenzie River Guide Service** (41594 Madrone Street, Springfield; 503-741-4882). **Northwest Whitewater Excursions** (Eugene; 503-342-1222) also offers whitewater trips on the McKenzie, Umpqua and Rogue rivers.

The Rogue River is one of the Northwest's most popular rafting spots. Whether you paddle your own kayak or float with a guide, this is the ideal way to see the Rogue's wild and scenic sections. Choose between one-day trips and overnight trips. Contact **The Galice Resort** (11744 Galice Road, Merlin; 503-476-3818), **Rogue River Guide Service** (Grants Pass; 503-582-0271), **Orange Torpedo Trips Inc./Grants Pass Float Co.** (Grants Pass; 503-479-5061) or **Rogue Wilderness Inc.** (Grants Pass; 503-479-9554). For further information on whitewater raft operators contact the **Oregon Guides and Packers Association** (P.O. Box 10841, Eugene, OR 97440; 503-683-9552).

Another way to tour (though not very ecological) the Rogue wilderness is via jetboats. **Hellgate Excursions, Grants Pass Jetboats, Inc.** (953 Southeast 7th Street, Grants Pass; 503-479-7204) offers two-to-five-hour scenic trips through Hellgate Canyon.

GOLF

When you're ready to hit the links in the Salem area try **Salem Golf Club** (2025 Golf Course Road, Salem; 503-363-6652), **Trysting Tree Golf Club** (Route 34 and Northeast Electric Road, Corvallis; 503-752-3027) or

Marysville Golf Course (2020 Southwest Allen Street, Corvallis; 503-753-3421).

Possibilities in the Eugene area include **Fiddler's Green** (91292 Route 99 North, Eugene; 503-689-8464), **McKenzie River Golf Course** (41723 Madrone, Springfield; 503-896-3454) and **Hidden Valley Golf Course** (775 North River Road, Cottage Grove; 503-942-3046).

In the Ashland-Rogue River area, try **Oak Knoll Golf Course** (3070 Route 66, Ashland; 503-482-4311), **Cedar Links Golf Course** (3155 Cedar Links Drive, Medford; 503-773-4373) and **Colonial Valley Golf Course** (75 Nelson Way Grants Pass; 503-479-5568).

TENNIS

The **Salem Parks and Recreation Department** (503-588-6261) operates public courts at Bush's Pasture Park (Mission and High streets), Cascade Gateway Park (2100 Turner Road Southeast) and Grant School Park (1350 Cottage Street Northeast).

Eugene Parks and Recreation (503-687-5333) offers public facilities at Amazon Courts (Amazon Parkway Court and 25th Avenue), Washington Park (2025 Washington Street) and Sheldon Courts (2445 Willakenzie Road). The **Willow Creek Racquet Club** (4201 West 13th Street, Eugene; 503-484-7451) is also open to the public.

BICYCLING

The Willamette Valley is paradise for bikers. Hundreds of miles of relatively flat, scenic bike trails will make your journey a pleasure. Extensive bike-support facilities are found in all cities covered in this chapter. Seldom congested, some of the best routes parallel beautiful rivers, parks and lakes. You can camp at hiker-biker primitive campsites in any state park or enjoy a comfortable bed and breakfast along the way.

A popular route follows the **Oregon Trans-America Trail** from the Dallas area near Salem south through the state's wine country to Corvallis. The trip, which parallels portions of the Willamette River, heads east from Eugene through the scenic McKenzie River Valley. Highlights include wildlife refuges and covered bridges.

Eugene's **Willamette River Recreation Corridor** offers five bridges which connect the north and south bank bike trails. The 12-mile loop from Knickerbocker Bridge to Owosso Bridge includes numerous parks, downtown Eugene and the University of Oregon campus.

Eight miles south of Eugene, the **Fox Swale Area** offers an easy-to-difficult eight miles of offroad trails ideal for mountain biking. Ride the Fox Hollow Road nine-and-a-half miles over the summit and down into the valley to BLM Road 14-4-44. Muddy during the rainy season.

From the town of Rogue River, east of Grants Pass on Route 5, head north eight miles along Evans Creek to Wimer and the glorious **Evans Valley**. It's a four-mile ride out Pleasant Creek Road at the covered bridge. Look for elk in the meadows.

Just north of Ashland at Talent, Anderson Creek Road heads west to Little Applegate Road and the **Applegate Valley**. This route returns to Jacksonville via Applegate Road and Highway 238. To complete the 40-mile loop back to Ashland pick up South Stage Road to the Bear Creek Greenway Recreational Trail. You can also enjoy the **Bicentennial Bikepath** that runs across Ashland and then continues north ten miles to Medford paralleling scenic Bear Creek.

For further information on cycling routes contact the **Salem Bicycle Club** (P.O. Box 7666, Salem, OR 97303; 503-362-1420), **Eugene Off-Road Cyclists** (P.O. Box 23625, Eugene, OR 97402; 503-485-8929) or the **Southern Oregon Cycling Association** (P.O. Box 903, Ashland, OR 97520; 503-482-1122). **Eugene Mountain Bicycle Resources Group** (503-686-4365) publishes *Mountain Bike Ride Guide* available at bike shops in the Eugene area.

BIKE RENTALS   To rent a cruiser or mountain bike call **Peak Sports** (129 Northwest 2nd Street, Corvallis; 503-754-6444), **Pedal Power Bicycles** (545 High Street, Eugene; 503-687-1775), **Sim's Cyclery** (925 North Central Avenue, Medford; 503-772-9220) and **The Adventure Center** (40 North Main Street, Ashland; 503-488-2819).

HIKING

From short ridgeline trails above the region's major cities to remote day hikes through river valleys, the Willamette Valley and Ashland-Rogue River area offer great possibilities.

SALEM AREA TRAILS   A great way to acquaint yourself with the Willamette River is to hike the **Riverfront Trail** (4 miles) in Willamette Mission State Park. This trail offers a secluded stretch of river.

The Loop Trail (7 miles) at Silver Falls State Park reaches all ten waterfalls along Silver Creek Canyon. Shorter hikes (less than 2.5 miles) can also be taken from roadside trailheads to the individual falls.

Salem's **Rita Steiner Fry Nature Trail** (.3 mile) offers a pleasant stroll through Deepwood Park, adjacent to the Historic Deepwood Estate.

On River Road South, a mile south of downtown, **Minto-Brown Island Park** has 15 miles of trails and paths.

EUGENE AREA TRAILS   Convenient to Eugene, the **Fall Creek National Recreation Trail** (★) (14 miles) is ideal for day hikes and overnight trips in the hardwood Willamette National Forest. Pristine Fall Creek is visible from most of the trail, which begins at the Dolly Varden Campground. The short Johnny Creek Nature Trail, a spur located off Road 1821, is ideal for the physically challenged. Wildflowers abound in the spring.

Eugene's **Mount Pisgah Arboretum** has seven miles of hiking trails. You can enjoy a lovely walk through oak savanna, a Douglas fir forest or along a seasonal marsh.

Pre's Trail is a Eugene memorial to the legendary Oregon runner Steve Prefontaine. This all-weather trail through the woods and fields of **Alton Baker Park** offers parcourse-style routes ranging from .5 to 1.5 miles.

The **Kentucky Falls Recreation Trail** (★) (4 miles) runs along Kentucky Creek through a forest of Douglas fir and western hemlock. Located 41 miles southwest of Eugene, it leads down 760 feet to the twin falls viewpoint; information, 503-268-4473.

ASHLAND-ROGUE RIVER AREA TRAILS   Try Medford's **Bear Creek Nature Trail** (3 miles), beginning at Bear Creek Park off Siskiyou Boulevard. A series of 25 interpretive stations points out more than 20 kinds of trees and berries as well as landmarks along the creek.

More than 30 trail systems are found in the **Illinois Valley Ranger District** surrounding the Cave Junction/Oregon Caves area. Trails run from half a mile to 15 miles. Possibilities include **Tin Cup Gulch**, the **Kalmiopsis Wilderness**, **Black Butte** and **Babyfoot Lake**; information, 503-476-3830.

Transportation

BY CAR

From Northern California, **Route 5** runs north over the border to Ashland and the Rogue River Valley. Route 5 also takes you southbound from Washington across the Columbia River into Portland. If you're arriving from the Northern California coast, pick up **Route 199**, which heads northeast through the Siskiyous into Southern Oregon and Grants Pass. Many other highways link the Willamette Valley with the Oregon Coast and central Oregon such as **Routes 126, 20** and **22.**

BY AIR

Two airports bring visitors to the Heart of Oregon: Eugene and Medford. In addition, the big **Portland International Airport** an hour north of Salem has convenient connections to all major cities.

Eugene Airport is served by American Airlines, Horizon, United Airlines and United Express. **Medford Airport,** near Ashland, is currently served by Horizon, United Airlines and United Express.

For ground transportation to and from the Eugene Airport call **Eugene Limousine Service** (503-746-1440) or **Airport City Taxi & Limo** (503-484-4142). In Medford **Courtesy Yellow Cab** and **Airport Limousine** serve the airport (503-772-6268). **Ashland Limousine** (503-482-3065) links the Shakespeare capital with the Medford Airport.

BY BUS

Greyhound Bus Lines serves the Willamette Valley and Ashland-Rogue River area. Local stations are: Salem (450 Church Street; 503-362-2428), Corvallis (153 Northwest 4th Street; 503-757-1797), Albany (108 Southeast 4th Avenue; 503-926-2711), Eugene (987 Pearl Street; 503-343-2578), Sweet Home (1225 12th Street; 503-367-3678), Grants Pass (460 Agness Avenue; 503-476-4513), Medford (212 North Bartlett Street; 503-779-2103) and Ashland (91 Oak Street; 503-482-2516).

BY TRAIN

Amtrak's "Coast Starlight" provides daily service to the Willamette Valley. Amtrak (800-872-7245) serves Eugene (4th Avenue and Willamette Street), Albany (110 West 10th Street) and Salem (13th and Oak streets). In the south the train arrives in Klamath Falls where **York Tours** (503-779-1068) provides connections to Medford, Ashland and Grants Pass.

CAR RENTALS

You'll find many of the major rental agencies at the airports in Eugene and Medford. In Eugene, airport agencies include **Hertz Rent A Car** (503-688-9333), **Avis Rent A Car** (503-688-9053) and **Budget Rent A Car** (503-344-1670). In Medford, try **Hertz Rent A Car** (503-773-4293), **Avis Rent A Car** (503-773-3003), **National Car Rental** (503-779-4863) and **Budget Rent A Car** (503-773-7023).

PUBLIC TRANSPORTATION

All the major Willamette Valley and Ashland-Rogue River cities have public transit systems. While there are bus connections to many of the smaller towns, you'll need to rent a car to see many of the rural highlights.

The Salem area is served by **Cherriots** (503-588-2877). For service in Corvallis, call the **Corvallis Transit System** (503-757-6998). In Eugene, the **Lane Transit District** (503-687-5555) blankets the city. Medford, Jacksonville and Ashland are served by the **Rogue Valley Transportation District** (503-779-2877).

TAXIS

In Eugene, **Airport City Taxi & Limo** (503-484-4142) can take you downtown. In Medford, call **Courtesy Yellow Cab and Airport Limousine** (503-772-6288).

CHAPTER ELEVEN

Vancouver and the Sunshine Coast

Mother Nature went all out in British Columbia, a province larger than California, Oregon and Washington combined. Stretched along the upper west coast of North America, the coastline is dotted by thousands of islands, only a few inhabited. Inland are thick forests, rugged mountain ranges and high deserts. The more remote northern regions contain vast, pristine wildernesses.

Bordered by the Pacific to the west, the United States to the south and the Coastal Range to the east, the southwestern corner of the province, including Vancouver, Whistler and the Sunshine Coast, contains scenic splendors unrivaled in Canada. The waters of the region, fed by heavy rains (60 inches annually in Vancouver, more at higher elevations), shape this land; the ocean, high lakes, mountain streams, broad rivers, inlets and fjords carve through alpine meadows and mold shorelines.

Nature has long provided for human needs here. Myriad Indian tribes, living in peaceful coexistence with the earth, thrived in the mild climate of the region for centuries, hunting and camping in verdant forests, fishing salmon-filled waters and traversing the many streams and rivers. Europeans made an appearance in the 1770s when Captain James Cook sailed through searching for the Northwest Passage and stopped to trade with the Indians. Britain didn't lay claim to the area until Captain George Vancouver's visit in 1792.

Stories of the incredible abundance of wildlife brought in trappers and traders; a string of posts established by Hudson's Bay Company soon followed, with a steady flow of settlers not far behind. Friction arose when American settlers moved in and sought United States government authority. Eventually, the boundary between the United States and British Columbia was settled in 1846 by the Oregon Treaty.

As the fur trade began to wane, the Fraser Gold Rush of 1858 was just gaining speed, so the stream of settlers continued. Logging took off not long after the gold petered out. Gastown, the first settlement in what is now Vancouver, grew around an early saw mill. The city's future was insured with the arrival of the transcontinental railroad in 1887 and, with its natural harbor, its importance as a shipping center soon became evident.

Industry in British Columbia is still largely based on what the land provides—logging, fishing and mining—with Vancouver the processing and shipping center. Since the Vancouver World Fair in 1986 that focused worldwide attention on all the region had to offer, tourism has grown to become the second major industry in the province. Add to this mix Swiss-style banking regulations that attract investment from around the world and you have a truly dynamic city.

Commonly referred to as the "gateway to the Pacific," Vancouver has long attracted waves of immigrants from the Far East, more recently from Hong Kong as people seek to leave the island before control reverts to China. The second-largest Chinatown on the continent is based here, as are strong Italian, Greek, French, Indian, Japanese and other ethnic neighborhoods. It is this comfortable, congenial mix of nationalities that gives the city its vital, cosmopolitan nature.

Whistler, 75 miles northeast of Vancouver, is close enough for a day trip from the city (though there's too much to see and do in just one day). With island-dotted Howe Sound to the west and the verdant Coastal Range to the east, there are enough sights along the picturesque Sea to Coast Highway to make driving the narrow, winding road slow but enjoyable. Parks and scenic pull-outs along the way are perfect for a picnic or stretch.

The first settlers to arrive in Whistler in the early 1900s realized right away the potential in the area's beauty, so it comes as no surprise that some of the first structures were built as vacation retreats, most geared toward fishing and hunting. Skiing began in earnest in 1966 with the opening of the Garibaldi Lift Company in Whistler. A stylized European village resort was constructed 12 years and $550 million later at the convergence of the Blackcomb and Whistler mountains. In its short time, this ski destination has gained a strong international reputation and is now among the top attractions in North America.

Boutiques and eateries line the cobbled walkways of Whistler Village that are often alive with street entertainers, from jugglers and clowns to dancers and musicians. The warmer months (June-September) are a favorite time to visit since crowds are minimal, prices for accommodation are drastically lower and there are so many outdoor activities to enjoy in the area's quiet alpine meadows, dense green forests and cool mountain lakes. However, even during ski season (November-May), you'll find no shortage of parking—a big problem at many resorts—because the main village of this carefully planned resort is built atop a massive underground garage.

With approximately 2400 hours of sunshine each year, the Sunshine Coast lives up to its well-deserved name. It is made up of small, quiet fishing and logging communities strung along a 90-mile coastline. These pleasant sights lie between Langdale, a short ferry ride from Horseshoe Bay in West Vancouver, and Lund, the gateway to Desolation Sound Marine Park. Another short ferry ride between Earls Cove and Saltery Bay connects the northern and southern sections of the coast. The ferry trips give visitors the sense that they are touring a series of islands even though the Sunshine Coast is firmly attached to the mainland.

The region is a gem for anyone who loves the great outdoors, with mild weather and enough hiking, camping and water activities—fishing, diving, canoeing, kayaking, sailing or simply lounging on one of many beaches—to please one and all. The locals, mainly loggers, anglers and artists, are friendly

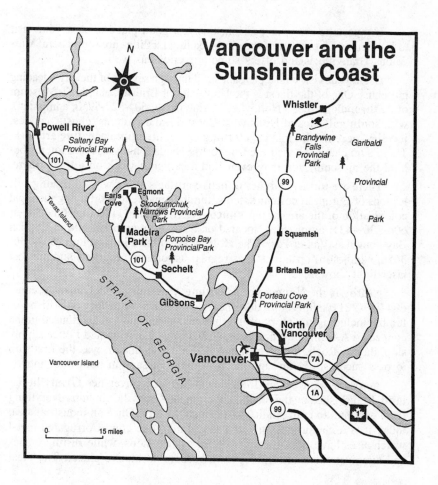

Vancouver and the Sunshine Coast

and upbeat, willing to share recommendations for what to see and do in their neck of the woods. Except for warm summer weekends, the Sunshine Coast is not yet inundated by tourists and retains a rustic, provincial air.

Southwestern British Columbia offers something for everyone tucked into a neat package; the urbane and worldly pleasures of Vancouver, the bustle and excitement of resort life at Whistler and the undeveloped, uncrowded scenic beauty of the Sunshine Coast. Simply put, it is a vacationer's paradise in the Pacific Northwest.

West Side/Granville Island

If museums are your passion, this is a good place to start your visit to Vancouver. A number of the city's leading facilities are found here. Marvelous Granville Island offers some attractions as well.

Begin your visit with a pleasant stroll through several of the city's leading museums. One of the finest is the University of British Columbia's **Museum of Anthropology** (6393 Northwest Marine Drive; 604-822-5950; admission), with sunlit galleries of Northwest Coastal Indian totems, chests, canoes, jewelry, ceremonial masks, clothing and contemporary native artwork. There's no charge to visit the true-to-life Haida long house and totems behind the museum; you may even find a carver at work on a totem there.

There are further samples of native artifacts along with intriguing collections of European costumes, tools, furniture and relics portraying the rapid colonization of the area at the **Vancouver Museum** (1100 Chestnut Street; 604-736-4431; admission), located on a small green peninsula in English Bay known as Vanier Park. The **H. R. MacMillan Planetarium** (604-736-3656; admission) upstairs stages regular astronomy programs and musical laser light shows.

Nearby is the **Vancouver Maritime Museum** (1905 Ogden Avenue; 604-737-2211; admission), documenting the maritime history of British Columbia including the glory of international steamship travel. Housed in the connected A-frame building is the Royal Canadian Mounted Police supply ship, the **St. Roch**, now a National Historic Site since it was the first ship to pass successfully through the Northwest Passage in both directions.

Across a short bridge from downtown Vancouver lies **Granville Island**. Refurbished by the federal government, Granville contains everything from parkland to craft studios to a cement factory. Once an industrial area, today it is a classic example of native funk gone chic. Corrugated-metal warehouses have been transformed into sleek shops, while rusting cranes and dilapidated steam turbines have become decorative pieces. The focal point is the **Granville Public Market**, a 50,000-square-foot collection of stalls selling fresh fish, fruits, vegetables and other goodies.

A quick stop at the **InfoCentre** (Johnston Street; 604-666-5784) to see the orientation film and pick up a map helps you focus on what you want to see and do. There are several **working studios** to view. Leave time for an informal, 30-minute tour of the **Granville Island Brewing Company** (1441 Cartwright Street; 604-688-9927), the first micro-brewery in Canada and home of the popular Island Lager. Of course, getting to the market is half the adventure: You can walk, drive or catch the **False Creek Ferry** (604-684-7781) from behind the Vancouver Aquatic Center (south end of Thurlow Street), or the **Aquabus ferry** from the Maritime Museum.

WEST SIDE/GRANVILLE ISLAND HOTELS

Throughout the year there are affordable rooms available at the **Walter Gage Residence** (5961 Student Union Boulevard; 604-822-1010), part of the University of British Columbia's conference center. Single and twin rooms in the dorm buildings are generally full of students during the school term, but "deluxe suites" (one-bedroom apartments with kitchenette and private bath) are always available. Guests can get a cheap meal in the Student Union Building cafeteria or head to the fancy Faculty Club for a meal. Moderate.

The **Vancouver Hostel** (1515 Discovery Street; 604-224-3208), the second-largest youth hostel in North America, enjoys a prime setting on English Bay across from lovely Jericho Beach. Housed in what was once military barracks, there is space here for over 300 hostelers in the many dorm-style rooms with shared baths; the few couple/family rooms go quickly. With fully equipped communal kitchens, laundry facilities, cafeteria and lounge with big-screen television, this is easily one of the fanciest hostels you could hope to visit. Budget.

The welcoming glass lobby full of greenery bustles with business people, the majority of the clientele at the **Executive Inn** (7211 Westminster Highway, Richmond; 604-278-5555). This quiet, friendly hotel near the airport has 18 standard rooms and 62 suites in pastel tones with breakfast bars, mini-refrigerators and modern furnishings in separate seating and sleeping areas. Rooms with jacuzzis or kitchenettes are also available. Moderate.

WEST SIDE/GRANVILLE ISLAND RESTAURANTS

The Kitsilano neighborhood, a long, narrow district that runs from around Burrard Street to Alma Street and features commercial corridors along 4th Avenue and Broadway, boasts many excellent, small restaurants. **Pistachio's** (1938 West 4th Avenue; 604-732-3114), with its easy ambience and fresh pasta dishes, is a budget-priced café that attracts a local crowd.

The top Thai restaurant hereabouts is **Bai Tong** (2042 West 4th Avenue; 604-734-8424), a trim dining room that combines intimacy with intriguing dishes. Open only for dinner, it offers several curry dishes as well as steamed trout with hot and sour sauce, squid in chili sauce and beef and chicken dishes. Highly recommended by local critics. Moderate.

Last time we stopped by **Sophie's Cosmic Café** (★) (2095 West 4th Avenue; 604-732-6810) diners were lined up outside the door. Inside, people were piling into naugahyde booths and gazing at the pennants, posters and antique toys that line this quirky café. There are tofu omelettes and high-fiber Belgian waffles for breakfast, and falafel burgers and Texas-style chili later in the day. Dinner gets downright sophisticated as Sophie cooks up Cajun prawns, poached oysters and chicken Rouchambeau. A scene. Moderate.

Set near the conservatory at the peak of Queen Elizabeth Park, the elegant **Seasons In The Park Restaurant** (Cambie Street at 33rd Avenue; 604-874-8008) enjoys sweeping views of the Vancouver skyline and the mountains towering above the North Shore. The seafood and Continental dishes are seasonal, and specials from the daily menu are always on a par with the outstanding view. Deluxe.

A just-for-fun diner is **Fogg 'n' Suds** (500 West Broadway; 604-872-3377), a fancified hamburger joint with relaxed atmosphere and a friendly crowd. You probably won't have time to try each of the 250 beers from around the globe, but it's a big event when a regular manages to fill that final slot in Fogg 'n' Suds stylized passport of brews. Budget.

Tandoori fans will appreciate the hearty East Indian fare at **Da Tandoor** (3135 West Broadway; 604-737-7333) where flavorful spices wake up those bored taste buds. Favorites from the authentic earthenware oven include leavened breads, lamb curry, India spice chicken and other tandoori specialties marinated in yogurt and spices. Dinner only; deluxe.

Another spot for a fine view of the city lights, this time from water level on the Granville Island Wharf, is **Bridges** (604-687-4400), one of the current hot spots of the dining elite who choose the refined elegance of the dining room, the relaxed bistro or the convivial pub. The fare here ranges from standard and nouvelle preparations of seafoods and meats to basic pastas and finger foods. Moderate to deluxe. Reservations recommended.

Inevitably you are going to end up on Granville Island. Should hunger strike while you're touring the shops and artist studios, check out the budget-priced food stalls at the **Granville Public Market**. Here you'll find a fish-and-chips shop, souvlaki stand, juice and salad bar, deli, even a fresh soup outlet.

WEST SIDE/GRANVILLE ISLAND SHOPPING

A strip of intriguing shops lies along **4th Avenue** between Burrard and Alma streets. Situated between Granville Island and the University of British Columbia campus, this is the Kitsilano neighborhood. Back in the '60s and '70s, it was a center for Vancouver's counterculture. Since then, time and gentrification have transformed it into a spiffy district of smart shops and comfortable homes.

The main draw on Granville Island is the **Public Market,** with rows of vendors selling fresh produce, flowers, pastas, wines, baked goods, seafood and meats, along with the section brimming with fast-food outlets proffering an international array of delectables. Other stops of interest include the **Kids Only Market** (1496 Cartwright Street; 604-689-8447), a mall full of toy stores, children's clothing shops and a tikes' beauty salon; **Christmas Presence** (1551 Johnston Street; 604-684-9922), a year-round showcase for yuletide ornaments and decorations; and the **Cartoon Corner Art Gallery** (1406½ Old Bridge Street; 604-683-8989), carrying limited-edition animation cells that go for a pretty penny.

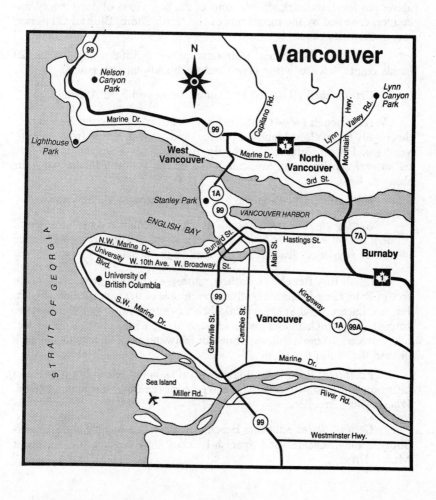

WEST SIDE/GRANVILLE ISLAND NIGHTLIFE

There is plenty of innovative theater to choose from on Granville Island at the **Arts Club Theatre** (604-687-1644), **Carousel Theatre** (604-669-3410), **New Play Center** (604-685-6228) and **Waterfront Theatre** (604-685-6217), with afternoon performances often followed by high tea.

WEST SIDE/GRANVILLE ISLAND BEACHES AND PARKS

Queen Elizabeth Park—Taking the place of two stone quarries that once supplied building materials for the city, this 130-acre park now features various ornamental gardens showcasing the indigenous plants of the coast along with two rock gardens that reflect the land's past. At 350 to 500 feet above sea level, the park affords some of the best views of downtown Vancouver, crowned by the mountains of the North Shore. Bloedel Conservatory rests at its peak.

Facilities: Restaurant, restrooms, picnic facilities, playgrounds, 20 tennis courts, lawn bowling lanes, and pitch-and-putt golf course.

Getting there: Located at Cambie Street and 33rd Avenue.

Wreck Beach (★)—Of the many beaches in and around Vancouver, this highly undeveloped (and unspoiled) sandy stretch across from the University of British Columbia on the tip of Point Grey Peninsula is the only *au naturel* spot in town. Students make up the majority of the sun worshippers here.

Facilities: Restrooms and restaurants nearby at the university.

Getting there: Located south of Nitobe Garden and the Museum of Modern Art off Northwest Marine Drive; a steep, twisting trail opposite the university residences leads from the road to the beach.

English Bay Beaches (southern shore)—Stretched around the north face of Point Grey Peninsula on the opposite side of the bay, Kitsilano Beach, Jericho, Lacarno and Spanish Banks beaches attract hordes of windsurfers, sunbathers, picnickers and swimmers but are spacious enough not to feel overcrowded. There's a heated outdoor saltwater pool at Kitsilano Beach in case the sea is too nippy.

Facilities: Restrooms, lifeguards (in summer), changing rooms and intermittent food stalls; restaurants and groceries nearby.   *Swimming:* Good. *Windsurfing:* Excellent.

Getting there: Kitsilano Beach is at Cornwall Avenue and Arbutus Street; Jericho, Lacarno and Spanish beaches are accessible off Northwest Marine Drive.

Downtown Vancouver

If your vision of downtown is an office world that rolls up the sidewalk at 6 p.m., get ready for a pleasant surprise. A beautiful harbor setting, intriguing historic districts, galleries and gardens sets downtown Vancouver apart from most cities.

The shining geodesic dome so prominent on the Vancouver skyline as you approach the city from the south was Expo Centre during the 1986 Exposition and is now home to **Science World British Columbia** (1455 Quebec Street; 604-687-8414; admission). Fascinating hands-on exhibits let you bend light, fondle a tornado, dance on a giant synthesizer keyboard and more. The **Omnimax Theatre** (604-875-6664; admission) upstairs features a variety of exciting films shown on the largest screen in the world.

There are numerous photo-worthy spots in **Chinatown**, which stretches along Pender Street between Carrall and Gore streets. North America's second largest Chinese community, this crowded neighborhood is particularly festive during holiday periods. Among the most remarkable sites is the extremely narrow **Sam Kee Building** (Pender and Carrall streets), listed in the *Guinness Book of World Records* as the skinniest building in the world at just six feet wide. Along the way you'll also see brightly colored, elaborately carved facades of buildings housing herbalists, bakeries, dim sum parlors, silk or souvenir shops and open-front produce stands.

A bit further on Pender Street is the old **Sun Tower Building** (★) (100 West Pender Street; 604-693-2305), which, at 272 feet, was once the tallest building in the British Empire and site of a daring escape stunt pulled off by Harry Houdini during the height of his career. Photographs displayed in the lobby chronicle the event.

Colorful **Gastown**, named after saloon keeper "Gassy" Jack Deighton whose statue stands in Maple Tree Square (Alexander and Carrall streets), is where it all began as the original townsite in 1867. This touristy heritage area of cobbled streets, Victorian street lamps and storefronts, charming courtyards and mews is chock-full of antique and souvenir shops and international eateries. On the corner of Cambie and Water streets is the world's first **steam-powered clock** wheezing out musical chimes on the quarter hour.

A few steps farther on Carrall there's a great view of the harbor from **Canada Place**, Vancouver's convention center and cruise-ship terminal. From the bow of this land-locked behemoth you can scan the waterfront, taking in the broad sweep of North Vancouver and the spectacular mountains behind it. There are arching bridges to port and starboard, ships at anchor in the harbor and an occasional ferry plying the narrow waterway.

Nearby, a glass elevator zips you up to the aptly named **Lookout!** circular viewing deck high atop Harbour Center (555 West Hastings Street; 604-689-0421; admission). With a tremendous 360-degree view of Vancouver and environs, plaques pointing out all the major sights, guides present to answer all questions and a brief multimedia presentation on the highlights of the city, this is one of the best places to get your bearings.

Housed in what was once the central courthouse, the **Vancouver Art Gallery** (750 Hornby Street; 604-682-5621; admission) has four floors of galleries showcasing the works of masters such as Goya, Picasso and Chagall alongside popular contemporary Canadian artists; the Emily Carr Gallery featuring many of her drawings and paintings of the coastal rain forests is a must see.

Robson Square (604-668-2830), just across the street below the current government offices and courts, is the site of frequent concerts and lectures and has a skating rink and fast-food court.

STANLEY PARK   Easily ranked as one of the most outstanding city parks in the world, 1000-acre Stanley Park (604-681-1141 or 604-738-8535) offers more recreational and entertainment options than you can imagine. Only the outer 20 percent of this green grove poking out into Burrard Inlet at the head of the downtown peninsula is developed for recreational use.

Within the park you'll find the **Vancouver Public Aquarium** (604-685-3364; admission) where you can view Bjossa and Finna, the orca whales, and the other 9000 or so varieties of marine life in the museum's numerous tanks. Then stroll through the tropical rain-forest room and listen to the birds chitter while peering at crocs or piranhas. An outdoor viewing platform on the west side of the compound allows free looks at the seal and beluga whale pools. Visits to the modest **Stanley Park Zoo** (604-681-1141) in the same vicinity are also free; however, there is a minimal fee to enter the **Children's Petting Zoo** to frolic with the llamas, goats and other little critters.

The best way to take in all the sights is to bike or hike along the divided six-mile **seawall promenade** (see "The Sporting Life" for more information). If you're pressed for time or just not up for the several-hour jaunt around the perimeter path, hop in the car and follow the one-way **scenic drive** signs from the park's main entrance off Georgia Street to hit most of the highlights.

Making your way around the promenade, you'll pass a statue of Lord Stanley, the rose gardens, the Royal Vancouver Yacht Club, Deadman's Island, the Nine O'Clock Gun, an array of Kwakiutl and Haida totem poles and the "girl in a wetsuit" statue next to the historic figurehead from the *S.S. Empress* of Japan.

Continue along the promenade to **Prospect Point Lookout**, at the far northern tip of the park, which boasts a great view of the **Lions Gate Bridge**. One of the longest suspension bridges in the world, it stretches over Burrard Inlet to the slopes of West Vancouver. Siwash Rock, the hollow tree and Second, Third and English beaches, extremely popular among sunbathers and water enthusiasts, finish out the seawall route.

To get to know the wild interior of the park, join one of the **summer nature walks**. Hikers will enjoy the miles of trails through thick coniferous forest while birdwatchers will probably prefer to perch quietly at the edge of **Beaver Lake** or **Lost Lagoon** to peer at Canadian geese, rare trumpeter swans and other waterfowl. For children there's the **Variety Kid's Water Park** (complete with slides, water cannons and a pint-sized, full-body blow drier), a miniature steam locomotive, pony rides, Kids Traffic School and a fire-engine playground.

DOWNTOWN VANCOUVER HOTELS

The **Travel InfoCentre** operates a free reservation hot line (604-683-2772 or 800-888-8835) to assist visitors in arranging for accommodations in all price categories. It's expensive to stay in the city, especially in the downtown core. If you bring your car, expect to pay an additional $10-$15

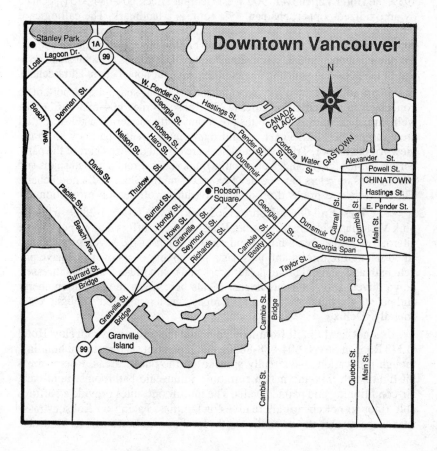

per day to park at most downtown hotels. You will also pay the Goods and Services Tax (7 percent) on short-term hotel accommodations; if this tax amounts to over $7, you can claim a rebate by filling out a form (available from your hotel) and presenting it at any Canadian Duty Free Shop or mailing it to Revenue Canada.

Located in the heart of the business and entertainment district of cosmopolitan Vancouver, the luxurious **Le Meridien** (845 Burrard Street; 604-682-5511) offers five-star accommodations at prices comparable to (and in some cases lower than) other top hotels in town, while assuring guests more for their money in terms of space and personal attention. Needless to say, rooms are elegant, with classical decor punctuated by a blend of antique reproductions and fine botanical prints; marbled bathrooms are enormous, with deep European-style tubs and separate showers. Personal service is the signature here. Ultra-deluxe.

Home away from home for the British royal family since it opened in 1939, the **Hotel Vancouver** (900 West Georgia Street; 604-684-3131), peaked by an oxidized-copper, château-style roof, is a landmark. The calling card of this posh property is Old World elegance. Rooms are spacious and well appointed with polished antiques, plump chairs, large writing desks and tall windows that open to the surrounding scenery. Bathrooms are a bit small (typical of the period in which it was built) but elegant nonetheless. Ultra-deluxe.

If prime downtown location and lots of room space are important to you, check into **Pacific Palisades** (1277 Robson Street; 604-688-0461). The well-furnished studios and suites are roomy with modern, pastel decor; all are equipped with kitchenettes, and many have breezy patios with grand views of the harbor. Triple-sheeted beds are turned down as part of the pampering service that includes pluses like thick robes, French milled soaps and other extras travelers have come to expect from the Shangri-La hotel chain. The ultra-deluxe prices drop drastically during off-season promotions.

The West End Guest House (1362 Haro Street; 604-681-2889), a bright-pink Victorian a block off bustling Robson Street, offers a more personable alternative to the area's hotels and motels. Each of the seven guest rooms filled with a mixture of antiques has a personality of its own. All have private bath and romantic four-poster brass beds with plush feather mattresses, down duvets and luxurious linens. Meals here, from the afternoon sherry and pâté to the multicourse morning repast, are a gourmand's delight. Gay-friendly. Deluxe.

It's not hard to tell from its layout that the three-story **Barclay Hotel** (1348 Robson Street; 604-688-8850) was at one time an apartment building, though renovations have really spruced up the public areas. Rooms are a bit tight, with mix-and-match furniture, minuscule bathrooms, mini-bars, air-conditioning and painted walls. The multiroom suites provide an affordable (though not cheap) alternative for families. Facing on Robsonstrasse near all the restaurants and boutiques, the location is its best attribute. Moderate.

Heritage House Hotel (455 Abbott Street; 604-685-7777) offers 110 rooms in an older brick building shaded by green awnings. Thoroughly renovated, the budget-tabbed rooms feature refrigerators, microwaves, wall-to-wall carpeting and contemporary furniture. Centrally located, the hotel is convenient to Gastown, Chinatown and major shopping districts.

The **Burrard Motor Inn** (1100 Burrard Street; 604-681-2331) has standard, motel-style accommodations at moderate prices in a good central location. A crotchety old elevator takes guests to upper-level, medium-sized rooms arranged in a quadrangle around the carport hidden under a rooftop garden. Furnishings are run of the mill, but parking is free, virtually unheard of in downtown Vancouver. There are a few kitchenette units available.

Offering six moderately priced rooms in a converted Victorian, **Gables Guest House** (1101 Thurlow Street; 604-684-4141) is a gay-friendly establishment facing Nelson Park. Furnished largely with Queen Anne-style furniture, the shared-bath rooms offer kings and queens. Some also sport decks. There's a lounge area for guests, a dining room where full breakfast is served and, in the summer, a barbecue area.

The budget-priced **Kingston Inn** (757 Richards Street; 604-684-9024) is an unusual find in downtown Vancouver. This 1910 wood frame with the large, beige awning and red neon sign was recently renovated inside and out to look more like a European bed and breakfast. The tiny rooms are clean and offer the bare necessities—vanity sink, dresser, bed, small closet—and a shared bath down the hall; seven rooms with private bath and television are larger. Continental breakfast is served in the lobby.

DOWNTOWN VANCOUVER RESTAURANTS

Dining in Chinatown is spelled dim sum. And the **Pink Pearl Restaurant** (1132 East Hastings Street; 604-253-4316) is a dim sum emporium, a cavernous dining room where black-clad waiters and waitresses roll out dozens of steam-tray delectables on trundle carts. You can dine at moderate cost on this finger food while enjoying the Chinese artworks that adorn the walls.

Closer to downtown is the **Snow Garden Restaurant** (513 West Pender Street; 604-682-8424), a Mandarin-style dining room. The menu includes an array of meat, fish and poultry dishes comfortably priced in a budget-to-moderate range.

They don't get many tourists in the quirky, hole-in-the-wall **Japanese Deli House** (★) (381 Powell Street; 604-681-6484), perhaps because of its location in a rundown section of Japan Town. Of the profusion of sushi shops in town, this low-key eatery continues to offer the best deal, with all-you-can-eat tuna, salmon, prawn and maki sushi accompanied by miso soup, tempura and teriyaki chicken. Budget.

Behind broad doors watched over by fierce Chinese guardian figures that scare away evil spirits, **Noodle Maker's** (122 Powell Street; 604-683-

9196) serves fine Chinese fare but is perhaps better known for the large interior pond full of koi that are called to dinner each day by gong and hand fed shrimp by the waitresses. Try to get a seat on the second level near the pond or waterfall for a fun, first-hand look at the fish feed. Moderate.

When wandering around Gastown, it's hard to miss the rotund, dancing monks touting their "scrumptious spaghetti, super salmon, ravishing ravioli and fabulous fondues" painted on the side of **Brother's Restaurant** (1 Water Street; 604-683-9124). Waiters in long, brown robes fit right in with the dark, monastical decor of this fun, family-style eatery. As promised, the food is good (especially the seafood and glazed barbecue ribs). Moderate.

Kilimanjaro (332 Water Street; 604-681-9913) has large picture windows looking out over Gastown, so diners can enjoy the bustle and lights of the area while feasting on authentic East African cuisine. Top picks here include *kuku paku* (coconut chicken), *kukuwa zabibu* (banana chicken), and prawns *piripiri* (tiger prawns in lime juice, garlic butter, paprika and Congo peppers), a specialty of Mozambique. African art and music and occasional weekend belly dancers round out the experience. Moderate.

When the wallet is plump and its time to indulge the taste buds, head for long-time favorite **The William Tell** (Georgia Court Hotel, 765 Beatty Street; 604-688-3504), poshly appointed in fine European art and a few antique crossbows in keeping with its name. Your gastronomic experience might start with Beluga caviar or lobster bisque, followed by veal loin in real morel sauce or Barbarie duck in juniper gin sauce. Items on the seasonal menu insert are always good choices, as are the extraordinary set meals presented in conjunction with shows at the Queen Elizabeth Theatre. Ultradeluxe; reservations recommended.

Bandi's (1427 Howe Street; 604-685-3391) is a charming home-turned-restaurant serving authentic Hungarian fare such as pork tenderloin, crunchy duck and red cabbage, marinated veal, robust goulash and peasant bread. On fine days the best seats in the house are actually outside in the garden. There's usually no problem finding a table at lunch, but reservations are recommended for dinner; deluxe.

If you're in the mood for Italian food, you can't go wrong by heading to one of Vancouver's five restaurants in the Umberto dynasty. The service and decor are impeccable and the food always tasty. Caesar salad, calamari, antipastos and pastas are always reliable choices. For al fresco dining on sunny days, we recommend the villa-style terra-cotta courtyard of **Il Giardino** (1382 Hornby Street; 604-669-2422). Check the phone book for addresses and phone numbers of other Umberto locations. Deluxe.

Café Fleuri (★) (Le Meridien, 845 Burrard Street; 604-682-5511), well known for outstanding Continental cuisine, also serves an incredible Chocoholic Bar from 6 to 10 each Friday and Saturday night that attracts hordes of sweet-toothed locals. There are 16-20 different chocolate items on the buffet (crêpes, fondues, cakes, covered fruits), the most intriguing being the chocolate pizza with layers of cake and mousse under shavings of white chocolate (the cheese) and toppings of sliced kiwi, strawberries, pineapple or other seasonal fruits. Moderate.

Humorous artwork and an upbeat decor set the tone at **Banana's Café California** (1044 Robson Street; 604-682-2411), the place to be seen among young professionals working downtown. The focus of the menu is contemporary Western cuisine with distinct Asian and Mexican influences. Come to feast on the variety of salads, steaks and seafood or just snack on nachos and sip fun drinks. Moderate.

Le Crocodile (818 Thurlow Street; 604-669-4298), an intimate bistro with romantic, candlelit tables, is the critics favorite for fine French cuisine at reasonable prices. The emphasis here is on hearty regional fare, lightly sauced in many cases and always beautifully presented. Particularly good are the roast leg of lamb in mustard seed sauce, grilled quail with spinach pesto and sweet breads with pink peppercorn sauce. Save room for a treat from the fresh dessert menu. Moderate to deluxe.

For more refined dining, turn to the **Monterey Lounge and Grill** (in the Pacific Palisades Hotel, 1277 Robson Street; 604-684-1277), a romantic spot with candlelit tables, soft piano serenades and expansive window views of the endless parade on bustling Robson Street. Best bet on the continental menu is the *prix fixe*, multicourse dinner that might feature such delectables as crab cakes, smoked-salmon mousse with toast and fruit, reddened snapper with polenta and chocolate pecan flan in bourbon cream. Moderate to deluxe.

Generous breakfasts and lunches attract a mixed clientele to the **Elbow Room** (702 Jervis Street; 503-685-3628). Located in a century-old brick building, this small Bavarian-style room is decorated with autographed photos of movie stars. Start your day with the lumberjack or English breakfasts, eggs benedict, pancakes or an omelette. For lunch try a Monte Christo, Reuben, clubhouse or shrimp sandwich. The owners say you have to have personality to fit in. Weekend breakfasts are popular with the gay crowd. Budget.

Tokio By The Bay (1752 Davie Street; 604-683-8744), a two-story, contemporary, glass-and-beam structure, takes full advantage of its setting and wonderful views of peaceful English Bay. Upstairs is a serene sushi bar where aficionados will find all their favorites. Downstairs is a yakitori bar serving calamari and yakitori grilled on flat stones heated over charcoal. Prices here are moderate for dinner and a bargain for lunches served on the weekends only.

Harajuku (1256 Robson Street; 604-685-5818) looks and feels more like a bar than a restaurant, probably due to the banquette seating, dim lighting and laser karaoke projection screens, but it's a great spot to grab an inexpensive, hot meal in an otherwise expensive area of downtown. Here you can sing along to classic tunes like "Traveling Man" or "Dock of the

Bay" or just be serenaded by the staff as you slurp steaming bowls of ramen or munch tidbits of sushi, shrimp and vegetable tempura. You'll probably have the place to yourself before 9 p.m., but expect a big crowd later for karaoke, drinks and snacks. Budget.

Don't miss **Quilirum West Coast Indian Restaurant (★)** (1724 Davie Street; 604-681-7044), a "longhouse" serving the native cuisine of the Pacific Northwest. You'll feast your eyes on Vancouver's most unique menu, then fill your belly with caribou stew, baked juniper duck, barbecued goat ribs or steamed smoked Alaska black cod. On the side are steamed fern shoots and wild rice. For dessert, how about cold raspberry soup or whipped soapallalie (Indian ice cream), washed down with a cup of juniper tea? Deluxe.

Tropika (1096 Denman Street; 604-682-1887) off English Bay offers a fine introduction to Malaysian cuisine. If you really don't know what you're getting into, order satay (marinated meat skewered and grilled over charcoal); if you've had some exposure, you'll appreciate the spicier starred selections. Moderate.

With it's bordello decor and prime Northwest haute cuisine, funky **Delilah's** (1906 Haro Street; 604-687-3424) in the West End is one the locals usually prefer not to share. As you arrive, you'll be handed a menu of the day's specials where you'll check off your selections—perhaps a tasty pheasant pâté, wild mushroom soup and salmon grilled to a turn. Next, sidle up to the bar for one of their famous martinis to keep you happy during the longish wait to be seated and served. Dinner only; deluxe.

DOWNTOWN VANCOUVER SHOPPING

There are enough shops in Vancouver to overwhelm even the most serious of the "I'd-rather-be-shopping crowd." Here are a few in the most popular shopping districts.

In Chinatown, the **Beijing Trading Company** (89 East Pender Street; 604-2736) carries an intriguing selection of herbs, teas and food products, while **Cheng Kiu** (8105 Main Street; 604-327-1381) is an emporium of Chinese vases, brassware and collectibles.

Nearby, Gastown is brimming with souvenir shops full of T-shirts, totems, maple sugar, smoked salmon and other regional items; **Canadian Impressions** (321 Water Street; 604-689-2024) seems to have the widest selection. Other stores worth visiting in the area include **Artemis** (321 Water Street; 604-685-8808) for fine antiques, rugs, statuary and other decorative art; **Mrs. Junko** (375 Water Street; 604-669-6306) for everything frilly, lacy and feminine; **Neto** (357 Water Street; 604-682-6424) for sleek leather fashions; and the **Inuit Gallery** (345 Water Street; 604-688-7323) for high-dollar North Coast Indian and Inuit art.

Another popular downtown shopping area is Robson Street. It's nicknamed Vancouver's Rodeo Drive because of the sheer number of see-and-be-seen sidewalk cafés and upscale boutiques. High-quality and high-priced stores include **Polo/Ralph Lauren** (604-688-7656) and **Alfred Sung** (604-867-2153) in Robson Fashion Park (1131 Robson Street) selling high fashion. There are also several souvenir shops scattered along the strip along with some fun places such as **The Love Shop** (121 A-1025 Robson Street; 604-669-6643) offering lingerie and adult toys, and the **Robson Public Market** (1610 Robson Street; 604-682-2733) with over two dozen retail stores.

DOWNTOWN VANCOUVER NIGHTLIFE

The **Vancouver Opera Association** (604-682-2871) stages productions about four times a year at the Queen Elizabeth Theatre and Playhouse (Hamilton Street between Georgia and Dunsmuir streets; 604-665-3050), also home to **Ballet British Columbia** (604-669-5954) as well as major theater productions and visiting musicals. The **Vancouver Symphony Orchestra** (604-684-9100) provides first-rate entertainment at The Orpheum (884 Granville Street), a multilevel vaudeville theater built in the mid-'20s that's worth a visit in itself.

There are hundreds of clubs, discos, cabarets, lounges, pubs and taverns in Vancouver; we touch on only a few popular selections here. **Richard's on Richards** (1036 Richards Street; 604-687-6794), the city's current "in" place, with its refined wood, brass and stained-glass decor, adult-oriented rock and live Top-40 bands on weekends, attracts an upscale business class.

A younger, wilder set frequents **Notorious** (364 Water Street; 604-684-1968), a self-dubbed "classic rock-and-roll party room" with dancing, darts, pool and pinball.

For an unhurried drink and quiet conversation, your best bet is the **Gérard Lounge** (Le Meridien Vancouver, 845 Burrard Street; 604-682-5511), a genteel gentlemen's-style club; this is the place to spot visiting celebrities as well.

Bridges (1696 Duranleau Street; 604-687-4400), a fairly subdued but trendy bistro on Granville Island, is fairly quiet and a good place to savor a glass of wine and the lights of the city dancing on the water of False Creek.

For laughs, the locals go to **Punchlines Comedy Theater** (15 Water Street; 604-684-3015) and to the **Hot Jazz Society** (2120 Main Street; 604-873-4131) for swing and modern jazz. The **Coastal Jazz and Blues Society Hotline** (604-628-0706) lists what's going on in the numerous jazz clubs around town.

Karaoke (sing-along) draws a big crowd to **Roppongi** (987 Granville Street; 604-685-9856), a slick Japanese-style nightclub aptly named after a pricey section of Tokyo.

Of the local gay haunts, **Celebrities Night Club** (1022 Davie Street; 604-689-3180) is open to both men and women, while the trendy **Gandy Dancer** (1222 Hamilton Street; 604-684-7321) reportedly reserves the dancefloor for men only at times. **Charlie's Lounge** (455 Abbott Street; 604-685-7777) offers soft jazz in a chandeliered room warmed by a fireplace and decorated with traditional paintings. Downstairs, at the same location is **The Lotus Club**, featuring country-and-western music played by a deejay. A mixed gay and lesbian crowd frequents the dancefloor at this contemporary lounge. Friday nights (women only) the club features Top-40 music. Cover. The third venue at this location is **Chuck's Pub**, where you'll find drag shows three nights a week. This male-oriented room offers a large oak bar, pool table, dart boards and contemporary music. A club with a southern mansion-style exterior, **Spunkey Disco** (1082 Granville Street; 604-688-1333) has a big dancefloor and full bar making it is a popular spot. Special line dancing and karaoke nights add to the fun.

Casino gambling is legal here, with half the profits going to local charities; for a little roulette, sic bo or blackjack action, try the **Great Canadian Casino** (2477 Heather Street; 604-294-1895) or the **Royal Diamond Casino** (1195 Richards Street; 604-685-2340).

DOWNTOWN VANCOUVER BEACHES AND PARKS

English Bay Beaches (northern shore)—Connected by Stanley Park's seawall promenade, silky English Bay Beach and broad Sunset Beach Park are prime candidates for a long, sunset stroll. Within walking distance of the city center, they are a favorite of business people out for a lunch break or there to catch the last rays after work during the week.

Facilities: Restrooms, changing rooms and intermittent food stalls; restaurants and groceries nearby. *Swimming:* Good.

Getting there: Off Beach Avenue on the southwest side of town.

Stanley Park—Beautiful Stanley Park is a green oasis in downtown Vancouver. Highlights include the aquarium and zoo, seawall promenade, children's water park, a miniature railway, scenic lighthouses, totem poles and statues, pitch-and-putt golf, shuffleboard, tennis courts, an evening gun salute (each day at 9 p.m.), open-air theater, a swan-filled lagoon and miles of trails through thick coniferous forest. Second and Third bathing beaches are extremely popular among sun lovers and water enthusiasts.

Facilities: Restaurants and concession stands, restrooms, showers and picnic facilities; information, 604-681-1141. *Swimming:* Excellent.

Getting there: Follow Georgia Street heading west through downtown to the park entrance.

North Shore

One of Vancouver's best features is its proximity to nature. Just a few minutes from the heart of town is this lush, green slope with scenic beaches, ecology centers and campgrounds. Easily reached by transit, this area also offers a great bird's-eye view of the metropolitan district.

There are several sights of interest on the North Shore, beginning with **Capilano Suspension Bridge** (3735 Capilano Road, North Vancouver; 604-985-7474; admission), a swaying footbridge stretched over the chasm 230 feet above the Capilano River; you'll pass through an amusement park complete with totem poles and souvenir-filled trading post to reach the bridge. Up the road a bit is the **Capilano Salmon Hatchery** (4500 Capilano Road, North Vancouver; 604-987-1411) where the public can tour free of charge and learn about the life cycle of this important fish.

Up farther still is **Grouse Mountain** (6400 Nancy Greene Way, North Vancouver; 604-984-0061; admission), the top of Vancouver, where visitors catch the Skyride gondola to the mountain peak complex to ski, hike, see the incredible high-tech mythology and history presentation about Vancouver in "The Theater in the Sky" or settle in for a meal at one of the restaurants.

NORTH SHORE HOTELS

Since 1985, the **Bed and Breakfast at Laburnum Cottage** (1388 Terrace Avenue; 604-988-4877) has been a breath of fresh air in North Vancouver, offering welcome respite for weary travelers. There are three posh guest rooms (each with private bath) on the second floor of the elegant, antique- and art-filled main house. Of the two housekeeping cottages on the grounds, the larger has two extra sleeping lofts making it suitable for families. The smaller, nestled in the prim English garden, is designed for romance. The food here is also a memorable experience. Deluxe.

The **Grouse Inn** (1633 Capilano Road; 604-988-7101), near the north end of the Lions Gate Bridge not far from shopping, dining and sightseeing spots, offers 74 tidy but plain, motel-style rooms decorated in earth tones. Standard rooms have the basics—full bath, queen bed, cable television, small table and chairs—though a few are set up as family suites and others are equipped with kitchenettes or waterbeds. Moderate.

NORTH SHORE RESTAURANTS

For that million-dollar view of the city and outstanding seafood to match, **The Salmon House On The Hill** (2229 Folkestone Way; 604-926-3212), perched on a North Shore hill in what is actually referred to as West Vancouver, fits the bill. The specialty here is fresh British Columbia salmon grilled over alderwood, but the shrimp-and-scallops brioche and veal are also worth trying. Lunch, dinner and Sunday brunch; moderate to deluxe.

Chesa (★) (1734 Marine Drive; 604-922-2411), yet to be discovered by the "in" crowd that tends not to stray from downtown, has built a solid reputation on extremely friendly service and moderately priced, delicious Swiss fare. Our favorite selection here is *emincé of veal a la Zurichoise* (sautéed morsels of veal, mushrooms and onion in a light, creamy, white-wine sauce), though the parfait of duck liver and chicken Ossi are also tempting. The garden decor and wicker furniture are conducive to a leisurely, relaxed meal.

Beachside Café (1362 Marine Drive, West Vancouver; 604-925-1945) offers outstanding dishes at moderate cost. The menu is an imaginative mix of such entrées as médaillons of turkey with shiitake mushrooms, stir-fry prawns in Thai curry, salmon wrapped in romaine lettuce, back ribs and lamb loin with cinzano and rosemary. The decor is a simple combination of white tablecloths, straight-back chairs and mirrored walls.

Strange as it sounds, **Capers** (★) (2496 Marine Drive, West Vancouver; 604-925-3316) is a waterfront restaurant tucked into the back of a health-food store. The accent, as you might have guessed, falls on quiche dishes, fresh seafood, pastas and vegetarian plates. There is an array of salad choices, and the views of Burrard Inlet are included in the moderate tab.

NORTH SHORE SHOPPING

Across Burrard Inlet in North Vancouver, **Lonsdale Quay Market** (end of Lonsdale Avenue) is a tri-level atrium mall on the waterfront. In addition to postcard views of the Vancouver skyline, this bustling shopping center combines trendy stores with a farmer's market. A great place to spend money, people watch and survey the shoreline.

NORTH SHORE BEACHES AND PARKS

Lynn Canyon Park—Though it's much shorter but slightly higher than the Capilano Suspension Bridge, there is no charge to venture out onto Lynn Canyon Suspension Bridge stretched 240 feet above the rapids of Lynn Canyon. There is also a fine ecology center in this pretty, 200-acre park.

Facilities: Restrooms, picnic facilities, nature trails and ecology center; restaurants and groceries nearby; information, 604-987-5922. *Fishing:* Fair.

Getting there: Located in North Vancouver at 3663 Park Road.

Capilano R.V. Park—Located under the north end of Lions Gate Bridge, this private venture is the closest camping option you'll find. While it's primarily set up for recreational vehicles, there are a few grassy tent sites; call ahead since these go quickly, and keep in mind that reservations (along with a deposit) are essential during the busy summer months.

Facilities: Restrooms, showers, picnic tables, playground, lounge, laundry, pool and whirlpool; restaurants and groceries nearby; information, 604-987-4722.

Camping: There 208 sites, 125 are RV hookups.

Getting there: In North Vancouver at 295 Tomahawk Avenue.

Whistler

One of Vancouver's best day trips leads to Whistler, a resort area famous for its skiing and après ski life. Snow lovers are drawn to the region's crystalline lakes and lofty mountains as well as its alpine trails and cosmopolitan ski village. Located 55 miles north of Vancouver, Whistler is considered by many to be one of North America's top ski areas. A number of British Columbia's best-known provincial parks also make the area ideal for fishing, windsurfing, swimming and, of course, loafing.

On your way up to Whistler, stop for a tour through the **B.C. Museum of Mining** (Highway 99, Brittania Beach; 604-896-2233; admission) which takes you deep into the workings of what was once the highest-yielding copper mine in the British Empire. The kids will enjoy panning for gold in the small pool set up for just that purpose.

As you're cruising farther up the Sea to Coast Highway, you'll pass a couple of sights worth a detour near the town of Squamish. First will be **Shannon Falls,** a high, shimmering ribbon of tumbling water immediately off the highway. Next you'll come to **The Chiefs,** the second-largest monolith in the world after the Rock of Gibraltar; on a fine day there will be climbers dangling all about the face of this mountaineer's dream.

One of the more interesting heritage sites in Whistler is at **Rainbow Park** (Alta Lake Road), the site of the area's first vacation retreat. This is also the best spot for a view of the valley and the Blackcomb and Whistler mountains.

For an in-depth look at the history of the area, visit the **Whistler Museum and Archives Society** (1101 Highway 99; 604-932-2019), a quaint museum with relics and artifacts and an interesting slide presentation.

North of Whistler past the logging and farming town of Pemberton is **Meager Hot Springs** (★), a series of pools, each varying in temperature, set in a pristine grove of evergreens. To get there, take Highway 99 to the Pemberton Meadows Highway and follow it north to Hurley River Road. After 45 minutes on this logging road, you'll come to the springs. It's possible to drive all the way through in summer, but a snowmobile trip is required to reach it during winter.

WHISTLER HOTELS

The **Whistler Youth Hostel** (Alta Lake Road; 604-932-5492) on Alta Lake is a convenient location for those arriving by train (which passes immediately in front of the hostel twice each day and stops on request). Accommodations are basic here, with men's and women's dorms and a few couple's rooms upstairs and a kitchen, dining room and gameroom downstairs overlooking the lake. Budget.

A nicer alternative is the **Whistler Lodge** (2124 Corrie Drive; 604-932-6604). You still need to provide your own food and bedding and will share cubicles with other hostelers, but this log lodge set above a quiet residential section offers lots of pleasant extras like a sauna and jacuzzi, barbecue and fire-pit off the large deck, ski-equipment locker, kitchen, laundry, game lounge and separate television/movie room. The budget prices are even lower if you reserve two-, three- or five-day packages; book well in advance for ski season.

If you seek an all-out alpine experience, you'll do well to choose **Edelweiss** (7162 Nancy Greene Way; 604-932-3641), a charming, European-style pension complete with window boxes and rosemaling on the chalet-like exterior. There are eight simply furnished guest rooms with private bathrooms and down comforters. A small guest lounge shares space with the sunny breakfast room where guests are treated to a hearty breakfast. The French and German proprietors, avid skiers, post a ski bulletin daily and provide free transportation to the ski lifts; there's even a whirlpool for post-slope relaxation. Moderate to deluxe.

The **Clock Tower** (604-932-4724), a landmark in Whistler Village, is one of many condominium complexes offering accommodations. Skylights brighten the angular studio bedrooms equipped with kitchenettes, long, narrow bathrooms and basic furnishings. Skiers will appreciate the ski lockers and sauna at the end of the day, and everyone will love the great location in the center of the village. Deluxe.

The **Fairways** (4005 Whistler Way; 604-932-2522) is farther from the lifts but has resort amenities like dining room, lounge, pub, fitness room, sauna, jacuzzi and indoor pool. Rooms are boxy, with basic, light-wood furniture, mini-bars and cramped bathrooms; some have built-in window seats to take advantage of the views. Request a corner unit or one with vaulted ceilings, which seem to be roomier and are the same price. Deluxe.

"Lifestyles of the Rich and Famous" dubbed the **Château Whistler** (4599 Château Boulevard; 604-938-8000), located at the base of Blackcomb Mountain, "Whistler's premier address" with good reason. The property is strikingly elegant and brimming with Old World charm. Guests enjoy inspiring alpine views from all 394 rooms smartly furnished with country-style wood furniture, double sleeper sofas, queen or king beds, mini-bars and large bathrooms. Ultra-deluxe.

Le Chamois (4557 Blackcomb Way; 604-932-8700), Whistler's newest full-service, luxury hotel, shares the same prime ski-in, ski-out location at the base of the Blackcomb runs. However, its smaller proportions (only 50 rooms) allow for a high degree of personal attention. The guest rooms are spacious, with big bathrooms, kitchenettes and designer touches evident throughout the decor; the studio rooms are especially wonderful, with two-person jacuzzi tubs in the living room area set before bay windows overlooking the slopes and lifts. Ultra-deluxe.

WHISTLER RESTAURANTS

"Never trust a skinny chef," is the motto at **Les Deux Gros** (★) (1200 Alta Lake Road; 604-932-4611), which the staff translate to mean the two fat guys. The focus here is on country French cuisine, and portions are generous indeed. The spinach and warm duck salad, steak tartare, juicy rack of lamb and salmon Wellington are all superbly crafted and presented, well worth the deluxe price. Located just about a mile southwest of the village, this is the spot for that special, romantic dinner. Open for dinner only.

With '50s pop-rock decor, plenty of booth seating and good old American favorites like roast turkey and stuffing, New York strip, gourmet burgers and baby back ribs, **Jimmy D's Roadhouse** (4005 Whistler Way; 604-932-4451) is a prime location to bring the family. Here again it fits into our moderate category, but residents regard it as the budget alternative to fast food.

To complete that alpine experience, you might want to head to **Chez Joël** (Whistler Village Square; 604-932-2112) for a cheese or meat fondue. Other picks from the far-reaching Continental menu include several healthy stir-fry and pasta choices. The wooden tables are a bit crowded here, and the bar is often packed, so this is no place for private conversation. Deluxe.

Araxi's (Main Square, Whistler Village; 604-932-4540), a bright and airy restaurant with congenial staff, has been a dependable favorite in town since the beginning. The menu features creative Northern Mediterranean cuisine with a heavy dose of Italian standards. The dining room is suitable for a quiet dinner for two, while the antipasto bar is best for a rousing drink with friends. Moderate to deluxe.

There are also several delis in the village, and the one the locals recommend most is **Hatto's Corner Deli** (Saint Andrews House; 604-932-8345) occupying a street-level corner on Sundial Place. Offerings here are gourmet soups, salads, sandwiches, pastries, cookies and other baked goods thrown in for good measure. On nice days there are plenty of tables set out front; otherwise you'll be lucky to get one of the few stools at the bar along the front windows. Budget.

Amazingly, there are five Japanese restaurants in little Whistler Village, and of those five, **Sushi Village** (4272 Mountain Square; 604-932-3330) is the one the locals most often visit. This place is busy, so service can be slow to a fault, but the atmosphere is serene, the decor clean cut and the food quite good, especially the tasty tempura and a la carte sushi items. Dinner prices fall into our deluxe category; lunch is a good deal.

Another romantic spot slightly removed from the bustling activities of the central village is **The Wildflower** (604-938-2033), an elegant restaurant decorated to echo the Old World charm of its setting in the Château Whistler. The award-winning chef focuses on fresh Pacific Northwest cuisine featuring organically grown regional herbs, veggies, fruits, eggs and meat. Seafood is also a specialty of the house, and the Sunday Seafood Brunch is a bargain, as is the breakfast buffet. Deluxe.

WHISTLER SHOPPING

Most of the great shopping in Whistler is done in the village, with top boutiques like **Polo/Ralph Lauren** (4182 Springs Lane; 604-932-6127) alongside specialty shops like **Christmas at Whistler** (4050 Whistler Way; 604-932-3518). Outdoor-lovers will appreciate the assortment of climbing gear and back-country equipment at **The Mountain Shop** (Delta Mountain Plaza; 604-932-2203) and **Escape Route** (#3-4241 Village Stroll; 604-938-3338). Chocoholics will be in seventh heaven at the **Rocky Mountain Chocolate Factory** (4190 Springs Lane; 604-932-4100).

Few artists call Whistler home, but the works of those who do are shown alongside contemporary pieces by well-known Canadian artists at the **Shepard Gallery** (4433 Sundial Place; 604-938-3366).

Native arts (primarily sculpture, jewelry and paintings) are exhibited at **Gaauda Native Fine Arts** (4599 Château Boulevard; 604-932-3382) in the lower level of the Château Whistler. As long as you're there, pop across the hall to **Zonda Nellis of Whistler** (604-938-2014) for distinctive and exclusive women's fashions.

WHISTLER NIGHTLIFE

You'll find a good selection of lounges, taverns and discos in Whistler Village (not surprising for a resort destination). The après ski scene is big everywhere, though one of the most popular spots is the **Longhorn Pub** (Charleton Lodge; 604-932-5999).

Rustic and rowdy **Garfinkel's** (4228 Village Stroll; 604-932-2323) concentrates on classic rock, while the glitzier **Savage Beagle Club** (4316 Skier's Approach; 604-932-4540) across the avenue features video pop hits and a comparable dance scene.

Buffalo Bill's (4122 Village Green Way; 604-932-5211) regularly brings in an array of live entertainment to whip things up on their big dancefloor.

The refined **Mallard Bar** (Château Whistler; 604-938-2430), with a large fireplace, soft piano music and expansive views of the Blackcomb Mountain base, is infinitely suitable for a quiet drink with friends.

WHISTLER BEACHES AND PARKS

Porteau Cove Provincial Park—This is a favorite among scuba enthusiasts because of its wooden-hulled minesweep ship and concrete reefs full of marine life located not far off the rocky beach. Porteau Cove, a long, narrow park stretched along the B.C. Rail tracks on the east shore of picturesque Howe Sound, also appeals to windsurfers.

Facilities: Restrooms, showers, picnic facilities, amphitheater, ecology center, divers' changing room and boat launch; restaurants and groceries nearby; information, 604-898-3678. *Fishing:* Excellent offshore. *Swimming:* Good. *Windsurfing:* Very good. *Diving:* Great.

Camping: There are 44 sites; there are also 15 walk-in sites.

Getting there: Located off Sea to Sky Highway 15 miles north of Horseshoe Bay.

Garibaldi Provincial Park—Named for Mount Garibaldi, its crowning point, this awe-inspiring park is made up of 480,000 acres of intriguing lavaland, glaciers, high alpine fields, lakes and dense forests of fir, cedar, hemlock, birch and pine. Thirty-six miles of developed trails lead into the five most popular spots—Black Tusk/Garibaldi Lake, Diamond Head, Singing Pass, Cheakamus and Wedgemont Lake.

Facilities: Restrooms, picnic tables, shelters, nature, bike and cross-country ski trails; restaurants and groceries nearby; information, 604-898-3678. *Fishing:* During the summer and early fall try for rainbow trout in Mamquam Lake (Diamond Head Area). *Swimming:* Very cold.

Camping: Permitted at Diamond Head where there is a hike-in shelter (seven-mile hike); you must bring your own gear. There are two hike-in campgrounds at Garibaldi Lake (four-mile hike).

Getting there: Located 40 miles north of Vancouver off the Sea to Sky Highway.

Brandywine Falls Provincial Park—The highlight of this small park is its 230-foot waterfall; a fascinating suspension bridge and winding nature trails are also close at hand. Perched alongside the highway, the sparsely wooded campsites can be a bit noisy at high-traffic times (weekends).

Facilities: Restrooms, picnic facilities, fire pits, nature and hiking trails; restaurants and groceries nearby; information, 604-898-3678. *Swimming:* Permitted in Daisy Lake.

Camping: There are 15 sites.

Getting there: Located approximately 40 miles north of Vancouver on the Sea to Sky Highway.

Sunshine Coast

The tourism boom has yet to hit the Sunshine Coast, which is rather surprising since nature has provided so much to admire here. With a 100-mile shoreline that stretches along the northeast side of the strait of Georgia, the Sunshine Coast is bordered by sandy beaches, secluded bays and rugged headlands, It reaches from Howe Sound to Desolation Sound in the north. This area is rustic, even a bit worn around the edges, but don't let that stop you. There are pleasant sites, plus a good number of artists in residence whose work is worth checking out.

As you leave the ferry at Langdale and begin to wind your way up the Sunshine Coast along Highway 101, one of the first areas of interest is the port town of **Gibsons**. Be sure to stop at **Molly's Reach** (Highway 101), for years the set for a popular Canadian television series. Displays at the **Elphinstone Pioneer Museum** (Winn Road; 604-886-8232) map the history of Indians and pioneers in the area. The museum also houses a massive collection of sea shells.

Next stop on the lower coast is the **House of héwhîwus** (Highway 101, Sechelt; 604-885-2273), or House of Chiefs, the center of government, education and entertainment for the self-governing Sechelt Indian band. Photographs and artifacts relating the history of the tribe are on display in the **tems swîya Museum**. Ask for directions to the totems and grouping of carved figures behind the complex.

If you have an interest in archeology, rent a boat and head north up the inlet from Porpoise Bay to view ancient Indian **pictographs** (★) on the faces of the cliff walls looming above the water.

From the trailhead near the town of Egmont, it takes approximately an hour to stroll the well-posted trail in to see **Skookumchuk Narrows**, a natural phenomenon of rapids, whirlpools and roiling eddies created by massive tidal changes pushed through the narrow inlet. If you arrive at low tide you can view the fascinating marine life trapped in tidal pools near Roland Point.

Taking the next ferry hop, from Earls Cove to Saltery Bay, brings you to the **Lang Creek Salmon Spawning Channel** (★) (Highway 101) about midway to Powell River. During the peak spawning season (October to December) you can get a close look at pink or chum salmon making the arduous journey upstream.

Nearby at **Mountain Ash Farm** (Nassichuk Road, Kelly Creek; 604-487-9340) the kids can play with little pot-bellied pigs, chickens, goats, sheep and other farm critters while you visit the country store for a look at local crafts and specialty foods.

Bird-lovers will be able to see past the wire-fenced compounds and enjoy the rusticity of the **Cranberry Lake Wildlife Sanctuary** (5570 Park Avenue, Powell River; 604-483-2122) with large pond, swampy creek and tall bush areas that attract swans, ducks, swallows, geese and other migratory birds.˙

The **Powell River Historical Museum** (Highway 101, Powell River; 604-485-2222; admission), an octagonal building just across from Willingdon Beach, houses a fine collection of regional memorabilia including furniture, clothing, utensils and logging equipment of pioneers and Indians along with a photo and print archive with material dating back to 1922.

For a further lesson in the history of the area, take the **heritage walk** through the Powell River Townsite to early 1900s homes, churches and municipal buildings of this old company town. Maps are available from the **Travel InfoCentre** (6807 Wharf Street, Powell River; 604-485-4701).

During the months of June, July and August you can take a free two-and-a-half-hour tour of the **MacMillan Bloedel Pulp and Paper Mill** (6270 Yew Street, Powell River; 604-483-3722), the life blood of Powell River. The tour gives you an inside view on the process of turning logs into lumber and paper products, from water blasting the bark off through forming pulp sheets to rolling the finished newsprint. No children under 12 permitted.

There's a great hilltop view of the "Hulks," a half-moon breakwater of ten cement ships protecting the floating logs waiting to be processed in the mill, at the **Mill Viewpoint** on Highway 101. Interpretive signs give a bit of history about the ships and the mill.

SUNSHINE COAST HOTELS

There are no big resorts or major chain hotels yet. Motels, inns and lodges are sometimes a shade worn but generally are friendly and inexpensive.

The recently opened **Gibsons Motor Inn** (963 Highway 101 #100, Gibsons; 604-886-4638) is easily one of the nicest alternatives we found on the Sunshine Coast. Big guest rooms feature pleasant pastel decor in shades of pink and green with dark-wood furnishings. There are several styles to choose from including rooms with kitchenette, jacuzzi and/or fireplace. There are even a dining room, pool, sauna and exercise room on the premises. Moderate.

The **Royal Reach Motel and Marina** (5758 Wharf Road, Sechelt; 604-885-7844) offers clean, basic accommodations in 33 simple rooms that are pretty much the same. Nondescript furnishings include two double beds, a long desk/television stand, plain bedside table and lamps, a mini-fridge, electric kettle and a small bathroom. Ask for one of the waterfront rooms that looks out over the marina and Sechelt Inlet. Budget.

Lowe's Resort (Madeira Park; 604-883-2456), a Pender Harbor institution since 1952, offers a range of accommodation options including three simple motel units, 14 cabins and plenty of tent and RV spaces among the permanent mobile-home units on the grounds. White paint, blue trim and flower baskets adorn the rustic, little housekeeping cottages furnished with vinyl couch and chairs, laminated table, blond-wood furniture and imitation velvet bedspread in the separate bedroom. The bathrooms are tiny. This is a suitable spot for families on a budget. The marina makes it a good choice for fishing and diving fans as well. Moderate.

With furniture that appears to be stuck in at odd angles to make it all fit, the motel-style rooms at the **Beach Gardens Resort** (7074 Westminster Avenue, Powell River; 604-485-6267) are nothing special, equipped with the basics. There are also cabins and kitchenette units available. What qualifies this as a resort are amenities such as the private marina, dining room, lounge, indoor pool, weight room and sauna. Moderate to deluxe.

Within moments of arriving at the charming **Beacon Bed and Breakfast** (3750 Marine Avenue, Powell River; 604-485-5563) and getting settled into one of the two inviting bedrooms or roomy downstairs suite, you'll begin to unwind and feel right at home. It's hard to tell whether to attribute this to the genuine hospitality or the cozy, down-home decor. Whatever the case, the congenial hosts, large hot tub, billiards room, great ocean view, proximity to the beach and thoughtful touches like plush robes and hearty, made-to-order breakfasts make this one of the most delightful lodging options in the region. Budget.

SUNSHINE COAST RESTAURANTS

Gibsons Fish Market (★) (1543 Gower Point Road, Gibsons; 604-886-7888), a hole-in-the-wall outlet on the main drag above the landing, does a booming business with tasty takeout fish and chips. It may not look like much, but there's usually a crowd lined up on the front sidewalk. Budget.

The **Harbour Café** (Gower Point Road, Gibsons; 604-886-7521) a few doors down is your best bet for breakfast. This multilevel, wood-paneled diner serves fine omelettes and pastries throughout the morning and afternoon; they also add a selection of burgers, soups and salads to the lunch menu. Budget.

The **Blue Heron Inn** (East Porpoise Bay Road, Sechelt; 604-885-3847), a delightful waterfront home-turned-restaurant on picturesque Porpoise Bay, is home to masterful creations. The daily menu uses fresh regional produce and seafood in the dishes. Though they don't advertise it, there are three cozy guest rooms upstairs, with romantic dinner and accommodations packages available with advance notice. Deluxe.

Folks over 21 can stop by the **Royal Canadian Legion Hall Branch 112** (Lily Road, Madeira Park; 604-883-9632) for a super-cheap supper of prawns or chicken and chips, Salisbury steak, Cajun chicken or juicy burgers. This is actually one of the nicest (and only) places in town to get a meal, but the bar inside means that only those of legal drinking age can enter. The salt-of-the-earth folks here might even let you in on a hand of cards or a fevered dart or shuffleboard game. Dinner only; budget.

The Eagles Nest (4680 Marine Avenue, Powell River; 604-485-2733), a little, woodframe house with country-cottage decor, is new in town and with any luck will be around for years to come. The talented chef serves up enormous portions of Continental favorites such as veal cordon bleu, eggplant parmigiana, penne al pesto along with daily specials like quail with rice and raisin stuffing in calvados-apple sauce. He prepares everything from scratch, so be prepared for a lengthy wait followed by mouth-watering rewards. Moderate.

The **Shingle Mill Restaurant** (6233 Powell Place, Powell River; 604-483-2001), situated at the tip of Powell Lake, has large windows on three sides so the views of this beautiful, pine-trimmed lake are not wasted. It's no surprise that they serve grilled B.C. salmon in this waterfront eatery, but the steak au poivre, chicken with feta and spinach in puff pastry, and fussilli primavera are unexpectedly good. Items from the dinner menu are available in the relaxed bistro. Deluxe.

SUNSHINE COAST SHOPPING

There is an abundance of artists living in small communities all along the Sunshine Coast, many willing to open their studios to tours available through the Sunshine Coast Arts Council (Pat Forst, S13 C1 North Road, RR1, Gibsons, BC V0N 1V0). You'll find fine representations of local art (pottery, woodwork, watercolors, jewelry, sculpture) at the **Show Piece Gallery** (280 Gower Point Road, Gibsons; 604-886-9213), the **Dream Shoppe** (5482 Trail, Sechelt; 604-885-1965) and **Gallery Tantalus** (4643 Marine Drive, Powell River; 604-485-9412).

Cranberry Pottery (★) (6729 Cranberry Street, Powell River; 604-483-4622), a working studio, offers functional and affordable handmade stoneware in varying designs and glazes.

For arts and crafts of Northwest Indians including masks, drums, totems and baskets, visit the Sechelt Indian Band's **Cultural Center Gift Shop** (Highway 101, Sechelt; 604-885-4597) and **téxémay** (★) (#69 7100 Alberni Street, Town Centre Mall, Powell River; 604-485-2060).

SUNSHINE COAST NIGHTLIFE

Along the Sunshine Coast you'll find slimmer after-hours pickings, limited primarily to friendly, no-airs local taverns and pubs that occasionally have a dance space, live music and great water views.

Best bets in the region include **Gramma's Marine Pub** (1552 Marine Drive; 604-886-8215) at the top of Government Wharf in Gibsons, the **Lighthouse Pub** (5764 Wharf Road; 604-885-9494) or **Wakefield Inn** (6529 Sunshine Coast Highway; 604-885-7666) in Sechelt, **Irvines Landing Marine Pub** (Irvines Landing Road; 604-883-1145) in Garden Bay and the **Marine Inn Pub** (4429 Marine Avenue; 604-485-4242) or the **Shinglemill Pub** (Powell Lake; 604-483-3545) in Powell River.

SUNSHINE COAST BEACHES AND PARKS

Porpoise Bay Provincial Park—One of the prettiest parks along the coast, Porpoise Bay has a broad, sandy beach anchored by grass fields and fragrant cedar groves. This is a favorite base for canoeists who come to explore the waterways of the Sechelt Inlets Marine Recreation Area.

Facilities: Restrooms, showers, picnic tables, playground, amphitheater, nature trails; restaurants and groceries nearby; information, 604-885-2261.   *Swimming:* Good.   *Fishing:* Excellent sportfishing and clamming.

Camping: There are 84 sites.

Getting there: Located northeast of Sechelt off Porpoise Bay Road.

Saltery Bay Provincial Park—Named for the Japanese fish-saltery settlement located in this area during the early 1900s, this lovely, oceanside park with twin sandy beaches enjoys grand views of Jervis Inlet, where sharp-eyed visitors often catch glimpses of porpoises, whales, sea lions and seals. Scuba divers flock to the park to visit the nine-foot bronze mermaid resting in 60 feet of water not far offshore from the evergreen-shrouded campground.

Facilities: Restrooms, picnic sites, fire pits and boat launch; restaurants and groceries nearby; information, 604-898-3678.   *Fishing:* Great offshore salmon fishing.   *Swimming:* Excellent.   *Diving:* Excellent.

Camping: There are 45 sites.

Getting there: Located off Sunshine Coast Highway 17 miles south of Powell River.

Powell River Canoe Route (★)—There are 12 fjord-like lakes interconnected by rivers, streams and 11 miles of hiking trails making it possible to make portage canoe trips of anywhere from three days to a week in this beautiful Northern Sunshine Coast recreational area. Best time to make the trip is between April and November; lakes at upper elevations tend to freeze, and roads are inaccessible during winter months. Obtain a map from the Sunshine Coast Forest Regional Office (7077 Duncan Street, Powell River, BC V8A 1W1; 604-485-9831) to plan your circuit.

Facilities: Toilets, picnic tables, hiking trails (the Inland Lake trail is wheelchair accessible); restaurants and groceries nearby; information, 604-465-9831.   *Fishing:* Permitted.

Camping: Permitted at any of the 20 recreation sites.

Getting there: Jumpoff point for the canoe route is Lois Lake, accessible by a restricted logging road that's 12.5 miles east of Powell River off Highway 101.

Willingdon Beach Municipal Campsite—The sandy, log-strewn, crescent beach bordered by wooded acres of campsites draws a big summertime crowd to this comfortable municipal site in Powell River. Some of the campsites are right up on the beach, while others in a grove of cedar are more secluded.

Facilities: Restrooms, showers, laundry, barbecue area, playgrounds, nature trail and seasonal food stall; restaurants and groceries nearby; information, 604-485-2242. *Swimming:* Excellent though unsupervised.

Camping: There are 69 sites, three-quarters with full hookups.

Getting there: Located immediately off Marine Avenue in the Westview section of Powell River.

Desolation Sound Marine Park—Made up of 37 miles of shoreline and several islands, this is the largest marine park in British Columbia. The waters here are very warm and teem with diverse marine life making the area ideal for fishing, swimming, boating and scuba diving. The park is wild and undeveloped, with magnificent scenery at every turn.

Facilities: A few onshore restrooms and numerous safe anchorages; information, 604-898-3678. *Fishing:* Excellent for cod and salmon. *Swimming:* Excellent. *Diving:* Excellent.

Camping: There are four walk-in wilderness campsites.

Getting there: Boat access only from the coastal towns, including Gibsons, Sechelt and Powell River.

The Sporting Life

BOATING, WINDSURFING AND WHITE-WATER RAFTING

With 5000 miles of sheltered water within easy reach, Vancouver and southwestern British Columbia afford many opportunities to get out on the water, be it in a yacht, powerboat, rowboat, canoe, kayak, sailboard, raft or sailboat. In Vancouver, rentals are available through **Pacific Quest Charters** (1512 Foreshore Walk; 604-682-2205) for sailboats and powerboats and **Windsure Windsurfing** (1300 Discovery Street, Jericho Beach; 604-224-0615) for sailboards, wetsuits and instruction.

Scenic floats and whitewater rafting are also immensely popular, especially on the Chiliwhack River 65 miles east of Vancouver and the Green River and Birkenhead River near Whistler. Tours are available through **Hyak Wilderness Adventures** (1958 West 4th Avenue, Vancouver; 604-734-

8622) and **Whistler River Adventures** (P.O. Box 202, Whistler, BC V0N 1B0; 604-932-3532).

CANOEING AND KAYAKING

Canoeing and kayaking are very popular on Whistler's five beautiful lakes and all along the Sunshine Coast, especially in Desolation Sound Marine Park and on the 50-mile Powell Forest Canoe Route which takes in eight breathtaking lakes and interconnecting forests. Maps for the canoe route are available from the B.C. Forest Service (7077 Duncan Street, Powell River; 604-485-9831). Canoe and kayak rentals are available through **Whistler Outdoor Experience Co.** (Château Whistler; 604-932-3389), **Sunshine Kayaking Ltd.** (RR4 S12 C18, Gibsons, BC V0N 1V0; 604-886-9760) and **Mitchell Canoe and Kayak** (9537 Nassichuk Road, Powell River; 604-487-4448).

SPORTFISHING

The tremendous variety in southwestern British Columbia waterways affords an array of exciting challenges for the angler. In the mountain country, they can fly fish or spin cast in high alpine lakes and streams for rainbow trout, steelhead, kokanee salmon or dolly varden, while those on the coast can go after chinook, coho, chum, pink and sockeye salmon and bottom dwellers such as halibut, sole and rockfish. Licenses for both fresh and saltwater fishing are required and regulations change frequently; the Recreational Fisheries Division (Department of Fisheries and Oceans, 555 West Hastings Street, Vancouver, BC V6B 5G3; 604-666-3271) can provide further information.

For charters contact **Coho Fishing Adventures** (104 East 9th Avenue; 604-324-8214) or **ABC Boat Charters** (750 Pacific Boulevard; 604-682-2070) in Vancouver, **Whistler Backcountry Adventures** (204-4000 Whistler Way; 604-938-1410) in Whistler and **Destiny Charters** (6865 Gerrard Street, Powell River; 604-485-5931) or **Blackfish Salmon Fishing Charters** (Henderson Avenue, Sechelt; 604-885-7977) on the Sunshine Coast.

SCUBA DIVING

A thick soup of microscopic plant and animal life attracts and feeds an abundance of marine life that in turn attracts divers in numbers that continue to grow. Add to this the array of wrecks and underwater sights (such as a nine-foot bronze mermaid) and it's easy to understand the popularity of scuba diving around Vancouver and the Sunshine Coast.

Dive charters, air and equipment rentals are available through **Adrenalin Sports Ltd.** (1512 Duranleau Street, Vancouver; 604-682-2881), **Odyssey Diving Centre** (2659 Kingsway Street, Vancouver; 604-430-1451), **Tidal Wave Diving** (Porpoise Bay, Sechelt; 604-885-3328), **Seasport**

Vancouver in Bloom

Rain is a common sight in this neck of the woods during the winter months, but the payoff bursts forth in the spring. Vancouver is a green, green city over-flowing with international parks and gardens that are a flourishing testament to the forethought of the city's founders.

Rose aficionados will want to stroll through the lovely **Rose Garden** of Stanley Park (604-681-1141), crowning glory of the city's parks. The fragrant collection in this mid-sized formal garden is sure to contain one or two specimens you'd like to have in your own yard. Late summer is the best time to visit for the full effect. The Rose Garden is near the park's entrance just off Georgia Street.

There's also a wonderful rose garden in Queen Elizabeth Park, but it is often overshadowed entirely by the star of the show here, the **Bloedel Conservatory** (604-872-5513; admission). Set at the crown of Little Mountain, the conservatory houses over 500 tropical plant species under a 70-foot-high geodesic dome.

With over 16,000 species, the award for variety goes to the **University of British Columbia Botanical Garden** (6501 Northwest Marine Way; 604-228-4208; summer admission). This 60-acre research facility is filled with exotic and familiar specimens separated into alpine, Asian, British Columbia natives, food, evolutionary and contemporary gardens.

VanDusen Botanical Garden (5251 Oak Street; 604-266-7194; admission) runs a close second with over 6500 species of plants from six continents divided into theme areas. It takes a full day (and a great deal of staying power) to make it through the entire 55-acre complex, but you can hit the major sites—the English hedge maze, the hanging garden, rock and stone gardens, Oriental and Canadian Heritage gardens, fragrance garden and herb garden—in two to three hours.

Nitobe Memorial Garden (1903 West Mall; admission during summer) on the University of British Columbia campus is an authentic Japanese strolling garden with teahouse. Narrow paths wind through 215 acres of serene rock and sand gardens, traditional Japanese plantings and across gracefully arched bridges over the still pond. Folks come here for the cherry blossoms in April, iris in June and flaming-red Japanese maples in October.

The jewel of Chinatown is the multimillion-dollar **Dr. Sun Yat Sen Classical Chinese Garden** (578 Carrall Street; 604-662-3207; admission). Designed and constructed by craftsmen brought in from China, this Ming Dynasty-style garden is the first such classical garden to be built outside China. Most of the elements, including the plants, architectural and artistic components, were shipped in from China.

Scuba (5567 Dolphin Street, Sechelt; 604-885-9830) and **Emerald Seas Diving Adventures** (4675 Marine Avenue, Powell River; 604-485-7637).

HELI-ADVENTURES

Helicopters, more easily maneuvered in rough back country, offer access to all sorts of sightseeing and sports opportunities including heli-picnicking, heli-hiking, heli-biking, heli-skiing, heli-rafting and heli-fishing. If the experts at **Mountain Heli-Sports Inc.** (604-932-2070) or **Vancouver Helicopters Inc.** (604-898-9688) don't offer the activity you're searching for, they'll know where to refer you.

SKIING

The majestic range crowning Vancouver's North Shore offers three fine ski areas within minutes of the city center. **Cypress Bowl** (P.O. Box 91252, West Vancouver, BC V7V 3N9; 604-926-5612), with 23 groomed runs on two lift-serviced mountains, boasts the longest vertical run of the Vancouver resorts along with night skiing and a variety of nordic and backcountry skiing trails.

The glittering string of lights visible each night on the North Shore across the inlet from downtown Vancouver marks the arc-lit runs of **Grouse Mountain** (6400 Nancy Greene Way, North Vancouver; 604-984-0661) where residents head after work to get in some slope time. The resort offers 13 runs and a variety of lifts.

Mt. Seymour (1700 Indian River Road, North Vancouver; 604-986-2261), with more novice runs than the other two, is the best bet for beginners or those looking to avoid hot dogs. The 20 downhill runs serviced by a network of tramways, chairs, lifts and tows are open for night skiing; there are also cross-country trails running throughout this provincial park.

Whistler Resort, located 75 winding miles northeast of Vancouver at the base of Whistler and Blackcomb mountains, is a world-class resort and one of the top ski destinations in the world. The resort offers over 200 marked runs and the longest lift-serviced ski runs in North America, with a drop of one vertical mile. The official season runs from late November through May, then starts again for glacier heli-skiing in mid June. The **Whistler Resort Association** (4010 Whistler Way, Whistler; 604-932-4222) can provide further information.

HORSEBACK RIDING

Closer to Vancouver you can make arrangements for rides through **Tall Mountain Riding Stables** (1301 Lillooet Road, North Vancouver; 604-980-0299). An hour outside the city in Brackendale, **Cheekeye Stables** (604-898-3432) arranges group trail rides through coastal rain forests.

In Whistler, you'll find plenty of scenic trail rides or relaxing hay or sleigh rides to choose from, ranging from an hour on trails near Whistler Village to overnight camping trips into high alpine reaches, available through **Layton Bryson Outfitting** (604-932-6623) and the **Whistler Outdoor Experience Co.** (Château Whistler; 604-932-3389).

For horseback riding on the Sunshine Coast, contact **Elphinstone Trail Rides** (556 Pratt Road, Gibsons; 604-886-7467) or **Valley Stables** (7561 Duncan Street, Powell River; 604-485-4145).

GOLF

There are dozens of golf courses and practice facilities in and around Vancouver, especially on the South Side in the suburb of Richmond. Courses open to the public include the **Fraserview Golf Course** (7800 Vivian Street, Vancouver; 604-327-3717), the **University Golf Club** (5185 University Boulevard, Vancouver; 604-224-1818), closest to the city core, and the **Mayfair Lakes Golf Course** (5460 Number 7 Road, Richmond; 604-276-0505).

In Whistler you can tee off amid the splendid terrain at the **Whistler Golf Course** (4010 Whistler Way; 604-932-4544) or the **Robert Trent Jones Jr. Golf Course** (4599 Château Boulevard; 604-938-8000).

Best bet on the Sunshine Coast is the **Myrtle Point Golf Club** (Highway 101, Myrtle Point; 604-487-4653). Other options include the **Pender Harbor Golf Club** (Sunshine Coast Highway, Pender Harbor; 604-883-9541) and the **Sunshine Coast Golf and Country Club** (3206 Sunshine Coast Highway, Sechelt; 604-885-9212), each nine-hole courses.

TENNIS

There are over 250 public tennis courts around town, available free of charge on a first-come-first-served basis with the exception of those at **Stanley Park,** where there is a minimal fee during warm weather months. Other parks with an abundance of outdoor courts include **Queen Elizabeth Park** (just off Camie Street, Vancouver), **Jericho Beach Park** (off Northwest Marine Drive) and **Kitsilano Beach Park** (Cornwall Avenue and Arbustus Street). The Parks Board (604-681-1141) can tell you of more locations.

In Whistler you'll find public courts at the **Myrtle Phillips Elementary School** (Whistler Village), **Alpha Lake Park** (north tip of Alpha Lake), **Meadow Park** (end of Camino Drive, Alpine Meadows, Whistler) and **Emerald Park** (off Highway 99, Emerald Estates, Whistler). For more information contact the Department of Parks and Recreation (604-932-5535).

On the Sunshine Coast You'll find public tennis courts at **Dougal Park** (Marine Drive, Gibsons), **Hackett Park** (Dolphin Street, Sechelt), the **Wakefield Inn** (6529 Sunshine Coast Highway, Sechelt; 604-885-7666) and **Town Site Park** (next door to the lawn bowling club on Marine Avenue, Powell River).

BICYCLING

Because of heavy traffic in Vancouver, cyclists are better off sticking to the protected 5.6-mile seawall path around the perimeter of **Stanley Park**, along the shoreside paths at **Jericho Beach** and **English Bay** and the pathways that parallel Chancellor and University boulevards and 15th Avenue on the scenic campus of the **University of British Columbia**.

Biking is popular in Whistler, especially mountain biking on rough alpine trails or paved trails around **Lost Lake** and along the **Valley Trail** which connects the village with the nearby residential areas, parks and lakes. Daredevils will probably go for **mountain descents**, often combined with a helicopter or gondola ride to the peaks without expending energy needed for zooming down the dry ski runs at ungodly speeds behind an experienced trail leader who knows how to run the slopes safely. **Whistler Outdoor Experience Co.** (Château Whistler; 604-932-3389) and **Backroads Mountain Bike Adventures** (P.O. Box 643, Whistler BC V0N 1B0; 604-932-3111) offer a variety of guided tours.

There is no protected bike path along **Highway 101**, the main artery of the Sunshine Coast, and the rocky shoulder drops off entirely at times, forcing bikers onto the highway. However, the moderately challenging trip from Langsdale to Earls Cove is popular nonetheless. The back country of the entire coast is laced with marked and unmarked **logging trails** leading off Highway 101 just waiting to be explored by intrepid mountain bikers; a detailed map of the trails between Jervis Inlet and Lund is available from the Powell River Travel InfoCentre (604-485-4701).

BIKE RENTALS   **Stanley Park Rentals** (676 Chilco Street; 604-681-5581) and **Recreation Rentals** (2560 Arbutus Street; 604-733-7368) are just a couple of the many rental options in Vancouver. For rentals in Whistler, turn to **Blackcomb Ski and Sport** (Blackcomb Day Lodge; 604-932-5888), **Mile High Sports** (Château Whistler; 604-938-2012) or **McConkey Sport Shop** (Whistler Express Base; 604-932-2311). For rentals on the Sunshine Coast, try **Taws Gun and Cycle** (4597 Marine Avenue, Powell River; 604-485-2555).

HIKING

SOUTH SIDE TRAILS   **Pacific Spirit Regional Park/University Endowment Land Trails** (★) (30 miles, all told) crisscross 1000 acres of parkland on Point Grey Peninsula offering easy-to-moderate hikes of varying length through this largely unmarked ecological reserve. Here you're more likely to run into a blacktail deer or bald eagle than another hiker. A map is available from the Greater Vancouver Regional Parks office (604-432-6350).

DOWNTOWN VANCOUVER TRAILS   **Stanley Park Seawall Path** (5.5 miles), carefully divided to accommodate both cyclists and pedestrians, is easily the most popular hike in town. There are also numerous paths that plunge into the thickly forested acres of the park.

NORTH SHORE TRAILS **Capilano Pacific Trail** (4.5 miles), in North Vancouver's Capilano Regional Park, passes from massive Cleveland Dam to Ambleside Park through sections of coastal rain forest and offers great views of the Lions, the twin mountain peaks soaring majestically above the dam.

Norvan Falls (9.5 miles) offers a more rugged, backcountry trek for the experienced hiker through the wilderness areas of Lynn Headwaters Regional Park. The shorter **Lynn Loop Trail** (3 miles) affords views of Lynn Valley and passes an abandoned cabin. Call 604-985-1690 for trail condition.

WHISTLER TRAILS There are trails in Whistler to meet all levels. **Valley Trail** (15 mile loop) is a bustling paved walkway/bike path/cross-country ski trail that winds through town connecting Alpha, Nita, Alta, Lost and Green lakes, the village and the various residential areas.

Lost Lake Trails (9 miles, all together) serve as cross-country ski trails during the winter and make for fairly level summer hiking paths through the forested area between Lost and Green lakes.

Singing Pass-Russet Lake (6.75 miles), an alpine hiking trail just behind Whistler Village, and the graded **Garibaldi Lake Trail** (5.5 miles), located off Highway 99 south of town, are prime options for experienced hikers interested in heading into the steep fringes of incredible Garibaldi Park.

SUNSHINE COAST TRAILS The **Soames Hill Mountain Trail** (1.5 miles), otherwise known as "The Knob" because of its appearance to passengers on ferries approaching Langdale, is a brisk stair climb to an elevation of 800 feet followed by expansive views of Howe Sound, the surrounding mountains and villages.

Smuggler's Cove Marine Park Trail (0.5 mile) is an easy walk leading from the parking lot off Brooks Road approximately six miles north of Sechelt to the cove once used to smuggle in Chinese immigrants and other contraband and now home to an array of seabirds.

Mt. Valentine Trail (approximately 1 mile) offers a short walk up a gravel path followed by a steep climb up a stone staircase leading to panoramic views of Malaspina and Georgia straits, Vancouver Island and the surrounding town of Powell Lake.

Inland Lake Trail (8 miles), just north of Powell River, offers a longer hike over a well-maintained circuit of boardwalks and bridges through scenic swamp areas and skirting lovely Inland Lake. The entire trail is wheelchair accessible, and several handicap shelters and fishing wharfs are along the way.

Transportation

BY CAR

From the West Coast of the United States, **Route 5** turns into **Highway 99** after crossing the Canadian border at Blaine and proceeds northwest through Vancouver's suburbs and into the city core where the name changes once again, this time to **Granville Street**. The **Trans-Canada Highway (Highway 1)**, connects Vancouver with points east in Canada.

Highway 99, referred to as the **Sea to Sky Highway** from Horseshoe Bay northward, picks up again in North Vancouver, hugs the rugged coastline and continues north into the mountains to Whistler.

Highway 101, the only major thoroughfare through the Sunshine Coast, connects Langdale to Earls Cove and Saltery Bay to Lund, the northernmost point of this long, transcontinental highway with southern terminus in Chile.

BY AIR

Vancouver International Airport (604-666-5551) services domestic charters and scheduled flights by Air BC, Air Caledonia, Burrard Air and Harbour Air. International airlines include Air Canada, Air France, Air New Zealand, American Airlines, British Airways, Cathay Pacific, Japan Air Lines, KLM Royal Dutch Airlines, Lufthansa, Qantas, Singapore Airlines and United Airlines.

Airport express buses operated by **Perimeter Transportation Ltd.** (604-273-9023) depart every 15 minutes or so from Level II of the Main Terminal building and stop at the bus station and most major hotels in downtown Vancouver. **B.C. Transit** (604-261-5100) buses also serve the airport; catch #100 from either terminal and then transfer to #20 at Granville Street and 70th Avenue, which will take you to Granville Mall in the heart of Vancouver.

BY BOAT

Between May and October, cruise ships call regularly at the terminal at **Canada Place** (999 Canada Place, Vancouver; 604-666-3226), an architectural stunner under Teflon-coated white "sails." **B.C. Ferries** (1112 Fort Street, Victoria; 604-685-1021) provides service between Vancouver Island and Tsawwassen (an hour south of downtown Vancouver), Horseshoe Bay (half an hour northwest of downtown) and Langdale on the southern Sunshine Coast and Earls Cove and Saltery Bay on the northern Sunshine Coast.

BY BUS

Greyhound Lines of Canada (150 Dunsmuir Street; 604-662-3222) offers service to and from the United States and throughout Canada. Their discount Ameripasses are good in the 48 contiguous states and throughout

Canada. **Maverick Coach Lines** (604-255-1171) also provides bus service from Vancouver to the Sunshine Coast and Whistler.

BY TRAIN

Via Rail Canada (1150 Station Street; 604-669-3050) provides rail service throughout Canada and connects with **Amtrak** (800-872-7245) to points within the United States. From North Vancouver, **B.C. Rail** (1311 West 1st Street; 604-984-5264) runs daily, round-trip service to Whistler. Intriguing whistle- and flag-stops along the way remind you of the casual nature of British Columbia.

CAR RENTALS

Car-rental agencies at Vancouver International Airport include **ABC Rent A Car** (604-276-0108), **Avis Rent A Car** (604-273-4577), **Dominion U-Drive** (604-278-7196), **Hertz Rent A Car** (604-278-5522), **Thrifty Car Rental** (604-276-0800) and **Tilden** (604-273-3121).

Budget Rent A Car (604-263-5555), **Discount Car Rentals** (682-2413) and **Dollar Rent A Car** (604-263-6148) offer free airport pick-up.

PUBLIC TRANSPORTATION

B.C. Transit (604-261-5100) governs Vancouver's expansive transit system, with buses, the SkyTrain and the SeaBus covering all the main arteries within the city and fanning out into the suburbs. Running on a 14-mile, mostly elevated track between Canada Place downtown and the suburb of New Westminster, the SkyTrain is a good way to see some of the major sights of the city. You can also get a great view of the skyline from the water aboard the SeaBuses that cross Burrard Inlet between downtown and the North Shore. The handy "Discover Vancouver on Transit" tour guide, day passes and timetables are available from Travel InfoCentres.

Glacier Coach Lines (604-932-2705), the local operator for B.C. Transit, runs five buses connecting Whistler Creek and Whistler Village every half hour. B.C. Transit is also responsible for transit service along the Sunshine Coast; for more information dial 604-485-4287.

TAXIS

Cab companies serving the airport include **Bel-Air Taxi** (604-433-6666), **Black Top Cabs** (604-731-1111), **Vancouver Taxi** (604-255-5111) and **Yellow Cab** (604-681-1111).

CHAPTER TWELVE

Victoria
and Southern Vancouver Island

I say, do you want a taste of veddy proper Britain without having to fly across the Atlantic? Then step into Victoria, a city of stately government buildings, picture-perfect lawns and fascinating glimpses of the British influence. Shorn, manicured and embellished, Victoria is called more British than Britain itself.

But have no fear: This is not stiff-upper-lip territory. Travel out of Victoria and you will find the rest of Vancouver Island an untamed land. Stretching 280 miles along the rugged Pacific coastline of Canada and the United States and occupying some 12,400 square miles, Vancouver Island is the continent's largest Pacific island. Most of this mass protects the lower mainland of British Columbia from torrential rains and gale-force winds of the open ocean. However, the island does cross the 49th parallel, the general boundary between the United States and Canada, and its southern one-fifth, including the city of Victoria, is on the same latitude as parts of Washington State.

Much of the island lies in its natural state with beaches, forests, mountains and meadows. Rains nurture thick, sometimes ancient forests, and over centuries the ocean has carved out sandy beaches. The area is a stunning contrast of the rugged, mountainous and relatively uninhabited west coast to sleepy seaside villages, farms and bucolic islands on the southeastern shore. On the west coast, winds and rains can be brutal. Mountains drop right into a raging Pacific Ocean. Many remote settlements or camps—too small even to be called villages—have scant road access and rely on freighters, boats or float planes to deliver everything from apples to asphalt.

Geography and the elements have conspired to make the southern part of the island a relative haven where farming, tourism and commerce thrive. A number of picturesque villages and towns are perched on the coast. The Malahat Drive offers fabulous views of Washington's Olympic Mountains and the Saanich Peninsula, which is dotted with small farms, orchards and forests.

For the most part, the island's climate is gentle, thanks to the warmth from the Japanese current. A majestic range of mountains divides the island into a dense rain forest on the west coast and the drier lowlands on the east coast. The eastern summers can be blissful with long, sunny days. The climate of Victoria and the southeastern part of the island is akin to that of the Mediterranean—dry, cool summers and mild winters. It is no accident that many Canadians choose to retire there.

Not all of Vancouver Island is so bucolic. The west coast is rugged with craggy mountains, a rugged coastline and often brutal weather. Starting in September, the winter rains start to pour, and blustery winds are not uncommon.

In contrast to the rugged side of Vancouver Island, Victoria emerges gracious and genteel. On the island's southern shore, this is the seat of the provincial government, but there is also a cozy and quaint look to the place. It overflows with flowers, the lawns graced with tulips, rhododendrons and roses, the windowboxes and hanging planters filled with geraniums and lobelia. Victoria's economy rests on the shoulders of government and tourism. Although heightened in summer, tourism is a year-round activity in this city.

Prior to settlement by white explorers, the island's people lived in harmony with nature. Natives lived in bands of the Nootka or Nuu-chah-nulth on the west, the Coast Salish to the south and east and the Southern Kwakiutl to the north. These people lived off the bounty of the land, principally the salmon, cedar and wild berries. Spanish explorers first came to the island in 1592, followed by Captain James Cook in 1778. Vancouver Island is the namesake of George Vancouver, British naval captain, who negotiated the island away from Spain in 1795.

In 1843 James Douglas, a representative of the Hudson's Bay Company, established a fort, named after the British queen, Victoria, where Bastion Square sits on Wharf Street today. Coal mining, fishing, logging and fur trading brought settlers to other parts of the island.

Fortunately, the island's wealth of wildlife has not all been hunted away. Home to several species of salmon, the waters surrounding the island make for excellent fishing and offer a supply of natural food for orca whales, sea lions and seals. These waters also contain a wide variety of sea birds. The mountains and highlands contain Roosevelt elk, black bears, black tail deer, marmots, wolves and cougars.

It's all waiting for you. Ta-ta!

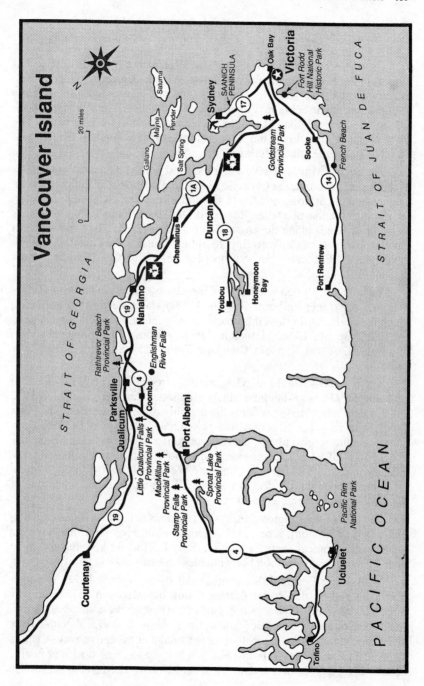

Vancouver Island

Downtown Victoria

Victoria combines a rich, British heritage with a relaxed lifestyle and climate of the North American West Coast. Winsome, gracious and colorful, the city comes alive with sights that illustrate its history, customs and ties with the sea. Sightseeing in Victoria veers in the direction of its British influence, its natural history and the residents' passion for gardening. The place to get information is the **Travel InfoCentre** (812 Wharf Street; 604-382-2127), on the Inner Harbour.

The **Scenic Marine Drive** along the coast is the best route to see views of the water, the coast, the Olympic Mountains and some of Victoria's most elegant homes. Starting at Mile 0, the end of the Trans-Canada Highway, (at the intersection of Dallas Road and Douglas Street), follow the signs as the drive winds along the coast. You pass through Oak Bay and Uplands Park, around part of Cadboro Bay, to Mount Douglas Park and the Saanich Peninsula. At Elk Lake, you can turn left onto Highway 17 to head back to Victoria.

Visitors get a good overview of the city by taking a **Tallyho Horse-drawn Tour** (Inner Harbour; 604-479-1113), whose steeds have been clip-clopping their way through the streets for 85 years. Other horsedrawn tours are **Black Beauty Line, Victorian Carriage Tours Ltd.** (Inner Harbour; 604-361-1220) and **Victoria Carriage Tours** (251 Superior Street; 604-382-8509).

The **Empress Hotel** (721 Government Street; 604-384-8111) is Victoria's unofficial central landmark facing the Inner Harbour. Opened in 1908 and recently renovated, it reflects the gentility of an earlier time. The Palm Court, with its magnificent stained-glass dome, is renowned for its afternoon teas and tropical plants. On the ground floor, you will find **Miniature World** (604-385-9731; admission), with more than 60 miniaturized illustrations of history and fantasy. Miniature World includes the world's smallest operational sawmill, two of the world's largest dollhouses and one of the world's largest model railways.

Just east of the Empress is **Crystal Gardens** (713 Douglas Street; 604-381-1213; admission), a one-time enclosed swimming pool that now is a glass-roofed tropical aviary with hundreds of colorful blossoms and more than 75 varieties of birds, plus wallabies and tiny monkeys.

Walk across Belleville Street, just south of the Empress Hotel, to a complex anchored by the **Royal British Columbia Museum** (675 Belleville Street; 604-387-3014; admission). One of the best on the continent, the museum focuses on the history of British Columbia—its land and people from prehistoric times to the present—in a personal and evocative way. Visitors sit among totem poles, walk inside a longhouse and learn stories of Native People struggling to survive once white settlers arrived. Museum guests also can walk down the streets of Old Town, plunge into the bowels of a coal mine and walk through the *Discovery*, a replica of the ship used by Captain Vancouver.

Part of the complex is **Thunderbird Park** (Belleville and Douglas streets), a postage-stamp-sized park covering only a quarter of the block. The park is the site of ten or so magnificent totem poles and a longhouse in which natives demonstrate the crafts of carving and beading during the summer.

Just behind the park and adjacent to the museum is **Helmcken House** (10 Elliott Street; 604-387-4697; admission), built in 1852 for pioneer doctor J. S. Helmcken. This is British Columbia's oldest residence on its original site. Rooms decorated in the style of the period are furnished with pieces brought around Cape Horn from England by Victoria's founding families. The library includes Dr. Helmcken's medicine chest and medical instruments.

From here you can take a detour (just a couple blocks south) to a Victorian Italianate cottage known as **Carr House** (207 Government Street; 604-387-4697). This is where British Columbia landscape painter Emily Carr was born in 1871 and lived her girlhood years. Historians have restored the home with period wall coverings and furnishings to look as it did when she lived there. Return north to the Inner Harbour.

The **Parliament Buildings** (421 Menzies Street; 604-387-3046) face Belleville Street, in the next block west of the Royal British Columbia Museum. The legislative buildings are Francis Rattenbury's architectural salad of Victorian, Roman and Italian Renaissance styles with 33 copper-covered domes. At night they are outlined with more than 3000 twinkling lights. A statue of Queen Victoria stands in front of the buildings, and one of Captain George Vancouver tops the main copper dome. Daily guided tours explain historic features and the workings of the provincial government.

Across the street is the **Royal London Wax Museum** (470 Belleville Street; 604-388-4461; admission), also designed by Rattenbury as the ticket office for the Canadian Pacific Railroad. The Acropolis-style building now contains wax sculptures of the Princess of Wales, President George Bush and some 200 other Josephine Tussaud figures. The likenesses of the American figures are lacking, but the Royal Family is very lifelike. You will want to keep young children out of the Horror Chamber with its gruesome depictions of decapitations and other methods of torture, but adolescents love it.

On the water side of the Wax Museum is the **Undersea Gardens** (490 Belleville Street; 604-382-5717; admission), a salute to British Columbia life below water. At regularly scheduled intervals, divers swim behind a huge window in the Inner Harbour to show and tell visitors (comfortably dry in the underwater auditorium) information about sea creatures within the province.

You can continue out Belleville Street by car, cab, bus or bicycle to picturesque **Fisherman's Wharf** (corner of Dallas Road and Erie Street), a working fishing pier. Moorage allows for up to 400 boats, but the little bay often is jammed with many more, tied up to one another. If the fishing fleet is in, visitors can buy fresh fish from the docks. A walk in the **James Bay neighborhood,** one of the city's more fashionable areas, takes you past several restored Victorian and Edwardian homes.

Continue back around the Inner Harbour past the Empress and the Travel InfoCentre heading north on Wharf Street to **Bastion Square** (off Wharf Street between Fort and Yates streets). In 1843–44, James Douglas established Fort Victoria here, but the buildings there now, including warehouses, offices, saloons and waterfront hotels, were constructed in the late 1800s, the city's boom period. The buildings, many of them red brick, have been restored and now house restaurants, shops and art galleries.

The **Maritime Museum** (28 Bastion Square; 604-385-4222; admission) is housed in a large, turreted building that was originally the Provincial Court House. The museum depicts British Columbia's maritime history from its early days to the present. It includes nautical charts, brassware from old ships, Navy uniforms and two incredible vessels—*Tilikum*, a 38-foot dugout canoe that sailed from Victoria to England at the turn of the century, and *Trekka*, a 20-foot ketch, sailed single-handedly around the world.

Walk over to Government Street and continue north to Johnson Street. Here you will find **Market Square** (Government and Johnson streets). Market Square incorporates the original Occidental Hotel, the choice of many Klondike gold miners in 1898, now a favorite area for shopping and dining.

Take Fan Tan Alley north another block to **Chinatown** (Government and Herald streets). In the late 19th century, Victoria's Chinatown was second largest on the continent, trailing that of San Francisco. The Chinese immigrants headed to British Columbia to work on the railroad and to mine for coal and gold. Approaching Chinatown from Government Street, you see the ceramic-tiled Gate of Harmonious Interest with two hand-carved stone lions standing guard. Fan Tan Alley, dubbed Canada's narrowest street, contains boutiques and artists' studios.

DOWNTOWN VICTORIA HOTELS

The problem with lodging in Victoria is the same as elsewhere in popular cities—it's expensive. Several luxurious hotels line the Inner Harbour. Several others charge luxurious prices for mediocre to shoddy rooms. Budget prices can be found, but those accommodations are often farther out from downtown. A toll-free **Tourism Victoria Accommodation Line** (800-663-3883) provides travelers with current rates and availability at a full range of places to stay in Victoria. Also contact **All Seasons Bed and Breakfast Agency** (P.O. Box 5511, Station B, Victoria, BC V8R 6S4; 604-655-7173) or the **Garden City Bed and Breakfast Reservation Service** (660 James Terrace, Victoria, BC V8Z 2L7; 604-479-9999).

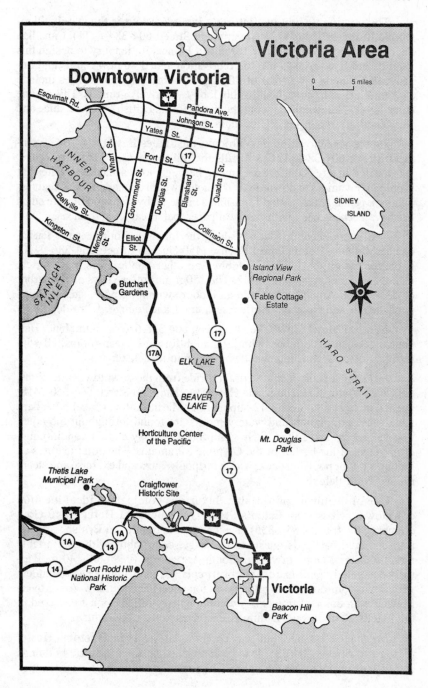

Victoria Area

0 ⊢──────⊣ 5 miles

SIDNEY ISLAND

N

HARO STRAIT

Downtown Victoria

Esquimalt Rd.

Pandora Ave.

Johnson St.

Yates St.

Fort St.

INNER HARBOUR

Wharf St.

Government St.

Douglas St.

Blanshard St.

Quadra St.

Bellville St.

Kingston St.

Menzies St.

Elliot St.

Collinson St.

Island View Regional Park

Butchart Gardens

Fable Cottage Estate

SAANICH INLET

17A

ELK LAKE

BEAVER LAKE

17

Horticulture Center of the Pacific

Mt. Douglas Park

Thetis Lake Municipal Park

Craigflower Historic Site

1A

1A

1A

14

14

Fort Rodd Hill National Historic Park

Victoria

Beacon Hill Park

The dominant sight in Victoria's Inner Harbour is the stately, Neo-Gothic **Empress Hotel** (721 Government Street; 604-384-8111). Canadian Pacific Railways commissioned architect Francis Rattenbury to design this magnificent hotel. A $45 million renovation added 46 new rooms and improved all others, for a total of 400 guest rooms. Other amenities include a swimming pool, sauna, health club, lobby and lovely grounds. This grande dame hotel is known throughout the world for its British-style elegance and wonderful afternoon teas. Ultra-deluxe.

Even after renovating its 50 rooms, the **James Bay Inn** (270 Government Street; 604-384-7151) still fills the bill for budget-minded travelers. It is located in a residential area among heritage homes and small cafés but is pretty convenient to downtown. The hotel, which opened in 1913, features light-oak paneling and period furnishings in the lobby. Guest rooms are small but have been updated with new wallpaper, paint, carpet and linens.

For luxury accommodations along the Inner Harbour near the Parliament Buildings, **Hotel Grand Pacific** (450 Quebec Street; 604-386-0450) is one of the city's finest. The lobby and other public areas feature rich, mahogany paneling and millwork. The 150 rooms offer views of the harbor or downtown. Amenities include an indoor swimming pool, sauna, whirlpool, health and fitness facilities, restaurant and lounge. Ultra-deluxe.

Admiral Motel (257 Belleville Street; 604-388-6267), on the Inner Harbour, is a very basic motel with 29 straightforward, clean rooms, all with refrigerators, 12 with kitchenettes. Moderate to deluxe.

Just a brisk walk or shuttle or ferry ride from the downtown attractions, the **Coast Victoria Harbourside Hotel** (146 Kingston Street; 604-360-1418) opened in 1991 and faces a 42-slip marina. Marine colors of teal blue, dark mahogany, original art and watery motifs are found throughout the hotel. The 132 rooms and suites, each with private balcony and air conditioning, offer views of the harbor or the Olympic Mountains. The hotel features an indoor/outdoor pool and deck, with whirlpool, sauna and exercise and steam rooms. Ultra-deluxe.

One of the most comfortable, luxurious hotels in an ideal location downtown, across from Eaton's Plaza, is the **Bedford Hotel** (1140 Government Street; 604-384-6835). The bellman in traditional British garb and a tri-cornered hat leads guests to the large, open lobby with comfortable rattan furniture. Done in vibrant Southwest colors, the hotel's 40 individually decorated rooms feature marble fireplaces, comfortable beds complete with down comforters and pillows, cotton sheets and window boxes overflowing with colorful flowers. A complimentary full breakfast is served in the hotel's Red Currant Dining Room. Deluxe to ultra-deluxe.

The place for basic, budget accommodations is the **Victoria Hostel** (516 Yates Street; 604-385-4511), sandwiched between historic buildings and offices in the downtown area. The recently renovated hostel features an all new interior including two kitchens, gameroom, lounge, eating area, library, bicycle-storage area and hot showers. The hostel offers 102 beds, dormitory-style, and three family rooms.

Swan's Hotel (506 Pandora Avenue; 604-361-3310) is a small, 30-room hotel in a restored, brick, heritage building along the harbor in downtown Victoria offering a colorful pub and restaurant. Each contemporary unit, ranging from studios to two-bedroom suites, features designer decor and includes a kitchenette, dining area, and original art on the walls. Deluxe.

If you want low-cost accommodations close to downtown but with more privacy than you'd find at a hostel, the **Cherry Bank Hotel** (825 Burdett Street; 604-385-5380), a hotel/rooming house, is a possibility. The full breakfast included with your room is the best part of the deal. The dining room is cozy, clean and attractive, which is more than can be said for the rooms, which, at their best, feature an eclectic mix of cast-off furniture, draperies and bedspreads. Budget.

Abigail's (906 McClure Street; 604-388-5363) is just four blocks east of downtown. This Tudor inn has a European ambience with colorful, well-kept gardens and a light, bright interior. The foyer features hardwood floors and an open oak staircase to the guest rooms. The sitting room is luxurious with hardwood floors, leather sofa, piano, game table, fireplace and fresh flowers. Each of the 16 rooms and suites features down comforters and antiques, and some have whirlpool baths, fireplaces and vaulted ceilings. Included in the room rate is an afternoon sherry hour in the library and a gourmet breakfast served in the dining room. Moderate to deluxe.

A truly hidden discovery for couples seeking a romantic getaway is **Humboldt House** (★) (867 Humboldt Street; 604-384-4044). It is so well hidden, it doesn't even have a sign out front—it looks like a private residence. A Victorian home built in 1895 and tastefully renovated in 1988, includes three suites. The library offers walls full of books and a fireplace. Guest rooms are individually decorated with stained glass, fireplaces and have whirlpool tubs. Guests can have breakfast delivered to their room via a two-way compartment, or dine with the rest of the patrons at the Beaconsfield Inn, a block away. Ultra-deluxe.

A large, old, Edwardian-style home, the **Beaconsfield Inn** (998 Humboldt Street; 604-384-4044) has the ambience of a gentlemen's club with heavy furnishings and original, dark paneling. Millionaire R. P. Rithet built it in 1905 as a wedding present for his daughter, Gertrude. The 12 guest rooms vary in charm, but all include down comforters and antiques. Many feature canopy beds, clawfoot tubs and fireplaces. Guests also can enjoy sherry hour in the library and a full gourmet breakfast in the kitchen, both included in the room rate. Deluxe to ultra-deluxe.

Dashwood Manor Bed and Breakfast (1 Cook Road; 604-385-5517), a gracious Tudor mansion built in 1912, sits next to Beacon Hill Park and offers unobstructed views of the Strait of Juan de Fuca and the Olympic Mountains. This is not the place to hang out and meet other bed-and-breakfast aficionados. Unfortunately, the only place for guests to mingle is a little office. Breakfast is make-it-yourself with ingredients provided in the kitchenettes in each of the rooms. Three of the 14 rooms have fireplaces. The grounds are impeccable, the rooms are clean, but industrial-grade carpeting in the hallways is grimy. Deluxe to ultra-deluxe.

DOWNTOWN VICTORIA RESTAURANTS

Rattenbury's (703 Douglas Street; 604-381-1333) is a middle-of-the road steak-and-seafood house. A simple, attractive interior greets diners at this restaurant in the ground floor of the Crystal Gardens. Salmon is the feature here in entrées such as poached salmon with lemon butter or salmon Wellington. The menu also offers prime rib, steaks and chicken entrées. In the summer, enjoy a salmon barbecue and al fresco dining. The food is good and plentiful and is definitely a draw for tourists because of the location. Moderate to deluxe.

Just outside downtown in the James Bay area is the **French Connection** (512 Simcoe Street; 604-385-7014), housed in a circa-1884 building that once was the home of a Hudson's Bay Company executive. The restaurant is quiet and intimate. The interior is painted in period color schemes that enhance the elaborate moldings and window trims. Start with the spinach crêpe appetizer. Entrées include rack of lamb, *boeuf borguinine* and seafood linguine. The food is carefully prepared, but service is reserved and formal. Moderate to deluxe.

James Bay Tea Room and Restaurant (332 Menzies Street; 604-382-8282) is a homey place with photographs of English royalty overlooking tables set close together with hand-crocheted tea cozies insulating every teapot. This place is popular with the older set. Afternoon tea is served daily. Dinner entrées include English beef stew and dumplings, Salisbury steak and roast lamb with mint sauce. Moderate.

Louie Louie's Diner (1001 Wharf Street; 604-382-1959), a tile-and-chrome establishment across the street from the Inner Harbour, is straight from the 1950s with juke boxes and neon signs. The menu features burgers, 'dogs and salads. Blue-plate specials include Cajun New York steak, shrimp creole linguine and a meatloaf dinner. Budget to moderate.

A charming and graceful Japanese restaurant is **Yokohama** (980 Blanshard Street; 604-384-5433). Its large sushi bar with an extensive menu is deemed the best place in town for such fare. The restaurant features authentic Japanese entrées as well as familiar favorites of shrimp tempura, sukiyaki and ginger pork in the main dining area or in private tatami rooms. Moderate.

The Keg (500 Fort Street; 604-386-7789) is an informal restaurant, one of the most popular, reasonably priced places in downtown. Its dark, barlike environs offer views of the Inner Harbour. Entrées include burgers, steaks and seafood. Try the Monterey chicken, a mesquite-grilled chicken breast topped with Black Forest ham and Monterey Jack cheese. Moderate.

Historic Bastion Square contains two of Victoria's best restaurants. **Camille's Restaurant** (45 Bastion Square; 604-381-3433) is romantic and elegant with brick walls, balloon curtains and linen tablecloths. This intimate restaurant prepares delicious French and Pacific Rim cuisine, such as Java chicken marinated in coconut milk and then glazed with ginger, lime and orange muscat. The breads and desserts are heavenly. Camille's also has an extensive wine cellar. Dinner only. Moderate to deluxe.

The other Bastion Square restaurant is **La Ville Di's** (26 Bastion Square; 604-388-9414). Set in an ivy-covered brick building, the atmosphere is cozy and friendly with soft lighting and classical music. Seafood, rabbit, beef and lamb entrées are prepared in a Brittany style. Try the *langoustines polinac*, tiger prawns with mushrooms and shallots in Calvados and Muscadet sauce, or the soufflé *de homard*, lobster soufflé with prawns. The restaurant features an extensive list of French wines. From May to October, more casual dining is available in the outside café. Deluxe.

Delicious Greek food, including moussaka, souvlaki and spanikopita, along with standard steaks and seafood are served at **Periklis** (531 Yates Street; 604-386-3313), a convivial, Taverna-style restaurant with dining areas on three levels and Greek posters on the walls. Greek and belly dancing draws big crowds on the weekends in winter and seven nights a week during the summer. Moderate.

The oldest French restaurant in Victoria, **Chez Pierre** (512 Yates Street; 604-388-7711), is still pleasing customers with entrées such as duckling in orange sauce, rack of lamb and fresh salmon in its pleasant, intimate, downtown setting. Moderate to deluxe.

A relative newcomer to the Victoria cuisine scene is **Siam Thai** (1314 Government Street; 604-383-9911), which serves up some of the best Thai food around. The atmosphere is dark and quiet, with soft lighting lending a bit of mystery to this ethnic eatery. Only fresh ingredients are used in the entrées, such as *larp gai*, diced chicken in spicy lime juice, onions and vegetables, or scallop *prik paow*, sautéed scallops with green-red peppers, onions, mushrooms and chili paste. Moderate.

Swan's (506 Pandora Avenue; 604-361-3310) offers a convivial ambience with huge vases of fresh flowers and a display of colorful local artwork against brick walls of the historic building that was once a grain warehouse. Entrées, such as bacon-wrapped tenderloin of beef in a brandied green-pepper sauce, are mouthwatering and colorfully presented in generous portions. Moderate to deluxe.

A traditional Chinese restaurant, in the heart of Chinatown, is **Don Mees** (538 Fisgard Street; 604-383-1032). Go through the door under the neon sign and walk up a long, red-carpeted staircase to the large dining area. The food here is good, portions are ample, and the presentation is upscale. Standard favorites are almond chicken, beef with broccoli and onions and sweet and sour pork. The Sunday dim sum is especially good. Moderate.

DOWNTOWN VICTORIA SHOPPING

Victoria's downtown is chock full of fascinating shops. Best buys are locally made candies, Indian-made sweaters, carvings and silver, British Columbia jade, weavings and pottery, books on Canada and goods imported from Britain. Shopping starts with tiny shops in the Empress Hotel and extends north on Government Street.

Roger's Chocolates (913 Government Street; 604-384-7021) is *the* place for connoisseurs of fine chocolates. Housed in a 1903 building with a tiled floor, dark-oak paneling and oak-and-glass display cases, the shop is full of Dickensian charm.

Even if you brought all your reading with you, stop at **Munro's Books** (1108 Government Street; 604-382-2464) to see this Neo-Classical heritage building with high ceilings and carved details, formerly the head office of the Royal Bank. It is one of the finest bookshops in western Canada. The shop holds more than 50,000 titles of Canadian, British and American works.

The purveyor of fine teas and coffees is **Murchies** (1110 Government Street; 604-383-3112) where you also can pick up some delectable pastries. This importer of teas and coffees also has one of the largest stocks of china, porcelain and crystal in the province.

For Battenburg lace, linen damask tablecloths, fine handkerchieves and natural-fiber lingerie, visit the **Irish Linen Store** (1019 Government Street; 604-383-6812).

For a look at another beautifully restored old building, stop by **The Spirit of Christmas** (1022 Government Street; 604-385-2501). It is located in an 1886 bank building with high ceilings, large, arched windows and dark-oak and glass display cases containing thousands of whimsical ornaments, music boxes, authentic German nutcrackers, Disney characters and collectibles.

Eaton's Centre (Government and View streets; 604-382-7141), a multilevel shopping mall in the heart of Victoria, has more than 100 shops and opens to an interior courtyard with a fountain under skylights and arches. Eaton's offers goods from all over the Commonwealth, especially china and woolen products.

The Canadian company that pioneered settlement of the west is the **Hudson's Bay Company** (1701 Douglas Street at Fisgard Street; 604-385-

1311). It still carries furs, the mainstay of trade in the early days, famous Hudson's Bay point blankets and top brands of English china and woolens, as well as contemporary works by local artists and artisans.

Fort Street between Blanshard and Cook streets is known as Antique Row with antique maps, stamps, coins, estate jewelry, rare books, crystal, china, furniture and paintings. **Victoria Limited Editions** (919 Fort Street; 604-386-5155), offers a large selection of china, crystal and collectors plates.

DOWNTOWN VICTORIA NIGHTLIFE

In the Empress Hotel, the **Bengal Room** (721 Government Street; 604-384-8111), with its high ceilings, potted plants and rattan furnishings, is fit for the Raj. It is a comfortable, old-money place for a drink.

Karaoke clubs are popular in Victoria. One of the best places is at the **James Bay Inn** (270 Government Street; 604-384-7151).

Rumours (1325 Government Street; 604-385-0566), a gay dance bar, features progressive music. Disco lights illuminate the dancefloor at this contemporary club with bare, black walls. Sunday is *déjà vu* night, featuring top hits from the '70s. There's also a pool room on the premises.

For a more cultured evening, Victoria has several options. The well-respected **Victoria Opera** performs at the Royal Theatre (805 Broughton Street; 604-383-9711). The **Victoria Symphony** (846 Broughton Street; 604-383-9711 tickets, 604-385-6515 information) offers concerts featuring international conductors and artists, from September through May.

Harpo's (15 Bastion Square; 604-385-5333) features an eclectic mix of music on different nights. The decor isn't much, but the nightclub does have a large dancefloor.

Sweetwater's (27-560 Johnson Street; 604-383-7844) offers contemporary rock music for dancing. Cover.

Victoria's pubs offer an alternative to the expensive price of having a drink in the hotel lounges. Some of these pubs feature beers made on the premises, while others stock a wide variety of local and imported beers and ales. Whether in historic buildings or cottage breweries, you also are apt to find a game of darts and a number of skilled competitors. One of the liveliest pub crowds is found at **Swans** (506 Pandora Avenue; 604-361-3310) where you can hear great local jazz combos several nights a week and see a changing and colorful collection of local and international art. It's housed in a restored heritage building.

Centennial Square arts center includes the original City Hall (1878) and the **McPherson Playhouse** (Government Street at Pandora Street; 604-386-6121). The playhouse is a restored baroque and Edwardian-style Pantages Theatre seating 800. It hosts stage plays, classical and pops concerts, dance performances, films and touring lectures.

Kaleidoscope Theatre Productions (520 Herald Street; 604-383-6183) presents musical cabaret entertainment.

A favorite spot for karaoke sing-alongs is the **Karaoke Club** in Paul's Motor Inn (1900 Douglas Street; 604-382-9231).

DOWNTOWN VICTORIA BEACHES AND PARKS

Beacon Hill Park—This sedate park near downtown, founded in 1882, contains forest, open grassy areas, ponds and Goodacre Lake, a wildfowl sanctuary. Among gardens blooming nearly year-round, you also will find one of the tallest totem poles in the world, lawn bowling, a 100-year-old cricket pitch and the Mile 0 marker of the Trans-Canada Highway, at the southwestern corner where Dallas Road and Douglas Street meet.

Facilities: Restrooms, picnic areas, tennis courts, playground, lawn bowling, baseball and soccer fields and children's wading pool; information, 604-385-5711.

Getting there: Along Douglas Street, only a five-minute walk from the Empress Hotel.

Victoria Neighborhoods

Beyond the heart of Victoria are some of the city's most important landmarks including a castle fit for a queen, the house where her majesty really stays on her visits. Your itinerary also features Victoria's major art gallery and a leading museum of Victoriana. If you have half a day at your disposal, just follow our lead.

You'll need your own or public transportation to head out east on Fort Street to **Craigdarroch Castle** (1050 Joan Crescent; 604-592-5323; admission). Robert Dunsmuir had the house built for his family after new coal deposits were found in 1869, making him, the overseer of the Hudson's Bay Company, British Columbia's first millionaire. Today, visitors can tour Craigdarroch, furnished in turn-of-the-century style featuring 39 rooms on five floors with stained-glass windows, intricate woodwork, original furniture and turrets.

Just a couple of blocks southeast of the castle is the **Art Gallery of Greater Victoria** (1040 Moss Street; 604-384-4101). One of Canada's finest art museums, this gallery features Canadian and Inuit art, European pieces from the 15th through 20th centuries, and the only Shinto shrine outside Japan plus a large oriental-art collection. The major part of the gallery is housed in Spencer Mansion, built in 1890, which features a dramatic staircase, Jacobean ceiling and a doll house with many intricate details.

Just a couple of blocks southwest is **Government House** (1401 Rockland Avenue; 604-387-2080), where the Queen of England and her family stay when they visit Victoria. It is the home of the Lieutenant Governor, the Queen's representative in British Columbia. When royalty is not visiting, the public can stroll through the formal lawns and gardens, complete with a lily pond and waterfall. Take a few minutes to explore Rockland Avenue, home of many mansions built during the 1880s and 1890s.

If you enjoy Victorian furnishings, you will want to see **Point Ellice House** (2616 Pleasant Street; 604-387-4697; admission), which contains British Columbia's most comprehensive collection of Victorian furnishings and art in its original setting. The house was built around 1860. Visitors also can stroll through a wonderful 19th-century garden.

VICTORIA NEIGHBORHOODS HOTELS

Clawfoot tubs in the bath, chocolates on the pillows, gourmet breakfast and waterfall-style beds are some of the attractions at the gay-friendly **Camellia House Bed and Breakfast** (1994 Leighton Road; 604-370-2816). A sunny deck, pleasant backyard and wicker furniture add to the charm of this circa-1913 home. This inn is convenient to the Oak Bay area. Moderate.

Oak Bay Guest House (1052 Newport Avenue; 604-598-3812) is a turn-of-the-century bed and breakfast that welcomes gays. Furnished with antiques and decorated with watercolors, the rooms offer garden views. Relax by the living-room fireplace or enjoy a book in the sun room. Deluxe.

If you don't mind student housing without frills, the **University of Victoria Housing Services** (P.O. Box 1700, Finnerty Road, Victoria, BC V8W 2Y2; 604-721-8395), just a few minutes north of downtown, offers 800 rooms, including breakfast in the residence dining room, from May 1 to August 30. Budget.

About one-quarter of the way from Victoria to Sidney in a quiet residential area on the edge of the park by the same name is the **Mount Douglas Park Resort** (4550 Cordova Bay Road; 604-658-2171). The contemporary lodge, built on the side of a hill, features large relief carvings of birds and marine life. Rooms are contemporary and comfortable. Suites have balconies with ocean or park views, and some have fireplaces and kitchenettes. Most rooms and some suites are moderately priced.

The Gorge Waterway extends northwest from the Inner Harbour. Here you will find a number of less-expensive motels. Hidden among the many motels lining Gorge Road, the **Coachman Inn** (229 Gorge Road East; 604-388-6611) is one that offers the most quality and service for your money. The motel appeals to families because of its video games room, indoor pool, twin saunas, restaurant and lounge. Just a few minutes drive from downtown, the motel offers a free shuttle in the summer. The 73 rooms are clean, decorated in light, cheerful colors and feature oak trim. Some rooms and 12 one-bedroom suites feature kitchenettes. Moderate. (Suites are deluxe).

VICTORIA NEIGHBORHOODS RESTAURANTS

For a truly English dinner or afternoon tea, meander out to Oak Bay to the **Blethering Place** (2250 Oak Avenue; 604-598-1413). There you will find the silver-haired set gossiping over hours-long tea, and families stopping by for supper. The fare includes crumpets, tarts, scones, cornish pasties, Welsh rarebit, steak-and-kidney pie, curries and decadent desserts. Budget to moderate.

The name, **Ceccone's Pizzeria & Trattoria** (3201 Shelbourne Avenue; 604-592-0454), implies a more casual atmosphere than you will find in this upscale bistro in the Shelbourne area. Soft lighting, decorator colors and window seats with cushions and pillows lend a feeling of intimacy. Ceccone's turns out wood-oven pizzas and calzones, pastas and other tasty entrées that are well worth the wait (up to 90 minutes on weekends—no reservations). Lamb chops stuffed with tomatoes, spinach and peppercorn sauce in puff pastry are to die for. Dinner only. Moderate to deluxe.

If you're hungering for borscht, schnitzel, pirogi or goulash, **Hungarian Village Restaurant** (1550 Cedar Hill Cross Road; 604-477-3023) in the Mount Douglas area offers these entrées along with full-bodied Hungarian wines in an intimate, brick-and-wood building with Hungarian pottery, candlelight and violin music in the background. Budget to moderate.

You will find a convivial atmosphere at **Six-Mile-House** (494 Island Highway; 604-478-3121), an 1855 roadhouse on the way to Sooke. The interior of this Victoria landmark is filled with brass, oak moldings and stained glass. The menu always features a seafood, chicken and pasta entrée, as well as hearty hamburgers. Moderate to deluxe.

The Aerie (P.O. Box 108, Malahat Drive, Victoria, BC V0R 2L0; 604-743-7115) is Victoria's newest, most elegant restaurant, sitting atop the Malahat summit. Located outside of greater Victoria on the way to Duncan, this eatery's dining room has a 23-carat-gold-leaf ceiling, with panoramic views stretching from the Gulf Islands to the Olympic Mountains. The menu changes, depending on availability of the very freshest local ingredients tracked down by Austrian-born owner and chef Leo Schuster. Entrées such as blackened Louisiana-style sirloin or pheasant breast in almond crust attract enough high-flying guests that a helicopter pad was added to the restaurant and 12-room guest house. Ultra-deluxe.

VICTORIA NEIGHBORHOODS SHOPPING

The municipality of Oak Bay features an array of boutiques and specialty stores on Oak Bay Avenue featuring designer clothing, English toffees, New Age toys and games, crafts and jewelry. Be sure to stop by the **Teddy Bears Picnic** (2250 Oak Bay Avenue; 604-598-5558) with a selection of toys appealing to the child in each of us.

Mayfair Shopping Center (a mile from downtown near Douglas Street and Finlayson Avenue; 604-383-0541) is one of the largest and most upscale shopping centers on the island. It contains more than 100 shops specializing in men's and women's fashions.

VICTORIA NEIGHBORHOODS NIGHTLIFE

In Oak Bay, east of downtown Victoria, the **Snug** (1175 Beach Street; 604-598-4556) at the Oak Bay Beach Hotel attracts locals and visitors alike. It has a warm, British atmosphere with plaster walls, dark-wood beams, a large bar and fireplace. In the summer, the balcony overlooks the ocean.

It doesn't take but a few minutes to drive out of the downtown area for an evening's entertainment. North of downtown in the Shelbourne area, **Ceccone's Pizzeria & Trattoria** (3201 Shelbourne Avenue; 604-592-0454), an intimate Italian bistro, features various jazz and blues groups who can be heard from the bar or the dining area every night.

VICTORIA NEIGHBORHOODS
BEACHES AND PARKS

Thetis Lake Municipal Park—Just five miles from the city center, this park offers opportunities for walking, hiking and solitude on more than 1600 acres of rolling hills, fir and cedar forest and lake frontage.

Facilities: Picnic areas and restrooms; restaurants and groceries nearby. *Fishing:* Good. *Swimming:* Good in summer.

Getting there: Located about five miles northwest of downtown Victoria off Highway 1.

Mount Douglas Municipal Park—On the east side of the Saanich Peninsula is this 500-acre park with forests of arbutus, fir and cedar, a beach and Mount Douglas peak. Visitors can drive a one and a half-mile paved route to a parking area and then hike a short distance to the peak where the view stretches in all directions.

Facilities: Picnic areas and rooms; restaurants and groceries nearby; information, 604-385-5711. *Swimming:* Good in summer.

Getting there: Located about five miles northeast of downtown Victoria off Highway 17 and Cordova Bay Road.

Saanich Peninsula

One of Vancouver Island's leading tourist attractions, Butchart Gardens, is the Saanich Peninsula's primary draw. This area also offers a host of other garden retreats featuring exotic fauna from all over the world. Traveling north from Victoria toward Sidney on Highway 17, follow the signs to **Fable Cottage Estate and World Class Gardens** (5187 Cordova Bay Road; 604-658-5741; admission). Here architecture resembles an elf's cabin with a stucco exterior, peaked roofs that come nearly to the ground, stone fireplaces and chimneys—all surrounded by pretty gardens. In addition to the enchanting Fable Cottage itself, this waterfront estate offers three-and-a-half acres of floral gardens dotted with figures of elves, dragons and other characters.

Continuing north on Highway 17, signs direct you to **Butchart Gardens** (800 Benvenuto Drive; 604-652-5256; admission), a must for anyone who ever dreamed of having a green thumb. Dating back to 1904, the industrious wife of the manufacturer of Portland Cement turned a quarry pit created by her husband into a fabulous sunken garden. Today, Jennie Butchart's project is a world-famous, 50-acre botanical showcase, which includes the Rose Garden, the Italian Garden, the Japanese Garden, the Star Pond and the Ross Fountains. The gardens, joined by a series of walkways, display masses of color and rare and exotic plants. See fantastic fireworks displays every Saturday night in July and August.

Returning south on Highway 17, you can stop at the **Horticulture Centre of the Pacific** (505 Quayle Road; 604-479-6162; admission) where perennial displays are all labeled. You walk on forest paths to see a fabulous display of Asian lilies, a rose garden with more than 100 kinds of miniature roses, a creek flanked with ferns and hostas and the rhododendron vale.

When Highway 17 intersects with Highway 1, head west on Highway 1 and follow the signs to **Craigflower 1850's Farmhouse Historic Site** (110 Island Highway; 604-387-4697; admission). Craigflower grew out of the requirement that in order to have a lease on Vancouver Island, the Hudson's Bay Company had to colonize it. Craigflower is one of four farms planned by the company. Some 25 families arrived from Scotland in 1853 to live on and work the farm. Visitors can tour the Georgian-style farmhouse built for bailiff Kenneth McKenzie in 1856, which contains furnishings and articles brought from Scotland. Craigflower Schoolhouse is the oldest school building in western Canada.

SAANICH PENINSULA HOTELS

Near Butchart Gardens, ferries and the airport, the **Best Western Emerald Isle Motor Inn** (2306 Beacon Avenue, Sidney; 604-656-4441) appeals to families because it is convenient and rooms have kitchenettes. No decorator interiors here, but the decor is functional. The 63 rooms, some of which are nonsmoking, are clean. Restaurant, whirlpool baths, sauna, health spa. Moderate.

SAANICH PENINSULA RESTAURANT

For seafood dishes like prawns, halibut and salmon as well as Greek specialties, try **Cordova Seaview Restaurant** (5109 Cordova Bay Road, Cordova Bay; 604-658-5227). Eight miles north of Victoria, this Mediterranean style eatery has a patio overlooking the Georgia Strait. Moderate.

SAANICH PENINSULA BEACHES AND PARKS

Island View Regional Park—On the eastern shore of the Saanich Peninsula, the weather has molded this relatively flat park with rolling sand dunes at the north end and a long, accretion beach at the water's edge. The beach, full of fine, white sand, is strewn with sculpture-like driftwood. The park offers view of Mt. Baker, de Haro Strait and the San Juan and Gulf islands.

Facilities: Picnic areas, restrooms and boat launch; information, 604-388-4421. *Swimming:* Good, but the water is cold.

Getting there: Located northeast of Victoria on the Saanich Peninsula off Highway 17 and Island View Road.

Elk/Beaver Lake Regional Park—Rolling hills, lush wetlands, tranquil forests and hilltop vistas surrounding Elk and Beaver lakes provide more than 1000 acres of habitat at this regional park for many birds, including owls, woodpeckers and ducks.

Facilities: Picnic areas, restrooms, boat launch; information, 604-479-2213; *Fishing:* Good for trout. *Swimming:* Good in warm weather.

Getting there: Located north of Victoria off Highway 17 and Beaver Lake Road.

Goldstream Provincial Park—This park provides two distinct vegetation zones—dry ridges with dogwood, lodgepole pine and arbutus, and wetter areas with 600-year-old Douglas fir, western red cedar, western hemlock, western yew, black cottonwood and big-leaf maple as well as many wildflowers. A salt marsh, where the Goldstream River flows into Finlayson Arm, contains mosses, lichens and liverworts. Each year, the river draws thousands of salmon returning to spawn. The river got its name after gold was discovered there, but the find was a small one.

Facilities: Picnic areas and restrooms; restaurants and groceries nearby; information, 604-387-4363. *Fishing:* Good.

Camping: There are 159 sites.

Getting there: Ten miles northwest of Victoria off Highway 1.

Esquimalt Area

Swing west of Victoria along Esquimalt Harbour to visit one of the region's most important landmarks, **Fort Rodd Hill National Historic Park** (Ocean Boulevard off the Old Island Highway; 604-363-4662), a 44-acre park of rolling hills, an open, parade-grounds area, woods and beach. The fort was built in 1895 to protect the entrance to the Royal Navy Yards in Esquimalt Harbor. It became a park in 1962. Visitors can see restored batteries and the restored Fisgard Lighthouse, the oldest lighthouse on the Pacific Coast, which features exhibits on shipwrecks and navigation.

Also in the Esquimalt Area is **English Village and Anne Hathaway's Cottage** (429 Lampson Street; 604-388-4353; admission). The village occupies five acres and includes replicas of William Shakespeare's birthplace and other English sites, such as the Garrick Inn and Plymouth Tavern. The replica of Anne Hathaway's Cottage is authentically furnished with 16th-century antiques and surrounded by colorful gardens of flowers and herbs. Tour guides are garbed in period costumes.

Southeast Island

Vancouver Island's southeast region is a great place to learn about the area's native heritage and logging industry as well as swim at surprisingly warm beaches such as those on Qualicum Bay.

The towns on the island's protected, southeastern shore tend to be more low key than the proper British Victoria. The town of **Duncan** is the site of a collection of some 60 totem poles, ten of which are along the highway and the others scattered about town.

This logging community is the site of the **British Columbia Forest Museum** (RR4, Trans-Canada Highway; 604-746-1251; admission) where you ride the rails behind a steam locomotive through a typical Northwest forest, across a trestle over Somenos Lake to the train station. Once there you can power yourself via an old-fashioned hand car or walk around the 100-acre park to see early logging equipment, the Log Museum exhibiting logging artifacts, the Tree Room with historic photos and displays explaining the life cycle of the forest.

Visitors have an opportunity to experience authentic traditions of the Cowichan people at the **Native Heritage Centre** (200 Cowichan Way; 604-746-8119; admission) in Duncan. Today, the Cowichan Band, with about 4000 members, is the largest group of native peoples in British Columbia. You can see carvers, jewelry-smiths and basket weavers at their work and watch women as they spin and knit authentic Cowichan sweaters. Succulent aromas will lead you to where fresh salmon is being smoked for the Friday and Saturday summer-evening feasts at the Big House Restaurant, which also offers interpretive dancing. An audio-visual presentation gives a sense of the Cowichan spiritual traditions so closely tied with the earth and nature. The center also includes a fine-art gallery and a smaller gift shop.

Chemainus is known as the little town that did. Instead of allowing unemployment to turn Chemainus into a ghost town when the local mill closed, residents hired well-known artists to paint murals all over the town. Yellow footprints on the sidewalks direct visitors past images of native chiefs, loggers felling huge trees and locomotives hauling logs through the forest. The murals have drawn tourists from around the world, creating a new industry there.

Nanaimo (★), population 53,000, is a hidden destination right under the noses of visitors who pass through it on their way from the ferry landing. The city's name grew out of its native title, "Snenymo" meaning "great and mighty people." White pioneers came to the area after large deposits of coal were discovered in 1851. The city was incorporated in 1874, and today, its economy rests on fishing, forestry, port business and tourism. For more information, contact the **Tourism Nanaimo InfoCentre** (266 Bryden Street; 604-754-8474).

The **Nanaimo Centennial Museum & Archives** (100 Cameron Road; 604-753-1821; admission) gives visitors an experience of the city's past by taking them through a coal-mining tunnel, a blacksmith's shop, general store, doctor's office and barber shop in a turn-of-the-century town, a restored miner's cottage, dioramas with an array of Coast Salish carvings, baskets and masks and a new area focusing on Chinatown. "Step Into History" is a self-guided, historical walking tour of Nanaimo detailed in a map available at the **Nanaimo Tourist & Convention Bureau Society** (266 Brydon Street; 604-754-8474).

The **Hudson's Bay Bastion** (just south of the Seaplane Terminal along the harbor), a 30-foot-tall building, was built on the waterfront in 1852 ostensibly to protect white settlers from the natives. But because the Indians proved to be peaceful, the fort really didn't protect anything. Since 1910 it has been a museum depicting Nanaimo's heritage.

In the Parksville-Qualicum area, you can visit **St. Anne's Anglican Church** (Island Highway to Wembly Street at Church Road, Qualicum; 604-248-3114), one of the oldest churches on the island. A group of 45 farmers in the area used oxen to haul the logs for building it. The log church features stained-glass windows.

The **Craig Heritage Park and Museum** (1110 East Island Highway; 604-248-6966) displays artifacts from the local area, including an old schoolhouse, fire engine and another period cottage.

The name of Qualicum Beach is derived from a native word meaning "where the dog salmon run." Visit the **Big Qualicum Fish Hatchery** (off the East Island Highway north of Qualicum Beach; 604-757-8412). During spawning season, you can watch the salmon thrashing their way upstream to lay their eggs. After the staff "milk" the salmon eggs, they are placed under controlled conditions for hatching.

Just a few miles west of Parksville is the little town of **Coombs** with its Old West look of boardwalks and hitching posts. In the summer, goats graze on the thatched roofs of some of the shops there.

West of Coombs is **Butterfly World** (Highway 4; 604-248-7026; admission) where visitors can see all stages of butterfly life, including egg laying and caterpillar rearing. The most colorful area is the tropical indoor garden where butterflies sip nectar, court and flit among colorful blossoms.

SOUTHEAST ISLAND HOTELS

The **Coast Bastion Inn** (11 Bastion Street, Nanaimo; 604-753-6601) is one of the most luxurious hotels in the area. Rooms feature wood furniture, designer color schemes and views of the water. The inn has a sauna, whirlpool and exercise room, restaurant, café and pub. Moderate to deluxe.

The **Dorchester Hotel** (70 Church Street, Nanaimo; 604-754-6835) offers oceanfront views from most of its 70 newly refurbished units with a Victorian theme. Built on the former site of the old Windsor Hotel and Opera House near the Bastion, the hotel also has a restaurant, rooftop garden and a library. Moderate to deluxe.

Surrounded by woods on three sides, **Beach Acres Resort Hotel** (1815 East Island Highway, Parksville; 604-258-3424) opens onto a large, secluded beach. The 60 beachfront or forest cottages or oceanview condominiums with kitchens are clean, comfortably furnished and some feature fireplaces. Amenities include an indoor pool, whirlpool, sauna, tennis courts, laundry, and a restaurant. Deluxe.

The **Island Hall Beach Resort Hotel** (181 Island Highway; 604-248-3225) is in downtown Parksville on nearly 1000 feet of sandy beach. This resort opened its doors in 1917 with 24 rooms. Now it has grown to seven beachfront buildings with 100 units, 28 of which have kitchenettes. Rooms are light and bright with a pleasing mixture of older and contemporary furnishings. The resort also features an indoor pool, sauna, whirlpool, tennis courts, restaurant, pub and lounge. Moderate to deluxe.

Once a private boys' school, the old-English, Tudor-style **Qualicum College Inn** (427 College Road, Qualicum; 604-752-9262) sits on five acres on a bluff overlooking Georgia Strait. Half the inn's 70 attractive rooms have water views, and some include fireplaces. Amenities include two nearby golf courses, an indoor pool, whirlpool, lounge, pool and beach access. Moderate to deluxe.

SOUTHEAST ISLAND RESTAURANTS

The **Lighthouse Bistro** (Seaplane Terminal, Nanaimo; 604-754-3212) is designed to look like a lighthouse built into a white, Cape Cod-style building with light-blue trim. The restaurant offers a great view of the harbor and entrées such as salmon with lemon butter sauce. Moderate to deluxe.

The **Bluenose Chowder House** (1340 Stewart Avenue, Nanaimo; 604-754-6611) is just a quarter mile from the B.C. Ferry Terminal. This eatery offers nautical charm as a backdrop to a variety of the freshest seafood, including prawns, crab, fish, clams and oysters. Moderate to deluxe.

The **Grotto** (1511 Stewart Avenue, Nanaimo; 604-753-3303) pegs itself as a Nanaimo waterfront tradition. It resembles a sprawling, wooden beach house surrounded by gardens of driftwood, shells and plants. Here you can dine on fresh seafood, pasta and stir-fry. Moderate to deluxe.

In Parksville, visit **Kalvas** (180 Moilliet Street; 604-248-6933), a large, log-beam building, for fine French and German fare. You can feast on East Coast lobster, fresh local crab and oysters. Lunch and dinner. Deluxe.

For English-style fish and chips, try Parksville's **Spinnaker Seafood House** (617 East Island Highway; 604-248-5532). The comfortable restaurant features a nautical theme, and the eclectic menu includes fresh seafood, pizza, hamburgers and salads for eating in or taking out. Moderate.

SOUTHEAST ISLAND SHOPPING

In Duncan, the **Khowutzun Arts & Crafts Gallery** (200 Cowichan Way; 604-746-8119) at the Native Heritage Centre offers one of the largest selections of authentic native arts and crafts on the island, including original paintings, jewelry, carvings, masks, rattles, drums, Cowichan knitted items and books on the culture and art of native Northwest coastal peoples.

Hill's Indian Crafts (138-4750 Rutherford Road in Nanaimo's Rutherford Mall; 604-758-4242) features Cowichan sweaters, small replicas of totem poles, carvings, jewelry and prints.

SOUTHEAST ISLAND NIGHTLIFE

Nightlife isn't as plentiful outside Victoria, but that doesn't mean you can't have an enjoyable time in some of the island's southeastern communities. Try Nanaimo's **Dinghy Dock Pub** (Protection Island; 604-753-2373) reached by a ten-minute ferry ride (information, 604-753-8244). The pub offers locally brewed beers and other spirits and spectacular views of Nanaimo, its harbor and Newcastle Island. Nanaimo also offers a handful of theater presentations, including the **Nanaimo Theatre Group, Yellow Point Drama Group, After Eight Dinner Theatre Group** and **Malispina College Drama Group** (information on all groups, 604-754-8474).

(Text continued on page 482.)

The Gulf Islands

Ready for some island-hopping? Whether you're into beaches, arts and crafts, birdwatching, dining or just plain looking around, there is something here for everyone. The Gulf Islands provide plenty of activities—swimming, windsurfing, scuba diving, beachcombing, boating, bicycling, hiking and horse-back riding—to suit families and outdoor enthusiasts of all abilities.

These islands are isolated places where residents enjoy a bucolic lifestyle. At sunset, basking like a group of sea turtles in the water, the islands are like shadows, amorphous shapes in muted shades of blue, mauve and gray stacked up behind one another. The islands, sisters of the San Juan Islands in Washington State, include mountain peaks, sandy beaches, and pastoral farms. The climate is Mediterranean-like—mild and dry. The archipelago includes almost 200 islands, but only five have a population of more than 250—Salt Spring, Pender, Galiano, Mayne and Saturna. **B.C. Ferries** (Victoria, 604-656-0757; or Salt Spring Island, 604-537-9921) plies the waterways between Tsawwassen, just south of Vancouver, and the Gulf Islands and Vancouver Island's Swartz Bay and the islands.

Salt Spring Island, named for a series of briny springs at the island's north end, is the largest with a population of about 7500. The first non-native settlers were blacks escaping slavery in the United States in 1859. Once supported by an agrarian economy, the island now thrives on tourism and the arts. In fact, the Gulf Islands are believed to be home to more artists per capita than most other regions in Canada.

The largest village on Salt Spring is Ganges, a pedestrian-oriented, seaside hamlet, where visitors flock to a summer-long arts-and-crafts fair, art galleries and the Saturday morning market.

Another attraction is Cusheon Lake, a popular, freshwater lake with a large swimming area—and the water is warm. The island also offers popular ocean-side beaches; Vesuvius and Bader's beaches on the island's west side have the warmest water. Because it sits at the edge of the forest, Bader offers much more privacy, but the sandy beach is small.

Pender Island, population 1500, is really two islands connected by a narrow, wooden bridge that affords splendid views of Browning and Bedwell harbours. Medicine Beach in Bedwell Harbour and Hamilton Beach in Browning

Harbour are popular picnic spots. The Driftwood Centre and Port Washington are locations of several galleries.

Birdwatching is a prime activity on the Gulf Islands. Cormorants, harlequin ducks, gulls, oyster catchers, turkey vultures, ravens and bald eagles are commonly seen. Other birds include tanagers, juncos, bluebirds, flycatchers, blackbirds and sparrows. Many of these birds can be seen in the island's parks.

Mouat Provincial Park (Seaview Avenue, Ganges on Salt Spring Island) is a pleasant, wooded park with views of the water and camping and picnicking facilities. **Prior Centennial Provincial Park** is near Bedwell Harbour on Pender Island. It features good fishing, swimming, boat launch, picnic areas and restrooms. The islands also are sites of several marine parks. One of the largest is **Beaumon Marine Park** on South Pender Island and sheltered by Bedwell Harbour. It includes upland forest, picnic areas, campsites and hiking trails.

If you are a diver, the Gulf Islands provide a number of good locations. Divers often see octopi, wolf eels, sea cucumbers, sea stars, sea urchins and sea pens. Shore dives include Vesuvius Bay on Salt Spring Island for sighting octopus and ling cod; Fulford Harbour opposite the ferry terminal with a shallow area perfect for seeing crabs and starfish; and Tilley Point on North Pender Island for interesting kelp beds. Near Thetis Island, the *Miami*, a steel- and coal-carrying freighter that sunk in 1900, is covered with interesting vegetation and marine life. The *Del Norte*, a 190-foot side-wheel passenger steamship that sank in 1868, is between Valdez and Galiano islands and appropriate only for more advanced divers.

Visitors can find a variety of accommodations on Salt Spring and Pender islands. The **Inn on Pender Island** (4709 Canal Road; 604-629-3353), a moderately priced, bed-and-breakfast facility with ten rooms, sits on seven acres of wooded tranquility near Prior Centennial Provincial Park where hiking, bicycling and beachcombing are in abundance. The **Plumbush Inn** (600 Walker Hook Road, Ganges; 604-537-4332) is a country-house bed and breakfast on nearly 1000 feet of private oceanfront that each unit faces. Moderate to deluxe. The **Applecroft Heritage Family Farm** (551 Upper Ganges Road, Ganges; 604-537-5605) is an elegant, 1893 family farm with breakfast concocted from the farm's organic produce. There are two units with whirlpool baths and one self-contained cottage. **Cusheon Lake Resort** (171 Natalie Lane, Ganges; 604-537-9629) features fully equipped log and A-frame chalets, some with fireplaces, an outdoor whirlpool, fishing, swimming and boating available.

SOUTHEAST ISLAND BEACHES AND PARKS

Bamberton Provincial Park—The warm waters of the Saanich Inlet make this park, with a 750-foot sandy beach, attractive to swimmers. The park contains many arbutus trees in a second-growth forest. The Saanich Peninsula, Mt. Baker and the Gulf Islands form the backdrop to water and mountain views from this park.

Facilities: Picnic areas, restrooms; information, 604-387-4363. *Fishing:* Good. *Swimming:* Good in summer.

Camping: There are 50 sites.

Getting there: Located northwest of Victoria off Highway 1 at the northern foot of Malahat Drive.

Newcastle Island Provincial Marine Park—11,000 acres of woods and sandy beaches on an island in Nanaimo Harbor afford views of Vancouver Island and the mainland's Coast Mountains. The park features sandstone ledges and sandy, gravel beaches. The area was a site for coal mining and sandstone mining in the mid-to-late 1800s.

Facilities: Picnic areas, restrooms, visitors center and snack bar in summer; information, 604-387-4363. *Fishing:* Good for salmon. *Swimming:* Good in summer.

Camping: There are 18 sites.

Getting there: In summer, scheduled ferry service departs from behind the Nanaimo Civic Arena off Highway 1, north of downtown. Cars are not allowed. For off-season ferry service, phone 604-753-5141.

Rathtrevor Beach Provincial Park—Located between Nanaimo and Parksville, this park's popularity lies within its sandy beach. There are also a wooded upland area, excellent birdwatching during the spring herring spawn and views of Georgia Strait.

Facilities: Picnic areas, restrooms, showers; restaurants and groceries nearby; information, 604-248-3931. *Swimming:* Good in summer.

Camping: There are 176 sites.

Getting there: Located about two miles south of Parksville off Highway 19.

Englishman River Falls Provincial Park—Forests of huge cedar trees surround a large, crashing waterfall in this lush park that encompasses 240 acres. Large groves of hemlock and fir also can be found in the park. A good time to visit is in autumn when the maple trees offer a colorful contrast to the evergreens.

Facilities: Picnic areas and restrooms; information, 604-248-3931. *Fishing:* On the river. *Swimming:* Good in summer.

Camping: There are 103 sites.

Getting there: Located west of Parksville off Highway 4.

Little Qualicum Falls Provincial Park—Although a neighbor to Englishman River Falls Park, this park is much drier. Consequently, visitors see more pine, Douglas-fir and arbutus trees in this park that straddles the Little Qualicum River. A must see are the impressive waterfalls splashing down a rocky gorge.

Facilities: Picnic areas and restrooms; information, 604-248-3931. *Fishing:* Good for salmon. *Swimming:* Good in pools or in Cameron Lake.

Camping: There are 91 sites.

Getting there: Located 11 miles west of Parksville off Highway 4.

Southwest Island

Whether you come by land or sea, southwest Vancouver Island is one of the Pacific Northwest's most accessible wilderness regions. With its national parks, wildlife and snow-capped peaks, this is a favorite getaway.

Board the **M. V. Lady Rose** (Alberni Harbour Quay; 604-723-8313) for a unique experience traveling the Alberni Inlet aboard a freighter, the likes of which have served the hidden, remote communities on the island's west coast for 50 years. Passengers on the day-long trips can see deliveries of fish food to commercial fish farms, asphalt shingles to individuals reroofing their homes and mail to residents of communities such as Bamfield, Kildonan and Ucluelet. Kayakers can be dropped off at the Broken Group Islands. Tourists should be forewarned that the boat is primarily a freighter, so don't expect a naturalist or interpretive guide with fascinating commentary.

Just outside Port Alberni at Sproat Lake, take the time to view a hidden attraction, the **Martin Mars Water Bombers** (★) (Lakeshore Road; 604-723-6225) owned by Forest Industries Flying Tankers Ltd., a private fire protection service. Although not regularly scheduled, and certainly not developed for tourists, the sight of the largest fire-fighting aircraft in the world dropping 5000 gallons of water on the lake in a test run is almost too impressive for words.

Pacific Rim National Park (604-726-7721), comprised of three units, protects the windswept and jagged west coast of Vancouver Island. The three parts of the park are distinctly different. The West Coast Trail can be traveled only by experienced hikers. The Broken Group Island unit can be reached explored by boat, canoe, kayak or dinghy. The Long Beach unit, the most accessible, includes a seven-mile-long sandy beach. There, you will find the Wickaninnish Centre, an interpretive center located between Ucluelet and Tofino. Here visitors can see powerful waves rolling up on the beach, watch nature presentations, participate in day hikes and view whales, seals and sea lions. There's also a restaurant with views of the surf and spectacular sunsets.

Most of the park includes a rocky shoreline that supports fascinating tidepools with barnacles, mussels, starfish, hermit crab and anemones. Sitka spruce thrive just behind the pockets of sandy beaches and the rocky outcroppings. Further inland are cedar, hemlock, fir and areas of bog and muskeg with pine and laurel. The forest floor is redolent with moss, ferns, huckleberry and salmonberry. The most popular wildlife here is the Pacific grey whale seen during spring migration between mid-March and mid-May. The park also offers sightings of sea lions, harbor seals, river otter, mink and a vast array of resident and migrating birds (see "Southwest Island Beaches and Parks" for more information).

The **Eagle Aerie Gallery** (350 Campbell Street; 604-725-3235) is as much a cultural experience as it is an art gallery. The building was designed by native artist Roy Henry Vickers and constructed by his brothers. The gallery is built in the longhouse style with adzed cedar paneling and massive totem cornerposts. Effective lighting, evocative subject material and a background of taped native chanting and drumming inspire a spirit of reverence unlike almost any other place.

SOUTHWEST ISLAND HOTELS

The **Barclay** (4277 Stamp Avenue, Port Alberni; 604-724-7171) with 88 rooms is one of the largest hotels in town. It features an attractive lobby, a coffee shop, dining room, pub and lounge. Accommodations are clean, fairly standard rooms and suites. Amenities include a heated outdoor pool, whirlpool, and sauna. Moderate.

Coast Hospitality Motor Inn (3835 Redford Street, Port Alberni; 604-723-8111) is one if not *the* best place to stay in town if you don't mind the absence of a pool. The lobby features comfortable seating in front of a fireplace. The motor inn offers 50 newly redecorated rooms in soft, attractive colors with firm beds and standard motel furniture. Moderate.

The **Canadian Princess Resort** (Ucluelet Harbor, Ucluelet; 604-726-7771) is unique in that 30 of its 76 rooms are aboard the ship of the same name (which serviced from 1932-75 as a hydrographic survey vessel). Consequently, these staterooms are small, and many share a bath. Three buildings contain 46 spacious, contemporary rooms and loft suites with fireplaces, decks and views of the ship and the harbor. The resort also includes ten fishing boats and a nautical-themed restaurant and lounge for guests. Deluxe.

Just a block from the Ucluelet marina is the **Thornton Motel** (P.O. Box 490, Ucluelet, BC V0R 3A0; 604-726-7725) with 19 rooms and suites with standard furnishings, some with kitchenettes. It is popular with the fishing crowd. Moderate.

At the **West Coast Motel** (Ucluelet Harbour, Ucluelet; 604-726-7732) views of the harbor from some of the 33 rooms make up for the rather standard motel decor. Nonsmoking rooms are available. Added advantages are an indoor swimming pool, whirlpool, sauna, squash courts and tanning salon. The dining room overlooks the harbor. Moderate to deluxe.

If you want a more personal experience, try **Chesterman's Beach Bed and Breakfast** (P.O. Box 72, Tofino, BC V0R 2Z0; 604-725-3726), which offers three private units, including a charming cottage, a spacious suite and a cozy honeymooner's room, on the beach by the same name. After a visit to the island's west coast, owner Joan Dublanko fell in love with the place. Her hospitality and tasty breakfasts match her enthusiasm. Moderate to deluxe.

The best thing about **Duffin Cove Motel** (215 Campbell Street, Tofino; 604-725-3448) is that it offers views of the ocean from a bluff a block away from downtown. Eleven suites and kitchen units with garage-sale furniture and two cottages with fireplaces on the beach are a winter storm-watcher's delight. Deluxe.

Ocean Village Beach Resort (P.O. Box 490, Hellesen Drive, Tofino, BC V0R 2Z0; 604-725-3755) is a nest of 48 comfortably rustic duplex and single cedar chalets on McKenzie Beach, a quarter-mile of safe, sandy beach facing the Pacific Ocean. The units feature an eating area with table and benches, sitting area and a sleeping area or separate bedroom and bath. The resort also includes an indoor swimming pool, hot tub and laundromat. A convenience store is open during the summer. Moderate.

Pacific Sands Beach Resort (P.O. Box 237, Tofino, BC V0R 2Z0; 604-725-3322) is one of the best resorts on the west coast. Located on Cox Bay, bordering Pacific Rim National Park, the resort offers 15 two-bedroom cedar cottages just a few feet from the beach and 43 housekeeping suites with contemporary furnishings, fireplaces and views of the beach and the ocean. Moderate to deluxe.

SOUTHWEST ISLAND RESTAURANTS

Little Villa Restaurant (3130 3rd Avenue, Port Alberni; 604-724-3612) is an all-around good eatery in a casual, bistro setting. It features seafood, prime rib, burgers and light meals in a casual, comfortable atmosphere. Budget to moderate.

Punjabi House (2800 3rd Avenue; 604-723-0940) is a small restaurant in the downtown area of Port Alberni. The interior is somewhat stark, but there are some East Indian prints on the white walls. Never mind that. What you will find is flavorful East Indian cuisine, such as curried lamb, tandoori chicken and chappatis, served with grace. Budget.

The **Harbour View Restaurant** (247 Hemlock Street, Ucluelet; 604-726-7474) on the second story of the West Coast Motel features large, log-beamed ceilings and panoramic views of the Ucluelet harbor and the mountains beyond. The menu features seafood, steaks, burgers and salads. The fettucine alfredo, baked in a casserole, is especially good. Moderate.

The **Maquinna Lodge** (120 1st Street; 604-725-3261) is housed in a fairly nondescript building in downtown Tofino, but the dining room offers splendid views of the harbor and kayakers returning at dusk. An equally distracting view is the dessert table with an array of baked-on-the-premises cakes, pies and cheesecakes. Entrées, such as two grilled pork chops, are carefully prepared and come in generous servings. Moderate.

Perched on a knoll above the harbor, **The Schooner Restaurant** (331 Campbell Street, Tofino; 604-725-3444) is a cozy place with excellent food. Knotty-pine walls and a nautical decor are the backdrop to an array of entrées such as salmon grenobloise in a tangy lemon-butter-caper sauce, or wienerschnitzel, pepper steak, ribs, salads and seafood, all carefully prepared and attractively presented. Dinner. Moderate to deluxe.

SOUTHWEST ISLAND SHOPPING

Ucluelet's **Du Quah Gallery** (1971 Peninsula Street; 604-726-7223) is a native-owned gallery featuring impressive carved masks with real animal fur and shredded cedar bark, fine jewelry, bentwood boxes and more.

In Tofino, the **House of Himwitsa** (346 Campbell Street; 604-725-2017) offers a good selection of native art including limited-edition prints, silver jewelry, weavings, carvings, beaded items and pottery. Nearby, the **Eagle Arie Gallery** (350 Campbell Street; 604-725-3235) features works by Roy Henry Vickers, a native artist who has found international acclaim for his works that integrate the contemporary and traditional.

SOUTHWEST ISLAND NIGHTLIFE

You won't find nightclubs on the rugged west coast. Some bars and lounges offer sunset views. The bar at **The Loft** (346 Campbell Street, Tofino; 604-725-4241) is not on the water, but it has a casual, nautical theme and lots of fishing tales told 'round its bar, attracting locals and visitors alike.

The bar at the **Maquinna Lodge** (120 1st Street, Tofino; 604-725-261) offers magnificent harbor views.

SOUTHWEST ISLAND BEACHES AND PARKS

East Sooke Park—This regional park is where the west coast begins. The 3500-acre park encompasses beautiful arbutus trees clinging to the windswept coast. You'll find small pocket beaches, rocky bays and islets for beachcombing and tidepooling. It features six miles of rugged coast trails and 30 miles of trails through forest, marsh and field with opportunities to view orca whales, sea lions, harbor seals, black bear, Columbian black-tailed deer and cougar. It has views of the Strait of Juan de Fuca and the Olympic Mountains.

Facilities: Picnic areas and restrooms; information, 604-478-3344. *Fishing:* Good for salmon.

Getting there: Located about 25 miles southwest of Victoria off Rocky Point Road on Becher Bay Road.

French Beach Provincial Park—Visitors have the opportunity to see whales in the spring from this mile-long, sand-and-gravel beach on the Strait of Juan de Fuca. The park also contains second-growth forest.

Facilities: Picnic areas and restrooms; information, 604-387-4363. *Swimming:* Good in summer.

Camping: There are 69 sites.

Getting there: Located west of the hamlet of Sooke off Highway 14 near Jordon River.

Pacific Rim National Park—Cliffs, islands, bog and beach are just some of the topography visitors discover at this vast, 158,400-acre park that is divided into three areas. The most accessible is Long Beach, a six-mile stretch of sand and surf between rocky outcroppings. The Broken Group Islands, more than 100 islands and islets in Barkley Sound, is popular with kayakers. The West Coast Trail, a demanding 47-mile stretch between Bamfield and Port Renfrew, follows a turn-of-the-century trail constructed to aid shipwrecked mariners.

Facilities: Picnic areas and restrooms; restaurants and groceries nearby Long Beach; information, 604-726-7721. *Fishing:* Good for salmon, also for some cod and halibut. *Swimming:* Good.

Camping: Scooner Campground offers 60 primitive walk-in sites right on the beach; pit toilets. At Green Point Campground there are 94 sites inland with beach access. Information, 604-726-4245.

Getting there: At Port Renfrew, access the park via Highway 14; visitors can enter the park by private flights into Bamfield or by driving on a logging road from Port Alberni to Bamfield; the *M. V. Lady Rose*, a mail boat that also takes passengers, makes trips to Bamfield, the Broken Group Islands and Ucluelet; Highway 4 from Port Alberni leads to Ucluelet and Tofino at Long Beach.

MacMillian Provincial Park—On the shores of Cameron Lake, this 336-acre park, available for day-use only, provides access to Cathedral Grove, a large stand of giant, old-growth Douglas fir. Some of the trees are 800 years old, and the largest are nearly 250 feet tall and nearly ten feet in diameter. These trees are believed to have survived a fire some 300 years ago because of their fire-resistant bark, nearly a foot thick on some of the trees now. Walking through this ancient forest can be a spiritual experience, but the area is so popular it is being "loved to death" by tourists.

Facilities: Pit toilets; information, 604-387-5002.   *Fishing:* Good.

Getting there: Located west of Parksville, about 11 miles east of Port Alberni off Highway 4.

Sproat Lake Provincial Park—On the north shore of Sproat Lake just west of Port Alberni, this park is a water enthusiast's paradise. The lake is warm and sunny. Visitors can walk a short distance through the woods to see prehistoric petroglyphs.

Facilities: Picnic areas and restrooms; restaurants and groceries nearby; information, 604-248-3931.   *Fishing:* Excellent for steelhead, trout and salmon.   *Swimming:* Excellent in summer.

Camping: There are 59 sites; pit toilets.

Getting there: Eight miles northwest of Port Alberni off Highway 4.

Stamp Falls Provincial Park—This park offers pleasant walks among the stands of cedar and fir, and an area for contemplation near the waterfall. Visitors can view salmon jumping up the fish ladders in summer and fall. Steelhead and cutthroat trout also invite anglers.

Facilities: Picnic areas; restaurants and groceries nearby; information, 604-248-3931.   *Fishing:* Good for steelhead, trout and salmon.

Camping: There are 20 sites; pit toilets.

Getting there: Located about eight-and-one-half miles north of Port Alberni off Highway 4.

The Sporting Life

SPORTFISHING

In the waters around Vancouver Island, salmon is king. Charter-fishing companies out of Victoria include: **Oak Bay Charters** (1327 Beach Drive; 604-598-3369), **Adam's Fishing Charters** (Inner Harbour; 604-370-2326), and **A-1 Charters** (Inner Harbour; 604-479-7640). On the west coast, contact **Alberni Pacific Charters Ltd.** (5440 Argyle Street, Port Alberni; 604-724-3112), **Bamfield Inn** (Bamfield Inlet; 604-728-3354) or **Weigh West Marine Resort** (634 Campbell Street, Tofino; 604-725-3277).

WHALE WATCHING AND NATURE CRUISES

The southern part of Vancouver Island is known for orca or killer whales, porpoises, harbor seals, California and Stellar sea lions, bald eagles and many species of marine birds. Watch also for the occasional minke whale, gray whale or elephant seal. For nature cruises out of Victoria, try **Seacoast Expeditions Ltd.** (1655 Ash Road; 604-477-1818) or **Ocean Ex-**

cursions (P.O. Box 156, Station E, Victoria, BC V8W 2M6; 604-598-8082). For a cruise aboard a 66-foot motor yacht to see bald eagles and sea lions, contact **Bastion City Charters Ltd.** (P.O. Box 413, Nanaimo, BC V9R 5N3; 604-754-8474). For nature cruises off the west coast, contact **Inter Island Excursions** (411 Campbell Street, Tofino; 604-725-3163).

KAYAKING

Kayaking is a favorite way to explore coastal areas of Vancouver Island. In Victoria, start with **Ocean River Sports** (1437 Store Street; 604-381-4233), **Sports Trade Mall** (508 Discovery Street; 604-383-6443) and **Victoria Canoe and Kayak Club** (355 Gorge Road West; 604-361-4238). On the west coast, there is **Tofino Sea Kayaking Co.** (320 Main Street, Tofino; 604-725-4222).

SCUBA DIVING

Diving is popular at the **Ogden Point Breakway**, an underwater Provincial marine park, on Dallas Road. The best shore access is at **10-Mile Point**, the underwater provincial marine park in Saanich. For a look at underwater west coast wrecks, try East Sooke Park between Victoria and Sooke.

For rentals and instruction, contact **Frank White's Scuba Shop** (1855 Blanshard Street, Victoria, 604-385-4713; and 2537 Beacon Street, Sydney, 604-656-9202), **Ocean Centre** (800 Cloverdale Avenue, Victoria; 604-386-7528) or **The Dive Shop** (9810 7th Street, Sidney; 604-656-0060). In Nanaimo, contact **Seafun Divers Ltd.** (300 South Terminal Street; 604-754-4813). In Port Alberni, see **Octopus Adventures** (4924 Argyle Street; 604-723-3057).

SURFING AND WINDSURFING

Elk/Beaver Lake Regional Park on the Saanich Peninsula is a prime windsurfing destination. For equipment in the Victoria area, contact **Active Sports Ltd** (1620 Blanshard Street; 604-381-7245), **Ocean Centre** (800 Cloverdale Street; 604-386-7528) or **Ocean Wind Ltd.** (2572 Sinclair Street; 604-721-1342).

BOATING AND SAILING

Boating and sailing is popular all around Victoria, the southeastern side of Vancouver Island and in the waters surrounding the Gulf Islands. The waters off the west coast are often too rough for relaxed boating, but some pleasure charters are available.

In Victoria, contact **Bosun's Charters Ltd.** (Bosun's Landing; 604-656-4935), **Clipper Yacht Sales** (975 Nicholson Street; 604-727-2596), **Clubsail Charters** (1327 Beach Drive; 604-592-2711) or **Seahorse Sailing School** (2324C Harbour Drive, Sydney; 604-655-4979).

In the Southeast, boats can be chartered from the **Anchor Marina Ltd.** (1721 Cowichan Bay Road, Cowichan Bay; 604-746-5424) or **Anglers Anchorage Marina Ltd** (933 Marchant Street, Brentwood Bay; 604-652-3531). Half-day, day-long or overnight trips are available aboard the *Meriah*, a 50-foot classic ketch through **Heritage Sailing Cruises Ltd.** (P.O. Box 57, Cowichan Bay, BC V0R 1H0; 604-748-7374). On the west coast, contact **Nootka Charters** (Tofino; 604-725-3318).

HANG GLIDING

For hang-gliding instruction, contact **Air Dreams Hang Gliding School** (3040 Carroll Street, Victoria; 604-383-1055) or **Hang Gliding Association of British Columbia** (933 Adderley Street, North Vancouver; 604-980-9566).

GOLF

Golf is very popular in Canada, and Vancouver Island is no exception. Around Victoria, try **Douglas Golf Lands** (5273 Cordova Bay Road; 604-658-5522), **Cedar Hill Municipal Golf Course** (1400 Derby Road off Cedar Hill Road; 604-595-3103), **Henderson Park Golf Course** (2291 Cedar Hill Road; 604-595-7946), **Olympic View Golf and Country Clubs** (643 Latoria Road; 604-474-3671), **Blenkinsop Valley Golf Centre** (4237 Blenkinsop Road; 604-721-2001), **Prospect Lake Golf Club** (4633 Prospect Lake Road; 604-479-2688), **Royal Oak Inn Golf Course** (4680 Elk Lake Drive; 604-658-1433) and the **Cordova Bay Golf Club** (5333 Cordova Bay Road; 604-658-4075). On the Saanich Peninsula, try **Glen Meadows Golf and Country Club** (1050 McTavish Road, Sidney; 604-656-3136). In the Parksville-Qualicum area, try the **Eaglecrest Golf Club** (2035 Eaglecrest Street, Qualicum Beach; 604-752-6311) or the **Morningstar Golf Course Ltd.** (525 Lowery Street, Parksville; 604-248-8161). On the west coast, there is the **Long Beach Golf Course** (Pacific Rim Highway, Tofino; 604-725-3332).

BICYCLING

Although Victoria's terrain is perfect for cycling, the city's streets and walkways are often very crowded, so there are no official bike paths, and many walking paths prohibit bicycles. One of the best bets for great views of the water and Olympic Mountains is Victoria's Beach Drive. Use caution, since it is winding and there is often considerable motor traffic.

BIKE RENTALS   For bicycle rentals, try **A-City Scene Rentals** (Inner Harbour; 604-384-1433), **Budget Rent A Car Victoria Ltd.** (727 Courtney Street; 604-388-4442), **Harbour Scooter Rentals** (843 Douglas Street; 604-384-2133) and **Sports Rent** (3084 Blanshard Street; 604-385-7368). In Nanaimo, try **Bastion Cycle Ltd.** (4196 Departure Bay; 604-756-1522).

HIKING

DOWNTOWN VICTORIA TRAILS   The **Greater Victoria Green-belt Society** is developing a trail system through the greater Victoria area. For more information, write 3873 Swan Lake Road, Victoria, BC V8X 3W1.

For an easy walk (just over 2 miles) around the Inner Harbour take the **Songhees Trail**. From there you can watch all kinds of water vessels, including float planes, passenger catamarans, fishing boats and yachts.

VICTORIA NEIGHBORHOODS TRAILS   The **Orange Trail** (3 miles) at Thetis Lake Park is a loop trail around both Upper Thetis and Lower Thetis lakes. The trail, part of which meanders alongside Craigflower Creek, is excellent for walking or jogging and is well marked.

The **Norn Trail** (2.5 miles) at Mount Douglas Park is an easy walk on a well-marked route with plenty of trees. It joins the **Birch Trail** to reach the summit of Mount Douglas. Hikers can access the Norn Trail from the Mount Douglas Park Resort.

On the **Island View Regional Park Loop** (3 miles), visitors can take an easy hike from the parking lot at Island View Park that loops through farmland along Island View Road, Puckle Road and Lamont Road and provides scenic seascapes from the beach.

The **Lakeside Route** (6.3 miles) at Elk/Beaver Lake Regional Park is a nicely shaded and well-groomed trail of wood chips and wooden bridges through the beaches surrounding Elk and Beaver lakes.

The **John Dean and Butchart Gardens Hike** (6 miles) provides views of Saanich Inlet, fertile farmland and orchards. The southern part of the trail winds through country lanes. The trail can be accessed at Butchart Gardens.

The **Goldmine Trail** (1 mile) at Goldstream Provincial Park is a dirt pathway that travels past a miner's spring and out to Squally Reach Lookout.

SOUTHEAST ISLAND TRAILS   For an easy walk in Nanaimo, take the **Harbourside Walkway** (2.5 miles) around the harbor with views of Protection Island and the Coast Mountains.

SOUTHWEST ISLAND TRAILS   **Gold Mine Trail** (just short of 2 miles) begins just west of the Pacific Rim National Park information center on Highway 4 for a nonstrenuous hike through a forest of amambilis fir, red cedar, hemlock, Douglas fir and red alder. The remains of mining machinery, including part of a dredge, can still be found on the beach.

South Beach Trail (just under a mile) starts behind the Wickaninnish Centre and winds through a stand of Sitka spruce. Side trails lead to rocky or sandy coves surrounded by headlands. At the far end of Lismer Beach, a boardwalk climbs over a bluff to South Beach. At the top of this bluff, the **Wickaninnish Trail** leads to the left, but continuing to the right takes hikers past groves of moss-enshrouded Sitka spruce and western hemlock.

The **Wickaninnish Trail** (3 miles) links Long Beach to Florencia Bay.
Hikers can access this trail via the South Beach Trail or from the Florencia
Bay parking lot. This trail is a part of the early Tofino-Ucluelet land route
that used beaches, forest trails and sheltered inlets to link the two towns
before a road was built further inland.

The most arduous trek on Vancouver Island is the **West Coast Trail**
(47 miles), stretching along the west coast. Hikers need to be prepared for
five to eight days traveling on an irregular slippery trail. There are tidepools,
fjord-like cliffs, opportunities to see Pacific gray whales, sea lions, harbor
seals, shore birds and sea birds. Access to the southern trailhead is at Port
Renfrew. The northern trailhead access is at Bamfield.

Transportation

BY CAR

Vancouver Island lies across the Strait of Juan de Fuca from the state
of Washington and west of mainland British Columbia. Victoria and the
southeastern communities are accessible from either. **Highway 14** runs from
Victoria through Sooke to Port Renfrew on the west coast. The **Trans-Canada
Highway** (Highway 1) goes from Victoria to Nanaimo. Highway 4 goes
from the Parksville-Qualicum area west to Port Alberni, leading to the west
coast communities of Ucluelet and Tofino.

BY FERRY

Ferries provide daily, year-round sailings to Victoria and Nanaimo. The
number of sailings daily usually increases in the summer, but it is advisable
to call for up-to-date schedules and rates.

Travelers wishing to depart from the United States can take Black Ball
Transport, Washington State Ferries or Victoria Clipper to Victoria. **Black
Ball Transport** (Port Angeles, WA, 206-457-4491; Victoria, BC, 604-386-
2202) takes vehicles and foot passengers from Port Angeles to Victoria's
Inner Harbour. **Washington State Ferries** (Seattle, WA, 206-464-6400;
Victoria, BC, 604-381-1551) takes vehicles and foot passengers on a scenic
route through Washington's San Juan Islands between Anacortes, WA, and
Sidney, BC, and buses take foot passengers to downtown Victoria from Sid-
ney. The **Victoria Clipper** ships (United States, 800-888-2535; Seattle, WA
206-448-5000; Victoria, BC, 604-382-8100) are 300-passenger, high-speed
jet catamarans that run year-round between Seattle's Pier 69 and Victoria's
Inner Harbour with stops in the San Juan Islands and Port Townsend, WA.
B.C. Ferries (Seattle, WA, 206-441-6865; Victoria, BC, 604-656-0757)

travels year-round from Tsawwassen, just south of Vancouver, to Swartz Bay, a scenic, half-hour drive by car or bus from Victoria.

BY AIR

The **Victoria International Airport** is just 20 minutes from Victoria in Sidney. Carriers include Air B.C., Horizon Airlines and Time Air. Airport bus service between downtown Victoria and the Victoria International Airport is provided by **PBM Transport** (604-383-7311). **Helijet Airways** (604-382-6222 in Victoria; 604-273-1414 in Vancouver) offers jet helicopter service into downtown Victoria from downtown Vancouver. The airport in Nanaimo, **Cassidy Airport**, is served by Air B.C., Burrard Air, Time Air and Tyee Airways. Pacific Rim Airlines serves the **Port Alberni Airport**.

Float planes offer a unique experience as they take off on the water and land directly in Victoria's Inner Harbour. **Lake Union Air** (206-284-0300) flies daily to Victoria from Seattle's Lake Union and to Tofino in the summer. **Kenmore Air** (206-486-8400) has a daily schedule to Victoria from the Seattle area in the summer only.

BY TRAIN

VIA Rail (800-665-8630) provides Vancouver Island rail service between Victoria and Courtenay, with stops at Nanaimo.

CAR RENTALS

Most major car-rental businesses have offices at Victoria International Airport. Rental agencies include **ADA Rent A Used Car** (604-388-5230), **Avis Rent A Car** (604-386-8468), **Budget Rent A Car** (604-388-5525), **Exotic Cars** (604-383-1444), **Hertz Rent A Car** (604-656-2312), **Island Auto Rentals** (604-384-4881), **Rent A Wreck** (604-384-5343), **Thrifty Car Rental** (604-656-8804) and **Tilden National Leasing** (604-386-1213).

PUBLIC TRANSPORTATION

Island Coach Lines (604-385-4411) has bus service between Victoria and other points on Vancouver Island. **B.C. Transit** (604-382-6161) provides local bus service from Victoria's bus terminal (710 Douglas Street). B.C. Transit and Victoria Regional Transit Commission offer public transit service to the disabled, called **HandyDART** (604-727-7811).

TAXIS

In the greater Victoria area, you will find **Airport Taxi** and bus service (604-383-7311), **Bluebird Cabs** (604-382-4235), **C & C Taxi** (604-384-2222), **Crown Taxi** (604-381-2242), **Empress Taxi** (604-381-2222) and **Victoria Taxi** (604-383-7111).

Index

Hotel and restaurant names have not been included here unless cited as a sightseeing or historical attraction. Trail names have also been excluded.

Area entries include Cascades and Central Washington; Columbia River and the Gorge; East of the Cascades; Heart of Oregon; Northern Puget Sound; Olympic Peninsula and Washington Coast; Oregon Cascades; Oregon Coast; Portland; San Juan Islands; Seattle; Southern Puget Sound; Southern Vancouver Island; Sunshine Coast; and Vancouver.

495

Hells Canyon National Recreation Area, 240, 243
Helmcken House, 461
Hendricks Park and Rhododendron Garden, 400
Hendrix (Jimi) grave, 71
Henry Art Gallery, 53
Heritage Museum, 302
High Desert Museum, 355
Highways. *See* Transportation *under area entries*
Hiking. *See* Trails *under area entries*
Hillsboro: sightseeing, 277
Hoh Indian Reservation, 152
Hoh Rain Forest, 148, 149
Hoko Archeological Site, 150
Holland Gardens, 108
Hood Canal, 65–66
Hood Canal Floating Bridge, 139
Hood River (town): hotels, 286; nightlife, 290; restaurants, 287; shopping, 289
Hood River, 284
Hood River County Historical Museum, 284
Hoquiam: hotels, 159; restaurants, 160; sightseeing, 157–58
Hoquiam's Castle, 158
Horseback riding. *See* Sports *under area entries*
Horticulture Center of the Pacific, 474
Hostels: British Columbia, 421, 438, 464–65; Oregon, 220–21, 331; Washington, 40, 42, 102, 140, 152, 165
Hotels 19, 22. *See also* Hotels *under area and city entries*
House of héwhiwus, 442
Hovander Homestead Park, 100
Howard Miller Steelhead County Park, 182
Howard Prairie Reservoir, 403
Hoyt Arboretum, 276
Hudson's Bay Bastion, 477
Humbug Mountain State Park, 329, 336–37
Husum: hotels, 286–87
Hyatt Reservoir, 403

Ice skating, 291
Illahee State Park, 70
Illinois River State Park, 410
Ilwaco: sightseeing, 164
Ilwaco Heritage Museum, 164
Independence: restaurants, 392
Index: restaurants, 193; sightseeing, 191
Indian Forest, 316
Indian Heaven Wilderness Area, 203

Indian Mary Park, 409
International District (Seattle), 36–37
International driver's license, 25
International Museum of Carousel Art, 267
International Rose Test Garden, 275
Iron Horse State Park, 196
Island Brewing Company, 421
Island County Historical Museum, 108
Island View Regional Park, 475
Issaquah: hotels, 71; nightlife, 73; shopping, 73

Jack Creek and Falls, 357
Jackson County Museum, 401
Jackson F. Kimball State Park, 372
Jacksonville: hotels, 404; nightlife, 408; restaurants, 405–406; shopping, 407; sightseeing, 401–402; visitor center, 401
James Island, 124
Japanese Garden, 275
Jarrell Cove State Park, 65
Jefferson: shopping, 392
Jefferson County Historical Museum, 138
Jeremiah Nunan House, 401
Jesse M. Honeyman State Park, 326
Jetty Island, 98
Jewell: sightseeing, 303
Jewell Meadows Wildlife Area, 303
John Day: hotels, 242; sightseeing, 240–41
John Day Fossil Beds National Monument, 241
Jones Island, 124
Joseph: hotels, 241; restaurants, 242; sightseeing, 239–40
Joseph Stewart State Park, 372

Kah Tai Lagoon Nature Park, 142
Kah-Nee-Ta, 349–50
Kalaloch Lodge, 152–53
Kam Wah Chung & Co. Museum, 240
Kanaskat-Palmer State Park, 77
Kayaking, 21. *See also* Sports *under area entries*
Keller Historical Park, 216
Kelley Point Park, 273
Kelly Creek: sightseeing, 443
Kennewick: restaurants, 230; sightseeing, 228
Kerby: sightseeing, 401
Kettle Falls: hotels, 222
Kirkland, hotels, 71; restaurants, 72; shopping, 73
Kite flying, 169
Kitsap Memorial State Park, 69
Kitsap Peninsula, 64–65
Kittitas County Historical Museum, 196

HIDDEN FLORIDA
From Miami to the Panhandle, from the Keys to Cape Canaveral, this award-winning guide combs the Sunshine State. 492 pages. $14.95

HIDDEN FLORIDA KEYS AND EVERGLADES
Covers an area unlike any other in the world—the tropical Florida Keys and mysterious Everglades. 156 pages. $7.95

FLORIDA'S GOLD COAST
The Ultimate Guidebook
Captures the tenor and tempo of the most popular stretch of shoreline in all Florida—Palm Beach, Fort Lauderdale and Miami. 192 pages. $8.95

DISNEY WORLD AND BEYOND
The Ultimate Family Guidebook
Unique and comprehensive, this handbook to Orlando's theme parks and outlying areas is a must for family travelers. 300 pages. $9.95

DISNEY WORLD AND BEYOND
Family Fun Cards
This innovative "guidebook you can shuffle" covers Orlando's major theme parks with a deck of 90 cards, each describing a different ride. $7.95

HIDDEN NEW ENGLAND
A perfect companion for exploring America's birthplace from Massachusetts colonial villages to the fog-shrouded coast of Maine. 564 pages. $14.95

HIDDEN BOSTON AND CAPE COD
This compact guide ventures to historic Boston and the windswept Massachusetts coastline. 228 pages. $7.95

FOR FREE CATALOG OR TO ORDER DIRECT   For each book send an additional $2 postage and handling (California residents include 8% sales tax) to Ulysses Press, 3286 Adeline Street, Suite 1, Berkeley, CA 94703. Or call 1-800-377-2542 or 510-601-8301 and charge your order.

About the Authors

Roger Rapoport, author of the Oregon chapters in this book, has written numerous other travel guides including including *Great Cities of Eastern Europe*. He has written extensively on the Pacific Northwest for such publications as *Outside* and the *Oregonian*. Formerly a travel writer at the *Oakland Tribune*, he is now editorial director for Ulysses Press.

Melissa Rivers wrote the introductory, Puget Sound/San Juan Islands and Vancouver chapters. She has collaborated on numerous guidebooks including *The Wall Street Journal Guides to Business Travel, Country Inns and Other Weekend Pleasures, Fodor's Bed and Breakfasts and Country Inns: The Pacific Northwest* and *Fodor's Canada*.

Archie Satterfield, a member of the Society of American Travel Writers, resides in Edmonds, Washington. In addition to the Central Washington and East of the Cascades chapters of this book, he has authored two dozen books on travel and history, including *Country Roads of Washington*. He has also written for *Mobile Motorist, Motorland, Pacific Northwest Magazine* and the *Chicago Sun-Times*.

John Gottberg has penned seven travel books including five Frommer's guides. The former chief editor of the Insight Guide series, he has been widely published in *Travel & Leisure* and *Islands*. A long-time resident of the Pacific Northwest and author of the Olympic Peninsula chapter, he recently joined the *Los Angeles Times* as its travel news and graphics editor.

Jim Poth, co-author of the Seattle chapter, is a native of the Northwest who spent 21 years reporting in the region for *Sunset Magazine*, where he became both bureau chief and senior editor. Jim recently founded Easy Going Outings, Inc., a recreational guide service based at the new Wild Iris Inn in La Conner, Washington.

About the Illustrator

Catherine Rose Crowther received her Bachelor of Fine Arts from the University of Massachusetts. She later ventured to California where she painted detailed ceramic jewelry for many years and discovered the joys of illustration. Her work appears in many books and magazines. She currently lives and works in Oakland, California.